CRAFTS OF AMERIC

CRAFTS OF AMERICA

Constance Stapleton

1817

HARPER & ROW, PUBLISHERS, New York
Cambridge, Philadelphia, San Francisco, Washington
London, Mexico City, São Paulo, Singapore, Sydney

Front cover photograph, clockwise from upper right:
Scherenschnitte with hen and chicks by Claudia Hopf; *Scherenschnitte* with girl and geese by Claudia Hopf; drape-molded redware plate by Lester Breininger; cobalt blue bottle by Hale Farm and Village; painted tin box by Lois Tucker; silver *concha* by Bill Bell; teddy bear by Joyce Sheets; brain-tanned leather purse with beadwork by Cathy Smith; Alaskan sealskin ball from Alaska Native Medical Center Craft Shop.

Back cover photograph, clockwise from upper right:
Painted hex sign by Ivan Hoyt; Alaskan wood mask from Alaska Native Medical Center Craft Shop; Alaskan grass basket from Alaska Native Medical Center Craft Shop; Hawaiian quilt by Deborah U. Kakalia; Alaskan willow root tray from Alaska Native Medical Center Craft Shop; *bulto* of Moses by Leo Salazar; cowboy hat by Manny Gammage, Alaskan sealskin yo-yos from Alaska Native Medical Center Craft Shop.

The author and the publisher wish to thank these makers for the loan of their handiwork for use on this book's cover.

CRAFTS OF AMERICA. Copyright © 1988 by Constance Stapleton. All rights reserved. Printed in the United States of America. No part of this book may be used or reproduced in any manner whatsoever without written permission except in the case of brief quotations embodied in critical articles and reviews. For information address Harper & Row, Publishers, Inc., 10 East 53rd Street, New York, N.Y. 10022. Published simultaneously in Canada by Fitzhenry & Whiteside Limited, Toronto.

Designed by C. Linda Dingler

Library of Congress Cataloging-in-Publication Data

Stapleton, Constance, 1930–
    Crafts of America.

    Includes index.
    1. Handicraft—United States.   I. Title.
TT23.S73   1988   680'.973   87-45671
ISBN 0-06-096079-5 (pbk.)

For Birch

Contents

Foreword by Ralph Rinzler   xiii
Introduction   xvii
Aklää Weaving   *See* Weaving,
    Norwegian-American
Autoharps   *See under* Musical Instruments
Banjos   *See under* Musical Instruments
BASKETS:
    Adirondack   1
    Alaskan   2
    The Amana Colonies   3
    Coiled Rye   *See* Skeps
    Low-Country Sea Grass   4
    Lummi Indian   6
    Maine   6
    Nantucket Lightship   7
    Pomo Indian   8
    Shaker   8
    Western Cherokee   10
    White Oak   11
Beadwork   12
Beehives   *See* Skeps
Bed Coverings, Knotted   14
    See also Crochet
Bed Ruggs   15
Besoms   *See* Brooms
BLANKETS:
    American Colonial   16
    Chilkat Dance Robes   18

Lummi Indian   18
    Rio Grande   *See under* Weaving
Boat Models and Half Hulls   20
    See also Pond Models
Bonework   21
    See also Carving, Alaskan *and* Scrimshaw
Books   22
Bookbinding   23
Boots, Western   *See under* Leather
BOXES:
    Bandboxes   24
    Shaker   25
    See also Petacas
Branding Irons   26
Brass   27
Brooms   28
Bultos   *See under* Santos
Candles   29
Canoes, Birchbark   31
Carousels   32
CARVING:
    Alaskan   34
    Bird   36
    Brasstown   37
    Cedar Fans   38
    Eagle   38
    Hawaiian   39
    Norwegian-American Figure   40

CONTENTS

Primitive   41

Tramp Art   43

See also Bonework

CHAIRS:

Bannister-Back   43

Ladderback   45

Mule-Ear, Thumb-Back, Arrowback, Fancy and Vermont Rocker   46

Shaker   48

Windsor   49

Chair Seats, Cowhide   51

Cherokee Crafts   52

Choctaw Crafts   54

Cigar-Store Indians and Figureheads   56

Clipper Ships   *See* Ship and Boat Replicas

Clocks   58

Clothing, Period   60

Coffin Guitars   *See under* Musical Instruments

Conchas   62

Coopered Items   64

Cornhusk Crafts   65

See also under Dolls

Cowboy Boots   *See under* Leather

Cowboy Hats   65

Crochet   67

See also Irish Lace, English Smocking and French Hand-Sewing

Crystal Painting   *See* Tinsel Painting

Decoys   67

DOLLS:

Alaskan   69

Apple   70

Cornhusk   71

Native American   *See* Carving, Alaskan

Porcelain   73

Rag   75

Other Doll Makers   77

Dower Chests   77

Dulcimers   *See under* Musical Instruments

Eggs, Decorated   79

EMBROIDERY:

American Surface   80

Colcha   81

Crewel   83

Cutwork, Hardanger, Hedebo, Netting and Teneriffe   84

Sampler   86

Exemplars   *See* Embroidery, Sampler

Fans, Cedar   *See under* Carving

FEATHERWORK:

Hawaiian   87

Native American   88

Fences   *See* Iron, Architectural

Fiddles   *See under* Musical Instruments

Figureheads   *See* Cigar-Store Indians and Figureheads

Firebacks and Stoveplates   90

Fireboards   90

Floorcloths   91

Flower Painting   *See* Rosemaling

Frakturs   93

Frames   *See* Graining

Frivolité   *See* Tatting

FURNITURE:

Adirondack   94

Chinese Chippendale   96

Country   97

18th Century American   99

Federal Period   100

Horn   101

Miniature   102

Norwegian-American   104

Scratch-carved and Painted   105

Shaker   107

Shenandoah   109

Southern   110

Spanish Colonial   111

Veneering   113

Willow   115

See also Dower Chests

Gameboards   116

Gametables   117

Gates   *See* Iron, Architectural

GLASS:

    Art   117

    Bull's-Eye and Leaded   117

    Hand-blown   119

    Lampwork   119

    Lead Crystal and Pressed   120

    Ohio   120

    Stained   122

Gold Liturgical Items   *See* Liturgical Gold, Silver and Pewter

Gourds   123

Graining   124

Grates   *See* Iron, Architectural

Guitars, Coffin   *See under* Musical Instruments

GUNS:

    American Long Rifles and Flintlock Pistols   126

    Southern Mountain Rifles   128

Hand-Sewing   *See* Irish Lace, English Smocking and French Hand-Sewing

Harpsichords   *See under* Musical Instruments

Hats, Cowboy   *See* Cowboy Hats

Hats, Straw   *See* Wheat-Weaving and Straw Hats

Hex Signs   129

Hides, Brain-tanned   *See under* Leather

Hope Chests   *See* Dower Chests

Hopi Crafts   131

Hornwork   132

Horse-drawn Vehicles   *See* Vehicles, Horse-drawn

HORSEHAIR:

    Twisting   133

    Braiding, Hitching and Weaving   135

Houses of Timber-Frame Construction   135

Inlay, Marquetry and Parquetry   136

Irish Lace, English Smocking and French Hand-Sewing   138

IRON:

    Architectural   139

    Cast   142

    Hinges   142

    Household   143

    Inlaid and Whitesmithing   145

    Nails and Latches   147

    Southwestern Colonial   148

    Tools, Locks and Cooking Utensils   150

Jerga Weavings   *See* Embroidery, *Colcha, and* Weaving, Rio Grande

JEWELRY:

    African-American   151

    Plains Indian   152

Kapa Cloth   153

Knifework   *See* Carving, Tramp Art

KNITWEAR:

    Qiviut Yarn   155

    Wool   156

KNIVES:

    Bowie   158

    Southern Mountain   159

Kraslice   *See* Eggs, Decorated

Lace and Netting   160

    See also Bed Coverings, Knotted *and* Irish Lace, English Smocking and French Hand-Sewing

Latches   *See* Iron, Nails and Latches

LEATHER:

    Brain-tanned Hides   161

    Cowboy and Western Boots   163

    Historic Reproductions   164

    Period Footwear   166

    Rawhide Bosals, Headstalls, Hobbles, Quirts and Ropes   167

Liturgical Gold, Silver and Pewter   169

Makouk   *See* Tatting

Marbles   170

Marquetry   *See* Inlay, Marquetry and Parquetry

Masks   *See* Totem Poles, Masks, Rattles and Dolls

CONTENTS

Moccasins, Beaded   *See* Beadwork

Molds for Baking   171

Murals   173

MUSICAL INSTRUMENTS:

Autoharps   175

Banjos   176

Coffin Guitars   177

Fiddles   178

Hammered Dulcimers   178

Harpsichords   179

Song Bows   180

Stringed Dulcimers   181

Ukeleles   182

Nails   *See* Iron, Nails and Latches

Needlework Tools   183

Netting   *See* Lace and Netting

Notch Art   *See* Carving, Tramp Art

Occhi   *See* Tatting

Oriental Pictures   *See* Tinsel Painting

Oyle Cloth   *See* Floorcloths

Painted Carpet or Canvas   *See* Floorcloths

Painted Grain   *See* Graining

Paper   184

Papercuts, Polish   185

See also Scherenschnitte and Silhouettes

Parquetry   *See* Inlay, Marquetry and Parquetry

Pearl Painting   *See* Tinsel Painting

Petacas   186

PEWTER:

Cast   187

Hand-forged   189

Liturgical Items   *See* Liturgical Gold, Silver and Pewter

Trade Items   190

Pipes, Ceremonial Stone   191

Pisanki   *See* Eggs, Decorated

Pond Models   192

POTTERY:

18th Century Stoneware, Earthenware and Salt-Glaze   194

Jugs, Churns, Pitchers and Ash-glazed   195

New England   197

Painted   198

Piedmont Stoneware and Earthenware   199

Salt-glazed Wares   200

Slip-Painting, Slip-Trailing, Sprigging and Tulipware   201

Slipware and Sgraffito   203

Spongeware and Spatterware   204

Puzzles   205

Pysanky   *See* Eggs, Decorated

Qualla Arts & Crafts   *See* Cherokee Crafts

Quillwork, Native American   207

QUILTS:

Amish   209

Hawaiian   210

Plains Indian Morning Star   212

Traditional American   213

Rakes   215

Rattles   *See* Totem Poles, Masks, Rattles and Dolls

Retablos   *See under* Santos

Reverse Painting   216

See also Graining

Ribbonwork, Native American   217

Rosemaling   218

RUGS:

Braided   220

Crocheted   222

Hooked   223

Ingrain Carpet   225

Navajo   *See under* Weaving

Patched   225

Rag   226

Summer-and-Winter Boundweave   227

Saddles, Western   229

SANTOS:

Bultos   231

Retablos and *Reredos*   234

See also Straw Inlay

Scherenschnitte   236

See also Papercuts, Polish

Schranks *See* Furniture, Country

Screens, Painted   237

Scrimshaw   239

Ship and Boat Replicas   240

Shoes and Boots   *See under* Leather

Shortbread Molds   *See* Molds for Baking

SILHOUETTES:

   Portraits   242

   Scenes   244

Silver, Hand-forged   245

Silver Liturgical Items   *See* Liturgical Gold,
   Silver and Pewter

Skeps   246

Skin-Sewing   247

Sleds   249

Sleighs   249

Smocking   *See* Irish Lace, English Smocking
   and French Hand-Sewing

Snowshoes   250

Song Bows   *See under* Musical Instruments

Spekulaas Molds   *See* Molds for Baking

Spinning and Dyeing   251

Spinning Wheels   253

Springerle Molds   *See* Molds for Baking

Spurs and Bits   253

STENCILING:

   Stenciling and Marbling   255

   Bronze and Gold   257

Stoveplates   *See* Firebacks and Stoveplates

Straw Hats   *See* Wheat-Weaving and Straw Hats

Straw Inlay   257

Tatting   258

Teddy Bears   260

Tepees   261

Theorem Painting   262

Tile   263

TIN:

   Cookie Cutters   264

   Household Items   265

   Lighting Fixtures   266

   Painted   268

   Pierced   269

   Southwestern   270

Tinsel Painting   272

Tomahawks   273

Totem Poles, Masks, Rattles and Dolls   275

Toys   277

   See also Gameboards *and* Puzzles

Tramp Art   *See under* Carving

Treenware   278

Trunks   *See* Petacas

Ukeleles   *See under* Musical Instruments

Utensils, Cooking   *See* Iron, Inlaid, and
   Whitesmithing *and* Iron Tools, Locks and
   Cooking Utensils

Vehicles, Horse-drawn   280

Wagons, Sheepherder   281

Wallpaper   282

Weathervanes   283

WEAVING:

   Cotton, Silk and Wool   285

   Household Linens   287

   Jacquard   288

   Linen, Ticking, Linsey-Woolsey and
      Calamanco   289

   Navajo   291

   Norwegian-American   293

   Overshot Coverlets   294

   Rio Grande   296

   Table Linens   297

   See also Crochet

Western Silver and Gold   299

Whalebone Carving   *See* Carving, Alaskan
   and Scrimshaw

Wheat-Weaving and Straw Hats   300

Whips   302

Wooden Molds   *See* Molds for Baking *and*
   Iron, Cast

Wycinanka   *See* Papercuts, Polish

Additional Resources State by State Who Sell
   Traditional American Crafts   305

Acknowledgments   329

Index   331

Foreword

Crafts of America will be controversial. The consumer will use and treasure the book. Research scholars may well be concerned about its impact on folk traditions. On the positive side, it should become a standard reference for four large and growing constituencies in our nation: collectors of folk art and craft, occasional craft purchasers who value the handwrought object, people restoring historic homes and seeking particular handcrafted items or the services of skilled craftsworkers and dealers in crafts and antiques who are ever seeking new sources. These will find the book a fascinating compendium of cultural data and present-day craftsworkers. On the other hand, some of my colleagues in folklore will point to the need to protect the traditional craftsworker, perhaps correctly. However, for the craftsworker whose livelihood depends on demand for his/her skills, the increased, better informed constituency which promises to develop from the availability of this unique reference work may well bring the additional revenue decisive to long-range continuity of waning traditions. History supports this optimistic position.

For thousands of years the arts and crafts of preindustrial societies have flourished because a nurturing bond existed between the creative endeavor of artisan craftsworkers and the strength and continuity inherent in the traditional community. The decline of direct contact with the traditional community, whose patronage for centuries shaped the esthetic and design values of the craftsworker, has been decisive. This more than any other single factor has influenced the craftsworker whose need to survive affects what is produced. Once the link to community is gone, other esthetic and economic systems come into play.

Each year fewer of the world's communities continue their dependency on local craftsworkers, as corporate interests reach into towns and villages, seeking new markets for their mass-produced merchandise. "The popular object has been accepted by the innovative individual because it saves him time, is more quickly produced or bought, and is easier to use than the traditional object—and also because it is new," Henry Glassie observes in *Pattern in Material Folk Culture of the Eastern United States*. Corporate self-interest combines with societal pressures influencing people in developing areas of the world to abandon tradition in the name of economic advancement. Gradually, the craftsworker seeks markets further and further afield. Some go on the road, selling to commercial establishments or through craft markets and fairs. They may depend on various kinds of catalog sales and direct mail orders. The role of crafts societies and government recognition has been important in supporting both the esthetic values and the economic viability of crafts globally. For more than a century, intellectuals on several continents who are concerned with cultural conservation have addressed this issue.

Van Wyck Brooks commented on the significance of American esthetic tradition in his introduction to Constance Rourke's *The Roots of American Culture:* "If this [tradition] could be shown to exist it might make all the difference for the future of our art and all the difference, meanwhile, for the creative worker. What would not our artists gain in maturity and confidence if they felt that they were working in [what Rourke referred to as] 'a natural sequence'?" Seeking the earliest roots of that "natural sequence," Rourke looked back to the crafts of early European settlement on these shores to note: "These arts were largely rural, as the life of the country was largely rural. All were in some sense folk-arts, descending by tradition from forms that had been developed by communal groups living for long in close identity."

Half a century before Rourke advanced these ideas, several independent movements had been launched with the dual purpose of reaffirming the importance of that "natural sequence" and validating the esthetic significance of American folk art and craft. Springing from the philosophy of work and life developed by Britain's Thomas Carlyle, John Ruskin and William Morris, the Boston Society of Arts and Crafts was established in 1897 under the chairmanship of Harvard professor and Ruskin correspondent Charles Eliot Norton. Committed to "beauty combined with usefulness," the Society was based on the British model which Morris had founded in 1888, as we learn from Allen Eaton's *Handicrafts of New England.* The success of the Boston group's exhibitions and education programs led to a national movement which laid the basis for the handicraft movement as we know it today. For the Boston organization's tenth anniversary, the National League of Handicraft Societies was formed in 1907. This ultimately grew to involve thirty-three states. It was dedicated to the circulation of craft libraries and lecturers, maintenance of a central reference library and publication of the magazine *Handicraft.* Next came the rural craft documentation and revival movements which gave rise to enduring institutions like the Southern Highland Handicraft Guild and the John C. Campbell Folk School, as well as to important publications like Allen Eaton's regional surveys of rural crafts: *Handicrafts of the Southern Highlands* and the previously mentioned *Handicrafts of New England.*

The American folk art movement and the establishment of the American and finally the World Crafts Council increased publication and exhibition activity, educating the public to the esthetic and functional advantages of traditional and contemporary crafts in today's world.

Beyond the United States, three important philosophical influences on the validation of crafts globally were the British potter Bernard Leach, the Japanese esthetician Soetsu Yanagi and his countryman the noted potter Shoji Hamada. From the post–World War I period into the 1960s, the three men maintained a dialogue focused on the problem of the survival of craftsmanship in an industrial society, or as Leach called it, a "counter Industrial Revolution," in his introduction to Soetsu Yanagi's *The Unknown Craftsman: A Japanese Insight into Beauty.* Not surprisingly their approach was taken from the British example set by Morris and Ruskin.

The first task for Yanagi was to find a word in Japanese to name the tradition he, Leach and Hamada sought to protect. No such word existed. In 1918, he created the word *mingei,* now a standard term. This he defined as "art of the people." Eight years later, the group founded the Japanese Craft Society, the *Mingei-kai;* six years later, in 1931, the magazine *Crafts,* or *Kongei,* was published; and finally, in 1936, the Japanese Folkcraft Museum, or *Mingei-kan,* was established.

Over the years, this trio struggled with the conflict between the need to support the "individual," or designer, craftsman in the face of the eventual disappearance, as they saw it, of the traditional, or folk, craftsman. They came to know the renowned American designer Charles Eames and explored the Scandinavian efforts by examining Skansen, the Swedish folklife museum, and the Danish industrial deisgners' approaches. Leach and Hamada toured the post–World War II United States, teaching and lecturing, as did others concerned with the crafts movement, to extraordinary effect: the pottery movement in the United States is a vigorous one which today boasts 100,000 producing potters. Their theory that the traditional craftsman, whose esthetic they revered, would eventually disappear to be replaced by the "individual," or artist, craftsman prompted Leach to write in the introduction to *The Unknown Craftsman:* "We can relate the work of the individuals to the magnificent communal creations of unknown, humble and usually illiterate artisans of past ages and draw inspiration from them." At the same time, Yanagi's subtle mind was concerned with his belief that contemporary artists and craftsmen were "overproud." With characteristic wisdom, he asserted in *The Unknown Craftsman,* "Take heed of the humble; be what you are by birthright; there is no room for arrogance." Throughout their 50-year collaboration, Leach, Hamada and Yanagi tested their theory, set in place lasting institutions like the *Mingeikan* and enriched the world crafts movement on both practical and philosophical levels.

Based on the work of this remarkable trio, Japan was the first nation to enact legislation to preserve traditional crafts. The Cultural Properties Protection Law of 1950 designates a particular craft as an "intangible cultural property" and honors individual highly skilled craftsworkers by naming them "Living National Treasures." The recipients receive government stipends to aid in improvement of techniques as well as to free them to train successors. The government Cultural Agency sponsors training programs and exhibitions to maintain a high level of public awareness and understanding of standards and to bring high status to crafts professions in the interest of encouraging the young to enter them.

Government recognition in other countries takes different forms. Concerned with the maintenance of high esthetic and technical standards, the Hungarians, in the post–World War II years, pinpointed the lack of interaction between folk craftsworkers and their own regional cultural communities as the problem. This they attributed to the interposition of middlemen in the marketing process as the demands for crafts shifted from local to urban-based consumers. Their approach, though not legislative, was similar in a practical sense to that taken by the Japanese. As explained by Gyorgy Domanovsky in *Hungarian Pottery,* since the early 1950s Hungary has annually awarded a Master's of Folk Arts to selected peasants in four categories: weaving, pottery, embroidery and general crafts. Working with cooperatives, these master craftsworkers train others to become "professional folk artists" in what the Hungarians now call "popular applied art."

In the United States, the National Endowment for the Arts, through its Folk Arts Program, established the Heritage Fellowship Awards in 1982. The program receives nominations annually from the U.S. public at large. These are reviewed first by the Folk Arts Advisory Panel and then by the National Council for the Arts. Senior artisans, musicians and dancers who have been selected are then brought to the nation's capital where tribute is paid at three events: first a Congressional reception, then a banquet and finally a performance before a live audience where each recipient speaks of major esthetic and philosophical influences. This performance is nationally broadcast over the public radio network. The chairman of the National Endowment for the Arts presents a certificate of tribute and honorarium to each fellowship award honoree. The National Heritage Fellowship Award program has awakened new interest in the regional folk cultural traditions of the United States by bringing national attention to exceptional craft and performance practitioners. Among the Heritage Fellowship Award recipients included in this book are: Bertha Cook (knotted spreads), George T. Lopez (*bultos*), Lanier Meaders (pottery), and Genevieve Mougin (lace).

In the light of this history, folklorists across the nation seriously concerned with the stewardship of traditional arts and their finest practitioners have an obligation to test the approach, factual content and impact on their cultural constituencies of Constance Stapleton's *Crafts of America*. The National Endowment's network of state folklorists needs to be vigilant on the regional level. Professionals at the American Folklife Center at the Library of Congress, the Arts Endowment and the Smithsonian Institution, concerned with the impact of policy on practice at the national level, are in a position to evaluate this book from both accuracy and policy perspectives. Some of the traditions and craftsworkers listed here are of no interest to the folklorist. But the author has developed reasonable criteria for inclusion, and these need not coincide with those of a folklorist. Clearly, much of what is here is important to folklorists who are concerned with material culture through either their research or their public sector responsibilities. It is these professionals, perhaps more than any others, who can help to determine whether the approach taken in a cultural catalog of this kind constitutes a risk worth taking.

Historians of folk art, collectors, dealers, craftsworkers themselves and, of course, the folklorists might all consider writing directly to *Crafts of America*, c/o Editorial Department, Harper & Row, 10 East 53 Street, New York, NY 10022. Let the publisher know:

nominations of crafts or craftspeople who should be included in future editions
where factual errors need correction
the reasons why a craftsworker included here should be left out in future editions
the book's impact on sales or customer attitudes
suggestions for restructuring the book to make it more useful

This suggestion has been discussed with the publisher because it is essential to consider the very real possibility that this book may well have the decisive affirmative educational impact of some of the strategies already tested in other nations as well as our own. If this proves to be the case, the book has the potential for service as another plank in a platform designed to strengthen and support the craft heritage which many of us agree forms the baseline of our nation's esthetic tradition and, as Rourke suggested, clearly is part of its "natural sequence."

If the book proves effective, and we all have a responsibility to participate in the judgment of that issue, the publisher should provide an improved and updated edition periodically, for *Crafts of America* can serve as a standard reference, an important economic and educational stimulus and a cultural catalog of signal importance and utility.

Ralph Rinzler

Smithsonian Institution
Washington, DC
January 1988

Introduction

If you wanted to find the best handmade cowboy hat in America, where would you start? At the library? Chances are you wouldn't find the subject in the card catalog (although the cowboy hat has become a worldwide symbol for freedom). At a craft fair? Top makers don't have to leave home to find business. How about a rodeo? Great idea, but how will you know which hat is best? Even if you see one that suits *you,* how will you find its maker so that you can order your own?

Multiply cowboy hats by several hundred crafts and several thousand makers and you will understand the challenges encountered in finding the best makers of traditional American crafts.

America's crafts, like its population, are rich in diversity. They are more available and more affordable than American antiques and art, and their value is appreciating rapidly, yet although there are national guides to antiques, inns and historic sites and homes, until now there has been no practical guide explaining what American crafts are and the traditions behind them. More than just Anglo-colonial crafts, which many have come to think of as traditional, American crafts also include native, buckaroo, ethnic and regional. Most included here—crafts like cowboy hats and boots, cornhusk dolls, tepees, tomahawks and banjos—are uniquely American. Others—like crewel embroidery, painted graining and Polish paper-cutting—have developed uniquely American characteristics. Some—Indian and Hawaiian featherwork, Alaskan carving and totem poles—evolved from spiritual traditions, while others—American, Amish, Hawaiian and Indian Morning Star quilts—created traditions all their own.

To the casual observer, *kapa, Chilkat, kachina, colcha, concha, bulto, mukluk, retablo, santo, Scherenschnitte* and *jerga* may not sound American, but they are. Most evolved from need: at first, the need to survive; later a need to make useful things beautiful; and in more recent years, the need to preserve tradition as well as to make or own a handmade object in a predominantly mass-produced world. The knowledge to create traditional American crafts, passed from one generation to the next, continues to enrich lives and communities, culturally, environmentally *and* economically. Small wonder that the word *craft,* rooted in the Teutonic *kraft,* originally meant "strength and power."

Criteria for Selection

To find the best traditional craftspeople in the United States, we decided to start at the top. We sent letters to experts in each field: directors and curators of museums, national parks, restorations, cooperatives, guilds, tribal museums, foundations, ethnic societies, the Smithsonian Institution, the American Folklife Center at the Library of Congress, national and state art councils, educators, collectors, artisans and editors of craft publications (see Acknowledgments) asking what crafts should be included and which makers were best. As nominations arrived, we mailed thousands of letters to craftspeople in all fifty states, asking for photos and slides of work; information regarding processes, materials, methods, finishes; and personal background, like how they came to their craft, why they continue and what they like best about what they do.

The response was overwhelming in quality and enthusiasm as well as in number: an average of twenty applications for each major craft, more for popular items like Windsor chairs. Some categories, like weaving, forged iron and tinsmithing, had so many qualified professionals that we decided to divide each medium into specialties so that more of the history, techniques and regional differences could be explored.

We soon discovered that the best craftspeople had much in common. Rather than resting on their reputations, they continued to search for: greater perfection within the parameters of their traditions; better methods, tools and finishes; historic details that would further unlock secrets of the past; and ways to pass on what they learned through apprenticeship programs, community education and publishing. The best were also quick to give others credit, even when it meant recommending someone whose work they considered better than theirs. But most exciting were the culture-bearing stories they told, like why cowboys wear spurs, why cowboy boots have pointy toes and underslung heels, why tepees face east, how the Kentucky rifle got its name, why Navajo weavers include spirit lines in their borders, why the American clipper could outrace any ship afloat, even how to tell where cowboys are from by the cut, shape and crease of their hats. That's when we decided that *Crafts of America* should be told through the words as well as the work of the best makers.

Because traditional crafts have traditions of shape, material and method, some candidates took themselves out of the running with their answers: basket makers who did not start a basket by chopping down a tree if that was the tradition; broom makers who didn't grow their own broomcorn; furniture makers who no longer used traditional tools. However, some crafts, like quilt-making, encompass as wide a range of traditions as types. For instance, American quilts are traditionally pieced and quilted by hand using traditional patterns, but Indian Morning Star quilt designs are never duplicated and are stitched on a sewing machine, a status symbol among makers. Hawaiian quilts, on the other hand, are made from folded material instead of scraps, which is why they resemble Polish papercuts, which are made from folded paper.

For some craftspeople, natural-born storytellers like Texans Bill Brett (see Horsehair Twisting) and Bill Bell (*Conchas*), the answers came easy; others, accustomed to letting their work speak for them, required months of interviews to arrive at what now appear to be simple answers. Bill Day sent a recording of song-bow music to make sure we could describe the sound accurately. When whip maker Curly Dekle couldn't put what he wanted to say in writing, he sent a tape full of stories about old-time rodeos and the days when Florida was open range.

Selecting the best rosemaler was easy: Karen Jensen was nominated by several experts, and her photos, slides and answers confirmed their praise. In other categories, like Shaker furniture, where several makers seemed equally proficient, we contacted experts once again to make sure the final decision was the right one.

Organization

Crafts of America is a sampler, written in easy-to-understand terms and told in the words of the makers whenever possible.

The book was initially organized by regions, but when this resulted in overlapping and repetition, it was reorganized by medium. This was the easiest approach for an author intent on telling a story from beginning to end, but not for readers intent on finding a single object like the cowboy hat. The last and final solution, organization by objects in alphabetical order with some media, like baskets, furniture, iron and tin, grouped for continuity, plus an index for easy reference, seemed the best approach.

To save space in the text, we devised codes for information common to most entries and listed them after the telephone number. Translation of code letters is as follows:

V = visitors welcome
R = retail
W = wholesale
C = catalog or brochure
S = shop
CC = credit cards accepted
MO = mail order

For more explicit terms on any of the above, please contact the craftsperson.

Prices are included for convenience only, and like everything else in life are subject to change with increases in material costs and the cost of living. Always confirm the price before placing an order.

Because the major craftsperson was the best of the best, runners-up were often almost as good, which is why we included them as Other Makers at the end of each entry. When a subject like Alaskan baskets contained so many varieties that each could not be explained through a single maker, we listed the makers at the end of the entry. In several instances, where makers traditionally sell through a cooperative or tribal museum (like the Hopi and Cherokee Indians) the outlet became the window for the subject. Secondary entries, shorter than major but just as important, are used to explain facets of a craft. At the end of the book is a state-by-state listing of additional sources, shops, galleries and tribal museums that specialize in traditional crafts.

Americans are a very mobile society, so despite our best efforts some of the addresses and telephone numbers may have changed since we went to press. If the address is no longer current try contacting the Postmaster at the maker's post office for a new address.

Since the 1960s, as Americans have become increasingly aware of the importance of quality in the environment and in the home, they have developed a new appreciation for tradition, history, handmade objects and the need to preserve the best of today for tomorrow. Nothing exemplifies this desire more personally than crafts.

Handmade crafts speak to the senses. Pick up a hand-turned pot and you can feel the hand of the maker in yours. Touch a hand-woven blanket and it responds. Follow the sun as it caresses hand-blown glass, transforming a room into a kaleidoscope of color, and you'll know what I mean.

INTRODUCTION

Traditional American crafts are cause for celebration. With one foot planted firmly in reality and the other reaching for the ideal plane, American artisans have, in their quest for excellence, created objects whose spirit and quality burst the boundaries of tradition and give new meaning to "Made in America."

If you want to believe that excellence is alive and well in America, read on.

CRAFTS OF AMERICA

Aklæ Weaving   *See* Weaving, Norwegian-American

Autoharps   *See under* Musical Instruments

Banjos   *See under* Musical Instruments

ADIRONDACK BASKETS

William B. "Bill" Smith grew up the youngest of ten children near Colton, New York, where his parents owned a small farm.

"My father worked in the woods," says Bill, "while my mother and the rest of us took care of the farm. We did everything the old way with horses and hand tools; raised, hunted, fished and trapped our own food. Indians from St. Regis Reservation used to come to our house to cut black ash trees, pounding them with a head axe, then separating the annual rings to make pack and clothes baskets. From the time I was a small boy until I was about 15 years old, I'd follow them around, getting in the way."

Bill married young, worked in construction and trapped in the winter. But the packbaskets he was buying "weren't made right," he says. "The splints were so thin that my traps kept going through the bottom. I told my wife, Sal, I could make a better basket, but she didn't believe it. So I cut down a tree and made four baskets to prove I could. People saw me making them on the front lawn and bought them as fast as they were finished. I've been making them ever since."

On his way to becoming a legend, Bill has been featured

Assortment of packbaskets: apple basket, diamond swirl basket and pineapple basket by Bill Smith

in *National Geographic* and on several television programs. His baskets, now made by the whole family, are sold in shops in the North Country of the Adirondacks and at the Museum of American Folk Art in New York.

"We use white and green ash for the standards," says Bill, "brown and black ash for the wrappers that go around the basket and white ash for parts that have to be strong, like the rims." Black and green ash are found in swampy areas, while white and brown grow on higher ground. "I look for trees 12 inches across the stump," he says, "with a trunk 10 to 12 feet long. Sometimes I chop a small cut on the north side to make sure the rings aren't too thin. If they're just right on the north, they're thicker on the south. If ash dries on the log, it can't be used, so we bring the tree home and lay it in the pond to soak. Then we pound it with a head axe. Pounding causes friction, which lifts the yearly ring and separates it from the tree. The splints are stored away in rolls and later soaked when it's time to use them."

Earlier Indians used rawhide or the inner bark of the basswood to make harness for the baskets, "but when I was growing up," says Bill, "they used webbing." His packbaskets are available with standard twill harness in 12- to 18-inch sizes (for $30 to $45) with the hard bottoms and cleats preferred by trappers; with regular harness, they range from 14 inches at $38 to 20 inches at $48; and in 18 inches with leather harness, $75. The Smith family also makes square and rectangular clothes baskets ($35 to $40), covered clothes hampers wrapped with bark ($45 and $60), melon baskets ($25 to $40), apple baskets ($40) and small Indian baskets with pineapple and diamond swirl designs woven into their sides ($25). The best way to break in any of the above is to sign up Bill as guide on a canoeing, hunting, fishing or hiking trip. You'll not only learn more than you ever knew about animal signs, tracks, trees, fish and birds, but you'll be entertained by one of the best storytellers in the Adirondacks.

Bill and Sal Smith
Smith's Adirondack Crafts
RFD 1
Colton, NY 13625
(315) 262-2436
V R S MO

Other Makers

Liana Haubrick, Streeter Road, Lempster, NH 03606; (603) 863-2758, makes 2½- by 1½-foot packbaskets with hand-woven straps.

J. A. Tomah, P.O. Box 1006, Houlton, ME 04730; (207) 532-6054.

ALASKAN BASKETS

Alaskan baskets, among the most beautiful in the world, have been called "songs made visible." Created from grass, roots and bark and used as tools for gathering, storing and preparing food, they were traditionally made by women, the gatherers. Men traditionally worked harder materials like whale baleen and ivory.

Baleen, the sievelike extension of the upper gum in plankton-eating whales, was once used for utensils, scoops and sled runners, shaved into boot insulation and split as fine as thread for knotting nets. When Yankee traders began buying baleen for products like corset stays, umbrella ribs and fishing rods, its value rose to $5 a pound, but as demand declined, baleen plummeted in price until a trader asked a man from Barrow to copy a willow root basket in baleen. The Barrow man did, breaking the age-old tradition that only women made baskets, and creating a basket unique to Alaska.

Similar in texture to human fingernails, fresh baleen is softened by soaking in water. It is then split into wide, narrow, round or flat rods, which are scraped to create shape and gloss, then stored in a cool place to prevent cracking. Baleen cannot be coiled small enough to start

Tray woven of split willow roots by Rita Young

when the sap begins to run. The roots are stripped, carved and hung to season and bleach. After weaving, baskets are decorated with dyed grasses and stems of maidenhair fern in a form of surface entwining called "false embroidery" because designs appear only on the exterior surface.

The strong geometric designs of the coiled willow root baskets made by Athabascans of the interior are woven directly into the coils. These baskets are fashioned from deciduous willow roots gathered in the spring from trees not more than 15 feet tall. The roots are split, scraped of bark, polished and bleached for the basket and dyed for the design.

Aleutian Island natives also decorate with false embroidery, but of silk floss instead of grass, and on baskets made of grass instead of roots. After gathering wild grasses in late summer, Aleuts hang them to dry to prevent mildew, then split each blade, sometimes as fine as thread, before making baskets in a twining technique that sometimes has as many as 1,300 stitches per inch.

Baleen baskets

a basket, which is why makers use a center core of ivory with holes along the outer edge through which strips of baleen are pulled. Woven in single-rod coiling in three variations: a spaced stitch weave with visible rods and close-stitch wide and narrow wefts. Baleen baskets are most often round with a lidded top crowned with a three-dimensional sculpture of an animal or bird. Sometimes they are decorated with contrasting bands of light baleen or opaque bird quills.

The finely twined baskets of southeastern tribes (the Tlingit, Haida and Tsimshian Indians) are made with young, pliable spruce roots dug by hand in the spring

Aleut basket by Nadesta Galley

2

Grass baskets made by Yupik Eskimos are coiled, sewn and decorated with dyed grass, fabric, animal parts (such as bird's feet and bird's bills) or dried seal gut exposed over the coil in squared designs created by overcasting. Larger coil baskets made on Nelson Island are started with a larger bundle of grass, while the smaller coil grass baskets from Hooper Bay are often as finely woven as baskets made by the Aleuts.

Sewn coil grass basket with dyed seal gut design by Mary Black

"The Eskimos also make lovely open-weave, loosely woven utility baskets, which are worn on the back while gathering murre eggs from the cliffs or used to carry fish," says Sharon Hobart of the Alaska Native Medical Center Craft Shop.

Birchbark baskets, made in regions where birches grow, were originally used to gather berries and carry water. After dampening to make it pliable, the bark is folded into square and oval shapes, which are joined with stripped willow root in an overcast stitch.

Baleen baskets as small as 4 inches wide begin at $400; root, from $300 to $600; grass, $200 to $800; and gut from $200 to $350.

Makers

BALEEN
Greg Tagarook, Point Hope, AK 99766.
Elaine and Alex Frankson, Point Hope, AK 99766.

BIRCHBARK
Katherine Cleveland, Ambler, AK 99786.
Edna Deacon, Grayling, AK 99590.
Belle Deacon, General Delivery, Grayling, AK 99590.

SPRUCE ROOT
Delores Churchhill, Box 5091, Ketchikan, AK 99901.

ALEUT
Agnes Thompson, Anchorage, AK 99502.

Margaret Lokanin, 1627 West 32nd Avenue, Anchorage, AK 99503.
Arlene Skinner, Kodiak, AK 99615.
Martha Matfay, Box 12, Old Harbor, AK 99643.
Gertrude Svarney, Box 197, Unalaska, AK 99685.

SMALL COIL GRASS
Cecilia Olson, Lena Smith, Anna Smart, Mary Friday, all of Hooper Bay, AK 99604.

LARGE COIL GRASS
Emma Isackson, Barbara Albert, both of Tununak, AK 99681.

SEAL GUT
Anna Beavers, Goodnews Bay, AK 99589.
Molly Pavila, Kipnuk, AK 99614.

BASKETS OF THE AMANA COLONIES

The Community of True Inspiration, or Amana as it was later known, started in Germany as a religious community whose members combined their worldly possessions, rented estates in the Province of Hesse, then set out to become self-sustaining by farming the land and making their own goods.

In 1842, four men were sent to America, where they bought land near Buffalo, New York, and set up six villages. Twelve years later, another group of four were sent westward to buy additional land 20 miles west of Iowa City, Iowa, where they established the Amana Colonies of seven villages. Each village had its own craftspeople, who made wagons, harnesses, furniture, fabric, kitchen utensils and baskets.

Their basket-weaving had all but disappeared in 1977 when Philip Dickel, a retired woolen mill employee who had learned the craft as a young man, showed Joanna Schanz how to grow willows and make the traditional Amana Colonies baskets.

"My husband and I had started a broom and basket shop in West Amana," explains Joanna. "When I asked Philip if he would tell me something about the Amana willow baskets, he said he would do better and show me. He gave me shoots to start a new patch, taught me how to harvest, sort the willows and make baskets. Each year from then on he helped with the harvesting and sorting until he passed away in 1981. I still feel his presence when I sit down and weave."

Cultivated black willows have more wood, making them stronger than wild willows, which have a higher percentage of moisture. Each Amana village had its own willow patch for making baskets, started from slips brought to Iowa from Germany and New York. Joanna picks her willow any time after the leaves fall off and before the buds appear. Green when picked, it eventually turns reddish brown. When peeled, it is white but mellows with age to a light brown or beige. Early basket weavers took their willow to the Middle Woolen Mill (the present-day Amana Refrigeration plant) and boiled it in huge vats of boiling water to peel off the bark, but Joanna does hers at home.

"My family is very understanding about my basket-weaving passion," she says. "They tolerate willows in the basement and in the water tanks, as well as my constant pursuit of wild willows along the roadside."

A unique feature of the traditional willow basket made in the Amana Colonies is its replaceable bottom rim. After a basket is woven, but before the handle is added, the basket is flipped over and a rim is woven on the bottom outside edge. This rim protects the bottom by taking the abuse of everyday wear and, when damaged or worn out, can be removed and replaced, extending the life of the basket. The apple-picking basket is unusual because its two handles are next to each other so that it can be worn on a picker's belt, freeing hands to reach the fruit. A large S hook can also be looped through the handles to hang the basket from a tree branch. A smaller version, the strawberry picker, is used in the same way.

For contrast and decoration, Joanna weaves wild and cultivated willow in various combinations into her baskets, and in the spring adds dogwood, lilac, mock orange, honeysuckle or other vines that she feels will add pleasing texture or color. Each spring and fall she teaches basket-weaving classes that begin with students picking willows

Round willow basket inverted to show removable rim

and end, after 12 to 14 hours of work, with completed baskets.

In addition to filling special orders, she repairs baskets and wicker furniture and works with her husband, Norman, a fifth generation woodworker, in the Schanz furniture business. The Schanz family has also revived the craft of Amana Colonies brooms, which come in many shapes and sizes including the famous West Amana side-liner whisk broom. Baskets range from $15 to $100, while brooms sell for $3 to $12.50.

Joanna E. Schanz
Old Broom and Basket Shop
West Amana, IA 52357
(319) 622-3315
V   R   W   C   S   MO

Coiled Rye Baskets *See* **Skeps**

LOW-COUNTRY SEA GRASS BASKETS

In the late 17th century, English plantation owners in the low country of South Carolina knew little about rice cultivation. In introducing this new crop, they depended on slaves for expertise as well as labor. Although in bondage, African-Americans in the region were highly self-sufficient. They grew their own food, built their own homes and taught their masters how to clean and winnow rice after it was hulled.

The baskets they made for the job, winnowing trays nearly 2 feet wide called "fanners," were used to separate

Joan Liffring-Zug

Apple picker, willow basket of the Amana Colonies by Joanna E. Schanz

the rice from the chaff. Made of black rush (also known as bullrush or needlegrass), bound with white oak splits or strips of palmetto butt, coiled and sewn with an interlocking stitch, baskets were produced in various shapes and sizes for agriculture, household and church needs, but not sold commercially until the 20th century.

"The baskets were called Gullah by the media, but not by the makers," explains Dale Rosengarten, author of *Row Upon Row, Sea Grass Baskets of the South Carolina Lowcountry,* the catalog of an exhibit of the same name organized by the McKissick Museum at the University of South Carolina. "Gullah is the name for the English-African creole language spoken by low-country blacks. In the past, some basket makers resented the term because they felt it implied they were backward. The term *sea grass* was current early in this century when the Sea Grass Basket Co. began buying baskets for resale."

Low-country baskets, one of America's oldest African-American crafts and considered by many the most noteworthy, are sold today at more than sixty family-owned stands along a 7-mile stretch of U.S. Highway 17 in Mt. Pleasant, in Charleston's Old City Market and the "Four Corners of the Law," at the intersection of Meeting and Broad Streets in Charleston. "Low country is an appropriate name for the baskets," says Ms. Rosengarten, "because the materials from which they are made, bullrush, sweetgrass and palmetto, are species from the tidewater region."

In the 1800s, Mt. Pleasant basket makers began making "show" baskets of sweetgrass, decorated with longleaf pine needles and sewn with split palmetto leaf cut from the center or heart of the Sabal palmetto (also called the cabbage palm). The butt, or stalk, of the palmetto frond from the low-growing saw palmetto (used by old-style makers, especially on the Sea Islands), though stronger, is less flexible and thus more difficult to prepare and is used today only by a handful of survivors of the Sea Island tradition. Bullrushes, originally found only in work baskets, are now used by Mt. Pleasant basket makers in the more delicate and decorative show baskets for added strength and variety.

Traditionally, the men gather the grasses (light-colored sweetgrass and thicker, darker bullrush) and women do the weaving. Started by tying an overhand knot in the center of a thick bundle of grass, the basket is built row upon row, each row of coil sewn onto the one before it with a strip of palmetto. A space for the binder to pass through the bundle is made with an awl-like tool called a bone, once the rib of an animal, but now more likely to be a teaspoon handle, a nail with a flattened end or occasionally part of a pair of scissors, an icepick, nailfile or

pocketknife. Started with a round or oblong base, the coil is pulled inward to build the side wall of the basket with pine-needle knots and secondary coils added for decoration. Baskets once carried on the head now have a wide variety of handles for carrying by hand. In addition to clothes hampers and sewing baskets, new forms in openwork, in-and-out baskets, covered cake trays and vases have been added.

Darcy Wingfield and McKissick Museum, University of South Carolina, Columbia, SC

Washpot basket by Mary Vanderhorst

Low-country baskets range in price from $2 to $5 for small items like Christmas ornaments and $20 to $80 for medium-sized baskets to hundreds of dollars for larger sizes. The highest price paid to date: $2,000 for a basket by Mary Jackson, now on display at the Charleston Airport.

Makers

Mary A. Jackson, 55 Cypress Street, Charleston, SC 29403; (803) 723-3229.

Mary Mazyck, 2189 Rifle Range Road, Mt. Pleasant, SC 29464; (803) 884-7155.

Henrietta Snype and her young daughter Latrelle, 1727 Highway 17 North, Mt. Pleasant, SC 29464; (803) 884-6978.

Annabell Ellis, 478 Egypt Street, Mt. Pleasant, SC 29464; (803) 884-0456.

Blanche Watts, 2726 Rifle Range Road, Mt. Pleasant, SC 29464; (803) 884-3895.

Mary V. Vanderhorst, 1721 Rifle Range Road, Mt. Pleasant, SC 29464; (803) 884-9807.

Lummi Indian Baskets

Although cedar bark is the main ingredient in their baskets, Lummi Indians also use bear grass, nettle fibers, cedar roots, wild cherry bark, cedar limbs, split cedar, fern roots, sweetgrass and rye grass. Each spring, Fran and Bill James visit logging areas to strip cedar bark from felled trees and dark cherry bark from trunks. Dried bear grass, which grows in the mountains, is used for decoration and in smaller baskets. It turns white after it's dried, as does reef net grass, grown locally. The Jameses wear long-sleeved garments and gloves when they gather nettle stalks, whose threadlike fibers are almost impossible to break.

Lummi Indian basket by Fran and Bill James

"Our people used to make string from nettle fibers or cedar bark for nets used in salmon fishing," says Fran. "We use the same string as weavers in our baskets. Overlapping strips of cedar bark are secured with nettle fibers, the top ends turned down around the lip and fastened." Most weavers use patterns that become their signatures. Fran's is an *X* of nettle fibers. Prices begin at $22.50. 4339 Lummi Shore Road, Ferndale, WA 98248; (206) 384-5292. V R W

MAINE BASKETS

The traditional Maine baskets made by Stephen Zeh are as practical and sturdy as the state that bred them. Made of supple, close-grained brown ash with hand-carved and bent rims and handles, they were created to do specific jobs well.

His potato basket's square handle, with a center thicker than its ends, has gentle curves in each corner just right for human hands. "In times past, handles were heavy enough for sitting so that workers could rest while picking," Stephen explains. "And when the basket was full and too heavy to carry, it could be dragged along the ground. Replaceable heavy splints called runners or shoes protect the bottom of the basket from wear."

His feather basket has a square handle as well, but a delicate one, more suitable to its task and load. Used by early settlers to hold the down as it was plucked from ducks and geese to make pillows and quilts, the basket has a cover that slides up the handle while feathers are put into the basket and drops of its own weight, freeing the hands for plucking.

His egg basket's swing handle drops onto the rim, where it is out of the way while gathering eggs and saves space in storage. Its sensuous "kick-up" bottom keeps eggs in the middle from getting crushed by distributing the weight of its contents outward. It's doubly strong because it has a double bottom made of two sets of eight uprights woven separately, then together, to form sixteen sets, or thirty-two uprights. It's lightweight and delicate looking, yet solid as a rock.

All of Stephen's baskets are made of brown ash, which has become increasingly difficult to find. "Many are dying from blight," says Stephen. "Growth rings of the last 5 to 10 years are too thin. Only one brown ash in a hundred is straight enough for a basket tree." Most are found on low ground near swamps and streams.

"When I get the tree home," he explains, "I peel the bark, then pound the entire length of its surface four or five times. This causes the fibers between the growth layers to be crushed and allows the growth layers to separate. Four to seven of these layers, 4 to 10 feet long, are torn off the log to produce rough splints, which are graded for weight and cut to width. The splints are smoothed by scraping with a drawknife, which produces a mellow finish with a pleasant wood grain effect. The finest are smoothed on both sides, then split again, producing a tough, flexible splint.

Joseph Dankowski

Swing-handle egg basket by Stephen Zeh

"Handles and rims use the same kind of wood, but it isn't pounded. The log is split in half with wooden wedges, then quartered, and the heartwood split out with a froe [a cleaving tool with a heavy blade at a right angle to the handle]. This piece is split again with the froe, then the sides of the piece are carved square with a drawknife on a shaving horse. This square stick [a radial section of the log with top and bottom parallel to the growth rings] is then split along the growth rings to form rough pieces for rims and handles, which are smoothed with a drawknife, carved, bent to final shape and dried." The result is a beautiful handle, made in the way of the old-time Maine basket maker, with the grain of the wood unbroken along its outer surface and what appear from the side to be neatly stacked layers of wood.

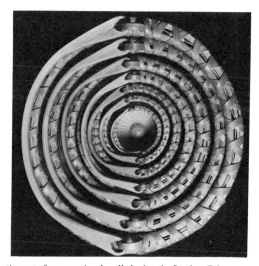

Nesting set of seven swing-handle baskets by Stephen Zeh

A trapper and outdoorsman, Stephen first taught himself how to make packbaskets for his own use, and later learned how to prepare materials and work with wood from Eddie Newell, a Penobscot Indian. Today, with his wife, Tammy, he makes baskets full time. The Maine potato basket is $325; the swing-handle egg basket in seven nesting sizes from 3- to 14-inch diameters runs from $195 to $375; and two-handled produce baskets are $289 for the half-bushel and $325 for the bushel. All are guaranteed free from defects in materials and workmanship.

Stephen Zeh, Basketmaker
P.O. Box 381
Temple, ME 04984
(207) 778-2351
R W C ($1) CC MO

NANTUCKET LIGHTSHIP BASKETS

Although similar to baskets made by a colony of Quakers on the mainland, Nantucket lightship baskets, made by men on board the South Shoal lightship 24 miles off Nantucket in the mid-1800s, were fashioned from rattan imported from the Philippines.

Woven on wooden molds in circular or oval shapes in many sizes and in nests of five to eight, the baskets have parts with barrel names like *staves* (vertical splints or ribs), *hoops* (rims) and *bottoms* (wooden boards into whose deep-grooved edge the staves are inserted). Delicate looking but sturdy wooden handles are fastened by "ears" of wood, brass or ivory. In retirement, many sailors continued to make these baskets on land. Over the years a lid was added, allowing baskets to be used as handbags. Woven in the same manner as the bottom, the wooden piece in the top is often decorated with scrimshaw, inlay or a carving made of wood or ivory. In the 1800s, the baskets took a week to make and sold for $2.50. Today they sell for hundreds of dollars and take months from order to delivery.

Nantucket lightship basket by Marilyn and Bill Rosenquist

Marilyn and Bill Rosenquist make traditional Nantucket lightship baskets, beginning by selecting and cutting the wood (pine for the molds, cherry for bases and oak or ash for ribs). Ribs are hand-cut, tapered, sanded and steamed to fit into grooves cut in the base, where they are dried and molded into shape. The basket is woven with rattan from the same tropical supply source used by the first makers, then fit with a rim. Lids made in the same manner as the bottoms are attached with hinges of leather wrapped with cane, and the handle attached with ivory knobs. After the cane is sealed with a fine coat of shellac, the basket is signed, numbered, dated and registered in the owner's name. Open baskets are $85; handbags in two styles are $300 without scrimshaw; also available in nests of seven ranging from 3¾ to 12½ inches in diameter. Scrimshaw decorations for tops are custom-made by Barry and Lisa Simon of Westport, Massachusetts, with cost determined by size and detail.

Marilyn and Bill Rosenquist
342 Moose Hill Road
Guilford, CT 06437
(203) 453-4512
R S MO

Other Makers

Michael Kane, 18½ Sparks Avenue, Nantucket, MA 02554; (617) 228-1548.

Bill and Judy Sayle, Washington Street Extension, Box 1233, Nantucket, MA 02554; (617) 228-9876.

Paul F. Whitten, Franklin Street, Nantucket, MA 02554; (617) 228-2480.

Four Winds Craft Guild, Straight Wharf, Nantucket, MA 02554; (617) 228-9623.

Pomo Indian Baskets

Pomo Indian baskets, considered by many experts to be the most beautiful in the world, are known for their form, design and fine stitchery. Although small, most often from 2 to 4 inches in diameter, they are meticulously made of two- and three-stick coil construction with a warp of willow sticks sewn in place with a weft of sedge root. (Sedge is similar in appearance to grass but has a solid rather than a hollow stem.) Most commonly bowl-shaped, they are decorated with feathers, beads, shells and abalone woven into the construction.

The Pomo weavers, represented by Pacific Western Traders, usually "work on order from collectors or dealers," says Herb Puffer. "Their feathered baskets range in price from $200 to $2,000 although pieces by weavers like Mabel McKay, which may take more than 2 years to make, command higher prices." Pacific Western Traders, P.O. Box 95, 305 Wool Street, Folsom, CA 95630; (916) 985-3851. V R C MO

Close-up of Quail Maiden basket woven in three-rod coiling of sedgeroot over willow sticks, with quail, pheasant and mallard feathers, clam shell disk beads and quail topknots, by Mabel McKay

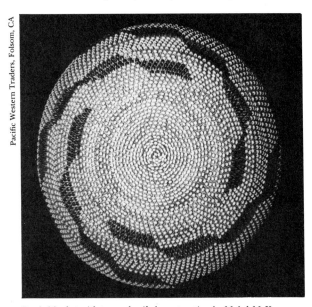

Beaded basket with two-rod coiled construction by Mabel McKay

SHAKER BASKETS

Shakers learned the art of basket-making from the Indians. Their first baskets were large and utilitarian, but as their supply of ash trees diminished, they made smaller and more delicate "fancy" baskets, celebrated for their excellence in construction and design, which were sold in Shaker stores in most communities. As the number of members in their sect declined, basket production ceased for a century until Martha Wetherbee, once resident basket maker of their Canterbury, New Hampshire, village, began making baskets on the original molds. Her hands-on experience coupled with research in the basket collections at Shaker museums enabled her to create remarkably accurate reproductions from old Shaker molds.

She starts with a tree. "The black ash (also known as the brown ash or basket tree)," she explains, "is a particularly unattractive tree that seldom grows straight and is usually found near a free-flowing stream. The ideal basket-making log is about 10 feet tall, 10 to 12 inches in diameter and free of knots. I set the log on the ground, shave off the bark and begin pounding. Using the back of a splitting maul, I strike the log with the same force one would use to split firewood. A 2- or 3-inch-wide section is pounded from one end of the log to the other, each new blow overlapping the previous one. I continue pounding until a year's layer of growth is loosened and can be lifted from the log. After 2 or 3 days of constant effort (and many sore muscles) the 10-foot log is as slender as a sapling and produces enough splints for about thirty baskets.

"For me, the most exciting part of basket-making is the woodworking part, the carving and shaping of hardwood for rims and handles. I carve them from ash or hickory, steam-bend them to shape, then lash them to the body of the basket. The perfect 'handle' tree looks young, tight and vibrant, should be knot-free, from 3 to 8 inches in diameter and cut at chest height."

Shaker baskets were made with simple, clean lines for specific uses. Because fruit seldom spoils or mildews in a ventilated container, the fruit basket ($129) has an arched bottom to allow air to pass through. Hardwood runners

Bottom of carrier basket by Martha Wetherbee

are attached with countersunk brass rivets to the inside and outside of the apple basket ($240), adding rigidity to its sturdy bottom. Heavy-duty baskets or "carriers" ($175) have hardwood runners on the bottom, interlocking at both the center and ends to form a lower framework. This keeps it off the ground, which in turn prevents the bottom from wearing out. The wood chip basket ($215, or $255 lined in leather), originally filled with a day's supply of wood for a Shaker stove, has skates lashed through the bottom with rawhide to keep the wood high and dry. Its handle runs lengthwise instead of across the width, allowing weight to be carried close to the body as a carpenter's box is held.

Other shapes include the Spoon ($85), Kittenhead ($66), Cathead ($85), the lined Deaconess used indoors for light duty ($330) and a nest of three Cat- and Kittenheads ($395). The cheese basket, 6 to 28 inches ($45 to $200), one of the few Shaker baskets not shaped over a mold, is woven freehand in a hexagonal weave of supercoarse brown ash splint.

Unlike the original Shakers, Martha does not expect her supply of ash trees to peter out. She's found that her answer to an unending supply lies in barter: "A basket for a tree is usually an agreeable trade. Converting a tree into baskets also gives a tree a second life because it will be cared for, admired and used for more years than it ever would have alive."

Martha Wetherbee's Basket Shop is usually open 9 A.M. to 5 P.M., Monday through Saturday, but call ahead to be sure.

Martha Wetherbee's Basket Shop
Star Route 35
Sanbornton, NH 03269
(603) 286-8927
V   R   W   C   S   MO

Apple basket by Martha Wetherbee

WESTERN CHEROKEE BASKETS

"Basket-weaving has been practiced by my people, the Cherokees, longer than there has been a recorded history of the United States," Mavis Doering will tell you. "Making baskets in their tradition gives me a feeling of closeness to my people and to the past. Although my baskets are utilitarian, I try to put special meaning into them and make them objects of beauty."

As a small child in eastern Oklahoma, Mavis watched her mother and grandparents make baskets, but she didn't become serious about basket-weaving until 1973 when she took classes sponsored by the Cherokee Nation. In the past decade, her muted-tone baskets decorated with Cherokee symbols, feathers, leather thongs and beads have been exhibited in museums throughout the United States and at the Kennedy Center and the Smithsonian Folklife Festival in Washington and used as Governor's Arts Awards and as promotion for the state in Oklahoma. Although she is now on the Board of Directors of the Indian Arts and Crafts Association of Albuquerque and the National Advisory Council of the Wheelwright Museum of the American Indian of Santa Fe, Mavis still forages for basket and dye materials in the small community of Christie, named for her maternal grandfather.

"There are two types of baskets traditional to my tribe," she says. "Plaited, made from wood splints with designs woven in their patterns, and double-wall wicker weave, made from round reeds like buckbrush (also known as coral- or winterberry) and honeysuckle." Other materials used include white oak and ash splints, cane and cattails.

Reed double-wall basket with mulberry, black walnut hull and black aniline dyes and leather fringes, tin cones and bells by Mavis Doering

Her dyes are also made from plants: blueberries; black walnut, hickory, pecan and almond shells; sassafras root and bark; sumac root and bark; huckleberries; pokeberries; elderberries; bloodroot; wild plum, cherry and peach leaves. Combined with one of several mordants (catalysts used to set the dye and also affect the color) like vinegar, salt, copper sulphate or alum, the dyes are boiled or soaked, then strained and stored in large jars for future use.

Reed and white oak splint double-wall basket with mulberry dye, Stomp Dancer design by Mavis Doering

"When I first started," explains Mavis, "I didn't realize our baskets were so different. All are double-walled and can be straight-walled or round, or round-on-square with a square bottom and round top. We start at the bottom, do the inside, then fold over the ribs and weave the outside wall until it is even with the basket bottom, then weave it into a rim."

Designs include the eagle—"the sacred bird of all Indian people because he soars highest. He faces east, the sacred direction to which ancient Cherokees prayed"; the

White oak splint basket with mulberry and blueberry dyes, Mountain Peaks design by Mavis Doering

turtle—"Legend says that Mother Earth is on the back of a giant turtle. When he moves we have earthquakes, lightning and landslides"; and the Circle of Life—"Indians believe all important things are created in the form of a circle: earth, sun, moon, seasons of the year and hours in a day." The Seven Clans basket is trimmed with leather fringes representing the moons of the year and seven guinea feathers representing the seven Cherokee clans. "Seven was a significant and sacred number," says Mavis. "There were seven counselors to the chief, seven honored women in the government, seven mother towns as clan headquarters and a seven-sided council house. Clan membership is inherited from one's mother and retained for life. Clan members are considered brothers and sisters. My son and I are members of the Wolf clan." Her most popular basket, called the Ganale, which means friend, has circles of people holding hands in friendship. The center of each figure is left undyed. It represents the heart of the Cherokee people reaching out to the people of the world. Prices range from $30 to $400 plus mailing.

Mavis Doering
5918 NW 58th Street
Oklahoma City, OK 73122
(405) 787-6082
R S MO

WHITE OAK BASKETS

Lestel Childress represents the fifth generation making baskets in his family; his wife, Ollie, is the third generation in hers. "We make them the same way they were made in the 19th century," says Ollie, "because as far as we're concerned, there isn't any better way to do it."

In early homes, baskets were made for gathering, storage, measuring, carrying and to barter for other goods. The Childresses' baskets have always been as good as money. Lestel's grandmother, Let Thompson, started her business by sending a basket to a woman whose name she found in the newspaper, with a note saying that if she liked it, she could pay what she thought it was worth in money or used clothing. The woman sent back a bundle of clothing with a thank-you note and the exchanges grew. After she had clothed the town, Lestel's grandmother had enough clothing left over to open a store. Ollie's family traded baskets for groceries. It seemed only natural when they married in the 1940s for Ollie to pay for her wedding dress with a basket. Today, Childress baskets are sold in stores like Marshall Fields, and because of their authenticity, in museum and antique shops as well.

Bushel feed basket with heartwood decorative trim by Lestel and Ollie Childress

"White oak is the best for a basket," says Lestel, "because it's the most durable. With proper care, a white oak basket will last several generations if not a century." Lestel and Ollie can make as many as three baskets a day, working under the apple tree in the front yard in the summer and in the kitchen during colder months. In addition to their own fifty styles, from baskets no bigger than a nut all the way to 2-bushel sizes, they can reproduce any basket from a sketch or photo. Their oldest style is the round basket but their most popular is called the gizzard, or withers, basket, "used to carry things up on the withers of a horse when ladies rode sidesaddle," explains Ollie. "It's called all kinds of names, like egg basket because the bottom is shaped to keep eggs from rolling around."

Lestel first selects a straight young white oak tree, preferably 6 to 8 inches thick and 6 to 7 feet tall, with a knot-free trunk and loose bark, growing on a southern slope. The timber is cut, then split into fleaches 1 inch square. After the bark is removed, these fleaches are cut into splits following the grain with a series of tools like wedges, froes, sledge hammers, mauls and axes, until the wood can be worked with a regular pocketknife. "The heartwood is used for handles and ribs," says Ollie, "and the lighter outer sapwood used for splits. The handles and ribs form the frames, while the ribs help shape the basket." For contrast, Ollie boils natural dyes from yellow root, pokeberries, green walnut hulls and bark from the white oak, "which makes a beautiful gray."

Although she now has arthritis, Ollie continues to weave. "It's part of me," she says. "When I'm making baskets, I never get tired. It seems to settle my nerves down. I feel great each time I finish one and sign the handle."

The baskets range in price from $18 to $125. When Lestel and Ollie have the time to do the work, they also sell splits by mail for $15 a pound.

Mr. and Mrs. Lestel Childress
Route 2
Park City, KY 42160
(502) 749-5041
V R W C MO

Other Makers

Scott Gilbert, G-H Productions, Route 1, Box 89, Adolphus, KY 42120; (502) 622-7497, makes white oak baskets in several styles.   C ($1 refundable with order)

Ken and Kathleen Dalton, Coker Creek Crafts, P.O. Box 8, Coker Creek, TN 37314; (615) 261-2157, have baskets in many American museums and private collections. From finding the right white oak tree to weaving the basket, only traditional methods are used. Prices are $30 to $500, with the average less than $100. Also available are white pine or oak basket molds in 6-, 8-, 10-, and 12-inch diameters ($60 to $100). R C MO

Earlean Thomas, Route 2, Box 261, Woodbury, TN 37190; (615) 563-4806, is a highly respected traditional basket maker. She has been making baskets since she was 6 years old, in the early years of the century.

BEADWORK

Beads arrived in America with Columbus, were used to buy Manhattan and became a common denominator of trade with the Native Americans. Bartered by all nationalities, beads were highly prized at first, less so as they became more common. Manufactured from colored capillary tubes cut in tiny pieces, beads were strung as necklaces and bracelets, sewn onto fabrics in designs or as decorative edges and sometimes woven or loom-beaded.

Crow beads, also known as China beads, were ¼ inch in diameter. "Real," or pony, beads were smaller, used with quillwork and sold by the pound, which is why they were sometimes called pound beads. Seed beads, often used with real beads, were smaller and came from Venice, while larger seed beads were imported from Bohemia, now Czechoslovakia. In addition to these glass beads, brass beads, known as iron beads, were also used.

As a young girl, Jeri Greeves (whose Indian name is Kia-Mah) worked in an arts and crafts shop near a reservation. "The Indians brought in exquisite beadwork to sell," she remembers, "but the owner didn't have money to buy it. I vowed if I ever had the money, I'd put together

Beaded belts

a proper showcase for their work and find them a more appreciative audience." More than two decades ago, she started the Fort Washakie Trading Co. on Wyoming's Wind River Reservation, seventh largest in land area in the United States, with the smallest number of Indians: 6,000 Arapahoe and Shoshone, half of whom make and sell handwork through her shop.

"The Shoshone create the finest beadwork in the world," says Jeri. "Since everything is one-of-a-kind, we usually suggest that people give us a specific idea of what they're looking for. We then mail them a descriptive list of what is in stock, and photos."

Her most popular bead items are jewelry: medallion necklaces ($45 to $95); belts ($250 up, depending on length, width and buckle); earrings ($15 to $30); hair combs and bracelets. Most frequently purchased by Europeans are moccasins in low and high-top styles (usually

Beaded medallion necklaces by members of the Shoshone tribe

Carolyn Hebb

Beaded moccasins

Carolyn Hebb

Old-style pipe bag with long fringe

worn by women to protect their legs from underbrush). "When I tell people the price for adult sizes is $175 to $300, they are surprised until I explain how they are made. Then, they buy more than one pair." Made with rawhide soles and brain-tanned deer or elk tops for adults, antelope for babies, the top is sewn to the sole with a welt in between, then turned inside out. "To keep from damaging the beadwork," Jeri explains, "the sole is dampened and the moccasin turned with a stick. They were originally stitched with sinew, but that dries, rots and needs constant repair, which is why we now use a good grade nylon thread. Each tribe once had its own designs: Arapahoe's were plainer, more geometrical, while Shoshone had sophisticated shadings and floral motifs. Certain colors had significance, but no more." Her own best advertisement, Jeri wears high-top moccasins year-round. "The leather breathes easily," she explains, "making them cool in summer and warm in winter."

Fort Washakie Trading Co., open 7 days a week all summer and by special appointment off-season, also car-

ries rawhide drums and shields, dance bustles, painted buffalo hides, cradleboards, bone breastplates (made of hair pipes, women's in vertical designs, men's in horizontal), as well as porcupine and deer hair head roaches worn in traditional dances. If visiting in person, try to attend one of the seven powwows and two Sun Dances held each summer next to the shop.

Geraldine Greeves
Fort Washakie Trading Co.
Wind River Indian Reservation
P.O. Box 428
Fort Washakie, WY 82514
(307) 332-3557
V R S MO

Other Makers

Nancy Brown Garcia, 179 Althea Street, Apt. 3, Providence, RI 02909, of the Narragansett Indian tribe, makes beaded jewelry, clothing and cradleboards.

Southern Plains Indian Museum Shop, P.O. Box 749, U.S. Highway 62 east of Anadarko, OK 73005; (405) 247-6221.

Marian Sanders, 1963 Balearic Drive, Costa Mesa, CA 92626; (714) 642-6595, makes beaded backpacks.

Hazel and Wallace Zundel, Shoshone Buckskin and Beadwork, 896 South 1000 East, Clearfield, UT 84015.

Beehives *See* **Skeps**

KNOTTED BED COVERINGS

Colonial knotted spreads have been made in the Blue Ridge and Appalachian mountains since settlers first migrated there from New England and Pennsylvania before the Revolution. A version of the embroidered spreads made in England and Scotland, they are made of cotton muslin with hand-tied fringe borders and embroidered with soft twist thread in designs of colonial knots (similar to French knots but named for the colonial period) and satin stitches.

Bertha Cook, 93 years old, of Boone, North Carolina, learned how to make knotted spreads from her mother and in turn taught her three daughters, who continue to make them. "My grandmother and aunts all made them," says Bertha, a recipient of the National Endowment for the Arts' Heritage Award (the American equivalent of being named a national treasure). "I've done all the old patterns," she says (some of which she estimates are 300 to 400 years old), "and invented a few of my own." She has always been quick to point out that knotted spreads should not be confused with candlewicking (embroidery made of soft heavy cotton like that used in candlewicks, a version of which was mass-produced by factories). "Colonial knotted spreads are entirely made by hand," she says. "They're prettier and last longer, too."

Bertha demonstrated her craft for 26 years at the Southern Highlands Handicraft Guild. She has made knotted table scarves, pillows and even a coat. She makes all the traditional patterns like Blue Bell (also known as Sweetbriar Rose) and Grape Wreath (which she also does in a Double Grape Wreath pattern), plus those of her own invention like Cinnamon Vine, named for the source of her inspiration, the vine climbing up the side of her porch. Hand-tied fringes, made of 4-ply carpet warp thread, are looped around a stick or wood dowel, then tied in a variety of patterns like Bow Knot, Colonial Braid and Crow's Foot.

To make a spread, Bertha places a piece of new muslin over a finished spread, which she has laid on her bed, then traces the design by rubbing a rag soaked in bluing over the top, which makes dots where the knots raise the material. Using an embroidery hoop to stretch the fabric taut, Bertha pulls 11 strands of white thread doubled in her needle through a ball of beeswax to stiffen the thread so it won't fray, then begins to twist and pull the colonial knots. Although it can take up to 2 months to make a single spread, Bertha estimates she has made more than a thousand in her lifetime.

"Some people can't give up smoking," she says with a grin. "Some people can't give up drinking. I can't quit knotting." There's only one thing she doesn't enjoy and that's ironing the finished spread. "It has to be pressed right side down," she explains, "on top of something soft,

Bertha Cook working on a knotted spread

Randy Johnson

and takes a lot of time." Bertha sold her first spread in 1916 for $25. They now cost $300. "But the muslin then cost 59¢ a yard," says Bertha. "It's now $5.29 and costs ten times as much to make the spreads. I could do a lot more with the $25 than I can with the $300."

In addition to making twin-, queen- and king-size spreads, Bertha also hand-ties canopies for four-poster beds. They can be purchased through Southern Highlands Handicraft Guild or from Bertha Cook or any of her three daughters listed below.

Mrs. D. W. Cook
Route 2, Box 187
Boone, NC 28607
R S MO

Other Makers
Mrs. Cecil Hartley (Wilma), 415 Belmont Drive, Bristol, TN 37620; (615) 968-9671.
Mrs. Mary C. Brown, P.O. Box 179, Boone, NC 28607; (704) 264-6285.
Mrs. C. E. Clay (Jackie), P.O. Box 293, Lansing, NC 28643.
Southern Highlands Handicraft Guild, Box 9545, Asheville, NC 28805; (704) 298-7928.
Village Antiques Shop, P.O. Box 493, Blowing Rock, NC 28605; (704) 295-7874.
Women's Exchange, 993A Farmington Avenue West, Hartford, CT 06107; (203) 232-8721.

BED RUGGS

Heavy bed ruggs, stitched with yarn and a large curved needle of bone or wood on a foundation of wool, twill, linen or linsey-woolsey, were used as the top layer on New England beds in the 17th, 18th and early 19th centuries. Of the fifty to sixty still in existence, more were found in Connecticut than in any other state.

"This does not mean they were made only here or that more were made here," says Jessie Marshall, a contemporary craftsperson who has the distinction of having made the first bed rugg since the last one recorded in 1833, "but only that perhaps Connecticut Yankees were less inclined to throw old things away."

Until the 1972 bed rugg show at the Wadsworth Atheneum in Hartford, Connecticut, many experts assumed that bed ruggs had been hooked. "One rug in the exhibition had been repaired by hooking," says Jessie, "which may have contributed to this conclusion. However, bed ruggs were needleworked, not hooked. Hooking leaves

no spaces between stitches on the underside of the rug, while needleworked rugs do."

After Jessie repaired a 1741 rug for the show, she wanted one in her 1751 saltbox house on the Boston Road in Coventry, "but I realized that even if I found one, I'd never be able to afford it, so I decided then and there I'd make one." Three years later, working evenings, she'd finished her bed rugg, made with hand-spun yarns and dyed with natural colors; its 70- by 80-inch size required 14,000 yards or 8 pounds of yarn.

Bed rugg by Jessie Marshall

After drawing a small pattern based on designs from several antique rugs—flowers interlaced with wandering vines, filling in open spaces with leaves, birds, grapes and small flowers—she enlarges it to fill the blanket. "Brightly colored animals, hearts and shell motifs were also popular," says Jessie, "as well as a double-handled vase at the foot of the design, from which the flowers and vines appear to grow, and adaptations of the tree of life. The shell was made from half circles set side by side in rows around the edge and stitched in three to four shades from dark to light tones in a flame-stitch effect."

Like 18th century needleworkers, she then applies the pattern with water-soluble color to a plain wool blanket

BLANKETS

Footstool cover, showing both cut (top) and uncut pile, by Jessie Marshall

Prices for Jessie's bed ruggs vary with design, stitch, colors and size, and start at $9,900. Hearth rugs made in the style of bed ruggs but usually stitched on linen, as well as cradle rugs and footstools run approximately $1.50 a square inch.

Jessie Marshall
3251 Main Street
Coventry, CT 06238
(203) 742-8934
R   MO

Besoms *See* **Brooms**

AMERICAN COLONIAL BLANKETS

In early Americans' personal inventories, bedding and bed curtains were valued second only to real estate. The average settler often had only one blanket, usually woven in tabby, a simple over-and-under weave that didn't require a great deal of wool to make. As sheep-raising increased and wool became more plentiful, blankets were woven in twill, with a diagonal line in the weave, producing a softer, fluffier nap and a warmer, more durable blanket. Made of two widths joined by a center seam, some blankets were left in their natural color, while others were decorated with banded stripes of dyed wool or woven in checks and plaids.

Fourth generation Vermonter Mary Worley taught herself to spin after she bought an old spinning wheel. "At the time there was no one around who could teach me," she says, "so I learned from an old English book." She later studied with the founder of the Marshfield School of Weaving, Norman Kennedy, whom Mary considers her "most important teacher and mentor. Our techniques are the same, but our choice of colors and work is often quite different."

Like many early American weavers, Norman came to America as an immigrant from Scotland. He learned to weave before he was 17 years old, but when he brought home the table loom he'd made, his father threw it out because he considered weaving a lower-class trade. Despite his father's disapproval, Norman repaired his loom and continued to weave. He earned his living as a tax collector by day, weaving at night and singing on holidays, until he was invited to represent Scotland as a ballad singer at the Newport Folk Foundation. From there he went to work for a Boston craft shop and then became master weaver at Colonial Williamsburg. Since 1975 he has taught tra-

foundation. ("I prefer stitching on wool because it handles easier than linen when sewing with heavy yarn.") She dyes the wool for the design before spinning, leaving the wool for the background stitchery and three sides of fringe in its natural color. Dyeing in late summer and early fall when plants are most available, she makes browns from black walnut hulls and lichens; yellows from goldenrod and onion skins; pinks, reds and purples from madder, cochineal and pokeberries; greens and blues from indigo; olive-greens from sheep laurel leaves; and soft gray-blues from privet bush berries.

To embroider, she uses two strands of yarn about 2 yards long doubled over through a blunt-edged needle with a large eye (finer spun yarns may require more strands). The most popular stitch was the running stitch, $\frac{1}{4}$ to $\frac{3}{16}$ inch long with a $\frac{1}{2}$-inch loop on top, in either cut or uncut pile or, for special effects, a combination of both. Other stitches used were the darning stitch, the knotted pile, the long and short stitch, the outline and the stem. Whatever stitch is used, it must completely cover the surface of the background for the result to be considered a bed rugg and distinct from other types of bed covers. Most needleworkers added initials and date at the head of the rug and sometimes the name of the recipient if it was a gift.

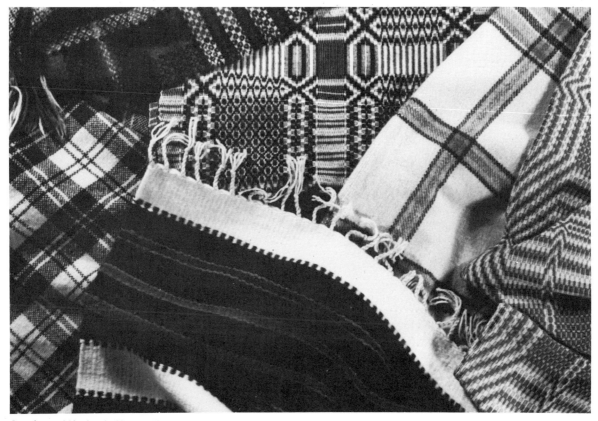

Coverlets and blankets by Norman Kennedy

ditional methods to hundreds of students at Marshfield. "Scottish immigrants brought weaving traditions to America," he'll tell you proudly, "especially to the Southern Highlands and Vermont, where large numbers of Scots settled in the late 18th and early 19th centuries."

Both Norman and Mary use antique equipment rescued from old barns, attics and homes. "The first time I set up an old loom," says Mary, who lives in an 18th century home full of centuries-old looms, wheels and quill winders, "it's as if that long-ago woman is standing behind me. Each piece has its quirks, but they're more than equipment. They're lovely things to look at and handle."

To obtain the bright, vibrant colors of early weavings, Mary uses only dyes with historical documentation, those used in the same period as the equipment. "All my blues are indigo," she says. "My bright reds to salmon tones come from a madder-roots technique given to me by an old tweed weaver. I crush, bake and boil the dried root before adding the mordanted yarn and boiling it. I use a

local plant for rust; black walnuts and butternuts for tans and browns and a yellow dye overdyed with indigo for greens. It's time-consuming, but Norman's instilled a need to do things well. The purity of techniques, dyes and equipment is important."

In recent years, Mary has received awards from the Vermont and New England Weavers' Guilds, including Best in Show, Best Blanket, Best Use of Hand-Dyed Yarns, Best in Four-Harness Weaving and Judges' Choice Award for Craftsmanship. She also set up and wove in a summer-long weaving exhibit at the Sheldon Museum in Middlebury.

Her wool blankets in several sizes and weights range in price from $95 for crib to $325 and up for double size. She also weaves overshot coverlets, tweed, toweling, shawls and specialized reproductions from museum pieces. In addition to blankets and coverlets, Norman weaves room-size carpets, tweeds of several weights, linens (including bed sheets) and tapestry woven rugs.

BLANKETS

Mary Worley	Norman Kennedy,
Mountain Road,	Master Weaver
Cornwall	Marshfield School
RD 2	of Weaving
Middlebury, VT	Plainfield, VT
05753	05667
(802) 462-2315	(802) 426-3577
V R MO	

Other Makers

Ellen Leone, Route 17, RD 2, Box 9, Bristol, VT 05443; (802) 453-3315, has a flock of forty sheep, which provides much of the wool used in her blankets. In natural, old red and indigo, in designs of 1-inch check and window-pane plaids and colorful New England plaids, they range in price from $120 for a couch throw to $400 for double size. Queen- and king-size may be special-ordered.

Betsy Bourdon, Scribner Hill, Wolcott, VT 05680; (802) 472-6508.

Chilkat Dance Robes

Ceremonial blankets made by the Chilkat Indians, the northernmost branch of the Tlingit tribe, are like no others in America. They are woven from the top down on a loose warp in a complicated tapestry weave, from the wool of mountain goats and shredded cedar bark, and their curvilinear design has a central totemic figure. The remaining surface is covered with clan symbols like those painted on house fronts, storage boxes and totem poles, particularly abstract animal designs and oval eye forms, which are difficult to weave and uniquely Chilkat.

After gathering the wool of mountain goats from low bushes where it collects as goats walk by, Chilkat women leave some of the wool in natural white and dye the rest

Chilkat blanket in yellow, blue-green, white and black

Alaska State Museum, Juneau, AK

in traditional Chilkat blanket colors: yellow from lichen, bluish-green from copper oxide and black from hemlock bark. The blankets are fringed on three sides with a longer fringe at the bottom and worn around the shoulders like a shawl. Jennie Thlunaut, a master of the fine art of Chilkat weaving who is credited with keeping the craft alive, taught several weavers before her death in 1986. Their names are listed below.

Makers

Anna Ehlers, 2524 Scott Drive, Juneau, AK 99801.
Ernestine Glessing, Homer, AK 99603.
Clarissa Hudson, Juneau, AK 99801.
Dorica Jackson, Ketchikan, AK 99901.
Doris Kybee-Grubber, Portland, OR 97208.

LUMMI INDIAN BLANKETS

After her mother died and her father drowned, Fran James went to live with her grandmother on an island with no running water and no electricity. "We raised 500 head of sheep," she remembers, "so I learned to spin young, when I was 9. My grandmother made socks and sold them for about 25¢ a pair. I used to sit on the stairs and help her. As a child I learned to weave and to make do with what I have."

Today with her son, Bill, she lives off the land by fishing and making baskets and blankets, many of which go to galleries, museums and collectors throughout North America.

The 12,500-acre Lummi Reservation where they live, on a peninsula 100 miles north of Seattle, Washington, and 15 miles south of the Canadian border, became the tribe's property in 1855 when the Point Elliot Treaty gained the United States more than one million acres of land and mineral rights and granted the Lummi hunting and fishing rights in their "usual and accustomed places." Recognized by early settlers for their expertise in fishing for all types of bottom fish and salmon, as well as for their methods of preserving food, the Lummi were also skilled weavers known for their decorated baskets and the ornate blankets that they made, wore and gave away at potlatches, large gift-giving powwows.

Fran, who was featured on a PBS documentary entitled "I Am Me," still digs her own clams and catches salmon in a gillnet. She is determined that the crafts of her tribe will live on and help future generations survive. Most mornings she spins, but during salmon season, she camps out on the beach until there is enough wind to move her

Lummi blankets made and modeled by Fran and Bill James

handmade boat, whose sail is a checkered tablecloth and whose rudder is an oar.

"The Lummi weavers once made fine weavings of material, but are no longer in operation," says Fran, "so I bought a loom from the tribe to keep my son going in the traditional arts. He's been weaving for more than 20 years. I've been spinning for over 50 years."

Bill and Fran barter blankets they make with owners of local flocks for wool. "The old blankets were made from mountain goat wool and dog hair," says Fran, "materials unavailable now. Today we make them the same way but from sheep's wool. Only the materials have changed. We use only natural wools and natural colors; we use no dyes."

After washing the wool in rainwater collected in an oak barrel to make it soft, they dry it on a clothesline, turning it as it dries, then card and spin it into skeins before washing it again. After they've done about a hundred pounds, Bill weaves it on one of his six looms. Using a twill weave characteristic of Northwest Indian blankets, in tones of creamy white with some black, brown and gray, the Jameses use traditional patterns, the most popular of which is a myriad of diamonds with a white warp and gray diamond weft, known as the Salmon Egg pattern. The next most favored design has three small dark stripes on all sides against a white background.

Although they do not have a shop, the Jameses supply a few shops in the Seattle area and do some wholesale and prepaid mail order commission work. The first blanket costs $500, two are $400 each and three or more cost $300 each. Fran also sells yarn at $1.75 an ounce. Fran and Bill also make Lummi baskets, which start at $22.50. Fran knits hats and ski socks at $22.50 each, and Bill makes Indian jewelry and beadwork.

Fran and Bill James
4339 Lummi Shore Road
Ferndale, WA 98248
(206) 384-5292 or 758-2522
V R W MO

Rio Grande Blankets *See under* **Weaving**

BOAT MODELS AND HALF HULLS

Ship and boat models serve for more than play or display. They are used to build ships, study nautical design and provide three-dimensional records of ships already built.

The earliest ship model in existence was built in the first century A.D. by the Egyptians. In 1650, the British Admiralty adopted a regulation stating that all naval ships had to be preserved in scale models (called Record Models) as well as plans (called draughts). In 1820 the U.S. Navy adopted a similar regulation. Since then, every contract for a full-size ship has called for a Record Model to be built and preserved. Most of these models are loaned to colleges offering naval architecture as a course of study (the largest collection being at the Massachusetts Institute of Technology in Boston).

Half hulls, which look like model ships sliced down the middle, are necessary in ship-building. Bruce L. Paton, who has been building ship and boat models since 1948, explains: "It has been common practice for several hundred years for shipyards to have detailed half-hull models of projected ships to be built because shipwrights, though experienced, often couldn't read technical plans. All they needed to build an entire ship was a carved, wooden half hull."

Bruce built his first model, of an airplane, at summer camp and later became Massachusetts Champion at

MODELS
BY
PATON

Model of 65-foot colonial sloop by Bruce L. Paton

model-building and flying. While attending MIT he financed most of his tuition by building model airplanes for the instructors and students to use in wind tunnels. After World War II, a friend left the Coast Guard with thirty-six contracts to build Record Models of ships built during the war and asked Bruce to help. He's been building ship and boat models ever since, for owners, collectors, naval architects, manufacturers and the U.S. Navy and Coast Guard.

Bruce takes pride in the fact that all his models are of museum quality, made of the best obtainable materials and can be expected to last at least a hundred years before deterioration is visible. No plastics (except for clear acetate windows) are used, and no lead or ferrous materials. All soldering is done with silver solder, and only the finest lacquers are used for finishes. Hulls are built up in lifts of clear, first-grade mahogany or basswood, then doweled and glued together with water-resistant glue. The surface treatment of all parts represents the appearance of the actual vessel.

Prices for models are based on a $30-an-hour rate, with a minimum price of $2,000. Prices are quoted based on line drawings and photos. Terms are 50 percent with the order and 50 percent on delivery, with 4 to 6 months for delivery.

Bruce L. Paton
P.O. Box 4331
Kingman, AZ 86401
(602) 753-5661
R S MO

Other Makers

George B. Armstead, Jr., 89 Harvest Lane, Glastonbury, CT 06033; (203) 633-7836, makes and repairs boat models.

Mystic Maritime Gallery, Mystic Seaport Museum Stores, Mystic, CT 06355; (203) 536-9685 or 536-9688.

BONEWORK

Bonework in this country has had two main groups of practitioners: Native Americans, since prehistoric times, and early immigrants from Scotland, Ireland and England. In the 17th century, many small tools were made of bone, from hooks for cleaning bobbins in spinning wheels to manicure sets for the gentry. Until the mid-1800s, combs, buttons, corset stays, shoehorns, needles, paper knives and spoons were made of bone. It was as large an industry as furniture and cabinetmaking.

"The most classic objects came from prisoner-of-war camps," says Bob Chadwick, one of the few people who works in bone in the United States today. "It was common practice for prisoners to carve or construct objects from animal bones to pass the time or to barter with captors for extra rations of food. Prisoners made articles like paper knives, penholders, broaches, chessmen, tiny solid Bibles and boxes. One even made a miniature guillotine with a decapitated man. Ironically, when plastics replaced bone, they were extruded to look like bone, including the grain texture."

Bob served a 7¼-year apprenticeship with his father, Robert N. Chadwick, a gun maker whose family has been making guns since before the Revolutionary War. "Old rifles, musical instruments and boxes were often inlaid with bone in the shape of fish, half moons and the like," says Bob. "The front sights on many gun pieces were made entirely of bone because they did not throw a glare the way metal sights did." Bob made his first bone box in 1971 on a very cold winter day in an unheated barn. After his box won first prize in a Lancaster County (Pennsylvania) Art Association show, "the surge of positive response from the public led to my becoming fully involved in the medium."

"My techniques are the same as those used for hundreds of years," he explains. "I use bison, cow and other large animal bones, which are naturally aged. The bison comes from Wyoming and the rest from Chester County farms. As long as bones are not associated with any historic or prehistoric artifacts, I can use them. Objects are put together with dovetail and butterfly joints, doweled construction and up to thirty coats of oil finish, which is pumiced off with a wax overlay."

Traditional bone boxes with lifting lids (5 by 3 by 1½ inches) range in price from $90 to $150, while larger boxes with dovetails and inlays are $175 to $425. Solid

Bone boxes, paper knives and shoehorns by Robert A. Chadwick

bone paper knives 7 inches long are $40, while those with bronze are $60. Shoehorns 8 inches long run $25.

Because he's as proud of his work in bone as his father's family is of their guns, Bob prefers making original pieces rather than reproductions that may become counterfeits. "When I'm asked to make objects with Libby Prison etched into them," says Bob, "I remember the time my dad bought some Green River cutlery and ground them to fit stag handles. The person he sold them to treated them with acid and sold them as original 1830 Green River trapper knives."

At the rate his traditional and contemporary bonework is being purchased by collectors, Bob needn't worry. The Chadwick name on bone is already as important as the Chadwick name on guns.

Robert A. Chadwick, Bone, Metal, Wood
325 Redpump Road
Nottingham, PA 19362
(215) 932-8637
R W S MO

BOOKS

A well-written book creates a world in the reader's mind. A perfect book engages the senses in subtle ways: colors please the eye; textures touch memories long forgotten; typeface gives voice to the text; and spaces on the page leave room for wonder.

Since she founded Janus Press in 1955, Claire Van Vliet has gained a reputation for creating books as perfect as is humanly possible. Janus, god of beginnings and balance, for whom her press is named, looks in two directions: to the future and to the past, a symbol Claire equates with traditional publishing. Making balanced and unified books whose parts illuminate one another takes patience, skill and time. She spent 5 years on *The Tower of Babel*, 3 on *The Circus of Doctor Lao* and has been working on *King Lear* (an edition with thirty-nine original woodcut illustrations) for almost 2 years. "I once printed a whole book in three colors in an edition of 250," she says, "and realized it should have been in two colors and on oriental paper. So I reprinted it. Fortunately, the type was still standing. I made the mistake because I thought I had to keep to a schedule. I have learned that books are only improved by delays."

Her most challenging project is "usually whichever one I am trying to figure out now, although larger books that span a long period of time have pushed me more than smaller ones simply because they were bigger problems

*Slipcase and binding of handmade book (*The Circus of Doctor Lao *by Charles G. Finney) by Claire Van Vliet*

that lasted a longer time." She designs the books, illustrates about one-third of them, designs and executes bindings and sometimes makes the paper.

Born in Ottawa, Canada, Claire graduated from San Diego State University and Claremont Graduate School, worked as a typographer in Germany and Philadelphia, apprenticed with John Anderson at Pickering Press in New Jersey and taught at the Philadelphia College of Art and the University of Wisconsin. She has produced more than 13,000 volumes, which include more than eighty titles, featuring the work of authors from Franz Kafka to poet Galway Kinnell (a Pulitzer Prize–winning neighbor). Her work is included in the collections of the National Gallery of Art, the Philadelphia Museum of Art, the Cleveland Museum of Fine Arts, London's Victoria and Albert Museum and the Museum of the Book in The Hague. Although Janus has received grants from the National Endowment for the Arts and the Vermont Council on the Arts for special projects, the press is entirely self-supporting, no mean feat in an age when numbers and speed outpace quality and beauty in the marketplace.

Claire's books (called chaste, eloquent, elegant, spare, sensual, haunting) are made to last, of handmade paper printed on hand-operated presses with hand-bound covers that don't buckle with age. After choosing the binding cloth and paper (the format of *From a Housewife's Diary* was decided by the width of the dishtoweling used as binding cloth; the texture of *A New Herball* changes each time a page is turned), Claire decides on ink and illustrations so that each facet complements and reinforces every other. The shape fits the content: a tall vertical format allowed the longest poems of *Bare Elegy* to be set on a

Opening of handmade book (The Circus of Doctor Lao *by Charles G. Finney) by Claire Van Vliet*

single page. Before constructing a dummy of the book, she sets the text, which helps determine dimensions and number of pages. "My thinking tends to be three-dimensional," she explains. "It is hard to separate the visual and word concepts. They seem to be inextricable." For *Aura,* a collaboration with Kathryn and Howard Clark of Twinrocker (see Paper), she used colored pulp for illustration and explored the possibilities of a large-scale continuous image in an unfolding colored paper pulp landscape. The one thing she hasn't done that she'd like to try is offset color illustrations for a letterpress book. "It's a chicken-and-egg process," Claire says of the way books develop. "Sometimes a text suggests visual ideas; sometimes a sequence of images makes me find the right author."

Her published books have ranged in price from $2.50 to $750. Standing-order patrons receive a 30 percent discount as well as extra items each year that are *hors commerce.* For list of current titles, send a self-addressed, stamped envelope.

Claire Van Vliet
The Janus Press
RD 1
West Burke, VT 05871
R   W   C   MO

Other Makers

Walter Hamady, The Perishable Press, Box 7, Mount Horeb, WI 53572.

Richard-Gabriel Rummonds, Ex Ophidia Press, Box 27, Cottondale, AL 35453.

Steve Miller and Ken Botnick, Red Ozier Press, P.O. Box 20013, London Terrace Station, New York, NY 10011.

Leigh McLellan, Meadow Press, 251 Parnassus 33, San Francisco, CA 94117.

David J. Holmes, Renaissance Press, 123 Cathedral Street, Annapolis, MD 21401; (301) 268-0523.

Bookbinding

Pamela Talin and her brother Jim, owners of Talin Bookbindery in Brewster, Massachusetts, hand-bind books as they were traditionally bound in the 17th and 18th centuries. In addition to gold-tooling, edge-gilding and marbling, they restore and preserve books and make blank books and slip cases for books. Prices range from $30 for a volume in a cloth cover to $200 for a leather cover with simple gold leaf to $500 for more elaborate productions. P.O. Box 314, 1990 Route 6A, Brewster, MA 02631; (617) 896-6444.

Boots, Western *See under* **Leather**

BANDBOXES

The first bandboxes were made for transporting ruffs: stiffly starched, frilled or pleated collars made of lace or muslin worn by both men and women in the 16th and 17th centuries. By the time ruffs went out of style, the lightweight covered boxes had become the favorite mode for carrying hats and wigs while traveling by stagecoach or carriage and keeping possessions (like bonnets, scarves, lace, ribbons and silk flowers) safe from dust at home. Made of pasteboard and sometimes wood, the round and oval, sometimes octagonal or even heart-shaped boxes were made in various sizes and graduated nests, which were painted with designs or covered with wallpaper. Some of the earliest bandboxes made in America were covered with imported papers, but as their popularity grew during the first quarter of the 19th century, American printers created bandbox papers with all-over block patterns or floral, historical, architectural and mythological designs, which were printed in long strips and glued on with the seam in the back. A fixture on the American scene until the mid-19th century, when they were replaced by sturdier leather versions, bandboxes were then banished to the closet and later the attic until they became valuable antiques. As an indication of their present value, an early bandbox of cardboard and painted paper, designed to hold trinkets, sold at the 1979 Garbisch auction for $7,250.

Heidi Mayer makes bandboxes from heavy posterboard, which she covers with hand-painted paper. "I dislike modern wallpaper," she explains. "After reading that old boxes were covered with hand-painted paper, I decided to block-print my own. Instead of woodblocks, I use potato

Bandboxes covered with hand-painted paper by Heidi Mayer

stamps, as early settlers would have done. The material is always at hand and easy to carve. I mix my own colors in subdued shades of russet, forest green, blue and mustard. These colors blend in nicely with antiques but look equally well in contemporary settings. I stamp the design in two or three different colors on a harmonizing background and sometimes overprint a second time with a contrasting color. This step is the most pleasing part of the process because I create something totally new and different each time." In the style of period makers who lined their boxes with newspapers, Heidi lines hers with antique paper: pages from worn-out books and almanacs that can't be repaired. "This way," she explains, "instead of being thrown away, the books gain new life and appreciation."

Heidi grew up in a family of German artists and craftspeople and learned to spin and knit before she was 5, when she was "promoted to making socks with five needles. My grandmother wound the yarn around a coin and I would sit and knit, dreaming how I would spend the money." She later became a skilled embroiderer and quilter and today still spins the yarn and knits sweaters for her family. She has also restored a 200-year-old house.

Her boxes, signed on the inside lid rim, "because I'm proud of the high quality and workmanship in every one," come in six nesting sizes, which can be purchased individually or in sets and ordered in assorted colors of russet, forest green, blue and mustard or one color only. Prices are from $10 to $20; $90 for the complete set. Heidi also makes a large box 9 by 7 by 6 inches for $28. For postage and handling, add $3 for orders under $20, $4.50 for those $20.01 to $50, $5.50 for $50.01 to $100 and $6.50 over $100.

Heidi Mayer
529 West King Street
East Berlin, PA 17316
(717) 259-0924
V (by appt.)   R   W   S   MO

Other Makers

Virginia Kent, 340 South Russell Street, York, PA 17402; (717) 755-8598, recreates 18th and 19th century bandboxes in tricorne, military bicorne, man's high hat and lady's bonnet shapes and fancy boxes in round, oval, heart, octagonal, tea caddy and fan forms, from posterboard covered with paper. Each is signed and lined with hand-colored reprints of fashion plates from *Godey's* or *Graham's Lady's Books,* poetry, sheet music, folk art drawings or "anything that strikes my fancy." She also conducts museum workshops and illustrated lectures.

Wallpaper-covered ladies' bonnet boxes and nest of heart-shaped trinket boxes by Virginia Kent

Lindsay E. Frost, Box A, Campbell Street, Avella, PA 15312; (412) 587-3990, makes bandboxes in twenty-four patterns and colors of wallpaper, lined with plain newsprint, in eight sizes.

Susan and Sven Miller, Open Cupboard, P.O. Box 70, Tenants Harbor, ME 04860; (207) 372-8401, make bandboxes and "minikins" hand-sewn from pasteboard, covered with document-print wallpaper and lined with actual 19th century newsprint.

Michelle Worthing and Nancy Yeiser, 2173 Woodlawn Circle, Stow, OH 44224; (216) 688-7788.   C (50¢)

SHAKER BOXES

Jack Lowell Johnson was born and reared on the small farm where he still lives, now with his wife and daughter, in the lower Licking River Valley, just below Cave Run

Round and oval Shaker boxes by Jack Lowell Johnson

Lake in Kentucky. His wife, Carolyn, a maker of honeysuckle and river willow baskets, grew up in nearby Morehead.

"I love the hills," says Jack, "and the plants and wildlife they produce. Woods have always been an important part of my life. As a child I cut, split, stacked and carried it by hand into the house where we used it for heating and cooking."

He made white oak pitchforks and rakes at first, then ladderback woven-bottom chairs, dough troughs, ladles and bark buckets. After seeing pictures of Shaker boxes, he read everything he could find on the subject, but his first attempt to make one was a dismal failure: "The box was lopsided and the wood split." He kept practicing, and 5 years ago took one to a show of crafts sponsored by the Kentucky Department for the Arts. "Everyone wanted one," he remembers. "Phyllis George Brown bought one as a gift for Robert Redford, the governor gave them to members of his cabinet for Christmas" and national magazines spread the word.

In the early 19th century, Shaker wooden boxes were handmade in various sizes and shapes for almost every household purpose. "Provide places for your things," Mother Ann Lee, the founder of the Shakers, told her followers, "so that you may know where to find them at any time, day or night." Large oval shapes, with carefully fitted removable lids, often made in nests of three, were cut with fingers lapping at the side in long narrow points fastened with handmade rivets. Oval shapes were used to store herbs; round ones usually held butter and cheese; while smaller sizes kept pills, sealing wax and wafers. To make them, thin wooden bands were bent around solid forms. When dry, bottoms were fitted to the bands and lids made to fit.

"Our boxes are made essentially the same way," says Jack, "but are not intended to be exact replicas because, like early craftsmen, we make them from materials at hand. Bands used for the sides are made from trees which we cut in the forest. They are not sawn at a mill, but split and worked into the bands by hand, then bent while still green. Once they're dry, we fasten them with solid brass nails and stain them with an oil base, then finish them in satin varnish and a coat of paste wax. Our Shaker-style boxes are made with poplar wood bottoms and poplar or maple bands. The carriers [open oval boxes with handles] are mostly pine bottoms with maple sides and oak handles."

While antique Shaker boxes now sell for hundreds and thousands of dollars, Jack's oval Shaker carriers, available in three sizes, are priced from $15 to $34.50. Oval boxes with tops are $18 to $35; nests of four are $98. Shipping

Shaker carrier box by Jack Lowell Johnson

charges extra. For price list, send self-addressed, stamped envelope.

Jack and Carolyn Johnson
Green Mountain Crafts
Route 1, Box 912
Morehead, KY 40351
(606) 784-9171
R   W   C   S   MO

Other Makers

Joe W. Robson, RD 3, Box 158, Trumansburg, NY 14886; (607) 387-9280, makes the intricately dovetailed boxes of fine line and light construction that the Shakers used for everyday tasks and storage. Primarily of native butternut, his smallcraft is also available in walnut and

© 1986 Jon Reis Photography

Shaker carrier box with handle by Joe W. Robson

black cherry and ranges in size from a candle box for $50 to a sewing chest for $130.

Charles Harvey, 201-C North Broadway, Berea, KY 40403; (606) 986-1653.

John Wilson, 500 East Broadway Highway, Charlotte, MI 48813; (517) 543-5325.

Frye's Measure Mill, RFD 1, Wilton, NH 03086; (603) 654-6581, housed in an old mill, makes and sells pantry, button, spice, sewing, game and wedding boxes, piggins and carriers.   C

Branding Irons

A brand was a mark of ownership burned into the hide of an animal with a hot iron to establish ownership and to discourage cattle rustlers. Branding was introduced to the Southwest by Hernando Cortés, explorer and colonial administrator of New Spain (who branded slaves and prisoners as well as cattle). Branding iron designs were the exclusive property of the owner and were registered with local officials. If a smith copied a brand not registered to the person for whom it was made, he was subject to fine.

Joan Neary

The "open safety pin," a Seidman family brand registered in New Mexico since about the 1930s. This iron is made by Frank Turley.

In designing brands, owners tried to find a combination of letters, numbers, symbols or pictures that could not be altered by thieves. Made with a handle, a round-sectioned shank and connecting rods, the brand (or stamp) ideally is tapered to a thinner edge where it is applied to the animal to make a cleaner line in the flesh with less blotching.

Makers

Frank Turley, Route 10, Box 88C, Santa Fe, NM 87501; (505) 471-8608.

A. G. Morgan, Route 2, Box 120A, Stockdale, TX 78160; (517) 996-3374.

BRASS

Of the five chandeliers in the second floor meeting room of Independence Hall in Philadelphia, only one is original. The rest were made by Ball and Ball in 1975.

"After we delivered them," says Whitman Ball, who took over the Exton, Pennsylvania, business from his father, "we lined up all five and asked Charlie Dorman, the curator, to pick the antique. It took him 20 minutes. Do you know how he recognized it? By the dirt in the candle cups."

When cabinetmakers say they use the finest brasses, chances are they order them from Ball and Ball, whose name has become the standard for quality in brass. If an object was ever made of brass, they have it or can duplicate it. It's no accident that their motto is, "The brasses for those who know the originals."

"The most fun part of this business for me," says Whit, "is making a copy of an original and then asking the customer to see if he knows the difference. Many firms like ours have product designers creating copies. To make a true reproduction of an original, all you have to do is copy it, not design it. That's why we say all of our designers have been dead for years." Although many other shops make cast copies with synthetic sand for molding, Ball and Ball uses a natural Albany sand because it picks up the finest details from intricate patterns.

Ball and Ball was founded in 1931 by Whitman Ball's father, William Ball, Jr., and his brother George, to provide a service to the antique trade, and the first catalog contained thirty-four different items. Their current 108-page catalog ($5) has more than a thousand items in over 1,500 sizes, the widest selection of quality reproductions available anywhere in the world, while their minicatalog contains specially marked items. Sectioned by periods, the catalog defines and illustrates what is appropriate for each period. For instance, the edges of William and Mary

Chinese Chippendale escutcheons by Ball and Ball

(1680–1710) and Queen Anne (1710–35) plates are hand-filed, as are the cast posts and drops; many are hand-chased, then struck with specially shaped chisels, using repeated hammer blows. Chippendale pulls and escutcheons (1740–65) have sand-cast backplates, bails, posts and nuts and hand-filed edges, like the originals. Ball and Ball's forty-eight styles of oval Hepplewhite pulls (1765–1810) are stamped from thin sheet brass in hardened steel dies and mounted with turned headposts threaded for round nuts.

Brass hardware by Ball and Ball

Ball and Ball also makes rosette pulls from the William and Mary through Hepplewhite periods, every conceivable kind of hardware (hinges, casters, feet, latches, locks) for furniture through the Victorian period and brass fittings for clocks, harpsichords, doors, cabinets, lamps and chests. Their chandeliers and lighting fixtures are made of solid brass, not plated, and the finest quality of hand-blown lead crystal. Electrified sconces have backplates large enough to cover outlet boxes, and electric wax or wood candles.

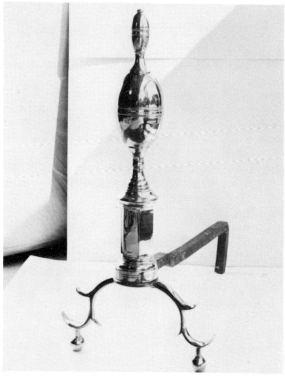

Brass andiron by Ball and Ball

Other brass products include sixteen styles of knockers ($32 to $65), bell pulls to mount on needlepoint ($32 to $48), letter knives ($9.75 to $11.75), a tobacco box operated by a coin ($420), doorstops, bells, hooks and everything for the fireplace including serpentine wire fenders. Their door hardware includes locks, bolts, hinges, knobs, keepers, keys and fittings for Dutch doors. All brass is available in polished bright or aged antique finish. Many styles are available in pewter, brass, tin, copper and forged or cast-iron finish.

Ball and Ball can also repair, copy or match almost any hardware item. "Hinges of all types, door locks, lights, lanterns, andirons, fire tools and furniture hardware can usually be repaired for less than replacement cost," says Whitman Ball. "We always quote in advance and leave the decision to the customer." Their showroom and museum of original brass and iron hardware, lighting fixtures and collectibles is open weekdays from 8 A.M. to 4:30 P.M. and on Saturday by appointment during the fall months.

Ball and Ball
463 West Lincoln Highway
Exton, PA 19341
(215) 363-7330
V   R   W   C   S   CC   MO

Other Makers

Horton Brasses, Nooks Hill Road, P.O. Box 95, Cromwell, CT 06416; (203) 635-4400, makes authentic brasses for periods 1680 to 1920. Showroom open weekdays 9 A.M. to 3:45 P.M.   C

James Chamberlain, P.O. Box 266, Williamsburg, VA 23187; (804) 898-2942. Send self-addressed, stamped envelope for price list.

BROOMS

Early New Englanders made yellow birch besoms (bundles of twigs attached to handles) in sizes large enough to sweep the floor and small enough to beat eggs, whip cream and scrub kettles. Most colonists used whatever material was available: corn shucks, husks, grasses, palmetto leaves, even the top fluff of the hemlock or pine. After broomcorn was introduced in 1700 by African slaves, many Americans, including Benjamin Franklin and Thomas Jefferson, grew their own, but it was Levi Dickenson, a Yankee farmer in Hadley, Massachusetts, who realized there was an industry waiting to be born. Despite the disdain of his neighbors, who thought that only Indians should make brooms, Levi began to manufacture and peddle them in New England and New York. Only 12 years later, American factories were turning out 70,000 brooms a year.

Like early broom makers, Susan and Paul Harris grow their own broomcorn. "This is no small task," Sue explains, "because spring planting and fall harvesting are done mostly by hand. Each spring when the soil warms, we plant the seeds, and by fall the corn is more than 12 feet tall. Hand-cutting several acres means we spend weeks in the cornfield, and more time bundling and hanging the stalks to dry in the barn. But it's worth the effort. There is no other way to have such a wide variety of color (russet, red and gold), and length of fiber. Materials of this quality are not commercially available. Each year, we fill the hayloft with enough corn to make brooms for the coming year."

Brooms made of broomcorn with hardwood handles by Susan and Paul Harris

Sue and Paul named their business the Continuum Studio and Craft Workshop because they are interested in preserving the continuing integrity of country skills. "Life here on our farm is marked by seasonal occupations just as it was in the beginnings of agriculture," says Sue, "and nothing is wasted. The chickens love the seeds, and whatever else is left of the broomcorn is used for mulch and fodder."

Hardwood handles selected for their strength are seasoned for at least a year, then sanded smooth and sealed to bring out the character of the wood and preserve it. To make brooms, seeds are stripped from the follicles by pulling the stalks through the metal teeth of a comb or saw. The broomcorn is skived (or shaved) to make bottom layers fit, placed around the handle, then soaked with water to soften the fiber. It is then placed in a harness rope hung from an overhead beam with a foot pedal attached to the bottom. Stepping on the pedal crimps the corn and tightens it around the handle, after which it is tied off with twine.

"Another method, similar to the Shaker broomwinder machines, is to run twine from a spool anchored under your feet," says Sue. "The corn is wrapped to the handle by inserting it while slowly turning the handle by hand, winding the twine around the binding. The twine can be taken over and under to produce a decorative weave. Many broom makers use this method because it is decorative and simple. For textural contrast, we use a basket-weave and specially grown Flint cornhusks woven into the bindings."

Short hearth brooms retail for $14 to $24; 5-foot-long brooms to sweep a floor are $18 to $40; and barn brooms start at $30. Whisk brooms come in two sizes, each $18.

Susan and Paul Harris
The Continuum Studio and Craft Workshop
3700 Emerson Road
Bloomdale, OH 44817
(419) 454-4553
R   C   S   MO

Other Makers

Joe Panzarella of High Point Crafts, RD 2, Sky High Road, Tully, NY 13159; (315) 683-5312, makes hand-wound brooms with finished hardwood and sapling handles using an 1800s Shaker broomwinder in wisp, round and flat shapes from $8 to $45; peacock and ostrich feather fans and dusters ($20 to $24); and four types of bellows ($40 to $48).

Kear's Broom Shop, Cartertown Road, Route 1, Gatlinburg, TN 37738; (615) 436-4343, makes forty-one kinds of brooms and three styles of walking sticks, from $11.50 to $30 a dozen, with a minimum order of six. For price list send self-addressed, stamped envelope.

The Old Broom and Basket Shop, West Amana, IA 52357; (319) 622-3315, uses three kinds of broomcorn (coarse inside, medium in the middle and fine outside) in whisk, pot and barn sizes and their famous sideline whisk broom.

Marie Weekley, 1108 Quincy Street, Parkersburg, WV 26101; (304) 422-6288.

Bultos   See under Santos

CANDLES

In 1630, tallow was in such short supply in New England that Governor Winthrop asked his wife to bring candles from England when she came. Because farm animals (whose fat was used for tallow) were also in short supply, colonists used deer suet, bear grease and fat from moose, fish and pigeons to make candles. Bayberry candles smelled the best but took buckets of berries and a great deal of work. Wicks, sometimes dipped in saltpeter to make the first few coatings stick, were made of loosely spun hemp, tow or cotton and, in some places, woven by children from milkweed down. Benjamin Franklin's father was a tallow and wax chandler, as are members of today's Walz family.

"We made our first tallow candles for a friend's antique shop," says Nancy, "and learned to make tallow from an elderly neighbor who rendered fat for soap. We use only beef fat, cut in small pieces, or ground up like hamburger, which melts faster. Beef fat is best because it's not good for anything else, whereas lard [the semisolid rendered fat from hogs] is used for cooking. We boil the beef fat over low heat until the cracklings or impurities separate themselves from the tallow and rise to the top. It's important to take the pot off as soon as it stops bubbling. If left on the fire, it will smoke and burn, which ruins the tallow. When done, the liquid is poured through a sieve. We keep tallow in solid blocks until used and feed the cracklings to the chickens."

When her first efforts filled the house with the smell of fat, Nancy moved the candle-making operation to the summer kitchen, where she, her husband, Ron, and their four children make candles just as the colonists did. They use two 2-foot-wide butchering kettles hung on trammels from cranes to swing them in and out over an open fire. One kettle is used for dipping and the other for replenishing. "We have to keep the dipping pot full so that it is the same depth as the candle's length," explains Nancy. From large bolts of cotton wicking hung on the wall, Nancy measures wicks for their 6-inch and 9-inch candles using two nails hammered into the counter. Whenever her children find a spare minute, they tie these strings onto walnut holders for the dipping process. "We made the first holders from pine," says Nancy, "but they cracked. The candles were heavy and bent the wood. Now we use only hardwood from our own backyard."

An ordinary paper clip is attached to the bottom of each string to weight the line during the first five or six dippings, or until the candles are about ¼-inch thick. Because each candle has to harden between dippings, the Walzes work a row of sixteen holders. "In perfect weather, we double-dip," says Nancy, "but if it's too cool or too hot, it doesn't work. Candle-making goes faster in cold weather. In summer months, the candles don't harden fast enough." The temperature of tallow is also important.

Tallow candles during dipping process by the Walz family

"If it's too hot, it melts what is already on the wick, and if it's too cool, the candles will be lumpy," says Nancy. "Between 140 and 150°F is ideal. If candles get too cold between dippings, they have spots that look like snowflakes. We've found the solution to this problem is to divide the number we're doing into quarters and finish each batch separately."

Tallow, which is soft and shiny like soap, lasts longer in a candle when it's mixed half and half with wax, which the Walzes find their buyers prefer. "The fifty-fifty mixture produces a soft lustrous candle," says Nancy, "which burns for 6 to 8 hours."

The 6-inch size is $2 a pair; the 9-inch, $2.50. Available in unscented dusty rose, heather blue, colonial blue, chocolate brown and natural cream as well as scented bayberry (an olive color), the candles are sold in shops nationwide, as well as at museums and directly by the Walz family. For shipping costs, add 5 percent plus $2.

The Walz Family
Smokehouse Country Crafts
8537 Hollow Road
Middletown, MD 21769
(301) 371-7466
R   W   MO

Other Makers

The Silvias, The Candle Cellar and Emporium, Box 135, South Station, Fall River, MA 02724; or 1914 North Main

Street, Fall River, MA 02720; (401) 624-9529, make hand-poured pure bayberry candles in antique molds 8 inches long in natural olive for $4 a pair plus shipping and handling.

Becky Rupp, Box 144, Brandamore, PA 19316, makes molded candles in many colors. Send self-addressed, stamped envelope for price list.

Cliff and Lois Sunflower, Bear Honey Farms, 2371 West Best Road, Bath, PA 18014; (215) 759-9655, make beeswax candles and ornaments and sell bulk wax.

Unicorn Candles at the Church of the Incarnation, 706 South Main Street, Telford, PA 18969, makes hand-dipped tapers using old iron pots and an antique dipping wheel just as the Pennsylvanians did years ago. In 5- and 10-inch lengths, a full ⅞-inch diameter base comes with a self-fitting fluted bottom. They are available in 100 percent bayberry, beeswax and stearine.

William and Virginia Laidman, 814 West Union Boulevard, Bethlehem, PA 18018; (215) 868-5315, make the Moravian star and beeswax candles for the Moravian Church.

Makepeace Chandlers, RFD 2, Box 342, Dover-Foxcroft, ME 04425, makes hand-dipped beeswax candles in 4-, 6- and 12-inch lengths in blue, rose, cream, sage and burgundy from $1.95 to $5.95 the pair, as well as pure beeswax, seamstress cameos, which are aids to keep thread from knotting and binding, and beeswax stove polish.

George Arold, P.O. Box 99, Hatfield, PA 19440; (215) 822-9630 makes hand-dipped candles.

The Shoemakers, RD 2, Box 212A, Oley, PA 19547, make hand-dipped beeswax candles in four sizes and six colors.

Low Country Candles, P.O. Box 266, McKinnon Airport Road, St. Simons Island, GA 31522-8266; (912) 638-4873, makes beeswax candles.

Country Crafts, Box 111, Landisville, PA 17538, makes Pennsylvania Amish candles.

BIRCHBARK CANOES

Henri Vaillancourt's birchbark canoes are said to be the most beautiful in the world. In the 20 years he's been making them with an ax, awl and crooked knife (an ingenious tool shaped like a farrier's knife, which he makes himself from used cold files) he's never made the same one twice.

"They vary in proportion and detail, depending on the materials used," he explains, "but they're all in the Malecite style, identical to those made by Indians in Maine and New Brunswick from about 1850 on."

Henri's canoes, like those of the Malecites, are known for their high degree of grace, sophistication, style, fine detail and craftsmanship. He selects his bark from prime white birch trees, chosen for their straightness, toughness of bark and freedom from blemishes. Most canoes are encased in a single sheet, which means the bark must be carefully removed from the woods as well as from the tree. Although some maintain that bark should be peeled in winter because it is harder, Henri has found "the difference if any between seasons, is slight. A good tree is good in any season. There's actually less risk in removing the bark in June and July because it peels more easily with less damage to the bark." After finding the right tree, he peels the bark, rolls it up, carries it out of the forest, takes it home and stores it until construction begins. Unlike hickory and elm bark, which absorb water, adding weight to a canoe, birch is high in resins and oils and highly resistant to water.

Henri makes both the flare-side (whose top is wider than its bottom) and the tumble-home (whose sides curve inward) in lengths from 10 to 20 feet, the most popular being the 16-foot length. Since he began making canoes professionally in 1966, at the age of 16, Vaillancourt has made more than a hundred, combining his day-to-day experience with ongoing research of archives, antique canoes in museums and private collections "and plenty of trial and error." Shortly after building his first canoe as a teenager, from an article in *Sports Afield,* he heard of and sent for a book entitled *Bark Canoes and Skin Boats of North America,* by Edwin Tappan Adney, which described how the Malecites had built theirs. Published by the Smithsonian, the book is in Henri's opinion "the best book on the subject. Anyone wishing to familiarize himself with details of construction should obtain a copy." Henri was so impressed with the sophistication of techniques used by Indians that he made a documentary film, *Building an Algonquin Birchbark Canoe,* available through the Trust for Native American Cultures and Crafts, which he co-founded.

For flexibility and strength, ribs and planking are split from selected cedar trees chosen for straightness of grain and freedom from knots, then shaved to required dimensions with the crooked knife. Gunwales (the upper edge of a boat's side where guns were once propped) are prepared from spruce and cedar in the same fashion. Thwarts (crosspieces used for rigidity and to keep the spread) are shaved in various fancy patterns in the Malecite tradition from either birch or maple and mortised into the gunwales. Bark is then sewn or lashed over the gunwhales (with the inner side out) using carefully selected black spruce roots whose whittled ends are threaded through holes made with an awl.

CAROUSELS

Birchbark canoe by Henri Vaillancourt

Decorations in the Malecite tradition include chamfering along the gunwales and thwarts, fancy carving on the thwarts, decorative stitching at the stem piece heads (the ends of a piece of wood beneath the bowsprit providing support or ornamentation), and double-curve motifs scraped into the rind (outer covering) of winter bark on the end flaps. "The bow and stem are often painted with the fiddlehead pattern," says Henri, "similar to the fiddlehead fern at first sprouting." When made with the refinements of the best Malecite canoes, construction takes from 400 to 450 hours and costs $400 a linear foot. Because of the scarcity of materials, Henri now makes only three canoes a season, signing each with his 6-inch-high fleur-de-lis mark on the bow. Each will last a minimum of 30 years, and with care, a lifetime.

Henri Vaillancourt
The Trust for Native American Crafts and Cultures
Box 142
Greenville, NH 03048
(603) 878-2944

CAROUSELS

"Carousels appeal to the fantasy of the impractical," says Bill Dentzel, great-grandson of Gustav Dentzel, America's first great carousel carver. "They open one small door to a part of ourselves that doesn't know where it's going, but exists and needs to be dealt with. Merry-go-rounds bring generations together and are also wonderful babysitting machines. Kids like the feeling of being detached from their parents."

After traveling the world, hiking the Himalayas, sailing the North Sea and Mediterranean, restoring tall ships and sailing vessels and earning a degree in political science and education, Bill began restoring antique Dentzel horses for his father's company in the mid-1970s. "I'd been around carousels all my life, but that was when I began to feel their magic," he says. "I found wood carving satisfying and painting fun because of the way it transforms wood into something almost real. Carousel woodworking is interesting because it is based on the geometry of the circle, not unlike constructing a big mechanical mandala of animals, kids and music."

In 1981 Bill designed and built a 14-foot-wide flying-horse carousel, paid for by the Mexican government and placed between a school and church in Ochuxclop, Chiapas, Mexico, a village without water or electricity. Seeing how its existence changed the attitude of the village, Bill has been dedicated to making small hand- or electric-powered carousels in a turn-of-the-century traditional style. Since then he has built three carousels and several dozen animals. His carousels with small mechanical chimes, actuated as the device turns, are reminiscent of the small machines seen in the mid-1800s but are made

Hand-carved giraffe for use on carousels, approximately 48 inches tall and 36 inches long, by William H. Dentzel, III

with better bearings, modern high-quality paints and glues and sturdier lightweight construction for portability.

Bill's great-great-grandfather Michael Dentzel built his first carousel in Germany in 1837 and supported his family by taking it to summer markets and fairs. In the 1850s,

Hand-carved tiger on rockers, approximately 48 inches long, by William H. Dentzel, III

A modified version of a Hershell-Spillman-style jumper, 46 inches long and 38 inches high including the base, by Richard Dawson

Michael sent his three sons to America on a sailing ship with a portable carousel, which generated so much business that Gustav set up shop in Philadelphia. As carousels evolved from manual to horse to steam power, the Dentzel carousel grew to 54 feet in diameter with seventy-two animals and four chariots. During the heyday of the merry-go-round, owners of electric trolleys extended lines beyond city limits to amusement parks to cash in on their popularity, but by 1920 the industry began to fade and during the Depression all but disappeared. Hand-carved animals were replaced by cast metal and eventually fiberglass.

Bill has taken the craft back to its American origins. He carves his figures from white pine, basswood and yellow poplar, paints them by hand or finishes them with gloss or satin varnish and does the metal and wrought-ironwork himself. To reduce weight and prevent cracking, the laminated body is hollow. His smaller animals are 3 to 4 feet in length and (not including stand), are strong enough for adults as well as children and can be custom-ordered in larger sizes. Prices range from $1,000 for medium-size unpainted animals to $4,800 for large painted animals. Stands with traditional brass poles are also available. To have an animal put on rockers adds $200 to the price. For more information and a drawing or photo of a specific animal, send $1.

"Today most carousel animals are bought by collectors, shop owners and shopping malls," says Bill. "Sometimes an individual will donate a carousel to a hospital or park." He'd like to see more merry-go-rounds in parks across America and to start small carousel-making companies in

Richard Dawson

A standing horse carved in the elegant realistic style of Gustav Dentzel, 50 inches long and 44 inches high, by Richard Dawson

third world countries. His other dream—to build a 22-foot-wide carousel on the waterfront of his hometown, Port Townsend—took a first step toward reality recently. Before shipping his latest carousel to Jalapa, Nicaragua, Bill set it up in Port Townsend and let the future voters try it on for size.

William H. Dentzel III
843 53rd Street
Port Townsend, WA 98368
(206) 385-1068
R   MO

Other Makers

In Bill Dentzel's opinion, horses are the most difficult to carve "because everyone knows what they look like and knows what he wants to see." Richard Dawson, 1511 North Cherry Lane, Layton, UT 84041; (801) 544-5480, makes three types: the larger standers that traditionally ride on the outside of the carousel, smaller prancers with front legs up in the air and jumpers with four bent legs and up-and-down movement. Carved from local pine, with sections joined and reinforced with dowels where additional strength is needed and no metal fasteners, the hand-carved animal is mounted on a black iron pipe with a brass sleeve and welded into place, then mounted on a simple base. Prices vary depending on style, size and detail. Standard sizes including pipe stand, standard base and oil resin finish range from $2,250 to $3,250. Traditional painting is $150 up depending on detail. A special stand

with design to complement the style is an additional $250 and includes oil paint finish.   V   R   S   CC   MO

William H. Dentzel, II, 1575 East Valley Road, P.O. Box 50026, Montecito, CA 93108, makes electrically operated carousels 6½ feet in diameter carrying four animals or 9 feet in diameter carrying eight animals of fiberglass, selling from $15,000 to $20,000.

Stanley Rill, P.O. Box 407, Port Townsend, WA 98368; (206) 385-6004.

ALASKAN CARVING

Eskimos believe that every living creature possesses a spirit or life force known as *inua*. To keep from offending spirits of their prey, hunters make beautiful weapons. The quarry's *inua*, appreciating good workmanship, then allows the weapon to capture the fish, mammal or waterfowl.

For aid in approaching their prey, hunters decorate their weapons with images of the prey's enemies. To protect themselves against wild animals and bad spirits, they

Ivory bears by Elmer Wongittlin

wear hand-carved amulets and, for added protection, carve and paint images on their boats, sleds, tools, utensils and houses. Because traditionally men were the hunters, they became the carvers of tools, utensils, weapons, charms and amulets made from ivory, walrus tusks and teeth, reindeer horn, whale bone, whale teeth and baleen, mastodon tusks and, less frequently, wood. In a craft continuum that has lasted thousands of years, Alaskan carving has grown from a tradition of making useful things beautiful to a means of economic survival and one of the most important primitive art forms in the world.

Ivory, traditionally used for utilitarian, ceremonial and decorative objects, continues to be a favorite material,

Whalebone carvings, including masks, figures and jewelry, by Stephan Weycouania

since only Alaskan natives can hunt, harvest and own unworked ivory (which can be sold only after it has been worked). New white ivory from the tusk of the walrus is recognized by its mottled inner core of beige and white and its outer surface, which can be polished to a brilliant sheen. Old ivory, found along the coastline, ranges in color from tan to brown, while fossilized tusks of the walrus and mastodon are dark brown with bluish overtones caused by exposure to minerals in the soil. To avoid splitting, ivory is seasoned (at least 2 weeks for small pieces and a year for larger) before cutting. Ivorywork, known as carving but not as sculpture, is done with a coping or hacksaw, file, graver and sandpaper.

Floyd Kingeekuk, Sr., began carving ivory when he was 10 and was proficient enough by the age of 12 to trade his bird carvings to the community store for a pair of boots. Known today for his finely detailed seals and the dolls that he makes with his wife, Amelia, Floyd like most masters is humble about his talent, considering it an inborn ability to be shared and passed on to future generations. To become even better at his craft, he often

Ivory seals by Floyd Kingeekuk, Sr.

studies animals on the ice. After carving a figure, he blackens the entire surface before etching, then removes the ink before highlighting. Many carvers specialize: Teddy Mayac of King Island is known for his birds; Nick Charles of Bethel for his masks; and Larry Matfay of Old Harbor for his models.

Although the market for harpoon rests and drill bows is slim, traditional objects like amulets, charms and spirit masks remain popular. "Amulets usually are in animal shapes and deal with maintaining a relationship with animals being hunted," explains Jeanne Dougherty of the Alaska Native Medical Center Craft Shop, "while charms are made in a number of shapes and used for different purposes."

Etched sperm-whale teeth by Peter Mayac and puffins by Teddy Mayac

Carved objects unique to Alaska include: puffins (sea birds with vertically flattened bills); ulu knives (semicircular knives used by women for cutting gut and removing blubber from seal and walrus hides); and wolf scarers (6- to 7-inch ovals with notched edges carved from whale baleen and attached to a rawhide or sinew string, which when twirled make a hissing sound, scaring dogs as well as wolves). Also available: totemic wood-carving by the southeastern Tlingit, Haida and Tsimshian Indian tribes. Wolf scarers are $15 to $25. While most carvings are $50 to $125 and up, those of master carvers like Floyd Kingeekuk begin at $450.

Makers

Floyd Kingeekuk, Sr., Savoonga, AK 99769.

Teddy Mayac, 10037 Marmot Circle, Anchorage, AK 99515.

Nick Charles, Box 36, Bethel, AK 99559.

Larry Matfay, Box 12, Old Harbor, AK 99643.

Isaac Koyuk, Anchorage, AK 99515.

Lincoln Milligrock, Nome, AK 99762, specializes in bracelets.

BIRD CARVING

Until 1968, Grace White was "just a Sunday artist married to a bird watcher." That's the year she gave Bill, a weekend whittler, a book on how to carve birds. "He was enthralled," she says. "He went down to his workshop with it under his arm and hasn't been up since."

Although they began with the idea of creating a collection of their favorite species, it wasn't long before their birds, carved by Bill and painted by Grace, had earned an international reputation. Sought by collectors, their birds have won many awards, been featured in the Smithsonian catalog and been exhibited at museums, galleries and Sapsucker Woods, the ornithology laboratory of Cornell University.

"Decoy carvers started the craft," says Bill, "and made decorative pieces and perching birds as a diversion during long winter months. When mass-produced decoys affected sales, decoy makers began carving birds as an art form. Our involvement stems from an interest in nature and wildlife, particularly ornithology. We carve only birds we have seen in their natural habitat. To date, we have completed 2,000 pieces, including 239 varieties and 175 species, although we've personally spotted more than 800 species."

Because *lifelike* refers to action as well as color and form, the Whites use many resources to develop technique and to study behavior, conformation and plumage. While

observing birds in their natural habitat, they take photos, make notes and sketch feather patterns, shapes and designs, movement and pose, noting how a bird moves its head, eats, walks and flies. They also research books and articles by noted ornithologists, examine paintings and drawings by famous artists and study taxidermy mounts and skins of game birds. Nearby colleges and environmental centers provide access to specimens of protected birds.

"Study skins," explains Grace, "are bird skins stuffed with cotton, then placed on a stick so they can be held for observation. However, they aren't lifelike mounts as in taxidermy, and conservation laws forbid having study skins or taxidermy models of anything but game birds."

Hummingbird on morning glory by Bill and Grace White

They use basswood because it is soft and close-grained and resists splitting. After drawing a pattern, Bill sketches it on a block of wood, then cuts the initial shape with a bandsaw. He carves the head first, then the body and the tail last, although if the beak is long and delicate, he sometimes leaves it until last to avoid breaking it. Details and feather patterns are drawn, then carved, with fine details and texturing achieved with a burning tool. After glass eyes are colored and inserted, legs fashioned from copper wire and attached to feet cast from lead or pewter, birds are mounted on wood to reflect the natural environment.

Birds up to the size of a robin are made full-scale, but

Red-winged blackbirds by Bill and Grace White

The Whites

Robin family by Bill and Grace White

feeder birds larger than robins are made slightly smaller than the stated field guide dimensions. "Birds are measured stretched out from tip of the beak to tip of the tail," says Grace. "Adhering to those dimensions sometimes makes the birds appear too large, and many collectors prefer something smaller than a museum piece."

In their "silent aviary" studio, Grace primes the carving using a series of thin washes of color to achieve depth of color and iridescence before painting details. She signs and dates each on completion. Birds range in price from $125 for a tiny kinglet to $1,500 for larger carvings or habitat groups. "The client is free to return it within 10

days if it doesn't meet his expectations," says Bill, "but we've never had a bird come back yet."

Bill and Grace White
995 Spring Lane
Chambersburg, PA 17201
(717) 264-7376
R W (limited) S MO

Other Makers

Al and Rita Calhoun, The Owl's Nest, Route 112-S, Moneta, VA 24121; (703) 297-5271, are known nationally for the birds that he carves and she paints.

Matthew Renna, 531 Poplar Avenue, Philadelphia, MS 39350; (601) 656-5375, carves birds from cypress, basswood and tupelo gum.

Tom Ahern, 110 Puggy Lane, Bethlehem, PA 18015; (215) 868-5840, creates exquisite wooden bird sculptures of basswood.

Kenneth L. Peiffer, Jr.

Red-tailed hawk by Bill and Grace White

Brasstown Carving

The John C. Campbell Folk School in Brasstown, North Carolina, was founded in 1925 to offer and demonstrate an education that was not just academic. Since then, it has become a rich source for traditional crafts of the region. The Brasstown carvers have become known for their lifelike animals and birds made from native woods like walnut, cherry and buckeye, ranging in height from 1½ to 9 inches. The John C. Campbell Folk School, Brasstown, NC 28902; (704) 837-2775. R W ($100 minimum) C ($1.50) MO

Carved bears by Hal McClure

CARVING

Other Maker

Ethel Hogsed, P.O. Box 5, Warne, NC 28909; (704) 389-8858, a former Brasstown carver, creates lyrical swans, ducks, squirrels, rabbits and some sea beasts from butternut, buckeye, wild cherry, basswood, black walnut and spalted (split) buckeye ranging in price from $5 to $250. Minimum $100 on mail orders.

Cedar Fans

During long winters at remote camps in Michigan, lumberjacks carved delicate three-dimensional fans and birds. They were made by cutting a large notch on each side of a block of white cedar, splitting the upper section into thin strips, then cutting smaller notches in these strips. After the wood was soaked to make it soft and pliable, the strips were spread apart and the small notches locked together to keep the fan or wing span permanently open. Glen Van Antwerp, fifth generation carver and descendant of Michigan lumberjacks, carves cedar birds for $12 to $35, fans on a handle or base for $35 to $150, and peacocks for $150 to $300. 912 Sparrow Avenue, Lansing, MI 48910; (517) 482-6258.

Peacock and grouse cedar fan birds by Glen Van Antwerp

Eagle Carving

The eagle, long a symbol of freedom and power, has always been a favorite of American carvers, especially since the bald eagle was named the national emblem in 1782. In nautical carving, eagles made proud figureheads and were carved into gangway boards, trailboards, billet heads (ornamental carving used in place of a ship's figurehead),

Eagle figurehead, 11 feet high with 16-foot wingspread, by Ron Beaulieu

paddle wheels and over the doors of pilot and custom houses. Eagles were also carved as freestanding sculptures and weather vanes, as ornaments atop gateposts and flagpoles and incorporated into the designs of mantels, boxes, presentation pipes, butter molds, mirror and picture frames (often with olive branches), arrows, flags, ribbons, shields and mottos.

Makers

Ron Beaulieu, 415 Columbus Avenue, Eastchester, NY 10709, specializes in eagles of all sizes made from pine, walnut, oak, mahogany and teak, ranging in price from $100 to $2,800.

Harold B. Simmons, Down East American Country, P.O. Box 503, Rockland ME 04841; (207) 594-0673, uses traditional styles and patterns of Maine ship carvers for his eagles.

Fred Grier, Shipcarver's Shop, Mystic Seaport Museum, Mystic, CT 06355; (203) 572-0711.

W. G. (Glen) Bean, 122 Battle Road, Yorktown, VA 23692; (804) 898-6146, carves eagles of white pine and

Carved eagle by Glen Bean

clear heart redwood. He also carves trail boards (curved and carved boards on the sides of the cutwater near the figurehead).

Roy L. Dupuy, 1301 Bumps' River Road, Centerville, MA 02632; (617) 775-2215, carves quarter boards (boards raised above the bulwark along a ship's quarter) as well as eagles.

HAWAIIAN CARVING

When he began carving, Rocky Ka'iouliokahihikolo'Ehu Jensen traveled to an adz pit 13,000 feet up in the mountains to select three stones of varying size, wrapped each separately to keep them from cracking during the descent and on his return home softened their edges by soaking them in vegetable juices. "It's a very subtle traditional process," he says, "but it works." After using an adz to break down and rough out the form, he defines carvings with a chisel and mallet, then a rasp, before sanding the surface by hand and rubbing the piece with kukui nut oil, which, in addition to being fragrant, is the symbol for light. Symbols and history are important to Rocky, founder and director of Hale Naua III, a society organized to perpetuate Hawaiian culture, history and religious traditions through the arts.

"In ancient Hawaii, art was created to uplift the mind and the spirit and meant to encompass all knowledge," he explains. "There were two types of carvers: functional, makers of tools, canoes, weapons, etc.; and ritual, those who carved the guardians, gods and ceremonial bowls. Symbols surrounding the images gave carvings identity, power and a mode of communication. In order to achieve the degree of master sculptor, one had to perfect his knowledge of symbols."

The hawk, most powerful of all totem images, is part of Rocky's personal symbol ("a black hawk striving upward toward the source" is a translation of his middle name), coupled with the "eye of Kane," creator of life and the original forest god. "It's important to recall what has been done in the past and to understand why," Rocky says. "Our word *akua* means 'from the back,' or 'those who have preceded you.' Our culture believes that each of us has three souls: the conscious and superconscious inside and the supreme conscious or mature parent who hovers over us like a guardian angel throughout our lives."

When he was 9, Rocky won his first art award, from the Honolulu Academy of Arts. After majoring in art at college on the mainland, he returned to Hawaii where he worked in construction and "began carving little things, *tiki*-like totems." He began researching his culture to give his son a traditional name. "As I became more aware of

"Wailua a'u" (My Two Souls), carving depicting the twin souls of man, the conscious and subconscious selves, by Rocky Ka'iouliokahihikolo'Ehu Jensen

the symbols and their meanings, I began to ask myself, 'Why are you here?' " Shortly after his great-grandmother came to him in a dream ("to scold me"), Rocky began to dream conceptually. "Sometimes the image of the carving was so vivid in my mind," he says, "that I felt like I'd done it before. One carving came in a series of dreams. I worked most of the week without sleep trying to keep up with it."

Since then, he has seen his carvings exhibited and included in private and public collections in the United States, won several major awards, organized workshops and seminars to teach Hawaiians their heritage, instituted the Annual Hawaiian Fine Arts Exhibit and established a branch of the Hale Naua to work with architects and developers.

Many of his carvings are made from found wood. His favorite, koa, is light to dark red like mahogany. "*Milo,* similar to rosewood, is light brown to purple to dark brown. *Wilwil* is white like balsa, with a tight grain and salt-and-pepper texture. *Kamani,* red like mahogany, with a wavy grain, is used for meat platters. *Kauila* was historically used for weapons, but I use it to carve hand-held images known as stick gods, or *kumuta'a,*" says Rocky.

CARVING

Each of his carvings is researched and has a definite name-essence. Although he does not sell his ancestral images unless he is commissioned to create one for a specific reason, he does create the national Polynesian god-images for sale. Prices range from $1,200 for small statues to $3,000 for medium to large and $5,000 upward for life-size. His bowls range in price from $750 to $3,000.

Rocky Ka'iouliokahihikolo'Ehu Jensen
Hale Naua III, Society of Hawaiian Arts
99-919 Kalawina Place
'Aiea, HI 96701
(808) 487-6949
V (by appt.)   R   MO

NORWEGIAN-AMERICAN FIGURE CARVING

When people see one of Harley Refsal's Norwegian-American carved figures, they tend to say something like, "I *know* that guy. He used to live down the road from my folks' place."

"Actually, most of my people are types, rather than specific personalities," says Harley, "inspired by those I knew as a child in west-central Minnesota. Our farm was one of the most old-fashioned in the county. The neighbors used tractors, but my father preferred a team of horses. We threshed instead of combining, used loose hay instead of baled, exactly the way my grandparents had done when they emigrated from Norway in the 1890s. My own experiences, the stories I heard while growing up, are a powerful source of inspiration for my carvings, which depict life in a traditional farming community. My work tells stories about clearing the land, washing clothes on the cookstove and getting a ride to school in a manure-spreader pulled by a team of horses."

Woman spinning and man carving, carved figures by Harley Refsal

Carved men with beards by Harley Refsal

The third generation in his family to work with wood, Harley still has the tomahawk he made from a peach crate as a boy. He didn't start carving until he became intrigued with the carved figures of peasants, laborers and fishermen that he saw while attending the University of Oslo. In the beginning, he used much detail, but as he progressed, he learned to convey character with fewer and fewer cuts. "That's what distinguishes this type of carving," he says. "Bold, flat knife cuts; about six cuts per pant leg. I used only large tools until I'd mastered the angular look of minimal cuts and deliberate, bold strokes that are not later smoothed out with sandpaper."

Three of Harley's characters evoke a strong sense of nostalgia among Norwegian-Americans: the *nisse,* and Ola and Per. "The *nisse* is a spritely elf that embodies the spirit of the farm and brings presents on Christmas Eve," explains Harley. "Treat him right and he takes care of you; deny his existence and prepare for the worst." (Harley recently carved a *nisse* on the "Prairie Home Companion" radio show, which makes Harley, in the opinion of host Garrison Keillor, the first live national radio wood carver.) "Ola and Per were characters in the longest running cartoon strip in the United States, which appeared in the Norwegian-language paper *Decorah Posten.* Ola, an all-around nice guy, and dapper Per, a tinkerer who sometimes can't put things back together, actually chronicle the Americanization of the Norwegian-Americans."

Harley's caricatures, which combine an American subject with a Norwegian carving style used by immigrants (whose work was known for its sense of humor and poignancy), have won many woodcarving trophies and awards in national and international exhibitions. Made of basswood, because "it's abundant, uniform to carve, takes detail well and most approximates the pine and birch used by Norwegians," his full-bodied characters are 6 to 12 inches tall and range in price from $100 to several hundred dollars for groupings. He also does busts and figures up to 24 inches tall on commission. A horse that he designed for *Wood Magazine* combines the clean-lined Scandinavian look with the powerful lines of the horses carved during the 18th and 19th centuries in Norway. "Carvers of that era frequently featured horses," says Harley, "because they were symbols of power."

Constantly on the lookout for "nicely wrinkled faces with good lines," Harley watches with a careful eye when he's with people, especially at the Norwegian-American Museum where he teaches and serves as volunteer guide. His best pupils? His young sons, Carl and Martin, fourth generation carvers who probably enjoy the stories as much as the work.

Harley Refsal
Route 5, Twin Springs
Decorah, IA 52101
(319) 382-9383
V (by appt.)   R   S   MO

PRIMITIVE CARVING

Like folk carvers of yesteryear, Dan Strawser uses only a pocketknife to make his eagles, lions, roosters, whimsical birds and human figures. And like itinerant carvers before him, he travels to follow his work. "However, early carvers wandered in search of work," says Dan. "After living in Berks County, Pennsylvania, for 42 years, I moved [to Tennessee] because my company transferred me. To keep my carving as creative as possible and not hurry it to get money to survive, I earn my living as an administrator."

Dan started carving in 1968 after being inspired by a local history course. "At first my style was heavily influenced by Schimmel, Mounts and Simmons," he says. "I still consider myself a student of theirs. I like their childlike naive approach in carving and coloration, but I've developed my own inner sense of feeling for color and character. My subjects come from memory: pictures I've seen,

Carved rooster by Dan Strawser

birds I'd like to see, anything that strikes my fancy. I try to make each carving one that I want to keep, an expression of joy, fun, life from my mind. I want each one to have a personality all its own in face, action, stance and character. Each must stand on its own and speak to those who see it. Sometimes this is achieved in the carving, sometimes the painting, usually a combination of both."

In 1968, Hattie Brunner, an antiques dealer in Reinholds, Pennsylvania, began selling Strawser's work, signed with his initials and the date, "as a good investment," says Dan, "because even then Schimmel's work was expensive. People bought my carvings because Hattie told them that someday they would be worth a lot of money." Today, Strawser's work is exhibited with that of Wilhelm Schimmel and Aaron Mounts in the Cumberland County Historical Society as well as museums and private collections in America and Europe.

Early Pennsylvania-German carvers created all kinds of fanciful animals, birds and figure groupings for amusement and decoration. Many carvings had their roots in the 18th century *putz*, or Christmas landscape, which illustrated Biblical stories and had a manger as focal point. It was set under or near the Christmas tree in a background of natural materials, and its foreground often included wise men, farms, villages, animals and a Noah's

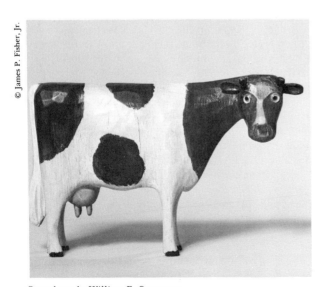

Richard J. Patrick

Carved animals by Walter Gottshall

© James P. Fisher, Jr.

Carved cow by William F. Oosterman

Ark. Dan's menagerie includes pigs, peacocks, sheep and storks.

He prefers working in sugar pine, but it's difficult to find in Tennessee, so he now carves figures from basswood, preferred by bird carvers for its close grain, which allows them to add feathers without worrying about the wood splitting apart. One of his most popular offerings, a sassafras tree with fourteen different hand-carved birds, is in the style of the early itinerant carver from Berks County known as Schtockschnitzler (cane carver) Simmons, who also used sassafras. "Sassafras grows wild in Tennessee," says Dan, "as well as in Pennsylvania. I collect it in the winter, tie it into shape and let it dry for 6 to 10 weeks." After carving, his figures are sealed with gesso, then polychromed for an age-old finish.

His figures range in price from $13 for a bird on a wire heart swing to $300 for a 20-inch-high eagle. Because his carvings are fragile, Dan prefers clients to pick them up at his studio. Otherwise they are shipped via UPS or Priority Mail with shipping and handling charges added to the price.

Daniel G. Strawser
409 Hay Long Avenue
Mt. Pleasant, TN 38474
(615) 379-0442
V R W C

Other Makers

Walter L. Gottshall, RD 1, Reinholds, PA 17569; (215) 678-1385, makes wonderful whimsical animals, as well as tramp art.

William F. Oosterman, 132 Pine Street, Oxford, PA 19363; (215) 932-2573, carves robust figures as sturdy and as strong as the people and traditions that inspire them: cows and horses that look up as if to ask why you're passing through their field ($25 to $125), angels ($50 to $200) and crèche figures ($175).

Norton Latourelle, 61 Water Street, P.O. Box 692, Newburyport, MA 01950; (617) 462-9735, carves happy birds and animals of pine, priced from $25, with most from $50 to $150. V R W C

Eleanor Meadowcroft, 25 Flint Street, Salem, MA 01970; (617) 745-6336, carves fanciful animals, some on wheels.

The Reverend Herman L. Hayes, 2630 Montana Avenue, Hurricane, WV 25526-1113; (304) 562-6411, does chain-carving, or objects within objects carved from the same piece of wood. These include balls within balls and animals or people inside cages. "People ask, 'How did you get that in there?' I say, 'I didn't. It's never been out.'" He won the 1979 Governor's Award for a ball game carving 14 inches across with 150 little spectators.

TRAMP ART CARVING

Tramp art, also known as knifework or notch art, is an intricate form of chip-carving, with notched edges built up in layers of inexpensive or found wood, rather than carved into more expensive stock. Started by itinerant American carvers in the latter half of the 1800s, tramp art was most frequently made of cigar boxes of cedar or mahogany that could be obtained for nothing or a few pennies. Wood from these boxes was cut with any sharp instrument into circles, squares, triangles, diamonds, hearts, stars, flowers, animals or patriotic and religious symbols, then built up pyramid fashion in layers glued or nailed in place and applied as decoration on everything from frames to furniture: mirrors, comb cases, boxes, hanging shelves, easels, miniatures, small-scale furniture, humidors, banks, clock cases, lamps or whimsical pieces crafted for the fun of it. Sometimes names, dates and letters were added to personalize a piece, or brass tacks used for ornamentation. As cigarettes became more popular than cigars and the number of cigar boxes declined, so did tramp art.

"It's definitely go for the Gothic, decoration on decoration and the reverse of minimalism, because in tramp art more is better," says Bob Self, who has been carving notch art since 1973. He saw his first piece of tramp art in an antique shop and a few years later decided to try the form himself. "The style appealed to me," he says. "Once I started, I stopped making any other form. The main feeling of accomplishment comes from the amount of notching in each piece, which always is more than necessary, sort of like icing on a birthday cake. It's a masculine form of knitting for the hyperactive man who has to be doing something with his hands. But if you expect instant gratification, it won't thrill you, because it takes patience and time."

Born in Trenton, New Jersey, Bob left school in the ninth grade and became a cameraman known for his special effects ("theater magic") on television commercials. He notches for relaxation, using traditional tools (a knife and bandsaw or matt knife and scroll saw) and scrap wood. He makes one-of-a-kind pieces because he gets bored making more than a few of anything.

Prices vary considerably. "Like the tramps of old," explains Bob, "I have charged as little as $1 for a very small frame and $300 for a pair of cactus lamps." The cacti are always made in pairs and no two are alike. Frames are made to fit subjects and are generally inspired by them. The frame of the moose is $90; a larger piece, with fewer notches, is $150. A rocket started in 1983, his largest piece to date, has four doors and many compartments and when finished will be a bar 8½ feet long.

"The concept of a whole environment of my notch art

Carved tramp-art frame of clear sugar pine, designed to emphasize moose subject, by Bob Self

comes naturally to me," says Bob, "as my home fills up with the stuff. If you've ever seen how lonely one piece of tramp art looks in a show or shop, you'll know what I mean. It's lonely, almost ugly in its aloneness, whereas a whole roomful takes on a totally different feeling. Think of a whole house and yard of it. Every inch covered with notches. A crackpot idea probably, but that's never stopped me yet."

Happily for collectors of tramp art, Bob has a permanent address. You can call him there Monday to Friday, 10 A.M. to 6 P.M.

Bob Self
230 West 10th Street
New York, NY 10014
(212) 675-4894
R   MO

BANNISTER-BACK CHAIRS

"When I discovered that a Queen Anne lowboy had been sitting in my grandmother's dining room," says Allan Breed, "there was no stopping my interest in furniture. I would go into people's houses and end up crawling under tables and chairs to see how they were constructed."

He began buying furniture that needed repair to learn more through restoration work and at the age of 20 volunteered to work without pay under Vincent Cerbone, the master restorer at the Boston Museum of Fine Arts. After the first summer, he was invited back to work for a salary, which he continued to do during breaks and vacations while he attended the University of New Hampshire.

"Working with Mr. Cerbone catalyzed my interest in furniture," says Allan, "and gave direction to my work. I was able to handle, examine and work on an endless variety of examples of the best early furniture available. The knowledge and excitement that resulted from this hands-on experience would have been hard to duplicate." After graduation, he became a restorer of antiques for dealers and historical societies "and learned cabinetmaking backwards by taking apart and reassembling the work of men who have long since died, leaving only their work as a guide." His venture into wood-turning came when he accepted a job no one else wanted: making 350 small fancy spindles for the restoration of the Sandown, New Hampshire, Meeting House. After thousands of more spindles, newel posts and chair parts, he began accepting commis-

Close-up of carved crest on bannister-back chair by Allan Breed

Bannister-back chair by Allan Breed

sions to make reproductions of 17th and early 18th century New England furniture and today is known for his superb bannister-back chairs.

"The chairs that I produce evolved from the wainscot chairs of the 17th century," he explains, "heavy paneled pieces with ornate carving derived from Renaissance embellishments. The bannister-back armchair is especially interesting because it combines the feel of the medieval pieces with the more flamboyant rococo style, and is a result of craftsmen interpreting and simplifying the more elaborate European styles. The chair has a certain powerful stance and feel to it that I don't find in later styles. Its almost royal look is closer to a seat of power, like a throne, whereas higher style Queen Anne or Chippendale styles (even though I like them) don't have that naive attempt at being high style that the early pieces do."

His bannister-backs, with their bold turnings, carved crests, Spanish feet and rush seats, have a centuries-old patina achieved by rubbing down oil paint. "The secret is in the mixing," says Allan. "I do a great deal of turning, and as much carving as possible, having bought several hundred carving tools from my former master at the MFA." Although originals are now selling for more than $10,000 each (if you can find them), Allan's bannister-backs sell for $1,100, in as great a number as a client desires. "Why not get what you want," he says, "in sets, even, for a fraction of the price?"

He accepts commissions to make almost any type of early furniture. "I usually use mahogany, cherry or maple," he explains, "and on the early maple pieces generally use a painted finish. Due to this variety, I have no catalog. I tell my customers that if they can find an example, I can make it. As a result, I do a great deal of work for people who collect early furniture but need a piece that is unavailable in the marketplace."

Allan Breed
Cabinet and Chair Maker
26A Cider Hill Road
York, ME 03909
(207) 363-6388
V (by appt. only)   R   S   MO

LADDERBACK CHAIRS

Arval Woody, a fifth generation chair maker whose family has been in the business for 150 years, makes indestructible chairs. To prove it, he likes to balance a chair on one leg, then jump up in the air and land on it full force.

The reason nothing breaks (including Woody) is that Woody's chairs are made without nails or glue. Chair posts are air-dried only, while ladderback slats and rounds are air-dried first then dried in a kiln. The chair pieces are then driven tightly together. As the posts continue to dry, they shrink onto the rounds, clamping them tighter and tighter with each passing year.

"I have a 75-year-old chair my grandfather made," says Woody, "and I can still jump on it without breaking it."

As a boy, Woody used to play in the sawdust in his grandfather's shop, a few hundred yards from the one he built for himself after World War II. His grandfather's shop was powered by a water wheel. Woody uses electricity, but has never found anything that works better than his 1873 mortising machine. He designed and built most of the machinery himself, including a post sander made of such spare parts as a wheel from an old lawnmower and the motor from a washing machine.

Each year, Woody spends a month to 6 weeks handpicking and processing the wood for his chairs (walnut, cherry, oak, ash and maple) in his own sawmill. Back slats are boiled 150 at a time in a 60-gallon drum in the backyard for 20 minutes, then bent into frames where they dry into curves. Posts and rungs are turned by hand. Before the chairs are put together, each piece is finished while spinning on a lathe, rubbed with oil to a sheen that surpasses several years of ordinary waxing. "With our oil finish," says Woody, "the beauty of the wood comes through and scuff marks can just be waxed off."

Scratching and chipping are rare. Although most of Woody's chairs are made for individuals, they've had use as well in schools (where they're able to handle any amount of use or abuse) and yacht clubs (because no amount of moisture can separate them). His most famous chair is a child's cherry rocker in the Smithsonian Institution. A pair in walnut, given to Caroline and John F. Kennedy, Jr., when they were children, are now in the Kennedy

Child's cherrywood rocker by Arval Woody

Library Museum in Boston. Woody's fairly famous too. He was featured in *National Geographic*'s "Craftsmen in America" and also in "Artisans of the Appalachians."

Woody's chairs are available in straight or rocking styles and range in price from $90 for a side chair in oak, ash or maple to $195 for a rocker in walnut or cherry. Two styles are available: the Betsy Ross (copied from a commemorative stamp) and the Colonial (with angel-wing slats and plain finials).

Woody ships smaller pieces by UPS, larger by truck, but recommends that one rocker or two straight chairs can be shipped most economically by bus. For a brochure showing all models, write. If you're in the neighborhood, stop by. The shop is 3 miles south of town on NC 226 near the Blue Ridge Parkway.

Arval J. and Nora N. Woody
Woody's Chair Shop
110 Dale Road
Spruce Pine, NC 28777
(704) 765-9277
V   R   C   S   MO

CHAIRS

Other Maker

David Barrett, Barretts Bottoms, Route 2, Box 231, Bower Road, Kearneysville, WV 25430; (304) 725-0777. C ($3)

MULE-EAR, THUMB-BACK, ARROWBACK, FANCY AND VERMONT ROCKER CHAIRS

Mule-ear chairs, also known as mountain or settin' chairs, have been the table chair of the Ozarks and Appalachians since colonial times. Shaved out each winter by generations of makers, bottomed with hickory bark or cornhusks, they were piled into wagons and sold up and down the valleys. Shaved chairs are made entirely with a drawknife from thin rivings of hardwood. The markedly bent rear posts, with the lower slat positioned to support the lower back, makes the chair extremely comfortable.

"The New England version was more quaint than comfortable," says chair maker Eric Ginette, "which is why I don't make them. The thumb-back, with deeply shaped bottom and small riven wood parts that exactly fit the human form, and flattened stiles that look like thumbs, is a more sophisticated version that became the favored table chair of New England. The old-style baluster turnings of the 1700s evolved into simpler two-ring legs with an H-stretcher, an easy bottom frame to assemble with a brace and bit. In the Sheraton period two rings grew to three to give the appearance of bamboo; the H-stretcher gave way to the box stretcher assembly of four rungs. The arrowback is similar to the thumb-back, but spindles flare out widely at the top like feathers on an arrow; flattened spindles carry the thumb-back shape across the back.

"After the war between the states, 'fancy' chairs appeared, nicknamed for their fancy paint jobs, with striping, multicolored stenciling and gold on the beads and vee's. All of these chairs were popular but did not mix with the better chairs of their day, which is why they're seldom mentioned in furniture books. They were too common and made no pretense of being art."

Eric Ginette became a chair maker because he was fascinated with the forms and fluid lines of chairs. His chairs, often referred to as green woodwork because the parts are taken directly from logs worked while green, lock together in a lifelong grip no glue can match as the posts shrink with age. Working as a carpenter and joiner since college days in the 1960s, Eric developed a reverence for old chairs that grew as he talked with old-timers who had made them. "I love old hand tools," says Eric, "both having and using them. For the small producer, hand tools are the only way these parts can be made. Once experience in their use is acquired, it's amazing how quickly and efficiently the old tools work."

He cuts native hardwood trees himself and splits them into rails in the forest. The rails are then riven with a froe and club into rough chair parts. The riven pieces are shaped with a drawknife on the shave-bench, then either steamed and bent to the shapes needed or turned on the lathe. The wood is worked green and unseasoned as it comes from the tree. Some parts like chair rungs are dried after fashioning, while other parts, like legs, are assembled green.

"The green parts shrink around the dry sections, locking together in an aggressive and durable way," says Eric. "I know my lifetime is far shorter than the life of my chairs. I often use milk paint for finish because colors produced by baked and ground clay, so characteristic of the 18th century, are impossible to reproduce with modern oil paints. The texture of milk paint gives a traditional chair the correct look and feel."

Eric's chairs range in price from $190 for a mule-ear to $225 for a Sheraton hoop-back to Windsors from $325 to a Sheraton settee for $650.

Eric Ginette
Cabot Chair Shop
RFD
Cabot, VT 05647
(802) 563-2558
V R C S

Other Makers

Brian Boggs, CPO 51, Berea, KY 40404; (606) 986-9188, has a reputation for making perfect mule-ear chairs from perfect hickory, with a good dark heart, no wind shakes (cracks along the growth rings) and medium growth. Seats are made of hickory bark, white oak splints or natural rush, all of which he gathers himself. He can also bottom in Shaker tape, cornshucks and rush (cattail leaves).

B. Terry Ratliff, Route 1, Manton, KY 41748; (606) 285-3740, makes mule-ear ladderbacks with hickory bark seats, as well as rockers and stools.

Mule-ear chair by Eric Ginette

New England thumb-back chair by Eric Ginette

Sheraton hoop-back chair, c. 1820–style, by Eric Ginette

Arrowback chair by Eric Ginette

Vermont rocker, early 1800s–style, by Eric Ginette

SHAKER CHAIRS

The Shakers, a small religious sect that lived and worked in nineteen communities from Maine to Kentucky, made chairs in all of their communities for their own use, but it was only at Mt. Lebanon that they made chairs of all sizes for sale.

Each settlement had style preferences. Enfield chairs were light and graceful, Canterbury were slightly heavier over-all. The Ohio Valley chair had graduated back slats with a flat top edge and gradually increasing curve, with inverted acorn finials. Some were tapered into what is known as mule-eared tops. Instead of cane or rush, most Shakers preferred weaving the seats and backs of chairs with tape called *listing*. The tape outlasted cane or rush and came in many colors, which could be used singly or in combination in a variety of designs. When chairs were not in use, they were light enough to be hung on pegs along the wall.

In 1978 when Lenore Howe and Brian Braskie tried to buy original Shaker chairs, they discovered they were expensive and rare. When they couldn't find authentic or well-made reproductions, they decided to make their own. After a year and a half of touring Shaker villages to study the furniture and talk with the remaining Shakers, they formed the North Woods Chair Shop.

Shaker furniture, forerunner of today's functional furniture, was known for its simple lines and solid beauty. In the mid-1800s, Shaker chairs sold for as much as $17

Enfield armchairs by Lenore Howe and Brian Braskie

because, like Shaker cupboards, tables and stools, they were light in construction yet extremely strong. They were also comfortable, functional, free of ornamentation and easy to clean.

Canterbury straight chair and Watervliet lowback dining chair by Lenore Howe and Brian Braskie

"It's not unusual for a Shaker chair to weigh only 5 pounds and last a century," says Lenore. "Our chairs, like the originals, are made by hand. They *feel* handmade. The tactile experience is as important to our customers as the visual or physical aspects of our work. There's only one difference and that's the size. Because people are bigger, the proportions of our chairs are slightly larger overall."

Named for the Shaker communities where they originated, North Woods designs include Enfield, Canterbury, Watervliet and Mt. Lebanon styles in chairs and rockers (from $295 to $495), a side table with hand-dovetailed drawer ($360), an ironing stool ($230), a children's chair ($225) and a low-back dining chair made to slide under the table ($205). Prices are for cherry and maple, FOB Canterbury, New Hampshire. Work in figured grains (like tiger maple, or bird's-eye maple) is custom and costs extra. Tapes are available in ten different colors and herringbone, checkerboard, basket-weave, diamond and radial weaving designs. Most orders are filled in 16 weeks. A 50 percent deposit is required at time of order, with balance due prior to delivery or shipping.

Brian builds the frames; Lenore finishes them in natural

cherry, medium brown, reddish brown or ebony with a hand-rubbed oil finish. Each piece that leaves their shop is signed, numbered, dated and registered in the name of the original owner.

Like the Shakers whose work they admire, Lenore and Brian take delight, as she says, in "being self-sustaining and independent. We've dedicated ourselves to the same standards they lived by and want to do work they'd be proud of, keeping quality first and foremost."

Lenore Howe and Brian Braskie
North Woods Chair Shop
RFD 1, Old Tilton Road
Canterbury, NH 03224
(603) 783-4594
V   R   C   MO

Other Makers

Tim Rieman, Box 402, North Lebanon, NY 12125, makes the Shaker tilter chair (whose rear legs are fitted with a socket to hold a device that allows the sitter to tilt back) plus several other styles.

Ian Ingersoll, West Cornwall, CT 06796; (203) 672-6334, makes a Mt. Lebanon rocking chair from steam-bent maple with interlocking tenons, signed with gold leaf decals to authenticate its origin. Shipping via common carrier freight collect.

Eric Ginette, Cabot Chair Shop, RFD, Cabot, VT 05647; (802) 563-2558, makes Shaker rockers in black cherry or sugar maple, finished in milk paint or a natural oil, whose canvas tape backs and bottoms contain a thick foam pillow for added comfort.

David Barrett of Barretts Bottoms, Route 2, Box 231, Bower Road, Kearneysville, WV 25430; (304) 725-0777, makes the classic Enfield side chair, the Ohio Valley chair with inverted acorn finials and the backed dining bench used in communal dining halls.

WINDSOR CHAIRS

From the time the first American version was made in Philadelphia in 1725, Windsor chairs have been at home in America. Called Philadelphia chairs at first, but known as Windsors as they worked their way northward into New England, American Windsors had more verve than their English cousins. The best were recognized by bold turnings, seats shaped to fit human bottoms, a wide splay in the legs and hospitable proportions. The earliest Windsors were large, while later versions had more delicate lines. Built with a solid plank seat, canted legs and spindled backs, Windsors found new interpretation in every period, from the bamboo turnings of the Federal era to the firehouse and kitchen styles of Victorian times. Pennsylvanians preferred ball feet, while New Englanders liked legs that flowed into gentle tapers. In the 1800s, long arrowbacks appeared in Pennsylvania and short arrowbacks gained popularity in Tennessee. While the English used oak, Americans created Windsors from a variety of woods, sometimes varnished but more often painted.

David Sawyer makes Windsors as they did 200 years ago, using the same materials and most of the same tools, "except that my lathe is powered by a motor instead of a foot." An MIT grad, Dave retired from engineering at the age of 28 and joined the Peace Corps before becoming a chair maker. "I use a bandsaw occasionally, but it's still 98 percent handwork, a lot of careful shaving, carving, turning, bending, fitting and finishing."

Seats are made of 2-inch pine planks, carved deep for comfort. Other parts are split from green wood following the grain, then shaved or turned. Dave used to bend backs from ash, "but it's getting hard to find bendable ash," he

Fan-back chair by David Sawyer

says, "perhaps because acid rain is slowing the growth and making the wood brittle." He now uses "oak for bending backs and ash for spindles. For comb-back spindles, I use ironwood [American hop hornbeam] for greater stiffness. Hickory would be good, but it doesn't grow here, but hard maple makes strong, crisp turnings. Some chair makers like soft maple or birch, but I find them too fuzzy and not hard enough. I like cherry on natural finish chairs because it's crisp."

Legs and posts are fitted to tapered sockets in the seat, then wedged for tighter fit, with glue added for extra insurance. Dave will provide chairs "in the wood" for $35 less, for those who want to finish their own, or finished in clear oil, but he prefers using milk paint (red, mustard, green, green-black, blue, brown, pitch black or black on red), "because that's the way period chair makers finished them. It unifies the design."

Prices range from $265 for an unfinished loop-back side chair to $560 for a comb-back with scroll-carved ears and knuckles in butternut, cherry and oak. A continuous arm settee for two costs $650, while a 10-footer is $1,455. In addition to the regular round bow back, plain ears and flat arms, options include carved scroll ears ($25), carved knuckles ($35), beaded bows ($10) and baluster turnings with shaved spindles from the colonial period or bamboo turnings from Federal times. High chairs can be made in any style for 85 percent of the full-size price, while rockers are $90 extra.

Oil-finished "natural chairs" with butternut seats, cherry turnings and oak backs ("a very pleasing combination," according to Dave) are $30 extra. For a brochure with drawings, photos and color samples, send $1 (deducted from order). Dave can also duplicate old Windsors or custom-build any style. Best of all, his chairs come with a lifetime guarantee "to outlast either myself or the original owner."

David Sawyer
RD 1, Box 107
East Calais, VT 05650
(802) 456-8836
R   C   S   MO

Other Makers

Eric Ginette, Cabot Chair Shop, RFD, Cabot, VT 05647; (802) 563-2558, makes a sack-back ($425), comb-back ($425) and continuous arm Windsor ($400).

James Lea, 9 West Street, Rockport, ME 04856; (207) 236-3632, makes continuous arm, bow-back, fan-back, comb-back and writing arm Windsors, high chairs and settees, in light or dark natural finishes as well as crackle finish, a five-step process that takes 2 weeks to complete but after a few years' use looks 200 years old.

Dan Mosheim, Box 2660, Red Mountain Road, Arlington, VT 05250; (802) 375-2568.

Robert Barrow, 412 Thomas Street, Bristol, RI, 02809; (401) 253-4434, specializes in Windsor chairs, especially Newport and Pennsylvanian styles.

Curtis Buchanan, 510 Locust Street, Jonesborough, TN 37659; (615) 753-5160. Free price list.

Mark Nelson, RFD Box 900, Starks, ME 04911; (207) 696-5281.

Peter Cullum, The Dovetail Joint, 1332 Harlem Boulevard, Rockford, IL 61103; (815) 965-6677, uses no electric power to make his furniture, but instead uses a foot-pedaled wood lathe.

Jeff Koopus, 1522 Maple Ridge Road, Harrison, ME 04040; (207) 583-4860, makes Rhode Island sack-back, Connecticut high-back and Nantucket braced-back armchair Windsors.

Jeffrey M. Fiant, RD 1, Golf Road, Reinholds, PA 17569; (215) 678-1828.   C ($1)

Peter Touhey, RFD 2, Box 113A, Eastman Road, Canaan, NH 03741; (603) 523-4465.

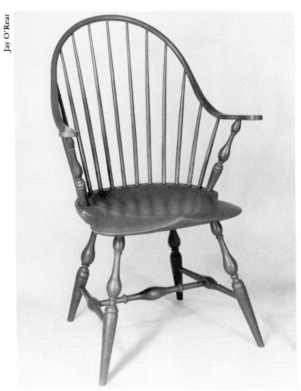

Jay O'Rear

Continuous arm chair by David Sawyer

Sack-back armchair by David Sawyer

Michael Camp, 636 Starkweather, Plymouth MI 48170; (313) 459-1190.   C ($3)

Stephen A. Adams, William J. James Company, Mill Hill Road, Denmark, ME 04022; (207) 452-2444, in addition to Windsors makes a comb-back courting bench.

Richard Grell, P.O. Box 2238, Hudson, OH 44236.

COWHIDE CHAIR SEATS

Cowhide has found more appreciation and uses in the Lone Star State than any place on earth. Anyone who raised cattle had hides, nothing was thrown away and a use was found for everything. Leather lasted longer than material bought in the store. All it cost was the time spent curing it. Cowhide was used for leggings (chaps, or *chaparajos*), laces, toe fenders (*tapedros*), boots, sandals, saddles, harness, rugs, ropes, gear, beds *and* chair seats. Old-timers in Texas believed that sleeping on cowhide would ward off or cure rheumatism. Chair seats of cowhide made sense: a natural material, leather was easier on the body than wood, more comfortable than splints or cane and didn't wear out like cloth.

"I don't know how far back cowhide-bottom chairs go," says Ronnie Fiedler, who learned to make them from his father, "but it's not unusual to get a chair seat well over 100 years old to recover. The average one lasts about 70 years. Cowhide chairs were more common in the South than in the North. The farmer was usually poor and used everything he had. Cowhide is strong, comes in many colors and thicknesses. The thickness of the hide depends on what climate the cattle was bred for. A fat cowhide is easier to clean. A poor hide takes twice as long to do and may tear while cleaning."

Ronnie gets his hides from a slaughterhouse, fresh and untreated. After hanging one over a fence rail 6 feet off the ground with the flesh side out, he spends about an hour slicing off all fat, meat and tissue with a 6-inch skinning knife. When he's through, the hide weighs 40 percent less than when he started. The hide is soaked in 8 gallons of water with a pound of Twenty Mule Team Borax Powder for an hour, then hung to drip dry for about 2 hours. The hide is then laid out in the shade with the flesh side up, rubbed generously with more borax powder, allowed to set for a day or two but not allowed to get too dry.

Handmade cowhide seat laced on to chair frame by Ronnie Fiedler

Cowhide stool seats by Ronnie Fiedler

CHEROKEE CRAFTS

The Cherokee, largest American Indian tribe east of the Mississippi, were peace-loving farmers who never lived in tepees, but built houses and raised crops. Quick to adopt the ways of the European settlers, the Cherokee also taught them how to grow and preserve native foods like corn and squash. In 1839, when the U.S. government forced the Cherokee to move to Oklahoma, nearly one-fourth of them died on the way from disease, starvation or hardship, but a small band of several hundred who hid out in the Smoky Mountains survived. Known as the eastern band of the Cherokee, they live along coves and roads on a 56,000-acre reservation where they teach their children the Cherokee language and sell crafts through the Qualla Arts & Crafts Center, a cooperative founded in 1946. Their baskets were admired as early as 1540 by none less than Hernando de Soto, who was exploring America at the time. They weren't for sale then, but they are now.

"In 1963, I was told that $10 was too high a price for one of my large baskets," says Eva Wolfe of Big Cove, one of the best-known basket weavers in the United States. Since then her baskets have been exhibited at the Smithsonian and won her a heritage fellowship from the National Endowment for the Arts, and now bring from $650 to $1,000. "At one time shops wouldn't even buy my double-weave baskets," says Eva. "Now they're in great demand." Eva specializes in one of the most difficult techniques of plaited basketry, the river cane double-weave, where one basket is woven inside another in one unbroken interlacing. Eva, her husband, Amble, and her son Jonah (one of their eleven children) gather cane by the truckload about four times a year. Eva cuts each stalk into four strips, then dyes some for contrasting color using bloodroot for reddish brown and butternut tree roots for dark brown. In addition to white oak and river cane baskets by other weavers, Qualla carries Joyce Taylor's baskets woven in mystical horizontal bands of skinned honeysuckle.

Qualla's most famous carver is Goingback Chiltoskey, known for his realistic figures and animals. Others include the husband-and-wife team of James and Irma Bradley, who also carve animals, and Davy Arch, who makes masks and strong mythological creatures from wood as well as pipes and fetish necklaces of stone. The most extraordinary carvings are by John Julius Wilnoty, whose powerful figures and pipes of local soapstone resemble pre-Columbian artifacts. The self-taught artist finds inspiration not in books but in his head: he sees the figure he wants to carve in his mind when he looks at a stone.

Qualla's other artisans include William Lossiah, who

"If I'm not going to use the hide right away," says Ronnie, "I can keep it in the refrigerator for weeks. I usually leave the hair on the hide because taking it off takes longer." Old-timers used to soak the hide for a week or so in a combination of oak ashes and water to make the hair slip, but Ronnie's found that freezing the hide several times causes the hide to start spoiling, at which point the hair can be almost wiped off.

He first cuts ½-inch strips around the hide three times, which provides enough lacing for the chairs that the hide will cover. Placing the hide over the chair bottom with a 3-inch overhang on all sides, he cuts three or four 1-inch slits in each overhang. With approximately 12 feet of lacing, he laces side to side, then front to back, pulling the laces as tight as possible and putting a half hitch in the last hole. The half hitch is easy to untie to tighten the laces, which is done twice a day for a week, depending on the weather, until the hide stops stretching.

Cowhide seats start at $30, depending on size. If you've never known the comfort of a leather seat and don't expect to inherit one in the Texas tradition, Ronnie also sells new hardwood (oak or ash) ladderback chairs, $55; sewing rockers, $75; large rockers, $95; baby rockers, $40; jumbo and double-jumbo rockers, $295 and $395; as well as stools from $25 to $40. Shipping extra. His shop is open 10 A.M. to 5 P.M. Tuesday through Saturday.

Ronnie Fiedler
The Hiding Place
P.O. Box 1255
Ingram, TX 78025
(512) 367-2584 or 895-4687
V   R   S   MO

River cane double-weave waste basket by Eva Wolfe

Cherrywood buffalo, 9 inches high and 14 inches long, by Goingback Chiltoskey

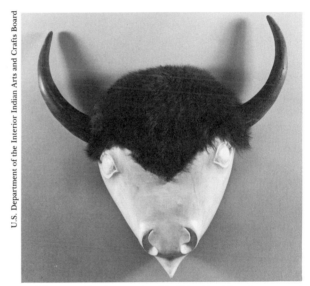

Buffalo mask of buckeye wood and buffalo skin, 17 inches wide and 18 inches high, by Davy Arch

"Inertia," 6-inch-high stone carving by John Julius Wilnoty

Medicine bowl of coiled and modeled earthenware with incised designs, 3½ inches high, by the Bigmeat family

creates objects rooted in his tribal past, like basswood drums, medicine sticks and tomahawks with leather-covered handles; and Alyne Stampers, whose fans, conjuring sticks, rattles, pipes and necklaces are recognized for their sophisticated bead- and featherwork. Also prized by collectors is the dark powerful pottery of the Bigmeat family. Built by the coil method and incised with designs, the pots are fired in an open pit. When soft woods are used for the firing, the clay turns dark from the smoke, while hardwoods, which create less smoke, turn it gray. Their effigy and medicine bowls (once used in healing ceremonies) are $50, water pipes (used in the council house) are $75 and large covered urns are $300.

The cooperative store, open year-round daily, from 8 A.M. to 8 P.M. in the summer months and 8 A.M. to 4:30 P.M. in the winter, carries a wide variety of Cherokee crafts, including small baskets at $3, beaded necklaces and bracelets from $2, hand-carved wooden dolls, double-weave sashes and Cherokee folk art.

Qualla Arts & Crafts Center
P.O. Box 277
Cherokee, NC 28719
(704) 497-3103
V   R   S   MO

CHOCTAW CRAFTS

In the 1830s, when the large and flourishing Choctaw tribe was moved by the federal government to Oklahoma, many evaded going, choosing to remain in their native Mississippi without legal status and earn their living by squatting the land and sharecropping. Though barriers of language and illegal status made life difficut for the Choctaw, isolation from modern life kept their culture intact.

They used to travel by foot for hundreds of miles to the marketplace in New Orleans to exchange baskets full of herbs, nuts and vegetables for their necessities. In more recent years, the Choctaw walked rural roads in their territory accompanied by a drumbeat to barter baskets for everyday needs. A typical transaction would be two basketloads of corn for a basket. Over the years, their colorful baskets became more prized for what they were than for what they contained. Prized by collectors, displayed in museums, they are still bartered, but now more frequently for money.

Baskets made by Choctaw women are woven from swamp, or river, cane, a tall native reed that looks like bamboo and grows in wet places. Green when cut, it ma-

tures to a rich creamy color. The cane is split four to six ways lengthwise with a pocketknife and the inner dull, stiff layer stripped away. Some shiny outside strips are tied into coils for later use while other coils are dyed every color of the rainbow, predominantly black, red, blue and yellow, but also green, orange, maroon, purple and even hot pink. Double-weave baskets in bold geometric designs are made for household use while more-open weaves are fashioned for specific tasks like sifting and winnowing. Sturdy white oak baskets are made by men for tasks demanding rougher use. The most unusual Choctaw shapes include: a large lightweight burden basket designed for balance against the back by use of a trump line (or band) worn across the forehead or chest and attached to a rope around the basket's bottom; and the elbow basket, traditionally used in weddings for the presentation of small gifts of money and ribbons.

In addition to weaving, quilting, pottery, blown and leaded glass, wood carving, toys, jewelry and baskets, the Mississippi Crafts Center is a prime source for *ishtaboli* equipment. *Ishtaboli* is an Indian game similar to lacrosse, played by any number of players with *kabucha* (stickball sticks) and a *towa* (a plaited leather stickball) to the beat of a drum. The object is to strike a single upright goal. *Ishtaboli* is more than a game; as dramatic as a dance, it's been called a form of religion, war, gambling and hunting, and it has been used to settle territorial disputes. The drums used for *ishtaboli* and ceremonial dances, of pine with hickory hoops and raw deerskin drumheads, are made in years when makers can bag a deerskin of sufficient size. If they can't, no drums are made until the following year.

Of interest to collectors are Choctaw beaded belts designed in white, black and sometimes turquoise beads on red velveteen or wool. The designs originally indicated the clan to which a wearer belonged so that one would not marry within one's own clan or family, which was considered a form of incest. "Today however," explains Martha Garrott, manager of the center, "sashes are worn by men and women for dress and have no more significance than wearing a Scottish tartan."

The center is also a source for the work of George Berry, one of Mississippi's few black craftsmen born in Oklahoma's Choctaw Indian area, whose magnificent carvings are done using only a pocketknife.

Open from 9 A.M. to 5 P.M. daily except Christmas and Thanksgiving, the center sponsors free craft demonstrations on weekends, March through September. Send self-addressed, stamped envelope for schedule and catalog. Crafts available by mail order include oak porch rockers ($140 to $200 plus shipping collect); thirty-five cookie

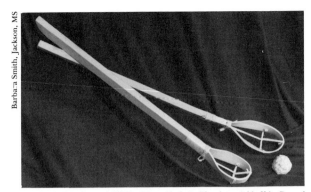

Traditional hickory stickball sticks and plaited leather stickball by Darryl Tubby

Mississippi Choctaw baskets: (top) winnower and sifter by Edna King, (left) storage or waste baskets by Nancy King, (right) burden basket by Jeffie Solomon and egg basket by Nancy King, (front) double-weave basket by Jeffie Solomon

Choctaw beaded sashes: (center) by Lela Solomon, (left and right) by Rosie Frazier

Walnut eagle carved by George Berry

55

cutters in stainless steel, copper and brass ($5 to $7); tree ornaments in copper and brass ($7 to $10); and Choctaw river cane baskets.

Mississippi Crafts Center on the Natchez Trace
  Parkway
P.O. Box 69
Ridgeland, MS 39157
(601) 856-7546
V R W C S MO

CIGAR-STORE INDIANS AND FIGUREHEADS

From the time Duncan Hannah's father, Pat, learned to carve from a Swedish neighbor, he whittled in his spare time. When he turned professional in the 1930s, Pat Hannah became known for his Matey, or Old Salt, figures, 6 inches tall. As a youngster, Duncan started carving small boats when he was 5 and turned professional in the fourth grade by selling his work to classmates. After a childhood of working with his father and accompanying him to shows, fairs and lumberjack roundups, Duncan earned a degree in economics from the University of Vermont.

"I'd always planned on being a partner with my dad," says Duncan, "but he died the year before graduation. I realized I liked turning a piece of wood into an object better than being in the business world, so I became a full-time carver. Since then, I've carved everything from 1-inch miniatures to 4-foot eagles, replacement parts for damaged antiques, business signs, life-size cigar-store indians and figureheads."

The figures that later became "cigar-store indians" began as "black boys." Originally created to attract customers to tobacconist shops in England during the mid-1700s, the figures were modeled after Jamaican slaves. As the tobacco trade increased between England and America, they became Indians and reached a height of popularity in the 1890s. Male figures were often sculpted in heroic poses, while Indian maidens usually had full figures, copied from prints and engravings of the period. Bolted into the ground, or on wheels so they could be taken into the store at night, some were later cast in metal to prevent theft. Figureheads, which graced ships under the bowsprit, were as much as 8 feet tall and 3 feet wide, made in separate sections and pegged together. The favorite subject was women: patriotic like Liberty or Columbia, but bare-bosomed as well. Other subjects were eagles, shipowners or a symbol that tied in with the name of the ship.

In addition to enlarging the line of Old Salts in (thirty-six styles), size (1 to 24 inches tall) and subject matter

Cigar-store indian by Duncan and Marilyn Hannah

(historical as well as nautical), Duncan has taken his father's place at Vermont's Lumberjack Roundup, taught carving at the Manatee (Florida) Art League and was the featured carver in the American Pavilion at the Montreal World's Fair. His most unusual commission to date was an ornament for a wedding cake: a Pittsburgh Pirate baseball player hitting the ball to his gloved bride.

He uses basswood for most objects because it has a true straight grain and doesn't split easily, but he prefers cherry or walnut for unpainted work. "I plan the work in advance," says Duncan, "because once it's taken away, the wood can't be put back. After drawing the pattern on the wood, I rough in the figure using an angled chisel-type tool for larger work, a gouge and ground-down knife for details, making sure the eyes carry the expression."

Cigar-store indian (left), replica of figurehead at Mystic Museum (center) and pirate figurehead (right) by Duncan G. Hannah

Just as his mother painted his father's carvings, Duncan's wife, Marilyn, paints his. He taught her on their honeymoon in 1970. With a large brush for fill-in work and a straight pin for finer details on small pieces, she works with oil paints and wood stains, which she buffs to a sheen when they're dry. Their two new partners, their children, Kristie and Ryan, who "learned the business from their playpens," now help with carving, selling and demonstrating.

Old Salts range in price from $15 to $90, while eagles from 18 inches to 4 feet are $90 to $500, depending on detail and size. His cigar-store indians cost $150 for the 2-foot size, $1,200 for life-size figures. Figureheads start at $225 for replicas and upward, depending on the amount of detail. "Ladies with beads, hats and feathers," says Duncan wryly, "are more expensive." Commission quotes on request.

Duncan G. Hannah
73 Killington Avenue
Rutland, VT 05701
(802) 775-1557
Summer address:
Route 30
Bomoseen, VT 05732
(802) 273-2783
V (by appt.)   R W C S MO

Other Maker

Ed Boggis, Old Church Road, Claremont, NH 03743, carves life-size cigar-store indians.   C

Clipper Ships   *See* **Ship and Boat Replicas**

CLOCKS

In the early days of the colonies, Americans copied, yet simplified, English clocks to make them more affordable, but even then only the wealthy could buy them. Most Americans kept time by the town clock.

The favorite style of the 18th century was the long case (also called the tall, or grandfather) clock made by hand with the case built around it. Most early tall clocks had 8-day brass movements, a few had 30-hour and the least expensive, for those who could not afford a case, was a wag-on-the-wall, whose weights hung free. When Connecticut makers began using wooden works, clocks became more reasonably priced. The Willard family, known for their innovations, created new styles: Simon invented the banjo clock, Aaron, the shelf clock, and his son Aaron, Jr., the lyre. Eli Terry's clocks had brass movements with standard and interchangeable parts in simple ogee cases and were best-sellers in England as well as the United States. But the most beautiful clock ever made in America, in the opinion of experts, was the girandole, designed by Lemuel Curtis.

Foster Campos was a cabinetmaker and finisher when he first met clock maker Elmer Stennes, who asked him what he thought of his clocks. "I told him they were beautiful," says Foster, "but the finishing was amateurish." Annoyed at first, Stennes later asked Campos to work for him temporarily, an affiliation that became a full-time one for 24 years. When Stennes died in 1974, Foster bought some of his mentor's tools and machinery and went into business for himself. Today, winner of numerous horological awards and a fellow of the National Watch and Clock Collectors Association, Foster makes twelve different clocks, including the banjo, the Curtis girandole and lyre, Willard and David Wood shelf clocks and a scaled-down Willard, which he calls a Grandmother, in mahogany or maple with made-in-America brass weight-driven movements. He does not make grandfather clocks. With one assistant and his son, Steve, he makes all cases and brass components.

"There are not many trades left where you can start a job and work at every step until it is complete," says the master clock maker, who signs and numbers each of his creations. "Every clock begins a new circle of friends. I take pleasure in knowing that my clock is a useful piece of furniture, meets a need and is also an investment in beauty that will return years of pleasure while increasing in value. I've paid two to three times the original price of clocks I sold while working with Stennes. That doesn't happen with a commercially made clock." He never minds

if customers change their minds about buying a clock. "Someone else will always want it," he's found.

Surrounded by clocks that he's made or restored in his Cape Cod workshop, Foster admits that it's the silence of an unwound clock that he hears, not the ticking or striking of the hour.

Because Foster keeps popular models in stock at all times, most orders can be filled within a few days. His clocks, which range in price from $500 for a miniature banjo to $2,500 for a girandole, may be purchased through museum shops at Old Sturbridge, Massachusetts, and Greenfield Village, Dearborn, Michigan, from well-known jewelers or directly from him. He also restores both cases and movements on all clocks.

Foster S. Campos
213 Schoosett Street, Route 139
Pembroke, MA 02359
(617) 826-8577
V   R   S   C ($2)   MO

Other Makers

Gordon and Christopher Bretschneider, Shoreham, VT 05770; (802) 897-2621, a father-and-son team, specialize in gooseneck or curved pediment top, flat top and arched or Willard-style top tall (grandfather) clocks, in mahogany with a hand-rubbed finish, 8-day movements, hour and half-hour strike and cable-suspended weights. The 7-foot-9-inch Chippendale is $4,500 plus movement, and the Willard, $5,500.

Martin F. Reynolds, 411 Village Road East, Princeton Junction, NJ 08550; (609) 799-1617, makes Eli Terry clocks in old curly maple, cherry and mahogany, as well as octagon clocks in oak or cherry with veneer inlays and school clocks in cherry, pine and oak.

Kilbourn & Proctor, Inc., 34 Curtis Street, Scituate, MA 02066; (617) 894-3260, makes 8-day weight-driven brass movements for banjo clocks and others similar to that made by Simon Willard in 1796; movements for Massachusetts shelf, grandmother and similar clocks; and New Hampshire mirror clock movements modeled on those of Benjamin Morrill of Boscowen, c. 1830.

Gerhard Hartwigs, Paupack, PA 18451; (717) 857-0111, makes movements for banjo and Terry clocks.

Robert Kunkle, 1628 Shookstown Road, Frederick, MD 21701; (301) 662-6545, makes clock movements to customer specifications for mantel, wall or tall case clocks. He also makes wooden clocks and parts and parts for

Replica of Lemuel Curtis's girandole clock (left), replica of Simon Willard's patent clock (center) and replica of Aaron Willard's shelf clock (right) by Foster Campos

Chippendale grandfather clock by Gordon and Christopher Bretschneider

antique music boxes. He also repairs clocks and watches, and can make any part if he has the specifications.

Ball and Ball (see Brass), 463 West Lincoln Highway, Exton, PA 19341; (215) 363-7330, can supply clock fittings such as hands, pendulums and finials.

PERIOD CLOTHING

Sewing is only one of the skills needed by seamstress Kathi Reynolds to recreate authentic period clothing for men, women and children. Since she began researching costume as a teenage guide at Wisconsin's Galloway House and Museum, Kathi has learned she also needs an in-depth knowledge of history, art, fashion, design, pattern-making, fabrics, colors, dyes, how fabric affects cut and how garments affect movement.

"Fashion plates were hypothetical ideas of what designers thought women should wear," the fifth generation tailor explains, "not what the average person actually wore. High-fashion styles were made for people whose servants could move for them. High-cut armholes prevent a woman from raising her arms. Stays restrict her sitting and food intake, and if she doesn't move sedately while wearing stays, she can faint. Today's woman has a larger rib cage, more muscles, a longer stride and more active life, all of which must be taken into consideration in the design and cut of materials."

Guiding a client toward appropriate fabrics is often necessary. "Before the invention of the cotton gin, cotton was a wealthy man's fabric because America sent cotton to England for processing," says Kathi. "The common man wore linen, wool and linsey-woolsey. Many high-fashion dresses were never intended to be washed or cleaned: 18th century gowns were worn over a chemise and 19th century dresses had detachable collars, cuffs and sleeves."

Aided in her research by a library of 200 books and periodicals and 800 antique patterns, which she has computerized for easy reference, Kathi has clothed participants from the skin out for reenactments, musicals, craft festivals, house tours, historic sites and living history events of the National Park Service. For one college anniversary she dressed fifteen women and twenty men with a total of seventy articles of clothing. The most time-consuming aspect is finding the correct materials. "Stiff silks are impossible to locate unless money is no object," says Kathi. "Some colors like pure browns and greens no longer exist. After computers began designing plaids with 30-inch repeat designs or odd color lines throughout, simple plaids became scarce. Achieving the color and fabric combina-

Double skirt and jacket bodice in Basque style with pagoda sleeves of the late 1850s to early 1860s by Kathi Reynolds

Civil War dress of 1863 by Kathi Reynolds

tions of the Victorians was never easy. Wealthy Victorians developed complicated construction and details to keep the emerging middle class from copying them. The late Victorian period remains the most demanding and expensive to cut and fit."

After deciding design, colors and details, Kathi drafts a basic pattern, which she makes in muslin and fits to the client before cutting the custom pattern and fabric. "I do everything as authentically as possible," she says, "including the way a pattern is laid on the fabric, the type of seam, finishes or lack thereof, sewing techniques, style of closing, fasteners, etc."

Once made, historic dress must be worn with the right underlinen and foundations (stays, corsets, bustles, and so on). "Colonial men's shirts were long, almost to the knee, and always covered by a jacket or weskit because shirts were considered underwear. An 18th century woman wore a very full, ankle-length chemise with sleeves

to the wrist or elbow under stays, then pockets and petticoats." Pockets were separate and worn under dresses.

Kathi can design from a client's ideas, photos or sketches as well as from her own research, fashion plates and patterns. Prices are based on labor and research. Complete outfits for women start at $350 plus materials, while late Victorian clothing (1870–1915) with more interior foundation work begins at $500. Earlier men's outfits (to 1790) average $400, but fitted suits from that time to 1910, as cut and fit become more important and labor intensive, start at $600.

Kathi Reynolds
330 North Church Street
Thurmont, MD 21788
(301) 695-5340
V R MO

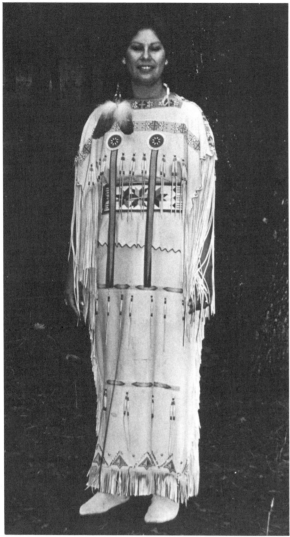

Buckskin dress with hand-sewn beadwork by Chlotiea Palmer

Other Makers

Chlotiea Palmer, Route 3, Box 189, Anadarko, OK 73005; (405) 247-3987, makes buckskin dresses as well as leggings and shirts for men with hand-sewn beadwork starting at $2,000.

Mrs. Eva McAdams, Warm Valley Arts & Crafts, Box 157, Ft. Washakie, WY 82514; (307) 332-7330, makes everything in buckskin from moccasins to dresses.

Mary Worley, Mountain Road, Cornwall, RD 2, Mid-

dlebury, VT 05753; (802) 462-2315, hand-weaves shawls, scarves and tweed capes ($175).

Carole S. Roberson, Buffalo Enterprises, 308 West King Street, P.O. Box 183, East Berlin, PA 17316; (717) 259-9081, makes period clothing, accoutrements, hats and uniforms.   C ($3)

Coffin Guitars   *See under* Musical Instruments

CONCHAS

As fur-trading declined, some Native Americans learned blacksmithing and silversmithing so that they could make objects to sell and trade. Round metal plates originally worn in the hair of Woodland Indians became belts or drops from belts on the dress of Plains Indians. After the Navajos adapted the Plains Indian belt, they decorated the plates (called *conchas,* Spanish for "shells") with Hispanic designs.

"The Navajo smiths took their basic forms from the Plains Indians," says silversmith Bill Bell, "and their mechanical processes and decorative ideas from the Hispanics. Hammering metal into shape, cutting with cold chisels, shaping with files, chasing and stamping designs are the same procedures used by Mexican blacksmiths on ironwork. The scalloped edges, crescent-stamp designs and holes around the border of *conchas* duplicate details found on door, furniture and trunk hardware. The reason there is so much similarity between the silver stamps and the stamped designs on Mexican leatherwork is that the blacksmith made the leather stamps and taught the silversmith how to make silver stamps."

Born in Houston, Texas, Bill spent much of his early life on his grandfather's ranches in California and Colorado while his journalist parents were on assignment. Before he moved to the Texas hill country and became a silversmith, Bill worked on Mississippi towboats, as a steeplejack and as a printer for the University of Texas Library. In 1973, a friend gave him a few metal stamps and showed him how to make his own. "I started making buttons from dimes," says Bill, "then a few hatbands. When I found a beautiful anvil, I took it as a sign that I was on the right path, and began acquiring more specialized tools. I took a big jump in making a large coin belt of eighteen old Philippine silver dollars, and my first hammered ingot buckle." The day he finished, Willie Nelson bought it and later gave it to Kris Kristofferson. Since then, Bill's *concha* belts have been featured in a television documentary and

Belts, buckles, conchas, *pendants and bracelets, together with the silver coins used to make them, by Bill Bell*

purchased by stars like Charlie Daniels, Dyan Cannon and Merle Haggard.

"Silver was scarce and expensive in the Southwest," Bill explains. "The main source was U.S. and Mexican coins, which were melted and poured into an ingot mold. The ingot was thick, so it was hammered to thin it. This hammering made it wider in diameter and hardened the silver as the molecules were compacted. It also gives a look and feel to the metal that can't be duplicated by sheet silver from a rolling mill. To release the pressure and keep the ingot from cracking, the ingot is reheated to a dull red, then quenched in water, which softens the silver. Hammering and annealing are repeated until the ingot reaches the thickness and diameter desired." Bill uses tools much the same as those used to make the first *concha* belts and makes his own stamps from old cold chisels and files. Hand-cut with a file, they are carefully annealed, carved and tempered to withstand the vigorous blows of the hammer used to drive them into the silver.

His *concha* belts range from large sizes weighing 40 troy ounces or more (made from sterling silver) to smaller sizes made from silver half-dollars, quarters and dimes. Ingots or coins are hammered flat and smooth, annealed, chased, stamped, domed, filed, sanded, polished, oxidized and custom-mounted on leather. Each coin belt comes with a matching buckle made from a hammered ingot. Unless a scalloped edge is requested, Bill leaves the coin edge as a reminder of its origins. Each is photographed and recorded so that the design is never repeated. Prices range from $400 to over $4,000. Bill also makes buckles in all shapes and sizes as well as bracelets, pendants and hatbands.

Bill Bell, Silversmith
Route 1, Box 144
Fredericksburg, TX 78624
(512) 685-3224
V (by appt.)   R   S   MO

COOPERED ITEMS

In the early days of America, anything that had to be carried from the well to the house, barn or town—especially if it was wet, fine-grained or heavy—traveled in a wooden bucket made by a cooper. From John Alden on, coopers were important links in a community's commerce. There were wet coopers and dry coopers, white coopers (who made smaller pieces) and traveling coopers (who made repairs). A ship's cooper was so necessary on a whaling vessel that his rank was just below that of an officer. As some of the tasks disappeared, so did names like *keeler* (a shallow tub used to cool milk), *noggin* (a pitcher) and *grease bucket* (a bucket filled with tar or pitch pine to grease the axles on wagons).

Rick Stewart, a fifth generation cooper born in 1960, still makes *piggins,* the all-purpose one-handled buckets used before the movable handle was invented. Similar to a small tub or pail, it has a handle-arm rising above the rim with a pierced hole for a rope loop. Its name came from Scotland, as did Rick's ancestors, who brought with them one of the oldest styles of coopering, the craft of fashioning water vessels from wooden staves.

Rick learned his trade by apprenticing with his grandfather Alex Stewart (who received the National Heritage Award, the highest honor a craftsman can receive from the National Endowment for the Arts). Using antique tools, the Stewarts make their vessels, buckets, churns and pitchers from hand-split cedar with white oak bands (also called locks), while larger items like barrels and furniture are usually made of oak or maple. Only one thing has changed: where Alex once used glass to smooth the wood, Rick now uses sandpaper.

When the first Stewarts arrived in the 1800s, they settled 6 miles east of Sneedville, Tennessee, 80 miles northeast of Knoxville, almost on the Virginia line. The ridges reminded them of Scotland, and they wanted to be near cedar trees, whose wood is used for its color, fragrance and resistance to insects. The best cedar must be free of knots and seasoned 1 year for vessels and 7 years for furniture. The log is split into bolts using a froe and maul (a hand-hammered blade and wooden club). After it is seasoned and dried, it is worked with a variety of tools, each designed for a specific task.

"If the bands don't fit right," says Rick, "they have to be taken off and refitted, because if their fit is wrong, they will split. When you hear them splitting you have to step away fast, because they pop off in all directions."

Piggins 6 to 10 inches in diameter cost $44 to $46; tubs 12 to 28 inches are $65 to $100; while buckets 8 to 12 inches sell for $58 to $62. Mugs are $20; butter molds, $22; butter churns, $78; cream pitchers, $24; larger

Assorted bowls, butter churns, tub, piggins and pitcher by Rick Stewart

pitchers, $45; while nut bowls 6 and 10 inches across cost $20 and $24. Rick also makes fork and spoon sets ($25), dough board and rolling pin sets ($12) and bread trays ($65 up depending on size). Not to mention furniture: a colonial baby cradle ($200), Appalachian-style baby cradle ($85) and doll cradle ($35), as well as custom pieces to order. He will also do antique repairs and restoration. Shipping costs extra.

Rick Stewart
Route 2, Box 328
Sneedville, TN 37869
(615) 733-2617 (days) and 733-4214 (evenings)
V   R   S   MO

Other Makers

John L. Stauffer, The Maine Bucket Co., 64 School Street, Auburn, ME 04210; (207) 784-6700, makes pine buckets with rope handles in 8- to 14-inch-wide sizes from $14.95 to $19.95, as well as butter churns for $28.

R. P. Raiselis, Strawbery Banke, Box 300, Portsmouth, NH 03801; (603) 433-1100, does museum-quality reproductions. His work is at Old Sturbridge Village in Sturbridge, Massachusetts, South Street Seaport in New York City and the Richmondtown Restoration in Staten Island, New York.

J. Richard Willis, Route 8, Box 230, Carthage, MS 39051, makes butter churns of cypress, oak or pine for $35 and sugar buckets for $25, both plus shipping.

The Cooper's Trade, P.O. Box 717, Williamsburg, VA 23187; (804) 566-1509, makes buckets, tubs, gunpowder kegs, piggins, churns and chests of cedar and oak. All prices FOB Lanexa, VA.

Bob Mantle, 20 South Ruby Lane, Fairview Heights, IL 62208.

Cornhusk Crafts

Early settlers threw nothing away. After they ate corn, they used husks to fill mattresses and braided, twisted and wove husks for chair seats, baskets, brooms, ropes and even horse collars. New doormats made each autumn in braided or shag styles caught mud at the door.

"The best husks come from field corn," explains Suse F. Cioffi, who makes cornhusk objects for museums and historical sites and to sell at craft events, "because they're larger, stronger, have better color and less shrinkage. Gathered when they are dry, usually after the second frost, coarse outer husks are used in mats and baskets, while softer husks close to the ear are better for dolls and decorations. Most articles are made from dampened husks, although doormats are best constructed dry."

© 1987 Vincent J. Cioffi

Cornhusk crafts: (clockwise from top) basket, mop, broom, doormat, chair seat and (in center) covered container and bottle by Suse F. Cioffi

In addition to authentic colonial cornhusk brooms, baskets, doormats, chair seats, toys and dolls, Suse also makes Indian masks, summer moccasins and bottles. "Indians used braided cornhusk bottles for storing medicines, seeds, salt and tobacco," she explains, "coating the bottles with melted beeswax to make them waterproof." For readers who prefer to make their own, Suse and her mother, Esta Fehrenbach, published *The Cornhusk Book*, which provides instructions for making all of the above ($4). 178 Maplewood Avenue, Bogota, NJ 07603; (201) 342-5972.   R   MO

Cowboy Boots   *See under* Leather

COWBOY HATS

"The cowboy hat evolved as a piece of equipment," Manny Gammage will tell you. "It shaded the eyes to see greater distances, kept rain, snow and sleet off the neck, sun off the face. A cowboy hat could put out fires or fan them brighter. Upside down it was a good water bucket. It's become a worldwide symbol of freedom because people who won the West were looked up to as being free thinkers and free-willed."

M. E. "Manny" Gammage has been making cowboy hats since he was 13 years old. When he decided to go into insurance instead of the family hat business, his father, a man of few words, told him, "You're nothing but a hi-roller," and sent him a hat spelling that out in block letters inside. "I wore it constantly," says Manny, "and even though I led my sales office for 5 years, I wound up selling more hats than insurance, so I came back where I belonged." Now patented and worn by the likes of Prince Charles, Princess Di, Bob Hope and Ronald Reagan, the Hi-Roller is Manny's best-seller.

"Hats all started with an open crown," he continues. "Creases were formed by how they were handled and improved upon. As areas picked up certain styles they became known by those names, like Carlsbad, Abilene, Ft. Worth, San Ann [San Antonio]. The most traditional style is the Rancher; the oldest crease, the Carlsbad, probably dating back to 1850."

Most cowboy hats are made of hare or beaver felt, not wool. The *X* marking indicates the percentage of beaver to hare fur (a 3X hat is 30 percent beaver). "Today some hats are labeled 15X and 20X," says Manny, "but I have yet to figure out how you can be 150 percent or 200 percent pure. When you're pure, you're pure. The belly hair made the finest hats because it was finer and made a thinner, tighter, tougher, more waterproof hat. The most popular color today is silver belly, which originally denoted the color of a beaver's belly. B-belly, which means the back of the beaver, is darker. Cowboys once had three hats: a silver belly for summer, a black for winter and cowboy gray for in-between seasons. Straw hats came into being in the 20th century."

Manny's hats are made by hand from beginning to end: trimmed, styled and shaped to the customer's satisfaction. "The first thing I do is look at their size, shape and style," says Manny, who wears a measuring tape around his neck, "because the shape of a head is considered in every step. The hardest part is hand-blocking; the blocks are as close to a pattern as you can get. The hat is molded by hand and placed on a crown iron where it's left until dry, when it's finished with a fine pouncing paper. The brim is ironed by hand; when flat, a rounding jack is used to cut it to

Hi-Roller cowboy hat with concha *band by M. E. "Manny" Gammage*

High Sierra cowboy hat with braided horsehair band by M. E. "Manny" Gammage

Carlsbad, or Hopalong Cassidy, cowboy hat by M. E. "Manny" Gammage

LBJ cowboy hat with tooled leather band by M. E. "Manny" Gammage

the desired width before pouncing. The hat is then hand-fit with a leather sweatband, the brim flanged on another mold, the interior lining and exterior trim hand-sewn with silk thread.'' Hatband selections include tooled leather, exotic skins, laced alligator, Indian beadwork, feather, rattlesnake (with or without the rattle), horsehair, braided leather, rawhide, ribbon, shotgun shells, silver, *conchas*, turquoise, Cavalry or woven bands.

"If you can imagine it, I can make it," says Manny. One customer wanted a hat to "scare women and children and start fights in Wyoming bars." He got a black beaver derby with a tooled leather band decorated with silver and turquoise inlay.

Compared with the cost of living, Manny's hats are a good buy. "A working cowboy would spend a month's wages ($10) on a hat. A century ago, a good beaver cost $100. Today's beavers are $190 to $225, while the 5X felts are $95 to $125." Available in whiskey, mesquite, silver belly, silver or cowboy gray, yellow, black and anything in between, the right hat will make a person "feel better, bigger and prouder," says Manny. "When I put the final crease in and turn around from my tea kettle, place that hat on an individual's head and watch him or her smile, it's worth more than gold to me."

M. E. "Manny" Gammage
Texas Hatters
5003 Overpass
Buda, TX 78610
(512) 295-HATS
V   R   C   S   MO

Crochet

Helen Deuel, who has been crocheting for more than 50 years, makes tablecloths and bedspreads of 100 percent cotton thread in natural shades that look like antique homespun as well as in sixty colors. Tablecloths are $100 and up depending on size and pattern, while bedspreads are $500 for full-, $750 for queen-, and $1,000 for king-size, depending on overhang and pillow allowance. To order, send dimensions of flat surface of bed or table and depth desired for overhang; plus a swatch of material, paint chip or name of dish pattern (to match for color); and weight and type of thread or yarn desired. Allow approximately 6 weeks for delivery. 2020 Kensington, Ocean Springs, MS 29564; (601) 875-4840.   R   MO

Other Makers

Sally Cox, Route 5, Box 132F, Ellijay, GA 30540, makes afghans and clothing of crocheted yarn.

Patricia Schurig, Generations in Crochet, 6994 Oakland Chase, Memphis, TN 38115, crochets baby clothes.

Crocheted tablecloth (foreground) in butterflies pattern and bedspread (background) in Victorian puffs pattern, both by Helen Deuel

Crystal Painting   *See* Tinsel Painting

DECOYS

Decoys, artificial birds made to lure wildfowl within shooting range, may be America's oldest folk art. Canvasback duck decoys found in Nevada during the 1920s are estimated to be more than 2,000 years old. The Indians used decoys to attract flocks of snow geese to save the Pilgrims from starvation. Although those early decoys were of woven reeds or bird skins stuffed with straw, decoys are now most frequently carved of wood.

Until the Migratory Bird Treaty was enacted in 1918 to protect shorebirds, and regulations were passed governing the number of ducks and geese that could be bagged, an individual could kill from 300 to 500 ducks

Canvasback drake decoy by Charles Spiron

Merganser decoy by Charles Spiron

Yellowlegs decoy by Charles Spiron

about an old hunk of wood that had been used to attract ducks so they could be shot." But as he talked to collectors and learned more about the lore of waterfowling, he began his own collection. After he discovered that few old decoys had survived and that they sold for $1,000 to $5,000 each, with rarer pieces selling for as much as $50,000, he set out to carve his own rig of hunting decoys, based on details he had read or heard about how old-timers did it.

"There were many fine carvers making decorative pieces," he says, "but there were few makers of traditional decoys, made for hunting or gunning." His first attempt took second place in a national competition. As a means of affording his new hobby, he sold a few decoys at shows and in 1978 was asked by Colonial Williamsburg to make a reproduction of a Nova Scotia merganser, the first reproduction from their folk art collection. He now carves more than twenty different styles of decoys and shorebirds for Williamsburg and several for the Winterthur Museum and the Smithsonian Institution.

To make a museum reproduction, Charles takes the original and copies every detail, including cracked paint, checked wood (cracked in a pattern of checks) and rusty nails. The copy and the original are then returned to the museum to be reviewed by a standards committee. Once approved, the copy becomes the standard and each future carving must meet the same specifications as the standard.

Charles reserves 20 percent of his time for creating original decoys after studying live birds in the wild. "It was the aim of the traditional carver to make the decoy as lifelike as possible in order to be a better lure," he says. "I feel these decoys are my best work. Every one has a different head position or body style, and each has a personality of its own." Over the past decade, he has made more than 3,000 decoys and nearly every species in North America.

Working alone in his small basement shop, using the traditional drawknife, spokeshave and a variety of hand knives, he carves each decoy by hand, using white cedar and pine. Most are hollow. The heads are carved separately, glass eyes added, then joined to the body before final finishing, sanding and painting. Priced from $125 to $750, his decoys may be purchased through Colonial Williamsburg, the Winterthur Museum or directly from him.

Charles Spiron
Currituck Decoy Company
800 Forest Hills
Goldsboro, NC 27530
(919) 735-5839
R   W   S   MO

in a single day. From the 1880s to 1918, professional hunters fed America and brought the development of the decoy to its highest form. Prior to 1918, there were hundreds of professional decoy makers. After 25¢ plastic decoys made hunters think twice about spending $5 for a hand-carved bird, makers turned to more profitable work. By the 1950s only a handful of decoy carvers remained.

When Charles Spiron attended a decoy show in the 1970s, he "could not imagine why anyone would care

Other Makers

William Massey, Route 1, Box 12, Massey Point, Waddington, NY 13694 (315) 388-5977 (winter address: Wekiva Resort, Route 1, Box 378, Sorrento, FL 32776), has been making award-winning duck decoys since 1929.

Duane Saylor, 99 Horney Road, Angelica, NY 14709.

Thomas Bonner, 812 Wagner Road, Mt. Vernon, IL 62864; (614) 244-3742.

Doris Lingle, Box 188, Route 2, Dongola, IL 62926; (618) 827-4288.

Will Kirkpatrick, 124 Forest Avenue, Hudson, MA 01749, makes one-of-a-kind shorebird decoys like those used by sport and market hunters from the early 1800s. C

Bob and Donna Paradis, Parker Mountain Decoys, RFD 2, Box 724, Center Barnstead, NH 03225; (603) 269-8881.

The Decoy Works, 2601 SW 122 Avenue, Davie, FL 33330; (305) 472-7910.

Laity Woodcarvers, 1674 Old Philadelphia Pike, Lancaster, PA 17602.

Randy and Pam Tate, Knot in Vane, 805 North 11th Street, DeKalb, IL 60115; (815) 758-2516.

The Bird Store, Route 1, Box 153, Tyner, NC 27980; (919) 221-8426.

Harry V. Shourds, 2023 South Shore Road, Oceanville, NJ 08230; (609) 399-0228.

Alaskan Dolls

Meticulously dressed Alaskan dolls mirror life, tradition and dress in Alaska. While some figures are carved entirely from reindeer horn or fashioned from coiled grass, the

Doll with ivory hands and face, dressed in walrus-gut kuspuk, *by Amelia and Floyd Kingeekuk*

majority of native dolls have stuffed leather bodies with faces made from bleached sealskin, ivory and occasionally wood, and are dressed in clothing made of hair seal, caribou, walrus and seal intestines. "Activity" dolls, posed singly or in groups, depict work, dance, hunting, sports and play, while others (especially those made by Dolly Spencer) are portraits of actual people.

Doll (left) with bleached sealskin face, dressed in walrus-gut kuspuk *(knee-length garment worn over parka like an apron) and traditional seal mukluks, by Josephin Ungolt; doll (right) with carved wooden face, dressed in ground squirrel parka and sealskin mukluks by Emma Black*

Makers

Dolly Spencer, Box 739, Homer, AK 99603.
Amelia and Floyd Kingeekuk, Savoonga, AK 99869.
Helen H. Smith, Hooper Bay, AK 99604.
Annie Alowa, Savoonga AK 99869.
Mary Pingayuk, Chevak, AK 99563.
Rosalie Panijak, Chevak, AK 99563.
Mary Nash, Chevak, AK 99563.
Caroline Penayah, Copper Center, AK 99573.

APPLE DOLLS

"I've always been interested in dolls," says Muffy Kashkin. "When we were small, my mother made dolls and dressed them for my three sisters and myself. As I grew up, I continued to make dolls I couldn't afford."

She took a course on doll-making and repair, and to earn money for college, worked in a nursing home. "Many of my apple doll faces reminded me of the elderly people I cared for," she says. "It was like working with real little people. But when they came out looking like some of my relatives, it was a little spooky."

In Orwell, the heart of Vermont apple country, she has many varieties to choose from. Her favorite is the Wolf River apple, which can weigh as much as a pound and measure 5 to 6 inches in diameter, "but any large variety will do, as the heads shrink while drying. I usually buy several bushel in the fall and store them in the basement." Since hollow apples dry faster and leave less chance for mold, Muffy starts by removing the core from the side that will be the back of the head (which is later filled with cotton). With a paring knife without a serrated edge, she begins the face by making a U for the nose, then slowly pares away on all sides except the top. After carving the eye sockets, she uses the point of the knife to make a line for the mouth, "usually smiling," she says. "To bring out the cheeks, I carve some away from the mouth area, and where I want prominent wrinkles in the forehead or around the eyes, I make shallow lines." Unlike many apple doll makers who wait for nature to add the details, Muffy finds she obtains more distinctive expressions by putting them in before the drying begins.

Once done, she soaks the head in a bowl of lemon juice for 15 to 30 minutes, making sure all sides are coated to

Chef apple doll by Muffy Kashkin

Elderly couple, apple dolls by Muffy Kashkin

keep it from turning brown, then pushes a hanger through the blossom and stem ends, bending the tip to keep the apple from slipping off and making sure the bent part is turned away from the face so it won't make a spot or a cleft chin. Like the early settlers, who learned to make apple dolls from the Indians, Muffy dries apple heads near her wood-burning stove "because the slower they dry, the more rounded and natural they become." Once they are dry, she adds eyes (peppercorns, allspice, beans, beads or any round object) and watercolors the face.

"When I first started making apple heads," says Muffy, "my husband turned on the stove, not realizing I'd left two in the oven. By the time I rescued them, they were partly scorched, but the burned part made them look ghoulish and added character, so I scooped out the mushy insides and turned them into grave robbers."

She makes body skeletons out of hangers, arms from wire, hands and feet from air-drying clay, for more exact detail "and because apple hands have a tendency to curl."

After building up the bodies with old sheets, stockings or gauze, she dresses them in styles from old catalogs, books or her own imagination. Hair is fashioned from lambswool and glued on. Her finished creations, 10 to 12 inches tall, sell for $20, while taller and more elaborately costumed dolls with miniature props like wire-rimmed glasses, tools and furniture may cost up to $120.

"The details take time," says Muffy. "I once hand-knit a piece of wool with common pins for a knitting doll to hold, then carved knitting needles from wood."

For those who would like to make their own, Muffy sells directions for carving the basic head ($3). To obtain a list of doll directions available and other apple-head creations, enclose a self-addressed, stamped envelope.

Muffy Kashkin
Goosehill Farm Crafts
Orwell, VT 05760
(802) 948-2561
V   R   S   MO

Other Makers

Deborah Doyle-Schectman, Waterman Hill Studio, P.O. Box 677, Quechee, VT 05059; (802) 295-1309, makes traditional apple dolls.

Stefanie Halwas, 232 East Lake Avenue, Freeland, WA 98249; (206) 321-1857, creates unique portraits of historical characters from $250 to $350 each, as well as a line of 9- to 12-inch dolls from $125 to $175.

CORNHUSK DOLLS

Native Americans used cornhusks to make moccasins, masks, mats, baskets, insulation and dolls. However, their cornhusk dolls were made not for toys, but as messengers to the spirits. Corn was more than a staple; it represented the mother of life. Although some Indian dolls did not have faces, when settlers learned to make their versions, they painted on faces because they used the dolls as toys for their children.

Lila Marshall had never seen a cornhusk doll until she was in her 20s. "I'd read about them," she says, "but I didn't start making them until 1955 when my husband died and I had to find a way to support my four children. I had no income; my only skill was handwork. I could grow corn in the field and get dynamite wire from people who worked in the coal mines. After they used dynamite to loosen the coal, the wire was thrown away. If you knew someone who worked there, you could get it free."

She'd always loved books and stories, so her cornhusk dolls had names from the very beginning: those of char-

acters in her favorite fairy tales, nursery rhymes or storybooks, like Goldilocks, Boy Blue, Jack and Jill and Tom Sawyer. Over the years her list of characters has grown to thirty-five. Every time a special order comes in for one not on her list, or she remembers scenes from her childhood, like a man plowing or mountain music makers, she adds another.

"There are now ten members of my family working in crafts from shucks," says Lila, "three daughters, three daughters-in-law and four granddaughters." Her most important outlet at first was the Southern Highlands Handicraft Guild. Now her work is sold worldwide.

"I make my dolls from white corn gathered in the fall as soon as the corn is hard," says Lila, "and use the inner husk because it's the finest. I store it in a dry place where it won't draw moisture, in a little building near the house where I also work in summer months. To dye cornhusks takes longer than dyeing cloth. I simmer them all day with salt added and sometimes let them set overnight. Before using, I dampen husks by dipping them in water to ease the brittleness. It makes them easier to use and stretches them like crepe paper. To make the head, I fold the shuck over, attach wire for the arms and wrap the shoulders and arms with narrow strips until they're the right size. I now use florist's 23-gauge wire for the arms and legs because it helps the dolls to stand up better and makes the arms more flexible." Hair is of cornsilk, and facial features are drawn with Higgins Drawing Ink and a fine penpoint. All clothes, trims and props are made from cornhusks, including spinning wheels and musical instruments.

Although her cottage industry now employs most of her family, Lila still enjoys going to fairs with her wares in summer months. That's when she sees the people who have been buying her dolls for the past 30 years and gets to meet their children and grandchildren. "Some have every character I've ever made," she says proudly, "but what I like most are the children. From about 4 years old to the teens, there's always a group in my booth, listening to my stories and telling me theirs."

To date, Lila's biggest seller has been her thirteen-piece crèche, which retails for $145. Her other dolls range in price from $10 to $20. The Marshalls also make Christmas decorations, wreaths, kissing balls (used at Christmas instead of mistletoe) and cornhusk flowers. For current price list, send self-addressed, stamped envelope.

Lila Marshall
Route 1, Box 218
Nickelsville, VA 24271
(703) 479-2518
R   W   S   MO

Cornhusk dolls depicting characters from fairy tales by Lila Marshall

Cornhusk dolls in nativity scene by Lila Marshall

Cornhusk doll in the Victorian manner by Jocelyn Mostrom

PORCELAIN DOLLS

From the time her two sons leave in the school bus each morning until they return in the late afternoon, Laurie Carlson plays with dolls—and makes a living at it.

"I used to enjoy making clothes for my dolls when I was young," says Laurie, now in her 30s, "but there was only one I really loved: a baby doll that my aunt dressed and gave to me when I was 3. I still have some of the clothes, but the doll was lost. I've never been able to find another like it."

While searching for a way to augment the family income, she began making dolls. "It was a way to combine all the things I like to do," she says, "like sculpt, paint and design." She went through more than 400 pounds of plaster before she produced a porcelain doll that satisfied her. Today, her wide-eyed baby and toddler dolls are bought by collectors and galleries as quickly as she creates them.

"The most beautiful dolls were always made of porcelain," Laurie says. "It's the ultimate material and the most

Other Makers

Jocelyn Mostrom, 16311 Black Rock Road, Darnestown, MD 20874; (301) 840-8409, makes exquisitely crafted cornhusk dolls in the Victorian manner, whose faces look like porcelain and whose dresses look like silk.

Barbara J. Briggs, Route 2, Box 420A, New Market, TN 37820; (615) 475-7187, makes traditional cornhusk dolls in colonial clothing trimmed with dry flowers.

George and Goldie Counts, 5324 Forge Road, White Marsh, MD 21162; (301) 256-3616; or Lost River, WV 26811; (304) 897-5570, make storybook cornhusk dolls in settings.

Mr. and Mrs. Allen Kilgore, 18 Orville Road, Baltimore, MD 21221; (301) 687-0430.

Judy Horn, 42 Breckenridge Parkway, Asheville, NC 28804.

Qualla Arts & Crafts Center, P.O. Box 277, Cherokee, NC 28719; (704) 497-3103, is a source for authentic Indian cornhusk dolls made by members of the eastern Cherokee tribe.

Native American Dolls   *See* **Carving, Alaskan**

Porcelain doll, 22 inches long, named Baby Marie, by Laurie Carlson

Porcelain dolls named Holly, Hannah and Darcy by Laurie Carlson

between two cultures at the turn of the century," include Camas, a barefoot Nez Percé Indian with feathers tucked in her braids, her brother Eagle and a lifelike papoose in a cradleboard.

Laurie's latest invention, composition dolls similar in appearance to those made by American doll makers at the turn of the century but made from a stronger formula, is cast in the same molds as the more expensive dolls. "So many of the porcelain dolls are bought by adults," she says, "that I wanted to make dolls that looked the same but that would be unbreakable for children to play with."

Sold mostly by mail order, Laurie's porcelain dolls retail from $60 to $300. Composition dolls cost a fraction of that price ($60 to $80). When dolls are purchased for children, Laurie often tucks in a set of paper dolls (sold separately for $2.50 in six designs). Her new line of muslin dolls, with hand-painted faces and wigs instead of yarn hair, sells for $40 to $50. For price list, send self-addressed, stamped envelope.

lifelike. Porcelain also retains its color over the years because it doesn't deteriorate like other materials."

Until the 1800s, American dolls were made at home or imported from Europe; there were no dolls in the shape of children until 1851, and most dolls were dressed as adults until the 1880s. Early porcelain dolls had painted hair, while those made later had wigs of hair, tow and sometimes sheepskin. A few had glass eyes and necks that rotated, but most heads were sold separately, to be attached to homemade bodies fashioned from muslin, with lower arms sometimes made of porcelain or leather.

Using the techniques of 19th century doll makers, Laurie designs her own patterns, sculpts heads and hands, then makes her own molds, which are cast in porcelain slip. After they are cured by air for several days or more quickly in the oven, she paints, fires and paints them again. Cloth bodies are sewn, stuffed and attached to heads, then each is dressed in clothing and hair that Laurie thinks suits the personality of the face. She makes baby dolls dressed in eyelet, fancy toddlers in lace-trimmed dresses with silk flowers in their hair, country schoolchildren dressed in calico and little boys in overalls. Her Native American dolls, which "represent Indian children caught

Porcelain Indian baby doll in cradleboard by Laurie Carlson

Laurie Carlson Dolls
234 East Houston
Gilbert, AZ 85234
V R W C S CC MO

Other Makers

MJA Porcelain Dolls, Sunset Drive, Hope Valley, RI 02832; (401) 539-2209.

Louise J. Tierney, 159 Old Main Street, Bass River, MA 02664; (617) 394-0684, makes dolls of fired porcelain polished to a satin bisque and china painted in several kiln-fired washes.

RAG DOLLS

Jimmie Cramer will never forget his first doll and the teasing he got from other children because he liked it so much. "It was a rubber baby doll," he says. "I played with it for years." Awhile back, he found the perfect mother to adopt his childhood playmate: a 3-year-old girl, who named her new doll Jimmie after its former owner.

Now in his 30s, Cramer is no longer teased for playing with dolls. His handmade folk dolls, fashioned from feed sacks and vintage materials; are sold at the Museum of American Folk Art in New York and snapped up by collectors as fast as they come from his needle.

"I planned on being an art teacher when I grew up," he says, "but somewhere along the way, my collections took over. When prices of antique baskets went up, I started making the shapes I wanted. Before I knew what was happening, I was in the basket business. I made the first cloth doll to hold a miniature basket in a display, but everyone wanted the prop instead of the product. I've never liked china dolls, only rag dolls, so I began researching them in books, photos and private collections. I've always appreciated antique hand-woven fabrics, so going into the doll business was a great excuse to indulge my addiction." He finds material at auctions, antique shops and flea markets, in the backs of worn-out quilts and the remaining parts of vintage clothing. He's also willing to barter a doll for old fabric.

The part of doll-making that he likes best is painting faces. "I never know if they're male or female until their faces are done," he says. "Their eyes talk. In many ways, they're like my children. I hold onto them as long as I can, and some I can't part with at all."

The bodies of his black-face dolls are made from feed sacks dyed with walnuts. The men sometimes have a shirt and tie but more often have homespun shirts with old-fashioned buttons, neckerchiefs and suspendered or

Black-face rag dolls made from feed sacks dyed with walnuts by James Cramer

drawstring pants. The ladies, dressed in calico or gingham, wear different styles of aprons and sometimes a ruffled fichu around the neck.

Because the Amish believed it was sinful to create graven images, which included photos and faces on dolls, Jimmie's Amish dolls, like many early dolls, have no faces. Their homespun bodies stuffed with wool or cotton are dressed in antique Amish fabrics, plain dresses and wide full-length aprons, with bonnets tied under their chins.

"They really don't need faces," explains Jimmy. "Shadows from their bonnets change their expressions constantly. This way, a child can imagine whatever expression he wants to see."

The folk dolls range in price from $28 to $65, depending on detail. From 14 to 20 inches tall, the faceless dolls each come with a small fabric cat. Jimmie also makes baskets ($20 to $55), folk art accessories and fabric Christmas-tree decorations: strings of stuffed homespun hearts ($15), a circle of five children ($26), lace-haloed

Rag folk doll with sunbonnet and cat by James Cramer

James Cramer
Route 1, Box 28A
Keedysville, MD 21756
(301) 432-6574
V (by appt. only)   R   C   S   MO

Other Makers

Way Back When, P.O. Box 15532, Fort Wayne, IN 46885.

Alice Knouss, 14 West Market Street, Bethlehem, PA 18018; (215) 866-0549, makes the Polly Heckewelder doll.

J. Sweetland, 4485 Buffalo Road, Churchville, NY 14428, makes clothespin dolls.

angels in homespun dresses ($6.50) or tiny homespun stockings ($2.50). His catalog of current offerings is $2.50.

The first doll he ever made sits on a nearby chair, her miniature basket still in hand, watching him work. At the rate success is finding him, Jimmie Cramer may never have to grow up.

Faceless Amish dolls by James Cramer

Appalachian doll called Jennie from up Turkey Hill, Farmer Allen's Daughter, by Ellen Turner

Other Doll Makers

Ellen Turner, Route 1, Box 156, Horse Shoe, NC 28742; (704) 891-8750, makes Appalachian People, with skeletons of wire padded with excelsior and cotton and covered with fabric; hand-painted faces and hand-sewn clothing of natural fabrics and calico; wigs of human hair, mohair or material; and accessories fashioned from dried flowers, twigs or fabric. From 25 to 32 inches tall, prices range from $80 to $425 for single figures, with prices for groups adjusted accordingly.

Margaret Paradise Spoor, 99 Beechwood Hills, Newport News, VA 23602; (804) 877-2228, makes "Penny" dolls fashioned from family favorites, in 6- and 12-inch sizes.

Master carver Bob Raikes, Raikes Originals, P.O. Box 82, Mt. Shasta, CA 96067; (916) 926-5607, makes all-wooden dolls jointed at the shoulder, elbow, neck, hip, knee and, occasionally, the wrist, as well as rabbits jointed at the shoulder and hip. No two are alike. Each is dressed in appropriate dress, designed and sewn by his wife, Carol, who also makes their wigs. Bob and Carol also make cloth-body dolls with hand-carved wooden heads and hands. Each is signed and dated on the back of the neck and

Hand-carved wooden rabbit dolls by Bob and Carol Raikes

Costumed papier-mâché dolls, called Swagman, Beast/Prince and Beauty, by Doris Rockwell Gottilly

comes with a certificate. From miniatures to 3 feet tall, they range in price from $50 to $500. For photo and information send $1.

Doris Rockwell Gottilly, 7905 Breda Court, Raleigh, NC 27606; (919) 362-7716, makes one-of-a-kind, costumed papier-mâché dolls, many of which resemble her children, who pose as models. An exception: the Beast/Prince, a gruesome hairy beast with tusks, whose removable head and clothing reveal a handsome prince dressed in silk. Beauty is a fair blond damsel dressed in silk and lace. The papier-mâché dolls, finished with four coats of gesso, have cloth bodies and include a line of marionettes and a 22-inch-tall Queen Adelaide. They are modeled after dolls and styles from the period 1810 to 1850, with hand-molded painted hair. Author of the book *Creative Doll-making*, Doris researches each period, "which is reflected not only in the clothes, faces and hairstyles," she says, "but also in the way people stand and hold their heads." She also makes ceramic dolls with handmade mohair wigs, as well as all-muslin dolls with painted faces and yarn hair. All are signed and dated. For information, send self-addressed, stamped envelope.

DOWER CHESTS

Of all Pennsylvania folk furniture, the painted dower chest was the most significant. Made by the Pennsylvania-Germans for girls 8 to 10 years of age to store dowries of blankets, linens and quilts before marriage, these six-board chests (four sides, a top lid and bottom) were usually 3 to 4 feet long and sometimes had drawers in the bottom. Kept in the main room or bedroom, the chest also became the receptacle for important family records: the names of the bridal couple and marriage date were painted on

Leight Johnson

Dower chest with tulips and unicorns painted by Virginia Jacobs McLaughlin

the top and *frakturs* for the wedding, baptisms and house blessings were often pasted inside the lid. Usually made by the father, the dower chest, forerunner of today's hope chest, was made of whatever wood was most plentiful, often tulip, poplar or white pine. If family members lacked artistic talent, they waited for an itinerant artist to come through town to paint the elaborate designs and symbols on the surface.

"The colors were the limited palette of the Pennsylvania-Germans," says Virginia Jacobs McLaughlin, who restores and paints dower chests in authentic colors, patterns and methods: "blues, barn reds, blacks to grays, mustard to gold, browns and dark greens. The front was

Leight Johnson

Dower chest with tulips and distelfink birds on front, thistles on sides and top, painted by Virginia Jacobs McLaughlin

often separated into two or three painted panels, arches, squares or rectangles, which could be horizontal or vertical and were sometimes repeated on the sides. Texture was as important as color and was achieved by painting a lighter color as a prime or base coat, then graining, marbleizing or mottling a darker color on top, using an assortment of everyday objects like feathers, combs, sponges, rags and corncobs. Although Europeans preferred realistic graining, most Americans worked fast, becoming more imaginative and flamboyant as the work progressed. The symbols also had meaning: unicorns were guardians of maidenhood; hearts represented love and marriage; tulips implied resurrection and regeneration; closed blossoms, virginity; open flowers, marriage; pomegranates for fertility; distelfink birds promised good luck; and because peacocks were thought to predict the weather, they represented future happiness. "In recent years," says Ginny, "couples giving chests to each other for anniversaries or to their children, often use symbols with special meaning, like farms, horses, angels, flowers, etc."

After graduating from college with a degree in art, Ginny worked as a display artist in Washington, married a career foreign service officer and lived around the world, mothering two sons and studying art each place she lived. When she opened an antique shop in Maryland near the Pennsylvania border and began restoring furniture, she began "to see how Pennsylvania designs were actually simplified translations of European techniques and patterns. Each piece taught me more, and whenever a homely chest came my way, I tried to give it new beauty with painted designs. Before long, my misfits were selling faster than the better antiques."

To paint a chest already owned by a client costs $400 to $800 depending on detail. Ginny also sells painted antique blanket boxes, or new dower chests (made by local cabinetmakers) in any size or wood, with mortise-and-tenon construction, dovetailed corners, plus moldings and feet of the desired period. Depending on the client's preference, Ginny can paint a chest as new or antiqued to look a century old. In the true spirit of the itinerant artist, Ginny also does signs, murals, grained woodwork, floorcloths, stenciling and portraits of today's owners in the style and dress of the period of their houses. In addition to *frakturs* on parchment, with hand-grained frames ($85 to $100) and fireboards on board or canvas ($150 to $200), Ginny also paints armoires, or wardrobes, and Bible and bride's boxes (smaller versions of the dower chest, made by the prospective groom as a gift to the bride, who used it to store sewing equipment and small treasures). For further information, send self-addressed, stamped envelope.

Virginia Jacobs McLaughlin
The Antique Cupboard
812 West Main Street (Box 114)
Emmitsburg, MD 21727
(301) 447-6558 or (717) 642-5142
V   R   S   MO

Dulcimers   *See under* **Musical Instruments**

DECORATED EGGS

The egg is the symbol for fertility and new life in many cultures. Decorated and given as a gift or as part of a tradition or ritual, it has added meaning. Eggs decorated at Eastertime are called *pysanky* by the Ukrainians, *pisanki* by the Poles. In Poland, eggs decorated by girls and women are placed in baskets of food to be blessed by the priest on Easter Saturday, and when a girl gives a boy a *pisanki*, it means that she accepts his proposal of marriage.

In Czechoslovakia, where Easter is the most joyous holiday of the year, eggs are exchanged to signal love, friendship, a new beginning and good things to come. Called *kraslice*, which means "beautiful or embellished eggs," they are given with the greeting, "Christ is risen," to which the recipient replies, "He is risen indeed." The most beautiful egg is saved for the one most loved. When *kraslice* are exchanged by members of the opposite sex, it is considered an agreement to become engaged.

"Eggs are tied on trees," says Kepka Hochmann Belton, a fourth generation Czechoslovakian-American whose family has continued to observe the old traditions, "or a single branch decorated with eggs is taken from house to house. In what is known as the 'switching' custom, a young man braids eight or more green willow branches in the shape of a switch, then decorates them with ribbons and flowers. This is called a *dynvaska*. When a young girl gives him her *kraslice*, he gives her a symbolic tap with his *dynvaska*."

Kraslice, intricately designed miniature works of art executed in brilliant colors by a wax resist process similar to that used in batik, represent an important tradition brought to America by emigrants from Eastern European countries. Kepka, known now as "the egg lady" in Kansas, remembers sitting at her grandmother's table decorating eggs. "We used to stick a spoon into a potato half," she says, "then bend it so the bowl was over the candle used

Goose eggs painted by batik method by Kepka Hochmann Belton

to melt the wax. Unfortunately, the wax caught fire when overheated and the candle produced carbon, which affected the colors." When she was named a master folk artist by the Kansas Art Commission, making her a teacher of apprentices, she circumvented dangers and injury by using a small alcohol burner whose temperature could be controlled and whose fuel cost less than candles.

After washing eggs in warm water with white vinegar, she pats them dry. Then, using a special mixture of beeswax and ink, she draws the sharp lines that separate the colors in her geometric designs. Using natural or commercial dyes, she works from light to dark, coating areas to be dyed with beeswax, which is later removed. When completed, holes are made in both ends, the yolk broken with a wire and both yolk and white blown out. The egg is heated for 10 minutes in the oven to dry the inside, then rubbed with butter for a dull finish or varnished.

"Czechs are superstitious," says Kepka. "Every shape and color has meaning. The eight-pointed star is a symbol for Christianity and resurrection. The butterfly means reincarnation, while the snake stands for protector, or the man of the family. Suns and daisies mean good fortune, and the ram's horn is for protection. Red is proud, heroic, a protection against evil, while green means growth, and yellow is for grain and gold."

A popular demonstrator at the Smithsonian's Folklife Festival, the National Dvořák Festival in Iowa and the Czech After-Harvest Festival in Kansas, Kepka sells decorated chicken eggs for $7 and goose eggs (which take twice as long to do) for $10. For those who want to do it themselves, her specially designed Egg Lap-Studio for

EMBROIDERY

Kent Meyerhoff

Chicken eggs (in middle) painted by batik method, duck eggs (around circumference) painted by colored wax method with raised relief by Kepka Hochmann Belton

working and carrying contains all necessary materials and tools for $50. On mail orders, add $3 for postage and handling of each kit and $1 for each egg.

Kepka Hochmann Belton
Kepka's Kraslice
1007 North Grand
Ellsworth, KS 67439
(913) 472-3008
R S MO

Other Makers

John J. Hejna, 4529 289th Street, Toledo, OH 43611; (419) 726-8387, makes *pysanky*. In simple designs without dye baths, his chicken eggs sell for $22 a dozen. Elaborate designs are $12 on chicken eggs, while decorated goose eggs are $7.50 to $30, and ostrich $120. His kits contain thirty designs, ten colors and beeswax ($12). Shipping extra.

Barbara Lally, RFD 5, Mountain Road, Goffstown, NH 03045; (603) 497-2198, sells *pysanky* and also teaches classes.

Marjorie Kopecek Nejdl, Ivanhoe Road, Route 2, Cedar Rapids, IA 52401, makes *kraslice*.

Mrs. Boris Tertichny, 227 North 9th Street, Keokuk, IA 52632, makes decorated eggs in the Russian tradition.

Evelyn Althaus, 35 Queen Street, Ephrata, PA 17522; (717) 733-3254, makes Pennsylvania-German scratch-decorated eggs.

Annie Morgalis. 300 Pine Hill Street, Minersville, PA

17944; (717) 544-4907, makes *pysanky* in the Lithuanian tradition.

Marion Rose, 1680 Main Street, West Warwick, RI 02895, *pysanky*.

Betty Baranko, Box 44, Fairfield, ND 58672; (701) 575-4976, *pysanky*.

Angeline Chruszch, Route 1, Box 48, Belfield, ND 58622; (701) 575-4690.

AMERICAN SURFACE EMBROIDERY

"American surface embroidery reflected American culture," explains Illoyna Homeyard, "in that it synthesized existing forms to reflect American needs, means and outlook. American needleworkers saw techniques, liked them and used them. Northern colonies drew heavily on English traditions; the South was influenced by France and the Orient; the mid-Atlantic by Sweden, Holland, Germany, England, France and the Orient; and the Southwest by Spanish and Native American. A rich, eclectic, innovative style evolved.

"After the Revolution, American embroidery became less utilitarian and turned from earlier, heavier Jacobean to painterly styles with delicate shadings, textures and more graceful, refined lines. Instead of mimicking styles of other countries, we began to create our own. Classically drawn, carefully composed flowers, landscapes, oriental garden themes, shepherdess bouquets and memorial scenes emerged in a mix and blend of motifs (like a Tudor rose and Pennsylvania-German tulips in a Chinese basket). Silk on silk was preferred, but wool never disappeared. It was typically American to mix fibers in the same piece. Silk was used with wool for contrast or when brilliance or a smooth effect was desired. Instead of heavy trunklike branches and stylized motifs, flower forms were arranged in a balance of imbalances in needle paintings whose stitches resembled brush strokes. Known as *opus quillarium* (in the style of the feather), long and short stitches were layered like the feathers of a bird. When completed, pieces were displayed as pictures.

"In the mid-1800s, when ladies' magazines taught readers how to create naturalistic colorations, realism became the desired form. Unfortunately, so much how-to by uncertain authorities caused American embroidery to devolve into an amorphous lump of padded work and unoriginality. At the time of the centennial, a sorting out took place. By the turn of the century and World War I, surface embroidery had reemerged as an art form. Designs depicted American flowers and subjects in colonial and classical themes. Wool reemerged as the primary fiber, with silk, cotton and metal threads in supporting roles. Pieces were more carefully composed, mature, vibrant and expressed a self-assured freedom of spirit."

Illoyna began embroidering at the age of 5 and by the time she was 8 had designed her first original piece. After graduating from Penn State, she joined the Peace Corps and has since been a social worker, floral designer and scientific illustrator. When an accident injured her arm so that she could no longer paint, she returned to embroidery, creating original and carefully researched traditional designs appropriate to their era and theme in stitches, fibers and coloration. Her one-of-a-kind renderings of classic garden themes in the forms of hangings, fire screens, pillows, chair seats, bell pulls and clothing are represented in collections around the world, and in kits through Creations, in Milford, New Jersey.

"I work in linen, silk or wool fabrics; cotton, linen, wool and silk thread," says Illoyna, "in needlepoint and whitework as well as surface embroidery. I use early design motifs: tree of life, vines, floral sprays, singleton flowers, in various stitches (up to 75 different stitches in more complex pieces) to create texture and mode, relying on

"Queen Anne Basket," typical American needlework blending of motifs and forms, by Illoyna Sotack Homeyard

chain stitch, satin, crewel, stem, long-and-short to form the painterly quality and raised work, with a range of other stitches for a bas-relief appearance, drawing on more than 600 stitches in our cultural heritage. I use chenille needles because the long eye and tapered shape afford more control over texture and direction of stitching with the least damage to fiber and fabric."

Illoyna's work is also available in miniatures as small as 2 by 3 inches up to 6 by 8 inches, stitched in cotton or silk with the same care, complexity and quality as the larger pieces. Prices range from $25 to $1,500, with most in the $75 to $200 range.

Illoyna Sotack Homeyard
2776 North Charlotte Street
Gilbertsville, PA 19525
(215) 326-7975
R MO

Other Maker
Jean Barnett, 3116 Mounds Road, Apt. 1, Anderson, IN 46013; (317) 649-2970.

"Jardinaire," example of opus quillarium embroidery, or needle painting, by Illoyna Sotack Homeyard

COLCHA EMBROIDERY

Although the Spanish word *colcha* means bed covering, the term is also used to describe a form of embroidery practiced in the Rio Grande Valley of northern Mexico and southern Colorado as well as the Hispanic embroidered textiles on which the self-couching *colcha* stitch is used.

"*Colcha* embroideries have the most spontaneous and whimsical designs among the Rio Grande textiles," says

Gordon Adams

Hand-spun, vegetable-dyed colcha *embroidery by Maria Vergara-Wilson*

Maria Vergara-Wilson, creator of a *colcha* in the Albuquerque Museum. "They exhibit a joyous indulgence in sinuous floral motifs, fanciful animals, religious and heraldic symbols."

Colchas are mentioned in New Mexican church records as early as 1743, and the dyes, fibers and spinning of the earliest *colchas* are tentatively dated 1750. Used in the church as altar cloths, altar carpets and wall hangings, and in the home as bedspreads, the wool-on-wool pieces used natural white *sabanilla* (see Weaving, Rio Grande) as a ground cloth and were embroidered with yarn made from the lustrous outer fleece of churro sheep.

"I have spent many hours learning to make a *colcha* similar to those made before 1820," says Maria—whose *colchas* and *jerga* weavings have won awards at the prestigious Spanish Market in Santa Fe every year since 1981—"weaving the ground cloth, experimenting with various fleeces to find the smoothest, most lustrous yarn. Hand-spinning and carding make the fibers slightly shiny instead of fuzzy and dull. When stitched in closely laid stitches, it creates a subtle reflective quality on the surface."

Maria spins yarn from unwashed fleece so that it will not lose its natural lanolin, then after harvesting local plants to make her dyes, dyes her yarn outside on a gas stove top. "Dyeing is one of the most delightfully creative processes in my art," says Maria. "I look forward to the abundance of colors that comes from plants each season. There are always subtle surprises (for instance, a very dry year makes colors more intense). I first mordant the yarn with mineral salts, which helps the dye to penetrate the wool, then boil the herbs to make a dye bath in which the wool is simmered."

Pre-1850 embroideries had large, simplified, chintzlike floral motifs, but as plain weave and twill cotton cloth replaced *sabanilla,* designs became more delicate and isolated. New stitches were used to depict stylized flowers with winding stems, insects, deer, sheep and birds, but the *colcha* stitch remained predominant. By the turn of the century, prestamped patterns displaced *colchas* until they were revived in the 1930s.

After tracing the design on the *sabanilla* in running stitches with black thread, Maria covers the surface with loosely laid *colcha* stitches, using fine yarn for floral parts, heavier in the background, beginning each piece of yarn with 3 to 4 running stitches because no knots are used.

"My embroideries are often pictorial," says Maria, "expressing traditional religious themes commonly the subjects of *reredos* or *retablos.* My weavings and embroideries

Jonathan Meyers/JAM Photography

Pictorial colcha *embroidery by Maria Vergara-Wilson*

come about as expressions of experiences I value, like the birth of a child, or a lonely hour spent in an abandoned pueblo. This small isolated village of La Madera where I live nurtures my creative energy. One hand is in the present while one reaches into the past. The old ways tell me who I am but the new forms give me a sense of individuality and creative freedom.''

Maria's weavings (*jerga*, weft-*ikat* and Rio Grande tapestries) and embroideries are sold through Bellas Artes Gallery, Canyon Road and Garcia Street, Santa Fe, NM; (505) 983-2745.

Maria Vergara-Wilson
Route 2, Box 46
La Madera, NM 87539
(505) 983-2745

Other Maker
Maria T. Lujan, P.O. Box 728, Espanola, NM 87533.

CREWEL EMBROIDERY

Although early colonial laws forbade the wearing of finery, none banned beautifying the home. Consequently, crewel embroidery, past its peak of popularity in England when the first settlers arrived in America, found new life and interpretation through the skilled needles of American colonists. As soon as women found the time, they embroidered crewel (which means twisted worsted yarn) on bed hangings, coverlets, blankets, chair seats, tablecloths and (where officials could not see) on their petticoats and pockets, which were made separately and worn under skirts. Simpler in design than English crewel, with more open space in the background, American crewel was lighter in feeling and also used simpler stitches. Faced with the need to make thread go further, frugal New Englanders replaced the English long-and-short stitch (also known as the Roumanian) with what became known as the New England laid, or economy, stitch, which kept most of the thread on the surface rather than wasting it on the back where it could not be seen. Usually done with a 2-ply worsted on any fabric but traditionally on linen or linen twill, American designs featured native birds, flowers, trees, animals, insects, corn and wild grapevines.

"The earliest American crewel was done in shades of indigo blue with no other colors," says fiber specialist Shelley Culhane. "Although linen was the favorite background, cotton was used more frequently in the South, as were dyed fabrics. Green was especially popular for backgrounds and embroidery. Southern designs also used flowers, trees and birds native to the region." Creativity could be more important than perspective. "Sometimes a thimble used to trace grapes and cherries was also used for apples," says Shelley, "so that they were all the same size in the finished piece."

In larger towns, cities and seaports, crewel yarn was bought in skeins imported from England, but in the country, thread was carded, spun and dyed at home with natural materials like goldenrod, black walnut hulls and butternut shells, producing rich, vibrant colors. As laws became less restrictive, crewel later appeared on outer garments like dresses, waistcoats, slippers and capes.

After earning her Master of Fine Arts in weaving and textile design, Shelley was an instructor at Mansfield State College, did dye work for the furniture curator at the Woodbury Strong Museum in Rochester and demonstrated and exhibited at Clermont, Robert Livingston's Hudson River estate. "I do all kinds of fiber work for museums, decorators and clients," she says, "from dyeing new material to matching and replacing antique fabrics to executing my own designs. Because different motifs and stitches were popular in various parts of the country,

Crewel valance embroidered by Shelley Culhane

I usually research each commission in the region where it will be used." She has designed crewel valances to co-ordinate with colonial upholstery on a sofa, curtains, bell pulls and footstools. Her most interesting commission to date was a bedspread for a period house furnished with authentic furniture. "The couple's hobby was birdwatching," says Shelley. "Using crewel in the style of 1760, I designed the spread with today's birds, in the owner's taste and interpretation."

In addition to crewel, Shelley also does needlepoint and flame stitch. Chair seats and church kneelers in flame stitch start at $100; in crewel, $150; less in sets. Valances start at $300, depending on fabric, design and size. Consultation fees on request.

Shelley Culhane
153 Richard Street
Rochester, NY 14607
(716) 442-8741
R W S MO

Other Maker

Elizabeth Creedon, The Sampler, 12 North Park Avenue, Plymouth, MA 02360; (617) 746-7077, does reproduction needlework for Winterthur and on commission, including complete bed hangings, curtains and wedding remembrances. Her popular HM 1773 potholder, used to serve tea, costs $110 when done by her but, like many of her designs, is also available in do-it-yourself kits. C ($1)

Authorized reproduction of the HM 1773 crewel potholder from Winterthur Museum by Elizabeth Creedon

CUTWORK, HARDANGER, HEDEBO, NETTING AND TENERIFFE EMBROIDERY

"As a child in Utah, watching my mother and grandmothers doing needlework," Denise Longhurst recalls, "it never occurred to me that the different threads or patterns they used classified their work by separate techniques. After I married and moved to Colorado, I discovered most people weren't even aware of them, and that many of these methods were becoming lost arts. I began researching and recording my findings."

The results became a book, *Vanishing American Needle Arts* (Putnam's), which includes brief histories, how-to instructions for beginners and numerous patterns, pictures and drawings. Denise now teaches techniques of embroidery at Utah State University, as well as half- or full-day sessions around the United States.

Cutwork, done on tightly woven cloth, is worked in designs slightly overlapping each other, with open spaces decorated with small bars. The simple version has no bars and everything connects; the Richelieu type is characterized by small picots (loops) on the side of each bar; while the Renaissance has bars but no picots. All types originated in Italy, so it stands to reason that the Italian type is the most difficult: after the threads are counted, some are pulled so that a design is woven between them.

"Danish hedebo looks similar to simple crocheted edging on towels," says Denise, "but it's worked with a needle and is much sturdier. Netting is hard to master. It uses one knot throughout. Designs form when you vary the size of the loop or the number of knots. It's actually an ancient method mentioned in the Bible and illustrated on Egyptian tomb drawings. Extremely rare today, there is a form of woven network popular in craft circles which imitates the older work where the background net is constructed first, then woven to form the designs. Hardanger, named for a city in Norway, is not difficult to do but elegant when finished. It combines the basic kloster block formations [a satin stitch worked in groups of five over four threads of canvas] with many other surface stitches in weblike designs over cut-away portions of the fabric.

"There is a lot of cross-over between methods. The satin stitch, for instance, is used on hardanger, cutwork and hedebo. Although each of the techniques originated

Fine linen decorated with Renaissance cutwork by Denise Longhurst

in a different part of the world, Americanization blended them. Teneriffe's weblike designs are thought to have come from an island in Spain, but the technique is similar to Brazilian point lace, daisy wheel medallions, polka spider webs, *nanduti*, Spanish sol lace and Paraguayan lace."

Prices of Denise's work vary according to the difficulty of the design and the materials requested. Each order comes with a brief history of the needle art and a signed verification of originality, with care taken to make each piece a little different. A framed piece of cutwork approximately 12 inches square is $145; 10-inch square or round pillows are $85. A bath towel, hand towel and matching washcloth in hedebo are $35. Using the ancient technique of netting, a doily 10 inches in diameter made completely of thread is $40, while a 6-inch doily with a circle of linen and 2-inch-wide netted edging is $30. A place mat and napkin set in hardanger is $20. *Vanishing*

Woven embroidery network by Denise Longhurst

Corner of hardanger table runner by Denise Longhurst

Teneriffe embroidery designs as pillowcase edgings by Denise Longhurst

EMBROIDERY

American Needle Arts is $17.95, plus $1.50 for shipping and handling.

Denise Longhurst
Vanishing American Needle Arts
P.O. Box 954
Mendon, UT 84325
(801) 753-7459
R S MO

Other Maker
Pat Benson, 326 15th Avenue South, Fargo, ND 58103.

Sampler Embroidery

Early samplers, or exemplars, recorded different stitches and embroidery patterns to demonstrate the

Original sampler by Joanne Harvey

Traditional wedding sampler by Sheila Barron Cox

needleworker's proficiency in embroidery. Because many samplers were made under the guidance of a tutor, a well-done sampler also demonstrated that a young girl's parents could afford to pay for her lessons. Joanne Harvey's shop, The Exemplarery, creates original samplers and is the authorized licensee for the Henry Ford Museum, the Daughters of the American Revolution, the Pilgrim Society, the Rhode Island School of Design Museum of Art and Winterthur, reproducing samplers from their collections.

"Artistry created by children often is laced with errors," says Joanne, "but we faithfully include mistakes as originally wrought to capture the feeling and spirit of the original needle worker. We do not alter, add to, delete or change any of the original designs. All samplers are worked on linen, some are a darker natural tone to reflect the hand-spun foundations sometimes used, others are hand-dyed using only natural vegetable dyes to mellow and complement the muted tones of floss." P.O. Box 2554, Dearborn, MI 48123; (313) 278-3282.   R   C   MO

Other Makers

Liz Chronister and Kathleen Brock, RD 2, Dillsburg, PA 17079.

Sheila Barron Cox, P.O. Box 6097, Rome, GA 30161, does marriage and birth samplers in counted-thread cross-stitch.

Gail Ray, P.O. Box 434, Hiawatha Circle, Chickamauga, GA 30707, does cross-stitch and counted cross-stitch.

Exemplars   *See* **Embroidery, Sampler**

Fans, Cedar   *See under* **Carving**

HAWAIIAN FEATHERWORK

When the 60-foot-long double-hulled canoe *Hōkūle'a* traveled from Hawaii to Tahiti in 1975 without modern sailing equipment, one of the ways the crew determined wind direction was by the feather banners attached to the masts. The feathers did more than tell which way the wind was blowing. In Hawaii, feathers have long been symbols of spiritual power and protection. High-ranking male chiefs donned long feather cloaks and feather helmets going into battle; royalty wore feathered robes of state. The higher the rank, the longer the cape.

"Enchantment was used in every phase of the work so that when the cape was completed, the chief was literally covered with magic incantations," says Lucia Jensen, whose feather capes are displayed in several important island collections. "That is why the capes and helmets were worn in battle; they were metaphysical shields that protected wearers from harm.

"The first mention of the all-feather cape was in the epic poem of Kaka'alaneo, a 14th century high chief of Maui. Before that, capes were made of *wauke* (bark cloth) and only partially covered with feathers. Larger feathers in browns, blacks and whites were used in the beginning, but as the style progressed, feathers became smaller. In the 18th and 19th centuries, when the capes became famous worldwide, feathers were only ½ inch long; when sewn on a net base, they looked like velvet. Ancient settlers used red feathers as the symbol for gods and chiefs, but yellow became the dominant color on the Big Island, red

the favorite on Maui, while capes on O'ahu and Kaua'i were made in a mixture of browns."

Most capes were made from the feathers of native forest birds, especially the red *i'iwi* and *'apapane,* and two types of blackbirds: the *'ō'ō* and the *mamo.* "The *mamo* has only two yellow feathers, one under each wing," says Lucia, who is also a research historian and genealogist. "They would catch the bird, pluck the two feathers, then let the bird go. It is said that the full-length yellow cape made for High Chief Kamahameha took many months and many hands to complete and contained the feathers of 100,000 birds.

"Anchored to a fishnet or net backing once made of *olonā* [fiber from a seawater-resistant shrub] but now of thin white twine, feather capes allow air to filter through and keep the body cool. The classical 18th century cape for high-ranking chiefs was ankle length. Prior to that the shorter rectangular shape was in vogue. Colors of helmets also represented tribal symbols; crests designated tribe and clan from each island. The crest followed an imaginary line to the ivory pendant hanging around the chief's neck, creating another magic circle of protection. Feathers were a precious commodity used in trade and to pay taxes and were never used frivolously."

Leis, worn around the neck or on top of the head like a crown, are made with feathers standing up or lying flat. Red feathers symbolized power and strength; yellow, superior intellect; and green, good health. *Kahili,* cylindrical shapes covered with feathers that are mounted on wooden poles, originally represented the guardian of the wind: Tawhiri in New Zealand, Kahili in Hawaii. They later represented sentries guarding the king, boasting insignia of royal rank with different designs for each family. Carried in parades on royal standards of koa wood, or held in

Feather cape with black feathers in large middle section, red on sides and bottom and bright yellow horizontal stripe by Lucia Tarallo Jensen

Kahili, Hawaiian featherwork by Natalie Kamahinaokalani'ehukapuaoka'iouli

cylindrical stands at ceremonies, they also designate islands and clans by their colors.

"The most satisfying aspect of creating featherwork is the awareness that it brings," says Lucia. "Each design has a metaphysical meaning; color and style were relevant to status in a totemic society. The ancients had a sense of order and design that we have yet to achieve."

Lucia's capes, made primarily of jungle fowl feathers in natural colors and of dyed goose feathers, take from two weeks to two months to make, depending on size. The smallest, a collar cape, is $400; the largest, $3,000. Her daughter, Natalie Kamahinaokalani'chukapuaoka'iouli, is one of the foremost designers of *kahili* on the islands.

Lucia Tarallo Jensen
99-919 Kalawina Place
'Aiea, HI 96701
(808) 487-6949
V R MO

Other Makers

Natalie Kamahinaokalani'ehukapuaoka'iouli, 99-919 Kalawina Place, 'Aiea, HI 96701; (808) 487-6949.

A. Ulu Seto, 929 Io Lane, Honolulu, HI 96817; (808) 847-2415, makes feather leis.

Mary Louise Kekuewa, 3779 Lurline Drive, Honolulu, HI 96816; (808) 734-5411, made the feather banners on the Hōkūle'a and is known for her leis.

Hattie Leong, 1491 Ainakea, Lahaina, HI 96761; (808) 661-3091.

Leimomi Perrera, c/o 562A Front Street, Lahaina, HI 96761.

Mrs. Sarah Kauainui, 89-363 Pua Avenue, Waianae, HI 96792.

NATIVE AMERICAN FEATHERWORK

Indians used feathers of native birds (turkeys, ducks, swans, prairie chickens, crows, owls, hawks and pheasants) to decorate their dress and gear. Although the hawk's feathers were worn for courage, the most sacred and highly prized were those of the eagle, whose tail and wing feathers were used to decorate lances, shields and bonnets. An eagle was never shot, but captured and killed by strangling, crushing or breaking its neck so that no blood was shed.

"The eagle was the chief of all birds, an emblem of strength and courage," explains Dixon Palmer, whose magnificent warbonnets are as highly prized by museums and collectors as by Indians. "The eagle's extraordinary vision and ability to fly to great heights inspired the Indian, filling him with hope and confidence of success and victory. Most Indians believe the eagle was created by their Supreme Being for its beauty and to provide special charms in battle. An eagle's feathers had to be earned by doing brave deeds."

The finest warbonnet had a trail of eagle tail feathers from head to ground, and a double-trailer bonnet had two tails, made of feathers from the right and left wings of the bird. Feathers and fluffs were left naturally white; the only color was in the beadwork. Warbonnets were not worn in battle, but at celebrations after battles. Indian braves danced a war dance before going to war and after their return. If victorious, they performed a victory dance.

Warbonnet with double trailer by Dixon Palmer

Today, dances are for entertainment and performed at social events called powwows. In Oklahoma alone there are one or two powwows almost every weekend.

"Today anyone can wear a bonnet," says Dixon, whose Indian name, Tsain-Sah-Hay, means Blue Hail. "Since the eagle is now protected, we dye turkey feathers to look like those of the eagle."

Dixon's warbonnets of feathers, plumes, rabbit fur strips, leather quills and beadwork have been made for entertainers like Willie Nelson, Jimmy Stewart, Chuck Connors, Loretta Lynn and a number of wrestlers like Wahoo McDaniel, a former University of Oklahoma football player who wears his bonnet into the ring because he is proud of his Indian heritage.

"Since I served in the armed forces during World War II with 511 days of combat," says Dixon, "I can wear my bonnet with great pride because I have earned the right."

Dixon and his three brothers began making their own feather costumes when they started dancing. Dixon, an accomplished war dancer since he was 12, has won many national titles in the more than five decades since. He worked at Indian City USA as head guide, managed Indian City Pottery and is now on the Board of Directors there. He lives on a farm where he raises Angus and polled Hereford cattle when he's not making feather costumes for his family and the world. He says, "I am most proud of my family and the fact we have learned to live in the white man's world and still retain our Indian heritage."

Although he is skilled at making dance bustles, shields, leggings, and vests, Dixon specializes in warbonnets. After cleaning feathers, he straightens them. When feathers are added to the bonnet, they must be perfectly balanced to hang right and flare out at the correct angle. His wife, Chlotiea, a skilled maker of buckskin clothing and tepees, does beadwork on headbands and rosettes, then fills in as model when Dixon makes final adjustments to the feathers.

Although Dixon's bonnet is white, clients often order them in school or tribal colors. He recently completed one for the HMS *Brave*, the Royal Navy's most modern ship, which features an Indian warbonnet on the crest.

Dixon's warbonnets range in price from $200 to $500 and take approximately 2 weeks to make. "My name is on the bonnet," says Dixon, "so I take my time to make them good. I want all of them to be A number 1."

Dixon and Chlotiea Palmer
Route 3, Box 189
Anadarko, OK 73005
(405) 247-3987

Other Makers

George Palmer, Route 3, Box 58C, Anadarko, OK 73005; (405) 247-6892, Dixon's brother, is one of the innovators in fancy war dance costume design in the Plains area. Several of his original ideas include the use of longer and more numerous hackles on the ends of each feather shaft in the neck and tail bustle, the swing bustle, the extremely long beaded dance harness and the knee-length leg furs.

Oklahoma Indian Arts and Crafts Cooperative, Southern Plains Indian Museum, Box 966, Anadarko, OK 73005; (405) 247-3486.

Fences   *See* **Iron, Architectural**

Fiddles   *See under* **Musical Instruments**

Figureheads   *See* **Cigar-Store Indians and Figureheads**

Firebacks and Stoveplates

Firebacks, cast-iron plates taller than they were wide, were placed at the back of a fireplace to protect the brick or stone, as well as to reflect heat into the room. Produced by American craftsmen through the 18th century, they usually had a raised crest or arch at the top. Patterns made from wood were pressed into moist sand, which created the mold into which the molten iron was poured.

Stoveplates, often mistaken for firebacks, were originally sections of five- and six-plate stoves made by German and Swedish emigrants in eastern Pennsylvania, New Jersey,

Replica of stoveplate, dated 1758 by American ironmaster Thomas Potts, 21 by 24 inches, by The Country Iron Foundry

New York and Connecticut. Such stoves could be dismantled and moved. As they were replaced by free-standing stoves, the square and rectangular sections were recycled as firebacks.

Makers

Pat and Charlie Euston, New England Firebacks, P.O. Box 162, Woodbury, CT 06798; (203) 263-4328, make six different firebacks ranging from a simple heart for $95 to larger, more elaborate designs up to $225. Hand-cast in Connecticut, price includes shipping.   C

Don Stoughton, The Country Iron Foundry, P.O. Box 600, Paoli, PA 19301; (215) 296-7122, makes more than a dozen designs in firebacks and replicas of six historic stoveplates.   C ($1 deductible from order)

Fireboards

Fireboards made from boards, wood panels, canvas or cardboard were used to cover fireplace openings when fireplaces were not in use. In early homes without dampers to open and close chimneys, fireboards kept out cold air when the fire wasn't burning, as well as birds, bats, insects and raccoons. Although cardboard was easier to cut and paint or cover, wood became the preferred material because it was sturdier, could be washed and didn't mildew in warm weather.

Cast-iron fireback, 22 inches high and 18 inches wide, in cavalier design, originally c. 1740, by Pat and Charlie Euston

Fireboard depicting inn, guest house and drover herding pigs to market, by Virginia Jacobs McLaughlin

Favorite subjects painted by owners or itinerant artists were pastoral or maritime scenes, vases of flowers, baskets of fruit and trompe l'oeil views of the fireplace itself, often with three edges painted to look like decorated tiles. Boards were also decorated with stenciled designs, pasted cutouts, fabric, wallpaper, papier-maché or combinations of paper and paint.

Cut to fit the opening, sometimes slightly larger, fireboards were leaned against the fireplace, held upright by molding or feet on the bottom edge or had slots cut to fit over andirons. As fireplaces fell into disuse, some fireboards had holes cut for stovepipes. A few were saved and hung on the wall, but most were discarded, sometimes even thrown on the fire.

Makers

Sandra B. Tarbox, 261 Hinman Lane, Southbury, CT 06488; (203) 264-8900, makes fireboards of wide pine boards held in place by battens, with handles and feet attached by screws if freestanding fireboard is desired ($200 to $600).

Virginia Jacobs McLaughlin, The Antique Cupboard, 812 West Main Street (Box 114), Emmitsburg, MD 21727; (301) 447-6558 or (717) 642-5142, creates fireboards of wide pine boards or canvas with original scenes that depict the owner's interests ($150 to $350).   V   R   S   MO

Tom Kelly, 3 Liberty Street, Mineral Point, WI 53565; (608) 987-2295.

FLOORCLOTHS

Early Americans liked floorcloths because they could make them at home in any color or design to match what they had or to imitate what they couldn't afford, like marble or even oriental rugs. Made of heavy canvas or sailcloth, stenciled with geometric designs or painted freehand, then sealed with several coats of varnish, floorcloths took extraordinary amounts of wear and tear, which made them ideal for heavily traveled parts of the house like entries, halls, stairways and dining rooms. More durable than woven carpets, thicker than linoleum but with a texture similar to summer matting, they were cooler underfoot in summer months, were not eaten by bugs, were easy to clean and could be recut without re-edging. When covered with carpet in winter months, they became a bonus layer of insulation. Popular from the early 1700s until the turn of this century, they were originally made by hand and eventually by factories where they evolved into linoleum.

After floorcloths (also called oyle cloths, painted canvas, painted duck or painted carpet) were rediscovered in the 1950s, museums, restorations and private individuals commissioned firms like Good & Co., Floorclothmakers, to recreate authentic patterns.

Like early makers, Nancy Good Cayford and Philip Cayford handcraft their floorcloths to order. Heavy canvas is cut, sized and specially treated for durability; oil-based paints are used for backgrounds and design application, then sealed with several coats of varnish in a satin finish. In addition to twenty historically accurate patterns and adaptations from pre-Revolutionary through Victorian times, Good & Co. can duplicate original designs or patterns from china, wallpaper or quilts in seventeen stock colonial colors or custom blends. Their most popular stock design is Dartmouth, adapted from a cloth in a 1793 painting; Rabbit Run was inspired by Dedham Pottery; Regina comes from a check design popular in the Victorian era; Grape Vine is art nouveau; Ebenezer is an 18th century design from the Ebenezer Waters House in West Sutton, Massachusetts; Sturbridge was inspired by

Wall-to-wall Regina floorcloth painted by Nancy Good Cayford and Philip Cayford of Good & Co.

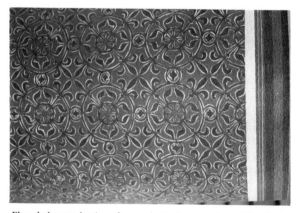

Floorcloth reproduction of an early linoleum made for John Quincy Adams's birthplace by Nancy Good Cayford and Philip Cayford of Good & Co.

an illustration in Nina Fletcher Little's *Floor Coverings in New England Before 1850* (a floorcloth made by Good & Co. in this pattern can be seen in the tavern at Old Sturbridge Village). Good & Co. floorcloths can also be seen in John Quincy Adams's birthplace in Quincy, Massachusetts, the Derby House in Salem, Massachusetts, and the Lloyd Manor, Lloyd Neck, New York.

While Nancy and Philip have discovered many patterns in primitive period paintings, they have found others right where they were left decades ago. When Nancy delivered a commissioned 10- by 40-foot marbleized runner to the Salisbury Mansion in Worcester, Massachusetts, she arrived just as they found two old floorcloths, one on top of the other, under floorboards of an unrestored room. The one on the bottom (c. 1830) is the second oldest in the United States and as soon as funds are raised will be recreated.

For all the work involved, the cost of floorcloths is surprisingly low: about $7 a square foot. They are available in sizes as small as 2 by 3 feet or as large as 12 by 14 feet and can be custom-ordered even larger. Sizes over 7 feet are seamed. Prices include shipping by UPS (unless otherwise requested). Sizes larger than 7 feet wide are shipped by freight. Orders should include check, money order or VISA/Mastercard number. Delivery is in approximately 4 to 6 weeks. A color catalog is available with samples of material used for $2. If you're in the vicinity, floorcloths can be seen in the Cayfords' store in Amherst, New Hampshire.

Nancy Good Cayford and Philip Cayford
Good & Co., Floorclothmakers
Salzburg Square
Route 101
Amherst, NH 03031
(603) 672-0490
V R W C S CC MO

Other Makers

Pemaquid Floorcloths, Route 32, Round Pond, ME 04564; (207) 529-5633, makes hand-stenciled canvas floorcloths in original and traditional designs, ranging from $5 to $8.50 a square foot depending on the complexity of the design. Because they mix their own colors, they can duplicate any piece of fabric, wallpaper or china. Workshop open by chance or appointment. R W C CC

Lynn Goodpasture, 42 West 17th Street, New York, NY 10011; (212) 645-5334, who teaches at Cooper-Hewitt Museum, custom-designs floorcloths for any decor.

Martha Berg, 2619 North 67th Street, Wauwatosa, WI

Alan P. Jacobs

Basket floorcloth, 6 feet in diameter, by Lynn Goodpasture

53213; (414) 771-2506, makes floorcloths, 2 by 3 feet for $35 with each additional square foot $4.

Janie Atkinson, 405 Stewart Avenue, Marietta, GA 30064; (404) 424-1156 or 998-8838, makes floorcloths at $10 a square foot.

Kathleen Livers, Hands and Hearts Stenciling, 2110 Cumberland, Rockford, IL 61103; (815) 963-8325, makes floorcloths and place mats, wall hangings and table runners using floorcloth patterns and technique.

Sherry Mason, P.O. Box 3305, Portsmouth, VA 23701; (804) 393-0095. C ($1)

Sandra Buck, Buck Mountain Stenciling, Maple Corner, Calais, VT 05648; (802) 229-9326.

Gladys Daniels Johnston, P.O. Box 151, Wayne, IL 60184; (312) 584-2491.

Toby Soule and Susan Martens, P.O. Box 185, South Freeport, ME 04078; (207) 865-4855 or 688-2294.

Raphaela, P.O. Box 441, Lyons, NY 14489.

June Bissell, Harris Road, Esmond, RI 02917; (401) 231-9145.

Sara Nolan, Teneriffe Mt. Road, RFD, Union, NH 03887; (603) 652-4488.

Flower Painting *See* **Rosemaling**

FRAKTURS

Germans who settled in Pennsylvania, Maryland, Virginia and Ohio brought with them a love of color, decoration and symbols, as seen in their embellishment of everyday objects. Tools were inscribed with hearts, butter was stamped with flowers, cookies were cut in hundreds of fanciful shapes and barns were painted with hex signs.

Traditional fraktur *in German by Beverly Weir*

Frakturs, inspired by medieval alphabets, had been used in Germany for centuries to inscribe family Bibles, church hymnals and religious books. In America, *fraktur* lettering was often taught at schools in German-American communities. Before long, the Germans' love of looking at beautiful objects won out over practicality. *Frakturs,* considered too nice to be kept in drawers or in family Bibles, were framed and hung up. From then on, an American

Colorful fraktur *with tulips by Beverly Weir*

folk craft that started as a way to record births, baptisms, weddings and deaths became a way to celebrate life and to include house blessings, birthdays, friendship, graduation and school and music awards.

Drawn on the best paper or parchment with a finely cut tail-feather quill from a crow or pheasant and india or drawing ink, the words of the record or sentiment were interwoven with colorful symbols from nature (flowers, trees, birds), fanciful designs (hearts, geometric shapes) or religious symbols (angels, crowns, clouds, devils). When *frakturs* were given as gifts, they were signed on the back by the donor, who in many cases was also the artist.

Beverly Weir studied German decorative arts for 3 years while living in Germany and has been painting *frakturs* since 1976. "My interest began," she says, "after I purchased my first original in Pennsylvania and began studying *frakturs* in collections like that of the Free Library of Philadelphia [one of the largest and most significant collections in existence, numbering more than a thousand]. I've gone on to collect about ten early examples."

Most of the *frakturs* that Beverly paints are custom work. "The person commissioning the *fraktur* usually chooses the paper, and when needed, I have old paper for special projects. After going through my sample books, the client chooses designs, colors, size, symbols, etc. In this way, every *fraktur* is original, although I can reproduce an old favorite when requested to do so."

Beverly can letter in German, but most clients prefer English. "Sometimes I paint symbols with meaning for the person's hobby or profession, like a kangaroo on a *fraktur* that went to Australia." Using size 000–0000 red sable brushes "with the finest points I can find, I paint with dry or premixed paint, to which I add a bit of gum arabic, a technique used on some of the early *frakturs*."

Beverly also designs bookplates and inscribes *frakturs* for books given as gifts. Prices start at $25 and go up according to size, detail and lettering, a bargain considering that 18th and 19th century *frakturs* regularly sell for thousands of dollars.

Beverly Weir
Frakturs from the Keeping Room
P.O. Box 405
Moorestown, NJ 08057
(609) 667-4712
V   R   C   S   MO

Other Makers
Trude Head, 109 West Main Street, Burkittsville, MD 21718; (301) 473-5055.

Virginia Jacobs McLaughlin, The Antique Cupboard, 812 West Main Street (Box 114), Emmitsburg, MD 21727; (301) 447-6558 or (717) 642-5142.   V   R   S   MO

K. Kerchner McConlogue, 701 Hunting Place, Baltimore, MD 21229; (301) 945-7441.

Frames   *See* **Graining**

Frivolité   *See* **Tatting**

ADIRONDACK FURNITURE

Of all rustic furniture, Adirondack was the most rugged, masculine and geometrical in design. Best known for its use in camps and hotels in the Adirondack Mountains, it was also made of swamp cypress in Florida, bentwood in the South, hickory in the Midwest and bent-twig slat styles by the Amish in western Pennsylvania. Made at home during the winter months at first, Adirondack furniture was later manufactured in Indiana and shipped all over the United States.

True rustic furniture in the Adirondack style was made of saplings with the bark left intact, the seats fashioned from wood slats, sticks or rush (although from 1940 on, the Old Hickory Company substituted caning and nylon webbing for woven splint seats). During the Victorian era, more elaborate styles emerged. Mosaic twig work on the surface was created by splitting twigs lengthwise, then nailing them on in intricate geometric designs, while what became known as Birchbark had sheets of birchbark applied to the surface, held in place by half-round twigs.

Rustic furniture looks simple until you realize that each

Adirondack settee by Ken Heitz

Adirondack cupboard in birchbark veneer with twig-work decoration by Ken Heitz

wood from 3 days to 2 weeks in a specially built kiln heated from a wood stove, which is also used to bend wood, although most curves are natural. The self-taught furniture maker spends fall and winter harvesting wood from his 20 acres at the foot of Starbuck Mountain in the Adirondacks, and estimates he has more than 5 miles of wood drying at a time.

"The pieces made by old-timers that lasted," he says, "were not nailed together but had mortise-and-tenon joints made by chiseling and drilling the ends to fit tightly together, then reinforcing by wooden pegs, which is how I build all my furniture." Tung oil is his only finish, with clear wood preservative added on outdoor pieces.

Ken is perhaps the only Adirondack furniture maker now creating birchbark pieces, which he considers "the greatest challenge to craftsmanship in my line of work. These case pieces must be designed because there are very few antique examples. I employ the same methods of construction as in my other pieces, and in addition use white birchbark, handmade boards, split pieces for bordering and twigwork for decoration."

Ken's chairs range in price from $150 to $200; tables, $125 to $500; settees, $350 to $1,200; beds, $300 to $1,500; and stools, $125. Most are custom-made.

Ken Heitz
Backwoods Furnishings
Box 161, Route 28
Indian Lake, NY 12842
(518) 251-3327
V   R   W   C   S   MO

piece of wood has a natural bend, which must match naturally with its counterpart on the other side (as in the arms of a chair). Half the work involves getting the trees out of the woods with the bark intact, cutting them to achieve the best forms, kiln-drying and stacking the wood to age, then cutting it once more to make furniture.

Ken Heitz originally tried spruce and balsam but found them "soft, full of pitch and knots. Pine is brittle and breaks." Hardwoods were more durable and had nicer natural curves, and most held their bark when dry, but oak and maple lost their bark *as* they dried. Ken now works mostly with ironwood, known locally as hop hornbeam, which is from the birch family. "With the bark on," says Ken, "it looks like cedar." He uses yellow birch and white ash as well as peeled poplar for framework, with cherry and birch for decorative trim. Wood must be completely dry before using. Since Ken cuts only green wood, and natural drying takes from 2 to 4 years, he "cooks"

Whimsical Adirondack bed by Ken Heitz

Other Makers

Bill Smith, RFD 1, Colton, NY 13625; (315) 262-2436, makes authentic Adirondack furniture.

Daniel Mack, Rustic Furnishings, 225 West 106th Street, New York, NY 10025; (212) 666-4277, makes rustic furniture of sugar maple or hickory saplings, with seats woven in Shaker-style cotton tape or 18-ounce canvas.

CHINESE CHIPPENDALE FURNITURE

From the mid-1700s through the early 1800s, Americans were smitten with anything Chinese: chinoiserie designs in fabrics, wallpaper and lacquered pieces; Chinese Chippendale architectural details in houses and gardens; and Chinese motifs in carving and furniture design.

"The ball-and-claw foot, the solid straight leg, cross stretchers on tables, the C-scroll, the cabriole leg, the yoke-shaped crest rail, fretwork bands and carving and the pagoda canopy all have their origin in China," says cabinetmaker Steven Knopp, who specializes in period furniture with emphasis on 17th and 18th century Chinese high-style Queen Anne and Chippendale. "The Queen Anne style is largely made up of Chinese influences brought to Europe by the Dutch, and I personally feel one of Thomas Chippendale's greatest contributions to 18th century furniture was his work in the Chinese style."

A fair amount of Chinese Chippendale was made in America, predominantly tables, display cabinets and chairs. Because it was usually made of fine mahogany and demanding to execute, therefore expensive, its ownership became somewhat of a status symbol. One of the favorite

Three-legged Chinese Chippendale table with ball-and-claw foot and grotesque mask at knee by Steven Knopp

Dining table in solid black walnut with carved brackets in Chinese Chippendale style by Steven Knopp

carved designs was the grotesque mask, dating back to the Greek theater and harvest games. "The mouth openings of these masks were unnaturally large and shaped like a bell-mouth," says Steven. "The design was used by Michelangelo. During the Renaissance and rococo periods, it was used in caricature form on keystones, consoles, backs of chairs, carved furniture and stove tiles. A grotesque-mask table, a transitional Queen Anne–Chippendale piece made in the Boston-Cambridge area in the early 1700s, is considered one of the rarest American antiques. Only one survived."

Steven, the oldest of three sons of a master mason, was involved in construction from an early age, spent summers working as a carpenter in northern California and studied architectural woodworking in Florida. It was there that he met Ed VanHoose, a pioneer in the American renaissance of traditional woodworking, who spent 8 years building a house with traditional joinery and hand tools. "I was part of its construction for the final 2½ years," says Steven. "I then apprenticed with a master boat builder and later spent 6 months restoring and rebuilding a Greek Revival house in Vermont." After two more apprenticeships with traditional furniture makers Rupert Hill and Robert Emmett, Steven opened his own shop in Asheville,

North Carolina, where in addition to traditional American furniture and accessories, he does period architectural joinery, from staircases to raised panel work, carving, sculpting and turnings, as well as repair and restoration of antiques.

"I am partial to carving," he says. "I enjoy tackling the most demanding, highly carved pieces and bringing to life a completed piece of fine furniture which did not exist before. I relish the challenge of doing jobs that others turn down for lack of skill or fear of the complexities involved. I strive for authenticity in design, the finest construction and finely executed work true in proportion and detail. I also harbor an intense interest in both traditional Chinese furniture and Japanese Tansu cabinetry (whose influence can be seen in what we call campaign chests)."

In his one-man shop (where he always maintains the practice of training an apprentice in the trade), he uses only the finest available first-growth hardwoods. All carving is done by hand. Completed work is hand-rubbed with a penetrating oil-varnish formula. Although most of his work is done on commission, approximate prices are: mahogany Chinese Chippendale dining table, $3,500; large Chinese psaltery table in solid black walnut with carved brackets, $3,000; transitional Queen Anne–Chippendale three-legged wall table with grotesque-mask carving on knees in mahogany or walnut, $1,850.

Steven Knopp, Cabinetmaker and Joiner
506 Merrimon Avenue
Asheville, NC 28804
(704) 258-2586
R S MO

Butternut corner cupboard by Rick Goehring

COUNTRY FURNITURE

American country furniture, fashioned by local cabinetmakers from regional wood, was often 25 to 50 years behind period styles, but because of its eloquent directness of character it often surpassed finer city pieces made of exotic, expensive woods. Built for function, sometimes for a specific use, country pieces copied period lines but usually omitted fancier details and more often than not reflected the personality of the maker.

"Country designs generally are simple, unpretentious and have a spirit of direct honesty," says cabinetmaker Rick Goehring. "Made to be used day in and day out, they are enjoyed for their ease of utility and unimposing beauty. They don't tire the eye with visual busyness and are easy to live with."

Born in Missouri and raised in the Midwest, Rick became "a country person by choice," and now lives in Dover, Ohio, an area where simple, stout furniture has been made for 150 years by Swiss and German settlers and their descendants. "My work," he explains, "which is of original design firmly rooted in traditional midwestern country furniture, happens to fall neatly into the historical style of the Amish, Mennonite, Zoarite and Moravian woodworkers of this region, especially my corner cupboards and chests of drawers."

Rick learned the techniques of construction through years of restoring antique furniture. Since then, his own creations have earned a reputation for fine proportion, careful grain-matching and clean execution. They have won several awards, including the Award for Excellence from Ohio Designer Craftsmen and a purchase award from the Ohio Arts Council. Rick considers himself "an interpreter of simple, finely crafted country furniture, a kind of bridge builder through whom familiar, accessible, richly personal and expressive pieces can be built.''

Most of his furniture is made to order. After discussing what a client desires, Rick designs a piece to fit a specific need and submits a scale drawing for approval (for a $50 drawing fee deductible from the cost). Once any necessary changes have been made, the client accepts and initials the drawing, pays a deposit (usually one-third), and a delivery date is set (often 12 weeks, but it can vary).

"I use locally grown domestic hardwoods," says Rick, "and a combination of machine and hand tools. Machines for rough ripping and planing, hand tools for joinery and surface finishing. Doors are always mortise-and-tenon joined and drawers always hand-dovetailed front and back. Surfaces are hand-scraped before hand-sanding and finished with oil, except for working surfaces like table and desk tops, which are varnished or lacquered." He prefers not to stain wood so that it can develop its own patina.

An arrowback rocker made of ash (also available in cherry and maple) runs $525, while a walnut trestle table is $900, a cherry chest of drawers with curly maple fronts is $1,400 and a butternut corner cupboard, $1,600. His shop is open Monday through Friday 9 A.M. to 6 P.M., other times by chance or appointment.

Ash rocking chair with ash splint seat by Rick Goehring

W. R. Goehring, Cabinetmaker
10327 Monroe Mills Road
Gambier, OH 43022
(614) 427-3379
V   R   S   MO

CENTRAL PENNSYLVANIA COUNTRY FURNITURE
Dan Backenstose, Jr., Spring House Classics, RD 7, Box 340, Lebanon, PA 17072; (717) 949-3902 (mail order, P.O. Box 541, Schaefferstown, PA 17088), began making furniture he couldn't afford to buy as antiques. Many of

Black walnut schrank (Pennsylvania-German wardrobe) with poplar as a secondary wood by Dan Backenstose, Jr.

his pieces are exact copies of early *schranks* (Pennsylvania-German wardrobes), hanging cupboards, splay-leg tables, chimney cupboards, linen presses and blanket chests. Made of the "poor man's cherry" (tulip poplar), walnut or cherry, pieces can also be ordered in mahogany or pine. All are available in rattail, butt, H or H-L hinges.
V   R   C ($3)   S

NEW ENGLAND COUNTRY FURNITURE
J. F. Orr & Sons, 215 Boston Post Road, Sudbury, MA 21776; (617) 443-3650, began as a family of cabinetmakers from four generations of craftsmen. Its wonderful

collection of tables (hutch and harvest), cupboards, wardrobes, chests, desks and chairs is made of wide, hand-planed New England white pine and cut nails, with mortise-and-tenon joinery, hand-beaded edges (indented lines cut into the edges), pegged-panel and frame construction, hand-applied finish and gentle colors. V R C

Other Makers

David T. Smith and Co., 3600 Shawhan Road, Morrow, OH 45152, makes country furniture and also does graining.

Christian H. Becksvoort, P.O. Box 12, New Gloucester, ME 04260; (207) 926-4608, is known for his desks, all of which have secret compartments and are finished with three coats of oil, sanded, wiped and polished by hand. His most popular is a classic cherry slant-top desk with bread-boarded writing surface over four large drawers ($2,375). It has an optional secretary top with two arched panel doors, two candle shelves, twelve pigeonholes, three main shelves and four side compartments for ledgers ($3,875). Many of his tables have secret compartments too.

Maynard House Antiques, 11 Maynard Street, Westborough, MA 01581; (617) 366-2073, can duplicate any country sofa or wing chair made in the period 1780–1820.

William James Roth, P.O. Box 355, Yarmouthport, MA 02675; (617) 362-9235, makes all kinds of tables, mirrors and beds from the William and Mary period to Hepplewhite.

Stephen A. Adams, Furnituremaker, Mill Hill Road, Denmark, ME 04022; (207) 452-2444, recreates period furniture from bannister-back chairs to country highboys. V R C

Meredith and Chris Miller, The Copper Rooster, RD 4, Country Place, Export, PA 15632; (412) 327-4392.

Stephen C. Staples, 32 Taunton Avenue, Route 140, Norton, MA 02766; (617) 285-4477, makes a wide variety of country furniture from native pine, maple, cherry and oak, finished with a mixture of oil and varnish or milk paint. Open 9 A.M. to 5 P.M. Tuesday to Saturday. V R W S

18TH CENTURY AMERICAN FURNITURE

Early American furniture makers created high-style masterpieces with broad expanses of highly figured woods, elegant details, vigorous turnings, beaded moldings and distinctive inlays. As soon as upper-class Americans started

Replica of Benjamin Franklin's quadruple music stand by Robert Whitley

building larger houses, the demand for large-scale furniture skyrocketed. In the 1700s, Philadelphia became famous for elaborate Chippendale furniture, Newport for blockfront styles and Boston for bombé kettle-shaped chests.

Today's owners and restorers of large buildings, whether individuals, historical societies or the federal government, when faced with the problem of finding the right furniture, often call Robert Whitley. Bob served as master conservator of Philadelphia's Independence Hall, where he restored much of the furniture and built four Queen Anne chairs for the Governor's Council Chamber. He also made an exact copy of Benjamin Franklin's quadruple music stand (designed so he could consult with other musicians without changing position) for Franklin Court; and the swivel-based Windsor armchair used by Thomas Jefferson when he wrote the Declaration of Independence (now at Graff House).

Like the craftsmen whose work he duplicates, Bob learned restoration and fine furniture-making by starting young. He followed his father to auctions and old homes in search of antique furniture, helped him disassemble pieces for repair and helped put them back together again.

"I was always surprised," Bob remembers, "by how much seemingly identical pieces varied. Each craftsman

Replica of Chippendale mahogany bombé chest by Robert Whitley

pers Ferry and George Washington's Headquarters (Morristown, New Jersey) or at his studio. Call for appointment.

The Robert Whitley Studio
Laurel Road
Solebury, Bucks County, PA 18963
(215) 297-8452
V   R   C ($4)   S

Other Makers

Michael Camp, 636 Starkweather, Plymouth, MI 48170; (313) 459-1190.

Marion H. Campbell, 39 Wall Street, Bethlehem, PA 18018; (215) 865-2522 or 865-3292.

Kerry P. Gagne, RFD 1, Box 38, Route 12, Fitzwilliam, NH 03447; (603) 585-2260.

N. Vandal, Roxbury, VT 05669.   C ($3)

left his mark whether he signed the work or not." Whenever a piece came through their shop, the Whitleys made a pattern, a practice that Bob has continued. Today he has more than 4,000 in his files. In 1952 he inherited his father's hardwood inventory and has been adding to it ever since. Cut to specification in flitches (tall, flat, thin slabs that retain the shape of the tree as well as its bark) to give Bob the widest choice of shapes and grain patterns, the wood is air-weathered, then seasoned for 2 to 6 years in heat-controlled storage rooms, where it is revolved and restacked to protect against uneven drying.

"I make furniture exactly as it was made in the 18th century," says Bob, "and use the same approach. Wood is selected for grain, color, density, matching and highest aesthetic value."

His Chippendale mahogany bombé bureau at $12,000 is a bargain when compared with the half-million dollars the original would cost if it were available. Those who covet one of the $100,000 Queen Anne chairs in Independence Hall can order their own for $4,200, while a matching mahogany Philadelphia highboy and lowboy are $35,000, a small price to pay when an antique you want belongs to a museum's permanent collection, was passed down to someone else in your family or is destroyed by fire. Sometimes even museums can't get the original. The presidential desk in the Kennedy Memorial Library may look like the one in the Oval Office, but it's a precise copy made by Whitley, after 3 days' patterning, photographing and taking rubbings of the original. His work may also be seen in The Hermitage in Russia, at Valley Forge, Har-

FEDERAL PERIOD FURNITURE

"After the Revolution, a rising spirit of nationalism caused English furniture to fall from favor in America," says James Lea, a third generation cabinetmaker. "Americans were determined to develop their own styles, but continued to be influenced by English designers: first by Robert Adams's neoclassical styles; later by George Hepplewhite and Thomas Sheraton, whose books were popular with American furniture makers."

Hepplewhite was primarily a designer and draftsman, but his designs went unrecognized in his lifetime. Only after his widow found his drawings and was persuaded by a friend to publish them in 1788, as the *Cabinetmakers and Upholsterers Guide,* did Hepplewhite's ideas become well

Hepplewhite sideboard with crotch mahogany veneer over white pine by James A. Lea

Sheraton bowfront chest of drawers with tulipwood case veneered with satinwood and Santo Domingo mahogany by James A. Lea

known. His furniture's classical shapes and graceful lines; square-tapered legs; elegant carving effects of draperies, feathers and vase-shaped forms; inlays of shells, bellflowers and eagles; and his chairs with shield-, heart- or oval-shaped backs brought new elegance to American homes.

"Sheraton, whose *Cabinet-maker and Upholsterer's Drawing Book* was published in 1791, had more originality and a greater feel for the material," says Jim, "perhaps because he'd been trained as a cabinetmaker. His chairs were almost always square-backed with lathe-turned reeded or fluted legs; his case pieces often had bowed or serpentine fronts. Compared to earlier periods, Federal furniture was light, airy and easy to move, quite different from the heavier, more massive styles of the colonial period."

Making furniture came naturally to Jim, who started at the age of 8, standing on an orange crate in front of a wood lathe he continues to use today. Although he earned a degree in chemistry and worked for 10 years in the finishing industry, Jim continued his study of American furniture. It wasn't until a friend died of a heart attack that Jim realized he wasn't happy in the world of business and resigned to set out in search of his own utopia. He found it in Rockport, Maine: a Federal home built in 1808, where he and his wife, Barbara, lived in two rooms while he restored it, doing the plumbing, wiring, masonry and carpentry himself. Today, he cuts the native woods he needs from his own woodlot, driving to Pennsylvania for walnut and cherry and to Ohio for tiger maple. Using only handmade joinery, antique hand tools and traditional

methods, he continues to learn and expects to be making his best furniture when he is 60 years old. "It takes that long to refine the technique," he explains.

He works in all periods, using traditional varnish and oil as a finish, and more durable finishes on dining room tables when desired. Of particular interest to collectors is his oxidized finish, a five-step process that took 30 years of research and experimentation with 18th century materials to perfect. When combined with traditional methods, tools and woods, the oxidized finish produces a time-worn, centuries-old look after only a few years' use. To prevent his work from being sold as antique, each piece is signed and dated.

His furniture, included in many collections of originals, is "built to be used daily and passed on for generations. I want it to last another 200 years. For that reason, I am satisfied with nothing less than perfection." A pier table is $1,500. Beds start at $1,250, while sideboards cost up to $4,500, depending on detail. Prices include all packing. Samples of finishes and stains are $5, refundable with order.

James A. Lea, Cabinetmaker
9 West Street
Rockport, ME 04856
(207) 236-3632
V (by appt.)   R   C ($4)   MO

HORN FURNITURE

"When I first saw a photo of a horn chair upholstered in leopard skin, I cut it out and pinned it to my studio wall," says Richard St. John, associate dean, Division of Art, at Wichita State University in Kansas. "I was working in clay at the time, but found myself wondering who made the chair, where, when. I found several books with photographs at the library, but no information about the maker. After contacting several curators who also couldn't tell me, I spent two years researching the life and work of the chair's creator, Wenzel Friedrich. To better understand the methods he used, I began making horn furniture myself; not to copy or duplicate his, but to try and match the level of craftsmanship he mastered so well."

Today, Richard is the leading expert on Friedrich and the prime maker of horn furniture in the world.

"Horn furniture began as a kind of western or cowboy folk art," he explains, "that was poorly designed, crudely constructed, with horns going in all directions. In the late 1800s through the turn of the century, a handful of master craftsmen made horn furniture. Friedrich's was unquestionably the finest. For 10 years he made some of the most innovative ever produced. His work won numerous gold medals and was owned by people like Queen Victoria, the president of France, Kaiser Wilhelm I, Bismarck and, of course, cattle barons. His standard armchair, upholstered in silk plush (velvet) or cowhide, sold in 1889 for $65; for an additional $2 to $5 he used fox, catamount or jaguar. Today one of his chairs in good shape when found can sell for as little as $300 up to $1,500, with an average near $750."

Richard purchases horns rough and sands them first with rough paper, then medium grit and finally fine, before buffing, steel-wooling and buffing again to a high sheen. He begins each piece by holding up horns to get a visual idea for the design, then tapes them together to get a better idea of proportions. After many drawings, he begins and works slowly. The most difficult part is making the horns fit together in a physically strong yet pleasing

Horn chair with cowhide upholstery and brass-nail trim by Richard St. John

design. All horns are fitted with oak plugs held in place with brass screws, which are cut off and filed down to appear as inlaid brass dots, requiring hours of labor. Each chair is designed so that it can be completely disassembled from underneath and easily reupholstered. The base of the chair, reinforced with steel pins, is hollow to eliminate extra weight. "My last chair, a large high-back," says Richard, "weighs less than 90 pounds." Another chair, made from both red- and black-tipped horns with an upholstered backrest held in place by an elaborate horn-structured back, took 500 hours of labor.

Friedrich, the originator of horn veneering, boiled horns, separated them into thin sheets which he pressed flat and dried. Used as decorative trim on the base of chairs and as covering for table tops, his veneering became a hallmark of his work. "Unlike Friedrich, I use a steam iron to heat and bend the veneer," explains Richard.

St. John's chairs sell for $6,500 and are guaranteed for his lifetime for structural strength. "Should the chair break down for any reason, it will be replaced at no cost to the owner," he says. "I do not sell to galleries or companies for resale. I don't make the furniture for money. If I had to lower the quality of craftsmanship to make a profitable venture, I would have no interest in making the furniture. After putting so much time and work into each piece, it is sometimes difficult to part with the work. However, each time I sell a piece it inspires me to get busy and make another to replace it."

Who buys horn furniture today? "Western collectors, people with western-style houses"—and, of course, cattle barons.

Richard St. John
Wichita State University
Box 67 Research
Wichita, KS 67208
(316) 689-3551
R

MINIATURE FURNITURE

Why do people collect miniature furniture?

"There are many theories," says Harry Smith, whose list of clients reads like an international *Who's Who*. "Something small is cherishable and also controllable. My personal theory is that a miniature world allows its owner to have a peaceable realm inside a world that seems out of control."

Harry's miniatures, known for their perfection of detail, in many cases cost more than the museum originals. The demand for his creations, called the best in the world, has

Miniature Boston Chippendale bombé chest, 3½ by 1⅞ by 2⅜ inches, by Harry W. Smith

Coe-Kerr Gallery, Schecter Me Sun Lee, Photographer

risen in recent years since his miniature mechanical objects (e.g., musical instruments that actually play) have been compared to Fabergé's intricate eggs.

"If it can be done full-size, I can do it in miniature," says Harry, whose personal credo of doing the best he can or not doing it at all won him a triple bypass last year. "My greatest enemy and competition is myself," he admits. "I'm constantly in pursuit of perfection and firmly believe the next piece will always be better."

From his first independent job, making miniatures for Marshall Field & Co., through an early mass-produced line sold nationwide through stores like F.A.O. Schwarz and I. Magnin, Harry, with the help of his wife, Marsha, has learned on the job. When he realized his creative needs were not being met, he stopped selling wholesale and started a mail order business, Barnstable Originals. His first show was on a card table in an Indiana grocery store, but in the 25 years since then, his work has been featured in half a dozen books and fourteen one-man exhibits in galleries and museums and is on permanent display at the Miniature Museum of Kansas City. His book, *The Art of Making Furniture in Miniature,* describes his work in detail and takes the reader through projects from the colonial to the Victorian period.

Each commission requires hundreds of photos, dozens of drawings, thousands of measurements and much co-operation from experts and museum curators. In the beginning, he simply reduced objects in size, aiming for his-torical authenticity, but as his eye and reputation grew, he learned he couldn't just reduce, he had to make visual changes as well. "It's what you can't see that makes a miniature come to life," he says, "because the eye will put in what isn't there."

The most difficult part is finding tools small enough to do commissions that range in scale from $\frac{1}{100}$ inch to 3 inches to the foot in size. His usual scale is 1 inch to the foot. He also makes his own hardware. His tools include calipers, iris scissors, tiny squares, dividers, steel rulers (marked in 64ths and 100ths of an inch), surgical and dental tools, #11 scalpel, micro chisels, files, jeweler's saws and miniature pliers.

"But the ability to work with tools is useless," he advises, "unless the eye is trained to appreciate proportion. Lighting is also important. The smaller the piece, the greater the amount of light needed." To ease eye strain, he works on a nonreflective surface.

He usually accepts commissions on a carte blanche basis without tight specifications, for serious art collectors who are more concerned with aesthetics than price. A Boston Queen Anne japanned high chest of drawers inspired by one in the Boston Museum of Fine Arts, recently had a selling price of $25,000 in a New York gallery. A complete room setting can cost upwards of $20,000. Although

Miniature Boston Queen Anne japanned high chest of drawers, 1⅞ by 6⅛ by 18 inches, by Harry W. Smith

Coe-Kerr Gallery, Schecter Me Sun Lee, Photographer

Harry usually deals directly with clients, three of his creations were carried in the Neiman-Marcus catalog, including a 2-inch-to-the-foot scale violin for $3,000.

Barnstable Originals
Studio of Harry W. Smith
50 Harden Avenue
Camden, ME 04843
(207) 236-8162
R   S   MO

Other Makers

Susan Rountree, 701 Powell Street, Williamsburg, VA 23185; (804) 229-0909, makes miniatures of furniture and toys from Colonial Williamsburg's Abby Aldrich Rockefeller Folk Art Collection. Her meticulously crafted and decorated miniatures and interiors range from $8 to $145.

Renee Bowen and James Hastrich, Route 1 South, Kennebunk, ME 04043; (207) 985-6279, create miniature country and Shaker furniture and accessories ranging in price from a sieve for $1.50 to a decorated chest for $275.

NORWEGIAN-AMERICAN FURNITURE

Norwegian immigrants to the United States continued to make furniture in the styles and traditions of their Viking ancestors: round *kubbestol* chairs made from logs; hutches called *fram skap;* three-sided hanging corner cupboards (*hjorne skap*); chests with curved tops; carved wooden plates often inscribed for wedding gifts; and *mangeltraer,* long one-handled mangle boards, flat on one side, carved on the other, once used to smooth damp linens. A *mangeltraer* was given to a woman as a symbol of betrothal and accepted as a sign of rejection if she refused it.

"The Norwegian people brought rich cultural gifts to America," says Phillip Odden, "and produced furniture that we have come to know as the Norwegian-American technique, using woods of the region and influenced by American techniques." Phillip, a descendant of Norwegian immigrants to the North Woods, grew up on a farm but didn't like the hours. After fire-fighting in Alaska, trapping and hunting in Montana and a stint with the Peace Corps in Nepal, he stopped in Norway on the way home and decided he wanted to be a woodworker. Because the school he wished to attend would accept him only if he spoke Norwegian, he went to Alaska with a tape recorder, where he hoped to find the necessary isolation to learn the language. His instructors didn't know he could only count in Norwegian until it was too late. After 2 years'

Kubbestol *with baroque acanthus design by Else Bigton and Phillip Odden*

studying wood-carving and cabinetmaking using hand tools and techniques of the 1850s, Phillip returned to Barronett, Wisconsin, in 1979 with a wife, fellow-student and now partner Else Bigton. Together they opened Norsk Wood Works in a converted feed mill near his family's farm. Since then, Phillip has won the first gold medal ever awarded in carving at the Norwegian-American Museum in Decorah, Iowa, where he teaches each summer.

"Else and I produce work pretty much on a fifty-fifty basis," says Phillip. She designs and makes paneled furniture and technical drawings and handles construction, while Phillip specializes in ornamental drawings and carving. They work in traditional woods of white birch and pine as well as basswood, butternut or, when requested, walnut, oak, maple and mahogany. They select rough-hewn wood, which they age for 1 to 3 years until the moisture content drops below 12 percent.

Phillip's acanthus designs in the Gudbrandsdalen style are especially effective on their *kubbestol*, made from a solid American linden log, which is hollowed, shaped with a slightly flaring back and seasoned for 1 to 2 years before carving. The carving takes from 150 to 300 hours. The only chair form found in the peasant's house, and reserved for the head of the house or guests, *kubbestoler* are decorated with a band or rim ridge around the chair at seat height. Phillip and Else's *kubbestoler* ($750 to $2,500 depending on size and carving) are available in the baroque acanthus leaf style or embellished with dragons and other mythical beings in the style of the medieval Vikings' stave churches. There is a removable seat for extra storage.

Their richly carved butternut chests ($450 to $600) are similar to those brought to America, with curved tops, a small inside compartment and, when requested, a family name and date on the top. Hanging corner cupboards with carved crowns, paneled doors and bottom shelf ($350) come in a choice of woods, all with solid wood backs. Ale bowls shaped like dragons ($450), carved plates ($25) in various sizes and designs and grandfather clocks ($1,650), often with the family name inscribed in the carved crown over the face, may be seen at Norsk Husflid, a shop owned by Phillip's parents, Highway 63, Box 87, Barronett, WI 54813; (715) 822-8747, or commissioned

Birch ale bowl in dragon shape by Else Bigton and Phillip Odden

directly from them. Send self-addressed, stamped envelope for brochure.

Else Bigton and Phillip Odden
Norsk Wood Works
Box 66
Barronett, WI 54813
(715) 822-3104
R   C   S   MO

Other Makers

Hans Sandom, 5347 Highland Road, Minetonka, MN 55343; (612) 934-3896, makes hand-carved Norwegian-American furniture in the baroque style. Prices range from $95 for a salt box to $1,800 for a black walnut grandfather clock.

Halvor Landsverk, Route 2, Box 22, Whalen, MN 55986; (507) 875-2539, has been making basswood *kubbestoler* since the 1930s, from $1,000 to $5,000 depending on size and amount of carving.

SCRATCH-CARVED AND PAINTED FURNITURE

There's a time warp in Peter Kramer's furniture that triggers memories of country cottages crowned with dormers, sunlight on wide plank floors and romantic evenings by the fire. Like nothing you've ever seen, yet similar to much you've imagined, its quiet colonial beauty is inspired by the needs of imaginary characters in a hamlet called Cloven Mill (not unlike the town where he lives). His original creations, made as if he were a cabinetmaker living in the year 1709, arise from the raw materials, not the drawing board.

"A sketch done at the drawing board deals only with the silhouette," says Peter, "yet much of the character

Hanging corner cupboard in pine, 31 by 14 by 14 inches, by Else Bigton and Phillip Odden

Scratch-carved flower design chest of drawers with drop pulls by Peter Kramer

or owned by museums." He was attracted to a look rather than a technique: the simple lines, hand-planed surfaces and worn edges of primitive and formal country furniture. After his first big sale to Bloomingdale's (where they liked his work so much they designed a room around it), Peter resigned as personnel manager of Radio Free Europe and moved to Washington, Virginia, a village of aesthetically pleasing, well-made structures in an area rich in natural resources. But like the heartwood center of the tree, with which Peter likes to work, his self-taught professional path has not been easily hewn. An accident that cost him three fingers slowed down the process "and forced me to image my actions before I do them," he says, "and to be more deliberate than rushed. Now when something is miscut or a board blemish develops, I let the design grow to incorporate it. Most of the time it adds character and the piece is better for it."

His structures emphasize joinery techniques as part of the design, abundantly revealing pegged dovetails and mortise-and-tenon joints. Drawers are reinforced with pinlocks (wooden pins driven vertically through dovetails):

dwells within that perimeter and throughout the depth." Each time a lumber shipment arrives at his workshop, boards are unloaded one at a time rather than by forklift, with the best set aside for special use. "It is here that the designs begin to have substance," he explains. "Some makers are concerned with how many pieces they will get from a board. My concern is how many boards I will have to go through before I find the piece."

The subtle ethnicity in his furniture comes not from a single tradition, but from his love of the amalgamations that resulted when two nationalities borrowed from one another, as when the French and English came together in the Connecticut Valley. Much of his work has scratch-carvings of trees, flowers, thistles and wheat, like those incised on furniture during the 16th and 17th centuries. In recent years, he has added painted designs to these carvings, further delighting clients.

"When a client says 'Do what you want to do' [with a commission], and they laugh when they see the completed piece, that makes me feel really good," says Peter.

Although he constructed his first stool at the age of 9, his family convinced him he could never earn a living working with wood. He began making furniture as a hobby because "the pieces I liked best were always too expensive

Wardrobe with carved doors, swan design and veined background pattern by Peter Kramer

surface hand-planing is slightly exaggerated to produce a sensuous feel; and wide boards are cherished for their special contribution to the overall look. Like space-conscious early Americans, Peter designs some pieces to be dual-purpose (hutch tables that open to benches) or easily disassembled (a cradle that can be taken apart and stored between babies). Upon completion, they are signed, colored when appropriate with a tung oil stain, sealed with a thinned shellac solution, then finished with varnish, which is wet-sanded smooth, and further protected with a hard paste wax. The effect is so authentic that his catalog opens with a disclaimer: "The furniture pictured within this portfolio is not antique nor is it reproduction. It is rather an interpretation of a period of furniture; they are my designs, which utilize the visually pleasing characteristics of the aging process."

His blanket chests range in price from $450 to $995; chests of drawers, $695 to $2,000; chests on frames, $2,200 to $3,800; corner cupboards, $1,500 to $1,800; cradle, $600.

Peter Kramer
P.O. Box 232
Washington, VA 22747
(703) 675-3625
Summer address (June through August):
P.O. Box 1139
Route 6A
Brewster, MA 02631
(617) 896-7576
V   R   C   S   MO

SHAKER FURNITURE

David Lamb was only 14 years old when he began a 3-year apprenticeship with master cabinetmaker Alejandro de la Cruz of Canterbury, New Hampshire. There he learned the techniques of hand joinery and construction as well as the philosophy of the master and his trade. Upon completion, he entered Boston University's Program in Artisanry (where in addition to his studies he spent 3 days a week at the Boston Museum of Fine Arts studying pieces on display and those in storage while writing seminar papers) and later learned the craft of carving from Alois Klein. In 1979, at the ripe old age of 21, he opened his own shop at Shaker Village in Canterbury, where he became the resident cabinetmaker. In 1986 he bought the home and shop of his former master, where he now lives.

"Working in one of the old Shaker shops and having

Shaker sewing desk by David Lamb

access to many Shaker pieces allowed me to reflect about what was done here and how it was done in the past," says David. "The spirit of those Shaker brothers permeates the village and has influenced me greatly. Shakers stressed perfection as a way of reaching a higher plane of existence. Work was a form of prayer, and timeless perfection the only acceptable goal."

The Shakers, who founded religious communities from Ohio and Kentucky to Maine, believed that furniture as well as life should be plain, simple, useful, practical and of sound construction without adornment. Made for "families" of thirty to more than a hundred, most pieces were designed to fit exact locations and to meet specific needs. Many sewing tables, desks and ironing tables were made for use by more than one person.

"The Shakers created a wide range of tables and case pieces," says David, "both freestanding and built-in, and were masters at combining framing elements, highly figured wood and joinery." They simplified drawer pulls, exposed dovetailing, put wheels on beds and narrowed cupboard doors. "Highly figured wood, often available only in small pieces, was resawn and matched for grain

FURNITURE

Shaker table by David Lamb

patterns and displayed in frame-and-panel construction, which also was a way of using short and narrow pieces of wood without extensive gluing."

David does all joinery, dovetailing and mortise-and-tenon joints by hand, using the finest hardwood available, including mahogany, walnut, cherry and figured maples, before applying finishes by hand. His hallmark is the precise way he fits doors and drawers, and the way his construction allows natural movement to take place in the wood without cracking as it dries.

"Although I follow original methods of construction where appropriate," he says, "I often have to utilize methods that allow for expansion and contraction problems caused by central heating. For instance, instead of nailing the molding on the bottom of a desk to the case, it is incorporated firmly into the feet because the grain on both parts runs horizontally. The case (which has a vertical grain) is then set onto this molding frame and screwed. However, holes at the back are enlarged to allow each part to expand at its own rate. Sometimes a client will ask for a specific object with the look or feel of Shaker that never existed. That's when the old inspires the new. Like the Shaker brothers, I feel a piece of furniture must be utilitarian, but proportion, grace and refinement are no less important. Designing for proportion is the most difficult part."

In addition to custom work in the major periods of American furniture, David also hand-carves architectural elements. Typical prices of his Shaker work are: bird's-eye maple bureau, $1,950; fourteen-drawer tall cherry chest (eight small over six large), $2,500; two-drawer side table, $450 in cherry, $500 in bird's-eye and curly maple; 7-foot-long trestle table, $1,200. Chippendale prices range from $850 for a side chair to $9,200 for a Connecticut highboy. A 50 percent deposit is required to confirm an

order, with the balance due at completion. Shop hours are Monday to Saturday, 8 A.M. to 5 P.M. and by appointment or chance.

David Lamb, Cabinetmaker
322 Shaker Road
Canterbury, NH 03224
(603) 783-9912
V   R   S   MO

Other Makers

Christian H. Becksvoort, Box 12, New Gloucester, ME 04260; (207) 926-4608, does most of the restoration for the Shaker community there. In addition to making every conceivable kind of Shaker furniture, he wrote the books *In Harmony with Wood* and *The Furniture at Sabbathday Lake*, creates ingenious built-ins and can reproduce any molding ever made.   C ($1)

Ian Ingersoll, Main Street, West Cornwall, CT 06796; (203) 672-6334, makes all Shaker shapes including clocks.

Joe W. Robson, RD 3, Box 158, Trumansburg, NY 14886; (607) 387-9280.

Shaker chest of drawers by David Lamb

Ian F. Edwards, 10 Saugatuck Avenue, Westport, CT 06880; (203) 544-8935.

Bill Scherer, 8267 Oswego Road, Liverpool, NY 13088; (315) 652-7778.   C ($1)

Dane Burkhart, RD 2, Box 467, Mohnton, PA 19540; (215) 775-4053 (shop), (215) 775-4446 (home).

SHENANDOAH FURNITURE

Mahogany was not a favored wood of the English and German cabinetmakers of the Shenandoah Valley because it was not indigenous to the region like walnut, cherry, poplar and pine. Oak was considered a "poor man's wood" during the 18th and early 19th centuries. Walnut was and is the favorite. It wasn't too hard or too soft; its color and patina seemed to improve with age. The main difference between furniture made in the region and that from port cities was not in the design but in the details.

"Shenandoah Valley furniture makers maintained the classical proportions seen on more traditional pieces but used greater freedom of expression in details," says Larry Crouse, a joiner from Shepherdstown, West Virginia. "They had a wonderful feel for proportion, the size of moldings, height of feet, etc., but they felt free to add their own touches. One Winchester, Virginia, cabinetmaker always applied a stepped bead of trim beneath the cornice on his cupboards, while an 18th century craftsman from Martinsburg, whose work I restored, applied his brasses diagonally instead of horizontally to fronts of drawers. Two hundred years later, we can still distinguish his pieces by the brasses, or holes left by them."

Secretary desk with paneled doors, Chippendale brasses and bracket feet by Lawrence Crouse

Drop leaf Queen Anne table with pad foot by Lawrence Crouse

After serving a 3-year apprenticeship with a Winchester cabinetmaker, Larry went into business for himself restoring antiques in the dirt-floored cellar of his first home, built by Hessian soldiers in the 1790s. He later bought and restored a small stone blacksmith's shop and now lives in a two-story log house moved log by log from Sharpsburg, Maryland, near the Antietam battlefield.

"I shun the terms Early American and reproduction," says Larry. "I recreate classic and authentic pieces exactly as they were crafted in the 18th and early 19th centuries. Much attention is given to construction. I use solid wood, handmade nails, the finest brass and old glass. All joints are hand-cut dovetails or mortise-and-tenon. I also use solid wood for the backs and bottoms of drawers. My favorite wood is walnut, which I cut locally, take to the sawyer and age here in my shop. When customers prefer,

Four-poster bed with Chippendale block feet and tester top by Lawrence Crouse

almost reverence that local people have for them inspires me to hope that someday when my signature is uncovered on a piece it will be appreciated in the same way.''

Lawrence Crouse, Joiner
Route 1, Box 6
Kearneysville, WV 25430
(304) 876-6325
V R W C MO

SOUTHERN FURNITURE

Southern pine, as it was known in the North, or heart pine as it was called in the South, used to be one of the most plentiful woods in the United States. It grew slowly in dense virgin forests and produced a fine-grained material with as many as 15 to 20 rings per inch compared with 3 or 4 in today's pine.

"Slow-growth yellow pine was once abundant in the South," explains furniture maker Craig Nutt, "but like chestnut, it has only come to be appreciated since it became unavailable. Although technically a softwood, every other ring is almost pure resin, which sets up hard enough to curl a chisel blade. Once used for building timber, slow-growth pine must now be salvaged from old structures, a labor-intensive process which puts its final cost in the range of walnut."

Two furniture forms made only in the South were the huntboard and the sugar chest. The huntboard was orig-

I also use cherry, maple, mahogany and old pine. All furniture comes in two 18th century finishes: beeswax or shellac, both hand-rubbed." Upon completion, Larry signs and dates each piece on drawer buttoms or inside cupboards.

Although he has never advertised, Larry's clients include the Smithsonian, the National Park Service and customers throughout the United States. His furniture has been displayed in several prestigious galleries as well as in Jay Rockefeller's office when he was governor of West Virginia.

Larry's catalog ($2) now includes several table forms: one-drawer bedsides ($195 to $225); tilt-tops; Queen Anne drop leafs ($925 to $995); harvests in turned or tapered legs and teas ($795); as well as two- and three-section Hepplewhite banquettes. His slant-front desk is $1,995, with secretary top (glass or paneled doors) $2,495; while his pencil-post bed in single-, double-, queen- and king-size can be had in five different headboard styles. His shop is open Monday to Friday from 8 A.M. to 4:30 P.M. and by appointment.

"Shepherdstown, the oldest town in West Virginia, was a mecca for fine craftsmen," says Larry. "The respect and

Walnut huntboard with satinwood inlay and heart pine as secondary wood by Craig Nutt

Walnut end table with satinwood inlay and cockbeading and heart pine as secondary wood by Craig Nutt

inally a 4-foot-high plank table, tall enough so that hunters could eat at it without removing their boots after the chase. It evolved into a form with drawers at each end and a central cupboard. Smaller than a sideboard, it was often placed in less formal areas like a back hall, porch or outside building where hunters congregated for breakfast. "More ornate huntboards were also made for the dining room," says Craig, "and today are preferred by owners of smaller homes where sideboards tend to overwhelm a room."

Craig's huntboard draws heavily on his research into Georgia Piedmont designs from 1800 to 1820. "Forms indigenous to this area [west central Alabama] closely resemble furniture from the Piedmont region," he says, "whereas furniture made in northern Alabama reflects styles from Kentucky and Tennessee." Made in walnut with satinwood inlay in a regional jonquil design, and heart pine as a secondary wood, it is constructed with pinned mortise-and-tenon joints and hand-dovetailed drawers. The dust boards, rather than being nailed, float in a framework similar to that in a frame-and-panel door.

"Makers of furniture outside the coastal centers made simplified versions of the high-style furniture of their era," says Craig, "with more emphasis on proportion and line." A fine example of this is his two-drawer end or bedside table made of heart pine with pinned mortise-and-tenon joints and hand-dovetailed drawers whose turned knobs are held in place with wooden pins; also his cherry corner cupboard whose nine-paned door is set with antique glass recycled from old houses.

Although Craig hasn't made a sugar chest yet, he has restored several and put aside materials for the job. Sugar chests, originally intended to store sugar and sometimes tea, coffee and spices under lock and key, were made only in the South. They were designed like small chests on legs, the tops opening to reveal one or more compartments; sometimes there was a bottom drawer. Still popular in the South, they're now more often used as liquor cabinets and end tables.

Craig is known for his adaptation of traditional designs, and his finely proportioned furniture has won the Governor's Arts Award, been exhibited in museums nationwide and been featured in national publications including *Fine Woodworking*. Craig sells directly by mail or through a local gallery, adjacent to his shop, which is open Monday to Friday from 8 A.M. to 5 P.M. He welcomes commissions.

Craig Nutt, Fine Wood Works
2014 Fifth Street
Northport, AL 35476
(205) 752-6535
V   R   C   S   MO

Other Makers

Charles Weston Phillips and Peter Garrison Drake, Phillips Drake, Treemont RFD 7, Lexington, VA 24450; (703) 463-7769, custom-handcraft furniture and restore and refinish antiques.

SPANISH COLONIAL FURNITURE

Early Spanish colonial furniture was simple, sturdy, rugged and most often made of ponderosa pine because it was plentiful and easy to carve. "Boards were thickly cut because tools were crude," explains furniture maker George Sandoval. To soften the furniture's massive proportions, makers decorated surfaces with carvings, "primarily the circular rosette (in concave rather than convex shape), the Spanish lion, pomegranates, feathers, shells and vines." Simpler forms included geometric patterns, chip-carving, gouged patterns and doors with open grilles. Chip-carving was widely used to add depth to carvings and for contrast on smooth surfaces. Because tools were handmade from scrap iron, surfaces were not smooth, but showed continuous adz marks, which became part of the furniture's tradition and charm. Iron was scarce. Instead of nails, makers cut mortise-and-tenon joints and fastened them firmly with dowels. When iron was available, hinges and hasps were cut and hammered out, but most doors swung on wooden pegs, with leather straps used for drawer pulls and door handles.

Methods changed after 1821 when Santa Fe Trail commerce brought tools, square-cut nails and machinery. After the railroad began shipping eastern styles, local furniture-making nearly ceased until the Spanish Colonial Arts Society encouraged a revival in 1930 and the state initiated a program to train woodworkers in the public schools.

George Sandoval, who became interested in woodworking from watching his Basque grandfather make furniture, entered the program at the age of 15 and has been making furniture "to be handed down from generation to generation" ever since. He carves by hand, uses dovetailing and pegged mortise-and-tenon joints and has never used nails and screws except on pulls and hinges, a detail appreciated by those in search of authenticity. Although his furniture is now in collections worldwide, George remembers back to 1955 when he was married with two small children, attending college full time, making furniture part time and having a hard time keeping ahead of his bills. "Until one day," he says, "a woman from Denver who had been searching in vain for traditional southwestern furniture stopped to pray for help in a nearby church named for San Felipe de Neri, my patron saint and protector. I was born on his birthday and named Jorge Felipe in his honor. Well, back in the fifties the only

Typical colonial New Mexican style of banco *(patio bench) by George Sandoval*

way to Santa Fe was north on Second Street past my shop. She saw my little sign saying Spanish Colonial Furniture, came in and ordered a houseful. The money paid the bills and kept us in beans and chili for a long while."

The descendant of a Spanish captain who came to America in the late 1600s, Sandoval creates furniture characteristic of that made in New Mexico during the 16th and 17th centuries: *mesas* (tables), *camaltas* (beds), *tarimas* (low benches or stools), *repisas* (hanging shelves or brackets), *varguenos* (desks), *trasteros* (cupboards), *bancos* (patio benches), *cajón de las donas* (a woman's storage chest), *rejas* (wooden grilles), *sillas* (side chairs), *sillóns*

Spanish colonial vargueno *(desk) in dark walnut finish by George Sandoval*

La Madera chest in pine, 31 inches high, 35 inches wide and 16 inches deep, replica of an early 19th century piece, by Southwest Spanish Craftsmen

(armchairs), high-backed royal dining chairs and doors. Like the woman from Denver, most clients come to his shop, look at photos and choose the style, size and finish. "Since everything is custom-made," says George, "most can be made larger or smaller."

He draws designs, then traces them on kiln-dried pine. Finishes are natural: hand-rubbed oil on raw wood or stained surface; tobacco brown, a warm butternut finish; mahogany, a reddish brown; medium or dark walnut; or Spanish gray or green: "The piece is stained brown," says George, "and when dry, a thin coat of gray or green oil-base paint is wiped on while wet." Prices range from $250 for a chair to $2,150 for a desk.

Although he's been a teacher, an artist-in-residence at Eastern New Mexico University and is now singled out for commissions like the carving and furniture for the University of New Mexico Law School building, the most satisfying part of his work remains the same: "Delivering a finished piece to a customer and knowing it will be enjoyed and useful for many years to come."

George P. Sandoval
3718 Second Street Northwest
Albuquerque, NM 87107
(505) 345-9442
V R MO

Other Makers

Southwest Spanish Craftsmen, Plaza Mercado, 112-116 West San Francisco, P.O. Box 1805, Santa Fe, NM 87501; (505) 982-1767, makes furniture based on pieces in the Museum of New Mexico collection of early Spanish colonial furniture and doors. Showroom open Monday to Saturday, 10 A.M. to 5 P.M.

Marco A. Oveida, Centinela Ranch, Chimayo, NM 87522; (505) 351-4755, makes traditional New Mexico Spanish colonial furniture.

Elidio Gonzales and Antonio J. Archuleta, El Artesano de Taos, Box 366, Taos, NM 87571; (505) 758-2449.

Frederico Armijo, 400 Rio Grande Boulevard Northwest, Albuquerque, NM 87104; (505) 247-8061.

VENEERING

Veneering is found in all periods of American furniture but predominantly in that made in urban centers. By sawing thin layers of fine or rare woods and bonding them to the surface of less expensive or more plentiful species, cabinetmakers were able to use woods displaying curly

Replica of 18th century chest of drawers, with mahogany and olive ash burls and Spanish wood as secondary wood, by Eugene L. Welker

figure, crotch figure, stumpwood and burl grains that could not otherwise be cut in large pieces; stretch the supply of rare woods; and create elaborate surface designs, double-mirror images and inlays as fanciful as the cabinetmaker wished.

"Although much of it has become thinner over the years from refinishing, early American veneer started out as thin as it could be hand-sawn, $\frac{1}{8}$ to $\frac{1}{10}$ of an inch," says Eugene Welker who, like early craftsmen, hand-saws his own veneer to $\frac{1}{10}$ inch. "It took considerable skill to do this and not have the saw blade come through the face of the wood."

Unlike early makers, who often veneered mahogany onto softwoods like pine or poplar, Eugene glues his veneers onto solid mahogany. "There's a lot of ugly mahogany around today," he explains, "but it's a very stable wood and makes an excellent, if expensive, ground for fine veneer."

Known for the custom period furniture he creates for designers, architects, other furniture makers and the public, Eugene specializes in veneering, using thick-sawn veneer and 200-year-old finishes, materials and techniques. His passion for making fine furniture didn't begin until after graduating from the California College of Arts and Crafts, when he was restoring antiques. "After corresponding with a friend, Peter Anthony Canepa, we decided to make period furniture," says Eugene. "We set up a small shop in Scotts Valley, California, and did everything with hand tools. When the operation evolved into a larger shop using machines, plywood, modern adhesives and spray finishes, I knew that wasn't what I started out to do and moved back to New Hampshire and the original methods of working with wood."

Hand-scratched moldings are his favorite because of their organic quality and subtle waviness. Eugene makes his own scratch-stock cutters from old saw blades. "For a piece of furniture, I don't need 5 miles of moldings," he says, "because most pieces require only 8-foot lengths. However, it has become increasingly difficult to find and obtain old tools and finishing materials, because they've become collectible, or obsolete. It takes time using these old tools and keeping them in top condition. To do the

Replica of 18th century secretary, in burl elm and cherry with oak and pine as secondary woods, by Eugene L. Welker

job right, we have to constantly sharpen plane and molding-plane blades, chisels, carving tools and fine-tooth dovetail saws. There's also much ongoing research. We can't just call up someone and ask, 'How did the old guys do it?' "

Eugene hand-planes every surface, even veneered. "This is possible because I don't use factory knife-sliced veneer, which is only $1/42$ of an inch thick. I use the same glue that's been around for thousands of years. I call it 'industrial strength Jell-O,' hot-hide glue. It's very strong and reversible, an important point in the construction of fine furniture because the joints can be steamed apart when necessary. Can you imagine the problems we'd have if Stradivarius had used epoxy in his violins? They'd have to be smashed apart to be repaired." For finishing, he uses several grades of shellac: seedlac, buttonlac, dewaxed garnetlac and dewaxed ultralight or superblond, and never uses grades treated with lye and bleach. In addition to his other skills, he also dyes and tools leather with 23-karat gold borders for inlaying into desk tops and backgammon game tables, with two point colors plus background, each point outlined in gold.

Replica of late 17th century William and Mary desk, with walnut and California laurel burl on oak ground and cross-grain walnut as moldings, by Eugene L. Welker

All furniture starts from a sketch or picture furnished by the client. Price is based on time and materials. A William and Mary desk on stand is $7,000. Chairs range in price from $1,500 to $3,500, and large secretary desks from $12,000 to $25,000. Terms are 50 percent down and balance on delivery.

Eugene L. Welker
RR 2, Box 947
Cornish, NH 03745
(603) 675-6295
V (by appt.)   R   MO

WILLOW FURNITURE

"One of the most interesting aspects of making and selling willow furniture," says Lynn Humphrey, co-owner with Bill Hoole of Settona Willow Co., "is sharing the stories and nostalgia of people when they see it. They remember sitting in a willow rocker on their grandparents' porch, or buying chairs from gypsies who sold them door-to-door.

"We saw our first willow chair sitting on the deck of a friend's cabin near Lake Tahoe. Bill decided to try and build one for us. It turned out just great. Friends and friends of friends wanted one, so that one chair became a hobby and eventually a full-time business. We decided to sell our house and T-shirt business and move to south-ern California. Bill worked day and night until he'd finished six chairs, which we piled on the roof of our van and took to the beach cities. We parked on the side of the road and sold chairs from Los Angeles to San Diego, for 3 months—a very *long* 3 months—until one day a man jumped out of his car and asked if we would sell our chairs at his craft show. We said yes, it was a huge success and we were in business."

Rustic furniture in various forms has been popular in the United States since the early 1800s: Gothic, a gnarly version made from rhododendron and laurel; Western, fashioned from wooden poles and rawhide; Adirondack, of unstripped hickory; and willow, the lightest and perhaps most lyrical.

"Early on," says Lynn, "we decided we wanted our furniture to last; to be sturdy and comfortable without sacrificing any of the traditional craftsmanship. Unlike antique willow, which lasted only a season or two, we feel that with proper care, ours will last indefinitely. We sell as many pieces for use indoors as outside, which I feel shows a big change in attitude toward willow furniture."

One or two mornings each week, Bill and Lynn go to the willow groves to gather material. Green willow is most pliable when first cut, so bendable pieces are used within 3 days. Bill builds the frames and bends the arm pieces, they both bend backs (a two-person job) and Lynn installs seats and builds tables. They trim the ends of all framing pieces, smooth rough spots and nub from the branches, then drill holes for the solid bronze, ring-shank boat nails.

Their standard line of twenty-five designs includes chairs, rockers, loveseats and chaise longues for prices ranging from $185 to $325. They also make fireside chairs, dining chairs, square and oval end tables and coffee tables. A 25 percent deposit is required when orders are placed, with the balance due on delivery.

Willow rocker by Lynn Humphrey and Bill Hoole

Two willow chairs by Lynn Humphrey and Bill Hoole

115

"We ship out-of-state orders," says Lynn, "but do all our own deliveries within 200 miles because we enjoy meeting our customers." It's even more fun to drop by. Bill and Lynn live with their daughter in a handmade house surrounded by flowers in a grove of trees. Their workshop is outside the back door and the fence and gate are made out of (could you guess?) willow.

Lynn Humphrey and Bill Hoole
Settona Willow Co.
41655 Magnolia
Murrieta, CA 92362
(714) 677-7909
V R MO

Other Makers

American Folk Art, P.O. Box 435, Marietta, GA 30061; (404) 426-6538, has been making traditional designs in golden willow for 100 years: chairs, loveseats, rockers, porch swings, beds, tables, baskets and children's furniture.

Shawn Mitchel Clark, 2144 North 1400 East, Provo, UT 84604; (801) 377-3381.

Carol Calderwood, Willow Works, P.O. Box 42, Magadore, OH 44260; (216) 628-2100, makes chairs from $80; sofas, $200; fern stands, $25 to $35; breakfast trays, $30; end tables, $70; of green willow. A 25 percent deposit is required on commissions. Free delivery within 50 miles of Akron. V (by appt.)

Pure and Simple, 117 West Hempstead, P.O. Box 535, Nashville, AR 71852; (501) 845-2251.

Noel Arrington, P.O. Box 402, Trevett, ME 04571; (207) 633-6654, makes twig furniture of bent alder and willow, Blue Ridge style, in adult's and children's sizes, shipped anywhere. R W

Jane and Don Miles, The Willow Place, 362 South Atlanta Street, Roswell, GA 30075; (404) 587-5541, make twig furniture in southern and Amish styles including tea carts, porch swings, baker's racks and four-poster beds. C ($2)

David Hand, 2020 Gunter Avenue, Guntersville, AL 35976; (205) 582-0373.

Gameboards

During the 18th and 19th centuries, board games were a major source of entertainment in America, especially at inns and taverns. Made from wood planks or old breadboards, some gameboards were dual-purpose so that checkers could be played on one side and Parcheesi on

Parcheesi gameboard by Randy and Pam Tate

Long checkerboard by Randy and Pam Tate

the other. Most were simple and colorful. The more elaborate boards were often painted by carriage, sign or itinerant painters, and sometimes hung on the wall between games as decoration.

Randy and Pam Tate make a wide range of boards including Fox and Geese, Ringo and Palm Tree, as well as American checkerboards from the 12- by 12-inch size to the longer 12- by 25-inch size that rests on players' knees. If you're puzzled by the number of squares in old checkerboards, Randy has the answer. "Canadian checkerboards were made with twelve squares across," he explains, "while American boards had only eight." Prices range from $40 to $100. Knot in Vane, 805 North 11th Street, DeKalb, IL 60115; (815) 758-2516. R C W MO

Other Makers

Beverly Stessel, P.O. Box 28, Costigan, ME 04423; (207) 827-8733, shop located at 19 Main Street, Milford, ME 04461, makes hand-painted 18-inch checkerboards, assorted 6-inch checker sets, 21-inch Parcheesi boards and handmade dominoes in a slide-top box with painted Vermont scenes.

Beverly Peet, 191 Sagamore Street, Hamilton, MA 01936; (617) 468-3440.

Robin Lankford, 15005 Howe Road, Portland MI 48875; (515) 647-6298.

Gametables

Cabinetmaker Sandra Pearl Pomeroy makes several types of gaming tables: a no-nonsense card table in walnut; a three-way dining, chess and backgammon table; a dual-use writing and backgammon table; and several types of backgammon tables with or without inlay and with cabriole or tapered legs; from $375 to $1,000. 101 Holt Road, Andover, MA 01810; (617) 475-7812.

Gates   See Iron, Architectural

Art Glass

Tom Buechner III, co-owner of Vitrix Hot Glass Studio, makes classical trail vases using traditional trailing technique with copper enamels picked up in clear glass, then encased in clear glass. They range in price from $30 to $70. 77 West Market Street, Corning, NY 14830; (607) 936-8707.

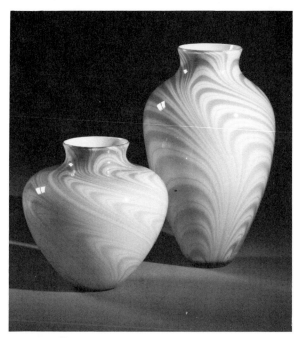

Classical trail vases by Thomas Buechner III

BULL'S-EYE AND LEADED GLASS

Before technology was available to make large sheets of glass, windows were made by the crown glass technique. Molten glass gathered on the end of a blowpipe was blown into a large sphere. A punty, or pontil rod, was then attached to the hot glass bubble on the side opposite the blowpipe. When the pipe was removed, a 2-inch hole was left in the sphere. The glass was then reheated, opened to a bowl shape, heated again and spun into a disk shape. The punty was cracked off and the bull's-eye disk annealed overnight. Window panes were cut from the perimeter. The center piece with the punty mark was either remelted or used in doors, sidelights or transoms.

"A hand-blown piece of glass full of bubbles and swirls has much more character than a piece of modern window glass," says Michael Kraatz. "Our leaded glass is unique because we not only design the panel but also make the glass, which is often decorated while molten on the blowpipe."

Michael started blowing glass at the University of Wisconsin in 1967 when the American studio glass movement was in its infancy. After he received his Master of Fine Arts degree and Susan Russell earned her degree in industrial design from Rhode Island School of Design, they

Bull's-eye glass disks in door by Susan Russell and Michael Kraatz

grooved lead bar that secures panes in stained-glass windows] has a much slower pace. We can pick and choose. It's a nice balance."

"It's also great fun to cut them up and piece them together into something larger," says Susan, "not unlike making a quilt."

Their work is installed in new and old homes all over the United States. In 1980 they were commissioned by the Museum of Fine Arts in Boston to make a series of leaded, diamond-pane casement windows for the reconstructed 1636 Fairbanks House on Boston Common.

Their most challenging commission was designing glass for a leaded panel whose decoration and overall design

Leaded glass door by Susan Russell and Michael Kraatz

moved to New Hampshire, where he built a glass studio and Susan had a woodshop nearby. It wasn't long before she was caught up in the excitement of the glass process.

"The laws of physics have a lot to do with the process of blowing and forming molten glass," says Susan. "Pushing those laws while you pursue an idea determines the outcome of each piece. Hot [2,000°F] glass is a gorgeous rose-orange like a sunset. The permanent color isn't apparent until the piece is cool. You don't really know what you've got until the next day. The result can be surprisingly good or unexpectedly bad."

"We were both drawn to the challenge of making glass for architecture," says Michael. "Each step has its own pace and rhythm. Making a decorated disk can be fast and furious. Decisions must be made quickly. You can't stand back. It's very physical and demands a great deal of teamwork and coordination with Susan. By contrast, cutting and fitting each piece into the lead came [the

had to have a Victorian flavor without using traditional Victorian motifs. "The client had heard about our glass but never seen it," says Susan. "She had Victorian furnishings in a modern barn-frame house. Our solution was three bull's eyes with flower centers made while the glass was molten. To do that, we had to figure out in the round what the finished product would look like flat."

Bull's-eye panes are cut to customer specifications and begin at $25 for the 6- by 6-inch size. "We can make panes as large as 10 by 12 inches but have found that the smaller sizes are more interesting and effective," says Michael. Leaded panels start at $100 a square foot.

"After working on a piece you get used to it," says Susan. "The specialness disappears until it is installed. Then you think, wow, this looks terrific, even better than I'd hoped. That's the magic. Turning an idea into a real thing, which looks good and pleases its owners."

Susan Russell and Michael Kraatz
Kraatz Russell Glass
Grist Mill Hill
RFD 1, Box 320C
Canaan, NH 03741
V (by appt.)   R   C   S   MO

Other Makers

J. Michael Doyle and Robert M. Lavery, The Cape Cod Bullseye Glass Co., 1780 Hyannis Road, Barnstable, MA 02630; (617) 945-3189 or 362-6808, make fine quality bull's-eye glass window panes.

Hand-blown Glass

Rochester Folk Art Guild's glass shop produces a wide range of hand-blown glass in clear and crackled texture, ranging in price from $10 to $40, available by mail order. Wholesalers can visit any time by appointment. For a schedule of retail sales and open house dates, send self-addressed, stamped envelope. RD 1, Box 10, Middlesex, NY 14507; (716) 554-3539 or 554-6401.   V   R   W   C   S   MO

Other Makers

Wheaton Village Glasshouse, Blasstown Road, Millville, NJ 08332; (609) 825-6800, makes hand-blown glass in lily pad designs.

Charles Gibson, Gibson Glass, Route 1, Box 102-A, Milton, WV 25541; (304) 743-5232.

Fluted vase 5 inches tall by Rochester Folk Art Guild

Lampwork

Glass was often decorated with applied glass threads and ribbons in the 19th century in America, using a technique called lampwork, still practiced by Gerard Lavoie. He begins by attaching long blowpipes to both ends of a lead crystal cylinder. Then, with gas-fired torches called "cross fires" (similar to Bunsen burners), the glass is heated evenly at 2,600°F. Ribbons of colored glass are then fused to the lead glass cylinder after it has been heated to the melting point. By blowing through the blowpipe, a symmetrical bubble is formed. Carbon rods are used to shape and sculpt the glass into various designs, many of which are inspired by those in *The Glass of Frederick Carder*, by Paul V. Gardner.

"Lampwork allows a glassworker a means of softening glass in small increments," explains Gerard, "instead of keeping hundreds of pounds in a liquid state." His most popular item, hand-blown Christmas tree ornaments "like Grandmother used to have," sell for $8 each or in sets of four for $30, while a treetop ornament 10 inches high

Variety of Christmas ornaments by Gerard Lavoie

is $20. Crystal candlesticks range in price from $18 to $30; vases, $6 to $10; cordial glasses, $10; perfume bottles, $20; and bells for $15 to $20. Gerard Originals, P.O. Box 531, Methuen, MA 01844-0631; (617) 686-6838. V (by appt.)   R   C   S   MO

Lead Crystal and Pressed Glass

Pairpoint Glass Works is one of the few glass shops in America working in off-hand full lead crystal. In addition to making flasks, decanters, lamps, vases, candlesticks, paperweights, ice cream plates and stemware in twenty different colors, they also create presentation pieces and can make matching or missing parts for chandeliers, old lamps and lighting fixtures.

Of special interest to collectors are their cup plates made of pressed glass in more than a hundred traditional designs and six different edge rings. When tea was served in cups without handles, and in saucers deeper than those used today, tea was poured into the saucer to cool and the cup placed on a cup plate to keep the tablecloth clean. Called "saucering," the custom originated in Europe and was practiced in America during the 1800s.

Pairpoint's blowing room is open to the public from 9 A.M. to 4:30 P.M. weekdays. Their factory store is open 9 A.M. to 6 P.M. year-round. 851 Sandwich Road (Route 6A), Sagamore, MA 02561; (617) 888-2344.   V   R   W   S   MO

OHIO GLASS

Some of the finest and most romantic American glass was made in Ohio in the first half of the 19th century.

Many collectors are surprised to learn that the same historical shapes and jewel-like colors continue to be made today at the glassworks at Hale Farm and Village of the Western Reserve Historical Society in Bath, Ohio.

In 1824, three enterprising men who felt that there was a market for glass in the rapidly developing lands of the Western Reserve, opened the Franklin Glassworks. Although it was a primitive facility, a very high-quality glass was produced there until the early 1830s when the glassworks burned down. In 1970 archeological digs conducted by Case Western Reserve University and the Western Reserve Historical Society uncovered the remains, which were moved to Hale Farm and Village. A glassworks modeled after the remains was built in an adjoining barn.

"We make functional forms of early Ohio glass that are true to our period, namely 1820 to 1850," says Kevin Rogers, their head gaffer. "Glassware is free-blown by the off-hand technique, which means it is produced by hand using hand tools as opposed to manufacturing glass by a mold process or machine. The only molds used are optic, which create a ribbed pattern on the glass surface. Using a basic mixture of sand [silica], soda, ash and lime, we recreate the traditional pattern-molded designs, shapes and patterns."

Glassblowers migrating westward from New Jersey, New York, Connecticut and New Hampshire brought designs with them. In later years, while retaining the best of the traditional designs, they added shapes of their own, now recognized as midwestern or Ohio glass. In addition to

Photo courtesy of the Western Reserve Historical Society, Hale Farm and Village, Bath, Ohio

Lily pad pitcher by Hale Farm and Village

Typical decanter in colonial style by Hale Farm and Village

came in every size from the miniature pitkin to the "grandfather" quart, but although chestnut flasks have been found in all the known pattern-molded designs, bottles were made only in the ribbed. Ohio glassware was also noted for its brilliant colors: ambers from honey to brown; greens from citron to olive; blues from cornflower to cobalt; and sometimes amethyst.

Kevin became an apprentice in 1978 at the age of 21, when "bored with my job and looking for something to do with my life." He was attracted to glass from the first day. "Glass is always moving," he says. "A glassblower must be constantly aware of what the glass is doing and about to do, then flow right along with it. Glass has a mind of its own. To be controlled, it must be coaxed. All the forming is done with hand tools, which become extensions of a gaffer's arms and hands. After years of working daily with the same basic style of glass, it becomes a sixth sense." This intuition helps when Kevin must re-create a piece of early glass. "There isn't much to go on at first," he says, "just a picture or two. Some pieces are relatively simple, but those that I'm most interested in producing are well designed and beautifully executed. They take much thinking as well as hours of trial and lots of error."

His glass bowls, saltcellars, compotes, flips, tumblers, decanters, cruets, pitchers, bottles, flasks and handled jugs

vertical ribbing, surface designs include circular threading, broken-rib, swirled and all-over diamond patterns. Salt-cellars are more angularly shaped than those from other regions and pitchers are more cylindrical and have short, straight-sided cylindrical necks. Robust sugar bowls come in voluptuous ogee and double-ogee shapes with defined (as opposed to rounded) shoulders, flaring flange tops and double-domed covers. Round chestnut-shaped flasks

Robust sugar bowl and creamer in ogee shape by Hale Farm and Village

Ribbed bottle by Hale Farm and Village

GLASS

sell for $9 to $26 in the Hale Farm and Village gift shop and at more than a hundred museums and shops in the United States. The shop also carries ironware ($3 to $35), pottery ($5 to $25) and textiles ($5 to $50). Open to the public May 1 through October 31, Tuesday to Saturday 10 A.M. to 5 P.M. and Sunday noon to 5 P.M.

Hale Farm and Village
The Western Reserve Historical Society
2686 Oak Hill Road
P.O. Box 256
Bath, OH 44210
(216) 666-3711
V   R   W   S   MO

Other Maker

Roberto Moretti, 53 Roland Park Drive, Huntington, WV 25701; (304) 523-4719, makes traditional glass.

Stained Glass

Gerhard Baut, fourth generation stained-glass maker, and his father, Eugene, who heads Baut Studios in Swoyersville, Pennsylvania, have created stained-glass windows and doors for churches throughout the United States. Gerhard, whose grandfather was a master in Louis Tiffany's studio, also has work included in the collections of the Smithsonian Institution and the Vatican Museum. Masters of the formalistic technique, creating painterly images in glass, they work from a palette of more than 3,000 types and colors of custom-made glass. The Baut Studios, Inc., 1095 Main Street, Swoyersville, PA 18704; (717) 288-1431.   V   R

Other Makers

Toland Sand, RFD 2, Box 422, Tilton, NH 03276; (603) 286-4589.

Barry and Cheryl Snowden and Bill O'Neill, Snowden-

"Transfiguration," stained glass by Gerhard Baut

122

Charles Noss

Stained glass in the Tiffany style by William S. Barash

O'Neill Studios, 137 West D Street, Encinitas, CA 92024; (619) 436-0632.

Penelope C. Starr, The Glass Depot, 193 Mill Street, San Rafael, CA 94901; (415) 456-9345.

Maryland Art Glass, 948 Sligo Avenue, Silver Spring, MD 20910; (301) 565-0466.

William S. Barash, 116 White Hill Road, Cold Spring Harbor, NY 11724; (516) 367-4405.

Gold Liturgical Items   *See* **Liturgical Gold, Silver and Pewter**

GOURDS

"We think of gourds as the clowns or fools of the vegetable world," says Priscilla Wilson, a former teacher who's now a full-time gourdworker. "Gourds inspire people to pun. Folks walk into our shop and say, 'Oh my gourd, I can't believe this,' or 'These are gourdgeous!'"

Priscilla first went out of her gourd over gourds in 1976 when she bought a few at a roadside stand. She planned on making one into a planter for her mother and bought some more for practice. She discovered "the impulse to make things from gourds was almost instinctive" and before long was growing her own in boxes and bottles, and trying to find better ways to clean them. "An uncleaned

gourd looks undesirable," she says. "People who don't know the outer skin comes off think it's rotten or not dried properly. If stored inside or in a protected place, it looks moldy. Out in the weather, the skin begins to peel like thin bark off a tree." She tried washing them in the dishwasher, coating them with oven cleaner and muriatic acid, and even ran them through a carwash before she found that the best way to get the outer crust off was to soak them in water or put them out in the rain. When the outer skin is saturated, she scrapes off most of it with a dull knife, then scrubs the remainder with a metal pot scrubber, cuts them open, pulls out seed and pulp, then sandpapers the inside smooth.

She resigned her job as teacher ("I wanted a happier life") and used her savings to rent a field ("I decided I'll never do anything special if I don't listen to the reckless part of me"). A lifelong friend and fellow teacher, Janice Lymburner, decided to join her in the venture.

"We knew nothing about farming," Priscilla explains. "I had to ask the owner how to use a hoe. I'd read somewhere that seeds come up faster if planted eye down, so we tried that. We didn't have a tiller. The weeds took over and the gourds didn't have a chance." But once they had mastered growing and carving gourds and took home ten times their investment from a country fair, they knew they were on to a "gourd idea."

Gourds grow wild in America and were used as dippers, bowls, funnels, rattles and musical instruments by pioneers and Native Americans. Egg basket gourds had such soft insides that eggs could be stored in them with leaves and moss on top to keep the eggs from freezing. The loofah, or dishrag, gourd was cut up for rags and sponges. "Gourds also make good salt and soda keepers," says

John Kollock

Bowl, dipper and colander gourds by Priscilla Wilson and Janice Lymburner

Gary Bogue

Turtle toy and puzzle by Priscilla Wilson and Janice Lymburner

Priscilla, "because they absorb moisture. The nest egg gourd was placed in nests to keep hens laying. No two are alike. They range from pale yellow to orange to dark rust with green veins. Some grow as big as a bushel basket."

Priscilla and Janice leave the gourds on the vines to dry and harvest in January when gourds are dry enough to store piled in open sheds. After cleaning, they dye, varnish and carve the gourds before cutting them open. "Dye lets the character of the gourd show through," explains Janice, "and gives a natural appearance."

In addition to the traditional gourd shapes, they make Christmas ornaments, Easter eggs, birdhouses, avant-gourd heads and masks, toys on wheels, puzzles, rattles,

Carved gourd containers with lids by Priscilla Wilson and Janice Lymburner

games and woven gourds (cut like a basket frame, then woven with natural materials).

Each January they hold a harvest party with a theme: Gourd Bowl; Once Upon a Gourd Gathering (with a Fairy Gourdmother); and Gourdcrafters Clearing House with giveaways all made from gourds. A museum next to their shop tells the history of gourds, and their traveling slide show takes schoolchildren and community groups from seed to finished product. To make sure others "have a gourd day," they give out instruction sheets with purchases of raw gourds and stock supplies for do-it-yourselfers.

Christmas ornaments are $4 to $10, natural utensils $4 to $16 and decorated containers $14 to $40. For a free brochure, send a self-addressed, stamped envelope. Located 5 miles east of Cleveland, Georgia, the shop is open Saturday from 10 A.M. to 6 P.M., Sunday from 1 to 6 P.M. and weekdays by chance or appointment.

Priscilla Wilson and Janice Lymburner
Gourdcraft Originals
P.O. Box 412
Blue Creek Road (Highway 255)
Cleveland, GA 30528
(404) 865-4048
V R W C S MO

Other Makers

Helen DuPree Park and her daughter Miriam Gruwell, 5201 Rock Springs Road, Lithonia, GA 30058; (404) 981-2878 or 981-5096, make gourd-head dolls, a form of early American folk art.

Aubrey Hamilton, 3530 Damien Avenue, Space 174, LaVerne, CA 91750, makes calabash pipes from the necks of gourds fitted with meerschaum top bowls.

Tony Joyner, 4015 North Avenue, Apt. 19, Richmond VA 23222, makes musical instruments from gourds.

Lucinda Ellison, P.O. Box 665, Jackson, MI 49204, makes gourd thumb pianos.   C

Sharon Barron, P.O. Box 123, Mentone, AL 35984; (205) 634-4767 or 634-4776, makes Gourdie dolls with funny faces, noses made from necks of gourds and burlap bodies.

GRAINING

During the 18th and 19th centuries, itinerant painters traveling America offered "economical painting"—plain and fanciful combinations of stains and grains that imitated fine woods, expensive inlays, carving, architectural details and rare materials like marble and tortoiseshell—created by layering a darker color over a lighter ground coat, then removing some of the top glaze to achieve depth. While European grainers preferred realistic treatments, most American artists disliked academic realism and worked fast, becoming more creative and abstract as they went along.

"Graining was popular," says Linda Lefko, a national expert who creates, teaches, writes and lectures on graining, "because it offered a wide variety of colors and trompe l'oeil textures and made inexpensive woods like pine, birch and basswood look like rosewood, mahogany, cedar, tiger and bird's-eye maple, woods that were prohibitively expensive and more difficult to obtain. While English and German grainers tended toward studied duplication of typical woods, American grainers took more liberties and were more imaginative. As a result, their finishes were both delicate and bold, amusing and stunning, and had more personality. Their great range of skill combined with creative license made their work more exciting and innovative than that of their European counterparts."

As a child, Linda became familiar with early grained furniture in her mother's antique business. After majoring in art in college she took classes in early American decoration with the same teacher her mother had studied under. "She spurred me on," says Linda, "in unorthodox techniques, making me want to know more about the original pieces." Working directly from originals at the Boston Museum of Fine Arts, Cooperstown, the Metropolitan, the Hitchcock Museum, and the Abby Aldrich Rockefeller Folk Art Collection at Colonial Williamsburg, Virginia, she tried to figure out how each finish was achieved. "Today's paints are different," she says. "I had to fudge around to find equivalents for what was used."

In applying graining to an object, Linda first sands the surface, then applies a base coat of flat oil paint in a bright color, sanding again before and after the second coat. She then mixes a graining glaze of two parts white vinegar (beer and whiskey can also be used) and one part dry powder paint pigment. "The old grainers used a bit of syrup or sugar in this mixture," Linda explains, "but I've found the addition of sugar leaves a buildup in the graining that can only be relieved by many coats of finish, so I no longer do it."

Using a variety of tools like rags, rolled-up or crumpled paper, sponges, leather strips, putty, corncobs, combs, plain or carved cork, feathers, cloth, potatoes, smoke and fingers, Linda plays with the glaze until she achieves the effect she wants. "Sometimes on something as simple as a frame," she says, "by the time I get to the fourth side I like the results so much that I wipe off the first three

Terry towel graining by Linda C. Lefko

with vinegar and do them over." After the vinegar glaze dries (about an hour) she uses shellac or an oil-based satin varnish, depending on whether hand-painted decorations will be added. "When the second coat is dry, I rub the surface with fine steel wool, then with paste wax. By combining colors and tools, possibilities are endless."

Linda teaches workshops in decorative painting at her studio and museums nationwide and also sells her own

Newspaper, sponge and comb grained pantry box by Linda C. Lefko

Chris Wright

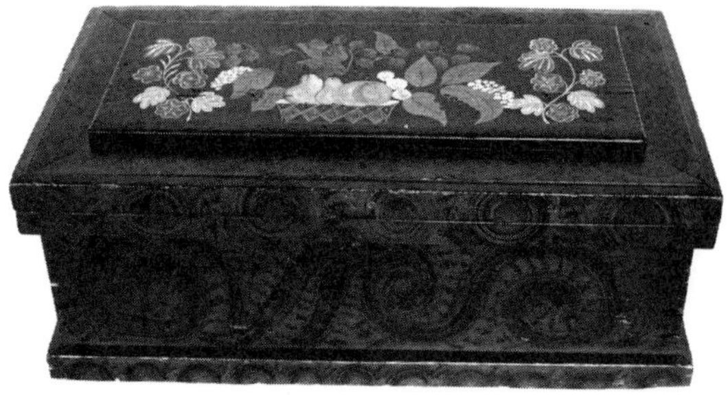

Coarse brush grained box by Linda C. Lefko

work. A grained frame costs as little as $25; commissions depend on size and time involved. Her work is so convincing that people often don't know it's there unless they try to use it. Visitors to the store at the Historical Society of Early American Decoration in Albany find that a grained mantel over a fireplace opening is actually just another wall.

Linda C. Lefko
Brookside Farm
2944 Corwin Road
Branchport, NY 14418
(315) 595-2722
V R MO

Other Makers

John H. Hill, Box 355, Unionville, PA 19375; (215) 347-2097, specializes in the scientific treatment of antique surfaces, filling in paint losses to conform to the original work. His clients include Winterthur, the Baltimore Museum of Art, the Smithsonian Institution and the National Park Service.

Malcolm Robson, 4308 Argonne Drive, Fairfax, VA 22032; (703) 978-5331, is a fifth generation grainer whose work is, as his company name, Robson Worldwide Graining, Ltd., implies, international.

Barbara Strawser, RD 1, Wernersville, PA 19565; (215) 693-6337.

David and Marie Gottshall, 210 East High Street, Womelsdorf, PA 19567; (215) 589-5239.

David T. Smith, 3600 Shawhan Road, Morrow, OH 45152; (513) 932-2472.

Roberta Taylor, 1717 Maywood Drive, West Lafayette, IN 47906; (317) 497-3111.

John Scott Nelson, Box 43, Peachum Road, Center Barnstead, NH 03225; (603) 776-7191, does graining similar to that used in Pennsylvania in the mid-1800s.

Sharon Sexton, P.O. Box 538, Worthington, OH 43085; (614) 888-2794.

Linda Podell, 207 Combs Avenue, Woodmere, NY 11598; (516) 569-0392.

Donna W. Albro, 70 Cranberry Drive, Duxbury, MA 02332; (617) 585-2062.

Marylou Davis, 165 Chapin Street, Southbridge, MA 01550; (617) 764-3828.

Grates *See* **Iron, Architectural**

Guitars, Coffin *See under* **Musical Instruments**

AMERICAN LONG RIFLES AND FLINTLOCK PISTOLS

The American long rifle, also known as the flintlock, Pennsylvania or Kentucky rifle, evolved before the Revolution and gained a reputation for accuracy and performance in both hunting and fighting. First made in the early 18th century by German and Palatine Swiss gunsmiths of Lancaster, Pennsylvania, it combined features of the German jaeger and English fowling piece.

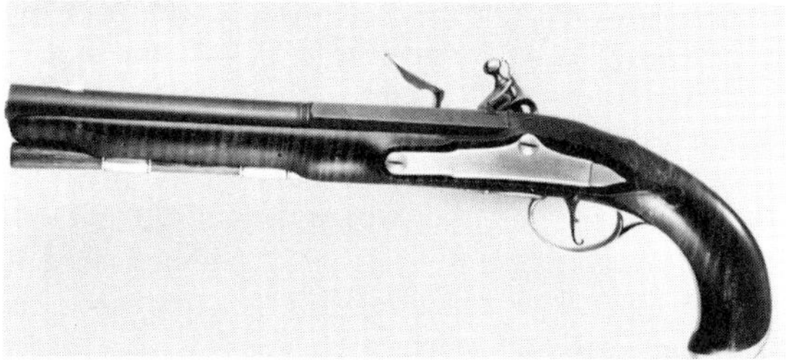

American flintlock pistol, .50 caliber, maple stock, by Mark Silver

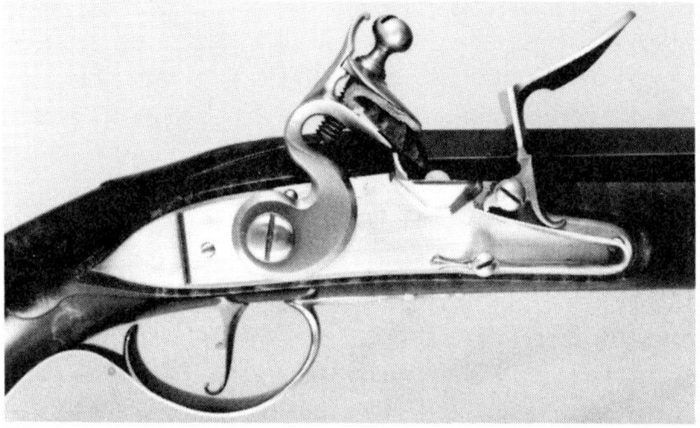

Closeup of American flintlock pistol by Mark Silver

American flintlock rifle, .45 caliber, maple stock, brass mounted, c. 1810 style, by Mark Silver

The barrel was long and octagonal; stocks were maple instead of walnut, and its patchbox cover was either of wood (1750–90) or an innovative sheet-brass box attached with a hinge. Stocks were often carved with scrolls, patterns, even animals, decorated with silver or inlay and proudly signed by the gunsmith. It became known as the Kentucky rifle, not because it originated there, but because of a ballad, "The Hunters of Kentucky," written about the Battle of New Orleans.

The golden age of American rifle-making lasted from the Revolution to 1830, when percussion lock and factory production put long-rifle makers out of business. "The American flintlock pistol, a type used by many American Revolutionary War officers," explains gun maker Mark Silver, "like most pistols made in 18th century America, showed English influence. In a very real sense, you can't draw a hard and fast line between England, the Continent and America when considering the handmade arms of America in the 18th century because America was just the most provincial region of Europe. As time went on more and more of an American style evolved, but not without the influence of Europe."

Mark began building long rifles as a hobby, worked full time with a nationally known expert, John Bivens, then went into business for himself specializing in 17th, 18th and 19th century sporting firearms. Since then, his work has been commissioned for many collections. A serious craftsman with a solid background in historical work, Mark prefers creating "my own designs for 18th century guns using the various American long-rifle schools as strict guidelines for architectural design, artistic motif and surface treatments, such as wood stains, varnish and metal finishes." Mark uses the most durable finishes available as long as they totally duplicate the appearance of 18th century craftsmanship. "My metal finishes such as color case-hardening, temper blueing and browning are accomplished by the same techniques used 200 years ago," he says.

Mark builds all parts himself with the exception of the barrel, which is custom-made by C. R. and D. E. Getz of Beaverton, Pennsylvania. Flintlocks (firing mechanisms) are assembled, fitted and polished by hand from available cast parts or totally handmade (which can nearly double the starting price). When brass mounts are used, the trigger guard and buttplate are made from castings like the originals. Other parts, such as ramrod pipes, nose caps, sideplates and patchboxes, are handmade as they were in the 1700s, with stocks made from a solid blank: usually of curly maple in America and walnut in Europe. Mark does all relief-carving as well as engraving on American pieces, but prefers to subcontract engraving on 18th century European guns. For iron-mounted pieces, he has rough forgings of his design made by Mark Bokenkamp of Powell, Ohio. Filing, detailing and relief-chiseling are followed by hand-polishing, a process that usually takes 24 hours to complete for a typical rifle trigger guard.

All guns are custom-made with a waiting period for delivery of approximately 18 months. Prices start at $3,750 for a relief-carved, engraved long rifle. Hours by appointment for "serious customers, students or builders only."

Mark Silver, Gun Maker
5640 Highway 614
Cedar, MI 49621
(616) 946-7616
R S MO

Other Makers

John Bivens, 622 2nd Street, Winston-Salem, NC 27108.

Judson Brennan, P.O. Box 1165, Delta Junction, AK 99737.

Mike Cox, Route 1, Box 232-C, Fayetteville, WV 25840.

Donald King, P.O. Box 208, Big Timber, MT 59011.

Jerry Kirklin, 1772, South Bates, Birmingham, MI 48009.

GUNS

Monte Mandarino, 136 Fifth Avenue West, Kalispell, MT 59901; (406) 257-6208.

Robert Harn, 228 Pensacola Road, Venice, FL 33595; (813) 488-3418.

Mark Bokenkamp, 10132 Liberty Road, Powell, OH 43065; (614) 889-0819.

James B. Stephen, P.O. Box 1116, Sonora, TX 76950; (915) 387-3076.

SOUTHERN MOUNTAIN RIFLES

The Kentucky and Pennsylvania long rifle was made for townspeople and more casual use. The workhorse rifle of American heroes like Daniel Boone, Davy Crockett and Sergeant Alvin York was the muzzle-loader, or southern mountain rifle. Entirely handcrafted, often by one person, it was plain and simple in design, made to be shot hard and put up wet.

After serving in Vietnam, Jim Moretz, then a professional photographer, set out to make himself a mountain rifle because the few on the market fell short of the originals. "I used every inlay known to man," he says ruefully, "and a brass patchbox the size of a country ham. The rifle was fine for hunting the flat fields of the Piedmont, but in the mountains where I live, hunting requires a fair amount of skill in tracking and stalking. Because it's impossible to shoot through hills, the average hunting shot

is about 40 yards. Toting a rifle that reflects more light than a Christmas tree is not the smartest thing to do. I realized that I'd created an object whose function followed form, not unlike putting a necktie on a Hampshire hog."

Dissatisfied with what he now calls his "Hollywood rifle," Jim began researching the territory, driving miles to see old mountain guns, talking to their owners, mailing slivers and splinters of old gun stocks to the U.S. Forestry Service to find out what woods and finishes were used, taking every course on metal that he could find. Before long he attracted a large amount of restoration work on old guns, which taught him even more.

"The southern mountain rifle has the basic appearance of the more familiar Kentucky and Pennsylvania long rifle," he explains, "but a much thinner and more graceful profile. Most stocks were walnut, cherry and curly maple; the barrels were usually octagonal. The lock, buttplate and all metal parts were usually made by hand, from wrought iron in the blacksmith's shop. Sometimes, but not often, the makers used brass or silver. The buttplate was more curved than in the Pennsylvania rifle, some say to shoot up and down hills. Patchboxes were made from sheet iron, usually in an elongated banana or oval shape, although I've seen some made of wood with a metal hinge. Mountain rifles had very little if any inlay, usually added as an afterthought and crudely done by the owner. Called a 'hog' rifle, because mountaineers let their hogs run wild

Southern mountain rifles: (top to bottom) Tennessee mountain rifle in the manner of Bean, North Carolina southern mountain rifle in the manner of Hughes, Northwest trade rifle and Allentown rifle with North Carolina influence by James L. Moretz

Cheekpiece detail of Allentown rifle by James L. Moretz

in the woods to get fat on acorns and chestnuts, then had to hunt them like wild game, the southern mountain rifle was extremely accurate.''

A few years ago, Jim closed his photography studio, built a house in the mountains on a dirt road and became a full-time riflesmith, using many of his grandfather's gunsmithing tools. Wood for stocks is cherry, walnut and curly maple cut in his woods and air-dried for several years. ''I usually custom-build each rifle to the buyer's requirements,'' he says, ''concentrating on function and authenticity. Wood is stained by the traditional method, with nitric acid, called aquafortis, which is also used to brown the metal. If I can't find suitable castings, I hand-forge needed parts from mild steel. I once made my own barrels, but now use a high-quality factory-made barrel for greater accuracy. I guarantee all work for a lifetime, mine or theirs, whichever ends first. When possible, I like to hand-deliver my guns and spend a day with the new owner shooting and cleaning the rifle. I prefer to build for a shooter or hunter rather than a collector, because that's the purpose of a rifle.''

Prices start at $1,000. Interested buyers should send $1.50 for photos and ordering information. Delivery time: 6 months.

James L. Moretz
Route 5, Box 66
Boone, NC 28607
(704) 264-4182 (to leave messages only)
R S MO

Other Maker

Steve Davis, P.O. Box 265, Centerville, TN 37033; (615) 729-5033.

Hand-Sewing *See* **Irish Lace, English Smocking and French Hand-Sewing**

Harpsichords *See under* **Musical Instruments**

Hats, Cowboy *See* **Cowboy Hats**

Hats, Straw *See* **Wheat-Weaving and Straw Hats**

Hex Signs

When Pennsylvania-Germans began painting hex signs in the southeastern corner of the state (Berks, Lehigh and Montgomery counties) between 1830 and 1850, the signs were meant to be purely decorative, ''chust for nice.''

''No one knows who painted the first one,'' says Ivan Hoyt, who has been painting them professionally for 15 years and has never repeated a design unless a client requested it. ''One theory is that hex signs appeared when manufactured paint pigments became available and farmers could mix these pigments with sour milk as a binder. In the beginning, they were geometric designs in red,

Cocalico star hex sign by Ivan E. Hoyt

Hill star hex sign with border of overlaid scallops by Ivan E. Hoyt

Double distelfink hex sign, symbol of good fortune, by Ivan E. Hoyt

black and yellow because that's what was available. Blue was seldom used because indigo was imported and more expensive. Farmers painted their own hex signs until the early 1900s, when itinerant barn painters added hexes to their stock in trade.

"Over the years, the distelfink has become the most popular symbol. Legend says that when the farmer saw the goldfinch bird pull the fuzz from the thistle seed to line its nest, and called it a 'thistlefinch,' his accent made it sound like 'distelfink.' Because this bird ate seeds from the thistle and cut down the number of weeds in the fields, the farmer had better luck with his crops, which is why the distelfink symbolizes good luck or good fortune. Another story says that God created the distelfink with all the colors He had left after creating the other birds.

"Tulips, another popular symbol, represent faith in yourself, what you do and in your fellow man. Pomegranates are for long life, fertility; the heart, a sign of love, romance, marriage. The scalloped border has two meanings: smooth sailing on the sea of life, or a life of ups and downs."

Ivan paints his hex signs on exteriors with exterior primers and paints. They range from 8 inches in diameter to 4 feet. Prices range from $15 to $150 with many options in between. Today, people use them both inside and out, often incorporating colors and symbols of their own preference. RD 2, Box 49D, Wapwallopen, PA 18660; (717) 379-3533.   V (by appt.)   R   C   MO

Hides, Brain-tanned   *See under* **Leather**

Hope Chests   *See* **Dower Chests**

HOPI CRAFTS

When the Spaniards arrived on the high, barren, sandstone mesas of northeastern Arizona, they were surprised to find Hopi Indians living in cities. Today, the 8,000-member Hopi tribe, one of the oldest communities in North America, are skilled dry land farmers who grow beans, melons, squash, cotton and corn (which is represented in all their ceremonies as Mother Corn). Culturally conservative and matrilineal, the Hopi have a rich religious culture with elaborate and ancient ceremonies, in which crafts have an integral part.

Their boldly patterned black, brown and red pottery is considered by many experts to be the best painted ware in America. Based on a tradition that goes back to pre-Columbian times, Hopi pottery is made by the coil method. Ropes of clay are formed, then layered in circles one on top of the other, the surface smoothed, dried and a coat of slip (a thin wash of clay applied as a glaze) applied. After the surface is polished with a smooth stone, a design is incised or painted. To fire, pots are placed on a grate, covered with broken potsherds, and surrounded with dried sheep manure, which is then burned. The best-known Hopi pottery, a decorated yellow-orange ware, is done in the style of Nampeyo, a distinguished Hopi/Tewa potter of the late 1800s. Another type, called white clay pottery, is made from red clay with a white slipped interior. Prices of jars and vases range from less than $8 for a 3- by 3-inch shape to $350 for a decorated one 8 by 10 inches, while bowls are priced from $1 for a miniature, 2 by 2½ inches, to $150 for one 5 by 12 inches. Undecorated pottery ranges from $12 to $175.

Hopi basketry, considered a sacred art, is learned by most young girls when they are initiated into the women's basket society. Wicker baskets, created with rabbit brush

Basketry plaque portraying butterfly kachina girl by Dora Sakeva of the Hopi Arts and Crafts Guild

Painted earthenware jar by Fannie Nampeyo of the Hopi Arts and Crafts Guild

or sumac, are colored red and black with natural or aniline dyes ($50 to $125), while yucca sifters are formed by plaiting yucca over a willow ring ($12 to $30). Coiled baskets ($70 to $1,000) made of yucca leaves and galeta grass have natural colors of green, yellow and white accented with rust-red and black obtained from vegetable dyes.

Kachinas represent powerful supernatural beings who have life-and-death influence over the lives of the Hopi. They bring blessings, rain and fertility in exchange for which the Hopi offer prayer feathers and corn pollen in various rituals. About 300 kachinas appear regularly and another 200 intermittently. To help children learn to identify them, figures carved in their likeness are given to children during ceremonies by masked dancers representing the kachinas. These dolls, which symbolize the perpetuation of all life forms, range from flat types, slabs of cottonwood with arms and legs painted on (sold for $15 to $55) to elaborately carved and decorated three-dimensional types with movable arms and legs ($50 to $800).

Weaving is traditionally done by Hopi men. For example, a groom's uncles make the wedding cape for the bride. Hopi designs are woven into ceremonial sashes ($350), wedding belts ($85 to $150), the black-and-white blankets made to be worn by children at weddings and

HORNWORK

Awatovi soyuk wuhti, kachina doll by Bruce Auguah of the Hopi Arts and Crafts Guild

the traditional manta robe worn by women at ceremonies. Fashioned of black woven material with red and green yarn cross-stitch down the right side, it is worn off the left shoulder and slit on the right side to above the knee ($400).

Hopi silver, an art form since 1890, is best known as overlay jewelry in ancient designs. For a catalog and price list, send self-addressed, stamped envelope.

Hopi Arts and Crafts Guild
P.O. Box 37
Second Mesa, AZ 86043
(602) 734-2463
V   R   W   C   S   MO

HORNWORK

"Because horn was often the only airtight and water-proof material," says hornsmith Delbert Brewster, "early pioneers used it to make containers for water, salt, rum, powder and tinder. Besides being cheap and available, horn was especially good for keeping powder dry because it was also fire-retardant and spark-resistant. Before mod-

ern bullets and shells, guns used round balls and black powder. People like Davy Crockett and Jim Bowie always carried a powder horn with their muzzle-loading guns. Horn was also made into ladles, spoons, knife handles, toys, charms and ceremonial objects. The Spanish, who introduced cattle into Texas, used powder horns. Southwest Indians scrimshawed bone and horn; while Eskimos and Northwest Indians used teeth, bone and mastodon ivory."

Delbert started carving pecans, wood and horns when he was 6 years old on a ranch in central Texas. "When I went fox-hunting with my dad," he says, "I loved the sound of the horn in the still night air. Texans also used horns like farm bells. My wife's Aunt Lillie told me that when her mother was ill, the children blew the horn until someone came by to ride for help. She said the horn was always blown a few times to bring the men in from the fields, and that continuous blowing meant an emergency."

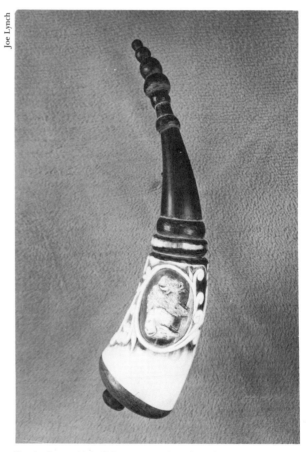

Powder horn with buffalo engraving by Delbert Brewster

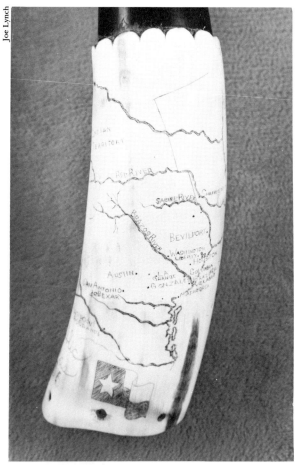

Hornwork map by Delbert Brewster

can be made because there's no erasing. The finished horn is rubbed with size 0000 steel wool and polished with paste wax. When I find horns with good color, a white outer layer and dark (preferably black) under layer, I do cameo or low-relief carving.''

To make powder flasks, Delbert boils horns and flattens them to have more area for scrimshaw. Stoppers in the small end are made of horn, bone or mesquite wood carved to fit the hole. The larger, butt-end plug is permanent and made of mesquite, also known as Texas ironwood. For a tight fit, Delbert boils the horn to make it pliable, then forces the plug about ½ inch inside, fastening it with small nails, wood pegs or mesquite thorns.

Well known in Texas, where he participates in the Texas Folklife Festival each year, Delbert's hornwork is on permanent display in the National Carvers' Museum in Colorado. An elementary school art teacher, he had never seen anyone carve horns and didn't know his designs were scrimshaw until he saw an Alaskan scrimshander in 1967. One of the few who know how to make a horn from horn that really blows, Delbert delights in making something beautiful from what others consider worthless.

In addition to his decorative powder horns, which start at $175, he makes knives of 440-C stainless steel with antler handles, which start at $175, as well as gunstocks and bolos.

Delbert Brewster
1107 Alpine Drive
Andrews, TX 79714
(915) 523-5335
R S MO

Other Maker

G. Atlee Crouse, RD Galen Hill Road, Reinholds, PA 17569; (215) 484-2214, makes articles like beakers out of horn.

Horse-drawn Vehicles   *See* Vehicles, Horse-drawn

HORSEHAIR TWISTING

"Up through the 1930s, nearly everybody in southeast Texas made their own horsehair reins and saddle girths," Bill Brett will tell you, "because there were lots of horses and damn little money. My grandfather braided horsehair and told me I was going to do it too. Been doing it ever since."

Delbert prefers working with horns from mixed breeds because longhorns are more than 3 feet in length. Here's how he describes the process: "When I first get horns, they are often dirty, don't smell good and take hours to clean. After boiling them in sulphur water to make them mothproof, I work them until they have no scratches. If an old horn is rough and weathered, I use a wood rasp, then scrape the horn with a knife. The horn must be so smooth that the ink won't go anywhere except where I cut, which becomes the design. Cuts don't show until ink is rubbed into them. I make a cut, ink, clean the surface with a damp cloth, then cut again. This process is repeated hundreds of times until the design is done. No mistakes

Bill Brett twisting horsehair

best to pull from the bottom end, not the cut end," he advises as he rolls it "from one side like a scroll to make it round." Spinning requires two people: one sits down and feeds hair into the spinner; the other turns the tarrabee and keeps it twisted. To insure a uniform size in the string, the hair must be fed evenly. "I once asked an old man how much to let out at a time," says Bill. "He stuck up his left thumb and said, 'That thumb knows,' which means after you've practiced enough, you don't have to watch your thumb."

For bridle reins, the string is twisted left to right until it's 60 feet long, then tied off and another started. The two are then twisted together to the left. "As long as you don't turn the end loose, it will stay together," says Bill, "but you can never leave the ends loose or they'll untwist. Tie them off with string until you get your knots tied. About the only knot that won't creep out of horsehair is a rosebud." The middle is held with a short smooth stick while the other hand doubles the end around to the tied end to redouble it. The four strings are then put together and twisted to the left and tied off. Doubling and redoubling the string makes a length of hair rope 10½ to 12 feet long. For a girth, two strings are twisted to 50 feet in length, put together and twisted back the other way.

The colors are the same as the horsehair: red, black, white or mixed. "You can't get too fancy with hair," Bill says, "because you have only three solids and nine color patterns to work with."

One of the oldest crafts in the world, horsehair twisting originated with the bedouins, a nomadic people with large animals that had to be controlled as they moved from one grazing area to the next. "Hair was the only fiber they could use," says Bill, "because every other fiber takes tools, equipment and a long preparation time. A Louisiana State University professor told me that whenever they needed a rope they'd stop, whittle a crude spinner, cut enough hair to make what they needed and throw away the spinner after they'd finished. The Moors took the craft to Spain and the Spanish brought it to America. The spinner, a simple homemade wooden tool, is called a tarrabee, and is made in the shape of an animal's shoulder blade, which is what they probably used on the desert. A hole is cut in one end and it's used with a pestle-shaped piece with a knob on one end."

After a horse's mane is at least 8 to 10 inches long, Bill cuts it, ties it with a string to keep it straight, pulls a few hairs at a time and lets the end fall bottom down. "It's

Alice L. Pate

Horsehair rope by Bill Brett

The best way to get Bill to twist horsehair is to raise your own and trade him two for one. That means, send him enough horsehair to make two of whatever you want. You get one and the other pays for labor. Now that Bill's down to only six or eight horses, that's the only way he can get enough hair to work with. If you don't own a horse or know one that needs a mane cut, reins run $150, girths $50, lead ropes $50 and a matching set of reins, girth and hatband is $200.

Bill Brett
P.O. Box 387
Hull, TX 77564
(409) 536-6950
R   S   MO

Horsehair Braiding, Hitching and Weaving

"For braided, hitched or woven hair," explains Rowdy Pate, "I gently pull about eight hairs, 24 inches long, from the hank, tie a hard overhand knot as near one end as possible, twist it into a strand, put half on each side of my right forefinger with the knot pointed out and my thumb and middle finger pressing down on the hair. I then catch it by the knot with my left hand and twist it as I pull it slowly out, then tie a knot in the loose end, which gives me a working strand. I lay my strands in a split mesquite stick the size of a pencil and tie it with twine. An eight-strand braid is braided in pairs, which are then laid side by side and sewn together in a solid color or any variation of different colors for pattern. Hitching is done by hitching strands around a twine string as it wraps

around the object to be covered. Horsehair weaving is made just like cloth." Box 581, Pearsall, TX 78061; (512) 334-2015.   R   S   MO

Other Maker

Gail Hought, 2680 Susan Road, McKinleyville, CA 95521.

HOUSES OF TIMBER-FRAME CONSTRUCTION

A dovetailed house? Why not? If you marvel at a mortise-and-tenon joint, imagine the daily delights of living in a house whose frame is built without nails.

Timber-frame joinery, used during the 17th and 18th centuries in America, was built to last, which is why old barns with three-quarters of the underpinnings removed

Close-up of timber-frame joinery by Ed Levin

Woven hatband by Rowdy Pate

Alice L. Pate

Richard Starr, Thetford, VT

Skeleton of timber-frame building by Ed Levin

won't collapse. As practiced in the United States, timber-framing became a unique blend of British, German, French and Scandinavian designs.

When Ed Levin built an addition to the 1790s Cape in which he was living, he decided to do it "the way it had been done." That meant massive posts and beams joined with wooden pins called trunnels (treenails) from fresh-cut wood. "At the time, in the late sixties and early seventies," he says, "there were no books on how to do it, so I used houses and barns as textbooks." He learned that "if buildings are built tight in the beginning, they will stay tight," and that "American barns are the unsung architectural giants of the American landscape." Learning as he went, he felled, peeled and hewed his own timber, worked up the wood by hand, then raised the frame with block and tackle, pick poles and commander (a mallet with a 30-pound head).

Since going into business in 1971 to build structures "inspired by that great period of American domestic architecture spanning the 17th and 18th centuries," the Dartmouth graduate has built a new frame for the bells in Boston's Old North Church, a curved hammerbeam roof for a stone building patterned after a 14th century English chapel and a five-story tower bristling with cantilevered projections. To build a replica of America's oldest house, the Fairbanks House, on Boston Common for the city's 350th birthday, Levin used a 7-foot, two-man pitsaw to prepare the posts and beams, as well as preparing 10,000 board feet of hand-hewn lumber, hand-riven clapboards and a thatch roof.

Although early settlers built frames of spruce, maple, pine, chestnut, fir, basswood, beech, hemlock, butternut and poplar, Ed prefers fresh-cut red oak. "It cuts like butter and is stronger than spruce or hemlock," which he recommends for barns and large utility buildings.

Because timbers are widely spaced and interior walls are not needed to support the roof in timber-frame structures, opportunities for solar heating devices and wide expanses of glass are endless.

"Most of our house frames are covered with stressed skin paneling," says Ed, "which provides exterior sheathing and an R-30 insulation, making them surprisingly energy-efficient and economical to heat." Decorative options include curved bracing and carved stop chamfers or finials. Working on one project at a time with two to four joiners, preparation takes from 6 to 16 weeks, depending on the size and complexity of the project.

After joinery is completed, timbers are planed and scraped, treated with tung oil finish and sent by truck to sites throughout the United States, where they are raised by crews of friends and neighbors or with four to six professionals and a crane.

"Rather than have stock plans," says Levin, "we offer both design and construction services, working closely with owners to develop designs which match their needs and dreams. Ballpark estimates are available without charge. A more refined estimate along with preliminary plans and elevations can be supplied for a small fee. Total design cost is usually less than 4 percent of the project cost. With framing, prices will range from $10 to $15 per square foot. The services of a solar engineer are also available to help create integrated solar designs."

Ed Levin
Upper Gates Road
RFD #2, Box 928C
Canaan, NH 03741
(603) 523-4812
R   C   S

Other Maker
Ted Benson, Benson Woodworking Company, Pratt Road, Alstead, NH 03602; (603) 835-6391.

INLAY, MARQUETRY AND PARQUETRY
When the National Trust for Historic Preservation decided to restore the 1870s parquet floor in the Decatur House in Washington, DC, Acting Director Vicki Sopher was told that no one alive would be able to do the job. She remembered a young craftsman named R. L. Heisey

Although inlay, marquetry and parquetry are different in application, they are similar in that they use small pieces of wood, ivory, brass, shell or other material to create designs. For inlay, the surface is cut and filled. Marquetry is small pieces of veneer set into one or more larger pieces to create a design that is glued to a solid backing and incorporated in a piece of furniture, used as a central decorative point on floors or framed and hung on the wall. Parquetry, though similar to marquetry, is cut from thicker wood, laid in patterns to contrast the grain (like herringbone) and is generally used on floors.

Rick had been working with wood for 10 years before opening his shop in Winchester, Virginia, but his first large commission presented a similar challenge: to build a breakfront bookcase adapted from one in the Heyward-Washington House in Charleston, South Carolina. "At the time, it involved more veneer and inlay than I'd done," says Rick, "so I went to see the original. It was almost 11 feet tall and more than 8 feet wide. The base was an inlaid double-serpentine shape whose doors were veneered with crotched grain and ribbon-stripe mahogany. The pedi-

Central motif of California state seal in floor of the Decatur House, Washington, DC, requiring nine kinds of $1/28$-inch veneer, by R. L. Heisey

whose marquetry and inlay work she'd seen, and asked if he'd like to put in a bid. The floor's 20 by 30 feet and prominent location would have frightened most, but Rick Heisey enjoys commissions that challenge what he knows and teach him more.

"I had to learn some new techniques," he says, "but the skills needed were the same as work I'd done on furniture. The most interesting part was studying the floor for clues to what tools, woods and techniques had been used. The central motif of the California state seal surrounded by a geometric design 52 inches wide required nine different kinds of $1/28$-inch veneer, which I installed and shaded with a burning knife. Three squares of the border had to be replaced, using $1/8$-inch veneer in six kinds of wood, while twelve kinds of wood were used in the $1/4$- to $5/16$-inch-thick banding."

Floor of the Decatur House by R. L. Heisey

Breakfront bookcase 11 feet tall, 8 feet wide, with inlaid double-serpentine base in crotched grain and ribbon-striped mahogany, by R. L. Heisey

137

ment had a great deal of marquetry and all the doors were embellished with ivory bellflowers. I rendered three full-scale drawings before I felt comfortable enough to start into the lumber. It took 900 hours of labor, required new tools, building new hand planes and a veneer press." When another client wanted a dining table of native Virginian woods, he used wide walnut boards for the top and designed a dogwood inlay, whose thinly sliced dogwood petals were scorched in hot sand to shade outside edges.

"The skills learned on the Decatur House floor now enable our shop to build and install new floors with the same sense of design and quality as our fine furniture," says Rick. "We just completed a living room floor with a diamond pattern and a central fleur-de-lis motif, which is repeated in the bay window as well as in the adjacent dining room and entry. Our latest product is an 8-inch inlaid block of cherry, maple and mahogany framed in creamy birch that can be interspersed with plain blocks to make subtle or bold floor patterns."

R. L. Heisey, Cabinetmaker, Ltd., specializes in high-quality custom furniture. Their inventory of unusual woods, many with special figures, enables them to build complicated pieces like the Charleston breakfront as well as smaller pieces, such as tilt-top tea tables from $200 to $350.

R. L. Heisey, Cabinetmaker, Ltd.
1011 Fort Collier Road
Winchester, VA 22601
(703) 667-3095
V   R   C   S   MO

Close-up of how Irish lace is made on a fabric backing, not in the hand, by Judith Brandau

IRISH LACE, ENGLISH SMOCKING AND FRENCH HAND-SEWING

Irish lace, English smocking and French hand-sewing have two things in common: their names are American terms for handwork techniques brought to the United States from other countries, and they are all incorporated in the creations of Judith Brandau. As she says, "I try to preserve the essence of these three interrelated branches of needlework in my designs inspired by Edwardian and Victorian styles, because these hand techniques were at their peak of popularity in those eras.

"Three different types of Irish lace were made in America," says Judith, "and not all are of Irish origin. Traditional Irish lace (also called Clones crochet after an Irish lace center) is the most difficult. Worked over one or more thick padding cords curved into three-dimensional motifs, it is sewn temporarily onto a back-ground fabric so that fine-mesh crochet can be worked around it. Irish appliqué lace uses the same motifs as traditional, but instead of crocheting around the design, the background is crocheted as a separate piece with the motifs sewn on top. Baby crochet is an American simplification without the padding, which gives a more two-dimensional effect. Crocheted around a rose or star center, it is made like little granny squares and joined as chains to make edging or into larger squares to make whole garments."

Smocking originated in England in the Middle Ages to make smocks, loose-fitting garments of linen or homespun that went out of fashion in the machine age but came back in style when Queen Victoria dressed her children in smocked clothing. "The English counted threads and gathered fabric on the back," says Judith, "then embroidered the front. American smocking omitted work on the back and connected stamped dots on the front with floss in linear designs and diamonds."

Victorian blouse with smocking by Judith Brandau

Judith, a second generation American of French ancestry, learned to sew as a toddler from her mother, a professional tailor who called French hand-sewing "plain sewing." "American seamstresses coined the term French hand-sewing," says Judith, "to describe fine handwork on Parisian couturier clothes." Judith learned to smock while recuperating from spinal surgery, and helped pay her college tuition through the sale of hand-smocked garments. While taking courses in textiles and art, she began drafting her own patterns, and lately has been editing smocking designs as well as creating lace designs for *Better Homes and Gardens*. A child's smocked dress and bonnet designed and made by Judith has been acquired by the Smithsonian Institution for its permanent collection.

When she was unable to find the lace she wanted, Judith set out to learn that skill, practicing with heavy thread to make pillows and working with finer threads until she was able to recreate authentic laces. She recently received a grant from the Pennsylvania Council on the Arts to teach apprentices.

"Whenever possible," says Judith, "I keep the authentic details, but because today's woman is of larger build and not corseted, it alters the cut. I work in natural fibers: cotton, silk, linen and ramie. French hand-sewing cannot be done on manmade fibers. Clients who want them must be content with machine sewing."

Her one-of-a-kind custom garments are priced from $100 to several thousand dollars, depending on the intricacy of the work, while collars and cuffs range from $50 to $150 and motifs cost between $5 and $35.

Judith Brandau
316 West Wayne Street
Butler, PA 16001
(412) 282-1584
R S MO

Other Maker

Marilyn Heller, RD 4, Box 70, Glen Road, Coopersburg, PA 18036; (215) 967-3795, does smocking on all garments and fabrics. Prices vary according to fabric and size.

ARCHITECTURAL IRON

How does a craftsman design an object that never existed in a traditional way?

"There are many levels at which a craftsman works," says Dimitri Gerakaris. "The simplest is as a skilled mechanic. The client says, 'Here's an example of what I want. Can you make one like it for me?' This is essentially what I did when the Boston Museum of Fine Arts asked me to forge hardware for the reconstructed Fairbanks House.

"Another level of skill comes into play when the craftsman is asked to interpret or design work as well as execute it for a traditional setting where nothing like it has existed. When Dartmouth College asked me to design and build a railing for a wheelchair ramp at Baker Library, the design evolved easily because there was other ironwork near the site to set the tone. I selected a Georgian motif already there in a rectangular mode and translated it to a rhomboid configuration to suit the angled railing. But designing ironwork for a turn-of-the-century bank in Stamford, Connecticut, presented a different challenge. Because I think the prevalent thin cold-bent stock combined with cast-iron decorative motifs of that era were insipid, I asked

High-necked lace blouse by Judith Brandau

One of two 10- by 11-foot grilles made for the Citizens' Savings Bank, Stamford, Connecticut, by Dimitri Gerakaris

myself, 'What if the best craftsmen of the day were asked to do the best they could? What would they have done?' I chose an overall form consistent with the era but emulated the solid detailing and techniques of the Renaissance period upon which American bank architecture was based.''

In 1971, two years after graduating from Dartmouth, Dimitri became a smith with primary emphasis on architectural and domestic commissions. After three years' working in a converted garage, he began building a stone forge with a medieval hammerbeam arched truss roof to allow headroom for large projects and space in which the intense heat of the forge could rise. He slated the roof, plastered interior walls, landscaped the exterior and has

been enjoying his aesthetically pleasing work space ever since. As founder, past president, director and editor for the 2,200-member Artist Blacksmiths' Association of North America, Dimitri lectures and conducts workshops worldwide. He works by commission only. Recipient of a Services to the Field Grant from the National Endowment for the Arts in 1980, he has had work exhibited at the Boston Museum of Fine Arts, the Smithsonian, the American Craft Museum and the National Ornamental Metal Museum.

He aims for perfection. After designing a hand-forged gate using ancient blacksmithing techniques, he made the lock and key by hand. When he was invited to design and build a monumental gateway to Eagle Square, across from

Detail of grille at Citizens' Savings Bank by Dimitri Gerakaris

Windswept Estate court gate by Dimitri Gerakaris

Dimitri Gerakaris
The Upper Gates Road, RFD 2
North Canaan, NH 03741
(603) 523-7366
V (by appt.)   R   S

the capitol building in Concord, New Hampshire, Dimitri found the challenge irresistible. "There was no direct precedent for an iron gateway of this magnitude," he recalls. "The restrictions were clear-cut. The gate had to visually unite the buildings of the historic district, replace a building fire-damaged beyond repair and be large enough to allow passage of a fire truck. The surrounding mid-19th century architecture was predominantly embellished with neoclassical motifs. I sought to bridge the gap between past and present by stylizing the elements. Rather than competing with nature, I constructed a fantasy tree. To make this 40- by 27-foot espaliered steel tree friendly, I added a gnome at child level hammering out the last detail, alongside a carved inscription that reads, 'Dedicated to the children of New Hampshire.' It took 9 months of intensive work. After it was assembled, I watched children of all ages clamber around the base of the tree and thought, 'What a great way to make a living!'"

Other Makers

Mark Bokenkamp, Bokenkamp's Forge, 10132 Liberty Road, Powell, OH 43065; (614) 889-0819.

Ned James, Mill River Hammerworks, 65 Canal Street, Turners Falls, MA 01376; (413) 863-8388.

G. Krug & Son, Inc., 415 West Saratoga Street, Baltimore, MD 21201; (301) 752-3166, has been in continuous operation since 1810, and is the oldest continuously working iron shop in America. They are capable of fabricating all types of ornamental iron for custom and historical restoration.

Nol Putnam, The White Oak Forge, P.O. Box 341, The Plains, VA 22171; (703) 253-5269.

Terry Steel, Blacksmith, North Road, Bridgton, ME 04009; (207) 647-8108, does creative traditional work, like making gates in the shape of a spider for writer Stephen King's residence.

Daniel Hurwitz, General Delivery, Brownsville, MD 21715; (301) 293-1168 or 432-2154, who made the gates at the Statue of Liberty, creates all kinds of ornamental iron on commission.

Cast Iron

Unlike wrought iron, which must be hammered by hand, cast iron is made by pouring molten metal into a sand mold. Before tin became available in the colonies, cast-iron cooking utensils were less expensive than those handmade of copper, brass and wrought iron. They also were durable, stood up well to heat and cold and didn't wear out. Once hot, cast iron retained heat, allowing cakes and bread to rise at a constant temperature; as it cooled down, it left a crunchy crust and a moist interior. Seasoned properly, iron didn't rust and contents didn't stick. Delicate and intricate parts could be made separately, then joined together. Combined with wrought iron, cast iron offered more flexibility in designing gates, fences, railings, hitching posts, urns, cemetery markers, furniture, architectural supports and ornamentation.

Lamb baking mold by The Country Iron Foundry

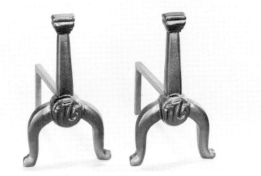

Andirons designed for a Philadelphia home by The Country Iron Foundry

Makers

The Country Iron Foundry, Box 600, Paoli, PA 19301; showroom, 1792 East Lancaster Pike; (215) 296-7122, makes baking molds, andirons, doorstops, footscrapers, banks, hitching posts, furniture and quoits used in lawn games.   C ($1 deductible from order)

Ray Zeleny, Windy Hill Forge, 3824 Schroder Avenue, Perry Hall, MD 21128; (301) 256-5890, makes fencing, shutter dogs (for holding shutters open), snow irons (also called snow birds) and wall washers (used for holding beams in walls) in old patterns.

IRON HINGES

"A hinge is simply a mechanical device with three basic parts," says Peter Renzetti, "the stationary part, called a rest or pivot; the pivot pin, or pintle; and the leaf, or barrel, which pivots on the pintle. Its earliest form was the snipe, or wire hinge, made from two wire staples, or cotter pins, that pivot at the loop end. After hinges developed a pintle and pivot, thousands of designs and patterns evolved, many of which were inspired by nature's forms, like horns, insects, flowers, trees and birds. There's no limit to design, but the function is basically the same. As skills and technology developed, more consideration was given to function, longevity, specific needs and space limitations."

To learn about colonial hardware, architectural students at the University of Pennsylvania go to Arden Forge, whose name came from the art colony where Peter was raised, and whose building was the site of the original Dilworthtown forge. A blacksmith by trade, a machinist by training, the self-sufficient Renzetti restored and reconstructed the 1735 stone building himself without tearing it down. In addition to doing most of the stone, concrete, brick and carpentry work, he also built the wood stove and carved the sign in the showroom.

"I was born with a hammer and a pair of pliers in my hand," he says, "and grew up in every garage in town." Born to two artists, a sculptor and an illustrator, Peter became fascinated by machinery at the age of 8, went on to learn tool-making, forged iron, industrial forging, dental instrument-making, silver- and goldsmithing, jewelry design, custom cabinetry, industrial and architectural model-building and sculpting before he went into business as a smith. Today, delighted that he makes a living at things he likes to do, he works with any metal but primarily iron, doing reproduction and restoration work on iron,

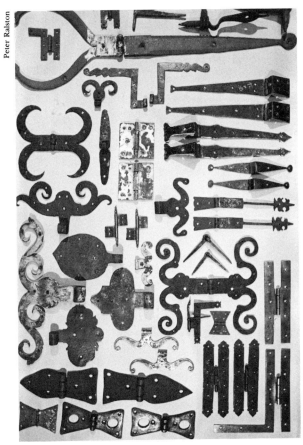

Peter Ralston

Assortment of Early American hinges by Peter A. Renzetti

Iron, by Albert H. Sonn (Bonanza Books), as a source of patterns for hardware. A client can then cite plate and page numbers, or supply us with a drawing and precise dimensions, or even the original to be copied. In addition to making every kind of architectural or domestic hardware, we also make rim locks in iron, steel or wood, weathervanes and carriage brakes and fabricate parts for antique cars. We take a great deal of pride in our craftsmanship and guarantee our work to be historically correct."

Using traditional methods, a large assortment of antique hand tools and several that he made himself, Peter hand-forges all hardware in mild steel but also has a good amount of wrought-iron stock for reproduction and restoration of historic sites and antique furniture. All objects come with a natural forged finish, with beeswax and linseed oil coating or a semiflat paint coating.

Most work is custom-ordered. In general, hinges range from $8 to $10 for a pair of hand-forged snipe hinges to $200 to $500 for ornate hinge sets of complex design or composition. H or H-L hinges start at $39 a pair; strap hinges, $35 a pair; butterfly and rattail hinges, $45 a pair.

"If we don't have what you want," says Peter, "we will make or find it for you." Showroom open Monday through Friday 9 A.M. to 5 P.M. and other times by appointment.

Peter A. Renzetti
The Arden Forge Co.
301 Brintons Bridge Road
West Chester, PA 19380
(215) 399-1530
V R S MO

Other Maker

Paul H. Spaulding, The Farmers' Museum, Inc., Lake Road, P.O. Box 800, Cooperstown, NY 13326; (607) 547-2593.

HOUSEHOLD IRON

Instead of turning heat up and down on a stove, early settlers raised and lowered pots over a fire with saw-toothed hangers called trammels, and swung them in and out with cranes. Rigs, cranks, turnspits and clock jacks turned the meat, while smoke jacks worked the chimney. Pans had long handles to keep hands from being burned, and tools had names describing what they did, like apple roaster, plate warmer, toaster and broiler. The connecting link for all the tools was not the hardware store but the village smith.

copper, tin, pewter, brass, bronze, lead, zinc and wood objects. His motto is: "If we can't fix it, it ain't broke."

His artistic, authentic ironwork can be seen in the Smithsonian, Plimouth Plantation, Winterthur, Eleutherian Mills, Hagley Museum and on Stephen Girard's Greek Revival house in Society Hill, Philadelphia. In addition to reconstructing old tools and architectural hardware for the National Park Service, he also makes latches, hinges and locks for antique dealers, restoration architects and builders.

"We have a large assortment of 18th and 19th century hardware available for restorations," says Peter. "It would be impractical if not impossible for us to catalog all the hinges we can make or supply as originals. We usually refer clients to the Bible of iron, *Early American Wrought*

Apple roaster by Ronald E. Potts

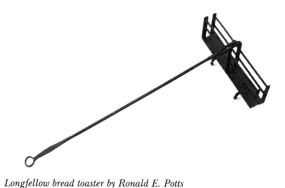

Longfellow bread toaster by Ronald E. Potts

Ronald E. Potts studied architecture, loved history, but never thought about becoming a blacksmith until he visited Colonial Williamsburg. Three years later, he quit his job and signed on as apprentice to John Allgood, the master smith in the colonial village. Now master of Chriswill Forge (named for his children, Christine and William),

Ron forges 17th and 18th century iron by hand using the same tools and techniques as colonial smiths.

"I could go twenty times faster and make much more money by using modern equipment," says Ron, "but I think preserving the craft is important. Once a craft has disappeared, the tools and techniques go with it. Besides, handmade iron is better than machine-made. In future years, my work will be more rare than that made in the colonial period because there are fewer blacksmiths now." He heats iron to 2,200°F in one of two coal/coke-fired forges, then hammers pieces into shape on an anvil. His wife, Bonnie Jean, helps with drilling, painting and merchandising, and their children handle booth sales when they go to fairs 120 days a year.

Wherever they go, they spend spare time exploring restorations to examine traditional iron firsthand. Their catalog now includes 350 objects. Prices start at $1.30 for hooks. They have ten types of sconces ($4.50 to $16), fifteen varieties of chandeliers ($25 to $90), twenty candlestands ($18 to $58), trivets ($15 to $22), andirons ($60), boot jacks ($10), puzzles ($6 to $8) and triangles (to call in children or farmhands, $10 to $22). They also make brackets, hooks, hinges, shutter dogs, latches, scrapers, brass-and-copper utensil sets and four types of Dutch crowns (circle and half-circle shapes with hooks for hanging pots, utensils or herbs). Their carefully researched wares include rush holders (lighting fixtures that burned meadow rush that was peeled, dried and dipped in tallow), splint holders (which burned wood splints of resinous pine) and Betty lamps (shallow metal containers used to hold melted oil or fat lit by wicks).

Each trip adds more. Their latest utensils include a bird spit (for cooking birds), plate warmers and grissettes (to

Virginia twelve-arm chandelier by Ronald E. Potts

hold melted fat for dipping rushes). For gentlemen who like to light their pipes the old-fashioned way with coals from the fire, Chriswill makes pipe tongs ($10).

"When I see something I've made at a restoration, I feel very close to the blacksmith whose work inspired it," says Ron, one reason he and Bonnie teach the history and craft of blacksmithing to fifth graders in Stark County, Ohio. "Children should know that history is more than presidents and wars," he explains. "It's being made every minute by people and they are part of it."

Ron Potts also does custom work of all kinds. Catalog cost of $2 is refundable on first order.

Ronald and Bonnie Potts
Chriswill Forge
2255 Manchester (State Route 93)
North Lawrence, OH 44666
(216) 832-9136
V   R   W   C   S   CC   MO

Other Makers

Michael J. Saari, Childs Hill Road, Woodstock, CT 06281; (203) 928-0257.

Walt Scadden, 22 Warren Street, Manchester, CT 06040; (203) 646-8363.

Tom Summers, The Forge, 14624 South Gallatin Boulevard, Brook Park, OH 44142; (216) 676-4647.

Robert Bourdon, The Smithy, Wolcott, VT 05680; (802) 472-6508.

Michael Snyder, P.O. Box 60, Harmon, WV 26270; (304) 227-4565.

David W. Osmundsen, Arrowhead Forge, RFD 2, Box 214, Belfast, ME 04915; (207) 338-2222.

Hayne & Son Forged Hardware, 76 Daniel Ridge Road, Candler, NC 28715; (704) 667-8888.

K & M Forge, P.O. Box 65, McConnellsville, NY 13401; (315) 245-0809.

INLAID IRON AND WHITESMITHING

"Whitesmithed objects have always been more prized than regular iron," says Thomas Loose, whose whitesmithing is often compared to that of Peter Derr, who worked from 1840 to 1860 near where Tom does now. "People could get regular iron anytime, but whitesmithing was saved for special things like utensils in a young girl's dowry."

During the process of heating and hammering iron, a black scale forms on the surface. When this scale is removed by filing, the metal turns silvery white. The metal

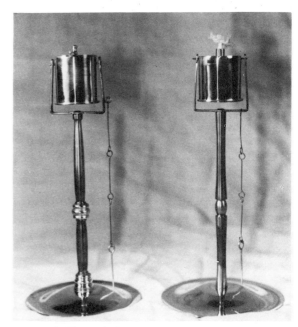

Fat lamps by Thomas G. Loose

is then further refined by polishing, incising, embellishing with other metals like copper and brass in overlay or inlay and cutting out iron to leave a design.

A ninth generation Pennsylvania-German in a long line of blacksmiths, Tom says, "My grandfather could make anything from iron, but although his work was good and useful, it wasn't fine like that of Peter Derr, who consistently took ordinary items a step further. I've made just about everything that can be made from iron, but the most difficult by far was a fat lamp in the style of Peter Derr. Although it had the basic shape of a Betty, or fat, lamp, its hinged lid in brass and copper had little turned knobs and a wick pick decorated with incised lines. He was a master, always in search of perfection."

With the advent of the industrial revolution and mass production, the whitesmith faded from the scene and the blacksmith's role changed dramatically. Instead of creating items for the home, blacksmiths spent most of their time repairing tools and shoeing horses. When Tom began blacksmithing in 1969, he asked his grandfather about techniques as he assembled his tools and equipment, a great deal of which had belonged to his ancestors. He also began collecting old iron. "Most of it was ordinary and made to serve a purpose," he says, "but one in a hundred was special, nicely done, sometimes with punch-

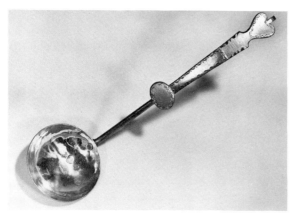

Ladle with heart handle by Thomas G. Loose

work, inlay or overlay. I decided I wanted my work to be like that: treasured and living on after me.''

Using the two basic tools of the blacksmith, the hammer and anvil, Tom makes authentic Pennsylvanian pieces, most of which are inlaid or overlaid with brass or iron in the old tradition. His most popular designs, used on blades

as well as handles of utensils, are the heart and tulip. Pennsylvanians also like blanket chest hinges and escutcheons in shapes of hearts, tulips, fish and birds. Pump handles, fireplace implements and andirons are sometimes decorated with sixteen-sided ball knobs, ''which serve no purpose except decoration,'' says Tom. Wedding-band hogscraper candlesticks, made from iron with a brass ring, are another popular wedding gift in his region. ''It's the same design as a hogscraper,'' explains Tom. ''If the base were on a wooden handle, it could be used to scrape hair off a hog in butchering. In fact, I've repaired old ones that still had hog hair in the push-up mechanism.''

His favorite type of customer tells Tom what he wants, then waits, giving him time to experiment as he goes. He recently delivered a seven-piece ladle set ordered 3 years ago, with copper inlay, overlay and designs of snakes and birds. ''My best work takes time, weeks of long days, trying to figure out the best way,'' says Tom. ''Luckily, iron can be reworked and mistakes don't have to be thrown away or burned like wood.'' He rewards himself for long winter days by working shorter shifts in summer so that he can go fishing.

Although he has no sign, no shop, doesn't advertise and is open by appointment only, clients continue to find him. His work (signed T. Loose) has been featured in the Smithsonian catalog and is shown annually at the Kutztown Festival. His wedding-band hogscraper candlesticks in four sizes range from $37 to $53; forks, $14 to $95; and food choppers in whimsical animal shapes, $20 to $27. Everything he makes is available in miniature as well as in graduated sizes. For a copy of his current catalog, send a self-addressed, stamped envelope.

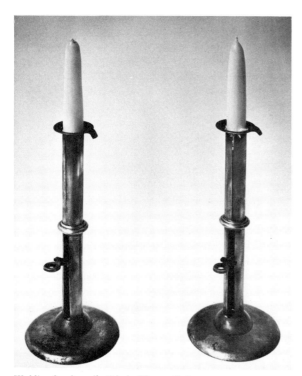

Wedding-band candlesticks by Thomas G. Loose

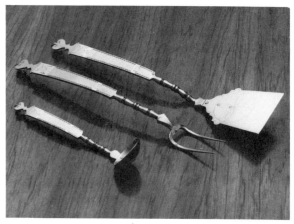

Three utensils—ladle, fork and spatula—of a seven-piece set by Mark Bokenkamp

Thomas G. Loose
RD 2, Box 2410
Leesport, PA 19533
(215) 926-4849
V (by appt. only)   R   W   C   MO

Other Makers

Mark Bokenkamp, Bokenkamp's Forge, 10132 Liberty Road, Powell, OH 43065; (616) 880-0819.

Paul H. Spaulding, The Farmers' Museum, Inc., Lake Road, P.O. Box 800, Cooperstown, NY 13326; (607) 547-2593.

IRON NAILS AND LATCHES

In the early days of the mid-Atlantic colonies, skilled labor was scarce and expensive. What settlers lacked in skill, they made up in nails. More nails went into a single room in a Virginia-style house built then than into an entire house built today. Because nails were costly and tedious to make, owners often set houses on fire before moving so they could gather up the nails from the ashes. To stop this destruction, Virginia passed a law forbidding the practice and offered each owner as many nails as the dwelling contained in return for not burning it down.

Assortment of iron nails of different sizes, shapes and heads by Woodbury Blacksmith & Forge Co.

Before 1790 nails were made by hand and were not manufactured in volume by machine until about 1830. Although Thomas Jefferson had two slaves making nails for buildings at Monticello, many families made their own nails over the fireplace from a supply of nail rods cut into short lengths, using tongs and a hammer. While the iron was hot, the maker drew out a point, tapered the shank, leaving thickness for the head, cut it to size, then inserted it into a "header," where the nub was hammered into a head with a few quick blows.

If the prospect of restoring a period house by such means sounds like work, consider the task confronting the state of Maryland in reconstructing St. Mary's City (c. 1634). Not one original building remained. Most of the work of rebuilding ten authentic structures was done at the site, but clinch nails, pintles to hang hinges and doors, as well as reproductions of original cockshead H-hinges were made by Woodbury Blacksmith & Forge Co. in Connecticut.

"Authentic restoration is our specialty," says co-owner Charles Euston. "We forge 17th, 18th and early 19th century hardware from mild steel or wrought iron, by hand and original methods." Their attention to detail has brought an ever-growing flow of clients including restorationists, the National Park Service, Minute Man National Historic Park, John Adams's Quincy, Massachusetts, birthplace and builders who dismantle, move and rebuild early structures.

In addition to rosehead and T-head nails (headed and pointed, as well as headed only) in lengths of 1 to 4 inches, Woodbury makes hardware, utensils, fireplace equipment, lighting devices and as many kinds of thumb latches as there were original colonies. Their Suffolk latches (which fastened American doors from the 16th to the 18th century) are forged from a single bar of iron, and consist of an upper and lower cusp with a thumb-press protruding from a slot in the cusp. The most common cusp design, 6 to 9 inches long, resembled a lima bean, while many of the most ornate styles were made in the Connecticut Valley. With filed accents, spade, arrow and heart motifs, some are as long as 30 inches ($34 to $70). Woodbury also makes spring latches; H, H-L, butterfly, Moravian, rattail and ram's-horn hinges; bolts, hasps, hooks, shutter dogs and five types of Norfolk latches (the successor to the Suffolk type).

Woodbury Forge was started by former investment banker Donald Goss on the Fourth of July, 1976, in a barn that was once a repair garage and warehouse. Former teacher Charlie Euston, who excavated a blacksmith shop for Sturbridge Village in Massachusetts and renovated an early smith's shop in New Jersey, is now co-owner. When

Suffolk door latch by Woodbury Blacksmith & Forge Co.

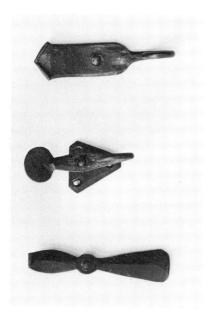

Shutter dogs by Woodbury Blacksmith & Forge Co.

famed blacksmith Donald Streeter retired a few years ago, he selected the Woodbury Blacksmith & Forge Co. to carry on his work. Since then, they have made arrangements to acquire his catalog, tools and patterns. With an extensive library on 18th and 19th century hardware and ironwork, a showroom with a full array of their products, and tea in the late afternoon, Woodbury Forge is as close to heaven as an iron connoisseur can get.

Woodbury Blacksmith & Forge Co.
P.O. Box 268
161 Main Street
Woodbury, CT 06798
(203) 263-5737
V   R   C ($2)   S   MO

SOUTHWESTERN COLONIAL IRON

Blacksmiths arriving with settlers in the upper Rio Grande Valley in the late 1500s had to be armorers, gunsmiths and locksmiths as well. In addition to household utensils, hardware, wagon fittings and tools for farming and mining, they had to know how to make and repair armor, chain mail, knives, lances, shackles, cuffs, chains, fetters and padlocks. Although armor was losing favor in Europe at the time, conquistadores needed it as protection from native weapons. The first Spanish expedition carried blacksmith tools, a dozen files for horseshoeing and 50 pounds of iron, for without shoes for their horses, exploration would soon cease.

"Iron was always scarce and constantly recycled," says smith Frank Turley, coauthor of *Southwestern Colonial Ironwork.* "Worn iron tires were a frequent source of wrought iron over the centuries. Made in varying thicknesses and widths to fit around wooden felloes (rims), spokes and hub, the tires were straightened and reworked into other items. Three of the forty-three *carretas* [small carts pulled by oxen] in the first expedition had iron tires, and records show they carried ten spares."

Because iron was scarce and expensive, colonists often substituted wood for iron in the making of grilles, handles and hinges. When iron was available, the snipe hinge was used on doors, trunks and shutters; the strap hinge for heavier weights; and the jointed hinge (rings joining leather straps) for even more economy in iron. Large wooden doors were bolted with *trancas* (crossbars), while heavy double doors were secured with the hinged, T-shaped *cerrojo.* Large nail washers called bosses, or *chatónes,* were added for decoration and extra strength. Thumb latches similar to those used in the East were more ornate in design, and locks were plainer than those in Mexico but often had pierced or filed edges.

Joan Neary

Hispanic chest lock and key by Frank Turley

Thumb-latch parts, disassembled, by Frank Turley

"Aside from some differences in overall shapes, southwestern iron often has unique edge-filed patterns," says Frank. "Workers in the Southwest also used small stamped designs, most frequently the crescent and asterisk (or stamped rosette) similar to those used by Navajo silversmiths. Most hardware designs show Hispanic and Indian influence."

After graduating from Michigan State in 1959, Frank came to blacksmithing "through the backdoor of horseshoeing." He apprenticed under five master smiths; was the first recipient of the Alex W. Bealer Award from the Artist Blacksmiths' Association of North America; restored colonial ironware and guns at the Museum of New Mexico where he was conservator; made hardware for the Missions of San Jose, California, and the Santuario de Guadalupe, New Mexico; and founded the Turley Forge Blacksmithing School.

Turley's hardware, normally forged of carbon steel or wrought iron, is often given a beeswax/turpentine finish baked into the hot metal surface. Before installation, pieces receive two coats of paste floor wax and are lightly buffed, or if needed, three coats of primer and paint for a more permanent finish.

"Iron is unforgiving," Frank will tell you. "One must really strike while the iron is hot. But I enjoy the immediacy of the work as well as the mind/body integration in the movement and process."

Frank's increased awareness of how relaxed body movement and proper breathing affect work and health is now offered in a course at the forge. Although he says he'll never publish a catalog because it would be "self-limiting and constricting," brochures are available on the school and the line of farriers' forging tools that he makes. All commission work is custom-designed for the job at hand. Hours are 8 A.M. to 5 P.M. Monday through Friday.

Frank Turley
Turley Forge
Route 10, Box 88C
Santa Fe, NM 87501
(505) 471-8608
V   R   MO

Hasp and cottered eye by Frank Turley

IRON TOOLS, LOCKS AND COOKING UTENSILS

The 18th century blacksmith had to be both more versatile and more specialized than any other artisan because every craft and trade, from carpenters and stone masons to silversmiths and surgeons, depended on the smith for tools, implements and hardware. While the rural smith often produced a little of everything, more skilled smiths tended to specialize as farriers, shipsmiths, locksmiths, gunsmiths, cutlers, armorers, architectural smiths or tool makers.

"In addition to agricultural tools and implements," explains Paul Spaulding, "the rural smith produced woodworking tools such as hammers, axes, chisels and drawknives, but lacked the facilities and manpower to produce quantities needed to meet the overall demand. He also often lacked the skill and materials necessary to produce finer, more delicate tools. Most blacksmiths' forges were too small to make larger tools, so a few shops specialized in making anvils, vises and forging tools used by other smiths.

"Colonial tool steel was very expensive, hard to forge and in limited supply. Instead of solid steel, most tools were made of wrought iron with a tool steel face or edge welded on, depending on the type of tool. Most edged tools, from small plane blades to broadaxes, were made of iron with a steel 'bit' welded on for the cutting edge. Tools that needed rigidity and strength, like knives, springs, saw blades and drill bits, as well as items too small to weld, were made of solid steel."

Before Paul became the smith at the Farmers' Museum in Cooperstown, New York, he apprenticed at Mystic Seaport Museum in Connecticut and was a consultant to Onondaga County, New York, at the recreated 17th century site of Ste. Marie de Gannentaha. Today, using designs, techniques and tools of the 18th and 19th centuries, Paul specializes in making tools from unalloyed tool steel of virtually the same composition as high-grade cast steel.

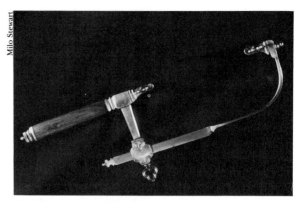

Jeweler's saw by Paul Spaulding

He works with original equipment in an 1827 stone blacksmith shop at the Farmers' Museum. The building has two stone forges, each equipped with bellows, anvil, leg vise, cone mandrel and stake anvil. The shop also has a tool bench, treadle metal/wood lathe, swage block (a shaping tool), post drill and tire bender. The forge makes small ornate carved tools and implements of 17th, 18th and 19th century design: chisels and gouges for woodworking; chisels for steel carving; tools and hammers for engraving, repoussé and chasing; drawknives; scorps; spokeshave irons; froes; hatchets; slicks; bow drills; and spoon bits. "We also produce household hardware and utensils," says Paul, "particularly whitesmithed cooking utensils and small decorative implements in small quantities."

In addition to producing a wide variety of ironwork for use in exhibits and craft areas of the museum and for sale at the museum's General Store, the forge makes iron for individuals, restorations and historical associations. Sales are retail only, although a 10 percent discount is given on large orders during the museum's off-season. Suffolk latches start at $25; strap hinges begin at $18 a pair; ram's-horn hinges, $70 a pair; whitesmithed cooking utensils, $20 to $100 each.

Cooperstown also has an apprenticeship program that stresses techniques of the 18th and 19th centuries, including advanced forging techniques, design, layout, forge welding, tool-making and finishing.

Paul H. Spaulding, Blacksmith
The Farmers' Museum, Inc.
Lake Road, P.O. Box 800
Cooperstown, NY 13326
(607) 547-2593
V   R   W   S   MO

Hatchet head, 18th century type, by Paul Spaulding

Utensil set by Paul Spaulding

***Jerga* Weavings   *See* Embroidery, *Colcha, and* Weaving, Rio Grande**

AFRICAN-AMERICAN JEWELRY

Stripped of their rights and possessions, African slaves had little to cling to but each other when they arrived in America. Although many African-Americans scorned or ignored their cultural traditions, segregated communities kept the old ways.

"Many early medicinal practices like wrapping herbs onto the body were translated into jewelry and other forms of adornment," says Cledie C. Taylor, jewelry designer, assistant director of the Children's Museum in Detroit, Michigan, and previously supervisor of art education in the Detroit public schools. "Originally, ears were pierced and earrings worn to prevent blindness; silver coins worn around the neck or ankle to protect against colds and arthritis; copper wire around the ankle for tuberculosis;

two nutmeg on a string around the neck for heart trouble. When metals were not available, African-Americans made jewelry of natural fibers, hair, found objects, shells, coins and seeds. A large palm seed, hardened and sliced, looks much like ivory."

Over the years, the cultural memory of African-Americans has had a strong impact on American design and style. A few of the results: Afro hairdos, shaved heads for women, multi-pierced ears, the use of coins and found objects in jewelry construction, the wearing of multiple chains and necklaces, bangle bracelets, dangle earrings for daytime wear, head pendants, ankle bracelets, toe rings, wide armlets, choker necklaces and wrapping, twisting and coiling techniques.

"Because there were no complete written languages," Dr. Taylor continues, "some symbols, like the Adinkira cloth pattern stamps of the Ashanti with developed symbolic meanings, have become a rich source of design elements, as have scar and ceremonial cuts once used on the skin for clan identification and protection against intermarriage. Another contemporary style, the pairing of bracelets (which gave the bangle its sound and name) is an outgrowth of the African proverb, 'One plus one equals three,' which refers to the procreative results of pairing."

Cledie had always been interested in art but did not discover crafts until after graduation from Wayne State University. Then curiosity about the process of niello (an alloy of silver and sulphur used to inlay or decorate metal) led her to metal and constructed forms.

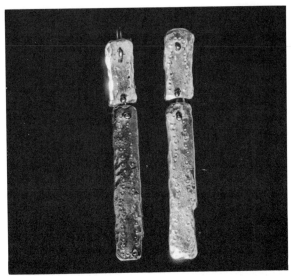

Hammered and forged gold rose earrings, with decoratively punched surface that parallels skin markings made by tribal scarring, by Cledie C. Taylor

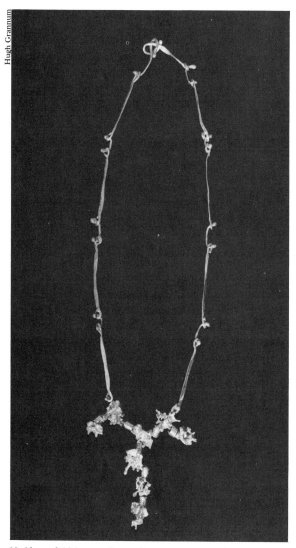

Hugh Grammum

Necklace of 18-karat yellow gold, gravity cast with constructed and fused chain, by Cledie C. Taylor

"My favorite method is construction," says Cledie. "The African-American traditions of twisting, wrapping and coiling are not only decorative, they're an economical way to build heavier shapes from thinner metals, which in turn keeps my work more affordable. I work in any metal, mostly silver with gems and gold in combinations of green, white, rose and yellow. I love yellow gold, especially 18 karat, which works like butter. Most of my jewelry is designed to be jointed, moving and sounding. It lives a life of its own, yet moves in concert with the wearer."

Cledie's knowledge of the shapes, symbols, practices and techniques of her African-American heritage, like the contextual language of her ancestors, is finding its own audience. Included in exhibits, publications and collections, it is worn by celebrities like Lena Horne, Beah Richards and Angela Davis. Most of her work has an historic prototype. A necklace of flat, round, silver disks in the collection of silversmith Ronald Pearson is a modern-day version of curative coins on a string, while a necklace of large open disks has its roots in African embroidery and brass breast medallions.

For all the work and thought that go into its creation, Cledie's jewelry is reasonably priced, especially since she will repair it for life. Gold earrings range in price from $100 to $300; gold necklaces from $300 to $450.

Cledie C. Taylor
1553 Woodward, Suite 201
Detroit, MI 48226
(313) 961-5036
R   W   S   MO

PLAINS INDIAN JEWELRY

Mitchell Zephier, the foremost Native American jeweler of the Northern Plains, stamps only his best work P.V.H., for Pretty Voice Hawk, the name he shares with his great-grandfather, a medicine man who dealt with the spiritual realm. To carry the name of an esteemed ancestor is an honor but also adds the responsibility for never misusing the name. Mitchell takes this personal commitment into his business as well. In his company, Lakota Jewelry Visions, he employs and involves as many Lakota (Indian for Sioux) as possible. When he first started making jewelry in 1973, he used only nickel silver (also known as German silver, an alloy of copper, nickel and zinc that actually has no silver content) because it was less expensive than silver and could be afforded by more of his people. He feels it is important that the Lakota know and preserve their craft heritage. "The Plains Indians created metal work before the Southwest tribes," he explains, "but for cultural and personal use rather than for sale like the Navajos. Everyone's work was considered fine art. Although it was made to be functional, it was also beautiful."

His first jewelry, made when he was 20 for the grandmother who raised him after his parents died, was a pair of earrings, whose buffalo figures were cut from nickels. The buffalo holds significance in his life as well as his designs. "Buffalo are noncompetitive," says Mitchell. "They work together as a herd to survive."

His work has been exhibited in many American mu-

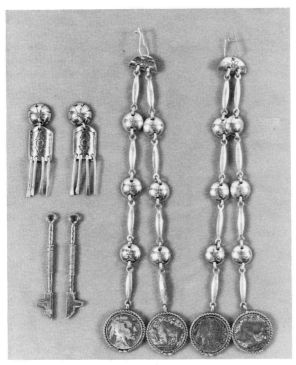

Silver pendant earrings made of Indian symbols and buffalo head nickels by Mitchell Zephier

Silver design of Indian on horseback with polished native stone inset by Mitchell Zephier

seums including the Smithsonian Institution, the Museum of the American Indian, Harvard's Peabody Museum and the Heard Museum in Phoenix. Today he works in all metals, but his catalog, "The Gift from Mother Earth," clearly defines his intent and direction. In both traditional and contemporary jewelry, Mitchell prefers natural value to precious metals and jewels. For settings, he cuts and polishes native stones like Wyoming jade, Tipi Canyon agate, blood jasper, rose quartz and red and black pipestone. To soften designs, he sometimes uses feathers, leather, horsehair and bear and eagle claws.

Most Zephier designs reflect movement and love of the earth (particularly the sacred places of the Black Hills of South Dakota). They symbolize a concept or tell a story or legend. "A necklace I made called My Song to the Four Directions best sums up my work," he says. "It shows a man with a pipe in his hand standing on a hill. He's on a vision quest, seeking guidance, direction, deeper meaning or a message." Another design, called All My Relations, refers not just to his family, but to animals and plants as well. Many designs feature animals: horses, antelopes, coyotes, deer, turtles, buffalo and eagles. "To

have the heart of an eagle," says Mitchell, "is to strive for higher knowledge, above ordinary things of life." Also important to him is how his jewelry moves when worn (for example, earrings should accentuate movement as a woman dances).

Mitchell Zephier's signed work ranges in price from $150 for a broach or pendant to $4,500 and more for *concha* belts. His production line includes pins and earrings from $9 to $45 and pendants from $20 to $80. He also makes armbands, rings, crosses, breastplates (pectorals), rings and bracelets. Catalog $4, refunded on first order over $100.

Mitchell Zephier
Lakota Jewelry Visions
P.O. Box 5158
Rapid City, SD 57709
(605) 348-0359
V (by appt.)   R   W   C   S   MO

Other Maker

Joe Begay, Old Town Artisans, 186 North Meyer Avenue, Tucson, AZ 85701; (602) 573-0181, a Navajo Indian, makes jewelry in the Navajo tradition.

KAPA CLOTH

Kapa, the Hawaiian term for *tapa,* or bark, cloth, is made from the beaten and felted inner white bark of the wauke plant (*Brousonetia papyrifera,* or paper mulberry) and decorated with various native plant dyes by several methods of design application.

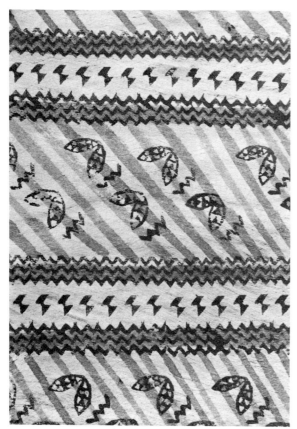

Kapa design of shark's teeth with little maile leaves by Hale Kuku O Moanalua

"Each Polynesian group has their own term for bark cloth," says Wesley Sen, who began research and experimentation in *kapa* a few years ago. "We learned much from Mrs. Mary Pritchard of American Samoa and Dr. Beatrice Krauss of the Lyon Arboretum. In ancient Hawaii, *kapa* was used to make receiving blankets for newborns, loincloths for men (*malo*), wraparound skirts for women (*pa'u*), blankets (*kapa moe*) and burial shrouds. *Kapa* consisted of four plain watermarked sheets with the fifth and top sheet decorated. Eighteenth century *kapa* used for everyday clothing was similar to bark cloth made in other parts of Polynesia except that it was not pasted together but sewn to make the desired size of cloth. The finer watermark *kapa* is similar to the *kapa moe* made in the early 1800s."

In summer, when days are dry and hot, the wauke bark is harvested, stripped from the stick and the outer bark peeled off. The white bark is soaked in sea water for ten

to twenty days until soft, when it is beaten on a smooth stone with a *hohoa* (round-grooved beater). After drying and bleaching in the sun, it is soaked in water and left damp in banana leaves to ferment. When the bark is soft and slimy, it is taken to a wooden anvil (*kukua*) and beaten with an *i'e kuku* (square-grooved beater) into a sheet of cloth. The finished material is dried in the sun and, after being beaten smooth, the soft *kapa* is decorated by using different methods like bamboo stamps (*ohe kapala*), cord-rubbing (*ahapi'i*) and bamboo lines (*lapa*).

"Through research," says Wes, "I developed *kukui* root dye from root shavings of the *kukui* [candlenut tree], which grows in abundance in the mountains above Honolulu. After the pulpy outer bark is scraped off, it is strained. For black, early Hawaiians used either this dye or *kukui* nut oil mixed with black soot from burned *kukui* nuts. Designs are cut into the inner side of bamboo strips with wood-block carving tools. To carve out beaters, we use a combination of ancient and modern tools: shark's teeth, basalt lava chips, iron files and a steel adz. Prior to the early 1800s, most designs were hand-painted with bamboo pens and liners. After the introduction of metal tools, Hawaiians invented bamboo stamps to print *kapa*."

In traditional village culture, the master craftsperson had relatives and friends to help with the labor-intensive work. Today, Wes is the chief craftsman of Hale Kuku O Moanalua, a group that makes and decorates *kapa* with traditional tools and techniques. This includes cultivation of the wauke, tool- and implement-making, collecting and preparing dyes, research, experimentation and preservation.

"I receive a real sense of closeness with nature through my work," says Wes. "It has helped me to appreciate what God has given to us to make a living. What I make comes

Kapa handbags by Hale Kuku O Moanalua

from the land and the land gets its life from God. What I make will also be returned to the land, continuing the timeless cycle of our islands.''

A sheet of watermarked, hand-stamped *kapa* 24 by 34 inches is $200; hula costumes made of *kapa* without watermark start at $50 for a *pa'u* (wraparound skirt). Wall hangings are priced by type of material and decoration. The work of Hale Kuku O Moanalua is for sale at the Bishop Museum, Kauai Museum, Mission House in Honolulu, Maui Museum and Volcano Art Center. Commissions are handled by Betty Harrison Interiors.

> Hale Kuku O Moanalua
> c/o Betty Harrison Interiors
> P.O. Box 4555
> Kawaihae, HI 96743
> (808) 882-7070
> R   W   MO

Other Maker
Pua Van Dorpe, Box 12435, Lahaina Maui, HI 96761.

Knifework   *See* **Carving, Tramp Art**

QIVIUT YARN KNITWEAR

If you know Alaskan symbols, you'll be able to recognize where an article of qiviut was made by its pattern. And if you buy an article made of qiviut, you'll know who made it by the name on the card enclosed with every piece of wearing apparel.

Qiviut? This strange word (pronounced ki-vee-ute) means "down" or "underwool" in the Eskimo language. In English, it describes the grayish-brown or mauve wool of that rare Arctic animal, the domesticated musk ox (which does not give musk and is not closely related to cattle). The only domesticated herd in the world lives in Alaska, and the only place that articles made from this rare textile fiber can be purchased is the Musk Ox Producers' Co-operative in Anchorage.

The wool, which makes lacy garments eight times warmer than wool by weight, grows close to the skin of musk oxen to protect them from wind and bitter Arctic temperatures. Protected by the long guard hairs, which swing like hula skirts when the animal runs, qiviut works its way through the outer guard hairs in the spring and hangs in untidy soft clumps until it drops off or is combed off by a herder. A grown musk ox produces from 4 to 6 pounds of qiviut a year, while a cashmere goat produces only 3 ounces of cashmere. However, qiviut is rarer than

Star cap worn with tunic by Musk Ox Producers' Co-operative

Bethel smoke ring or nachaq *by Musk Ox Producers' Co-operative*

Hip-length tunic, or taqmaq, *by Musk Ox Producers' Co-operative*

cashmere, while comparing favorably with it for softness, warmth and lightness.

After the qiviut is cleaned and spun into strong yarn, it is distributed by bush-plane mail to 150 to 200 knitters in thirteen villages, where it is knit in seven different village or area patterns. Mekoryuk has a triple-harpoon pattern derived from a 1,200-year-old ivory harpoon head; Shishmaref, a star design taken from a beaded mukluk (or boot) top; Marshall, a geometric pattern taken from a woven grass basket; and Unalakleet, a wolverine pattern derived from a mask. Knitters work at their own speed and are paid for finished garments by the number of stitches in the work. Items are then washed, blocked, labeled, packaged and marketed, both retail and wholesale.

The co-op's most popular item is the *nachaq*, a circular Eskimo scarf worn as a mantilla, as a cowl or draped around the shoulders, for $95. Unlike lace or silk, qiviut does not slip off. Other items include a hip-length tunic, or *taqmaq*, for $350; berets and caps for $55 to $85;

scarves, $135 to $195; and stoles, $210. Each item is enclosed in a plastic bag or a box with a gold card signed by the knitter and marked with the sign of the village where it was made.

While only the finest, lightest cashmere can pass through a finger ring, all qiviut scarves can, including the 6-foot-long muffler. Another advantage to qiviut is that it doesn't smell like wool when wet. Unlike other animals, the musk ox has no sweat glands. If you buried your head in its fur when it was wet, you would smell only water.

The Musk Ox Producers' Co-operative, the only place that sells these rare garments, prefers to be known as OOMINGMAK, which in the Eskimo language means "musk ox" or "the bearded one." Their shop is open Monday through Friday from 10 A.M. to 5 P.M. year-round and on Saturdays during the summer and Christmas season. They accept VISA, Mastercard and American Express.

Musk Ox Producers' Co-operative
604 H Street
Anchorage, AK 99501
(907) 272-9225
V R W C S CC MO

WOOL KNITWEAR

"My great-grandmother kept a flock of sheep on their farm in the Missouri Ozarks between 1880 and 1910," says Catherine Cartwright-Jones. "She had no spinning wheel, so a neighbor did the spinning in return for a share of the wool. With all she had to do, she still knit socks for her thirteen children. My grandmother said they used to beg for longer, more fashionable stockings, but she refused to knit them past the knee because they wore out too soon."

The spinning and knitting skills skipped two generations until Catherine's husband taught her to knit in 1969. "I studied weaving as a pictorial arts major at UCLA," says Catherine, "and found traditional textiles satisfying. I personally dislike anything not basically useful. Wool makes sense. Sweaters make sense. I like that. I also like meticulous detail. Repetitive manual things allow me to daydream and sort life mentally while my fingers are busy. My work aims at the ideas of the preindustrial revolution cottage knitters of the 18th century. I use real wool (mill-spun if affordability is important) and patterns from 16th, 17th and 18th century peasant textiles. Many farms near where I live have a small flock. People bring me raw fleeces or carded batts to spin. If I have a fine healthy staple, I sort and clip, take several locks in hand, tease gently and

Hand-knit sweaters in traditional patterns, of hand-spun wool in hand-dyed colors, by Catherine Cartwright-Jones

Stockings and leggings in traditional patterns, of hand-spun wool in natural colors, by Catherine Cartwright-Jones

spin worsted wool. This is the hard-wearing glossy yarn made from fibers all lying the same way. I spin S-twist, ply Z-twist for 2-ply yarn. If the client wants a classic Nordic, I will either hand-dye the yarn or seek a black fleece to complete the pattern. When a client brings a carded batt, I spin 'woolen' yarn. This is loftier, warmer yarn, but not as durable. Woolen yarn is spun from fibers carded every which way. The microspaces of this tangle are more insulative. I wash all my wool in cool water with mild detergent (shampoo is dandy) and rinse in cool water with vinegar to bring out the glossiness.''

Catherine knits sweaters, caps, mittens, vests and stockings in "guaranteed historical" designs and patterns brought to America from small towns in Norway, Sweden, Germany, Denmark and Austria. A family in Iowa recently commissioned sweaters for all the great-grandchildren in patterns the great-grandmother brought with her from Norway, in two colors of gray and white wool from their own sheep.

"Homespun sweaters are more tactilely impressive than photogenic," she says. "My husband's brown quarterbred merino socks may look irregular, but they feel like faerie. People get saucer-eyed when they touch hand-knits and gasp, 'I never knew wool could feel like this!' "

Catherine's knits in millspun or homespun, your fleece or hers, are priced as follows: women's sweaters, $50 (small, millspun) to $240 (large, homespun); men's, $55 (small, millspun) to $310 (XL, homespun). Extras include: $15 for cardigan style, $15 for raglan sleeves and $8 for pewter buttons. Women's vests range from $25 (small, millspun) to $140 (large, homespun), while men's are $30 (small, millspun) to $180 (XL homespun). Other items include: mittens ($12.50 to $50), caps ($7.50 to $30), stockings ($25 to $100) and leggings ($12.50 to $50). Catherine also makes pure silk sweaters for those with allergies.

If you want to design your own sweater, send $2 for a kit with fifty patterns and yarn samples. A "knit-to-fit" kit with ten custom-made sweater designs is $1, and a catalog $1.50 with a self-addressed, stamped envelope. Sweaters are guaranteed to fit or are reblocked free. "I also hand-spin fleeces for hand or machine knitters for $5 an hour," says Catherine, "and chart new patterns at the same rate. If someone must have orlon, I'll use it, but I'll snarl about it."

Catherine Cartwright-Jones
4237 Klein Avenue
Stow, OH 44224
(216) 688-0303
V (by appt.)   R   W   C   MO

Other Makers

The Ladies Aid of the Methodist Church, % Diane Calder, Chebeague Island, ME 04017, makes fishermen's mittens and sells them for $22 (postage included) as a fundraiser. Fishermen prefer mittens because they allow more movement of fingers, and wool because it holds warmth when wet. Made of 3-ply natural fisherman yarn, they are knit large, then shrunk until they are matted and dense, half again as heavy as worsted weight.

Alice Stough, Route 1, Box 405, Millstone, WV 25261; (304) 354-7531, does traditional knitting and spinning.

Unique 1, 2 Bay View Street, Camden, ME 04843, specializes in sweaters hand-knit from 100 percent natural Maine wool.

The John C. Campbell Folk School, Brasstown, NC 28902; (704) 837-2775, has handmade sweaters, vests and hats of vegetable-dyed yarns.   C ($1.50)

Bowie knife by William Moran

BOWIE KNIVES

An early colonist was seldom without his knife. He used it for defense, hunting and skinning hides, as well as for preparing and eating food. Each nationality brought its own style of knife to America, and it was not until the Bowie knife that a truly American knife came into being. Used by Colonel James Bowie before his death at the Battle of the Alamo, and probably invented by his brother Rezin, the Bowie knife was made of heavy, single-edged steel with a slanted point. It was from 9 to 16 inches long and so well balanced that it could be thrown with great accuracy. Originally designed for the frontier as a weapon and tool, the Bowie knife was used by heroes like Davy Crockett and Buffalo Bill.

"Until the Bowie," says William Moran, a founder and now president of the American Bladesmith Society, "most European types had large guards to protect the hand from being struck by another's blade. The Bowie almost always had a guard but it was small: just large enough to keep the hand from sliding down the blade. Although many think of the Bowie as a weapon, because it was used by both sides in the Civil War, it was actually a camp or trail knife. Usually worn on the belt, sometimes stuck under the belt or hung in a sheath like a sword, some had elaborate inlays while others were plain, depending on the taste and purse of the owner. After 30 or 40 years, its use died out until World War II, when it was used for jungle fighting in the South Pacific. It remained popular through the Korean and Vietnam Wars."

Bill, who has been called the greatest bladesmith of the

20th century, made his first knife in the blacksmith shop on his father's farm in 1935 when he was 10 years old. In 1945, when he couldn't find a large camp knife in the stores, he began making them professionally.

"From the 1940s until about 1968," he says, "there was only a handful of bladesmiths in America making custom knives. Today there are hundreds. Knife-making has become an American art form." Credited with being the first in the United States to make Damascus steel, which alternates hundreds of ultrathin layers of iron and steel, Moran hand-forges classic knives from the finest tool steels (containing vanadium, which gives a finer grain structure and makes a tougher blade). Handles are made of curly maple, rosewood, stag horn, ivory or ebony, often inlaid with silver wire work.

"To forge a blade takes great skill, knowledge of steel and heat ranges," he says. "Great care must be taken not to overheat the steel. I use a technique known as hammer-hardening or packing. After the blade is forged almost to the finished shape, the blade is hammered at a rather low heat with rapid, light blows. This causes the grain to be better aligned and the steel to be more compact. After forging to shape, the blade is ground by hand close to its finished size, then heat treated so that the edge will be much harder than the back. All my regular steel blades are triple-drawn, which gives the same result as super-chilling and adds greatly to the quality. The blade is then ground to its final thickness and goes through six polishing operations, all freehand, to achieve a mirror finish. After the handle is shaped, sanded and polished, the sheath is cut from the finest strap leather and stitched by hand."

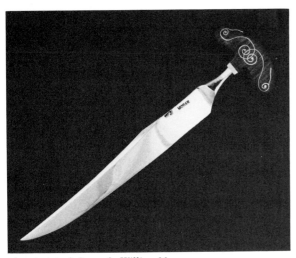

American push dagger by William Moran

Moran's Bowie is bound to become an American tradition. "Most Bowie knives were designed for chopping," says Bill. "Mine work better because I've designed what I think is a better handle to fit the hand and modified the overall profile for more balance, forging better tapers from the guard to the point with better grind angles from the back to the edge." His knives start at $360, while his Bowies range from $800 to $6,500.

William F. Moran, Jr.
P.O. Box 68
Braddock Heights, MD 21714
(301) 371-7543
V (by appt.)   R   S   MO

SOUTHERN MOUNTAIN KNIVES

John Gwaltney makes his blades the old-fashioned way: by hand from old saws in a one-man shop. Hunting knives are made from old circle saws once used in sawmills. "Saws used to cut logs into lumber," John explains, "had to be of the finest high-carbon steel to take a fine edge and hold it, because one small flaw could cause a fatal accident."

Blades that have to be more flexible than strong (like those used to fillet meat and fish) are fashioned from old two-man cross-cut saws. "The older the better," says John. "These knives have been made in the mountains for hundreds of years. They used to just break the blade from an old saw and fasten it to an oak or hickory handle." John makes his in nineteen styles plus "custom within

reason," with handles that "feel good in the hand" of thirty-two different types of wood from all over the world, including many native woods like walnut, curly oak and maple, bird's-eye and fiddleback maple, dogwood, persimmon, cherry and osage orange ("a nice hard yellow").

John started making knives for something to do after he retired. "The knife maker was always the most popular man in town," he'll tell you, "because he made something everyone needed." But in the decade since he started his second career, he has discovered that "knives are becoming more popular than guns with collectors because their money holds its value, and knives are worth even more when they're not used." John's knives have won a whole box full of blue ribbons, best-in-shows and purchase awards, and two are part of the permanent art collection of the State of Georgia.

His best-sellers are: The Pride of Hiawassee ($105, named for his town at the foot of Jonathan Mountain in northern Georgia), with a blade that dips a little at the end; The Bearskinner ($125), with a raised tip and a long, slender, curved blade; Larry's Favorite ($95), a small neat knife designed for fit and grip; and Hunter's Dream ($105 to $125), which has "a little hook at the tip to unzip the hide. Cutting through the hair on the skin is what dulls a knife. This works from the backside and cuts from the underside out."

The best part of his work is making "something new out of something old and seeing it finished. I spend at least 2 days of my life making each knife," says John, "and since it's the only life I've got, I want it to amount to something. I don't like to be rushed." He seldom is, especially by those who have been searching for a certain

Hunter's Dream knife with gut hook, full tang, blood drip and thumb notches for nonslip grip by John Gwaltney

Assorted knives and trailblazer hatchet by John Gwaltney

Lace and Netting

LACE

Lace maker Genevieve Mougin, who was awarded a National Heritage Fellowship from the National Endowment for the Arts, makes needle lace in designs "straight out of my head." Using only a sewing needle and fine linen thread, she builds her lace knot upon knot, beginning with a center ring of 20 stitches and working outward in concentric designs in traditional repetitive motifs. Although she is now in her 70s, Genevieve continues to make lace about 8 hours a day.

The finer the thread, the larger the piece, the higher the price. An 8-inch doily in size 30 thread costs $20, but in size 100 thread it will run $100. 1708 Mississippi Boulevard, Bettendorf, IA 52722.   R   MO

Elena Cola makes bobbin lace on a tubular pillow in a fitted basket held in her lap. A lace pattern is attached to the pillow, pins stuck into the pattern and the thread wound around them. In a process of weaving, twisting and pinning, she works with twelve to forty bobbins, usually doing different patterns on three pillows at a time.

Made from white or ecru linen thread in size 70 to 100 or DMC cotton in size 70 in all colors, her doilies range from $5 to $35, handkerchiefs are $25, and collars, $20 to $40. Pins and Bobbins, 12215 Coit Road, #237, Dallas, TX 75251; (214) 233-6441.   R   V   MO

NETTING

Netting, a craft that began with fishnets, became popular in the colonies to make lacy coverings for the tops of four-poster beds when heavy curtains and canopies were not needed to keep out the cold. The earliest netted canopies, which may date from 1765, are distinguished by their long points. Martha Washington made netted

shape all their lives. "All they have to do is draw a picture and I'll make it." Sometime back, a couple asked him to choose the two best knives he had, then let their son select the one he wanted. " 'This is going to be an heirloom,' they told him," says John, " 'Never use it. Pass it on to your children.' It made me feel good that something I made will live on in the lives of others."

He also makes three sizes of hatchets ($75), with blades also made from old saws and with handles like the knives that "are practically indestructible." The handles are epoxied, bolted and lined with guards and butt caps of brass, with the guards silver-soldered in place. Each comes with a hand-sewn leather sheath and is guaranteed to be free from defects in workmanship and material. "If they're used and not abused," says John, "they should last a lifetime."

Of special interest to collectors is the Knife Record-Keeping Book with room for 500 entries, small enough to carry in the hip pocket. "A lot of men buy knives without telling their wives or recording their value," John says. "This is a way of making sure a widow doesn't give away their investment." Visitors by appointment only. For current price list send a self-addressed, stamped envelope.

John Gwaltney
Gwaltney Knives
Route 3, Box 458
Hiawassee, GA 30546
(404) 896-4550
V   R   C   S   CC   MO

***Kraslice   See* Eggs, Decorated**

Assortment of lace doilies in original patterns by Genevieve Mougin

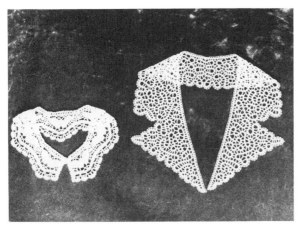

Bobbin lace collars by Elena Cola

fringe for her counterpane spreads; Thomas Jefferson made detailed drawings for netted edges on curtains for Monticello; and *Godey's Lady's Book* printed instructions for netted purses, shawls, hairnets and covers trimmed with tassels for horses' ears.

Margery Burnham Howe, author of *Deerfield Embroidery*, makes netted canopies in patterns used at old Deerfield. She can also copy other old canopies and made one for the Longfellow House in Cambridge, Massachusetts, from a 1917 photograph. She has made canopies for many historic sites including the American Museum in Britain and the White House. Each can have as many as 39,000 knots exclusive of tassels and takes a minimum of 90 hours to

Netting canopy by Carter Canopies on Sheraton field bed by James Lea

complete, using a mesh stick as a gauge and tying knots with a steel netting needle. 4 Lorita Lane, Northfield, MA 013601 (413) 498-2007. R MO

Other Makers

Mrs. H. L. Coffey, Route 2, Box 770, Boone, NC 28607; (704) 264-3197.

Virginia Goodwin, P.O. Box 36603, Charlotte, NC 28236.

Laura Copenhaver Industries, Inc., Rosemont, Marion, VA 24354; (703) 783-4663.

Carter Canopies, Route 2, Box 270G, P.O. Box 808, Troutman, NC 28166; (704) 528-4071.

See also Bed Coverings, Knotted

Latches *See* **Iron, Nails and Latches**

BRAIN-TANNED HIDES

The Plains Indians used the brain of the animal to tan deer, elk, buffalo and moose hides. Legend says that each animal has exactly enough brains to tan its own hide. Done entirely by hand and requiring many hours of intense labor, brain-tanning creates a snow-white hide with no grain or epidermis. Soft, supple, comparable to velvet in texture and pliability, it is considered the finest leather in the world. It is also incredibly strong because the fibers are stretched, not broken as in chemically tanned hides.

Growing up in the sacred land of the Plains Indians, listening to stories told by original settlers, elders and relatives on Sioux reservations, Cathy Smith has spent her life researching western and Plains Indian material culture. Adopted by a Lakota family, she now lives with her 12-year-old daughter on a ranch homesteaded by her grandfather in South Dakota's Black Hills. "Much of my knowledge was gained from apprenticeships, working on and restoring original artifacts and studying artifacts in European collections," she says. "Unfortunately, most of the pre-1850 Indian material culture collected is in museums in Europe, as there were few museums in this country at that time and Indian material was not then considered valuable." In 1974, Cathy founded the Medicine Mountain Trading Company as a center for the study, preservation and production of 18th and 19th century North American Indian art forms. Using traditional tools, techniques and materials, she makes items and garments that are entirely wearable and usable.

Cathy's work has been commissioned by the Museum of Indian Art, the Denver Art Museum, the Smithsonian's

Kiowa boots (moccasins with high tops) with rawhide soles, using smoked, brain-tanned leather and decorated with old seed beads, by Cathy Smith

lishing Co.). "Quillwork has always been a holy or sacred art," she says, "and traditionally must be approached in that context. The beads we use are the originals traded during the 19th century. Made in the glass factories of Venice, they are quite different in color value and size variation from modern beads, which greatly affects the authenticity of a piece. My partner, Stan Dolega, and I make clothing, accoutrements, weapons, tools, beadwork and quillwork on a commission basis for many collectors, museums and galleries, as well as props used by contemporary western art painters."

Her museum-quality clothing for women includes partially beaded moccasins ($150); quilled moccasins ($350); boots ($250, with beads, $375); and brain-tanned dresses ($450 to $1,500). Men's garments include deerhide leggings sewn with sinew, whose inside edges are stained with red ochre, trimmed with quilled strips and pony beads ($275 to $800); brain-tanned buckskin coats with buffalo collar and pewter buttons ($500); buffalo hide jerkins in stained yellow ochre with a buffalo hunt scene painted in pictograph with earth pigments and pony-beaded rosette ($425, or $324 without rosette and painting). Accoutrements include a three-sided pouch, c. 1860, with two sides of smoked moose hide with quilled floral patterns and a third side of native mink with the fur out. It is fringed in brain-tanned buckskin with a drawstring top, and its structure is based on an animal scrotum ($350). Knife

Cooper-Hewitt Museum and the Boston Museum of Fine Arts. In addition to creating traveling lecture displays for the international "Circles of the World" exhibit sponsored by the Denver Art Museum, she wrote the chapter on quillwork for the *Third Book of Buckskinning* (Rebel Pub-

Garments by Cathy Smith: (left to right) men's leggings, buffalo jerkin, buckskin coat, wool coat, quilled society shirt, buckskin shirt and buckskin vest

Man's vest with leather front embroidered with porcupine quills in floral design by Cathy Smith

sheaths range from $45 to $250; pipe or tobacco bags, $40 to $250; saddles, $500 to $800; and porcupine tail hairbrushes with quilled seam, partially beaded for $38. Color catalog $3.50. On inquiries, state tribal preference, time period, colors or desired modifications.

Cathy Smith
Medicine Mountain Trading Company
Box 124
Sturgis, SD 57785
V   R   C   S   MO

COWBOY AND WESTERN BOOTS

Although most western gear evolved from that of the vaqueros who worked longhorns on the Rio Grande plains in the early 1800s, boots began as a combination of the

Handmade custom-fit cowboy boots with pointed toes and undershot heels by F. W. "Dutch" Leopold

plain leather, high-topped boots used by southern planters, eastern military men and cavalrymen. During the heyday of the cowboy after the Civil War, when large numbers of stray cattle abandoned by ranchers gone to war had to be rounded up, the cowboy boot as we know it came into being.

"My grandad was making them in Odessa in 1872," says F. W. "Dutch" Leopold, whose family has been making cowboy boots in Texas ever since, "and he learned it from somebody else in the 1860s. Out here, boots are a functional tool, not a cosmetic accessory. Westerners didn't walk; they rode. Pointed toes helped get their feet in the stirrups faster; undershot heels kept the foot from going through the stirrups; and high tops protected their legs." Boots were originally very plain with little or no extra stitching. Fancy details were later added by performers in Wild West shows and movie stars.

After studying accounting for 3½ years, Dutch (whose name was then Bob Grissom) "knew that wasn't what I wanted to do. I bugged Henry Leopold to take me on as an apprentice. After a year Henry agreed but made it clear he wasn't looking for a partner, that after I learned I'd have to be on my way. I worked for 2 years without pay, then started buying tools for my own shop." When it came time to leave, after 10 years, Henry wanted him to carry on the business. Dutch became Henry's partner and adopted son, taking the name of Henry's father as his own. "I sold all my property, bought the boot shop from Henry and leased it back to him for the rest of his life.

"Real cowboy boots," says Dutch, "are custom-fit and handmade. The main thing is the quality of the fit. The best have an understated elegance and are finely crafted of the finest materials." Dutch (who wears an apron that says "You want it when?" given to Henry by a customer who'd waited 6 years) spends about 3 weeks on each pair, makes twenty-five pair a year and no longer takes orders, only referrals from existing customers. "No sense making them for New York cowboys," he'll tell you, "when there are working cowboys and ranch people who need them more."

Like Henry, who Dutch thinks was the best boot maker who ever lived, Dutch believes a boot maker should be "a complete worker" and know how to do everything: "fitting, which is making the uppers and lasts, inlays and fancy stitching; and bottoming, which gives the boot foundation and shape and has much to do with the way a boot fits and wears." His most rewarding work is making orthopedic boots "because they require so much knowledge. The most difficult I ever made were for a man who blew off his heels when he fell on his shotgun."

Dutch's 12-inch-top basic boot in kid or calf with three rows of stitching costs $1,000. Water buffalo and caribou can be had for the same price, but kangaroo, retan, shark, snake, lizard, elephant, ostrich, sea turtle, anteater and alligator run higher. Extras include brands, monograms, stitching, overlays, wrinkles, toe flowers, higher tops, mule ears, toe tips, heel spots and wings.

The good news is that all boots are guaranteed against flaws in workmanship and there is now only a 2-year wait. The bad news is that because exotic leathers are subject to flaws and deterioration they are not guaranteed; and price is determined at the time of delivery, *not* at the order date.

F. W. "Dutch" Leopold
Leopold's Boot Shop
Route 1, Box 667
Morgan, TX 76671
(817) 622-3235
V   R   MO

Other Makers

John A. Weinkauf, Desert Leather, P.O. Box 2295, 100 Landing Lane, Carson City, NV 89701; (702) 882-5900, in addition to making some of the best western boots in the country, also makes lace-up boots. These have been around as long as pull-ons but have been used more in Nevada and Idaho.

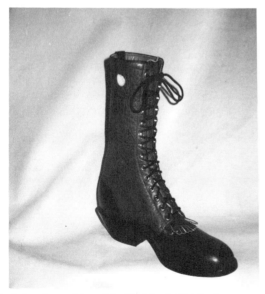

Black French-waxed lace-up boot by John A. Weinkauf

Charlie Dunn, 2222 College Avenue, Austin, TX 78704; (512) 443-4447, is a fifth generation bootmaker known for his perfect fit. Now 88 years old, he's made boots for many of the all-time greats.

Jim Bowman, Route 1, Box 79, Ruckersville, VA 22968; (804) 985-2794.

Ray Jones, Box 215, Lampassas, TX 76550; (512) 556-3192.

HISTORIC LEATHER REPRODUCTIONS

"The leather bottle was used in kitchens, taverns and by travelers because it was so durable," says Steven Lalioff, who specializes in historic leatherwork. "The leather was made watertight by lining it with pitch [the smooth tar that remained after the alcohol and turpentine were extracted from pine resin]. Owners of colonial taverns encouraged rowdy customers to use pitch-lined mugs and saved the more breakable wood, pewter and crockery for more genteel guests. Pitch-lined leather couldn't be used for hot liquids because it would melt, but it was easily mended by pouring boiling water over the crack."

Steven grew up loving antiques so much that he was the only kid in high school to take woodshop six semesters in a row. "I made things I couldn't afford to buy," he says, "and refinished antiques I picked up at auction." At the age of 16 he went to work part time as an historic interpreter at Connor Prairie Pioneer Settlement, a reconstructed (c. 1836) village in Noblesville, Indiana. He later studied history and folklore at Indiana University. When a friend told him about an opening at Colonial Williamsburg, he called, made an appointment for the next day and took off, driving 750 miles to get there. His apprenticeship in colonial leatherwork brought his skills and interests together. He returned home to Indiana and opened his own business.

Today, using authentic patterns copied from American originals and traditional construction methods, he hand-stitches vegetable-tanned leather in the saddlestitch or double-running stitch with linen cord, making leather items from the earliest days of the colonies, like: blackjacks ($20), hand weapons filled with lead shot c. 1850–80; men's buckled garters to keep long stockings from slipping ($5); cannisters (c. 1820) used for breakables while traveling ($20 to $65); dice cups used in all types of games ($10); formal belts of full-grain steerhide in widths ½ inch to 2 inches, embossed on an 1866 creasing machine and hand-stitched to solid brass buckles ($8 to $25); plus three styles of saddlebags ($175 to $300).

Trunk of rawhide over wood by Steven M. Lalioff

Replicas of holsters, c. 1850–80, by Steven M. Lalioff

His willingness to make any historic leather object has increased his stock of designs to over a hundred, most with a story. His 1751 wallet is embossed with *The Ranger,* a ship captured by John Paul Jones during the French and Indian Wars, while an 1836 wallet copies one used during Harrison's presidential campaign and bears a likeness of Harrison on one side and his campaign symbol of a log cabin and cider barrel on the other ($15 each). His portmanteau ($100 to $250), which means "to carry the coat" in French, comes in two styles: the oval from Williamsburg, c. 1750, and the 1800 flat bottom after one in Ohio Village. He has an infinite variety of styles, sizes and periods of trunks ($100 to $300), but specializes in 1750–1850 construction with papered or painted interiors, covered with leather and trimmed with brass tacks, handles and hasps (although iron hardware can be special-ordered). His buckaroo leather includes cowboy cuffs c. 1880 for roping and branding ($25 to $40) and chaps to protect the legs in bushy terrain ($150 to $300). Homeowners searching for period fire buckets to hang on the hook next to the stairway in period homes have the best news of all. Steven not only lines them with pitch but also oil paints choice of background color and the family name or crest ($150 to $200). He also has dozens of styles of hunting pouches ($50 to $250), once used to store flint and steel for starting fires, lead balls, compass, knife and tools; and twenty different types of holsters ($40 to $75). All work guaranteed. Inquiries must include self-addressed, stamped envelope. For photos of work, include $1 refundable with order.

Steven M. Lalioff
Traditional Leatherwork Company
14311 Bryn Mawr Drive
Noblesville, IN 46060
(317) 773-5389
V   R   S   MO

Hunting pouch and horn by Steven M. Lalioff

LEATHER

Other Maker

Theresa McMahon, Route 1, Box 497, Mechanicsville, VA 23111; (804) 353-2424, apprenticed at Colonial Williamsburg, makes harness, military accoutrements, hunting bags, game bags, officers' haversacks (17th to 19th century), 17th century military gear and 18th century leather pocketbooks.

PERIOD FOOTWEAR

Shoes worn by early Americans were entirely handmade and identical in shape. Known as straights, each "pair" was made to fit the larger foot and built around a wooden last, or form, measured to fit the foot. Leather for the soles and heels was placed over a lap-stone and pounded with a hammer to compact the hide and increase its durability. For each pair, between twenty-five and thirty pieces of leather had to be carefully measured, cut and trimmed, then sewn by hand with waxed threads of hemp or flax using boar's bristles instead of needles.

"The quality varied greatly," says cordwainer D. A. Saguto, who reproduces period hand-sewn boots and shoes. "In the late 1700s, a man might wear out one or two pairs annually, each of which could cost two-thirds of a tradesman's weekly salary."

In the early 1600s, men's shoes were made with round openings at the sides, and if stylish, with large ties added in the front. The close shoe had no such openings and was made for everyday life. Early overshoes, known as clogs, galloshoes and pattens, were worn by both sexes. Bagging shoes, start-ups, cockers, or ockers, and batts were the sensible leather boots and shoes worn by working men in the 17th century, while quail pipe boots, pantables and footwear with Polony heels, cabbage shoe strings and slap soles were favored by the upper classes. After 1640,

Farmer's boot worn in the third quarter of the 18th century, made by D. A. Saguto

jackboots worn by military and post riders were painted with molten pine resin and tallow to harden the leather. As stiff as casts, they were impossible to walk in but protected legs from swords or from the weight of a horse keeled over from death or fatigue. Thick soles and high heels were stitched on, as were the bottoms of most shoes until machine-made wooden pegs and nails became available in the early 1800s.

"When the profile lathe was invented," says Al, "cordwainers no longer had to use straight shoe lasts, but they were reluctant to invest in a right and left last for each pair, which is why the use of straights continued through the Civil War. As the United States became the world leader in the invention of machinery to mass-produce footwear, cordwainers were forced to do repair work or go out of business."

Al became interested in historical footwear while he was in high school. After graduation, he opened his own leather goods shop and studied historical techniques of shoe-making with E. W. Peterkin, the leading American authority. By 1975 he was spending so much time "haunting museums that housed collections of old shoes, working with historians and costume specialists and making 18th century styles for historical reenactors' feet" that

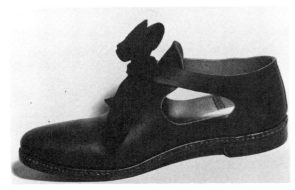

Man's cordwained shoe of the early 17th century by D. A. Saguto

he decided to specialize. He now makes "authentic replicas of footwear from Roman styles through the mid–19th century, in each case trying to replicate the actual manufacturing processes used in making the original object. My shoes and boots are not fanciful creations, but buildings in a technical sense, based on antique objects and confined to the technology available in that period. My concept of perfection is to preserve the process as well as the end product."

In addition to the hundreds of shoes he has made for museums and historical organizations, both here and abroad, Al has worked as a footwear and shoe-making consultant for the Smithsonian Institution and the National Park Service and written an English translation of *L'Art du Cordonnier,* the earliest technical account of hand shoe-making. His shoes cost anywhere from $200 up and are priced according to the degree of authentic detailing required. "A typical pair of shoes for the 1770s can take from 8 to 15 bench hours of work," says Al, "and longer for boots. When research is involved to collect data for a particular style or type, it also factors into the cost."

D. A. Saguto, Cordwainer
4406 Glenridge Street
Kensington, MD 20895
R   S

Other Maker

Butch Myers, J. R. Myers Company, 6507 Horsepen Road, Richmond, VA 23226; (804) 288-9380, specializes in 19th century cordwainery and makes men's military brogans c. 1860.

RAWHIDE BOSALS, HEADSTALLS, HOBBLES, QUIRTS AND ROPES

Intermission movies at the Marlboro Country Music Concerts feature two men: Will Rogers and Rowdy Pate, a 6-foot-6-inch cowhand from Pearsall, Texas, whose parents and grandfathers were ranch folks. Rowdy is also one of the most popular attractions at the Texas Folklife Festival, where he spins tales while weaving rawhide and horsehair.

"There was no way I could be anything except a cowhand," says Rowdy, who got the name as a little boy because he was "very loud and a shade reckless. My favorite toys were a piece of broken rawhide rope and rawhide thongs to tie knots in. By the time I was 15, I could make just about anything I needed. Most country people worked

rawhide because even if they did get to town there wasn't any spare money to waste on something you could make yourself.

"Flint hides dried without salt or any other treatment are best for most braiding jobs," he says. "I dry mine in the shade. Summer hides are best because they have less hair and the hide seems firmer. I soak mine in a weak lime-water solution until the hair slips, then lay the hide on a flat board and scrape off the hair with a dull knife, wash the hide good and stretch it in the shade again until I'm ready to use it."

His main tools are a sharp knife, a deer horn fid (large tapering pin used to open strands of rope before splicing), a jack-plane to skive thongs down to an even thickness and lots of elbow grease. For a softer finish on gear like reins, thongs are dampened and rubbed with saddle soap, then pulled around a limb or fence rail until dry, or rubbed with tallow and beat with a wooden mallet to break the

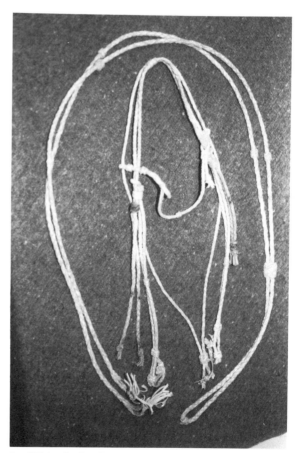

Rawhide headstall and reins by Rowdy Pate

LEATHER

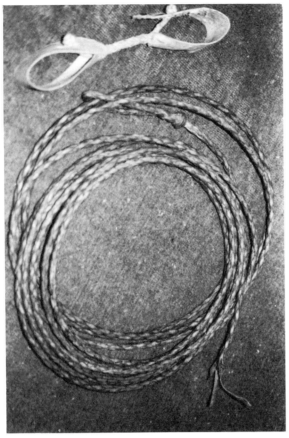

Rawhide rope and hobbles by Rowdy Pate

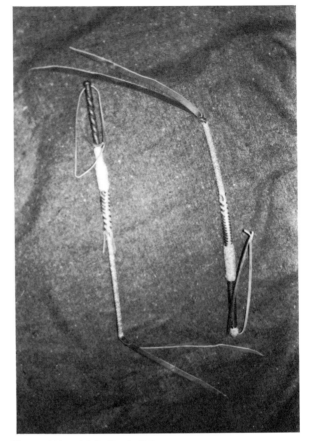

Two rawhide quirts by Rowdy Pate

fibers. Before cutting, he dampens the hide to make it flexible.

"A white or light-colored cow 2 to 3 years old is best for a rope," he says. "I trim the blank until I have a round, then start the string or thong on the outside edge, cutting around and around until I reach the center. A 12-inch circle makes about 40 feet of ⅛-inch thong, but to make a rope 25 feet long requires a strip 160 feet long, because four lengths are braided around a fifth, which is the core."

A bosal is the part of a hackamore that goes around the horse's nose. (A hackamore is similar to a halter, but the bosal fits close and is used for breaking and training horses.) "I make mine with a twisted rawhide core," says Rowdy, "a little more than ½ inch thick when it's twisted right. Six or eight strands are braided over the core, turned back and worked through the first braids." Headstalls, the parts of a bridle that hold the bit in the horse's

mouth, are made from 500 feet of string ⅛ inch wide braided in six-strand, half-round braids with sliding knots on each side instead of buckles.

"Hobbles are put on horses so they can do anything except run away," Rowdy explains. "Rawhide hobbles in brush country are made from a strap of rawhide 4 inches wide and 3 feet long. After soaking in water, edges are doubled over to the center with the flesh side in so they won't hurt the horse as he travels. One end is slit for a button hole, and the other split into four or more strands and tied in a knot for a button. A quirt is a riding crop with a stiff rawhide core on a brass handle with thongs braided over it and a double tail or popper on the bottom end. A common quirt goes for about $35, although I've made one with thirty-two strands for $145. A rope sells for $250 up depending on the length. My bosals are solid rawhide, natural color, made only for people that use them, so most go for a quart of Jack Daniel's or a good hide or a sack of hair for braiding.''

Rowdy Pate
Box 581
Pearsall, TX 78061
(512) 334-2015
R S MO

Other Makers

David Stewart, P.O. Box 970, Alturas, CA 96101; (916) 233-4756, makes braided rawhide reins, quirts and lariats.

Mr. and Mrs. Ted Schaeffer, Box 508, Beach, ND 58621; (701) 872-4276, make braided bridles and do other saddle work.

LITURGICAL GOLD, SILVER AND PEWTER

As a boy, Randy Stromsoe's favorite activities were drawing and hammering double-headed railroad nails into miniature swords on an anvil. At college, his jewelry teacher told him, after seeing his first creation, ''You are a craftsman.'' But it was a class trip to master silversmith Porter Blanchard's studio in 1970 when he was 20 that put Randy on the right path.

''It was like walking back in time,'' he remembers. ''His workshop was a magical, comfortable place full of tools I'd never seen, hundreds of hand-forged hammers, a drawing room full of renderings and photos, almost-finished tea sets, large altar candlesticks. I was enchanted and in awe of this 84-year-old man in his leather apron who had trained most of the silversmiths in Los Angeles. He let us take turns hammering a piece and on our way out pulled me aside to ask if I would like to be his apprentice. I switched my studies to night classes and started the next day.''

During his intense 4-year classical training with Blanchard, Randy helped make elegant 14-karat-gold cups and platters, sterling wine cisterns large enough for three bottles, fluted and scalloped sterling trays 2 feet wide and 3 feet long, silver teakettles complete with burners, 3-foot-long gold and silver fish platters and 2½-foot-long punch ladles that held 3 cups of liquid. From Blanchard, Randy learned the techniques of hollowware, one being a special buffing process that makes pewter as bright as sterling; and from Porter's son-in-law Lewis Wise, he learned flatware. Both men bequeathed tools to Randy that he cherishes and uses in his work today.

One of the few master silversmiths in the United States who rigorously adheres to classical disciplines in metal-

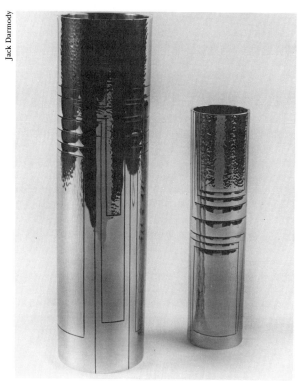

Candlestick/flower vases of polished pewter by Randy Stromsoe

smithing, Stromsoe continues to make each piece entirely by hand. Since he went into business for himself in 1974, his work has been commissioned by some of the great names in show business and by jewelry firms like Cartier. The State Department continues to give his tankards, letter openers and paperweights as gifts of state. In recent years, his liturgical pieces in gold, silver and pewter have earned him a special niche in the world of metal as well as in the hearts of those who commission them.

''A few years ago,'' Randy explains, ''the Pope asked churches to commission and buy quality, traditionally hand-crafted liturgical pieces. Throughout history, the best that man could offer was placed on the altar. It used to be gold, then silver plated with gold. Some chalices are gold inside, but most church work reflects the period of architecture in the building. I've made tabernacles, processional crosses, altar candlesticks, paschal candlestands, flagons, ciboria and patens in all dimensions and metals, but the most exciting work is chalices. When a priest is first ordained, the family usually buys a chalice as an ordination gift, but most often from a catalog. Throughout his priesthood, he dreams of the chalice he'd really like to have. Every priest who has commissioned a

Jack Darmody

Pewter chalice made bright as sterling by special buffing process by Randy Stromsoe

chalice knows the exact size, shape, metal and number of ounces he wants his chalice to hold. I find it exhilarating and satisfying to bring those dreams to fruition, and as in all my designs, try to create something timeless."

Randy continues to make all the fabulous objects once crafted by Porter Blanchard, and objects of gold like hand-forged baby spoons and wedding anniversary goblets, but he also makes a simple pewter goblet for $120 and a pewter bottle coaster for as little as $55. His shop is open 10 A.M. to 5 P.M. weekdays except Tuesday.

Randy J. Stromsoe
Stromsoe Silversmiths
P.O. Box 8
Harmony, CA 93435
(805) 927-8455
R   S   MO

Makouk See **Tatting**

MARBLES

Bud Garrett's father made marbles from chunks of flint pecked out with a file in Free Hill, Tennessee, an isolated community founded by free blacks before the Civil War. He then placed the roughed-out shapes under a small waterfall where over a period of weeks or months their edges were turned round and smooth.

Jed Dekalb

Robert "Bud" Garrett taking a shot during National Rolley Hole Marbles Championship

As a young man, Bud invented his own system of producing marbles that replicated the action of a waterfall and natural basin but speeded up the process. Now in his 70s, Bud's known as a blues singer and guitarist elsewhere in the South, but in Clay County, Tennessee, where natives have played "rolley hole" for generations, Bud's known for his perfectly crafted marbles.

Rolley hole, a marbles game once common in the South, is now played in only a few rural counties along the Tennessee-Kentucky state line, where families have handed down marbles, playing strategies and enthusiasm for the game since the early 1800s.

"Grown-ups lost many a crop playing rolley hole," says Bud. "They'd play marbles when they were supposed to be weeding corn. Some would play half the night, and instead of going to work the next day, keep on playing."

Smooth manicured dirt yards used as playing areas were once found near schools, country stores, in barns, basements, woodlots and old roadbeds, and until only recently, on the courthouse square in Celina, Tennessee. A factory in Celina has four marble yards, and nearby Standing Stone State Park is the site of the National Rolley Hole Marbles Championship held each August. Day and night between the rainy spring season and the fall frost, men and boys gather to play rolley hole, a game with elements of pool, golf and croquet that requires shooting skill and strategy. Two players challenge a second pair, with each player using one marble. The yard, approximately 25 by 40 feet, has three holes spaced evenly down the center. Both players on each team must travel up and down the three-hole course three times, rolling marbles into the holes, while doing everything to keep their opponents from scoring. A good match can last more than an hour.

Glass marbles would be shattered by the powerful shots in the game, but high-grade chert nodules (flintrocks), weathered from limestone bedrock, hand-turned by Bud, are guaranteed for life and usually last longer. After blocking them out with a file, he places the marble blank in a small basin of abrasive stone against an electric-powered grinding wheel. A third piece of abrasive stone is hand-held against the flint. As it gets rounder, it becomes smoother. When perfectly round, it feels slick all over. The marbles must be turned slowly to avoid heat buildup, which weakens them. Finished marbles, never less than ⅝ inch or more than ⅞ inch in diameter, are made to fit the grip of different hands. Completed with a thin coat of Vaseline to add to their luster, they sell for $5 to $20 depending on quality and color. Most are gray. Some are yellow, white, red or black.

The best way to buy one of Bud's marbles is direct from his home in the Free Hill community near Celina (where he was born and continues to live) or at local tournaments. If you can't get down that way to buy and try your own, and want to know what an all-American marble looks and feels like, you can mail order. Write for a price list, or tell him what you want and he'll mail it COD. Best of all, if one of his marbles ever breaks, he'll send you a replacement in return for the pieces—free.

Robert "Bud" Garrett
P.O. Box 261
Celina, TN 38551
R   MO

Other Makers
Jody Fine, 1800 4th Street, Berkeley, CA 94710; (415) 845-4270, makes glass marbles.
Steven Maslach, 44 Industrial Way, Greenbrae, CA 94904; (415) 924-2310, makes glass marbles.

Marquetry   *See* **Inlay, Marquetry and Parquetry**

Masks   *See* **Totem Poles, Masks, Rattles and Dolls**

Moccasins, Beaded   *See* **Beadwork**

MOLDS FOR BAKING

Springerle, a pale, hard, lemon-anise cookie from Germany; spekulaas, a rich, spicey cookie from Holland and central Europe; and shortbread from Scotland—have two things in common: each receives its design from a wooden mold before baking (springerle by pressing the mold into the dough, spekulaas and shortbread by pressing the dough into the mold), and all three types of molds were brought to America by immigrants who continued to make them.

"In German dialect," says Don Dillon, who carves all three types, "*springerle* means 'small jumping horse.' The horse was the sacred animal of Wotan, king of the Nordic gods. During celebrations at Julfest and Winter Solstice, animals were offered as sacrifice. Those who could not afford to sacrifice real animals baked tokens of dough in the shapes of animals as their offerings."

Springerle cookie mold in horse design by Don Dillon

When springerle molds began to be used at other times of the year, subject matter grew to include people, houses, birds, flowers and fruit as well as animals. Carved from boards ranging in size from 1½ by 2 inches to 2 by 4 feet (used during village festivals), or on cylinders shaped like rolling pins, springerle molds can have a single design or several.

"I began carving springerle and spekulaas molds while serving in the army in Germany, after my wife became interested in them," explains Don. "Carving cookie molds is the opposite of relief carving. Using the incise, or intaglio, method, each design is carved in reverse into the mold so that when the design appears on the cookie, it will be positive. I use over 450 gouges: about 100 continually and the rest occasionally. The Germans used pear and linden wood most often, but in America pear trees are much smaller and do not provide much usable wood. The American wood most similar to linden is basswood, which is what I use. After the wood is kiln-dried to 7 percent moisture content, I place a pattern on the raw wood, carve out the design cavity, then carefully carve designs into the cavity. In early times, the molds were left unfinished because their only use was functional. [When used they were dusted with powdered sugar to prevent sticking.] Unless specifically requested not to do so, I stain, finish and sign each mold, because today people like to use them as decoration between bakings, instead of burying them in a drawer. The shortbread molds originally used the Scottish thistle as a design. We added the tree and pineapple [the early American symbol for hospitality]. To use, the shortbread dough is packed into the cavity, then knocked out onto a cookie sheet for baking."

When Don retired from the army as a lieutenant colonel in 1979, he became a full-time carver. "As my carving became more interesting," he says, "my army career became less enjoyable. Being involved with the worldwide transportation of material was challenging, but creating wooden molds is more personally satisfying."

A large horse spekulaas mold from an early 1800s pattern is $40; a cat mold from the same period is $27; a long multiple-design board is $20. Other designs include George and Martha Washington at $17 and $18 each; shortbread molds 7¾ inches in diameter at $18 each; a 5½- by 6-inch Pennsylvania-Dutch heart springerle board

Springerle cookie mold in cat design by Don Dillon

Shortbread mold with Scottish thistle design by Don Dillon

at $17; smaller 2½- by 3½-inch designs of distelfinks, tulips and edelweiss at $9.75. Each mold comes with a recipe and historical background. A catalog of all designs is 50¢. Shipping charge of $1.50 on all retail mail orders.

Don Dillon
D. D. Dillon Carvings
850 Meadow Lane
Camp Hill, PA 17011
(717) 761-6895
R W C MO

Other Makers

Gene Wilson, 321 Lebanon Avenue, Belleville, IL 62221; (618) 233-7689, hand-carves the three types of molds mentioned above plus plunger-type butter molds in solid cherry, butter stamps, cookie stamps and gingerbread hornbook molds.

Carl Forslund, Peart Street at the river, Grand Rapids, MI 49503.

MURALS

"A mural shouldn't overpower a room or look like a mammoth painting on the wall," says David Wiggins, who has gained a national reputation for his murals since he apprenticed with his father in 1961. "It should add to or complement what's there and provide a sense of place. A mural should also be appropriate for the setting and take into account the architectural features of the room. Style is everything. Color is something I can't even talk about, but it's the essence."

Like the best decorative painters of the past, David likes to "handle it my way. It's an intimate thing and requires a dynamic balance between the client, myself and the work. The client lays out what he has in mind, I show him slides and photos of work I have done and listen to his ideas. We then explore options within that context. A preliminary sketch tends to limit my creativity, spontaneity and the ability to take chances, which I feel is essential to the success of the project. Besides, an arch that seems like a good idea in the beginning may not achieve the right balance in the overall mural."

More practical than wallpaper, which tears and stains, murals can be made to fit the space, tell a story, include the history of the family or town, add architectural elements (like niches for depth, friezes to lower a ceiling or widen a room, windows and doors for interest on an empty wall), create marble at a fraction of the cost, and be executed in any style, color or period desired by the owner. New Englanders loved them in the early 1800s because they weren't as expensive as imported wallpapers and could be washed.

Master muralist Rufus Porter was credited with bringing New England out of its puritanical past with his bold, colorful murals at a time when decoration was considered the image of the devil. Porter began murals as David does, at the far horizon. Painting directly on plaster or a prime coat of paint, David builds from the sky downward to below the horizon to establish the main light source. "Trees are silhouetted against the horizon," explains David, "then the distant landscape, after which I lay out areas of land, dividing wall spaces into mountains, lakes, cliffs, orchards, working with broad brush strokes, sponges and washes until walls are covered. The middle ground is then developed with points of interest like houses, boats, cattle, often reduced to simple forms and stenciled in." Some objects are symbolic: anchors represent hope; doves, purity; grapes, plenty; willows, immortality; eagles, freedom; and a broken branch, death. An arch is often used as a transition from one thing to another. The fourth stage, or foreground, nearest the viewer is painted last,

Mural of river scene with boat in distance by David Wiggins

Primitive landscape mural of hillside scene by David Wiggins

with the main trees, stones and bushes with large roots and trunks to the mopboard or wainscoting.

"About halfway through," says David, "when I feel comfortable and open to suggestion, the client and I discuss what is happening and future direction. Much of the energy from that encounter session appears in the final rendering. I am then left alone to develop the color and form that I think best enhances the execution."

With a personal reference, David gives the first consultation gratis if the site is within easy commuting distance. If not, he charges a daily per diem plus expenses. A room mural can cost from $5,000 to $30,000, depending on its size, complexity and the number of surfaces involved. In the tradition of early muralists, David also stencils walls and floors, grains woodwork and furniture and restores murals.

David Wiggins
RFD 2, Box 420
Tilton, NH 03276
(603) 286-3046
R

Other Makers

Gerard Wiggins, 65 Lafayette Street, Arlington, MA 02174; (617) 641-4083, who is also David's brother, specializes in more citified techniques and styles.

Christopher Gurshin, P.O. Box 616, Newburyport, MA 01950; (617) 462-7761.

Monica Halford, 850 El Caminito, Santa Fe, NM 87501; (505) 982-4175.

Virginia Jacobs McLaughlin, The Antique Cupboard,

Country village mural with fanciful trees in foreground by David Wiggins

812 West Main Street (Box 114), Emmitsburg, MD 21727; (301) 447-6558 or (717) 642-5142.   V R S MO

Candy Thun, 3 Edwunds Court, Plymouth, NH 03264; (603) 536-1355.

Autoharps

Although few had the money to buy a harp in the 19th century, most could afford a factory-produced autoharp, which became America's favorite instrument in the 1890s. The autoharp was used to teach harmony in schools and became a favorite of American folk musicians in the 1920s. Maybelle Carter, credited with the rise of the autoharp as a performer's instrument, developed a melodic style of playing with her arms crossed over the instrument as it was clasped to her breast.

Back of autoharp showing inlay by Tom Morgan

Autoharp by Tom Morgan

Simple chords are played by strumming the autoharp's strings with the fingers or a plectrum. Strings grouped to make three-note chords are anchored at the lower end by metal pins hammered into the frame, then brought up over a small wooden piece called a bridge on the face of the instrument and into the tuning pegs. Chord bars are suspended above the strings so that when a bar is pressed it automatically makes a chord as the harp is strummed.

Tom Morgan's handmade autoharps, with carved spruce tops and rosewood backs and sides, have a pre-stressed hidden truss for added strength and small f-holes in the graduated and braced top to increase tone ($1,000). Their balanced, melodious, full-bodied sound lends itself to recording because it has no harsh overtones, which is why his instruments, called "the best in the world," are used by entertainers like Arlo Guthrie, Mike Seeger and John McCutcheon. Tom Morgan, Route 3, Box 204, Dayton, TN 37321; (615) 775-2996.   V (by appt.)   MO

BANJOS

Invented by slaves trying to recreate the long-necked lutes they'd known in Africa, the banjo, a cross between a drum and a stringed instrument, is uniquely American. The happy sound of fingers or picks plucking and strumming its strings played an important role in the development of mountain, country, ragtime, jazz and bluegrass music and became an integral part of minstrel show and riverboat entertainment. The earliest banjos had relatively long necks, large round heads made of wooden hoops covered with animal skins, gut strings, no soundholes and no frets (metal bars across the neck).

"I learned to pick a five-string banjo at the age of 7 or 8, using a borrowed banjo," says Dave Sturgill, "but when I was 11, the owner wanted it back. Having nothing to

Banjo with inlaid resonator (front view), designed for bluegrass playing, by David A. Sturgill

Banjo designed for old-time clawhammer playing by David A. Sturgill

play, I made my own from a packing crate and a tin can, which I still have. An old tom cat unwillingly sacrificed his hide for the head, but he's made better music on my banjo than he ever did on the fencepost. That was in 1925 and I've been making instruments ever since. At least 1,500 of all types, and repaired about 6,000. I play all of them. I've never copied other instruments except for making a few violins on the Stradivarius pattern."

When he finished high school during the Depression, Dave took off on his bike to see the world, going 550 miles in the first 3 days. After a winter spent milking fifty cows by hand, he switched to hitchhiking, playing music in clubs whenever he needed money, and crisscrossed the United States many times. In 1938 he settled down in Washington, DC, studied electrical engineering for a year and went to work for the telephone company. Five years later, married and a father, suffering from ulcers, living on babyfood and eggs, he was advised by the doctor to find a hobby. He began making violins. After he'd made and given away more than a dozen, only 14 months from retirement, he quit his job and headed back to the hills of North Carolina, where he worked for a small musical instrument company before opening his own. Since then, with his sons John and Dan as partners, he's made instruments for some of the all-time greats, won awards for his playing and craftsmanship, participated in and judged fiddlers' contests and lost his ulcers.

Like Grandpa Jones on the TV program "Hee Haw," Dave plays clawhammer style, the backs of his fingernails striking down on the strings. Drop-thumb banjo is played with the fingernails, but the thumb drops to play the other strings too. Flailing is strumming the strings with the fingers and playing more chords than individual notes. Dave and his sons make all styles of banjos: the more primitive mountain style, which usually has five strings; the plectrum style with four strings and long scale, played like a guitar with a flat pick; the tenor with four strings and a short scale; the old-time with five strings and open back; and the bluegrass with five strings and resonator, which constrains the sound and reflects it back.

"The majority today have five strings," says John, "but back in the twenties more had four. The fifth peg, patented in 1858, was popularized by mass marketers to increase sales by making the banjo easier to play. The fifth string is not noted and is played as a drone, or counternote, to what you're playing. The fretted fingerboard came into being in the early 1900s."

Handmade primarily in curly maple but also available in black walnut, cherry and mahogany, the Sturgills' banjos range in price from $200 to $2,500. They also make guitars, mandolins, Appalachian dulcimers, hammered dulcimers, balalaikas, autoharps and violins. For those who want to make their own, the Sturgills sell a kit for a 6-inch-head mountain banjo for $49. If you want to use your own wood and tomcat, check out *Foxfire 3*, which features Dave explaining how to make a banjo. The Sturgills' shop is open evenings, weekends, holidays or by appointment.

David A. Sturgill
Skyland Musical Instrument Co.
Route 1, Box 211
Piney Creek, NC 28663
(919) 359-2280
R S MO

Other Makers

Leonard and Clifford Glen, Route 1, Box 197, Sugar Grove, NC 28679; (704) 297-2297, make handsome fretless banjos of walnut or cherry in the early five-string form that are extremely playable and have excellent tone. They are also well known for their dulcimers.

Arlin Moon, Route 2, Box 415, Holly Pond, AL 35083; (205) 796-2473, makes such good banjos that one is in the Smithsonian Institution.

Tom Morgan, Route 3, Box 204, Dayton, TN 37321; (615) 755-2996, makes banjos for bluegrass from mahogany, maple, cherry or walnut with a three-ply rim, cast bell metal tone ring in arched or flat head, laminated resonator, as well as an open-back model like that used by John Hartford.

Coffin Guitars

The mountain-style, square, or coffin guitar was made by rural American musicians who wanted to build a guitar but lacked the skills needed to curve the sides. Scott Morgan first saw one at the C. F. Martin Company Museum when he was 12 years old, but he didn't build one until

Barbara Atwood

Banjo with inlaid resonator (back view), designed for bluegrass playing, by David A. Sturgill

Coffin guitar by Scott Morgan

Back of coffin guitar by Scott Morgan

he was 24, in 1979. Since then he has built several and has been playing lead with his in concert with his family group, The Morgans, known for their old-time and blue-grass songs. Comparable in sound to the old Martin guitar, his rich-toned coffin guitars, made of spruce and rose-wood, are like traditional guitars in every way except the shape. Route 3, Box 204, Dayton, TN 37321; (615) 775-2996.   V (by appt.)   R   MO

Fiddles

Ever since English, Irish and Scottish immigrants brought their fiddles to America, fiddles have played an important role in folk, country and western music. Arlin Moon made his first fiddle when he was 17 years old, in 1930. "If you wanted to play a fiddle, you made it," he says. In the years since then, he's made fiddles, banjos and mandolins for some of the top country musicians in America. "A fiddle is good if it sounds good," he says. "Bad if it sounds bad." His sell as fast as he makes them. Although one of his banjos was exhibited in the Smith-sonian Institution, his favorite instrument to play is the fiddle, "because I can hear all the double tones and listen to the rolls." Route 2, Box 415, Holly Pond, AL 35083; (205) 796-2473.   V   R   MO

Other Makers

Royce Cleveland, Route 1, Maysville, GA 20558.

David A. Sturgill, Route 1, Box 211, Piney Creek, NC 28663; (919) 359-2280.

Hammered Dulcimers

One of the first instruments brought to America was the dulcimer; not the stringed or fretted version, known as the Appalachian dulcimer, but the hammered dulcimer, a rhythm and melody instrument shaped like a shallow wooden box strung with wires and sounded by striking or plucking. Moderately popular until the 1930s, it made a major comeback at the Newport Folk Festival in the 1960s. Although in some areas of the United States the dulcimer is only plucked, it is usually struck with mallets like a percussion instrument, its strings tuned to pitches so that musical notes are sounded as well as percussive rhythms. It's no accident that the hammer dulcimer re-sembles a portable piano without dampers; the hammer action of the piano is a sophisticated development of the hammered dulcimer principle.

Hammered dulcimer showing delicately carved wooden leaf inlay in sound holes by Sam Rizzetta

"It's a magical-sounding instrument that sounds like a giant music box or a cross between bells and a harp," says Sam Rizzetta, whose award-winning hammered dulcimers are a favorite of entertainers and considered the finest made in America.

Sam's dulcimers have been exhibited at the Smithsonian Institution; featured in documentaries, records and magazines; and have won the Governor's Award in West Virginia where he lives and works. The Rizzetta Standard, a large dulcimer with over three chromatic octaves, and other custom models are made by hand, one at a time, while his portable Dulcetta and Augusta models are produced in multiples in small batches. One of his trademarks is a delicately carved wooden leaf inlay in the sound hole. Priced from $300 to $5,500, all come with tuning wrench, hammers and instructions. Write for current price list. P.O. Box 510, Inwood, WV 25428; (304) 229-3166.   R W   MO

Other Makers

Tom Fellenbaum and Jerry Read Smith, Fellenbaum Dulcimer Workshop, 205 West State Street, Black Mountain, NC 28711; (704) 669-8950.

David Boyt, Route 4, Box 354, Neosho, MO 64850; (417) 451-5495, makes dulcimers of native woods: walnut, cherry, ash, maple or oak.

HARPSICHORDS

The harpsichord, preeminent keyboard instrument of the baroque era, is unique among keyboard instruments in that it plucks rather than strikes its strings. An important religious and secular instrument for centuries in Europe, it was built to order by American furniture and cabinet-makers much as they would make a chair or a chest. Smaller and more delicate than a piano, the harpsichord has a dry, brilliant sound, softer than a piano's, less resonant than a harp's.

"Composers often wrote for and conducted from the harpsichord," says David Holmes, artisan-in-residence at St. John's College in Annapolis, Maryland, "but from 1790 until 1903, when Arnold Dolmetsch built a few harpsichords at Chickering Piano Co., the instrument fell out of fashion. When John Challis began building harpsichords in 1930 they once again became the product of the artisan instead of the factory. His apprentice William Dowd continued the tradition and with Frank Hubbard laid the groundwork in research that has since made the American harpsichord the world standard."

The smallest and least expensive harpsichord, called the virginal (from the Latin *virginalis,* "of a young girl"), was the standard house instrument in early America, often the first instrument purchased for a young daughter. Many of the old string dulcimers made in Appalachia were patterned after the virginals, but because mountaineers lacked the sophistication to make keyboards and other action parts, they omitted these mechanisms and designed an instrument whose strings were plucked by hand.

"Early American spinets were fairly crudely made," says David, "and were small domestic instruments comparable to today's uprights. Pianos were definitely status symbols. The middle class had spinets, the upper middle class, harpsichords. The double harpsichord was the Cadillac of the group. At the time of the Revolution one cost £40. In today's dollars, that would be about $18,000 to $20,000. The clavichord, on the other hand, is a small, private instrument that can be carried under the arm. It has a quiet sound, yet lively presence, great for practice because it has a wide range of capability. The virginal's strings are at right angle to the keyboard; the spinet's at a 30-degree angle; the harpsichord's are parallel. The clavichord's strings, though similar in position to those of the virginal, are struck from underneath."

A former motion picture and television cameraman, David was building 1- and 2-ton racing sailboats when he decided to try making musical instruments by the same method: learning the skill by reading books over and over until he felt he had done it himself. He began with classical guitars; built several harpsichords, a positiv pipe organ to fit in a Toyota and a two-manual harpsichord used in the State House for the 200th anniversary of the signing of the Treaty of Paris; restored the 1806 Broadwood pianoforte in the Hammond-Harwood House; and re-

Spinet by David J. Holmes

Double manual harpsichord by David J. Holmes

Portable fretted clavichord by David J. Holmes

cently made a positiv to accompany a baroque singing group of which he is president.

Although his favorite wood is mahogany because "it works well under tools, is stable and doesn't shrink or swell with the weather," he works in fifteen to twenty different woods. "Each has its own purpose," says David. "The wrestplank, the heart of the instrument, which holds the tuning pins, must be strong, so I use oak (or beech when I can get it). Bridge, nuts and jack registers are pear because it's pretty, predictable and has fine grain. When veneered, case sides are poplar; if not, solid walnut. The keyboard is basswood. Keys are made of cow bone, the sharps skunktailed in ebony/bone sandwich construction."

Each instrument is made to conform as closely as possible in materials and dimensions to the best examples of antique instruments. The result is a finished product with the responsive action and full tone of the originals, yet the stability of temperament and action demanded of the concert stage.

Small triple-fretted clavichords are $1,850; virginals, $3,850; basic spinets, $5,000; single-manual harpsichords, painted without veneer, $7,500 to $8,000; double harpsichords "with everything," $18,500; and the positiv $25,000. David also makes Irish knee harps for $500.

David J. Holmes
123 Cathedral Street
Annapolis, MD 21401
(301) 268-0523
V   R   MO

SONG BOWS

A song bow is shaped like a shooting bow but is strung with wire to make music and played like a jaw, or Jew's, harp. Also known as a music bow, mouth bow, sambow, tune bow, jazz bow, bowharp, strummin' bow or pick-n-bow, it can be placed against the mouth and plucked with the finger or a small pick, stick or paddle; or vibrated by a player's breath as in whistling. While some say the song bow came to America from Africa, others credit the Cherokee Indians with introducing it to early settlers. A favorite folk instrument in the Ozark and Appalachian Mountains, the song bow has a happy twang and is most often used to play folk music.

"Our oldest daughter, Ellen, saw one in Arkansas where she was studying different types of music," says Bill Day, whose bows are considered the ultimate by players, "and told me how they were made. I cut down a shellbark hickory tree and kept working with a drawknife and vise until

I flexed a piece to suit me, then carved a tuning peg and strung it with 20/1,000 piano wire. It worked real good. People seemed to get a kick out of seeing and hearing the pick-n-bow, so I started making more of them to sell."

Bows can be made of any straight-grain wood like hickory, ash, white oak or cedar, but Bill prefers walnut "because it looks better." He says, "A bow can be of any dimension, but it should be made to flex right. If the flex is stiff it will have a high tone; if it is limber, it will have a low tone. They can be any length, but those 3 feet long have the best sound. Shorter than that loses some of the tone."

Tools used to make music bows are the same as those used to make shingles: a froe (a cleaving tool with a heavy blade set at a right angle to the handle), a knobmaul and a homemade shaving horse. The wood, cut 3 feet long, 1¼ inches wide and ¼ inch thick, has a double thickness about 4½ inches long on one end, where a hole is drilled for the 4-inch-long tuning peg. After the wire is threaded through a small hole in the other end of the bow, it is pulled through a guide loop, then through the tuning peg and tightened until there is a 3- to 4-inch space between the wire and bow.

To play, the end opposite the tuning peg is placed against the open lips and a pick used either flat or edgewise to pluck the wire. Tones are made by changing the cavity of the mouth with the tongue or using resonators like gourds or hollowed pieces of wood. Folklorist Bill Caswell, who has performed with Day at Dollywood, Tennessee, six to ten times a day, says, "There is something about the true mountain sound of Bill's bows that absolutely mesmerizes the audience."

When the bows weren't selling as fast as he thought they should, Bill started making wooden bowls, originally "in the living room, but after I made a few holes in the carpet, my wife decided I should have my own shop." He mastered bowls the same way he learned how to make song bows: he "just started chopping." He makes both bowls and bows by hand. His pick-n-bows sell for $20 each, while his bowls (see Treenware) range in price from $20 to $200.

A former county commissioner, farmer, firefighter and rail-splitting champion, Bill Day now makes a bowl a day, selling them by word of mouth and at the Indiana State and Gatlinburg (Tennessee) Fairs. It's easy to find his booth. Just follow the sound of the song bow.

Bill Day
Rural Route 1, Box 64
West Lebanon, IN 47991
(317) 893-4390
V   R   S   MO

Other Maker

Rick Stewart, Route 2, Box 328, Sneedville, TN 37869; (615) 733-2617 (days) and 733-4214 (evenings).

STRINGED DULCIMERS

The word *dulcimer,* derived from the Middle English *dowcemere,* the Old French *doulcemer,* the Latin *dulce* and the Greek *melos,* means "sweet song." A musical instrument with wire strings of the same length stretched over a long slender sound box that is played with a pick or a quill, the plucked dulcimer, like its name, evolved from several cultures and is uniquely American.

Appalachian, Kentucky and mountain dulcimers (also called "delcymores" by mountaineers) have no set size, pattern or standard, which means that they can be made of whatever wood is available in any shape that pleases the owner. Ideal for playing ballads, folksongs and hymns, dulcimers have a soft mellow tone and are easy to tune and to play.

Robert Mize, who wrote the directions for making dulcimers in *Foxfire 3,* says anyone can learn to play one in 15 minutes. "If you can pick out a tune on the piano with one finger," he says, "you can play a dulcimer, because the frets are like the white keys. There are no sharps or flats. Each fret is a note of the scale. The range of the fingerboard is fourteen frets or two octaves. The first string carries the melody while the drone strings carry the beat and rhythm."

If you prefer a dulcimer made of a single wood, Mize says cherry or maple is nice, but the best, most mellow

Atteberry/Indianapolis Star

Song-bow maker Bill Day demonstrating proper playing technique

Stringed dulcimers in elongated hourglass shape with scroll and shamrock sound holes by Robert Mize

tone is achieved by using a combination of two or more woods, preferably black walnut for the back and sides, with chestnut, butternut, gum or sassafras for the top, because "different woods make different sounds." He uses cured, kiln-dried solid lumber. "The lumber from different trees of the same species will vary in color and texture, as will the grain, depending on where and how it is cut from the log."

Most important is construction. He uses an elongated hourglass shape with three, four or five strings. The shape and size of the sound holes have little effect on the sound, so he makes them in scroll, cross, shamrock, heart and diamond shapes. Keeping as close to the traditional dulcimer as possible, he uses no fancy inlays, veneers or plywood and makes wooden keys from Brazilian rosewood. After three coats of sanding sealer lacquer and three coats of finish lacquer, his dulcimers are hand-rubbed, waxed, signed, dated and registered. Guaranteed for a year against defects in materials or workmanship, the standard model sells for $175 (with delivery 2 to 3 weeks from date

of order), while custom-made curly cherry, curly maple or burled walnut runs $250. Mechanical tuners must be custom-ordered and cost $15 extra. Shipping is by UPS with a wall display bracket and instruction book included.

Like a fine violin, a well-made dulcimer will improve in tone quality with age and playing. "I don't make seconds and never let a bad one out of the shop," says Bob Mize, only one of the many reasons his dulcimers have been given as state gifts to world dignitaries and exhibited at the Smithsonian. With his wife, Maude, son, Stephen, and daughter, Jane Mize Jones, all involved in the business, Bob is the only one who cannot play the dulcimer. "I have no rhythm," he admits, "and I prefer making dulcimers to playing them."

Robert R. Mize
Route 2, Box 288
Blountville, TN 37617
(615) 323-8489
R   MO

Other Makers

Warren A. May, 110 Center Street, Berea, KY 40403; (606) 986-9293, makes traditional Appalachian Mountain dulcimers in three- and four-string models in mahogany, yellow poplar, walnut, cherry, Kentucky red maple or fancy maple and in natural knothole and teardrop shapes, priced from $175 to $300, with 2 to 3 weeks for delivery. Special orders on request.

J. Richard Willis, Route 8, Box 230, Carthage, MS 39051.

Edward and Anne Damm, Great Lakes Dulcimers, 118 Ledgelawn Street, Bar Harbor, ME 04609; (207) 288-3102, make dulcimers and children's harps.

Tom Fellenbaum, Fellenbaum Dulcimer Workshop, 205 West State Street, Black Mountain, NC 28711; (704) 669-8950, makes hourglass and teardrop stringed dulcimers with three, four or five strings in spruce, cedar or redwood tops for a rich mellow tone. He also makes guitars and bouzoukis.

Robert D. Hutchinson, North Country Dulcimers, RD 4, Box 269, Dambach Avenue, Valencia, PA 16059; (412) 625-9232.

Ukeleles

The four-string *ukelele* (a word that means "jumping flea") is an Hawaiian interpretation of the five-string Portuguese *machete da majao* brought to the Sandwich Islands in the late 19th century. Although it's also known as the Hawaiian guitar, it's smaller and has fewer strings. "It's a so-called musical instrument," Will Rogers once said, describing its twang, "which, when listened to, you can't tell whether one is playing on it or just monkeying with it."

Most often heard accompanying hula dancing, the ukelele was first introduced to the mainland in 1915 during the Panama-Pacific Exposition in San Francisco, became popular with collegians in the 1920s and more widely known in the 1940s and 1950s because of the playing of Arthur Godfrey on radio and television. The instrument has an all-wood belly and was traditionally strung with gut but is now most often made with wire or nylon strings.

Makers

David Gomes, P.O. Box 5, Kapa'au, HI 96755; (808) 889-5100.

Kamaka Ukelele, 550 South King Street, Honolulu, HI 96813; (808) 531-3165.

Douglas Ching, 1229-C Waimanu Street, Honolulu, HI 96814; (808) 537-6451.

Nails *See* Iron, Nails and Latches

Needlework Tools

Like old-time turners, Bill Schmidt turns his needlework tools freehand without the aid of forms, patterns or templates. His partner, Diana Andra, who is responsible for the development and production of their tatting shuttles,

Shuttles for tatting by Diana Andra

assists him in making crochet hooks ($6.50 each, or a set of six in a velvet-lined cherry or walnut case for $59); knitting needles (maple $6, rosewood $8 a pair); four sizes of functional or decorative thimbles, including topless tailor's thimbles ($3.50); tatting shuttles ($8 to $12); lace bobbins ($3.50 each, $7 a pair); darning eggs ($7) and gauges used to measure handmade hooks and needles ($3.50). William Schmidt and Diana Andra, 704 West 4th Street, Mansfield, OH 44906; (419) 525-0776 or 526-2056. R W S MO

Netting *See* Lace and Netting

Notch Art *See* Carving, Tramp Art

Occhi *See* Tatting

Oriental Pictures *See* Tinsel Painting

Oyle Cloth *See* Floorcloths

Painted Carpet or Canvas *See* Floorcloths

Painted Grain *See* Graining

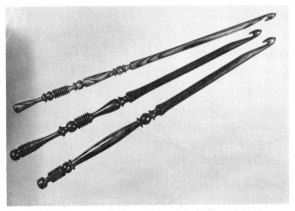
Crochet hooks in range of styles and woods by William Schmidt

PAPER

The making of paper by hand ended in America near the turn of the century when the speed and consistency of machines outpaced human hands. However, machine-made paper's consistency can be aesthetically boring, which is why in 1928 Dard Hunter began to handmake paper again. The success of his mill was cut short by the Depression, and no one established another hand mill until Kathryn and Howard Clark founded Twinrocker in 1971.

"We wanted to make paper in traditional ways," says Kathryn, "but decided to do what could best be done by hand: limited editions of paper for particular projects; developing new techniques; and collaborating with artists, fine book printers, bookbinders, calligraphers, conservators and designers who needed special papers. We wanted to push the craft to unknown artistic ends and allow the artistic image to begin in the paper. The core of Twinrocker is making the 'anonymous' sheet, one that is incomplete and must be used by someone. Aesthetically alive, like the bud of a flower, it anticipates what is to come."

The Twinrocker logo and watermark, two rockers back to back, is an appropriate symbol for the Clarks. They met in Detroit, Michigan, while Kathryn was studying print-making and Howard, a mechanical engineer, was designing machinery for a manufacturer of materials-handling equipment. When Kathryn began working as a lithographer in San Francisco, printing limited editions for a famous artist, she became more and more convinced that the sheet of paper was as important as the image on it. Handmade paper from Europe was difficult to get, so

Kathryn Clark putting pulp into mold to make paper

on April Fools' Day 1971, Howard began building a Hollander beater in the basement of their apartment and the Clarks began making artistic and archival papers by hand. The next year they moved the operation to Brookston, Indiana, where Howard designed and built a mill.

"We had no teachers," says Kathryn, "but the good thing about learning on your own is that you shape it yourself and it's yours. When people came to us to learn, we learned together."

They made a shaped paper for William Wiley's *Mask* from colored cotton rags and old chicken feathers, and in 1973 nearly went bankrupt learning to make 3- by 4-foot sheets for Jim Dine's print *The Red Banana*. But it was a first; no one had made paper that large before. In 1981 when Robert Rauschenberg exposed sections of paper as an integral part of the design in his *Arcanum Series*, the paper he used was Twinrocker's.

After 10 years of developing new techniques, teaching, giving hundreds of lectures and workshops throughout the United States, and training thirteen apprentices, "We decided enough universities were offering courses and we no longer had to assume that responsibility," says Kathryn. "Our goal now is to keep the handmill in operation long after we're dead. To help it grow in the community, we bought another building and began training local people."

Paper is made from plant fibers beaten into pulp, a process requiring knowledge of fibers, cooking procedures and beating, which determines hardness, softness, rattle, printability, opacity, transluscency, folding/tearing strength and shrinkage while drying. Light beating produces coarse, soft paper ideal for casting sculpture; much beating makes finer, stronger, harder sheets for books. Twinrocker makes paper in the Western tradition from many combinations of fibers, in smooth to loft-dried finish (which is quite rough), in thicknesses from .004 inch to very heavy board weight, in any size or shape from the smallest imaginable to 4- by 8-foot sheets. They also create custom or toned portrait watermarks.

There is always a large selection of art, watercolor and book papers on hand sold by the sheet. For a sample swatch, send $3. Priced according to the hand mold on which it is made, paper ranges from $3 for a sheet of 12- by 18-inch antique laid text weight to $225 for a sheet of 48- by 96-inch wove heavy art weight. For custom orders there is a $100 setup fee and a $500 minimum. Twinrocker also sells the supplies they use: ready-to-use beaten pulp in 5-gallon pails or unbeaten fibrous form by the pound. For a comprehensive primer on paper, send for their catalog. For information, call between 8 A.M. and 7 P.M. 7 days a week.

Kathryn and Howard Clark
Twinrocker Handmade Paper
RFD 2, Brookston, IN 47923
(317) 563-3210
V (by appt.)   R   C   CC   MO

Other Makers

Rosemarie Huart-Wourms, 4876 Harlou Drive, Dayton, OH 45432; (513) 256-6050, makes stationery in soft, subtle colors packaged in a handmade paper folder, four envelopes with notepaper $12, plus shipping and handling.

Margaret Rhein, Terrapin Paper Mill, 2318 Nicholson Street, Cincinnati, OH 45211; (513) 662-9382, creates high-quality, all-cotton handmade papers in a variety of sizes, shapes, colors and weights as well as elegant blank books in a number of styles.

POLISH PAPERCUTS

The word most often used to describe the style, execution and color selection in Polish papercuts is *brilliant.* Cut in many folds, sometimes in a single color and at other times layered so that colors reinforce the design or challenge each other, Polish papercuts have a verve that evolves from creating new designs rather than repeating traditional motifs.

Known as *wycinanka,* Polish papercuts originated as a folk art in the 18th century and were used to decorate homes for festive occasions, particularly at Eastertime. As new cuts were made, old *wycinanki* were hung on the walls of barns for the cattle to enjoy. Villages tried to outdo

one another in the use of colors and intricate designs. As the craft was passed from generation to generation, Polish paper-cutting developed an electric quality equal to dynamic tension in sculpture. The major development in Polish paper-cutting since immigrants brought it to America has been in size. Keeping pace with the dreams and expectations of its artisans, *wycinanki* grew larger and more expressive.

When the Balch Institute for Ethnic Studies wanted to show how Polish paper-cutting was influenced by life in America, they chose the work of Jaga Ruta to exhibit. Born in Lodz, Jaga graduated from the University of Warsaw and the College of Art in Lodz and taught drawing, painting and sculpture. In addition to designing stained-glass windows, mosaics and jewelry for an international chain of stores, and patterns for the textile industry, Jaga translated *wycinanka* designs into embroidery patterns, which were later incorporated into a book. Since arriving in the United States in 1971, she has decorated Boehm porcelain, designed paper for Gibson Greetings, Inc., and worked on the restoration of several churches and residences.

Jaga's designs are much like looking into the center of a magic kaleidoscope. The longer and more closely her designs are examined, the more they reveal. Geometrics become dancers, thistles have faces, blades of wheat become a menorah. Her colors glow with the intensity of a well-executed stained-glass window. Her designs incorporate people, animals, flowers, both naturalistic motifs and geometric figures called *gwiazdy,* which means "stars." Each color and symbol has meaning: a rooster, a new day; birds, love and caring; flowers, happiness; trees, freedom.

"Nepponese," papercut by Jadwiga Ruta

"Love Story," papercut by Jadwiga Ruta

"Daisies," papercut by Jadwiga Ruta

"Iris Hybrids," papercut by Jadwiga Ruta

Jaga also does stained glass, tapestries and mosaics on a commission basis.

Jadwiga Ruta
12326 Medford Road
Philadelphia, PA 19154
(215) 632-4641
R W S MO

Other Makers

Kati Ritchie, 1704 Ashland Avenue, St. Paul, MN 55104; (612) 644-8005, sells *wycinanki* for $5 for a small card to $375 for a large framed wall piece.

Magdalena Nowalka-Gilinsky, 4474 MacArthur Boulevard, NW, #4, Washington, DC 20007, does *wycinanki* on commission.

Parquetry *See* **Inlay, Marquetry and Parquetry**

Pearl Painting *See* **Tinsel Painting**

Petacas

Petacas are leather-covered boxes, trunks and chests used by early Hispanic-Americans. Although the chest had

Petaca (Spanish colonial pine chest) covered with steer rawhide, lined with reproduction newspaper and decorated with 1880 rodeo poster, by Steven M. Lalioff

Yellow represents spirituality; orange, attraction; red, love; purple, royalty; and blue, health.

"When creating these paper cutouts," says Jaga, "peasants used dyes from herbs on specially glazed paper, often black on white or vice versa, with other colors used for detailing. The technique, which graduated from a folk art to a recognized art form in the 19th century, involved a piece of paper folded two, four, eight, or sixteen times. I introduced six as a different folding pattern, and use any color that works well in the design. To date, I have created more than 200 copyrighted designs. Unlike peasants who used large sheep shears centuries ago, I use very small manicure scissors, with gift-wrapping paper for the designs and a heavier gauge poster board for the background."

Her completed 16- by 16-inch designs are $100 framed.

Petaca covered with hand-stamped leather and with more than 200 handmade nails by Victoria Adams

a board bottom, the boards were not nailed together, but instead were sewn into pockets of leather. The joints are essentially sewn leather and flexible to withstand the rigor of travel by ox-drawn carts and mule trains. Like contemporary luggage, it was made in less and more expensive forms. The *petaca* by Steven M. Lalioff, a reproduction of one used in the 1860s, is a pine frame covered with steer rawhide, with tanned leather edges and brass tacks, lined with reproduction newspaper and a rodeo poster. The more ornate hand-tooled leather chest by Victoria Adams after one in the Folk Art Museum, Santa Fe, New Mexico, is trimmed with more than 200 handmade nails, a silver lock and corners and a painting inside the lid by Buckeye Blake of Augusta, Montana.

Makers

Steven M. Lalioff, 14311 Bryn Mawr Drive, Noblesville, IN 46060; (317) 773-5389.

Victoria Adams, Silversmith, 2801 South Old Stage Road, Mt. Shasta, CA 96067; (916) 826-3291.

Star Tapia, Route 6, Box 01, Aqua Fria, Santa Fe, NM 87501.

CAST PEWTER

As part of its 350th birthday celebration, Boston recreated a colonial village on the Common and peopled it with families and tradespeople who might have lived there in the 1600s. It contained only one woman artisan: pewterer Lydia Holmes.

"A female pewterer would have been unusual in the early days of Massachusetts," Lydia says, "because a woman couldn't become a pewterer unless her father had no sons or her husband died and left her the business."

Lydia's path to pewter began as a child when her brother found an early latten spoon in a Plymouth sandbank. "Latten was the predecessor of pewter. Made from a mixture of metals, latten looked and tasted like brass. It was coated with tin to resemble silver, but the tin wore with use, and unlike pewter, latten couldn't be melted down and reused."

Her father took the spoon to his father-in-law, Ellis Brewster (a direct descendant of the Pilgrim Elder), who surprised him by giving him a bronze spoon mold that had been in the family for at least five generations.

"It was unusual for a family to have their own mold," says Lydia. "Molds were so rare they were bequeathed in wills. Most spoons were made by a pewterer who traveled from town to town, which is why so many people had the same pattern in tableware. Once my father's interest was piqued, he started collecting spoon molds, one of which turned out to be a 1690 mold of the only spoon ever recovered from an archeological site in the Plymouth area" (the Joseph Howland House in Kingston, Massachusetts).

Spoon molds from the collection of Pilgrim Pewterers

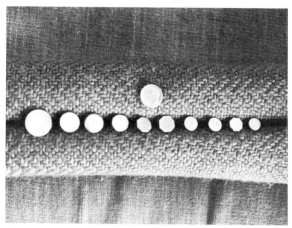

Shank buttons by Pilgrim Pewterers

To protect the inner surfaces of her molds from the molten pewter, Lydia first smokes them by holding the molds over a candle flame. She then pours the heated pewter into the upright mold held in a wooden vise (a technique known as gravity casting because the pewter falls by its own weight). After the spoon or button is formed, it is hand-ground, buffed and stamped with the touchmark *L* for Lydia, to distinguish it from an antique or reproduction. Spoons range from $6 to $12, while buttons cost $1.10 each.

Lydia and Evan Holmes
Pilgrim Pewterers
Sudbury Road
Stow, MA 01775
(617) 568-8838
R   C   MO

The collection has since evolved into Pilgrim Pewterers, owned by Lydia and her husband, Evan, who use original antique molds to produce "not reproductions, but modern originals" of five antique spoons and ten different shank buttons dating from the late 1600s to the early 1700s. All five spoons have a rattail, an extension of the handle under the bowl to provide strength.

"Spoons were all-purpose utensils," says Lydia. "They had to be large enough for serving, small enough for eating. Pewter was too soft for forks; the tines broke off. When people needed a knife, they used the end of the spoon. Pewter was the poor man's silver. The wealthy used silver from England, while the poor used wooden spoons. The English pewter guilds would not allow raw tin (the prime ingredient for pewter) to be exported to the colonies and sent only broken English pewter, which the colonists melted down and remade. That's why many early pieces were not signed."

American pewter was harder, thinner and lighter than the English, looked more like silver than Sheffield plate and cost one-tenth as much as silver. It could be melted down and remade. Its value was constant, which in an age of barter meant that it was as good as money. American pewterers also could sell their wares for less than imports because they didn't have to pay tax, freight or middlemen.

Pilgrim Pewterers' formula of 95 percent tin with small amounts of copper and antimony has *no* lead, which means their spoons can be used for eating and serving. "It's a treat to eat with a pewter spoon," says Lydia. "The soft feeling of the metal coupled with its warmth makes eating a very tactile experience."

It takes as many as ten castings to create a perfect spoon.

Martha Mae Emerson

Hurricane oil lamps with pewter base and solid brass burner by Ted and Cheryl White (pewter lamp design © 1984 Ted White)

Other Makers

David Jones, Prop., Three Feathers Pewter, 245 Collins Avenue, Columbus, OH 43215; (614) 221-5768.

Ted and Cheryl White, Stoneham Pewter, RFD 1, Stoneham Corners, Box 656, Brookfield, NH 03872; (603) 522-3425, make candleholders, snuffers, cordial glasses, napkin rings, bells, matchboxes, and hurricane oil lamps.

Hampshire Pewter Company, 9 Mill Street, P.O. Box 1570, Wolfeboro, NH 03894; (603) 569-4944, decorated a Christmas tree on the Ellipse in front of the White House in 1983 and has reproduced objects for the Metropolitan Museum of Art. For a catalog of more than 125 items, send $2.

Jay Thomas Stauffer, 707 West Brubaker Valley Road, Lititz, PA 17543-0707; (717) 626-7067.

Village Pewter, 320 West Washington Street, Medina, OH 44256; (800) 922-1946.

Ship's decanter, goblets and cordial glass by Rebecca Hungerford

HAND-FORGED PEWTER

"From what I've read," says Rebecca Hungerford, Kansas City, Missouri's only pewtersmith and a member of the American Pewterers Guild, "there were no early pewterers farther west than St. Louis. That's because Kansas City was founded about the same time pewter went out of fashion."

Becky started working with pewter in high school, earning money by making and selling pewter pins. After graduation from college, she apprenticed in Frederick, New Brunswick, to learn fabrication, lathe work, soldering techniques and how to make her own molds.

"I love the softness of pewter," she says. "When I design a piece, I consider how highlights will enhance it." Traditional pewter is especially appealing, she thinks, "because 17th and 18th century styles caught the spirit of the metal. It wasn't overworked with embossed designs."

For concentric forms, she makes molds of hardwood because "it won't compress or change during the spinning process like softwood." Starting with a flat disk of pewter, which is held next to a form on the lathe, Becky guides the metal with a wooden stick held in each hand. Wood absorbs some of the frictional heat caused by the speed of the lathe (700 rpm). "Changing the direction of the metal takes leverage, strength and muscle," says the 5-foot-2-inch smith. "To get a nice even wall all the way up, it's necessary to stay in control. Otherwise, it wrinkles like piecrust. If pewter is pushed too far or too fast, it will thin out and break."

Becky also turns on the lathe (cutting through a solid

piece of pewter to create a shape). Stems and handles are solid cast to give objects extra weight. For cast pieces, she creates her own vulcanized rubber molds for centrifugally poured pewter. She solders and welds sections together, then files and buffs the object.

"The colonial smith cast most of his pieces and parts," she says, "and used an 'apprentice-powered' lathe to skim off the rough exterior of the cast pieces." Early pewterers scrubbed pewter with sand, but Becky uses fine steel wool or a Scotch Brite pad to apply a satin finish. This polishing also makes joints invisible. Unlike colonial pewterers who "would add any metal that would melt, even lead shot" when they couldn't get enough tin, Becky's Pewter Shop uses only the finest lead-free pewter composed of 92 percent tin, 1 to 2 percent copper and 6 to 7 percent antimony. It is comparable in quality, she says, to the best 18th century pewter.

Her carefully researched pieces include a ship's decanter whose wide bottom and low center of gravity keep it from tipping over ($138); a ship's sconce that keeps its balance in stormy seas ($66); and chargers (large plates that were originally made of wood) for $48. Her early inkwell, true to its origins, instead of being open all the way down has only a small depression on the top. "That surprises people, who forget that colonists mixed dry powder with water to make ink," Becky explains. Complete with quill, it sells for $24. Jefferson cups are $14. "When Jefferson didn't like the style of a pair of goblets given to him as a gift, he redesigned them," says Becky, "then asked a local smith to melt them down and make eight new cups without stems and handles."

The Pewter Shop offers similar services as well as custom

Five-piece tea or coffee set with walnut handles by Rebecca Hungerford

Mug, candlestick, candle snuffer, vase and hurricane lamp (partially hidden) by Rebecca Hungerford

design work, repair and engraving services. For a copy of their brochure of more than fifty items, including seventeen Christmas tree ornaments, a dozen larger bas-relief animals, tea sets, bowls, goblets, trays, buttons, figures, frames and candlesticks, send a self-addressed, stamped envelope. Shop is open Tuesday through Thursday, 10 A.M. to 6 P.M., and on Friday and Saturday, 10 A.M. to 5 P.M.

Rebecca Hungerford, Pewtersmith
The Pewter Shop
21 Westport Square
Kansas City, MO 64111
(716) 753-5255
V   R   W   C   S   MO

Other Makers

Woodbury Pewterers, 860 Main Street South, Woodbury, CT 06798; (203) 263-2668, make bowls, candlesticks, coffeepots, mugs, tankards and teapots.

David Weber, 320 West Washington Street, Medina, OH 44256; (216) 725-8545.   C

J. Thomas Stauffer, 707 West Brubaker Valley Road, Lititz, PA 17543-0707; (717) 626-7067. Send self-addressed, stamped envelope for catalog.

Jack Davis, Ranier Metalcraft, P.O. Box 44382, Tacoma, WA 98444, spins brass, copper, pewter, aluminum, gold and sterling; lamps, candlesticks and bowls made from wooden molds; soldering, casting and polishing.

Pewter Liturgical Items   *See* **Liturgical Gold, Silver and Pewter**

PEWTER TRADE ITEMS

Most people know that the Indians traded Manhattan for a handful of beads, but few know that the tribe was just passing through and didn't own the island. The Europeans, however, learned a valuable lesson: Indians loved trade items. Salt, metal cooking pots, clay pipes, knives, fish hooks and axes, tiny bells, colored beads, tomahawks and match coats (a cloak of coarse wool) brought food and furs in exchange, but small effigies were easier to carry.

The inventory of pewtersmiths Jim and Barbara Strode contains several of these trade items, including kissing otters (originally made of silver) and several sizes of turtles and beavers. Crosses were made in many sizes and styles as trade items and gifts for the Indians and included the Cross of Lorraine brought into the Northwest Territory from the French district of Lorraine and a fleur-de-lis pendant, also popular in the Northwest Territory.

The Strodes saw their first brass mold used to gravity-cast pewter spoons while visiting East Coast restorations in the 1960s, and bought their first spoon mold 2 years later. They now produce a 19th century cup plate (used to hold the cup when coffee was poured into the saucer to cool), a pap boat (for feeding semisolid foods to infants

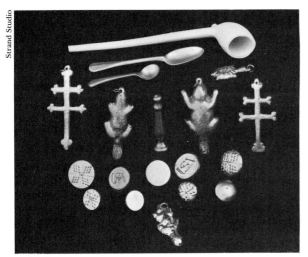

Assortment of pewter trade items, including pipe, spoons, crosses and buttons, by Jim and Barbara Strode

and invalids), a 2 $\frac{7}{16}$-inch beaker rum cup with a 4-ounce capacity, a 2-inch pipe tamper and a child's whistle. Their pewter is a lead-free, nontoxic alloy of 95 percent tin, 3 percent copper and 1 percent each of antimony and bismuth.

"Our pieces are gravity cast," says Barb, "then filed and polished by hand. Most of the spoons, all of the buttons and the 8-inch dinner plate are cast in brass molds dating from the late 18th and early 19th centuries." Each piece is signed with an acorn (their touchmark) and a consecutive number for that style in that year (if the piece

Assortment of pewter spoons, plates, bowls, candlesticks and candle snuffer by Jim and Barbara Strode

was cast in an original mold). "We also include research on each of the pieces and on the mold in which it was cast," says Barb.

Their twelve spoon styles include: Queen Ann and Trifid II tablespoons cast in molds made by Josiah Miller, who worked in New England between 1725 and 1775; fiddleback; sunburst; midrib; demitasse; bird (a neoclassical style made in an original mold with wooden handles: a bird engraved on the front of the handle and the back of the bowl, plus two crowns and a lion on the back of the handle); as well as a sealtop teaspoon dating from the late 16th century. Their plates include an 8-inch one cast in an original mold and a porringer. Six button shapes include two sizes of Continental Army, plus plain and domed in various sizes.

All pieces are available in one of three finishes: satin, antique or dark. Prices are based upon the quantity of metal, time used for production and whether the mold is an original or a reproduction. Mail orders are billed for the amount of the order plus postage at the time of shipment.

Jim and Barbara Strode
3766 Sheridan
Saginaw, MI 48601
(517) 777-6625
R W C MO

CEREMONIAL STONE PIPES

When Native Americans met to discuss war or peace, to purchase a bride or to settle land disputes, a ceremonial pipe was used to solemnize the occasion. Because the pipe was a passport for safe travel, early traders soon learned to "trade on the pipe." After a pipe was placed on the ground between two parties, each side would place what they had to trade in a pile beside the pipe. When everyone was satisfied, each group gathered up their new possessions and left. The same system was used for ransoming or exchanging captives.

Smoking the pipe was a sign of willingness to discuss an issue and was used as the formal act of accepting an agreement, much as we sign and seal a contract. However, when the settlers coined the term "peace pipe," they didn't realize that such a truce lasted only until the visiting party was out of sight of the camp in which the smoking took place. Except for when a brave fasted, prayed or meditated, smoking was something shared with others and the spiritual powers of the universe. Indians smoked tobacco to bring peace, blessings and friendship, stop evil and storms and to gain protection.

The simplest and oldest form was the tube pipe, made of bone (usually a section of leg bone from a deer, antelope or bison) wrapped with sinew to keep it from cracking and from burning the fingers. Elbow pipes with an L-shaped stone bowl and separate wood stem were popular in the Plains, while a T-shaped style, called the Plains, or Sioux, had a projecting point in front of the bowl. A rarer disk pipe, associated with the Iowa, Oto and Osage, is characterized by a small-bore bowl surrounded by a large, flat-topped disk. The micmac was a blunter, chunkier model used by the Plains Ojibwa, the Plains Cree and the Blackfoot tribes.

Pipe stems were usually straight and made of wood like ash and sumac, whose soft, pithy core was easily removed. Some stems were thin and flat, others round. They could be plain or highly decorated with braided porcupine quills, horsehair, feathers, fur and colorful materials like beads. Decorating with red feathers instead of white was a sign of war. Ornate pipe stems were used as ceremonial dance wands in the brotherhood or adoption ceremony of the Dakota and Pawnee tribes.

Some bowls were made of pottery and wood, but the most popular were made of stone like steatite, catlinite, argillite, shale and limestone, which was soft enough to carve, yet not damaged by heat.

Long before the white man reached the northern plains, Native Americans of many tribes were traveling as much as a thousand miles by foot to reach the sacred pipestone quarries of southwestern Minnesota. A widespread legend among the Indians was that catlinite or pipestone, a soft red layer between the layers of hard quartzite, was made from the flesh and blood of their ancestors. A well-made catlinite pipe bowl was worth a horse in trade. The site

Carved 8-inch stone pipe by John Julius Wilnoty

of the quarry was sacred ground where Indians met in peace. When the federal government acquired the land from the Dakota for Pipestone National Monument, it was decreed that all Indians might continue to quarry there.

Today, third and fourth generation pipe makers using ordinary hand tools quarry and carve pipes like those of their ancestors. After squaring up a block of stone with a saw, the maker scribes the outline, saws a pipe blank and drills it. The pipe is then shaped with files, rasps and knives, sanded smooth and finished with beeswax.

The shop in the Cultural Center at Pipestone National Monument sells dozens of styles of pipes ranging from a Plains style with a feather decoration to one with elaborate inlayed lead designs. The shop also has a wide variety of carved animal effigies such as turtles, owls, bears and buffalo.

Pipestone Indian Shrine Association
Pipestone National Monument
P.O. Box 727
Pipestone, MN 56164
(507) 825-5463
V   R   W   C   S   MO

Other Maker

John Julius Wilnoty, Qualla Arts & Crafts Center, P.O. Box 277, Cherokee, NC 28719; (704) 497-3103. Also sold through Medicine Man Craft Shop, P.O. Box 256, Cherokee, NC 28719.

Pisanki   *See* **Eggs, Decorated**

POND MODELS

Toy boats are for play, models for display, but a good pond model, as finely crafted as a full-scale vessel, can be

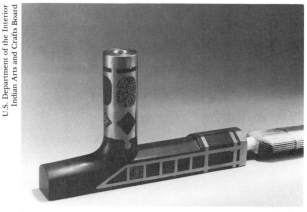

Santee Sioux pipe bowl and stem of catlinite with lead inlay, pine, paint and leather

Sandbagger by Michael deLesseps

Channel Cutter A by Michael deLesseps

used, played with, displayed *and* teach a child how to sail.

"Pond models are not as intimidating as big boats," says Michael deLesseps, who learned to sail before he rode a bike, made his first half hull when he was 12 and has been making sailboats, pond models and sailing toys all his life. "Nothing teaches the rudiments of sailing like experimentation and observation. The premise of a pond boat and a sailboat is the same, so a child can learn while he plays, but without the risks and responsibilities of a larger boat."

Enjoyed alone, a pond boat can transform an ordinary pond into a private world; when shared, it can open lines of communication on more than one level. "I treasure the note a father wrote to me after spending an afternoon at a pond with his son and one of my boats," says Michael. "He said he never realized how much his son knew about sailing, but that he also learned things about his son as a person that he had never known, that touched him deeply." Until 1981, Michael commuted weekly to New York City and a career in advertising. "But then my values changed," he explains. "I was tired of being away from home. I'd made boats for other people's kids for years and decided why not do full time what I enjoy doing most?"

Michael's pond models, built to order just as they do in working boatyards, are all based on traditional vessels but modified slightly for better performance on a smaller scale. Built to last, each is made by hand, from rough carving to the finely sanded and painted hull. Hardwood spars are turned with proper taper and finished with stain and varnish bristol fashion. All jibs and mainsails are hand-cut, numbered and sewn from real sailcloth, which sheds water; does not rot, mildew, sag or wrinkle; and outlasts cotton, which absorbs water, adding weight and in turn adversely affecting performance. The headstay is sewn into the jib and made of tough $^3/_{64}$-inch leech line, with small parts and fittings of solid brass.

"We build them the way they used to," says Michael, whose boats have been purchased by many prominent American collectors. "No magic, just hard work." The 22½-inch-long Sandbagger, the classic American sailing toy, is modeled after the sloop-rigged small boats used by East Coast fisheries. Distinctly American, its hull, center-board and rig influenced the design of yachts and work boats for more than 40 years (with stand, $150). His most popular model is the 16½-inch English Channel Cutter A ($200); while the Cutter B, his largest production boat, 36 inches from bowsprit to boom, with a hull 24 inches long, is the most difficult and time-consuming to make ($800). Custom sailing models average $20 per inch, depending on the complexity of the model. His latest model, a radio-controlled, electric-powered, 31-inch launch that's "beautiful at hull speed and produces an almost perfect quarter wave", is designed after the 1891 Atlantic Boatworks launch in the Mystic Seaport Museum. It's carved from one block of basswood, with mahogany deck and hatches, and a two-channel radio control.

In addition to building custom half hulls, Michael repairs old sailing toys and pond models and also provides parts for those who wish to make their own repairs.

Michael deLesseps
The Dockyard
P.O. Box 74
South Freeport, ME 04078
(207) 865-3465
V (by appt.)   R   C ($2)   S   MO

18TH CENTURY STONEWARE, EARTHENWARE AND SALT-GLAZE POTTERY

Jugtown Pottery, 3 miles northeast of Route 705 in the "dark corner" of Moore County in North Carolina's Piedmont, looks much as it might have in the 1700s when the area was settled by potters from Staffordshire, England. A cluster of log cabins nestled in a stand of pines just off the road and the fragrance of wood-burning fires inviting passersby to come in and visit, attract thousands annually from all over the United States and many foreign countries. Before the end of the last century, there were nearly fifty potteries in this 20-square-mile area, many making whiskey jugs, which is how the area got its

Candlesticks by Jugtown Pottery

Jug by Jugtown Pottery

name. Today, there are only eleven potteries, the best known of which is Jugtown.

Owner Vernon Owens, descendant of generations of potters, threw his first pot when he was 4 years old. "By the time I was 8," he says, "I was turning ashtrays and flowerpots for my daddy's shop." But it wasn't until he was in his late 20s that he decided to make pots his career. "I like being involved in the whole process of making pottery," he says, "from digging the clay to meeting the people who buy and use the pots."

Today, with three potters and five other workers, Vernon makes functional objects for everyday living just as his ancestors did in the 18th century. Native clay is dug, dried, ground to a powder, mixed with water and blended in a pug mill, then stored in the earth floor of the pottery. Vernon takes a ball of this clay, throws it on the moving wheel and shapes it with his hands as it turns. After the object is formed, it is set aside to dry on long planks, then fired to harden, glazed and fired again. Some pots are fired in groundhog kilns (kilns dug into the ground), where firing by pine and hardwood slabs produces a reduction atmosphere that affects the glazes and colors of the finished objects. Objects that require a more stable color (like dinner sets) are fired by oil. For durability, all the kitchenware is fired at a low stoneware temperature (2,200°F). Higher temperatures are used for stoneware, which is glazed with salt and decorated with cobalt blue designs of birds and flowers. Jugtown still makes a small amount of orange earthenware pieces such as candlesticks, vases and large urns.

Jugs, jars, bowls, batter bowls, candlesticks, candle saucers, churns, dinner and tea sets, coffee and teapots, mugs, vases, baking dishes and pie plates come in various sizes and natural hues with honest names like White Woodsmoke, Blue Ridge Blue, Mustard Green, Cinnamon, Tobacco Spit and Frogskin. For those who have never seen it, Frogskin is a speckled surface that can vary from olive to very dark green. The glaze is made from Albany slip clay mixed with water. After the pot is dipped in this mixture, it is fired and at the climax of the firing process salt is added.

Jugtown wares, ranging in price from $5 to $50, are for sale on the premises every day from 8:30 A.M. to 5 P.M. except Sundays and holidays. Although they do not sell wholesale or by mail, their wares can also be purchased at the Greensboro Historical Museum and the Raleigh Art Museum. For a brochure and map showing locations of neighboring potteries, send a self-addressed, stamped envelope.

Jugtown Pottery
Route 2
Seagrove, NC 27341
(910) 464-3266
V R C S

Tea set by Jugtown Pottery

JUGS, CHURNS, PITCHERS AND ASH-GLAZED POTTERY

Before they went across the street to school each morning, Cleater Meaders and his eight brothers and sisters used to set out all the newly turned pots their father had made the day before—"about a hundred," says Cleater. "And if it looked the least like rain during the day, we knew we had to run back home and put them all back in the shop before they got wet."

After school they hauled wood to burn in the kiln and shared the chores. Cleater's job was to hook up the mule to the pug mill to break up and mix the dry clay with the water and sand and make enough clay to use the next day. "When I was a child," says Cleater, "my father instilled in me the desire to learn to make pottery. Just watching and listening to him made all the difference in my life. He built a platform where we could step up and watch him turn. When he went to lunch, he let us use the wheel. We always knew when we'd done something good when he glazed the pieces. If he left them alone, we knew they weren't good enough to go in his kiln. It didn't take us long to realize if we had our own kiln we could make our own money, so we dug one out of the bank in front of the house. Then we made a display stand out of a big box and put it between the road and his shop so the customers saw ours first. We did real good until my father caught us using his wood instead of cutting our own."

In the rural area of Georgia where they lived, jugs were a necessity, along with butter churns and milk pitchers. Before glass jars became available, jugs were used to store all liquids including whiskey.

"Back then," remembers Cleater, "a person carried his own jug to buy moonshine and paid according to the size. I remember one preacher who wanted us to make him a gallon jug that really held 1½ gallons." Some of their best customers were bootleggers. "When the revenue officers saw hundreds of gallon jugs in the yard one day, but not the next, they'd ask who bought them, but my father would only say he didn't ask names. If people had the money for jugs, he sold them."

When *Foxfire* magazine wanted to explain how to build a wood-burning groundhog kiln, they documented Cleater's latest, built on the old family farm in Cleveland, Georgia. "The way we make pottery hasn't changed much since my grandfather started," he told them. "We still use an ash glaze called Tobacco Spit, the result of using wood ashes in the mixture, but instead of ground-up glass, we use whiting, a dust made from Georgia marble, and Albany slip, which acts as a base and gives it a full, shiny-smooth coat."

Their best-sellers are the face, or head, jugs, whose

195

Jug with corncob stopper in 2-gallon size by Meaders Folk Pottery

origins are unknown. "There are several ideas as to how they were first made," says Cleater. "The logical reason is that during the winter, when potters gathered at a shop to talk, they started putting faces on jugs. Another was to keep small children from bothering the menfolks' favorite tonic. They sometimes reflect how a potter felt when he made them, but in general, they're more grotesque than pretty. When a man asked me recently to make him an ugly face jug, I could tell him truthfully, 'Mister, I've never made a good-looking one.' " Regular 1-gallon jugs sell for $20, with $15 for each additional gallon up to 4 and a 5-gallon jug for $100. Face jugs are $50.

The Meaders family has become a tradition in Georgia pottery. Cleater and his cousins Lanier, John Rufus and Edwin work independently, yet stay in close contact with each other. Meaders pottery was the subject of the first documentary produced in the Smithsonian's Folklife Monograph-Film series. The Smithsonian has also exhibited their work.

"There's something about working with clay," Cleater will tell you, "that just won't let go."

Meaders Folk Pottery
Route 1, Box 389
Byron, GA 31008
(912) 953-3830
V R S MO

Grape vase 20 inches tall by Meaders Folk Pottery

Face jug by Lanier Meaders

Other Makers

Lanier Meaders, Route 1, Box 578, Cleveland, GA 30528; (404) 865-3971, is most famous for his face jugs, which sell for $75.

Edwin and John Rufus Meaders, Route 1, Cleveland, GA 30528.

NEW ENGLAND POTTERY

Earthenware and stoneware made and sold at the Potter's Shop at Strawbery Banke on Portsmouth, New Hampshire's harbor have the look and feel of another time. Generous-sized pitchers, healthy bean pots with grabbable lids, three-handled mugs, chamber pots and milk pans created by today's resident potter, Ellsworth H. (Bud) Wheeler, are made with the same techniques used in New England between 1720 and 1800. Hand-thrown on a wheel, glazed and fired to 1,800°F, many are similar to those produced by Samuel Marshall in the mid-1700s at a nearby site, while others are a result of research at Boston's Museum of Fine Arts. The one important difference is that these contain no lead.

"I am one of a series of potters going back to that period," says Bud. "I produce functional stoneware in the style of the 19th century, reproductions of 17th and 18th century earthenware and one-of-a-kind pieces in stoneware."

Three handles on a mug may seem superfluous today, but when they were made originally, "people did not wash anything much including themselves. They didn't understand the transmission of disease and didn't mind sharing utensils in public houses and communal dining areas. A

Milk pans with wide flaring sides by E. H. Wheeler

three-handled mug was easier to pass from one to another. Many potters sold wares from wagons in areas where there was no local potter. If one handle broke, the mug was still usable. When potters caught on to planned obsolescence in the 18th century, the three-handled mug disappeared."

Milk pans with wide flaring sides were used to hold milk while the cream was skimmed from its surface. "Bean pots evolved from simple, open crocks or storage jars," Bud explains. "Lids were added to keep beans from drying out while cooking. With the development of an iron oven, a handle was added to retrieve the pot from the back, probably with a hooked poker (hence no need for two handles). I refined the handle and put two on larger pots for ease in carrying them hot from the oven, then enlarged the knob of the lid. Earlier potters stacked pots on top

Pitcher and beanpot by E. H. Wheeler

Beanpots and mug by E. H. Wheeler

of one another in the kiln, which is why early knobs were flatter."

Known for his functional, understated forms and conservative decorations, Bud was the 17th century potter at the Marketplace on Boston Common during the city's 350th birthday celebration, and at the Museum of Fine Arts exhibit "New England Begins." His pottery has been exhibited and sold at the Boston Museum of Fine Arts, the Smithsonian and at Plimouth Plantation Museum.

Though his life today is quite different from that of a university professor of biological oceanography, which he was until he became a full-time potter in 1977, Bud sees similarities. "As an oceanographer, life aboard ship followed a rhythm without becoming routine. The sea always changes; one activity leads to another. There's a rhythm to working with clay as well. Efficiency demands a logical progression of tasks, but it's more pleasing because a one-man shop is mine to control. I feel very much at home here. I like being part of the fabric of a place with discernible history. The perspective helps me understand where my efforts fit in."

In stoneware, tankards are $18, two-handled bean pots, $45; one-handled bean pots, $32. In earthenware, 17th century ale jugs are $28, three-handled mugs $15. In 18th century styles, pitchers are $35; milk pans, $35; plates, $25; tankards, $12; and chamberpots, $25. Shipping costs vary with order size and destination. Bud also accepts commissions in earthenware reproductions. Shop hours are 9:30 A.M. to 4:30 P.M., Tuesday through Saturday.

E. H. Wheeler
Wheeler Pottery
Strawbery Banke, Box 300
Portsmouth, NH 03801
(603) 436-1506
V   R   W   S   CC   MO

Other Makers

Northwood Stoneware Pottery, Route 5, Box 458, Northwood, NH 03261, a cooperative, makes 18th and 19th century slipware in white or matte glazes decorated in bird and flower cobalt blue designs.

Paul D. Lynn and Kathryn Woodcock-Lynn, Woodstock Pottery, Woodstock Valley, CT 06282; (203) 974-1673, make 18th and 19th century redware in the style of Thomas Bugee, who lived in nearby Quasset.

Rowantrees Pottery, Blue Hill, ME 04614; (207) 374-5535.

Gerard T. Beaumont, Beaumont Pottery, 393 Beech Ridge Road, York, ME 03909, traditional shapes, salt glaze with blue decoration.

PAINTED POTTERY

D. X. Gordy, fifth generation potter, "born and raised in clay," has been making pots professionally since 1930. He wanted to be a painter or sculptor, but quit school in the seventh grade to work with his father, W. T. B. Gordy, owner of a large-ware pottery in Meriwether County, Georgia. Two women had the greatest effect on his work: his mother, who taught him sketching; and Mother Nature, who taught him proportion, form and balance.

As a child, D. X. (Dorris Xerxes) began putting rocks in his daddy's kiln "to see what happened." Experimenting with rocks to see what colors and glazes they produce has been an ongoing delight for D. X. His lifetime of records has made him a master of the art and earned him an international reputation for rich earth-tone glazes: celadons, grays, blues, browns and even jet black. After gathering rocks, he crushes them in a pulverizer, washes, calcines (heats to below melting point to reduce moisture and oxidation), then grinds them to a powder with porcelain stones he made himself. "I like to find a rock that has gone unnoticed for a million years and change it into something beautiful that will be noticed, admired and enjoyed for another million years," he says.

A hallmark of D. X.'s pottery is the nostalgic hand-painted scenes "with no beginning and no end" that he paints around his pots. He gathers all materials for clay and glazes within 100 miles of home and never prices anything until it comes out of the kiln. If it's not up to his standards, he takes off his name and sells it for less.

Half-gallon pitchers, 8-inch quart jars and 10-inch-wide bowls sell for $20; tall cylindrical and barrel-shaped mugs for $5; tea sets (teapot, creamer, sugar bowl, extra bowl, eight to ten cups and saucers) for $50. Hand-painted

Sample of pottery whose hand-painted scene has no beginning and no end by D. X. Gordy

scenes double the price. Write or phone ahead. His pottery is 8 miles north of Greenville, 18 miles north of Warm Springs and 25 miles north of Callaway Gardens.

D. X. Gordy
Route 3, Box 54
Greenville, GA 30222
(404) 927-6669
V   R

PIEDMONT STONEWARE AND EARTHENWARE

"The traditional handmade earthenware and stoneware that we make," says Mary Farrell of Westmoore Pottery, "is what would have been found in colonial and early American homes, with an emphasis on pottery used in North Carolina during the 18th and 19th centuries. Some was made here, some came from New England or Pennsylvania, while others, particularly pieces with blue in the pattern, were brought here by settlers from England and Germany. However, most of the shapes we make originated here in the Piedmont area. Our slip-decorated redware was definitely influenced by the Moravian Germans who came here from Pennsylvania. However, colors used in the Piedmont are more subtle. Instead of just the strong yellows and reds, we use more creams, browns, greens and oranges. Our slipware is heavily decorated but without

Decorated plate, covered pot with handles and a vase by Mary and David Farrell

sgraffito designs scratched into the slip. Another difference is that the slip-trailing designs in this part of the country were nearly always put on with a cup."

Westmoore's earthenware (also known as redware) and stoneware are made in traditional southeastern shapes, glazed with nontoxic glazes and, except for the salt-glaze pots, are ovenproof and dishwasher safe. All are handmade at the potter's wheel. Two uniquely Piedmont shapes are a tall kraut jar (for sauerkraut) in a cylindrical shape with a heavy flanged lip, and a candlestick with a cup at the top of a tall stem.

Westmoore also makes salt-glaze Bellarmine jugs, 6 inches to 1½ feet tall, with a bearded face and a medallion on the roundest part of the form, similar to those dug up at historical sites like Williamsburg and Jamestown. "Because we fire partly with wood," explains Mary, "they come out of the kiln in a whole range of colors from gray to light brown."

As a child, Mary visited Jugtown with her mother. She began making pottery at the age of 17 while at college, where she was encouraged to make nonfunctional objects when she wanted to make plates. As soon as she graduated, she signed on as an apprentice at a pottery. Her husband and partner, David, spent 6 years of his adolescence building Plasticine cities, then studied sculpture because he enjoyed working with clay as a sculptural form. From the time he discovered that clay would stretch on the wheel, he's been making pots. "Researching and making traditional pottery," he's found, "is a wonderful way to combine my interest in history with my work."

They met while apprenticing at Jugtown and in 1977 started their own business nearby, where they have been master craftsmen for a National Endowment for the Arts apprenticeship program. The authenticity of their work

Assortment of pots, pitchers and a vase by Mary and David Farrell

Heavily decorated plate by Mary and David Farrell

has made it a favorite of collectors. It also is used by a number of museums and historic sites like Old Salem and the Hezekiah Alexander House in Charlotte.

Their wares for the table include plates, mugs, cups, saucers, bowls, butter dishes, custard cups, pitchers, batter bowls, candle saucers and candlesticks. For baking they have covered casseroles, ramekins, pottery tube pans, pudding molds and three styles of pie plates (plain, with handles or with fluted edge). They also make cannisters, butter crocks, flasks, churns, ring jugs and storage jars.

In the tradition of Jugtown potters, Westmoore Pottery offers only limited mail order but has a shop that is open from 9 A.M. to 5 P.M. Monday through Saturday year-round. They close on major holidays and for vacation from December 24 through January 17 and the last 2 weeks of July.

Mary and David Farrell
Westmoore Pottery
Route 2, Box 476
Seagrove, NC 27341
(919) 464-3700
V R S MO

Other Makers

Ray and Susan Allen, Popcorn Studio, 2031 Nelson Lane, Murfreesboro, TN 37130; (615) 896-9167.

Jensen Turnage Pottery, 8529 Hicks Island, Lanexa, VA 23098; (804) 566-1989, potters for Williamsburg.

SALT-GLAZED WARES

When brine-soaked ship timbers were used to fire kilns near Westerwald, Germany, in the 1500s, potters noticed that their pots became covered with a thin transparent glaze. Because it was known that lead glazes were not good for the health, they began to drip brine, and eventually rock salt, into the kiln during firing to produce the pebbly glaze sometimes called orange-peel texture.

"Glaze is actually a thin skin of glass," says Jack Beauchamp, who with his wife, Heather, owns Salt O'Thee Earth Pottery. "Glass is made from sand [silica] and heat. Sand melts at 3,600°F, but when a flux is added, like lime [calcium], the silica melts at a more manageable temperature [2,400°F]. For conventional glazes, these ingredients are mixed with water and applied before firing. Salt-glazing, on the other hand, is done all at once in the kiln. Clay already contains silica, which becomes reactive when heated to 2,250°F. When salt [sodium chloride] is added in the burner box at this temperature, it vaporizes instantly, carrying the flux [sodium] to melt the silica in the clay, creating a thin, extremely hard and durable glaze that's impervious to acids and alkalines."

In the 1700s, the best clay deposits for salt-glazing came from New Jersey and were shipped to Pennsylvania and New England by canal boat. After vast deposits of clay were found in the Ohio River Valley, it made more sense

© Jerry Anthony, Photographer. Photo Courtesy of the Western Reserve Historical Society, Hale Farm and Village, Bath, Ohio

Pitcher in 1-gallon size with slip-trailed grouse design by Heather and Jack Beauchamp

Crock in half-gallon size with handles and double grouse design by Heather and Jack Beauchamp

brushed blue slip) and slip-trailing (the drawing of lines with a slip cup). It takes 8 hours to load the kiln, a 48-cubic-foot catenary arch cross-draft kiln they built behind their studio; 24 hours to fire to a cone-8 temperature (2,282°F); another day to unload, price and pack.

Their rarer items include large flat-bottomed harvest jugs, used to take water to workers in the field ($75); round canteens ($75); and bundt cake pans ($20). Their bowls range in price from $12 to $48 for a set of four and are also available in a cutout fruit bowl ($25) and pedestal style ($35). Covered bean pots are $25; pitchers come in quart ($20) and half-gallon ($28) sizes. They make a full range of utilitarian wares like pie plates ($15), bread pans ($18 to $20), soufflé ($15) and baking dishes ($20 to $38); but their most beautiful forms are handsome jugs and jars ranging in price from $20 to $90, some in sets of four with covers, which can be used as a cannister set. For price list, send self-addressed, stamped envelope.

Heather and Jack Beauchamp
Salt O'Thee Earth Pottery
71456 Bates Road
Guernsey, OH 43741
(614) 439-1936
V (by appt.)   R   W   S   MO

and more profit to make wares at the source, especially for a market headed westward. By the mid-1800s, there were as many as fifty potteries in Akron, known as Stoneware City until manufactured glass containers replaced stoneware.

After earning their bachelor's degrees (Heather's in ceramics and Jack's in art education), the Beauchamps settled in the Guernsey–Bird's Run area of Ohio, where they've made traditional salt-glazed functional ware ever since. "We prefer salt-glazing," says Jack, "because it shows the true character of the clay and the fire. The pots are flashed [kissed] by the flames in the kiln, forever recording their experience there." It's a high-quality, low-quantity operation. They believe that you can tell a good potter by his feet, meaning that if a potter takes time to put a good foot (bottom) on a piece, the more visible parts (lip, shoulder, neck) will also be good. "Pots have the same parts as people," explains Jack. "One reason pottery traditions are so strong is that they are deeply rooted in everyday life. Pottery is a life style more than a business. It's part of everything we do."

After 15 days of making pieces, Heather and Jack spend a week decorating with blue cobalt slip and a brush (called

SLIP-PAINTING, SLIP-TRAILING, SPRIGGING AND TULIPWARE

When collectors had to pay over a thousand dollars for a single piece of Weidner-made Oley Valley redware, they asked college professor Gerald Yoder if he would consider

Tulipware charger with Jacobean jug and pitcher by Gerald H. Yoder; jug and pitcher thrown by apprentice Henry Van Duren

Pennsylvania-German tulipware dish and Jacobean slip-painted mug, crock and pitcher by Gerald H. Yoder

reviving his family's pottery business. In 1980 he did. Since then, his tulipware has been presented to the World Federation of Lutheran Churches by the Lutheran Church of America and his Jacobean pottery given to President Reagan by Chester County.

"The first Oley Valley redware was made by my ancestor Georg Adam Weidner sometime before 1745," says Gerald. "Georg's heart-shaped apee cake dish is now in the Metropolitan Museum of Art. Apee, sometimes called apiece, is a very dense, somewhat dry cake. His dish was unglazed biscuitware. Mine is the same shape, but glazed tulipware."

Using the same native earthenware (redware), tools (a rolling pin, goosequill, sgraffito implements) and materials (meerschaum slip and colored engobes) as his ancestor, Gerald builds pottery by the primitive slab or drape process, just as pioneers did between 1683 and 1820. His techniques include sgraffito, slip-painting, slip-trailing and sprigging.

"I am constantly involved in research," says Gerald, "because I try to introduce a new traditional line annually. As a professor, I taught others that which I learned. As a potter, I am able to practice what I taught, but I'm learning all the time. The most surprising lesson for me was how to color my clays. Engobe is essentially a clay that has been colored. Oxides are added to white clay to produce color: vanadium powder produces yellow slip; copper oxide makes green; and cobalt oxide creates blue. Slip is clay diluted with water to the consistency of heavy cream. Meerschaum is an off-white liquid clay that is gray in its greenware, or raw clay, state but fires white. The primitive method of applying slip, as used by the Penn-

sylvania-Germans, is called slip-trailing, done with an instrument called a gourd. The steady flow of slip is controlled by placing the thumb over the hole in the gourd. Slip-painting is done with a brush and is more deliberate. The design and style of my work is influenced by the Jacobean period and is similar to 17th century Staffordshire."

Whereas sgraffito is scratched in and below the surface, bas relief is similar to flat sculpture, as on a coin. Sprigging is a technique for bas relief. Gerald's German Renaissance sprigged bas-relief pottery has a cable-edge rim with either a Staffordshire or tulipware center (tulipware is the official pottery of the Pennsylvania-Germans). In addition to tulip and thistle edges in bas relief, Gerald also makes an edelweiss border in honor of his Swiss ancestry. Oley Valley biscuitware has a tulipware center with an antique biscuitware edge. "Perfecting a monochromatic biscuitware and antiquing the rims of some plates to produce the dark rims found in museums were two other lessons learned through research," says Gerald. His Swiss pierced pottery is made with a tulipware center and a Swiss-type pierced border. His latest traditional design, Burgundy Lace, is a combination of tulipware and slip-painting.

His exquisite lacelike designs derived from Pennsylvania-German and German medieval folk art motifs usually include tulips, the tree of life, unicorns and the distelfink, the symbol for good luck.

The best news for collectors since Gerald Yoder brought Oley Valley redware back into production are his prices, which range from $1 for a dollhouse miniature plate the size of a nickel to $150 to $200 for his elegant chargers (or serving plates). Oley Valley redware is for sale at the Smithsonian, museum shops nationwide and from his studio, open weekdays from noon to 5 P.M. or by appoint-

Jacobean redware by Gerald H. Yoder

ment. For information, send a self-addressed, stamped envelope.

Gerald H. Yoder
Oley Valley Redware
RD 4, Box 317
Fleetwood, PA 19522
(215) 944-0227
V   R   W   C   S   MO

Other Maker

William T. Logan, Oley Valley Blueware, RD 5, Box 5095, Fleetwood, PA 19522, former apprentice to Gerald, now makes the country blueware formerly done by Yoder. Price range $10 to $175.

Cavalier on horseback by Lester and Barbara Breininger

SLIPWARE AND SGRAFFITO

Lester Breininger "was just a collector" until he bought an old pottery dog in 1965 and asked the local art teacher if he would duplicate it.

" 'No,' he said, 'but I'll show *you* how to do it,' " Lester remembers. "It took the whole night and didn't look that great, but it was the most wonderful fun in the whole world. The next night I made a rooster and started some Christmas plates for each of my children."

Before he knew it, the ninth generation Berks County Pennsylvania-Dutchman was in the business of making 18th and 19th century slip-trailed and sgraffito redware. The soil in most areas of Pennsylvania is fairly high in iron, which means that even yellow gray clay will turn red during firing. Slip, a liquid clay that fires yellow, is applied with a slip cup, which has one or more holes outfitted with quill tips. Sgraffito (scratching or incising designs into a layer of slip) is done by Lester's wife, Barbara, a talented artist. After the clay is dug, it is "slurped up" with water to remove lumps, then stirred to a smooth consistency. As water rises to the top, it is poured off. When the clay feels like putty, it is ready to use. Some of the Breininger plates are thrown, but most are drape-molded.

"After rolling the clay into slabs," explains Lester, "I cut a plate the size I want to work on with a plate cutter, a small wooden disk. It's slip-trailed while flat, then draped on a mold. We now have a collection of twenty old molds dated from 1824 to 1881, which means we make them the exact shapes and sizes of the pottery made then."

After shaping, the edge is trimmed with a knife, then *coggled* with a tool that looks like a pastry crimper to create a serrated edge. Once dry, the bottom is sponged to make it smooth, signed with their name and dated. What es-

pecially endears their work to collectors are messages scribbled on the bottom telling what happened that day (like "School is out") or thoughts that came to mind (like "To love and be loved is the greatest joy on earth").

Ever since they went into business, in 1965, Lester has continued to add to his knowledge through experimentation and research. Some of his best clues have come from shards contributed by people who find them in archeological digs and backyards. "I like to try and figure out how each old piece was made," says Lester. "I can get forty new ideas from one fragment."

The slip-trailed plates cost from $3 for a 4-inch ABC to $95 for a 22-inch platter with squiggles, while sgraffito ranges from $4 for a 4-inch design with birds to $110 for a special edition farm scene. Other tableware includes bottles, jars, bowls, tumblers, candlesticks and crocks. Their menagerie of animals now includes cats, horses, cows, goats, lions, turtles and birds. They also make banks (birdhouses, apples, eagles, beehives, cats, pigs and old-fashioned round types), flowerpots, whistles, rattles, Christmas tree ornaments (animals made from old cookie molds), six authentic Betty (or grease) lamps, nests of plates starting with 1-inch sizes "that look like little teardrops" and whimsical items like eggs and duck families.

The one event customers never miss (and come from all over the country to attend) is the Breiningers' Porch Sale, held the third weekend in August, from 8 A.M. to 5 P.M. each day. That's when they drape the porch with bunting and invite the world in for mint tea and homemade cookies. In 1985 they got a new flag and introduced a new plate by Lester. He'd seen one auctioned at Pennypacker's for $4,400 with a dozen lines and went one better: his had thirteen. That year some lucky customer

POTTERY

Primitive lion by Lester and Barbara Breininger

got home, turned his newly purchased plate over and found the inscription, "Our 20th year! Imagine!"

Lester and Barbara Breininger
476 South Church Street
Robesonia, PA 19551
(215) 693-5344
V (by chance or appt.)   R   W   C   S   MO

Other Makers

Turtlecreek Potters, 3600 Shawhan Road, Morrow, OH 45152; (513) 932-2472.

The Long Family, 237 Bridge Street, Phoenixville, PA 19460; (215) 933-3080, early American, German and English folk pottery.

Carl Ned Foltz, RD 1, Box 131, Reinholds, PA 17569, Pennsylvania redware.

Becky Mummert, 30 Fish and Game Road, East Berlin, PA 17316; (717) 259-9620.

SPONGEWARE AND SPATTERWARE

Bybee Pottery is the oldest existing pottery west of the Alleghenies. Located in the small rural town of Bybee in the southern hills of Madison County, Kentucky, it was founded by the Cornelison family, whose members have been making pots in the same old log building since 1809, and whose sales records show it was a thriving industry as early as 1845.

Walter Cornelison, the fifth generation to own and operate the business, with his wife and their children, Paula, James and Robert (or Buzz), makes pots from the same

clay used by Kentucky's first settlers. For 2 or 3 weeks each year, in August when the water table is down, the Cornelisons open-pit-mine their annual supply of 100 to 120 tons of clay. So pure that it doesn't have to be blended with any other form of clay or chemical before use, it is mixed with water, then ground in an old pug mill before being stored in an ancient vault, where it is kept moist and pliable until needed.

In 1860, when local potters began slip-glazing their wares, Bybee started using four parts Michigan slip to one part Albany, a formula used to this day. They made large-ware at first, but as its use diminished, started making dinnerware. After World War II, they stopped using the old beehive kiln and built a shuttle kiln, which is fired for 16 hours three times weekly by thirty-three natural gas burners to 2,200°F, or a cone-6 temperature, then cooled for 24 hours before opening.

Bybee's production is 10 percent cast, 45 percent turned and 45 percent jiggered. "Anything that can be made on a potter's wheel can be made on a jiggering wheel," says Buzz. "Our flat dinnerware and straight-sided mugs are jiggered in plaster forms on the wheel. Very moist clay is thrown into the center while the wheel is spinning, then shaped with a wooden wedge."

Bybee's well-crafted, nontoxic stoneware, true to its traditions yet safe for all baking and serving needs, comes in 120 generous shapes and a choice of ten colors (for a price list send a self-addressed, stamped envelope). But what people drive miles to get is Bybee's spongeware.

Pitcher and mugs by Bybee Pottery

204

Covered soup tureen by Bybee Pottery

Sponge and spatter dinnerware originated in the Orient and was taken by East India Company sea captains to Europe, where it was imitated by domestic potteries. Spatter was the finer, soft-paste porcelain made in England for the American trade. Its colors were brighter than sponge and its designs more formal, often with a center flower or figure. Sponge, made by American potteries in the mid-1800s, was country style, utilitarian pottery used every day. Its patterns were spattered, daubed or sponged on in small and close or large and free patterns, sometimes all over, sometimes in borders and designs, usually in one color on white or buff, but sometimes in whole rainbows of color as well. Bybee's spongeware (also called speckled) is available in an all-over pattern in blue on white, blue on sand, brown on sand, and other colors by request.

Teapot by Bybee Pottery

Their wares include almost every kind of pottery used in the home. Spongeware runs slightly higher than all-over colors. Teapots are $9 plain, $13.50 in sponge; covered bean pots run $6 and $9; 4-inch ramekins in several styles are 75¢ to $2.25; a 3-quart covered soup tureen is $15 and $22.50; 1- and 2-gallon punch bowls, $10 to $30; cuspidors, $4 to $6.75; mugs, $1.50 to $2.25; and pitchers from $4 to $9. Bybee does not ship or mail. Orders are picked up by the customer after notification of completion. Visitors can see the pottery made Monday through Friday from 8 A.M. to 4 P.M. at the pottery, Highway 52E on Old Irvine Road, 8 miles from Richmond, Kentucky. The salesroom is also open on Saturday from 9 A.M. to noon and 1 to 4 P.M.

For those who can't get to Kentucky, Cousin Ron Stambaugh's shop, aptly titled Little Bit of Bybee, at 2244 Taylorsville Road, Louisville, Kentucky 40205; (502) 458-8717, carries a complete line of ware and he ships. Send a self-addressed, stamped envelope for a catalog.

Bybee Pottery
P.O. Box 192
Waco, KY 40385
(606) 369-5350
V R C S

Other Maker
Bastine Pottery, RR 3, Box 111, Noblesville, IN 46060; (317) 776-0210, make stoneware with cobalt blue spatter. C ($1.50)

PUZZLES
The solitaire puzzle, also called the hermit's or priest's game, was popular with monks during the Middle Ages. Spanish conquistadores reported seeing Indians play it with arrows stuck in the ground; in Europe, the puzzle

Solitaire puzzle by Bunchgrass Folk Toys

Indian leather puzzle by Bunchgrass Folk Toys

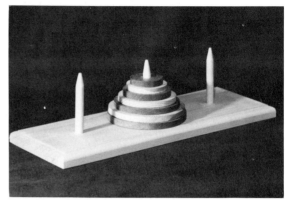

Pyramid puzzle by Bunchgrass Folk Toys

was played on ornate boards. The traditional version has a cross-shaped field of play with thirty-three positions. Pegs are placed in all holes except the middle. The only move allowed is a jump, horizontally or vertically but not diagonally, after which the jumped peg is removed. Play continues until only one piece remains. The reason the puzzle has remained popular for centuries is that winners can seldom remember how they won and keep trying to win again.

Other puzzles *look* difficult but once the solution is known are actually quite simple. The Indian leather puzzle, adapted by pioneers, consists of a strip of leather with two slits and a doubled thong through a hole at one end. The object is to remove the thong without removing the wooden beads on each end (whose diameter is larger than the hole). The answer is to go in reverse: pull the strip through the hole and remove the thong.

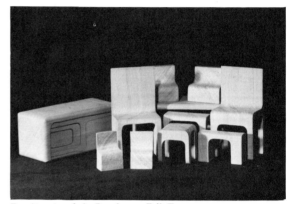

Furniture puzzle by Bunchgrass Folk Toys

Any parent will tell you that one of the best ways to keep children amused on long trips is with puzzles and games. In 1980, while preparing for a trip to Florida, Kay and Dick Shew, short of funds, decided to make duplicates of the wooden puzzles, toys and games their children enjoyed and sell them at the town's annual Christmas sale. Sales were brisk and Bunchgrass Folk Toys was born. As soon as they returned from Florida, they began research in earnest—in libraries and by talking with older people about favorite childhood toys.

"We constructed many items and put them to the *true* test," says Kay, "our homegrown testing laboratory of three boys aged 7 to 11. We also watched reactions of their playmates and adult guests." Today, their cottage industry in the Palouse area of southeastern Washington, 10 miles from Washington State University where Dick teaches, is a family enterprise. When Dick's not teaching,

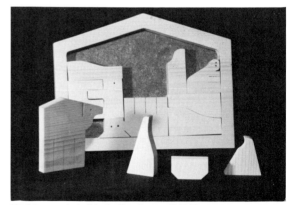

Nativity puzzle/crèche by Bunchgrass Folk Toys

he fires up the wood-burning stove in the converted chicken-coop shop and starts cutting wood. Kay and the boys help with sanding; she does the finishing, packaging, marketing and bookkeeping. Their handmade puzzles, games and toys of oak, pine, fir, mahogany, alder, walnut and birch, finished with a nontoxic penetrating oil, are sealed in plastic bags, which also contain historical information and directions.

Their Solitaire puzzle is $4.50; their Indian Leather puzzle is $3. Other puzzles include the Nine-Square ($7.50), Pyramid ($8.50), Kindling ($7), Horseshoe ($3), Houdini ($4) and the Box of Nine ($8). Both the Furniture puzzle ($9) and the Creche ($14) can be played with as toys. Every time the Shews go to another fair or hear about another puzzle, the list grows. They recently added the Nail, Love's Knot, Shoe, Fishing Pole, and Mountain Misery puzzles.

"We try everything at least once," says Kay. "The most pleasure comes when I see the light in a child's eye. Even better is the universal smile when people recognize the rubber band pistol or shotgun. Many in their 50s and 60s tell us how they made them as children and cut up innertubes for ammunition." Bunchgrass also makes tops, tic-tac-toe games and rice-stuffed juggling balls. Write for an up-to-date price list and free catalog.

Kay and Dick Shew
Bunchgrass Folk Toys
Route 2, Box 147
Pullman, WA 99163
(509) 397-3222
V (by appt.)   R   W   C   S   CC   MO

Other Makers

Stave Puzzles, Inc., Main Street, Norwich, VT 05055; (802) 649-1450, sells puzzles hand-cut, one piece at a time, by an individual artist from the finest 5-ply laminated hardwoods with African ribbon mahogany on the back. C

Tucker-Jones Tavern Puzzles, 9 Main Street, Setauket, NY 11733.

Pysanky   See **Eggs, Decorated**

Qualla Arts & Crafts   *See* **Cherokee Crafts**

NATIVE AMERICAN QUILLWORK

Before Europeans brought beads to America, Indians decorated clothing, moccasins, tomahawks, ritual robes and cradleboards with the teeth and bones of animals and the quills of porcupines. Although animals had to be killed for teeth and bones, each porcupine carried a ready supply of 30,000 quills up to 5 inches long and ⅛ inch thick, which grew back after plucking. Most Indians preferred to use their wits to obtain quills without killing off the source of supply. Tricky business, since quills are the porcupine's first line of defense.

"One way," says lawyer Clyde Hall, an internationally recognized Indian craftworker, "is to clamp the porcupine in place with two forked sticks: one around his neck and the other on top of his tail. An easier method is to throw a blanket over the porcupine, let him shoot the quills, then pick them out of the blanket." Once obtained, quills are washed, dried, sorted and dyed. To soften and make them easier to use, they were soaked in water or held in the mouth. Quills were flattened by pulling them through the teeth or with a variety of homemade tools.

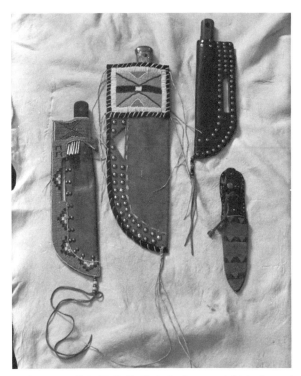

Knife cases by Clyde M. Hall: (clockwise from top right) leather and brass tack; bead, buckskin and small brass tack; cut bead with tin cone jingles; and buffalo rawhide with tacks, wool cloth and beaded top

Shoshone split horn bonnet, 1890s style, by Clyde M. Hall

highest in the sky," Clyde explains, "and lives in the air, which is why their feathers have spiritual significance. They are thought to take prayers to the Great Spirit, or Mystery Da-Ma-Uppa, which means "Our Father" in Shoshone. Although eagles are an endangered species, Indians can use their feathers; but in traditional pieces created for non-Indians, they use turkey feathers painted to look like those of the eagle." One of his most spectacular pieces is the split-horn bonnet headpiece worn by honored men of the Northern Plains, made of buffalo horns mounted on buckskin, decorated with rare materials and ermine fur ($1,500).

Quill prayer wheels ($35), worn in the hair on the heart side or attached to the breastplate, are circles divided into four sections representing the seasons and races of man. "The circle stands for continuity, the universe and life without end," says Clyde. "Everything in nature is round. Only the rock is square, which is why it represents the power to destroy."

Clyde first became interested in Shoshone/Bannock crafts at the age of 16. While majoring in fine arts at college, he studied Indian styles, clothing and utensils and made drawings. Before long, he found that he enjoyed making them more than researching them. "Indians designed objects for a use or a function," says Clyde, "but even the simplest tools were designed for form and line and embellished beautifully. Porcupine quills interested me in particular because they were used as decoration only in America. My main interest is in recreating and restoring objects from 1830 to 1890. I make large pieces like pipe bags, paint pouches, traditional dance equipment, gun and knife cases, as well as *parfleche* work [painting on Indian-worked rawhide]." Using the centuries-old wrap technique, he dyes and flattens quills, then wraps them in rawhide, which is twisted between each quill. "Originally, Indians used roots, berries and plants for dyes," says Clyde. "They later unraveled trade blankets and boiled them to abstract dyes, but by the 1860s they were using anilines."

Many of his designs use eagle feathers. "The eagle flies

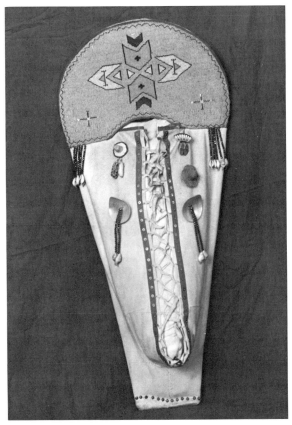

Beaded babyboard with hand-tanned buckskin cover by Clyde M. Hall

A wrapped-quill fringe for a pipe bag is $100. Beaded work includes Sioux and Shoshone decorated tomahawks ($300 to $400), a large pipe bag from the early reservation period ($600) and a cradleboard ($800 in cloth, $1,000 in hand-tanned buckskin). "A child feels very secure in a babyboard," says Clyde. "It helps him to grow straight and strong. But now instead of being strapped to the shoulders, they are more frequently held in the arms or leaned against a support." With inquiries, send a self-addressed, stamped envelope.

Clyde M. Hall
P.O. Box 135
Fort Hall, ID 83202
(208) 237-2142
R S MO

Other Makers

Cathy Smith, Medicine Mountain Trading Company, Box 124, Sturgis, SD 57785, has done commissions for the Smithsonian's Cooper-Hewitt and the Boston Museum of Fine Arts. She wrote the chapter on quillwork for the *Third Book of Buckskinning* and is completing a book on quillwork.

Janice Galipeau, Wabanaki Arts on the Penobscot Indian Reservation, P.O. Box 453, Old Town, ME 04468; (207) 827-3447, specializes in porcupine quill jewelry.

Nancy Brown Garcia, 179 Althea Street, Apt. 3, Providence, RI 02909.

AMISH QUILTS

Although the Amish are known as the "plain people," their quilts have a dynamic tension, created by combining subtle color combinations within strong geometric forms, that is simple yet complex.

"Their clean lines have a peaceful vibrancy and subtle energy that is refreshing and pure," says Racheal Alexander Scott, whose Amish quilts are in as much demand as the antique bed coverings she admires. "I can sit and look at Amish quilts for hours and never tire of them."

When the Amish arrived in Lancaster County, Pennsylvania, from Switzerland in 1727, they formed farm communities that, like themselves, were self-contained and self-sufficient. Today, members dedicated to religion, family and community continue to live in the world but not of it, in spare houses, without luxuries, telephone, electricity or indoor plumbing, and driving horse-drawn buggies instead of cars. They dress in quiet colors devoid of pattern so as not to call attention to themselves or to

Pine Tree quilt top by Racheal Alexander Scott

set themselves apart from their communities. Their love of color surfaces in their gardens and in their quilts. Like stained-glass windows set in a stone wall, their quilts glow with an inner light of colors relating to one another in geometric forms (squares, triangles, diamonds) set in wide borders, sometimes with inner borders containing smaller squares at the corners. Usually pieced at home and quilted with friends and relatives at quilting bees, frolics or sisters days, Amish quilts were known for their fine quilting, as many as 20 stitches to an inch, in designs of feathers, flowers, vines, baskets, wreaths, chains and scallops, traced onto the material with pencil or chalk using templates of cardboard, tin or wood.

Racheal's mother, who taught her to quilt, "used prints beautifully," says Racheal, "but I'm not a little flower person. I prefer to see my flowers growing. When I was in high school, I began quilting in solids, playing colors against one another, after studying the art of Joseph Albers and Franz Kline. But it wasn't until I worked in a shop that sold antique quilts that I began using traditional patterns and began quilting full time."

The earliest Amish quilts were made from old clothing dyed with natural materials. "When I studied weaving, I became intrigued with natural dyes and began searching for fabrics with the same intensity to use in my quilting. When I can't find them, I dye materials and sometimes the entire quilt top to achieve the right feeling."

Like quilters of yesteryear, she also pieces by hand. "I

Sunshine and Shadow quilt by Racheal Alexander Scott

The most difficult quilt she's made was in the honeycomb pattern known as Grandmother's Flower Garden, composed of hundreds of pieces less than 1 inch square. Although Racheal makes quilts in all the traditional Amish patterns (bars, diamond in the square, stars, baskets, Irish chain), her favorite remains Sunshine and Shadow because "I love to play with the colors and pieces." Although her quilts have been exhibited in museums and galleries from New England to Mexico, Racheal never makes a quilt she wouldn't want to sleep under.

Made in 100 percent cotton fabrics with backing brought to the front as binding, they can be made with cotton batting if preferred. All are custom-made and range in price from $150 to $200 for crib-size to $400 to $500 for full-size.

Racheal Alexander Scott
RFD 3, Box 679
Putney, VT 05346
(802) 387-4219
V (by appt.)   R   MO

Other Makers

Sara Miller, Kalona Kountry Kreations, RR 1, Box 266, Kalona, IA 52247.

Lizzie Stoltzfus, 400 South Ramona Road, Lebanon, PA 17042.

Mabel Kauffman, 79 Circle Drive, Manheim, PA 17545; (717) 665-5736.

Nora Martin, c/o Verne Hoover, Route 1, Box 267A, Mifflinburg, PA 17844; (717) 966-2350.

Elizabeth Fisher, Route 340, Ronks, PA 17572.

Katie Stoltzfus, 184 Quarry Road, Leola, PA 17540.

Gail E. Hurn, 3 Lincolnwood, Evansville, IN 47715, sells quilts from Amish quilters in Pennsylvania, Indiana, Ohio, Kentucky, Tennessee and Iowa.

like to be as exact as possible," she explains. "Stitching by hand makes more concise corners and angles. And caring for my two children, I can piece anywhere. I enjoy planning each quilt, playing with the colors within the pattern. I work most often with purples, from red to blue, offsetting them with reds, blues and grays and a minimum of green."

HAWAIIAN QUILTS

Hawaiian quilts, the most dynamic and dramatic in the world, are not pieced like other quilts but made of whole cloth. Unlike the missionary wives who taught them to sew, Hawaiian women did not wear fitted dresses whose sewing left scraps of cloth. Hawaiian garments were cut full, wrapped around the body and used all the material. Cutting whole cloth into scraps and sewing them back together again seemed like a waste of time, so ever since 1820, when needles, thread, scissors and quilting first arrived on the missionary brig *Thaddeus*, Hawaiians have changed the rules to suit themselves.

Diamond in a Square quilt by Racheal Alexander Scott

Hawaiian flag quilt by Deborah U. Kakalia

Because quilts were not needed for warmth, they evolved as an art form instead of a necessity. First to go were the repeated designs and geometrical squares. Instead, the fluid designs of the Hawaiian *kapa kuiki* (quilted coverlet) come from flowers, fruits and leaves, accented by contour quilting that follows the appliquéd design's edges like waves. Traditionally, only two plain colors of sharp contrast are used, except for the Lei Ilima and Hawaiian Flag designs, which use more. Originality has always been encouraged. Some quilters destroyed patterns so they could not be copied; those who stole another's design were made to feel embarrassed or ostracized.

Deborah U. Kakalia, one of the islands' most popular quilters and teachers, had never seen an Hawaiian quilt until 1958 when the hospital where she worked had an exhibit. "They were so beautiful," she remembers. "As the fourteenth child in my family, I knew I wouldn't inherit a quilt, so I decided to make my own and give them to my children. I asked the owner if she would cut some quilts for me (which she did for a fee) and began to teach myself." Since then, Debby has created more than 200 original patterns, written the book *Hawaiian Quilting as an Art* and seen her quilts displayed at every major Hawaiian celebration as well as in mainland museums.

Designs are created by folding paper or material in eighths (like paper-cutting), then cutting through the eight

Living Room Lights of the Palace, traditional quilt by Deborah U. Kakalia

White Ginger quilt by Deborah U. Kakalia

thicknesses. Debby uses 100 percent cotton fabrics because they are easier to work with, and prefers not to prewash because it tends to fray edges on intricate designs. With the help of her husband, David, she pins the design color onto the background, then bastes. "I like the appliqué stitch best," says Debby, "and use between 10 and 12 stitches an inch. I also use the chicken-feet embroidery stitch; when cross-stitch is used, the edge is not turned under. Quilting 8 to 9 stitches an inch, in rows no less than ½ inch apart, starts at the center and ripples outward like ocean waves. The closer the rows, the flatter the surface."

Red and yellow, once royal colors, are now those of the state. The quilts of each island are often made in the colors of its symbol. For instance, Maui's Lokelani (rose of heaven) is two shades of pink, while Nihau's Pupu (shell) is two shades of blue because the shell comes from the sea.

Debby's quilts cost from $300 for crib-size to $2,000 for king-size. She also will cut and baste quilts ($20 to $170), appliqué ($40 to $180), pin-baste ($12 to $80) or quilt only ($150 to $1,500). For those who want to make their own, her book costs $9.10 including postage, and pattern kits with six designs and quilting charts are $8.10. Pillow kits in a large range of patterns and colors cost $25 plus $3.50 postage. For a price list, send a self-addressed, stamped envelope.

Deborah U. Kakalia
1595 Elua Street
Honolulu, HI 96819
(808) 841-7286

Other Maker

Elizabeth A. Akana, The Hawaiian Quilter, 46-334 Ikiki Street, Kaneohe, HI 96744; (808) 247-5358.

PLAINS INDIAN MORNING STAR QUILTS

After the Indian wars were over and tribes were moved to reservations, missionaries began teaching the Indians occupational and domestic skills, including quilting. The Plains Indians of the Gros Ventre, Sioux, Assiniboin, Mandan Hidatsa and Cree tribes on reservations in Montana, Idaho and the Dakotas used colors and designs distinctly their own, made significant changes in the social and functional aspects of quilting and became the only Indians to use quilts for both artistic reflection and tribal ceremonies.

Ignoring the subdued colors and conservative patterns

Eagle Star quilt by Mary Red Feather, Sioux, from the Florence Pulford Collection

War Bonnet Star quilt by Regina Brave Bull, deceased, Sioux, from the Florence Pulford Collection

of the white settlers, the Plains women used bright solid colors in dynamic, almost electric geometric patterns. Their playful, innovative designs, inspired by their dreams, hopes and visions of the world around them, often told the story of natural occurrences like storms, seasons and sunsets. Nearly all the designs incorporated the morning star, used for centuries as decoration on tepees, shields and clothing. Stars are considered evidence of the revered spirit known as Wakan Tanka, "The Great Holy," or "The Great Mystery." Camp criers once wakened tribes by riding through on horseback crying, "Arise, come see the morning star," which was the promise of a new day or a new life. Incorporated into the morning star theme are other Indian symbols like birds, tepees, arrowheads and sometimes eagles, the messenger to the heavens and a symbol of the bravery of those who die for their tribe or for their country.

Quilts have become an integral part of tribal customs from birth to the grave. When a baby is born, a quilt is made. If a young boy goes up to the mountain to have a vision, he may wrap himself in a quilt made by his grandmother. Quilts are used for tribal meditation and as burial shrouds, given to celebrate weddings, personal honors, graduations, recovery from illness and homecomings, given as favors at Giveaways (the Plains version of a potlatch) and as a way of saying thanks to friends, family and loved ones.

Unlike the white settlers, who favored quilting bees, Plains Indian women consider quilts personal statements to be made alone at home, sometimes with a mother or daughter. And contrary to easterners' preference for hand-piecing, most Plains women piece by machine (whose ownership is considered a symbol of prestige), but quilt by hand, using Indian motifs or an overall stitch resembling clouds.

The quilts had always been made for home use or given away as gifts until 1968 when Florence Pulford, of Los Altos, California, was invited to a Giveaway and saw the quilts for the first time. Although the women were reluctant at first to sell their handiwork, the money helped the local economy. Florence founded an organization, Art of the Plains Indians, arranged museum exhibits nationwide to gain recognition for the quilters and their work and now acts as their sole agent, returning all profits to them. She spends much of the year traveling to reservations, encouraging the quilters, whom she pays in advance.

The quilts, which come in no set sizes from small to large, are priced from $100 to $4,500 and are for sale through the Marjorie Cahn Gallery, which also sells museum-quality crafts from the Plains Indians, like fancy-dancer figure dolls, moccasins, deerhide skins,

Indian Heads quilt by Emma King, Sioux, from the Florence Pulford Collection

shields, quillwork and Elks Feet and Dew Claw baskets. Photos and slides are available for a $10 refundable deposit, plus $3 shipping and insurance.

Marjorie Cahn Gallery
P.O. Box 2065
Los Gatos, CA 95031
(408) 356-0023
V (by appt.)   R   MO

TRADITIONAL AMERICAN QUILTS

Thrifty early Americans found ways to recycle almost everything. Scraps of material were saved, cut up and pieced together for quilt tops, first in random piecing, then in designs. By the time a young woman married, she was expected to have made thirteen quilt tops for her dower chest: twelve for everyday use and one for her bridal bed.

"The Log Cabin pattern was an early favorite," says Mary Louise Brion, "because small bits of fabric could be combined in a wide range of contrasting colors. Narrow strips of light and dark fabric were stitched around a solid center so that half the block appears light and the other half dark. The blocks were then integrated in a larger

Carl Doney, Allentown, PA

Pieced sampler quilt by Mary Louise Brion

materials, the kits are available nationwide in more than seventy-five designs that can be made into a pillow, framed for the wall or expanded into a quilt, using one repeated design or all seventy-five different patterns. Local favorites are Moravian storybook quilts and the Star of Bethlehem, an eight-pointed star with many variations. Known as the Lone Star in Texas, it is composed of many 45-degree-angle diamonds, eight of which meet in the center and radiate into larger diamonds.

In addition to traditional designs, Mary Lou custom-designs museum-quality quilts stitched entirely by hand. The only quilter to have two designs chosen for the thirty-square Bicentennial Friendship Quilt exhibited throughout the United States, Mary Lou was commissioned by President Carter to make a baby quilt to be given as a gift of state to King Hussein, and by the local Republican Committee to create a wall hanging for Nancy Reagan. Two of her designs have been magazine covers.

After the design and colors are decided, Mary Lou draws the pattern, makes the patchwork and quilting templates, then washes fabrics to remove chemical finish, adding a cup of vinegar to the final rinse to set colors before marking and cutting. "For everyday quilts and for those in a hurry," says Mary Lou, "I have also developed a method of strip-piecing that can be done by machine."

A finished quilt, generous enough to fit a queen-size bed or eliminate the need for a dust ruffle on a double averages between $500 and $700. A brochure with pic-

design of light and dark. In early settlements, the finished top was quilted to a backing and filled with whatever was available for insulation: old cotton or wool, feathers, even pine needles, leaves, moss, cornhusks, and later, cotton batting. Stitches had to be close together to hold the insides of this fabric sandwich in place because hand-stuffed wadding had a tendency to shift."

When Mary Lou made her first quilt in 1950 the few quilting books on the market were picture books with a minimum of instructions, so she wrote, illustrated and published *Creative Quilting,* a favorite of beginners. Since then, she has written four more workbooks, started classes, formed a guild and started the business Creative Quilting, a one-stop source for stitchers and buyers. Creative Quilting sells fabrics, batting, workbooks, patterns, templates, notions, hoops and quilting frames. She's even devised a simple solution for those who can't make up their minds which pattern they prefer or who are intimidated by the thought of making a large quilt: kits ($12). Consisting of one square in a single design and complete with

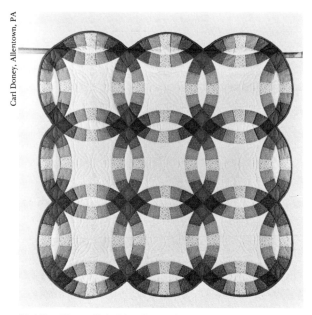

Carl Doney, Allentown, PA

Wedding Ring quilt by Mary Louise Brion

Carl Doney, Allentown, PA

Baltimore Bride Square and Border quilt by Mary Louise Brion

tures and descriptions of twenty quilts is available for $3.50, which is refunded on the first order. For those who aren't sure what they want, Mary Lou suggests that they visit in person and browse through an album of finished quilts for ideas. Her shop is open Monday, Tuesday and Thursday from 10 A.M. to 4 P.M., Wednesday from 10 A.M. to 9 P.M. and Saturday by appointment.

Mary Louise Brion
Creative Quilting
415 High Street
Bethlehem, PA 18018
(215) 868-0376
V R W C S MO

Other Makers

The Freedom Quilting Bee, Route 1, Box 72, Alberta AL 36720; (205) 573-2225, makes hand-stitched quilts in fine cotton calico and ginghams, backed with muslin and filled with dacron in the Bear's Paw design, the Coat of Many Colors, Grandmother's Choice and Grandmother's Dream, ranging in price from $65 for a baby's quilt to $340 for king-size. V R C CC

Ethel Santiago, 706 Palm Ridge Road, Immokalee, FL 33934, does Seminole patchwork.

Darlene R. Scow, 1396 Hollowdale Drive, Salt Lake City, UT 84121; (801) 942-4333, makes bed quilts and

wall hangings, hand-appliquéd or pieced and hand-quilted.

Kae Gamble and Jan Knox, Heartwood Quilts, P.O. Box 563 Z, Newmarket NH 03857; (603) 659-2542, make hand-quilted 3-inch-thick quilts, from a 38- by 38-inch wall hanging for $80 to king-size for $350.   MO

The Quiltery, Benfield Road, RD 4, Box 337, Boyertown, PA 19512; (215) 845-3129, represents forty quilters who custom-make quilts by hand, from $165 up, all sizes. Owner Marjorie Cannon Groff says "most are done 10 stitches to an inch." They also quilt owner's tops. V (appt. only) C ($1)

Rural Arts & Crafts Cooperative, P.O. Box 227, Parkersburg, WV 26101; (304) 422-5493, does traditional patchwork and quilting.

Appalachian Craftsmen, Inc., P.O. Box 559, Barboursville, WV 25504; (304) 736-0003, does traditional patchwork and quilting.

Nina Grimes, 918 First Avenue, Salt Lake City, UT 84103.

RAKES

Earl Allen makes rakes the way his family has for three generations: of hardwood, with three bows and twelve teeth. "The teeth are hardhack," says Earl, "the rest of the rake is white ash, which is very strong because here rakes are used mostly for haying. Uncle Del used to make them part white birch but it's hard to find trees with no 'cat faces,' which weaken the stales [the 6-foot-long handle]. I select trees from my woodlot that are good and straight, saw them in my mill, trim the tree, cut off the bark, square it up, then saw it into lumber. The boards are cut again for the size of the stales, inserted by hand into a handmade machine with a handmade cutting blade. The teeth have to be hand-held and put through the machine once each way for each tooth because one side is sloping and the other, smaller side keeps the teeth from going straight through. I make the bows the same day I get the wood, bend them into three different sizes directly on drying racks, let them set a day or so, then use them. Heads [the part that goes crossways from the stale] are bored to hold the teeth, and the stales are dried on a rack. The teeth are tumbled smooth in a handmade tumbler. Hitting against each other makes them smooth. The bows are fastened with small brads, the teeth glued in place. I do not use finish on any part of the rake."

Because of their size, Earl's rakes (which cost only $10) cannot be shipped and must be purchased from him when he's demonstrating his craft at places like Cooperstown

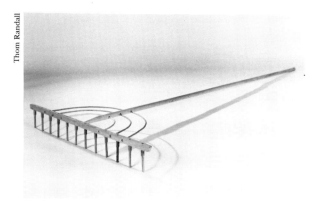

Thom Randall

Wooden rake by Earl L. Allen

Farmers' Museum or at his farm, a mile off Route 8 on Edwards Hill Road. It's worth the trip. When he's not making rakes, Earl makes maple syrup in the spring; in fall months uses his team of horses to move hunters and fishermen into the deep mountains; and in between builds houses from old barn materials.

Earl L. Allen
P.O. Box 41
Bakers Mills, NY 12811
(518) 251-2707
V R

Rattles *See* Totem Poles, Masks, Rattles and Dolls

Retablos See under Santos

REVERSE PAINTING

Reverse painting, as the name implies, is the opposite of regular painting, which is built up from larger masses to smaller details. "In reverse painting on glass, objects in the foreground must be painted first, with successive details added until the furthest distance is reached," explains Marianne Picazio, a professional reverse painter since 1949. "At the same time, since the clear glass side faces out, the picture is a mirror image whose lines in black or brown must be drawn in reverse as well."

Americans preferred reverse paintings framed as art and as decoration on clocks and mirrors. The most popular subjects at first were heroes, battles, historic scenes,

buildings, landscapes and, during the Adams period, classical themes. Before 1900, going west (trains, wagons, riders) was popular, and after 1900, monuments (Statue of Liberty, Washington Monument). Although decals and transfers eventually replaced reverse paintings in the marketplace, clock makers, antique dealers and collectors have been steady clients for Marianne ever since she graduated from the Vesper School of Art and became an apprentice to a restorer in Boston.

"I'd decorated furniture," she says, "so when he showed me how to paint dials and glasses for clocks and mirrors, it came naturally. One of the first pieces I did was for Tiffany's, a moon dial with a logging scene on one side, ships on the other and moon faces. Two years later I went into business in partnership with my husband, whose specialty is painting dials."

Since then, she has done work for Colonial Williamsburg, Old Sturbridge and Shreve, Crump and Lowe, as well as for leading auctioneers and antique dealers. Her main source of research information is the records she has kept of work she has reproduced or repaired since she began, augmented by visits to important clock collections.

"The part I like best is reproducing a well-executed original glass," says Marianne. "The biggest problem is poor atmospheric conditions that affect drying and sometimes require repainting." While some clients want glasses that show their homes, coats of arms or even their grandchildren, "one ordered a glass depicting a woman's head with the iris of the eye left clear so that the pendulum could be seen swinging, Another, commemorating events in a man's life, included his purchase of three Rolls-Royces, which he parked next to his Christmas tree."

Reverse painting of Spanish galleon by Marianne and Edmund Picazio

Reverse painting of Old State House, Boston, by Marianne and Edmund Picazio

Most glasses have borders of stenciled-in bronze powders (applied on varnish) or 23-karat gold leaf (applied to glass with a gelatin size). "Gold leaf is very delicate and difficult to handle," says Marianne, "requiring a gilder's tip and much expertise because it can disintegrate into particles with the slightest motion."

Price is determined by size of glass, patterns, gold work and details. Mirror glasses range from $75 to $300; steeple clocks, from $30 to $40; Terry pillar and scroll clocks, from $125 to $160; and sets of top and bottom glasses, from $175 to $300. Basic dials range from $20 to $50, but others must be seen to be quoted because they can be small with a minute track, or be "an elaborate moon-phase grandfather clock with Roman numerals, Arabic figures, a minute track, date dial, hemispheres, monthly phases, name, place, corner decorations, flowers, raised gold leaf, miniature pictures, a moon disk painting with the moon faces, country scenes and seascapes or anything in between." Add to that the choice of backgrounds (wood, iron, zinc, marble, glass) and materials (lacquer, enamel, ink, gold leaf, bronze powders, varnish), and it's easy to understand why the services of Marianne and her husband, Edmund, are in such demand that they've never had to advertise.

Marianne and Edmund Picazio
P.O. Box 1523
Buzzard's Bay, MA 02532
(617) 888-6267
R   MO

Other Makers

Allean Mix, 3205 Perry Street, Mt. Rainier, MD 20712; (301) 927-2126.

David and Marie Gottshall, 210 East High Street, Womelsdorf, PA 19567; (215) 589-5239.

Ralph and Mariette Berry, Durgintown Road, Cornish, ME 04020; (207) 625-3324.

Ingrid Sanborn, Helige Ande Arts, 85 Church Street, West Newbury, MA 01985; (617) 363-2253.

Monica Halford, 850 El Caminito, Santa Fe, NM 87501; (505) 982-4175, specializes in southwestern styles.

Cindy Burleigh, 7 Sheffield Road, Winchester, MA 01890.

NATIVE AMERICAN RIBBONWORK

During the 17th and 18th centuries, ribbon was a rare trade item, saved for important occasions such as signing peace treaties or awarding medals to Indian chiefs. However, in 1797 when ribbons became unfashionable on European dress, the French began to use them in trade with the Indians.

"The Indians loved color and appreciated new materials," says ribbonworker Shalah Rowlen, a descendant of Pawnee, Oto, Potwatomi, Sac and Fox tribes. "Until then, their dress decorations had been made of natural materials like hides, porcupine quills, shells, bones, dried berries, fruit pits, grasses, cornhusks, raffia and even the spines of bird feathers. As soon as the Indians had access to ribbons and glass and porcelain beads, they used them."

U.S. Department of the Interior Indian Arts and Crafts Board, Southern Plains Indian Museum and Crafts Center

Friendship blanket by Shalah Rowlen

Shawl of woolen fabric with border of satin ribbonwork and hand-tied fringe by Shalah Rowlen

Ribbonwork (also known as ribbon appliqué) is a form of decoration applied to clothing worn by Indians in the eastern and midwestern United States. The brilliant borders and bands in contrasting colors of silk, satin and moiré ribbon are used on ceremonial blankets, dance aprons, costumes, shawls, leggings, shirts, skirts, breechclouts (similar to dance aprons but longer), and sometimes on cradle bands, saddle blankets, collars, cuffs and moccasin flaps. Shalah first learned of ribbonwork when her father asked her to restore some family costumes.

"The work was exquisite," she says. "A dance apron owned by my aunt had a floral design worked in green, purple, blue and red, while the one belonging to my mother had a geometric design. I wanted to know more about ribbonwork, how it came to be, what the colors and patterns meant." She discovered that early dated specimens were rare because of the perishable nature of the materials. As she questioned older tribe members and researched in libraries, museums and books, she learned that colors had meanings (for example, white stands for peace and health, purple for sorrow, red for war) and tribes were known for specific designs.

"Woodland tribes used floral and leaf patterns," she says, "whereas Sac and Fox (two tribes that merged) preferred more stylized botanical designs." In recent years, she has incorporated more geometric designs in her work, such as those used by the Navajo, Zuni and Hopi tribes "because they stand out more. My favorite work is done with three or four shades of blue (which signifies sky and water), orange and red (for the sun), brown (for the earth), with accents of bright pink and green."

Since she developed an interest in ribbonwork and appliqué in the late 1960s, Shalah's creations using both beads and ribbon have been exhibited in museums and galleries throughout the United States, featured at the Smithsonian Festival of American Folklife in Washington, DC, and become popular with Oklahoma Indians, whose favorite social activity is attending weekend powwows. Today, Shalah makes costumes for the Sac and Fox, Pawnee, Kickapoo, Kiowa, Comanche, Cheyenne and Oto tribes, as well as shirts, vests and shawls. In addition to selling strips of ribbonwork 2 yards long and 8 to 10 inches wide in taffeta (three colors, $15 to $25) and satin (three colors, $25; four colors, $30 up), Shalah makes dance aprons (16 inches wide by 18 inches long) in solid color wool or polyester ($25 up), decorated in taffeta or felt, lined or unlined. Ceremonial blankets, half red and half blue (with the red worn over the heart), are made in wool and broadcloth, with the price determined by size, material and the amount of ribbonwork. Shalah also does special-order beadwork for fan handles, gourds (shaken in time to the drum) and dance canes (staffs used by the priest during a Native American Church meeting). For more information and price lists, send a self-addressed, stamped envelope.

Shalah Rowlen
P.O. Box 533
Meeker, OK 74855
(405) 279-3343 (8 A.M. to 5 P.M. weekdays)
R S MO

ROSEMALING

Rosemaling (which means "flower painting") originated in rural Norway in the 18th century and came to America with early settlers. At first used as a substitute for and in combination with carving in churches, rosemaling soon

Rosemaling on small trunk by Karen Jenson

Small traditional cupboard built by Orville Loftners with rosemaling by Karen Jenson

Norway and is involved in starting a museum in Milan, Minnesota, and a Minnesota rosemaling festival. Her commission work has included liturgical pieces, storefronts, ceilings and walls in a bank and drugstore and panels used in place of stained glass at a Bible camp.

"American rosemaling is more spontaneous than Norwegian," says Karen. "I almost never tell students 'This is correct' and 'This is wrong' because rosemaling is very personal. I often feel as though it is coming through me from somewhere else. I look at work I've completed and sometimes can't believe I've done it."

Unlike early craftspeople who made paint from curdled milk and blood, Karen paints backgrounds with three coats of oil-base semigloss enamel, sanding after each coat. "I then apply a glaze of artist's oils mixed with a medium of two parts boiled linseed oil and one part turpentine for the lasuring [framing]. I like to use blue on blue ground, burnt sienna on red ground and blue and sienna on white ground, gently patting the surface with a paper towel dipped in turpentine for a marbled effect (which can be varied by using a wide brush, plastic bag, fur or feather). Lasur may look like wood, fabric, stippling, marble or carving and is used as a frame for the design itself. It should be very subtle."

became popular for use on wooden objects like dowry chests and ale bowls, then on furniture, ceilings and walls.

The craft developed a language all its own, with various styles named for the Norwegian regions where they originated. The Rogeland style was known for its precise patterns, while the Hallingdal form was celebrated for its bold colors, symmetrical designs and strong outlining of flower motifs.

Karen Jenson, who lives in the Norwegian-American community of Milan, Minnesota, began rosemaling in 1972 and works in the Telemark technique, recognized for its transparent effects and free-flowing, asymmetrical combinations of *C* and *S* shapes entwined with flowers. Depending on the object's use, the design may also include farm or nautical scenes, mythological dragons, unicorns and mermaids, as well as Christian symbols.

When she started, Karen set three goals for herself: "To get my gold medal in the National Competition held at the Norwegian-American Museum in Decorah, Iowa; to be invited to teach there; and to get to Norway," all of which she achieved in a few years by working at her craft from 10 to 12 hours a day. In addition to her business, she teaches classes, conducts rosemaling tours to

Sugar tub with rosemaling by Karen Jenson

Once the background is dry, Karen does the rosemaling. "I never know in advance what the design will be," she says. "I play with shapes and forms, aiming for balance in composition and color. If I like the results, I build around them. If not, I wipe it off." After the piece is dry, she applies three coats of polyurethane varnish, sanding lightly after the first two coats. When desired, gold leaf is added after the lasuring and the rosemaled design over it.

Her shop ("open anytime I'm home") carries items like 22-inch plates ($175), hanging cupboards ($450), large cupboards ($4,000) and covered bowls with gold leaf ($450). Karen also restores (but will not repaint) old pieces and creates custom work.

Karen Jenson
Karen's Krafts
Box 6
Milan, MN 56262
(612) 734-4715
V R C S MO

Other Makers

A. Eldred Arntzen, 15 Ridgewood Road, Windsor, CT 06095; (203) 688-9144, does rosemaling in the Telemark style. Bowls, plates, trinket boxes and wooden articles range in price from $10 to $75. Arntzen is an instructor at the Fletcher Farm School for the Arts and Crafts, Ludlow, Vermont, during the summer months.

Dolores Peterson, 1261 North 4th Street, Fargo, ND 58102; (701) 293-8140.

Marika Krause, 805 Butler Pike, Broad Avenue, Ambler, PA 19002.

Gudrun Berg, 1212 Conger, Olympia, WA 98502; (206) 943-4380, works in Hallingdal, Telemark, Rogeland and what is known as West Coast rosemaling, a flower form more brilliant in color and found only on the west coast of Norway. Her husband is a woodworker and their specialty is large trunks.

Billie Nelson, Route 2, Box 27, Galesville, WI 54630; (608) 582-4277, does rosemaling in the symmetrical Rogeland style, priced from $15 to $300.

Nancy Ellison, Route 2, Box 197, Hayfield, MN 55940; (507) 477-3569. For paint samples, send $1 with a self-addressed, stamped envelope.

Nancy Morgan, 4709 Cody, West Des Moines, IA 50265; (515) 225-0702, decorates smaller objects for the home.

Judy Nelson, 1709 East Lake Street, Minneapolis, MN 55407, excels in the use of traditional color and fine detail.

BRAIDED RUGS

The first braided rugs were probably made of grasses, but early Americans' favorite material was leftover wool. Braided rugs were a great way to use up old stockings and clothing remnants, but the best rugs were always 100 percent wool, braided to be reversible and joined with linen thread. Usually round or oval, sometimes in straight parallel braids, strips were sewn together in longer strips, wound in balls, then joined together in braids of three to twelve strands.

When Julie Ryan began searching for the well-made braided rugs she remembered, to decorate homes of clients in her decorating business, she found that some were too flat, others made of manmade fabrics, some used fillers and none were joined correctly. Her answer? Make them herself. Her firm, Jugtown Mountain Rugs (named for the mountain in New Jersey where she spent summers as a child) has grown to a cottage industry workshop of fourteen artisans.

"At first, the rugs were made from wool coats and dresses purchased at rummage sales," says Julie, "but now we purchase all our wool new as needed. Our one-of-a-kind signed and dated rugs are hand-braided and hand-laced, four layers thick. [To make a braided rug four layers thick, a 3-inch strip is folded in half and then in half again.] They are laced together with heavy linen cording and completely reversible, which cuts down on cleaning and lengthens the life of the rugs. There is no filler used in our rugs, and the only machine-sewing is to piece together the strips to change colors of the wool."

The biggest problem encountered in homemade rugs—

Hand-braided, hand-laced, four-layer-thick braided rug by Jugtown Mountain Rugs

not lying flat—is eliminated by the thickness of Jugtown rugs. They are so heavy, they can't do anything else.

Their price list with twenty colors asks customers to check color preferences and suggests they also indicate which colors they do *not* want. "In the traditional rugs our grandmothers made," says Julie, "colors were determined by what old clothing was available, but in today's color-conscious world a single color can upset a total scheme." Different areas of the United States have decided color preferences, she's found: "The Northeast likes darker colors, barn reds, dark blues, tans, plaids and tweeds, while California and westerners like pastels, and Florida and southerners lean toward beiges and whites with touches of color like peach or purple."

To show the high quality of wool used and the thickness of the rug, Jugtown offers a sample braid in return for a $5 deposit. "These braids do not represent the colors of an entire rug," says Julie, "as we cannot construct a 12-inch braid using more than a few colors." Since they've been in business, one fourth of their customers have requested a braid.

Ovals from 3 by 5 feet to 10 by 14 feet range in price from $225 to $2,100, while round shapes 3 to 10 feet in diameter are $135 to $1,500. Scraps left over from the braided rugs are now hand-woven with a linen warp into rag rugs that range in size from 3 by 5 feet for $135 to 8 by 10 feet for $720. Custom-woven rugs are $12 a square foot, while custom-braided rugs are $18 a square foot.

Braided flannel mat made using a "lost" technique flat-braid and assembly method by Diana and Dennis Gray (design © Rafter-Four Designs)

Jugtown Mountain Rugs
21655 Circle Trail
Topanga, CA 90290
(213) 455-2828
V (by appt. only)   R   C   S   CC   MO

Other Makers

Judy Jarrow, 1419 Harvard Avenue, Salt Lake City, UT 84105; (801) 583-1433, makes braided rugs and footstools as well as woven rugs in hit-and-miss design (where the colors are added at random) at $12 to $15 a running foot, while her wool/wool blend braided rugs are $20 a square foot for round, oval or heart-shaped.

Dick and Betsy Houser, 147 Lorraine Court, Berea, KY 40403; (606) 986-9747, make wool/wool blend braided rugs for $22 a square foot.

American Rug, Box 493, Pittsfield, IL 62363; (217) 723-4560, makes wool braided rugs in hit-and-miss or pattern designs. Wool is hand-dyed, hand-cut, hand-folded, hand-braided and hand-laced.   C ($1)

Marylee Forgey, Break-A-Day Country Store, RFD 10, Box 168, Loudon Road, Concord, NH 03301; (603) 224-7232, braids rugs for a clientele worldwide at $19.50 a square foot. Rug-braiding has been taught at the store since 1948, first by Marylee's great-aunt and now by her.

Rafter-Four Designs, P.O. Box 3056, Sandpoint, ID 83864-9548; (208) 263-6217.

Lisa Jarrow

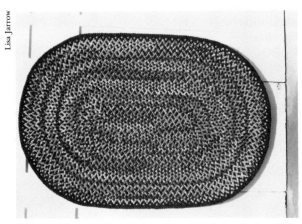

Braided oval rug in hit-and-miss design using black and vibrant color mix by Judy Jarrow

CROCHETED RUGS

Although braided, hooked and woven rag rugs were eventually manufactured, some rugs—knitted, crocheted, fabric tapestry, Amish knotted and Swedish and Bohemian braids—could be made only by hand, which is why many of the techniques were lost except in families with a rug-making tradition.

"Great-grandmother crocheted rugs during the Depression for pin money," says Diana Gray, whose cottage industry Rafter-Four Designs makes all of the rugs mentioned above, "and her mother custom-braided rugs for clients. The family remembers her braiding rugs so much larger than the room they had to be folded against the wall as she worked." Diana and her husband, Dennis,

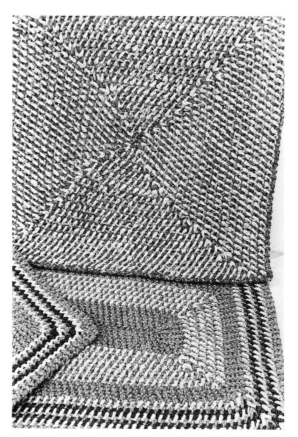

Bohemian braid rugs by Diana and Dennis Gray (design © Rafter-Four Designs)

Fabric tapestry rugs in poinsettia pattern (top) and primrose pattern (bottom) by Diana and Dennis Gray (design © Rafter-Four Designs)

began making crocheted rugs as a family business, then researched and redeveloped several of the "lost" methods.

"Crocheted rag rugs were made from single strips of fabric with a large wooden hook carved from wood," explains Diana, "in simple rounds or ovals in the hit-and-miss technique [in which colors are added at random]. During the Arts and Crafts movement [1890–1915] they became more of an art form and were planned in spirals, double-spirals and a wide variety of patterns. Fabric tapestry rugs combined the methods used in crocheted rugs with flat-wrapped rugs [a basket-making technique], using two to five strips simultaneously to create reversible patterns. Needlecraft writers termed the technique 'tapestry crochet.' Now called fabric tapestry, they are similar in weight and texture to braided rugs because they contain several layers of fabric. A 6-foot-round rug takes 80 yards of fabric, more than a mile of rag strip." After strips are

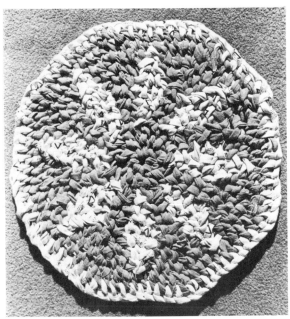

Amish (also known as Navajo) knotted rug by Diana and Dennis Gray (design © Rafter-Four Designs)

although they appear knotted on both sides they are only one knot thick.''

These fifth generation rug makers crochet rugs in fifteen shapes in six basic surface designs. Only the fabric tapestry, Bohemian braid and Swedish braid are available by mail order. For those who wish to make their own, Diana has written instructions for making all of the rugs mentioned. For an information sheet, send a self-addressed, stamped envelope. Catalogs (one for custom rugs, the other for rug-making supplies and how-to books) are $2 each, credited to the first order. Prices on custom rugs are highly varied and depend on the technique used, how elaborate the pattern is and if it is made of cotton or wool. A 24-inch rug is $35; more elaborate rugs cost up to $1,000. The shop at 334 North First Avenue in Sandpoint, Idaho, can be reached at (208) 263-6217.

Diana and Dennis Gray
Rafter-Four Designs
P.O. Box 3056
Sandpoint, ID 83864-9548
R   C   S   CC   MO

cut by hand, they are folded, then folded again, making each strip six layers thick, resembling a cord of fabric with no raw edges. Rugs are worked in rounds from the center outward.

Swedish and Bohemian braids are also known as toothbrush rugs because they were once made using the notched handle of an old toothbrush. Swedish braid is made by pulling a single fabric strip through loops with a notched instrument, creating a tight surface and spectacular sunburst effects that appear braided on one side and knotted on the other. Because the braid is created with a single strand laced into the previous round and braided around itself, they are extremely durable. Bohemian braid (also called beggar's), which looks like a woven basket, is made by braiding a single strip of fabric around itself with a notched stick.

The typical knitted rug is rectangular, but circular ones can be made by knitting wedges together. "One type of coiled, knitted rug is known as a Shaker Circle," says Diana, "probably because one can be traced to the Oneida Shakers, who made the most elaborate of this type. Round rugs knit in narrow strips joined in circles were combined with crochet for special effects, often finished with a crocheted border or joined with the stockinette stitch to be reversible. Amish knotted (also called Navajo knotted) rugs are made from strips in a technique similar to macramé;

HOOKED RUGS

Primitive hooked rugs were made of narrow strips of material hooked through a backing with a #1 crochet hook carved of wood, bone or porcupine quill, forged from iron or even bent from a nail. Before burlap feed sacks became common during the 1840s, backings were made from meal and sugar bags. Women would wash and cut

Joan Schumacher

Hooked rug with basket of apples design with leaf border by Gail F. Horton

them to size, then draw designs on with charcoal. Animals, still lifes, scenes, flowers, geometrics and nautical subjects were popular themes, as were messages like Welcome, Good Luck, Call Again and Home Sweet Home.

As clothing was worn out or outgrown, it was cut into narrow pieces, sewn together in longer strips, then rolled into balls until enough material had accumulated for a rug. If additional colors were needed, fabrics were dyed with natural materials like black walnut husks, fruit, flowers, leaves, berries, mosses, onionskins and sometimes brick dust.

"As a very young child, I used to cut, sew and roll material into balls for my grandmother," says Gail Horton. After graduation from college, Gail read an article about hooked rugs, took out every book on the subject from the local library and taught herself. "Primitive rug makers were not concerned about perspective and careful shading," she says. "Most designs were done in red, black and purple, the clothing colors of the period. In the 1870s a tin peddler named Edward Frost made tin patterns and sold preprinted rug designs along his route, which increased the availability of designs but robbed them of their spontaneous charm and truly personal nature."

The average woman hooked two rugs each winter. Done correctly, a rug 2 square yards in size could take 3 solid weeks to hook. Longer loops further apart made the work go faster, but narrow strips looped low gave a more finely textured surface. Cutting loops made the surface softer but decreased the life of the rug. To increase the longevity of their handiwork, many homemakers kept rugs upside down except when company came to call.

Fred G. Hill

"Canterbury Shaker Village," hooked rug by Suzanne and Cleland Selby

"Rug-hooking poses the same problems and challenges of planning and executing as painting a picture," says Gail, a talented artist. "To begin, I research an old design or draw an original, then color-plan the rug with a full-scale drawing of the chosen design. This is then transferred to the primitive weight burlap, and I plan my dye scheme for the colors desired. After I search through available wool for appropriate materials and purchase what is missing, I dye the wool, cut and sew a binding to the burlap, cut the wool in ⅜- to ½-inch strips and begin hooking. When finished, I trim the excess burlap and whip down the binding."

Her rugs, made from 100 percent wool, cost $55 a square foot. A full-scale color workup costs $20, deducted from the price of the finished rug. A photo or detailed description is necessary for commissions, with 50 percent down upon approval of the workup.

Gail Fischer Horton
The Queen Anne Parlour
727 First Street
Greenport, NY 11944
(516) 477-0631
V (by appt. only)   R   S   MO

Other Makers

Marion N. Ham, Quail Hill Designs, 1 Fairview Road, Clark, NJ 07066; (201) 388-8611, publishes a catalog containing over 400 designs for hooked rugs for $6.75 including postage and handling. She sells the patterns stamped on burlap, hemmed and ready to hook. Write for information on her summer workshops in Quail Hill, Limerick, Maine.

Joan Schumacher

"Spike and Alice," hooked rug by Gail F. Horton

Suzanne and Cleland Selby, The Aged Ram, P.O. Box 201, Essex VT 05451; (802) 878-4530, third generation rug hookers, create one-of-a-kind hooked rugs as well as commissioned story or memory rugs like the one pictured of Canterbury Shaker Village. Planning and execution of custom rugs depend upon the detail's complexity and overall design but would involve about 8 months to a year to complete. Costs depend upon size and design. The 4-by 6-foot Canterbury Shaker Village, for instance, costs approximately $1,500.

Peggy Teich, 9292 North 60th Street, Milwaukee, WI 53223.

Ingrain Carpet

When the National Park Service needed ingrain carpet like that ordered by Mrs. Lincoln in 1858, for Abraham Lincoln's home in Springfield, Illinois, they gave two samples of carpet woven in the mid-1800s to Jacquard weaver David Kline and asked him to reproduce it. "The ingrain carpet available today didn't feel like the old yarn spun by mulespinners," says David, "which was made on an old-time frame for spinning wool." After much research, he found two mills in the United States still making the yarn, then wove 87 yards of flat-woven, double-cloth, woolen carpet. He used a geometric and floral design of red with three shades of olive green for Abe's bedroom and dining room, and a maple leaf pattern of natural,

blue, red and green for the sitting room. His carpet may also be seen in the 1840 House in Baltimore, Maryland. Woven on a Jacquard loom, his 2-ply wool reversible ingrain is 36 inches wide and runs $90 to $140 a square yard. David Kline, Family Heir-Loom Weavers, RD 3, Box 59E, Red Lion, PA 17356; (717) 246-2431.   V   R   MO

Other Maker

Constance LaLena, 2851 Road B½, Grand Junction, CO 81503; (303) 242-3883, makes ingrain carpet in geometric designs on a hand loom, 36 inches wide, using 100 percent wool in a variety of colors. She will also design a pattern in the style of the 18th and early 19th centuries.

Navajo Rugs   *See under* Weaving

Patched Rugs

Patched rag rugs, closely related to appliquéd patchwork quilts, consist of layers of wool fabric or felt stitched to a backing. Traditional patterns include shingle or scallop, woven strip and dollar or penny rugs. Modern patched rugs are also made using a number of modified quilt patterns. Whatever the shape of the scraps, the button-hole stitch is the traditional method of securing patches to the backing material. Because stitching is exposed on the surface, patched rugs are not as durable as

Courtesy of J. David Allen & Son

Inlaid carpet woven in geometric and floral design, red with three shades of olive green, for restoration of Abraham Lincoln's home in Springfield, Illinois, by David Kline

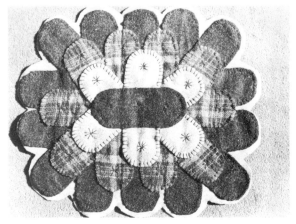

Patched rug in shingle pattern by Diana and Dennis Gray (design © Rafter-Four Designs)

other rag rugs. However, they are easy to make, lend themselves to a wide variety of patterns and are ideal for color accents.

The Rafter-Four Designs shop, at 334 North First Avenue in Sandpoint, Idaho, (208) 263-6217, in addition to making patched rugs also sells supplies, patterns and instructions. Diana and Dennis Gray, Rafter-Four Designs, P.O. Box 3056, Sandpoint, ID 83864-9548.   R   C   S   CC   MO

Rug in variation of brick-and-block pattern with fringed ends by Rastetter Woolen Mill

RAG RUGS

The most common floor covering before the Revolution was the rag rug, made from worn-out clothing, stockings and linens cut into strips, wound in balls and, after enough material had accumulated, woven with a linen warp into a rug.

"Today, only 5 percent of our customers, mostly Amish, bring in their own material," says Tim Rastetter, a fifth generation weaver whose family has been hand-weaving rag rugs since the 1870s. "Preparing material, figuring out how colors will look after weaving, has become a lost art," says the owner of Rastetter Woolen Mill, on Route 62 between Berlin and Millersburg in Ohio. In 1973, Tim took over the business on a 3-month trial basis from his grandfather Ralph Aling. Now in his nineties, Ralph still comes in every day to weave. There's only one thing older on the premises and that's the carding machine: built in 1862, it is the oldest one operating in an American business. It was first powered by water at Tim's great-great-

Rug in variation of brick-and-block pattern with fringed ends by Rastetter Woolen Mill

grandfather's mill on Doughty Creek, and later by steam, gas and electricity.

Rastetter rugs and carpets are hand-woven of wool or cotton rags in traditional weaves of hit-and-miss, block, pebble, chamois check, solid colors or honeycomb, which is a loose, rough weave. "Most rag rugs have 12 warp threads per inch," says Tim, "but honeycomb has only 2 warp threads per inch, which makes the material go up and down around the warp, creating a very thick rug and interesting texture." Hand-woven on small looms by twelve weavers, taught by Tim and his grandfather, the rugs are made in widths up to 3 feet wide (which can be seamed for room-size) with warps of 8/4 or 4/4-ply cotton or 12/3 linen, which is the same thickness as the 8/4 cotton but more durable. Their most popular rug, the brick-and-block pattern originated by Ralph's grandfather Simon Troyer, is made by running two different shuttles for the block design and a separate pattern on the warp. After Ralph demonstrated weaving at the Smithsonian in 1971 and they exhibited the rug, it was renamed The Smithsonian. (Prices range from $9 a yard for 27-inch widths to $37 a yard for 36-inch wool with a linen warp.)

Although Tim's weaving was featured in the Washington Craft Show sponsored by the Women's Committee of the Smithsonian, he likes designing best of all. "Sometimes he has trouble choosing his own clothes," says his wife, Maureen, their business manager, "but he has a great eye for warp and rag combinations." The sixth generation, their children, Vanessa and Timmy, has been on the job since 1979, when they were 6 and 4 respectively, washing wool, restacking inventory and helping at folk festival demonstrations.

The Rastetters' other products include braided rugs, coverlets (overshot and double-weave), place mats, down comforters and pillows and old-fashioned wool comforters. "We're one of the few companies left making comfort batting," says Tim, "which is lighter than down (that needs ticking to hold it in) and has no definite life. A wool comforter is extremely warm and can be recarded for generations, whereas down has a limited life, depending on how it's used." In addition to refilling down comforters and pillows, Rastetter's also washes, cards and restuffs wool comforters and sells raw wool. "Some people like to spin it raw," says Tim. "It's also beneficial for foot problems and used to soften skin." For a price list, send a self-addressed, stamped envelope. The mill is open 12 noon to 5 P.M. Tuesday through Saturday, June through December, and Wednesday through Saturday, January through May.

Rug in variation of brick-and-block pattern with fringed ends by Rastetter Woolen Mill

Rastetter Woolen Mill
State Routes 39 and 62
Star Route, Box 42
Millersburg, OH 44654
(216) 674-2103
V R W C S MO

Other Makers

Mrs. Marion C. Edens, Route 9, Box 242, Greeneville, TN 37743; (615) 638-4951, weaves wool rugs on a cotton warp in any color and size at $5.50 a square foot.

Anita Miller, 182 Ridgefield Road, P.O. Box 643, Wilton, CT 06897; (203) 762-9235, makes custom-designed, color-coordinated rugs in the Swedish style at $16 to $100 a square foot.

Susan Bradley, Silver Street, RFD 1, Box 231, Sheffield, MA 01257; (413) 229-2031, makes cotton rag rugs and table mats with 8/4-ply cotton warp in custom-dyed colors. Hit-and-miss on a natural warp rugs are $10 a foot (29 inches wide), while custom colors are $12 a foot.

Coker Creek Handweavers, P.O. Box 8, Coker Creek, TN 37314; (615) 261-2157, makes rag rugs in hit-and-miss or matched border pattern at $18 a running foot for a 28-inch width to $24 a running foot for a 42-inch width.

Sara Hotchkiss, 25 Forest Avenue, P.O. Box 4213, Portland, ME 04101; (207) 773-5474, weaves rugs in a traditional tapestry technique called dovetailing (the same technique used by the Navajos) in patterns of squares, diamonds and stripes with knotted, twirled or bound edges, at $15 to $22 a square foot regular, more for custom designs.

Kay and Ron Loch, Heritage Rugs, Lahaska, PA 18931; (215) 794-7229, hand-weave wool rugs in any size up to 15 feet wide by any length on antique hand-built looms. Prices range from $155 for one 4 by 6 feet to $1,460 for a 15-foot square, plus shipping and handling.

Minnie B. Yancey, Innisfree Weaving Center, Inc., P.O. Box 469, Berea, KY 40403, weaves rugs with a 100 percent cotton warp at 10 threads per inch with a weft of wool strips cut 4 inches wide. When woven, strips roll into thick 1- to 2-inch ribs up to 15 feet wide in any length.

Mary Beth Burkholder, Perfectly Warped, 419 South Market Street, Troy, OH 45373; (513) 335-3795, weaves cotton and wool or all-cotton rugs.

Black River Junction Co., P.O. Box 263, 15 Main Street, Nicholson, PA 18446; (717) 942-6651.

Julia Brown, 4516 Hucks Road, Charlotte, NC 28213.

Carolyn and Vincent Carleton, 1015A Greenwood Road, Elk, CA 95432; (707) 877-3540.

SUMMER-AND-WINTER BOUNDWEAVE RUGS

"Summer-and-winter weave is considered to be a distinctly American weave," says Dianne Carol Roach, "made in America from about the time of the Revolution. Since the patterns possible on a four-harness loom are limited, it probably was the work of a professional weaver rather than that of a member of a colonial household, since most home looms were limited to a maximum of four harnesses. Summer-and-winter weave stands alone as an American accomplishment in textiles, our one contribution to the vast store of weaving knowledge."

Boundweave rug by Dianne Carol Roach

Summer side of summer-and-winter rug by Dianne Carol Roach

Winter side of summer-and-winter rug by Dianne Carol Roach

What early Americans liked most about summer-and-winter rugs was their reversibility. Unlike the overshot weave, which had smaller areas of background, summer-and-winter could have large areas of color. Because one side was predominantly light and the other side dark, the light side was used in summer months with the dark side turned up in winter, which is how the design got its name.

Dianne had planned on being a painter until she walked into the textile room at Moore College of Art in Philadelphia. "The mystique of the yarns, colors and designs captivated me from the start," she says. Since 1982 she has concentrated on the two-tone summer-and-winter weave because of its flexibility. "I wanted to experiment with shaft switching [changing the threading of the warp while it remains on the loom]," she says, "to explore specific but complex relationships of color and design. I chose the boundweave technique because it produces a durable fabric. It can also be applied to a variety of weaves, providing the weaver with additional design flexibility." Boundweave construction is a method of warp and weft interlacement that gives rugs a ribbed surface with a two-sided weft-faced finish. Summer-and-winter is only one of a variety of weaves suitable for boundweave.

After deciding design and colors, Dianne does a detailed drawing, then a color workup with a mixture of dyes and gouache before beginning the actual weaving. "The most challenging part of my job," says Dianne, who works mostly on commission, "is working out a design for a particular space, so that the finished rug is a melding of what the client wants as well as an aesthetic statement that pleases me and is true to my artistic direction. Rugs are my specialty. I love them. They can set the tone and mood of a room and become family heirlooms to hand down to future generations. At times in the work, something very special happens, but there are also moments when something stands out more than I expected. For instance, the luster of the yarn can throw off the total composition. But I've found in more than 10 years of weaving that when things don't work out as planned, if I keep looking ahead, that even mistakes lead to something better. In recent years, people have been hanging my work on the wall, where the image confronts the viewer vertically instead of horizontally. This has prompted thinking on my part about the visual impact of my work and what directions its further development will take me."

In addition to creating rugs for private and corporate clients, Dianne has designed dress fabric for M. Lowenstein and Sons and carpets for the Lee Carpet Company. Her work is in private and corporate collections throughout the United States. Her summer-and-winter rugs, made in double-threaded, double-sleyed linen warp and 100 percent wool weft, are mothproof and colorfast, and range in price from $600 to $5,000 or $65 to $110 a square foot.

Dianne Carol Roach
7401 Carroll Avenue
Takoma Park, MD 20912
(301) 270-6981 or (202) 232-5325
R S

WESTERN SADDLES

"A working cowboy is usually more particular about his horse and gear than the car he drives," Jim Lathrop will tell you. "A custom saddle must fit both the rider and the horse. People aren't made the same and neither are horses. Thoroughbreds have high withers, whereas the withers on most quarterhorses aren't as high and prominent."

He should know. He started as a Montana cowboy at the age of 16 and made his first saddle when he was 25. A lifetime member of the Professional Rodeo Cowboys Association, Jim quit the rodeo circuit in 1974 to become a full-time saddle maker. He earned a national reputation for his western saddles in Montana. Jim says that even after more than 30 years, "each saddle is just as hard to make as those I made 20 years ago. A lot of my soul goes into every one." Although he's never advertised, customers come from as far away as Kuwait. "But the majority of my work is for repeat customers," says Jim. "Working cowboys, riders who want show saddles for pleasure-riding events, and their sons and daughters." Some come to his shop to browse through his album, but he can usually tell what people want by talking to them, and has "taken many a saddle order on napkins and matchbook covers."

Only the best materials and workmanship go into his handcrafted saddles: saddle trees (a handmade wooden frame covered and laced with rawhide) custom-built to his specification; matched skirting leather sides, the best oil-tanned latigo and lace leather, plus heavy three-quarter wool skins for lining the saddle skirt.

"*Skirting* and *sides* are trade terms that indicate the tannage of the cowhide," says Jim. "Skirting is a heavier leather used for saddles and western horsegear. Each saddle uses 13- to 15-ounce sides. Each side is half a cowhide, and approximately 2½ sides are used on each saddle. Three-quarter wool skins [the heaviest wool for saddle use] are quality sheepskin linings that cover the skirts between the saddle and the saddle blankets." His base-price saddle (all plain or rough side out) at $1,350 is made of the same material as the one costing $2,200.

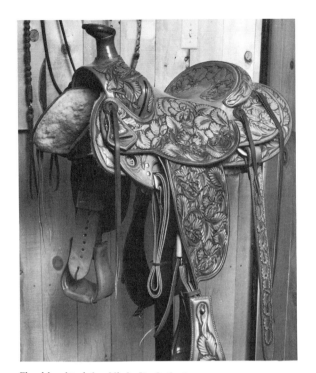

Floral hand-tooled saddle by Jim Lathrop

Silver buckstitched saddle by Slim Green

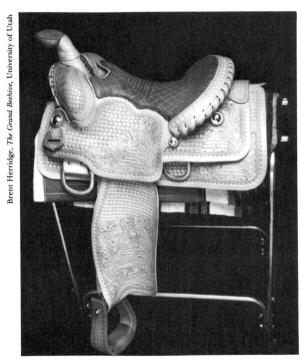

Beehive saddle by Glen Thompson

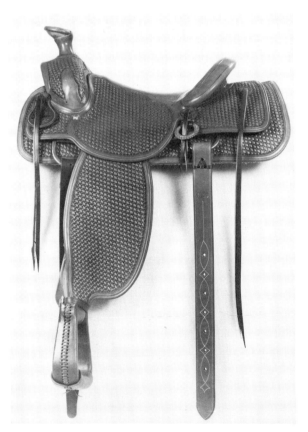

Basketweave-stamped saddle by Charles Weldon

230

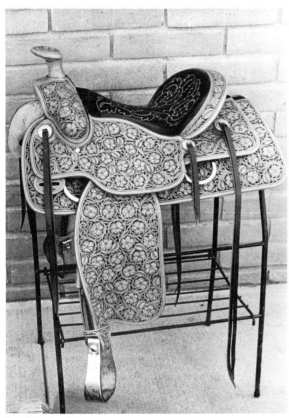

Saddle by Don King

"The variables that increase the price," explains Jim, "are flower stamping [tooling] and the amount of silver used. The stamping on each saddle is different, depending on the customer's preference, and can add from 4 to 5 days' labor." Each custom saddle takes from 5 to 15 days to complete. He refuses to cut corners or to compete with production-line saddles or those made for price competition. "Using premium material and craftsmanship will give a customer at least 25 to 35 years of daily use," Jim believes, "and with care, more."

No machinery touches the custom saddle. The saddle-maker sews the parts separately and with a small splitter thins the lace strings. After piercing holes through the leather with an awl, Jim sews all other parts by hand with waxed linen thread and two needles, passing them back and forth in a saddle stitch. There are three basic types of rigging (hardware and leather parts that hold the saddle on the horse): full double dees (stainless steel shaped like *D*s); flatplates (usually of brass); plus rigging in the skirt. All are fastened to the tree with leather and screws. Upon

completion, Jim hand-rubs the leather with pure neat's-foot oil (to soften and prolong the life of the leather), a saddle butter compound and lanolin, then proudly bolts a silver plate with his name on the front of the seat.

"A good custom saddle is really a work of art," he says, "in addition to being a practical and functional piece of equipment."

Jim Lathrop Custom Saddles
Box 4468
Bozeman, MT 59772-4468
(406) 587-2765
V R S MO

Other Makers

Slim Green P.O. Box 88, Tesuque, NM 87544; (505) 982-2092, has been making saddles since the early 1930s and has never made the same one twice. Using hand-selected A-1 leather and saddle trees made to his specification, he carves saddles to sit flat on a horse's back and shapes the seat to protect the horse's withers and keep the rider from sliding around. His tradition of leaving an unfinished letter in a monogram or name stems from Indian lore of leaving a space for bad spirits to escape. His clients have included John Wayne, Errol Flynn, Slim Pickens, Robert Redford and Ralph Lauren. One of his rodeo saddles is in the National Cowboy Hall of Fame.

Glen D. Thompson, 149 South 7200 East, Huntsville, UT 84317; (801) 745-2313, recipient of the 1984 Governor's Award for Folk Art, is known for his made-to-order leather ground seat saddles (in which the seat is built of six layers of custom-shaped leather) with trees of sugar pine. Prices start at $700.

Charles Weldon, Weldon Ranch, Blue Creek, Billings, MT 59104; (406) 248-2555, uses heavy saddle skirting, plain or with basketweave-stamping, floral or carved designs. Saddle trees and hardware are handmade in Oregon. Base price is $1,250.

Don King, King's Saddlery, 184 North Main Street, Sheridan, WY 82801; (307) 672-2755 or (800) 443-8919, was selected six times to make the Professional Rodeo Cowboys Association World Championship saddles and has also made and donated hand-tooled roping saddles to the Champion All-Around Cowboy at the Sheridan, Wyoming, rodeo.

BULTOS

Religion was the backbone of existence for early immigrants in New Mexico. Spanish settlers named their children, villages, mountains and rivers for saints and prayed to them daily. Because the mountainous terrain made it difficult for them to acquire religious symbols from their native lands, they created their own.

Santos (saints), which stood near the altar and in *nichos* (recessed altars in adobe walls), were made by carvers (*santeros*) in each village. They were made from local woods, in two forms: *retablos*, or figures carved into boards; and *bultos*, three-dimensional figures of Christ, the holy family and the saints, from sizes small enough to hold in the hand to life-size. They played an integral role in daily life, and the demand for them kept image makers working full time until the Catholic Church labeled their work pagan and replaced it with imported plaster and gilt figures. Non-Spanish immigrants, not understanding the significance of the saintly figures, compared them to statues in European churches and considered them crude. During the 19th century, as access to trade routes improved, many *santos* were replaced with plaster forms. As

Bulto *of St. Francis of Assisi by Leo Salazar*

Bulto *of Moses with tablets by Leo Salazar*

the need for carved wooden *santos* diminished, the number of *santeros* declined until *santos* gained new appreciation as the honest expression of religious folk art they'd been all along.

Leo Jorge Salazar, whose *bultos* are among the finest in America, began carving in 1966 at the age of 33, when a leg injury kept him from his job as a heavy equipment operator and foreman for a construction company. The Taos native had always admired the work of his friend, the well-known carver Patrocinio Barela. "After watching him," Leo remembers, "I picked up a piece of wood and started carving. He had his style, and over the years, I've found mine. My tools are simple: a wooden mallet and two chisels" (one of which he inherited from Barela). Just as Leo once went with his friend Pat into the mountains and over the mesas in search of stumps and fallen limbs, he now goes with his sons, fifth generation *santeros* who began carving when they were 5 and 6 years old.

"The wood I use is cedar," explains Leo. "I can visualize

the *santo* as it sits in the tree. I enjoy the aroma as I carve cedar under the tree in my backyard." Now a respected *santero*, Leo carves 8 to 10 hours a day and says he "would rather carve than do any other kind of work. My home has become my gallery. I have a shop in my backyard where my sons and I carve. People call or mail orders, but most come to our house, sometimes busloads at a time in summer months. I like that because I enjoy meeting new and interesting people."

Salazar's work is now included in more than a dozen books and many private and public collections, including the Smithsonian, the Vatican and the Museum of American Folk Art. His repertoire includes forty saints as well as Old and New Testament subjects. Most tell a story: Moses with arms raised, beard flying, holds a tablet in one hand; St. Peter casts a net; St. Martin of Siguenza

Nacimiento in Portal bultos *by Marco A. Oviedo*

holds a broom. But of all the saints, St. Francis of Assisi is Leo's favorite. "He was kind like Jesus," Leo explains, "and would never let anyone be poorer than he."

Winners of awards for 12 years at the Spanish Market in Santa Fe, Leo's *bultos* range in price from $100 for 12-inch figures upward. His sons, Leonard, Michael, Ernest and David, now in their teens and early twenties, have won three awards for their *bultos*, while David has captured two for his *retablos*. Prices for their *bultos* begin at $50.

Leo Salazar & Sons
P.O. Box 1035
Taos, NM 87571
(505) 758-8490
V S R W MO

Other Makers

Felix A. Lopez, P.O. Box 3691, Fairview Station, Espanola, NM 87533; (505) 753-2785, creates *santos* from cottonwood and paints them with natural pigments (soot, boiled walnut shells, indigo, raspberry and cherry juice, native clays) in the soft warm tones used by early image makers.

Marco A. Oviedo, Centinela Ranch, Box 3A, Chimayo, NM 87522; (505) 351-4755, creates carved images in the style of colonial New Mexico that are painted by his wife, Pat, with natural pigments.

Eluid L. Martinez, 221 Villeros Street, Santa Fe, NM 87501; (505) 982-2214, is a seventh generation *santero* in the Lopez family of Cordova. He is author of the book *What Is a Santo?*, and his aspen *santos* are included in many private and public collections.

Theresa Sanchez Martinez

Bulto of San Antonio de Padua by Felix Lopez

233

Orlinda and Eurgencio Lopez, Box 107, Cordova, NM 87523; (505) 351-4820, carve *santos* from aspen and cedar, which they sell in their shop. They also carve special orders, with smaller items taking a few weeks, larger, up to 3 months.

Orlando Romera, Route 1, Box 103, Santa Fe, NM 87501.

Felipe Benito Archuleta, Route 4, Box 43, Santa Fe, NM 87501; (505) 982-1433.

George T. Lopez, P.O. Box 27, Cordova, NM 87523; (505) 351-4374.

Horacio E. Valdez, P.O. Box 98, Dixon, NM 87527; (505) 579-4351.

Joseph T. Sanchez, P.O. Box 62, Torreon, NM 87061; (505) 384-2206.

James Sanchez, Route 1, Box 164-B, Espanola, NM 87523; (505) 753-2893.

Luisito Lujan, Nambe, NM 87501.

Fred Vigil, 1107 Canyon Road, Santa Fe, NM 87501; (505) 983-9511.

Enrique Rendon, P.O. Box 131, Velarde, NM 87582; (505) 852-4532.

Anita Romero Jones, Route 2, Box 246-D-18, Santa Fe, NM 87505.

Max Roybal, 608 Third Street, SW, Albuquerque, NM 87102.

Jose Benjamin Lopez, 63407 El Alamo Street, Espanola, NM 87532.

Eulogio and Zoraida Ortega, P.O. Box 676, Velarde, NM 87582; (505) 852-2290.

Retablo in needlework by Monica Halford

RETABLOS AND *REREDOS*

Santos (saints) carved or painted on boards are called *retablos*. They were used as objects of faith and devotion by Catholics in New Mexico and displayed as art by others.

"We also refer to religious paintings on tin, glass, hides, tiles, straw and embroidery as *retablos*," says *santera* (carver) Monica Halford, whose work is in the Albuquerque Museum. "I've made *retablos* in needlepoint and on brass and copper as well. When we include more than one religious painting, we refer to it as a *reredo* (or *tabla*), which is used as an altar backdrop or altar screen."

Like early settlers, who painted their favorite saints on flat pieces of wood when they couldn't afford to buy a *bulto* from the local image maker, Monica made her first *retablo* of St. Pasquale (patron saint of cooks) on tin for her kitchen. A friend saw it and asked her to make one of St. Anthony, who is Monica's favorite saint. "He's the patron saint for salvation, money and a good marriage,"

Altar backdrop with La Conquistadora (in center), St. Ysidro (on left) and St. Francis (on right) by Monica Halford

she explains. "He also helps find lost objects. In return for his help, you must always donate money to his poor."

Monica began sketching and studying early *retablos* in museums, churches and books and discovered that a perfect background was "old doors with five panels, just enough to include the five most popular images: St. Joseph, Jesus of Nazareth, Our Lady of Sorrows, St. Francis and St. Anthony." When she had made three door/*retablos* for a local restaurant, twelve tile *retablos* and murals of Our Lady of the Immaculate Conception for the Immaculate Heart of Mary Seminary and a series of tin *retablos* for the Museum of New Mexico shop, she was in business. "I've always been affected by *retablos*," she explains. "I feel a closeness to the old ones and love and respect *retablos* made by others. They are a part of our heritage which goes back to the late 1500s."

Monica's ancestors arrived in New Mexico in 1594 with the first colonists. "That's 26 years before the Pilgrims landed at Plymouth," she says proudly. Now in her 50s, mother of five and grandmother of four, Monica is known for her use of subtle colors like those of the 17th and 18th centuries ("Mine look old, but they have a touch of Monica").

When working on wood, she sands each panel, then coats it with gesso, sanding between each coat: one coat for an aged look, three to four for a porcelain finish. She sketches the figures, then paints handsome faces on her saints because "It makes it easier to pray to them." Monica seems to know each of them personally. "San Pancracio is the patron saint of money and business," she'll tell you, as if talking about a friend. "Santa Monica loved wine and always had a good supply of it. San Simon is dressed like a gambler and has to be paid for favors in liquor. His candles can always be lit by cigars." She also collects *dichos* (sayings) lettered on her work. Her favorite: "*No sera en diablo pero apesta asufre,*" translates "He may not be the devil but he smells like sulphur."

The first year she entered one of her doors in the prestigious Spanish Market in Santa Fe, it won first prize. Since then she has captured awards for her work on tin and glass and in 1987 won the Tillie Galbadon Stark Award. "I feel the energy of the saints very much in my work," says Monica. "I'd like my *retablos* to comfort those who buy them whether they believe in the saint or not. I want them to bring love and peace wherever they hang."

Monica Halford
850 El Caminito
Santa Fe, NM 87501
(505) 982-4175
V R MO

San Acacio bulto/retablo *carved by Marco A. Oviedo and painted by Patricia Trujillo de Oviedo*

Light the Way retablo *by Manuel Lopez*

Other Makers

Marco A. Oviedo, Centinela Ranch, Box 3A, Chimayo, NM 87522; (505) 351-4755.

Manuel Lopez, Route 2, Box 21-d, Hernandez, NM 87537; (505) 753-9769.

Efren and Angelina Martinez, 1127 Maez Road, Santa Fe, NM 87501, do *retablos* framed in tin.

Charles M. Carrillo, 217 Mesilla, NE, Albuquerque, NM 87108; (505) 268-0620, does *retablos* on native pine.

Linda Martinez de Pedro, P.O. Box 505, Chimayo, NM 87522.

SCHERENSCHNITTE

Initially, paper-cutting began in China where papercuts were used as embroidery patterns. Later papercuts were used in Europe to make the borders on watercolored pictures of the saints look like Florentine embroideries. The German version, *Scherenschnitte* (which means "scissors cuttings"), was used to decorate religious documents like marriage certificates. In the hands of Pennsylvania-Germans, paper-cutting grew to be used on birth certificates (*Taufschein*), love letters (*Liebesbrief*—given as marriage proposals), shelf paper, doilies (often cut from the paper used to wrap fruit), bookmarks, paper dolls and decorations on mantels, Christmas trees and Easter eggs. German Catholics used pictures of saints and religious symbols, while German Protestants preferred words and quotes from the Bible.

"Paper-cutting was also very popular with children," says *Scherenschnitte* artist Claudia Hopf. "They would cut simple flowers, animals, people, geometrical snowflakes and all their valentines."

Scherenschnitte: *"The Brementown Musicians" by Claudia Hopf*

Scherenschnitte is cut from a single piece of paper in a continuous design, with one to three folds for repeats in the overall pattern and no glueing or over-pasting of paper, then painted. The most difficult part is cutting larger pieces, learning how to handle or manipulate the paper without tearing it. "I first do a skeletal sketch," says Claudia. "By careful planning, I know where portions will touch or overlap to cause 'bridges' in the work and thus strengthen it."

Trained as an artist, Claudia became involved in restoration work at the Farmers' Museum, Inc., in Cooperstown. When her husband was curator at the Pennsylvania Farm Museum, she saw her first *Scherenschnitte*: an old birth certificate with a lacy border. Research led to practice, and within 10 years she was scissors-cutting full time.

"I was drawn to its simplicity," she says. "Until then, I was involved in paintings with complex colors. Paper-cutting contains the most basic of design elements. By cutting away pieces of a sheet of white paper, there was a sharp contrast between paper and void, positive and negative. Pure and simple, the design was easier to see and I was no longer tempted to erase."

After exploring many possibilities, she started painting

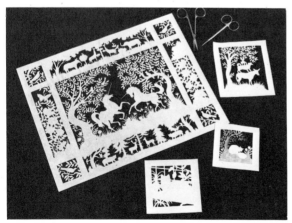

Scherenschnitte *in process: cutting scissors displayed with uncolored works by Claudia Hopf*

her pieces, but with a limited palette of earth tones (yellow ochre, cadmium red, Prussian blue and burnt sienna) like those used by 18th century artists. Today, her colors are brighter, but most of her work continues to tell stories from folk tales or the Bible. Her favorite is the Peaceable Kingdom. "Some days I draw sheep, others pigs or cows," she says. "All the animals in my cuttings have loving natures and friendly faces."

Claudia's work has been featured in the Smithsonian catalog and in an American Folk Art calendar and translated into cards and stationery. She has also researched and documented the history of the craft in America and Europe, written two books on the subject and in 1980 represented the Pennsylvanian tradition at the International Scissors-Cutting Forum in Washington.

Scherenschnitte is now her family's cottage industry. After Claudia designs pieces and transfers them to paper, her son, Perry, cuts and antiques the paper for an ivory look. Claudia then paints the paper-cutting with watercolors, using a magnifying glass for fine details. Her husband, Carroll, then mounts the work on velour paper and makes the frame, decorating it with the distemper or vinegar graining technique. Prices range from $40 for a 3- by 3-inch *Scherenschnitte* up to $2,500 for one 22 by 34 inches. Laser-cut *Scherenschnitte* designs, which are cut many at a time, sell unframed for $2 to $3.

Claudia Hopf
13 Mechanic Street
Kennebunk, ME 04043
(207) 985-4654
R S MO

Other Makers

Walter Von Gunten, 3414 Tiltree Road, Hattiesburg, MS 39401; (601) 268-6964, uses black papercuts so fine that his *Scherenschnitte* look like pen-and-ink drawings.

Trude Head, 109 West Main Street, Burkittsville, MD 21718; (301) 473-5055, makes exquisite *Scherenschnitte* in the German tradition and language (with translation in English on the back of antique or grained frames).

K. Kerchner McConlogue, 701 Hunting Place, Baltimore, MD 21229; (301) 945-7441, creates more primitive, whimsical *Scherenschnitte,* with messages in English.

Carol Maxwell, Principia College, Elsah, IL 62028; (618) 374-1134, uses knife on glass, the technique used by Italians during the Renaissance, as well as Swiss methods.

Papercuttings by Alison, 404 Partridge Circle, Sarasota, FL 33577; (813) 952-0763 or 957-0328.

Martha Link Walsh, 779 East Main Street, Branford, CT 06405; (203) 481-3505.

Schranks   *See* **Furniture, Country**

PAINTED SCREENS

Baltimore summers are steamy and hot. Before air-conditioning, residents of brick rowhouses had to leave doors and windows open in warm weather for air to circulate. Unfortunately, the solution created a new problem: passersby could see in. To protect their privacy, Baltimoreans started painting colorful scenes and designs on the outside of the wire mesh in their screen doors. That way, passersby saw only the surface painting, while those inside saw only the screen.

"William Anton Oktavec, a produce store owner, started the practice locally in 1913," says screen painter Dee Herget. "Instead of keeping his produce outside in the sun where it would spoil, he put it inside and then, to attract customers, painted an advertisement for his fruits and vegetables on the screen. After his idea caught on, William Oktavec taught most of the early screen painters in the city."

Although screens were painted in other parts of the

Scherenschnitte: *"Friends Are Like Jewels" by Claudia Hopf*

Painted screen of pastoral scene with pond and swans by Dee Herget

"Potted Plants," painted screen by Dee Herget

United States and sold ready-made by a Detroit company as early as 1874, the only American city where screen-painting is alive and well today is Baltimore. Born of necessity, continued for love of tradition and color, the painted screen has become a trademark in East Baltimore, where thousands exist.

"Scenes are usually serene, pastoral and bucolic," says Dee (whose motto is: "You can see out but they can't see in"). "The most popular contains a cottage, garden, trees and a pond that *always* has at least one swan floating in it. Other favorites include street scenes, waterfalls, forests, hunters, Swiss chalets, boats, lighthouses and waterfronts, although I have also painted mugs of beer, sandwiches and flowers." When house owners have all the screens painted, they usually repeat the same scene on all, rather than choosing a variety.

Dee had worked for 13 years at City Hall handling complaints before a hearing problem forced her to quit. Realizing that she missed contact with the public, she took lessons in screen-painting from Ben Richardson, a retired professional, and after a month of practice, started advertising in the classifieds. Although she has painted screens from a 12-foot-high scaffold, she usually paints them at home. During her busy season (March through June), she often completes as many as fifty a week. Customers can choose from her portfolio of twenty designs or supply their own. Using a combination of oil, acrylic and enamel paints, Dee paints each screen, then seals it with clear varnish. When kept out of the winter sun and cleaned with soap and water, an average screen with normal use won't need to be touched up for at least 5 years.

"Almost everyone who sees my work tells me how they grew up with painted screens and how much they love

"Dream Castle," painted screen by Dee Herget

them," says Dee. "At first I thought they'd appeal to older people, but I sell more to the young, not just for windows, either. They use them on campers, for room dividers and frame them for the wall."

Although Dee is credited with the revival of interest in screen-painting and her work has been exhibited at City Hall and the Baltimore Museum of Art, she hasn't raised her prices. The average painted screen still sells for $15 to $30, in her designs or yours. (Shipping costs additional.) "If they want it and I can do it," she says, "I will."

Dee Herget
Screen Art
910 Sue Grove Road
Baltimore, MD 21221
(301) 391-1750
R S MO

SCRIMSHAW

Scrimshaw, the decorating of whale ivory, bone or shells with intricate carvings or designs, is a uniquely American folk craft first done by Eskimos and later by seamen on whaling vessels. A sperm whale with a 20-foot-long jaw and up to fifty teeth provided a ready source of supplies. Between whales, scrimshanders would soak a whale's tooth or bone in brine, scrape it clean, polish the surface with sharkskin or ashes, cut the design with knives or sail needles, then fill in the etched area with India ink, dye, soot, tobacco or berry juice. Nautical scenes and women were favorite subjects, often copied from *Harper's Weekly* or Godey illustrations.

"Scrimshaw's a one-shot deal with no room for error," says Gerry Dupont, whose work won the Award for Excellence in 1983 and 1984 at the Mystic International competition. "It's much like photography. One only knows what one has after the process is completed."

After Gerry sands the tooth or ivory smooth, he buffs it to a high gloss, then brushes ink over the entire surface. The design is then penciled in. "As I scratch away," he explains, "I go through the ink into the piece itself, making minute canals that retain the ink. When the etching is complete, it looks much like a drawing on a blackboard. The piece is again covered with ink and buffed clean. The surface should be altered as little as possible and feel smooth to the touch, not full of deep gouges to hold the ink."

Known for the painterly tonalities in his work, Gerry admits to being a crosshatch fanatic, proud of his velvety blacks, halftones and quartertones, obtained through the

Three-masted schooner putting out to sea, scrimshaw by Gerry Dupont

choice of stylus, angle held and pressure used. "The scene should be correlated with the shape of the tooth," says Gerry, whose specialty is harbor scenes. "I try to recreate history as it was. For that reason, I research collections of old photos, not engravings, which are other artists' interpretations. People relate to a ship's home port. Seeing a ship next to a dock with people and buildings gives scale and adds weight to the scene because the eye is consumed by a number of things rather than one focal point." Scenes also display his talent for minute lettering on a ship or sign. "Most artists do it after completion. I do it first, without magnifying glass or lenses."

Born in Fall River, Massachusetts, Gerry saw his first scrimshaw in his teens and thought he could do better but didn't try until after graduating from Southeastern Massachusetts University, where he majored in commercial art and visual design. While playing bass in a rhythm and blues group, he answered a wholesale jeweler's ad and contracted for a paid apprenticeship. "That's when

239

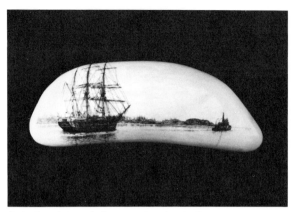

Scrimshaw design of schooner and tugboat by Gerry Dupont

I got a feel for what I could and couldn't do," he recalls, "and progressed to the techniques I use today."

"One of the hardest aspects of the craft," says Gerry, "is that teeth are convex. To create the illusion of straight or curved lines often means doing the opposite." He likes doing tight precise lines and the challenge of ambitious scenes but feels "there's a certain futility doing one-of-a-kind pieces as far as exposure goes. The same etching on one plate could produce 200 limited prints and provide 200 times the exposure for one-twentieth the work. Almost like a counterfeiter who's made an exquisite $20-bill plate and sells it without printing a single bill." However, this rarity is particularly enticing to collectors, who are now willing to pay an additional $500 to $1,000 in return for a promise from Gerry that he will not duplicate the work on another piece. His scrimshaw ranges in price

from $150 to $5,000 depending on size, amount of detail and subject matter. Because scrimshaw by law cannot be sold over state lines, buyers must travel to Massachusetts or provide the tooth or ivory for Gerry to etch.

Gerry Dupont
P.O. Box 117P
South Dartmouth, MA 02748
R   S   MO

Other Makers

Barry and Lisa Simon, 175 Division Road, Westport, MA 02790; (617) 636-3011, descendants of whalers and scrimshanders, scrimshaw a wide range of materials including antique and fossilized ivories. Jewelry ranges from $12 to $60, and much of their work is in color.

Susan Ford, 137 NW 80th, Seattle, WA 98117; (206) 284-5310 or 784-7672, does exquisite scrimshaw of Northwest wildlife on fossil walrus artifacts, and portraits of Native American tribes other than those of the Northwest.

Judy Yost, 5041 Camelback Place, Kingman, AZ 86401; (602) 757-3325, scrimshaws registered African ivory, mostly elephant, fossilized Alaskan walrus ivory and wild and domestic salvaged bones.

C. Milton Barringer, P.O. Box 562, Palm Harbor, FL 33563; (813) 785-0088, purchased the stock of a whaling station in Chile in the 1960s. It included a large number of whale teeth, which he has been using ever since. His work has been presented to many world figures and is exhibited in the British Museum of Natural History. Price list available and Certificate of Exemption, which allows him to sell the teeth.

Brian Kiracofe, Baltimore Scrimshanders, Light Street Pavilion, Harborplace, Baltimore, MD 21202; (301) 659-9494.

Daniel Kiracofe, Boston Scrimshanders, 175G Faneuil Hall Marketplace, Boston, MA 02109; (617) 367-1552.

Gary Kiracofe, The Island Scrimshander, Mackinac Island, MI 49757; (906) 847-3792.

Marcy Pumphret, 333 Old Harbor Road, Chatham, MA 02633.

Daniel A. Van Der Maas, 2205 Gring Drive, Wyomissing, PA 19610.

Harbor scene showing schooner returning to port, scrimshaw by Gerry Dupont

SHIP AND BOAT REPLICAS

"American clippers were the ultimate sailing ships," says Melbourne Smith, who designed and is building a replica of the 180-foot-long *Sea Witch,* most famous clip-

Replica of the 180-foot clipper ship Sea Witch *by Melbourne Smith*

Replica of Pride of Baltimore *by Melbourne Smith*

per of all time. "The *Sea Witch*'s records coming home from China—74 and 77 days—have never been beaten. No other ship ever came close."

Melbourne, who built the topsail schooner *Pride of Baltimore* in the city's inner harbor and was master on her maiden voyage to Bermuda, also designed and built California's tall ship *Californian,* an 1850 revenue cutter used by the Revenue Marine Service to collect taxes and stop smuggling and the slave trade. He is currently designing for the state of Pennsylvania a replica of Commodore Perry's flagship, *The Niagara,* used in the Battle of Lake Erie. "The first and only time an entire British fleet was defeated," says Melbourne. "Perry captured the whole fleet. *The Niagara* was built in a hurry from green wood and carried twenty guns on deck, each weighing a ton. You can't have a warship without guns, but that weight is dangerous and exceeds minimum stability requirements. We'll probably cast the guns in aluminum, which is one-third the weight of iron, and anodize them. The original ballast was probably stone, slag, shale or iron, a main cause of lake fever because of dirt and stagnation in the bilge. I recommend lead because it is clean, can be taken out, washed and put back.

"You can't really replicate a ship; you can only build examples of composites. We don't know what color *The Niagara* was, but we do know that most of that type were painted black. We don't know the length of individual spars, but we know the average of many others and can use examples of the best, not longer or shorter or halfway. We also must use rot-resistant materials and employ modern techniques when advantageous. The *Sea Witch* will have a rosewood keel instead of oak, because it's denser and more resistant to rot and borers.

"It's also important to know where a ship is going and what it will do. The 100-foot *Globe* we built for Sacramento originally took missionaries to the Sandwich Islands and forty-niners around the Horn, but its replica is a floating storeship used as a landing platform for tourists and will never go to sea, which meant we could save money by building a flat bottom. The 15-foot *Federalist* I just designed was originally sailed up the Potomac as a gift to George Washington; its replica will be put on a cart and pulled by horses as a form of touchable history in the Maryland schools for 5 years and then go to a museum. I can build the best ships in the world, but performance depends on what people do with them." Smith recently designed and built two skipjacks, which dredge for oysters under sail, part of the last working sailing fleet in America. "A cheap, easy-to-build boat invented at the turn of the century. To restore one would take years, cost twice as much and you'd end up with nothing better because it

Replica of Californian *by Melbourne Smith*

would be rotting out as fast as you put it back together.''

Called America's leading builder of replica ships, Melbourne is a designer, builder, illustrator, book designer, marine artist, writer, researcher, navigator, compass adjuster, former sailing master and shipyard owner. When pressed to explain how he learned to do so many things well since he left school at 14 and went to sea as a Royal Canadian sea cadet, he says he "learned everything by hanging around the wrong bars,'' and discovering the writings and drawings of John W. Griffiths, who designed the first American clipper ships. More concerned with the next job than with praise, he takes pride in always being on time, on schedule and on budget with no cost overruns. "They're all good investments," he says of the ships he builds, "for education, sail training, sea experience and promotion. *Pride* logged 150,000 miles in 9 years and did great things for Baltimore.''

Price range is from $455,000 for the *Pride of Baltimore*, built in the 1970s, to $1,000,000 for *Californian*, $2,000,000 for *The Niagara* (it's twice as large and more complicated) to $18,500,000 for the *Sea Witch*.

Melbourne Smith
P.O. Box 54
Annapolis, MD 21401
(301) 268-5804

Other Makers

Carl G. Hathaway, 7 Algonquin Avenue, Saranac Lake, NY 12983, and John B. Spring, Indian Lake, NY 12842, build Adirondack guide boats.

Plimouth Plantation, Plymouth, MA 02360; (617) 746-1622, makes Indian log canoes.

Mystic Seaport Museum, Mystic, CT 06355; (203) 572-0711, reproduces traditional boats not built elsewhere and types from their collection. Recent boats have included a Herreshoff dinghy, Rangeley Lake boats, Rushton double-ended pulling boats, Delaware River tuckups, New Jersey Melonseeds and Marblehead dory-skiffs. They are sold through the Curatorial Department, and prices have ranged from $2,000 to $5,000, with sailing types at the high end.

The Carpenter's Boatshop, Branch Road, Pemaquid, ME 04558; (207) 677-3768, makes the Monhegan Island skiff ($410), Pemaquid dory-skiff, Grand Banks dory, Swampscott dory, Herreshoff dinghy and the Muscongus Island Peapod ($2,400), of northern white cedar over oak frames, with copper and bronze fastenings and, when appropriate, mahogany transoms and rails. One set of spruce oars is included in the price.

Edmund A. Cutts, Cutts & Case, Inc., P.O. Box 9, Oxford, MD 21654; (301) 226-5416, builds wooden boats up to 65 feet long.

P. Conner, Crockett Bros. Boatyard, 202 Bank Street, P.O. Box 369, Oxford, MD 21654; (301) 226-5113, builds wooden boats up to 60 feet long.

Graham Ero, Church Street, Still Pond, MD 21667; (301) 348-2296.

Rick and Cameron Pratt, Box 2209, Port Aransas, TX 78373; (512) 749-4396.

Shoes and Boots *See under* **Leather**

Shortbread Molds *See* **Molds for Baking**

SILHOUETTE PORTRAITS

Silhouettes, practical portraits for those who could not afford the more expensive miniatures and oil portraits, were in vogue from 1760 to 1860, when the daguerreotype and later the photograph took their place in American frames. The work of a first-rate silhouettist not only cost less but was more valued than the work of a third-rate painter. Also known as shades or shadow portraits, they were cut freehand from black paper or traced with the help of a machine called a camera obscura and mounted on a white background. Silhouettes were also painted on glass, paper and plaster and used as designs on china and jewelry.

The liveliest and most personable were cut freehand.

Family silhouette portrait cut freehand by Lonita Straus

August Edouart, a French silhouettist who did some of his best work in America, did not consider the machine-made silhouettes to be art. Those of Charles Willson Peale, according to Raymond Lister in his book *Silhouettes*, "were machine-cut and are generally poor, even allowing for the normal shortcomings of mechanically produced profiles."

Silhouette of young boy in period dress cut freehand by Lonita Straus

"American presidents up to and including Abraham Lincoln all had their silhouettes made," says silhouettist Lonita Straus. "As a child, I was fascinated by those in women's magazines and learned how to cut them while in training to become an art teacher. We were taught that silhouettes were not art unless they were cut freehand without drawing guide lines. I seemed to have an aptitude for cutting them and found the talent a distinct asset in rearing my family." When Lonita found herself alone in

Anniversary silhouette cut freehand by Lonita Straus

midlife, a friend asked her to cut silhouettes at the 1964–65 World's Fair in New York. It was there that it became her profession. Since then, she has traveled the United States cutting silhouettes at fairs, festivals and museums. She has also written a book on methods of silhouette-cutting with special emphasis on the therapeutic value of such a hobby for the handicapped.

"Silhouettes are essentially character studies," says Lonita. "Although eyes and smiles don't show, they are as recognizable as are one's shadows. Adult profiles remain the same unless and until a person develops a double chin. Silhouettes have many advantages: they are more memorable than a photograph, cheaper than the average haircut and don't show wrinkles.''

Working with a small sharp scissors and black-plated paper gummed on the white side (which she orders 5,000 sheets at a time), she cuts mostly on the white side to preserve her eyesight and checks for accuracy on the black side as she goes along. ''Having the paper gummed makes pasting quicker and less messy than using a glue pot,'' she's found. Upon completion, the silhouettes are mounted on medium-weight bristol board in 7- by 9-inch and 8- by 10-inch sizes to fit standard-size frames. ''The bristol board does not buckle easily and tends to retain its whiteness better than lighter paper.''

In the manner of the classic silhouettists, Lonita cuts on folded paper, which produces two silhouettes. The original, facing the same direction as the sitter, is $7 while the copy is $3. If you can't get to Texas, Lonita will accept a mail order based on a profile photo, but only if the sitter's head is as large as a quarter.

Lonita Straus
121 Avenue M, #113
San Antonio, TX 78212
(512) 822-2382 or 494-3998
R S MO

Other Maker

Joyce A. Yarbrough, P.O. Box 28967, St. Louis, MO 63132; (314) 569-0774.

SILHOUETTE SCENES

The silhouette has provided a form of instant recognition from Ice Age cave drawings to Greek pottery to shadow plays to today's road signs, corporate logos and inkblot tests. Silhouette illustrations in children's books have long been popular because they cut printing costs and also because they communicate information quickly on a very basic level, allowing children to fill in from their imaginations what is not spelled out.

Silhouette scenes were a favorite form of artistic expression of German-American women because, unlike painted pictures in watercolors and oils, silhouette scenes or cutwork could be done with only paper and scissors. Professional silhouette portrait artists often included details that captured a subject's home and surroundings or reflected his profession.

''But it's interesting to note,'' says cut-worker Elke Dorr, ''that silhouette portraits, done primarily by men, fell out of favor, while scissor-cutting, done mainly by women, continued. Cut-work, a combination of the two, has had periodic revivals, especially in the art nouveau period and in the 1920s, when painted silhouettes were used in advertising as well.''

Born in Germany, where she lived until she was 8 years old, Elke moved to the United States in 1956 when her mother married an American. Now married herself, Elke lives on a farm in Maryland's Middletown Valley, settled by Germans in the 1700s. ''One of the most satisfying aspects of my work,'' says Elke, ''lies in the fact that I'm creating something which reflects not only where and how I live, but is also reminiscent of my own German background. I derive great satisfaction pursuing a craft practiced in America's early years, which serves as a reminder of the rich folk art heritage bequeathed us by our German, Swiss and Polish ancestors. In my work, I try to capture the feeling of rural life. The country activities in my cutting are minus the machine-age technology of 20th century life. They picture country life as it was a century ago: raking hay by hand, gathering eggs, using a hand pump

Pastoral scene, silhouette cut by hand by Elke Dorr

Pumping water at well, silhouette cut by hand by Elke Dorr

Hanging the wash, silhouette cut by hand by Elke Dorr

at the well. Many of my cuttings include small animals and almost always a bird or two.''

Composition is especially important to silhouette scenes. Figures must capture the character, the landscape must accurately record the forms of nature, and negative and positive values must balance so that one does not overpower the other. ''Balance can be tricky,'' says Elke, ''and requires thinking in the negative. I begin by sketching out an idea, simplifying details in order to capture the essence, then cut a practice piece from plain white paper, going back to the drawing board to work out elements of the design. Even then, it can look completely different when cut from the black. Because each piece is cut by hand, no two are identical. I constantly vary details, such as leaf shapes on trees, adding or subtracting animals and sometimes customizing a silhouette scene with the family homestead or pet.''

Scenes are mounted on ivory mat board and set in frames finished with a painted grain, ''which falls somewhere between purely fanciful and simulated wood grain,'' says Elke. Prices range from $28 to $55 depending more on the intricacy of the piece than the size. For further information, send a self-addressed, stamped envelope.

Elke Dorr
Country Cuttings
9022 Mt. Tabor Road
Middletown, MD 21769
(301) 293-2035
R S MO

Other Maker

Martha Link Walsh, Branford Craft Village at Bittersweet Farm, 719 East Main Street, Branford, CT 06405; (203) 481-3505, uses silhouette scenes in designing invitations, announcements, stationery, logos and advertising. Her cutting of three churches on the New Haven green was included in *Three Centuries of American Folk Art*, while another was Branford's bicentennial symbol.

HAND-FORGED SILVER

Although New York silversmiths were influenced by more ornate Dutch and French designs, most early American silversmiths followed English designs while developing their own style of strong, clean, slender lines, the best of which has never been equaled.

Under England's colonial policy, Americans were supposed to trade only with England, but Yankee traders preferred to sell for the highest price, which meant they were often in possession of illegal coins like Spanish or Dutch silver dollars. Instead of burying treasure like the pirates, they converted their pieces of eight to legal plate, which could be openly displayed, never traced and, if stolen, identified and gotten back. Because it was expensive, silver was usually owned only by the well-to-do and nearly all silver objects were made to special order. Some popular items then were known by now-unfamiliar names like caudle cups (two-handled cups for hot caudle, or posset), dram cups (with shallow two-handled bowls) and suckets (spoons with fork tines on the ends of handles).

Unlike early silversmiths, who were often engravers, clock makers, bell founders, cabinetmakers, blacksmiths and tinsmiths as well, Peter Erickson of Gardner, Massachusetts, works only in sterling, but like them, he makes all pieces by hand. After serving a 5-year apprenticeship with his grandfather George Erickson, who had been a master craftsman for more than 60 years, Peter took over the business in 1976.

''Working as a silversmith,'' says Peter, ''gives me a great deal of satisfaction and pride. Looking at a completed piece, knowing the time and effort involved, makes it all worthwhile. My grandfather's patience and skill were the dominant factors in my development as a silversmith. I

Hollowware cream pitcher and sugar bowl by Peter Erickson

Assortment of serving spoons by Peter Erickson

his first taste of luxury the morning his wife replaced his earthen porringer and pewter spoon with a china bowl and a handmade silver spoon. If you've never experienced the difference in eating with a piece of handmade silver, it may be time to do so. Peter has ten different spoon patterns ranging in price from $35 for a lemon fork to $300 for larger serving pieces. He takes commissions for flatware and hollowware like Paul Revere bowls. He does not have a brochure but his shop is open Monday to Friday from 8:30 A.M. to noon and 1 to 5 P.M.; on Saturday from 9 A.M. to noon.

Peter Erickson
Erickson Silver Shop
39 Green Street
Gardner, MA 01440
(617) 632-0702
V   R   S   MO

Silver Liturgical Items   *See* Liturgical Gold, Silver and Pewter

SKEPS

Skep? "People have forgotten the word," says skeppist Rolla E. Chandler, "but the minute they see one, they know it's a beehive. That's because the skep has become the symbol for honey. Its shape is used for honey containers made of clay and banks and string holders cast from iron. Mormons also use the skep to signify a thrifty hard-working community, which bees certainly are."

Honeybees are not native to North America. Europeans

am very proud to be able to continue the business he started in 1932.''

With the exception of gold, silver is the most malleable of all metals, and next to platinum, the most ductile: 1 ounce of silver can be beaten to a thickness of 1/10,000 of an inch. But pure silver (1,000 parts fine) is too soft for everyday use. Coin silver (900 parts fine) was long preferred for tableware until the sterling standard was set at 92.5 parts pure silver to 7.5 parts copper for durability.

Peter works on as many as a dozen pieces of silver at a time. Starting with a flat copper pattern and a bar of silver, he cuts the metal and shapes a piece by repeated hammering and heating, which stretches and strengthens the silver. This tempering is what distinguishes hand-wrought silver from commercial machine-made pieces. Designs are sketched on the handle with a scratch awl, the bowl curved, or "bowled up," and the handle bent to the proper shape. Finishing is a series of processes that remove unnecessary marks and polish the final product.

Benjamin Franklin, known for his frugality, said he got

Detail of a skep under construction by Rolla E. Chandler

Collection of skeps by Rolla E. Chandler

prised to learn that *he* makes the skeps and not the bees.

It takes from 6 to 7 hours to make the average skep. Rolla feeds locally available materials like rye straw and cattail leaves through a short section of cow's horn to make coils. He binds these with strong twine (although chair-caning and blackberry bramble can also be used) threaded through a thin, homemade needle of steel, bone or horn. A finished skep sells for $45 if picked up in person, $5 extra for UPS when ordered by mail. For those who don't care for bees or hives, Rolla also makes 10-inch-wide coiled-rye dough baskets, which sell for $30 (plus $5 UPS). Enclose self-addressed, stamped envelope with inquiries.

Rolla E. Chandler, Skeppist
2047 Manchester Avenue
Cardiff-by-the-Sea, CA 92007
R S MO

SKIN-SEWING

When Yankee whalers arrived in Alaska, the first skin-sewn articles they purchased or bartered for were parkas and fur boots, called mukluks. Once warm, they were impressed by the fact that the skin boats used by natives were stronger, more flexible and more secure than any wooden craft they'd known. Kayaks built from hand-carved driftwood, fastened with pegs and lashed with wet rawhide before being covered with skin, weighed one-third as much as wooden craft, didn't freeze and were nearly unsinkable, a decided plus in the cold waters of the North. The *umiak*, a larger, dory-type boat 35 to 40

Fur hat from Alaska Native Medical Center Craft Shop

with a taste for honey brought them here in skeps, dome-shaped hives that look like an upside-down basket. Traditionally woven in coils of long-stemmed rye straw bound with string or twine, skeps are also made of native grasses, leaves and even cattails. Ranging in size from 10 to 16 inches in diameter and as tall as they are wide, sturdily built skeps weigh from 4 to 6 pounds and will last for years if kept dry.

Unlike humans, who know that a skep is a home for bees, honeybees don't make the association without bait. "Honeybees won't go into skeps of their own accord," says Rolla, who has raised bees for more than 30 years. "To entice them, a beekeeper will tie a small section of bee comb to the top of the skep to get the bees to stay." Bees also like lemon balm, thyme and borage, separately or combined with honey.

For its annual supply of honey, a colonial family kept ten to fifteen skeps. Each fall they would harvest honey from half of them, then winter the remaining bees until spring when new swarms would be lured into the old skeps. Americans used skeps for many years until they realized that bees could be managed just as easily in hollow logs, called gum beehives, which didn't require as much work. After the movable-frame beehive came into use in the mid-1800s, gums and skeps were not used as much, because some states banned producers from keeping bees in containers without movable frames, and skeps necessitated sulfuring the bees to remove the honey. Skeps are still used in Europe, though, because straw and grass are more plentiful and cost less than lumber.

"Most people today purchase skeps as decorative or historical items," says Rolla, who demonstrates his craft at festivals and fairs, where spectators are constantly sur-

feet long and used for whaling, was built in a similar fashion. Covered with split walrus hide, it could carry up to 2 tons of weight yet was light enough to be carried by only two people.

Skin-sewing, a craft partnership between men who hunt the game and women who sew the skins, has kept Alaskan communities fed, clothed and sheltered for thousands of years. Nomadic tribes lived in tents of caribou hides; clothing was made from hides; rain slickers from intestines. Until the Migratory Bird Treaty banned making products from birds, skilled Alaskans also made feather-light, toasty warm parkas from the feathered skins of puffin, loon, goose, duck, cormorant and murre. Since the Marine Mammal Act went into effect, only Native Americans have the right to kill whale, walrus, polar bear and seal.

Today, parkas are most often made of caribou or Siberian reindeer, but they're also made of bear, fox, muskrat, ptarmigan, beaver, squirrel, marmot or mink. Thicker winter pelts are more valuable, Sometimes color changes with season: squirrel skins change from red tones to gray in the fall; arctic fox becomes white in winter.

"The Athabascans of the interior use a lot of caribou and moose skins, which they smoke to cure," says Jeanne Dougherty of the Alaska Native Medical Center Craft Shop. "They make elegant smoke-tanned moosehide slippers trimmed with beaver or local furs and with beaded toes. When their slippers come into the shop they smell good enough to eat."

Anaktuvuk-style caribou skin masks, male and female, from Alaska Native Medical Center Craft Shop

Traditionally stitched with reindeer sinew, whose suppleness stretches with movement, parkas slip over the head, are usually as long as the fingertips and have hoods edged in wolverine ruff, which resists frost. Depending on the region where they're made and the materials available, parkas are decorated with designs, insets, hanging strips of fur and sometimes beadwork. The fur is most often turned inside for warmth. Women's and children's parkas are sometimes worn with a knee-length garment of cotton or gingham with a ruffled bottom, called a *kuspuk,* which protects the parka like an apron.

Rain parkas are fashioned from horizontal strips of the intestine or gut of sea animals, a translucent material also used for windowpanes in sod houses. "When opened, the seal intestine is usually 4 to 5 inches wide," explains Mrs. Dougherty. "Dried, pieced together and sewn with grass or sinew, gut is a lightweight protection against wind and rain, and ideal for riding in kayaks. St. Lawrence Islanders use walrus gut, which is winter-cured and more opaque. White like the snow, it's preferred by hunters." When rain parkas arrive at the shop, Jeanne unrolls, then sprays them with water to restore moisture. "Humidity is greater in village homes," she explains. "If kept in a drier atmosphere, they could dry out and crack."

Mukluks, soft boots of sealskin or reindeer with thick, stiff soles made from bearded seal, are made in heights from ankle to just below the knee, stitched with sinew, decorated with inserts of fur, leather from caribou legs, feather tufts in the seams and sometimes beadwork ($157 up). Slippers ($40 up) are most often made of hair seal (ribbon, spotted, ring and ooruk seals), trimmed with beaver, wolf or fox, with side-linings of sheared caribou fur and inner soles of arctic hare, a densely pelted winter-killed rabbit. Leather masks range in price from $35 to $75, with the more detailed ones over $100. Parkas start at $1,500; rain parkas, from $400; *kuspuks,* $12 to $18 for children and $25 to $45 for women.

Alaska Native Medical Center Craft Shop
3rd and Gambell, P.O. Box 7-741
Anchorage, AK 99510
(907) 279-6661, Ext. 150
V   R   MO

Makers

Annie Alowa, St. Lawrence Island, Savoonga, AK 99769.

Amelia Kingeekuk, St. Lawrence Island, Savoonga, AK 99769.

Ruthelle Kingeekuk, St. Lawrence Island, Savoonga, AK 99769.

Angela Larsen, Nome, AK 99762.

Mary Ahnangnatoguk, General Delivery, Kotzebue, AK 99752; (907) 442-3378.

Charlotte Douthit, Box 5569-0, Wasilla, AK 99687.

Rita Blumenstein, Box 3402, Palmer, AK 99645.

SLEDS

American clippers were the fastest ships afloat from the time of the Revolution until the Civil War, so it stands to reason that when a wooden sled was designed for speed, it too was called a clipper. Built close to the ground, with a rope attached for tugging, wooden sleds were being made by eleven commercial makers in the northeastern United States in 1849, but they were not made by machine until 1861. Many clipper sleds were made at home, which accounts for the wide range of sizes, colors, designs and names found on antique models. Decorated with stenciled horses, hand-painted landscapes and brightly colored flowers, they often carried the name of the owner or the image he wanted to convey, like General Grant or Captain Kidd.

The fastest way downhill on a clipper was to "belly slam" or "belly flop." A rider would take a short running start at the top of a hill, then jump on, landing on the stomach, grab the front handles with the hands and keep the knees bent, feet up in the air. To turn right, a rider leaned to the right, digging the toes of the right foot into the snow. If seated, the rider sat "Indian style" with crossed legs. To reduce friction and make the sled go faster, metal edges were scraped of rust and the sled put outside to turn cold, then water was poured on the runners to produce a thin layer of ice.

Dave Bleil's favorite winter sport as a child in Erie, Pennsylvania, was sledding, but he never saw a clipper-style sled until he was browsing through a flea market as an adult. As soon as he moved from an apartment into a house, he started producing them.

"My sleds are of hardwoods," says Dave, "mainly oak,

Infant's box sled in oak with detachable box by Dave Bleil

and structurally more sound than the commercially made sleds of the 1800s. Unlike the originals, which were held together with nails, I use a wedged mortise-and-tenon joint, making the cross-braces and sides one solid unit. Each sled is stained and varnished to a pleasant satin finish, and some are stenciled in dark red paint with the figure of a horse or an eagle."

His large 42-inch-long oak clipper sells for $60 plain, $65 stenciled with a horse. The smaller 32-inch size is $50 in oak, $55 in cherry or walnut and $60 stenciled with an eagle. The oak baby clipper, also 32 inches long, has an infant seat (with a cutout heart on the back) fastened on by four screws that are easily removed when the child learns to do without it ($75).

Since he went into production in 1976, Dave's greatest surprise has been to find that 50 percent of his sleds are bought by adults to be kept. "Few people can forget the sleds they had as children," says Dave. "When they see the sleds, they start reminiscing about their childhoods. Sometimes they still have their sleds and I get to see another original."

Delivery 2 to 4 weeks after order. Shipping $5 extra on each item. For information send self-addressed, stamped envelope.

Dave Bleil
446 Surrey Drive
Lancaster, PA 17601
(717) 569-7918

Other Maker

The Colonial Keeping Room, 16 Ridge Road, RFD 1, Fairfield, ME 04937; (207) 872-6493.

Sleighs

At the turn of the century, before motorcars, horse-drawn sleighs and cutters were the preferred means of transportation during winter months. A small version

Clipper sled in oak, 42-inch length, with stenciled horse, by Dave Bleil

Kip Brundage

Baby sleigh by C. H. Becksvoort

called the baby or child sleigh was popular well into the 20th century.

Early child sleighs were handmade. Backs, sides and snow deflectors were added, then pillows and upholstery. Made all over New England, and by factories after the mid-1800s, baby sleighs evolved like the larger horse-drawn models and began to add refinements like bent-wood, metal braces and pinstripes.

The body of C. H. Becksvoort's snow glider is two pieces of solid, reinforced hardwood bent to produce a nice curve in the back and finished in multiple coats of hand-rubbed, polished lacquer (dark royal blue, green or ma-roon) with a gold leaf pinstripe in natural black walnut or oak sealed with a clear protective finish ($2,200). For flexibility, the undercarriage and runners are made of ash or oak and mortised and tenoned for strength. Angle reinforcements, braces and runners are solid brass, while bells are cast brass. The handle dismounts for storage, and the upholstery is of wide-channel (ribbed) construction in soft, oil-tanned leather with a seat belt. Although the snow glider is 16 inches wide, 38 inches high at the handle and 48 inches long, it weighs only 22 pounds. Box 12, New Gloucester, ME 04260; (207) 926-4608 V R C ($1) S MO

Smocking   *See* **Irish Lace, English Smocking and French Hand-Sewing**

SNOWSHOES

Like the Native Americans before him, Carl Heilman "works with the strengths of a tree" in making snowshoes. "They worked with nature, using its strengths to their advantage," he says, "rather than trying to change nature to suit their whims."

After selecting and cutting each white ash tree, he splits it into sections, allowing the length of the frame to follow the vertical grain of the tree. After the bow is shaved to final dimensions with a drawshave, the frames are steamed, then bent around forms, with the bark side on the outside edge. Working the frames by hand this way gives the shoe the best possible strength-to-weight ratio. Before final assembly, frames are coated with varnish to keep water from deteriorating the mortised joints. The shoes are then laced with a fairly tight traditional weave, which allows as much flotation (staying on the surface) as possible. (The closer one stays to the surface of the snow, the greater the speed.)

High-quality handsplit wood-frame snowshoes are durable, strong and lightweight. With a tight traditional weave, they will outperform aluminum-frame snowshoes of comparable size in most snow conditions.

"I make ten different styles," says Carl. "The shorter bearpaw styles are best for bushwacking, mountaineering and backpacking, while the longer styles with a tail are mostly for deep snow and fairly level areas. All the shoes have their toes turned up for easier walking in fresh snow.

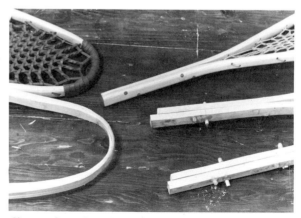

Close-up of snowshoe ends by Carl Heilman

"The Alaskan [10 by 58 inches] and Ojibwa [11 by 63 inches] are the two largest styles. They were originally designed for breaking trail in the deep dry powder snows in central and northwest Canada. The Maine [12 by 48 inches] and Cross Country [10 by 46 inches] styles are good general-use shoes. My Adirondack style [11 by 40 inches] is a nice walking shoe that is designed along traditional lines. It has a flowing diamond shape, a slightly squared toe and a fairly long tail. Green Mountain Bearpaws [9 by 37 inches], Trailpaws [9 by 31 inches] and Catpaws [8 by 26 inches], though, are the shoes I recommend most. The Green Mountain Bearpaws are the largest that I suggest for general use. Trailpaws and Catpaws are the most popular styles and are designed for backpackers, cross-country skiers and mountaineers. With Catclaw binding and supertough urethane lacing, they are the same weight as similar size aluminum-frame shoes and are excellent for bushwacking as well as trail use. Superlight Racing Catpaws [8 by 25½ inches], made to minimum United States Snowshoe Association racing specifications, are balanced for minimum heelslap on the track. The 5½- by 20-inch Kitty Paws are for children weighing up to about 50 pounds.

"If you own only one pair, choose the smallest shoe for the snow conditions in your area," says Carl. "The smaller Bearpaws are perfect for skishoeing [combining cross-country skiing and snowshoeing in the same day]. Snowshoeing is easier than other winter sports. If you can walk, you can snowshoe, and it doesn't require extensive lessons or special trails or clothing."

Prices range from $85 for Kitty Paws laced with neoprene, to $246 for Ojibwas laced with traditional rawhide or the high-tech combination of urethane lace in the middle and Hytrel-coated wire in the toe and heel sections. The advantage of nylon-reinforced neoprene is that it doesn't ice up or sag when wet and isn't appetizing to mice, all drawbacks of rawhide. Urethane and Hytrel are supertough modern materials that are several times more durable than neoprene. Bindings are $16 for Beck Special neoprene bindings, $65 for Carl's Catclaw, a specially mounted crampon that provides traction when needed yet is removable for downhill glissade. If you want to make your own, Carl's book, *Crafting Techniques for Handsplit Snowshoes,* says it all ($5.50 plus $1 postage).

Carl E. Heilman II
Box 213A, Route 8
Brant Lake, NY 12815
(518) 494-3072

Assortment of snowshoes by Carl Heilman: (rear, left to right) Adirondack, Kitty Paws, Catpaws, Trailpaws, Adirondack; (center) Catpaw, Kitty Paw, Trailpaw (standing); (front) Ojibwa

Other Makers

Henri Vaillancourt, The Trust for Native American Crafts and Cultures, Box 42, Greenville, NH 03048; (603) 878-2944.

Levine and Susie Williams, General Delivery, Hughes, AK 99745, make traditional snowshoes from birch and babiche.

Song Bows *See under* **Musical Instruments**

Spekulaas Molds *See* **Molds for Baking**

SPINNING AND DYEING

To become self-sufficient and independent of England, the colonists had to make their own cloth. By 1644, the 3,000 sheep in the Massachusetts Colony were so valuable to the economy that they were protected by law. None under 2 years could be sold to kill; if a dog killed a sheep, the dog's owner had to hang it or pay twice the value of the sheep. In areas where tobacco was the unit of exchange, a yard of homespun was worth 6 pounds of tobacco, and a pair of knit stockings, 12 pounds. A good spinner could do six skeins of yarn a day, an equivalent in foot action to walking 20 miles.

"Which is why I use both feet," says Michelle Reilly, who specializes in hand-spun and hand-dyed variegated

Blanket woven from hand-spun yarn displayed on the back of its source

wool yarn. "When I used only one foot, the calf of my leg got so big it wouldn't fit into my boot. Now I can do ten skeins in 8 hours before I tire."

Michelle purchased her first two Romney Marsh ewes to chew down the overgrowth on her farm and for her two children to raise and enjoy. As her flock grew to more than sixty and became consistent winners at fairs and festivals, members of three large guilds in her region began to buy her wool before it was processed. Customers visit her Triple "R" Farms and select the sheep whose wool they prefer. When a customer orders an article of clothing knit from the wool, the finished product is delivered with a picture of the sheep that furnished it.

"Most breeders raise one kind," says Michelle, "but we have several breeds, which provides a wide range of wool textures, from soft and fluffy to very shiny, sturdy fibers and a variety of natural colors: gray, brown, black and white." Although the majority of shearing is done in the spring, Michelle also shears in November. The fleece is rinsed in warm water to remove dust and half the lanolin and, when color is desired, dyed using natural or acid dyes.

"At present, the majority of our wool is acid-dyed," says Michelle. "Natural dyes have a tendency to fade in washing or light. When leveling-acid dyes are set with white vinegar, they do not bleed, are more resistant to fading and leave the wool soft and light, whereas natural dyes leave it slightly harsh."

The wool is rinsed once again, dried and carded by pulling it between two wire-toothed boards to separate, straighten and open up the fibers. It can then be spun to any thickness or diameter, woolen or worsted, single-strand or plyed. "Spinning is much like painting," says the former art teacher. "It involves molding a fiber and

combining colors in ways that will enhance a garment." The yarn is measured and skeined off, washed in scalding hot water with Ivory Snowflakes, then rinsed twice. "This insures that the yarn is shocked and there will be no change in the quality of the wool," she says, "and that no color bleeding will occur. It is then blocked [stretched] to insure an even twist and dried. All yarn that we sell is ready to knot or weave and wear."

Prices for finished wool are $2.75 to $3 an ounce, or about $11 for a 4-ounce skein. Michelle will also spin a customer's wool fleece to specification at a cost of $2.25 an ounce. Sweaters and garments are priced according to size, weight and pattern, and range from $50 to $250. When yarn is in stock it is shipped within the week. Otherwise delivery can take up to 4 weeks. If the order is over $100, there is no shipping charge. Shop hours are

Spun yarn with carding implements by Michelle Reilly

Monday to Friday, 9 A.M. to 2 P.M., Saturday, 9 A.M. to 5 P.M. or by appointment.

Michelle Reilly
Triple "R" Farms
Route 1, Box 355
Rohrersville, MD 21779
(301) 432-2009
V R W S MO

Other Makers

Nancy Ellison, Route 2, Box 197, Hayfield, MN 55940; (507) 477-3569, spins wool from gray, black and white sheep, as well as mohair from Angora goats, from $1.50

up an ounce. Send self-addressed, stamped envelope and $1 for samples.

Mrs. Marion C. Edens, Route 9, Box 242, Greeneville, TN 37743; (615) 638-4951, sells hand-spun and vegetable wool yarns.

Catherine Cartwright-Jones, 718 Cloverdale, Waterloo, IA 50703; (319) 234-1502, will hand-spin fleece and also knit anyone's fleece into a garment. Send self-addressed, stamped envelope for prices.

American mohair wool is available through Susanne Beutz, The Fiber Farm, Route 4, Box 140, Milaca, MN 56353; (612) 983-2371, who raises Angora goats in Minnesota. Available in soft heathered colors (green, blue, yellow, pink, rust, heather, coral), natural black and white, wool is hand-carded and spun of 60 percent wool and 40 percent mohair. A skein, priced at $8, weighs approximately 3½ ounces and is 125 yards long. A special two-ply sock yarn in white only, spun with nylon thread for strength, sells for $8 a skein. By mail order, raw adult mohair is $8 a pound and kid hair $12 a pound, plus shipping. For current price list of kits for hats, mittens and washed and/or dyed fleece, send self-addressed, stamped envelope. R W S MO

Spinning Wheels

Like early makers, George Jischke makes no two wheels alike because each is made to fit the size, needs and personality of the spinner. There are two types of wheels: the smaller treadle, at which the spinner sits, spins and stores in one continuous operation; and the larger "walking" wheel, at which the spinner stands and walks while spinning, then stores in a separate operation. However, there are many styles, many of which have European names but definite American and regional characteristics: the Saxony (also called the flax, Dutch or low Irish wheel), popular for centuries because of its durability; the Welsh (similar to the Saxony but with a tension screw on top of the table instead of within the table); the tall three-legged Irish Castle wheel (whose driving wheel is higher than the bobbin and flyer); the gossip (also known as the courting, mother-and-daughter or lovers' wheel), which is two-handed to increase production by one person; the small sturdy cottage wheel (also called the parlor or Scottish upright) with two or four posts; the Connecticut chair wheel, built like a chair frame, with three wheels instead of two for faster spinning, less treadling and more control.

George can make any of the above, or any kind of wheel from a sketch or a photo. He also modifies and repairs wheels, makes distaffs for new and old wheels and makes four types of hand spindles including the traditional drop and Navajo. Flintridge Woodshop & Fibers, 121 Woodcrest Road, Sister Bay, WI 54234; (414) 854-2919. V R W C MO

Springerle Molds *See* **Molds for Baking**

SPURS AND BITS

"Spurs help a rider signal the horse," explains Forest Fretwell, who in addition to making exquisite spurs and bits, owns 3,600 acres and works 20,000 acres with his brother. "A rider uses his legs and spurs to move, turn, stop a horse and start setting him down. You slow a horse by pulling back, motioning him with your body, touching him with your spurs, lifting his front end so he'll set down harder with his hind end and really stop."

At the age of 14, when Forest wanted a pair of spurs with silver mounting, he knew the only way he'd get them was to make them himself. Taking an old harrow tooth (spikes dragged over the ground by a tractor to break up clods of dirt), Forest split it down the middle with blacksmith tools on his father's forge and made a pair of spurs he still wears. He made his first engraver's block in similar fashion by mounting his plate and vise on the metal base of a swivel chair. Since then, he's made hundreds of elegant spurs and bits whose construction and design are even more important than their beauty.

To the uninitiated, the parts of spurs and bits sound like a foreign language, but for those who use them, knowing how each part works and why can make a difference in keeping a horse happy and improving communication between horse and rider.

Suzi Hass, Ellison Bay, WI

Welsh-style spinning wheel made by George Jischke

Silver spur by Forest Fretwell

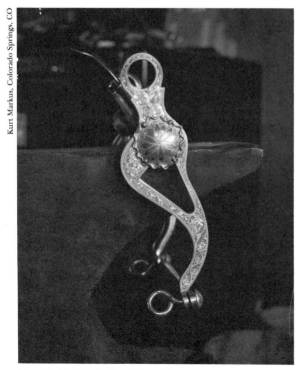

Bit with sidepieces by Forest Fretwell

American spurs (also called pricks, grappling irons, hell rousers and can openers) evolved from the Moorish style gaff, a prong attached to the back of a rider's boot by a leather strap and used to spur or urge a horse forward. The Mexicans added a spiked wheel called a rowel (sometimes up to 8 inches in diameter) to the point, plus chains and pendants. Texans preferred simpler, more functional spurs with shorter shanks, larger, wider bows and smaller, blunter rowels, until the late 1800s when it became the fad to make them in the shape of ladies' legs, longhorn heads or playing-card symbols. Early Californians, on the other hand, liked theirs fancy and decorated spurs and bits with engraving, coins, *conchas*, inlaid and overlaid silver. Their spurs had larger rowels, instep chains, chap guards on the shank to keep chaps away from the rowel and jinglebobs that made a jangling sound and locked the rowel in place, giving the rider more control over a bucking horse.

Bits fit inside a horse's mouth and are controlled by the reins. The oldest is the snaffle, a mouthbar hinged in the middle with round or D-rings on each end. More complicated bits have sidepieces (also called cheeks or shanks) designed for specific uses (for a cutting horse, for example) or named for place of origin (such as United States, Nevada, San Ramon or the ornate Santa Barbara). The slobber bar, which connects at the bottom, keeps sidepieces in balance and alignment. The spade bit has a piece that presses up against the horse's palate (variations include the full Spanish, Santa Barbara, spoon, frog, half-breed and its modifications, the Mona Lisa and Salinas). Some bits have crickets (also known as pacifiers), notched rollers that help calm a nervous horse, usually made of copper "to help a horse moisten out and slobber more," says Forest. The reason Forest's custom bits wear longer is that he squares the U-shaped end of the mouthpiece where it is attached to the cheekpiece. "When this isn't done," he explains, "a bit can wear out in one season."

Mounted decorations are soldered to the base metal. Silver overlay is bonded to the entire surface. For the more complicated inlay, the pattern is drawn on the base metal and cut away with a chisel and hammer to a depth equal to the thickness of silver used. The edges are undercut so that after the silver is placed in the groove, they can be hammered down to keep the inlay in place. For those who prefer, spurs and bits can be personalized with a monogram, silver *conchas*, gold eagles, jewels or any type of metal. Bits range from $175 to $450, spurs from $250 to $300, depending on design and decoration.

Forest E. Fretwell
Box 211
Jordan Valley, OR 97910
208-583-2361
R   MO

Other Makers

R. M. Hall, 119 North 3rd Street, King City, CA 93930; (408) 385-5650, author of *How to Make Bits and Spurs,* has been making them for more than 50 years, of cold-rolled steel, soft iron and sterling silver.

Carl D. Hall, Route 1, Box 41, Comanche, TX 76442; (915) 356-3598 has made more than a thousand spurs since 1963.

Dick Wagner, Flying W. Quarter Circle Ranch, 9917 East Pershing Boulevard, Cheyenne, WY 82001; (307) 634-3428, makes simple brass or copper inlay in steel spurs for $160 a pair and in steel up to $350.   (by appt.)

Gordon Hayes, 6905 Sycamore, Atascadero, CA 93422; (805) 461-3297.

Jerry "Gotcheye" Gaston, 211 North Cedar, Seymour, TX 76380; (817) 888-2315.

Gene Peterson, Almont, ND 58520; (701) 843-7641.

Roger A. Ayres, Route 1, Box 87, Canyon, TX 79015; (806) 655-0663.

Jerry D. Cates, 5235 Slope, Amarillo, TX 79108; (806) 383-6030.

Mark Dahl, Box 55, Deeth, NV 89823; (702) 752-3475.

Mark Drain, SE 3211 Kamilche Point Road, Shelton, WA 98583; (206) 426-5452.

R. F. Ford, Box 407, Knickerbocker, TX 76939; (915) 586-6447.

Elmer Miller, Route 6, Box 6319, Nampa, ID 83651; (208) 466-2870.

Robert Schaezlein, 1146 Clement Street, San Francisco, CA 94118; (415) 221-6923.

Earlon Shirley, Box 1238, Tahoka, TX 79373; (806) 998-5407.

STENCILING AND MARBLING

Stenciling, once called the poor man's wallpaper, in recent years has become an architectural and decorative bridge to other periods. Duplicating materials that no longer exist or whose cost would be prohibitive, stenciling creates illusions, transforming painted surfaces into inlaid floors, carved wooden panels, tin ceilings, stone friezes, antique wallpaper and elaborate plaster details. Marbling, or painting surfaces to look like marble, often costs a fraction of the real thing, gives the appearance without

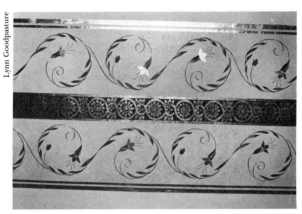

Lynn Goodpasture

Stenciled design adapted from historic sources for living room ceiling by Lynn Goodpasture

the weight or expense and is a way to match or patch antique marble. The Corinthian columns in the Franklin dining room of the State Department in Washington, DC, look like marble, but in reality are painted, because the weight of real marble would have taxed the existing structure.

"When the AT&T Building [built 1913–16] was restored and modernized by Equitable Life Assurance Company," says Lynn Goodpasture, "an entire bank of elevators was moved. Large areas of Sheetrock installed to fill the void were not compatible with the beautiful old marble already there, so I was brought in to marbleize fifty-three Sheetrock wall panels to match the marble. However, my most challenging project to date was achieving a trompe l'oeil effect on the vaulted ceilings in the lobby of the Crown Building on Fifth Avenue in New York City. After upscaling Peter Sari's watercolor designs to appropriate size for the repeat pattern, I translated the design to stencils, then determined the changing cast shadow so that the effect would be convincing. The hardest part was painting them in an unheated lobby in the dead of winter."

Trained in the fine arts, Lynn graduated from the Corcoran School of Art, where she also worked as studio assistant to painter Gene Davis. Lynn later became assistant to Cile Lord, coauthor with Adele Bishop of *The Art of Decorative Stenciling,* before going into business for herself, offering custom designs for floors, walls, ceilings, furniture, screens and floorcloths. Today, she works in a wide stylistic range from authentic period designs to original contemporary interpretations, in direct hand-painting and gold leaf as well as stenciling and marbling.

"Stenciling combines art, design and function and al-

Lynn Goodpasture

Sample of painted marble by Lynn Goodpasture

lows me to use my skills in a practical way," says Lynn, who also teaches stenciling privately and at the Cooper-Hewitt Museum, the Smithsonian's National Institute of Design. "I find marbling attractive because it is a form of painting in which composition, light, color, line and intention are major factors. Both have limitless possibilities for interpretation."

For stenciling, Lynn researches the appropriate period of art and design, carefully measures the surface to be painted, then works out the design on paper. After the

Lynn Goodpasture

Marbleized dictionary stand by Lynn Goodpasture

client's approval of the design, she traces and cuts stencils, mixes colors and proofs stencils on paper before presenting them once again to the client for approval. She works with Japan paints with a dry brush technique in circular strokes to achieve thin veils of color, letting the ground color show through. "This allows the stencil print to look painterly and variegated," she explains, "not solid and static. When marbling, I establish and paint the ground color, sanding between coats; apply clear glaze medium to the surface with a rag, roller or brush; then float areas of color mixed in a clear glaze medium on the surface glaze. Texture is created by removing colored glaze with textural materials like paper, rags, sponges or feathers, and adding texture with colored glazes in the same fashion. Veins are then cut through to the base color with solvent and a fine paintbrush. The entire surface is sealed with several coats of varnish sanded between coats with wet sandpaper." As an independent contractor, Lynn executes projects for architects, designers, homeowners and other painting companies in all period styles of decor and contemporary design.

Lynn Goodpasture
42 West 17th Street
New York, NY 10011
(212) 645-5334

Other Makers

Jane Bolster, 151 Waterloo Avenue, Berwyn, PA 19312; (215) 644-1344, an expert in early American decoration, does a limited amount of commission work.

Adele Bishop, 1963G Quail Ridge Road, Greenville, NC 27834; (919) 756-0429.

Rosemarie McDonald, 52 Fairlawn Drive, Rochester, NY 14617; (716) 544-1295.

Joyce Holzer, 62 Kahdena Road, Morristown, NJ 07960.

Carolyn Hedge, Long Pond Road, Plymouth, MA 02360.

Astrid Thomas, 21 Mast Hill Road, Hingham, MA 02043; (617) 740-1668.

Teresa A. Skoog, RD 4, Boyertown, PA 19512; (215) 367-0554.

Candy Thun, 3 Edwunds Court, Plymouth, NH 03264; (603) 536-1355.

Laurie Cozza, 47 Washington Avenue, South Nyack, NY 10960; (914) 358-2860.

Linda Podell, 207 Combs Avenue, Woodmere, NY 11598; (516) 569-0392.

Sandra Tarbox, 261 Hinman Lane, Southbury, CT 06488; (203) 264-9933 or 264-8900.

Virginia Jacobs McLaughlin, 812 West Main Street (Box 114), Emmitsburg, MD 21727; (301) 447-6558 or (717) 642-5142. V R S MO

David Wiggins, Hale Road, Tilton, NH 03276; (603) 286-3046.

Nora Papp, 573 North Division, Carterville, IL 62918.

Donna W. Albro, 6677 Hayhurst Street, Worthington, OH 43085; (614) 436-1248.

Bronze and Gold Stenciling

American craftspeople enamored of oriental lacquerware, French tole and ormolu furniture invented their own techniques to decorate tin and furniture. They worked freehand, with stencils and with combinations of handwork and stenciling. After applying primer and two to three coats of background color dried and sanded smooth, Astrid Thomas, master craftsman of the Historical Society of Early American Decoration, Inc., traces the design on the prepared surface. When the size (glaze or filler) reaches the proper tack (stickiness), she applies finely

Reprinted courtesy of Historial Society of Early American Decoration

Stenciled 30-inch sandwich-edge Gothic tray with black background and central bouquet of Victorian flowers by Astrid Thomas

ground metal powders with a soft sable bright brush, a velvet bob or soft charcoal stump. "After the design is complete, I apply three coats of gloss varnish, sanding between coats. The final coat of varnish is hand-rubbed with pumice oil. I then remove specks by rubbing the surface with rottenstone and oil, which produces a soft, mellow sheen." 21 Mast Hill Road, Hingham, MA 02043; (617) 749-1441. C R MO

Other Makers

Joyce Holzer, 62 Kahdena Road, Morristown, NJ 07960.

Carolyn Hedge, Long Pond Road, Plymouth, MA 02360.

Jane Bolster, 151 Waterloo Avenue, Berwyn, PA 19312; (215) 644-1344.

Teresa Skoog, RD 4, Boyertown, PA 19512; (215) 367-0554.

Stoveplates   *See* **Firebacks and Stoveplates**

Straw Hats   *See* **Wheat-Weaving and Straw Hats**

STRAW INLAY

Felix Lopez never thought about being an artist until after the death of his father, when the funeral service (the *velorio*) was held at Santa Cruz Morada, a meeting place for a religious order of laymen.

"The chapel had not been used for a wake in a long time," says Felix. "For 3 days, my family and friends prayed and sang *alabados* [religious hymns sung without musical accompaniment]. It was spontaneous, beautiful, sad, joyous. The culture came alive for me. The energy was incredible. I felt death, life, love, sharing, faith, beauty

Straw inlay cross with flower pattern by Felix A. Lopez

Straw inlay cross with a variety of designs by Felix A. Lopez

and an overwhelming sense of the past. That energy propelled me to create. My life has not been the same since."

He began working in clay, but when he decided to create a face like those on the *santos* he had seen during the wake, he chose wood as a medium. Two years later, he started painting his *bultos* with natural pigments in the soft warm tones of the early image makers, then taught himself to do straw inlay. Today he is one of the few artists in America creating works in this medium.

Straw inlay, the painstaking practice of shaping and fixing mature wheat straw in designs or mosaics, originated in North Africa and passed from the Moors to the Spaniards, who brought the craft to New Mexico.

"It's easy to see why straw was used instead of metal," says Felix. "It was free and it glitters like gold." Early settlers used straw inlay to decorate crucifixes, boxes, sconces and furniture.

Like the early settlers, Felix uses the materials at hand. His wood is gleaned from the woodpile, the mountains and along rivers, his straw from a nearby farm store. His delicate flowers, sunbursts, symbols and geometrics are never planned ahead. "I have no idea at all," says Felix. "I just start cutting straw and the pattern eventually appears." He cuts the wood with a regular pocketknife, then picks up and inserts the straw with a 4-inch-long, thick, needlelike tool he found one day in the garage. His favorite wood is pine because "It's soft, perfect for carving and cuts easily." Although early backgrounds were most often colored black or brown, Felix also does pieces in the less frequently found "off-red, almost pink" as well as blue.

"In the old days," Felix explains, "craftsmen used piñon pitch, which was heated and dissolved for use as glue to hold the wheat straw in place. Mutton fat or candle wax put on afterwards served as a varnish or sealer, but today we use glue and a matte varnish."

Felix's work is now in the collections of the Museum of International Folk Art in Santa Fe and the Albuquerque Museum. In 1984 he was awarded a National Endowment for the Arts Fellowship and in 1987 was selected as one of thirty artists featured in "Contemporary Hispanic Art in the United States," an exhibition organized by the Corcoran Gallery of Art in Washington, DC. But his greatest delight was in being selected to restore the religious art in Santa Cruz Church, built by the early Spanish settlers in 1733. The parish has since commissioned Felix to create additional art for the church, where he's always worshiped.

"I like to challenge myself," he says, "attempt something more difficult and not be afraid to create something more complex or on a larger scale." In addition to his art, Felix teaches Spanish and German at Espanola Valley High School, but plans to retire soon to carve full time. "My art has made me a more tolerant person with a healthier outlook on life," he says. "I have learned to be more generous and loving. Doing what I do takes me back in time to when things were not as complex." His straw inlay crosses begin at $100; his boxes at $300.

Felix A. Lopez
P.O. Box 3691
Fairview Station
Espanola, NM 87533
(505) 753-2785
V R S MO

Other Makers
Joseph and Krissa Lopez, Felix's son and daughter, same address as Felix Lopez above.

Star Tapia, Route 6, Box 01, Agua Fria, Santa Fe, NM 87501.

TATTING

Tatting—handmade lace formed by looping and knotting a single strand of thread into rings, semicircles and chains with a small hand-held shuttle—looks fragile but is actually very strong. Unlike knitting and crocheting, where each stitch is dependent on the next and easy to undo, tatting once knotted is difficult to take apart.

Although the finished product looks complicated, tatting is made up of variations of one knot called the double-

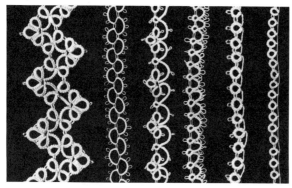

Variety of tatted borders by Doris Finch Kennedy

Tatted bookmark and Christmas ornament by Doris Finch Kennedy

Tatted wedding crown by Doris Finch Kennedy

stitch, which is done in two parts: an overknot and an underknot. Each is a half-stitch. When all the knots are pulled together in a circle, these floats loop up to form picots, made by allowing a length of thread to "float" between one hitch knot and the next.

"Most people over 30 years of age recognize tatting even if they don't know how to do it," says Doris Finch Kennedy, who learned to tat from her grandmother, taught textiles at Syracuse University and received her Ph.D. in textiles from the University of Tennessee. "Like myself, many watched their grandmothers' fingers making lacy trims, doilies, baby booties and bonnets with the tiny shuttles. Although I knew how, it wasn't until I was teaching high school home economics in a small farm community in Kansas that I found the time necessary to perfect the skill and to gain speed."

Known as *frivolité* in France, *occhi* in Italy and *makouk* in the Orient, the word *tat* is thought to derive from the Scottish *tate* meaning "tuft" or *tat* meaning "tangle," or the English *tatters* because tatting originally was sewn together from bits and pieces of fabric to form patterns. Popular in Europe in the latter part of the 18th century, tatting came to America with the early colonists. Interest lapsed from the late 1700s until the 1850s, lasted until the early 1870s and surfaced again in this century from the 1920s to the 1940s and most recently in the 1970s.

The three-piece shuttles, made of two pod-shaped blades, pointed at each end, are oval on the outside, flat on the inside and joined with a short, thick piece in the center. They can be made of any material, such as wood, tin or bone, that feels comfortable in the hand and can be shaped to make the work go faster and easier. Most shuttles are no more than 3 inches long and ¾ inch wide. They are usually 2½ inches long and joined just tightly enough to keep the thread from running out too quickly. Tatting with two shuttles to achieve scallops, straight lines between ovals and circles and more intricate designs is a more recent development.

"All items that I make at present are of 100 percent cotton thread," says Doris. "The finer the thread used, the more delicate the work, the higher the price of the item. Lace edges ¼ to 3 inches wide in ecru or white are from $12 to $80 a yard, while wedding crowns 4 to 6 inches in diameter and 2 to 3 inches high in ecru or white are $50 to $85. Items can be delivered in 1 to 6 weeks, depending on the complexity of designs and amount needed."

In 1984 Doris completed a 5-year study of textiles in Tennessee in which she documented, photographed and studied 1,000 textiles and collected old photographs of weavers and their home sites with Sadye Tun Wilson. Their efforts are compiled in a 496-page book entitled *Of Coverlets, the Legacies, the Weavers,* containing 400 pattern drafts, 550 pictures of coverlets and available for $70 plus postage.

Doris Finch Kennedy
1263 School Lane
Nashville, TN 37217
(615) 367-0268 (9 A.M. to 2 P.M., 4 to 9 P.M)
R   W   S   MO

Other Maker

Gail Digman, 821 McIntosh Street, Wausau, WI 54401, makes tatted snowflakes in twelve patterns for $3 each and butterfly doilies for $40 each, plus $1 handling. Minimum order $25.   R   MO

TEDDY BEARS

While in the South to settle a boundary dispute between Mississippi and Louisiana in 1902, President Theodore "Teddy" Roosevelt refused to shoot a bear cub during a

Timeworn Teddies—Woebegone, Sailor and Boat, Begonia—by Joyce Sheets

hunting expedition. "I draw the line," he was quoted as saying. "If I shot that little fellow, I couldn't look my own boys in the face again."

After seeing a Clifford Berryman cartoon about the incident, entitled "Drawing the Line in Mississippi," Morris Michton, owner of a Brooklyn, New York, toy and candy store, made a toy bear and placed it in his window with the sign "Teddy's bear." When Michton wrote to the president to ask if he minded, he received a handwritten reply saying, "I don't think my name is worth much to the toy bear cub business, but you are welcome to use it." As the teddy bear became the Republican president's standard instead of the eagle or the elephant, its popularity grew to such an extent that a decade later Butler Brothers bought all of Michton's bears in return for credit in plush. (Butler Brothers and the teddy bears were later absorbed by Ideal Toy Company, the world's largest doll manufacturer.)

"The traditional teddy bear looked different from the later, chubbier models," says Joyce Sheets, who makes both kinds. "He had a movable head, and legs and arms with longer, thinner limbs designed for sitting, not walking on all fours like a real animal. Made of brown plush, the bear had a hump in his back between the shoulders and embroidered paws, mouth and nose. His nose was also longer, which gave him a more solemn expression."

Like the original, Joyce's bears have old shoebutton-type eyes. The smaller (14-inch) size has sawdust-filled limbs, and the larger (20-inch) bears have growlers inside that make a noise when they are tipped back. Although antique bears had felt paws, Joyce makes hers of wool because "today's wool looks like the antique felt, whereas contemporary felt is synthetic, fragile, balls and wears through too fast." She machine-stitches bodies, but hand-

Traditional teddy bear by Joyce Sheets

stitches details like face and paws with heavy black cotton floss, her favorite part of the job.

"I love watching them come to life," she says. "They almost talk. Each one seems to have something to say once he has his face. They have the same effect on strangers. I always find customers peering into their faces. When they find the one they relate to, they almost smile in recognition."

Joyce's husband, Bob, son, Jason, and daughter, Josie, all help in the family business, called Pleasant Walk Folk. Their traditional bears include 14-inch Becky and Ben: dressed in a faded ribbon, they're $50 each. Otherwise, Becky wears a loose-fitting, puffed-sleeve dress of aged fabric and a straw bonnet decorated with ribbon and flowers, while Ben wears a checked romper suit fastened with old buttons ($75). The 20-inch growler bears are $80. Theodore, with hand-knit sweater and wool knickers, is $125, as is his mate, Althea, in dress and straw hat. The newer, chubbier models are gold plush and 16 inches tall. Dressed in a ribbon, they sell for $50; with hand-knit sweater, $70; with sweater and backpack or matching cap, $80.

New members of the Pleasant Walk Folk family include Genevieve, a 12-inch-long sheep pull toy on wooden platform with wheels ($60) and Miss Sarah and Thomas: Sarah is a 20-inch-tall cloth doll whose dress is made with antique buttons, tatting and lace; Thomas is the cat who sits in her lap ($60). Prices include shipping. For descriptions and price lists, send a self-addressed, stamped envelope.

Judi Quelland

Althea and Theodore, teddy bears by Joyce Sheets

Joyce Sheets
Pleasant Walk Folk
11025 Pleasant Walk Road
Myersville, MD 21773
(301) 293-2726
R W C S MO

Other Maker

Laura Turner, 131 Church Street, New Windsor, MD 21776; (301) 875-2850, makes teddy bears from synthetic furs, vintage furs and German mohair for $15 to $80 depending on size and materials. Dressed, a pair 16 inches tall sells for $140 or $70 each, while 8-inch corduroy jointed bears are $15.

TEPEES

As the Plains Indians followed buffalo herds for food, they used the skins to make clothing, moccasins and tepees, in which they lived. The skeleton of a tepee was three poles, 25 feet or more in length, lashed together at the top to form a tripod. Tepees always faced East. With one pole to the East, one to the North and one to the South, the East pole became the left-hand side of the door opening.

From thirteen to seventeen poles were then leaned against the tripod to form a circle. The West pole, last to be set in place, had the buffalo hide covering tied to it. This covering, of fifteen to eighteen buffalo skins cut and fit together in a semicircular shape, was brought together in front and fastened with wooden pins, with a space at the bottom for the opening, and the bottom fastened to the ground with pegs. Flaps at the top, adjusted by two poles on the inside, became a flue, which changed as the wind changed so that the fire would draw properly. Tribal tepees were decorated to commemorate a battle or important event in the history of the tribe; others were decorated with symbols of the owner's choosing.

"Since there are no buffaloes now," says Chlotiea Palmer, "our tepees are made from canvas or sailcloth: from 80 to 100 yards. They take a week to 10 days to complete on a heavy-duty machine, sewn with thread impervious to sun. Today most of my orders are from museums, Indians and hobbyists. Tepees (also spelled tipi and teepee) are still the Indians' mobile home."

They have also become an art form of the Plains Indians. The one pictured, a reconstruction by Chlotiea of one that belonged to a Kiowan named Never Got Shot, was made from dictation by the daughter of the former owner. Top and bottom areas of Indian red are separated by

Tepee Never Got Shot, made by Chlotiea Palmer, painted by Dixon Palmer

talent as painting,'' says theorem painter Lisa Kearney, ''because instruction books were available for beginners. Itinerant artists added the skill to their offerings, and young ladies learned theorem painting as part of their cultural education along with embroidery and needlepoint. Although it was applied to linen, silk, satin and paper as well, velvet became the preferred background because it added to the quality of overall softness and depth, which is part of a theorem's charm.''

Subjects most often pictured were baskets and bowls overflowing with colorful fruits and flowers; sometimes butterflies and birds. Less common still lifes included landscapes, Biblical scenes, figures and memorials.

''Mourning pictures became very popular after George Washington's death,'' says Lisa. ''Originally executed in embroidery, they were stylized in theorem with weeping willows, tombs, churches, ships and villages. Some surviving examples combined the two: embroidered compositions with painted faces. Sometimes a date appeared on the tombstone; at other times it was left blank to be filled in later, especially when a woman artist painted a theorem as a personal memorial to herself.''

After an outline sketch of the subject was transferred to transparent paper, the pattern was reduced to a set of stencils, numbered and used in a sequence of overlays. Cut from architect's linen or transparent paper, made by coating drawing paper on both sides with a mixture of copal varnish and spirits of turpentine, the hollowcuts were recoated when dry with pure varnish. Despite its mechanical aspects, the craft required skill.

black lines, with a blue sun at the center back. A large elk holds a red pipe in its mouth and within its long neck is a red and white heartline. Eight buffalo, seven black and one red, are all males but one. The first and last also have red heartlines. A tepee 15 feet wide costs $350 (not including poles); prices go up to $550 for one 22 feet in diameter.

Chlotiea Palmer
Route 3, Box 189
Anadarko, OK 73005
(405) 247-3987

Other Maker

Blue Star Tipis, 300 West Main, Missoula, MT 59802; (406) 728-1738.

THEOREM PAINTING

Theorem painting, a stencil craft that became popular in the 1820s, was also known as velvet or formula painting because a theory or formula for balance in the composition had to be devised before stencils were cut.

''It was faster than embroidery and didn't take as much

Theorem painting of basket with flowers by Lisa Kearney

Theorem painting of basket with fruits and flowers by Lisa Kearney

"Mixing paint is an important factor," explains Lisa. "It should be a creamy consistency and not too thin or it will blot the background or cause colors to run into each other. Pigment is applied sparingly with a bristle brush, a scrub or a cloth-covered finger. After the first application, a poonah brush is used to pull the color across the velvet, shading from dark to light. The stencils are never colored in completely. Otherwise, the beauty of each shape is lost and highlights are not established."

A graphic illustrator when she saw her first theorem at the Abby Aldrich Rockefeller Museum in Colonial Williamsburg, Lisa soon mastered the technique and began creating originals as well as reproducing early theorem

paintings. These have been sold at Williamsburg, the Museum of American Folk Art in New York and Sturbridge Village in Massachusetts.

"I've always enjoyed objects that give me a feeling of the past," she explains, "especially from the 19th century. I feel a part of me is very much in the past although I live and breathe in the present."

A completed theorem, especially when it is an old design, is dipped in coffee or tea solution or both to create the illusion of age. "I wrinkle the velvet first so that when it is submerged in the solution it will grab along the creases, which creates muted effects," says Lisa. Ranging in size from 10 by 12 inches to 26 by 32 inches and in price from $50 to $450, the theorem paintings on cotton velvet or velveteen are all done in oil paints. They may be purchased unframed, in antique frames or in custom frames made of walnut, tiger maple, pine, or oak and with grained or gilded finish. Lisa also teaches ongoing weekly classes at her studio, a course lasting 6 months. Color photos sent on request.

Lisa Kearney
31 Chimney Drive
Bethel, CT 06801
(203) 792-6126
R   C ($3.50)   MO

Other Makers

Rosemary Rister McDonald, 52 Fairlawn Drive, Rochester, NY 14617; (716) 544-1295, is the licensee for theorems at Colonial Williamsburg.

Marie Palota, RD 2, Box 293, Stockton, NJ 08559; (201) 996-2885.

Carol Frederick, Box 54A, Candia Road, Chester, NH 03036; (603) 887-2879.

Sandy McMillan, Box 96, Milton Mills, NH 03852.

Mona Rowell, 101 Townsend Street, Pepperell, MA 01463; (617) 433-6288.

Marjorie Yoder, North Street, Box 181, Morgantown, PA 19543; (215) 286-9445.

Donna W. Albro, 6677 Hayhurst Street, Worthington, OH 43085; (614) 436-1248.

Betty Hieba, 316 Mercert Street, Munhall, PA 15120.

Theorem painting of basket with fruits and birds by Lisa Kearney

Tile

Eileen Anderson specializes in hand-pressed, hand-painted earthenware clay tiles, used as architectural ornament for fireplaces, moldings, friezes, murals and house

Hand-pressed earthenware 6- by 6-inch tiles by Eileen Anderson

numbers, as well as mirrors and tables. Newly formed tiles are trimmed, dried, bisque-fired and then glaze-fired to 2,050°F. With a brilliant and varied pallette of glazes, the creative possibilities of style and design are endless. Red Clay Tile Works, 75 Meade Avenue, Pittsburgh, PA 15202; (412) 734-2222.

TIN COOKIE CUTTERS

One summer, after a hitch in the navy and 1½ years in college, Charles Messner of Denver, Pennsylvania, helped a tinsmith fix a roof and fell in love with tin. He apprenticed for 6 years, then went into business on his own, outfitting his shop with antique tools bought from retiring tinsmiths. As he installed rain gutters and downspouts, designed and repaired objects for local farmers, Messner began researching early American tin.

"Two hundred years ago," he'll tell you, "when household equipment was needed, the order was given to a tinker, who made everything from stove pipes to corn driers. The earliest tin was made in Berlin, Connecticut, but when it got cold there during the winter, tinsmiths came south to Philadelphia to earn money."

In 1960, Messner ran an electric drill bit into his left hand, severing a nerve in his forefinger. While recuperating, he made cookie cutters for his wife, bracing them against his stomach with his right hand.

"I started collecting patterns from anyone who would let me copy theirs," he says. "I now own 400 different designs but make about 70 on a regular basis. All are patterned after those used by Lancaster County families for three and four generations." One, a fighting gamecock, is the same as an antique that sold for $1,025 at auction, the only difference (besides age) being that Charlie's bears his trademark.

Most of his designs are based on the cone and series-of-cones patterns. In addition to making 4,000 cookie cutters a year, he makes lanterns and cutters for Ephrata Cloisters and is a featured craftsman at the Kutztown Pennsylvania-Dutch Festival. In his gray shingled barn, one of the oldest buildings in town, he makes cookie cutters ($2 to $12), pie cutters to vent pie shells ($2), comb boxes ($7), matchboxes ($6.50), candle molds ($20 to $32), pierced heart-shaped cheese molds ($17 and $19), two-piece swivel-jointed candle snuffers that reach up to chandeliers and down into smoke chimneys ($2.50), galvanized fruit driers ($32), funnels with handles for making funnel cakes ($4.25), navy grog cups ($6.75), pierced lanterns ($27 and $30), bun trays ($9), teakettles ($25), round and oval tinder boxes ($8), fireside roasters (copper $150,

Miniature tin cookie cutters by Charles Messner

Various tin lanterns by Charles Messner

tin $85), Revolutionary and Civil War canteens ($13)—to name a few.

Since going into business in 1948, he has expanded his list of products to include thirty different types of lighting devices, spittoons, camp kettles, peddlers' horns and speaking horns, ladles, dippers and flasks. Watering cans and fruit dryers are made of galvanized steel; a few items are copper. Lighting devices are made of copper and terne (sheet iron or steel plated with an alloy of three or four parts lead to one part tin, used as roofing material), but "anything that comes in contact with food is made with hot-dipped tin plate," says Messner, "which has not been made in the United States since 1969. The demand wasn't there, so factories stopped making it. I buy it whenever I find it, but hot-dipped tin plate is getting scarcer every year."

Advertising is by word of mouth. Retail business (with limited wholesale) has been so good there's never been time to print a catalog. His shop, near Route 272, just 3 miles from Exit 21 on the Pennsylvania Turnpike, is open daily except Sunday from Thanksgiving to Christmas only. The rest of the year is by chance or appointment.

Charles Messner, Tinsmith
515 Franklin Street
Denver, PA 17517
(215) 267-6295
V   R   W   S   MO

Other Makers

Hammer Song, 221 South Potomac Street, Boonsboro, MD 21713; (301) 432-4320, makes more than fifty cookie cutters, for $3.75 up.   C ($2)

Bob and Gail Tomson, Natural Metals, 2232 McDowell Road, Jackson, MS 39204; (601) 372-5159.

TIN HOUSEHOLD ITEMS

Bruce C. Panek, the tinsmith at Ohio Village in Columbus, Ohio, produces faithful copies of household items used in the mid-1800s: lighting devices, cooking utensils and storage containers, as well as military accoutrements like cups, canteens, Bible boxes and cartridge-box inserts (tin liners inserted into leather pouches to keep powder dry). Using tools from the same period, he cuts all pieces by hand, forms them on stakes or with machines that bend, bead, insert wire or shape the metal and heats soldering bits over a charcoal fire. His shop at the Ohio Historical Society is one of the few working tin shops in the country using this original method of firing.

"Tin plate is not pure tin," Bruce explains. "It is tin-

Tin kitchen cannisters by Bruce C. Panek

coated steel. When rust appears on tinware, it is because the tin itself has worn away and exposed the base metal." He prefers the shiny or semimatte finish over terne plate (sheet iron or steel plated with an alloy of three to four parts lead to one part tin, commonly used for roofing).

"The appearance of all tin plate 'softens' with age," he says. "The shine eventually becomes more matte and gray, developing a sheen similar to pewter."

Bruce first became interested in metal at the age of 11 when an artist offered to teach him the basics of pewter-work. When Ohio Village opened in 1974, he became the tinsmith's apprentice and since 1976 has been operating the shop with the assistance of volunteers.

In addition to berry pails (2-quart size, $12), match-boxes ($6), candle boxes ($25), candle molds ($8 per tube), wash pans ($18), coffeepots ($35), colanders ($22), tea

Tin document box by Bruce C. Panek

TIN

Tin coffeepot by Bruce C. Panek

cannisters ($12 to $15), graters ($4 to $6), document boxes ($15 up), five-part spice boxes ($35), 10-inch gooseneck coffeepots ($65) and reflector ovens, known as tin kitchens ($125), he makes Betty lamps ($15), kerosene lights in many styles (average $30) and two-candle electrified hanging lights ($70) on special order. Items such as hat boxes and Bible boxes are custom-made to fit contents and must be special-ordered.

The tin shop also does a large trade in reproductions of canteens, cups and cartridge box inserts modeled on those used in the French and Indian Wars, the American Revolution, the War of 1812 and the Civil War. Custom orders by mail, phone or in person are available on most items. Hours 9 A.M. to 5 P.M. Wednesday through Sunday from April through November. December hours are from 12:30 to 9 P.M. Wednesday through Sunday.

Bruce C. Panek, Tinsmith
Ohio Village
Ohio Historical Society
I-71 and 17th Avenue
Columbus, OH 43211
(614) 466-1500, ext. 360
V R S MO

Other Maker
Philip B. Kelly, 2389 New Holland Pike, Lancaster, PA 17601; (717) 656-6115.

TIN LIGHTING FIXTURES

Early settlers made lighting fixtures of iron, pewter, pottery, glass and china, but once they discovered the advantages of tin, hundreds of new styles evolved. Sturdier than pottery, glass or china; less expensive than pewter, brass or silver; tin devices were shiny and bright, didn't need polishing and could be made to order by tinsmiths who traveled rural America through the first quarter of this century.

While the wealthy could afford lighting fixtures of brass, silver or crystal, the majority of early American homes had iron, pewter or tin. But despite their greater popularity and numbers, few early tin devices survived. Considered cheap and therefore disposable, tin was discarded as soon as more durable, less expensive, machine-made metals (like galvanized metal and aluminum) arrived on the scene.

Joseph Messersmith of Chadds Ford, Pennsylvania, once earned his living restoring and reproducing old leaded glass windows at places like the Smithsonian, Winterthur, Old Salem Village in Winston-Salem, North Carolina, and Greenfield Village in Michigan. In 1958, when his neighbor Andrew Wyeth asked if he could make a palette out of metal, Joe discovered tin. Shortly after that, Wyeth's wife, Betsy, asked Joe to make a tin chandelier for her like the one in Washington's headquarters nearby.

Cone-shaped chandelier of tin by Joseph Messersmith

Replica of tin lighting fixture, c. 1790, made of 133 pieces by David L. Claggett

Joseph Messersmith
Murphy Road, Route 4, Box 566
Chadds Ford, PA 19317
(215) 388-6920
R   S   MO

Other Makers

David L. Claggett, 3N041 Woodview Drive, West Chicago, IL 60185.   C ($3)

The Saltbox, 3004 Columbia Avenue, Lancaster, PA 17603; (717) 392-5649.

Authentic Designs, The Mill Road, West Rupert, VT 05776-0011; (802) 394-7713.

Gates Moore, River Road, Silvermine, Norwalk, CT 06850; (203) 847-3231.

Jim DeCurtins, 203 East Main Street, Troy, OH 45373; (513) 335-2231.   C ($1)

Gerald Fellers, 2025 Seneca Drive, Troy, OH 45373; (513) 339-8164.   C ($1)

Hammerworks, 75 Webster Street, Worcester, MA 01603; (617) 755-3434, makes lanterns, chandeliers, door hardware, fireplace accessories and architectural ironwork.

Heritage Lanterns, 70A Main Street, Yarmouth, ME 04096; (207) 846-3911.

D. R. Williams, Village Lantern, Box 8A, Union Street, North Marshfield, MA 02059.

When the Wyeths bought Brinton's Mill and reshingled the roof, they gave the old tin roofing to Joe, who cleaned it up so that he could pound it into usable pieces.

Since then, he has acquired a national reputation for his authentic chandeliers, sconces and lanterns. He can't figure out how tin ever fell out of favor. "Tinware is straightforward and satisfactory stuff," he says, "with its own homely charm, a friend to pine and homespun, redware pottery and the poorest sort of blown glass."

His tools are shears, scribe, solder iron, anvil and pliers. After using the scribe to trace the pattern, he cuts the pieces and solders them together. Age alone provides the finish. No chemicals are used to produce artificial effects. Each piece is produced to order. The only problem that Messersmith has that didn't face his predecessors is how to hide the electric socket when clients want a piece electrified. One customer wanted to be able to use a candle *or* an electric bulb interchangeably. After hours experimenting, Joe invented an electric socket that could be unscrewed. The imitation candles on his electrified sconces, lamps and chandeliers are made with an actual coating of candle wax. And for those who prefer them, in addition to the aged tin finish, bright pewter and dull black are also available. Sconces range from $15 to $45, chandeliers from $160 to $225 and lanterns from $48 to $160.

In addition to his tinwork and leaded glass, Joseph also reproduces early punched tinwork like that found on pie safes. Hours by appointment only.

Tin lighting fixture by Authentic Designs

PAINTED TIN

Unlike wood, which was hard to clean, or iron, which was heavy, tin was light, bright and durable. Less expensive than pewter, tin had the beauty of silver at a fraction of the cost. Homemakers loved it. Decorated, they loved it more.

"Country tin-painting is a distinctly American art that had its beginnings in the 18th century when tinsmiths first started plying their trade in Connecticut," says Lois Tucker, who paints using the techniques and designs typical of early American tin shops. "Most tinsmiths designed and flowered pieces from their own imaginations. Although they got basic ideas for flowers from imported ceramics and prints, they mostly ad-libbed. As apprentices finished their terms and started their own businesses, tin shops sprang up throughout the northeastern United States. Few decorators signed their work, but the few signed pieces found have helped identify the type of flowering done by certain shops. From 1790 to the 1840s they made coffee- and teapots, tea caddies, cannisters, trays (called waiters), candlesticks, snuffers, snuffer trays, cases for knitting needles, tin trunks (both rectangular and oval in a variety of sizes), sanders, sugar bowls, creamers, syrup pitchers, mugs, cups, match safes, sconces and sugar shakers or flour dredgers, with trunks and waiters the most common and most popular. Homemakers bought

Ornate painted tin tray with elaborate border by Lois Tucker

Simple painted tin tray with plain border by Lois Tucker

Tin deed box by Lois Tucker

Tin deed box, side view, by Lois Tucker

so much from traveling peddlers that one journal reported a dealer who made $10,000 in one year from selling and trading painting tin."

Like the original decorators, Lois uses varnishes and japan paints with square-tipped quill and striper brushes. "The one major difference is that I use metal primer as a base coat," she explains, "so that my work will be in better condition 100 years from now than the antique pieces I find now. Originals did not use metal primer, although their paints were oven-baked to help them adhere to the tin. To survive, tinware had to be kept away from dampness, soot and cooking fumes of stoves and fireplaces and generally not be misused."

Backgrounds were usually black, but white, yellow, red and asphaltum (a rich transparent brown) were also used. Asphaltum produced a wide spectrum of colors from dark amber to shades of purple, and a black-glass, shiny, partially transparent surface, depending on the percentages used and the number of layers. "Border designs for the tops of trunks or the edges of trays are typically painted with just one stroke," says Lois, "most often in yellow, although other colors would be used on borders when lighter backgrounds were used."

Before Lois started painting tin in 1970, she collected it as an antique dealer. "I always liked it," she says, "so I decided to learn how to do it. Since then, I've received several A awards from the Historical Society of Early American Decoration, Inc., and am now certified as a country painting teacher." The most tedious part, she's found, is priming and painting the background color. "The fun is painting the design and the brushstroke borders. Practicing the brush strokes is essential, and similar to learning to play a musical instrument. If you do not practice for many hours, you can't expect to be very good."

Unlike the early makers of flowered tin, Lois signs and dates all her work—"L. Tucker and the year. Where I sign depends on the piece. I usually sign in an inconspicuous place where it will not be readily worn off, like the back of the flange on a tray rather than on the bottom." Prices range from $50 to $500 depending on the size of the tinware and the type of decoration. All are protected with a hand-rubbed varnish finish.

Lois Tucker
Box 429
North Berwick, ME 03906
(207) 676-4429
R   MO

Other Makers

The Cuklas of Hammer Song, 221 South Potomac Street, Boonsboro, MD 21713; (301) 432-4320, make crystallized tin, a 19th century technique that actually crystallizes the tin, producing unusual effects after being coated with a wash of color. They've also made tin decorations for the Smithsonian's Victorian Christmas tree, six-candle pineapple chandeliers, tea caddies, trays and coffeepots.

Pierced Tin

A pierced tin lantern was safer to carry into the barn than a candlestick because its rough surface kept hay and straw from sliding through the holes and reaching the flame; inside the house, the fanciful designs cut into its sides cast magical patterns of light around the room. Used as panels on pie safes and cupboards, pierced tin let air circulate around stored food, yet when the rough side faced out, insects were not as apt to crawl or fly in. On objects like foot and bed warmers that came in contact with the human body, the rough side was often turned in.

Pierced tin panels by James Palotás

269

Pierced tin lanterns by James Palotás

After two decades of collecting and making pierced tin, James Palotás went into business full time in 1976. Using old tinsmith's punches, he can recreate rare patterns in a wide range of sizes, duplicate missing antique tins or custom-design new ones. "Tin was originally available only in 10- by 14-inch pieces," Jim explains, "which is why most old pie safes and cupboards were made to fit this size panel. Although the original coke tin is no longer available, we can finish tin to look as bright as the original coke tin was when new, or antiqued, tarnished, or even pitted and rusted." HC31 Proctor Star Route, Box 321, Williamsport, PA 17701; (717) 478-2010. R C ($3) MO

SOUTHWESTERN TIN

When they could not get silver to decorate their churches in colonial New Mexico, Spanish friars used tin to make crosses, stations of the cross, *nichos* (niches to hold statues) and candelabra. Tin gained new popularity as a decorative medium after 1846 when the U.S. Army began bringing supplies to the territory in large, square, 5-gallon tin containers, which sold for 2¢ apiece after

they'd been emptied of supplies like lard, lamp oil and coffee. New Mexicans quickly recycled the metal to make boxes, chandeliers, sconces and picture and mirror frames for their homes.

"Unlike the utilitarian coke tin used in the eastern United States," says Angelina Delgado Martinez, New Mexico's leading tinsmith, "these cans had to be cut up, flattened and pieced together. A lot of old pieces still have the original trademarks on them. We later used roofing terne plate because it was more durable and wouldn't rust. Its lead content made it softer and easier to shape, but eliminated its use for eating utensils." Angelina continues to use 8-pound lead-coated roofing terne for everything except Christmas ornaments, which are created from a light, shiny, uncoated tin.

Angelina began her apprenticeship in tin at the age of 12, with her grandfather Francisco Delgado and her fa-

Sconce on cross by Angelina Delgado Martinez

Santo Nino de Atocha nicho *by Angelina Delgado Martinez*

ther, Ildeberto "Eddie" Delgado, in their studio at the corner of Canyon Road and Delgado Street in Santa Fe. "They urged me to take my time," she remembers, "to go slowly and to learn well. They believed '*Paso que dure y no recule,*' which means 'Haste makes waste.'" While other girls practiced sewing fine seams, Angelina learned to cut patterns, bend, engrave and make smooth soldered seams in tin. By the time she graduated from Loretto Academy, she was doing custom work. After she married and gave birth to four children, tin became more of a hobby until she was widowed in 1960. Then, to support her family, she taught first grade at Our Lady of Guadalupe School and depended on her "tin money" for extras like vacations. "It was during this period," she says, "that I knew my work was improving because it was getting more notice and was more in demand." It was not until she remarried in 1971 that she could afford to return to tinsmithing full time. With the encouragement of her husband, Efren, a *santero,* or carver of religious figures, she began producing award-winning pieces that are now in the collections of the Albuquerque Museum, the Museum of International Folk Art and the Museum of the Americas in Madrid, Spain.

Using her father's bench and her grandfather's handmade scorer, crimper and bending brake (a tool that turns edges and makes channels to hold glass and mirror), Angelina makes all pieces by hand without machinery of any kind. Unless she's making a pair of objects, she measures with her eye. To keep the tin from warping, she works both sides simultaneously. Her generations-old patterns are sometimes improved with her own additions, like the hearts she added to a tin mirror frame of her grandfather's

design. "I like to add birds and hearts to his patterns," she explains. "He was devoted to the Sacred Heart and St. Francis, and loved hearts and birds." Soldering is the most time-consuming part of the process, especially when some of her work contains more than a hundred sections. "But nothing is difficult if you like to do it," says Angelina. "I thank God every day for giving me the health and talent to continue the family tradition." Of the eight boys and three girls in her family, Angelina is the most active tinsmith, but in the next generation, her two sons Paul and Vincent Younis have become artists in their own right.

Angelina thought that winning New Mexico's highest honor, the Governor's Award, would be the highlight of her career, but when she did in 1984, she realized "it was just another step. I told those present that I hoped my father and grandfather were present in spirit to see what's been done with the little they had to work with," she says, "but secretly thought, if only my father could see me now!" Angelina's work ranges in price from $2.50 for a Christmas ornament to $1,200 for a large chandelier, depending on size and detail.

Tin mirror made of one hundred separate pieces by Angelina Delgado Martinez

271

TINSEL PAINTING

Angelina Delgado Martinez
1127 Maez Road
Santa Fe, NM 87501
(505) 473-0024
V (by appt.)   R   MO

Other Makers

Paul Younis, 1127 Maez Road, Santa Fe, NM 87501; (505) 473-0024.

Vincent Younis, 1127 Maez Road, Santa Fe, NM 87501; (505) 473-0024.

Emilio and Zenaida Romero, 1027 Houghton Street, Santa Fe, NM 87501; (505) 983-8850.

F. Bonifacio (Bone), 7222 Vivian, NW, Albuquerque, NM 87104; (505) 821-4476.

TINSEL PAINTING

Tinsel painting, a popular American folk craft from 1850 through the Victorian period, was a form of transparent reverse painting on glass enhanced with the crinkled foil that once lined tea boxes (one reason the technique is sometimes referred to as oriental pictures). The tinsel paper applied to the back, to simulate mother-of-pearl and gold, made the pictures glisten with what appeared to be an inner light, which is why they were also known as pearl or crystal paintings.

Beatrice Hoffman had been painting in watercolors and oils for 25 years before she read about tinsel painting. "I was intrigued by the effects I could get," she says, "and was having great fun experimenting until my husband asked, 'What are you going to do with all these?' So one spring morning, I took them to a gift shop, sold them all and have been making tinsel paintings ever since." Her tinsel work has been exhibited in many museums and historic sites like Winterthur in Delaware and been purchased by collectors including the Queen of Thailand. In addition to classes in her studio, she teaches at Landis Valley Farm Museum in Pennsylvania and in Florida during the winter months.

Period designs were usually combinations of fruit, flowers, birds, butterflies and animals, worked out on paper before copying on glass. Several of the most popular had a focal point (like birds in a fountain or a compote full of fruit) encircled by a wreath of flowers, while more ambitious designs introduced historical and religious themes, even portraits, into their composition. While English artists added paper and textiles, Americans confined tinsel painting to transparent paints backed with foil to illuminate and intensify the colors. Although the tech-

Tinsel painting of bouquet with assortment of flowers by Beatrice H. Hoffman

nique was taught in boarding schools and used by Civil War soldiers while they were recuperating in hospitals, tinsel paintings were never made commercially during the 1800s. Tucked away in the attic at the turn of the century, they regained some measure of popularity in the 1930s and again during the Bicentennial, but the expense of restoring peeling paint deterred most collectors from buying them.

Bea likes to plan designs inside the frame. "It's best to put it all on paper first so you know where you're going," she advises. "It's also easier to correct mistakes on paper than on glass. I use pictures or greeting cards in any combination, design my own or copy an old design. The glass should be cleaned on both sides with a nonscratching cleanser (not liquid because it leaves a residue), rinsed and dried with nonlint paper towels."

After laying the design under the glass, she traces it with India ink and a cro-quil pen and point, then paints in the background with household enamel ("that's what they used in the 1800s") and a size 00 brush. "Usually black, white or off-white, but you can use any color."

Tinsel painting of bowl with fruits by Beatrice H. Hoffman

When it is dry, she trims any mistakes, then paints the design with oil paints in three principal colors: alizarin crimson, Prussian blue and Indian yellow, using burnt umber or sienna for shading. For background sparkle, she crinkles aluminum foil, using the dull side because it has a patina similar to tea papers, or thin light tinsel paper imported from Japan.

Unlike period tinsel paintings, which go for prices up to $1,000, Bea's cost $20 for one 4 by 5 inches, $24 to $40 for one 5 by 7 inches, $30 to $60 for 8 by 10 inches and $65 to $75 for 11 by 14. Oval sizes are available for $125 to $500, depending on the design and frame. Both rectangular and oval designs are available in antique or reproduction frames and plain or bent glass. Commissions accepted for original designs or reproductions.

Beatrice H. Hoffman
2300 Aaron Street, Condo #105
Regency House
Port Charlotte, FL 33950
V   R   C   S   MO

Other Maker
Loretta Banks, Highland Avenue, Milton Mills, NH 03887; (603) 652-4488.

Tinsel painting of floral arrangement of roses by Beatrice H. Hoffman

TOMAHAWKS

Tomahawk was an Algonquian word for a clublike weapon with a spike or stone ball attached to its head, used in battle but especially useful for removing scalps. The term was transferred by the English to the hatchets with iron heads manufactured by Europeans for trade and sale to the Indians. When Indians made peace with their enemies, they sometimes buried their tomahawks, giving rise to the expression, "burying the hatchet."

"Tomahawks are perhaps one of the most uniquely American of all historical items," says Mark Bokenkamp of Bokenkamp's Forge. "To my knowledge, no other culture combined a smoking pipe with a hatchet. The tomahawk was used as a sign of personal power and importance, as a tool and a weapon, a symbol of peace and of war, as a religious adjunct and as a pipe. It was a popular trade item for about 300 years, with very elaborate examples awarded to chiefs of tribes at treaty ceremonies. Today they are special-ordered for competition throwing and showing at muzzle-loading rifle matches." Today, one of Mark's tomahawks, 18 inches long, made of silver and iron, costs about $800.

In addition to tomahawks, smith Bokenkamp ("Please

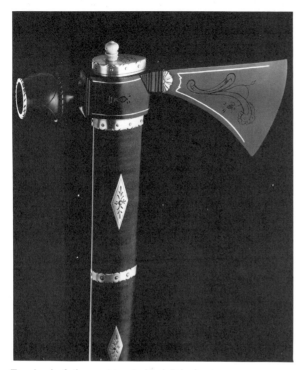

Tomahawk of silver and iron by Mark Bokenkamp

Most of Mark's work is done on commission. "Smaller jobs are often sent along with a bill, while larger or more specialized items require a 30 percent deposit. Large projects may require a design fee and periodic payment based on percentage of completion." Bokenkamp's Forge is open to customers from 8 A.M. to 5 P.M. Monday to Friday by appointment.

Tomahawk with stone head and leather-covered handle by William Lossiah

remind readers that a smith is a person, a smithy is a building") makes flintlock rifles, wrought-iron gates, fireplace equipment, knives and a whole line of antique reproduction hardware and lighting devices.

"Most of my work is forged from mild steel," he says, "but for the purist I can occasionally find enough true wrought iron (which hasn't been produced in this country for three decades) for some small jobs." He uses hammers and tools identical to those used by blacksmiths for hundreds of years. Finishes are varnishes, wax or oils, depending on whether the piece is forge finished or whitework and on how it will be used.

"While we think of iron as a static material, in the heat of the forge it becomes a very plastic one," says Mark. "At temperatures approaching 2,000°F, it can be worked in much the same way as a sculptor shapes his clay. The ultimate finish can show the scale formed by the heat of the fire, be left with the mark of the hammer blows or be filed and polished to a surface so bright that it appears to be chrome plated. The rough hammer marks can be replaced with delicately filed moldings and engraved designs rivaling the grace of silver. It is this multifaceted personality of the material which I find so intriguing."

Mark Bokenkamp
Bokenkamp's Forge
10132 Liberty Road
Powell, OH 43065
(614) 889-0819
V   R   MO

Other Makers

William Lossiah, Qualla Arts & Crafts Center, P.O. Box 277, Cherokee, NC 38719; (704) 497-3103, a Cherokee, makes tomahawks with stone heads and leather-covered

Sioux-style tomahawk with lazy-stitch dangle by Clyde M. Hall

handles decorated with leather thongs, beads and feathers, for between $100 and $500.

Stan Neptune and Janice Gallipeau, Wabanaki Arts on the Penobscot Indian Reservation, P.O. Box 453, Old Town ME 04468; (207) 827-3447, make simpler versions with stone heads and carved handles.

Clyde M. Hall, P.O. Box 135, Fort Hall, ID 83202; (208) 237-2142.

TOTEM POLES, MASKS, RATTLES AND DOLLS

Totem poles, one of the great craft traditions of the world, display the coats of arms and symbols of family honor of the Northwest Indians, an extremely complex cultural group living along the Pacific coast from the mouth of the Columbia River to Yakutat Bay, Alaska. Carved monuments in cedar that depict mythological and contemporary events in the family or in the life of the owner, they are proud reminders of what was and must continue to be. From the Ojibwa, *nintotem* means "my family mark," while its stem, *ote*, means "to be from a local group."

"Totems were used in many ways, like welcoming members of the tribe to the potlatch feast, and as houseposts on the large communal dwellings where related families lived," says Chief Don Lelooska, who has carved totems as tall as 145 feet, "but they were used in ostentatious ways as well. The Northwest Indians were rich in resources and raw materials. They lived in the midst of enormous trees with dense undergrowth in a land with long wet winters and timid summers, which gave them leisure time to carve."

Don's mother, Shona-Hah ("Gray Dove"), matriarch of the family, was born in Oklahoma's Cherokee Nation, where her father, He-Killer, taught her to carve. Her realistic dolls made as teaching devices are in many museums and private collections. Carved of basswood and dressed in traditional Indian dress of skins, fur, wool and bark, her "little people" sell for $650 to $2,000. Her three sons are all well-known carvers whose work is in museums worldwide. Lelooska ("He who cuts against wood with a knife") made his own carving tools, which he uses to create

Totem pole by Don Lelooska

Makah clam digger doll by Mary (Shona-Hah) Smith

Owl sculpture by Don Lelooska

eloquent totems, human and animal figures, ceremonial bowls and intricate masks. Kwunkwa-dzi ("Big Thunder") sold his first carving before he turned 10 and is known for his imposing red cedar masks of Hoh-Hox, the mythical cannibal bird. His large carved feast bowls are focal points of many collections. Tsungani ("He who excels") is a gifted ceremonial dancer who specializes in objects used by the old healers like rattles, frontlets, staffs and shamen's masks.

Ceremonial masks showing mythic figures of the clans and the supernatural world are used in the ceremonies to illustrate stories behind the dances to the uninitiated. Many masks are 6 feet long, while others open up to reveal other masks. Their price (from $300 to several thousands of dollars) is determined by size, type and intricacy of design.

Rattles were used to tame some of the dancers being initiated, and by shamen (medicine men) during healing rituals. "They were used much as a modern speaker uses the gavel," explains Lelooska. Made of alder and maple, they are round and can have very complex interlocking figures carved into their surfaces. Starting at $300, they

"The Foolish Sun," mask by Fearon M. (Tsungani) Smith

are used in the traditional dances. Staffs, called talking sticks, are used by chieftains and shamen to formally address the tribe. "Made like slender totem poles, they can be quite simple or include crests of the family," says Don, "while a frontlet, a small forehead mask worn at the front of a headdress, with a trail of ermine skins down the back, is often inlaid with shell and trimmed with sea lion whiskers."

Totem poles today are often used as architectural accents. Although the average is 10 feet tall, the Lelooska family can make them any height or design. One recently commissioned for a Japanese client featured a crane.

The Lelooska Family
5618 Lewis River Road
Ariel, WA 98603
(206) 225-9522
V R S MO

Other Maker

Stan Neptune, Wabanaki Arts on the Penobscot Reservation, P.O. Box 453, Old Town, ME 04468; (207) 827-3447, carves totem poles any size from 18 inches to 30 feet, from poplar beaver cuttings as well as basswood or cedar. Poplar and basswood sell for $120 a foot, while cedar is $175 a foot.

Jack-in-the-box by Rochester Folk Art Guild

TOYS

The Rochester Folk Art Guild began in 1957 with a single potter's wheel in the basement of a member's home. Since then, the nonprofit educational organization has grown to include workshops in pottery, weaving, glassblowing, ironworking, graphic arts, woodworking and clothing design. They now own and operate a 300-acre working farm 50 miles south of Rochester, New York, whose land provides essential staples and where a flock of sheep grows wool for the weavers' looms.

Although guild artisans work 7 days a week year-round, the farm is open to the public only during two openhouse weekends, usually in June and September. All other sales are through four or five large retail shows in the northern and southern tier regions of the state, and by mail order. Each craft area operates somewhat independently of the other, particularly in marketing. No overall catalog is available except in wood toys and graphic arts, which are also their more traditional products.

For the parent who doesn't have time to make the toys he or she treasured as a child, the guild's line of thirty-four can be a godsend. Remember the whirly—the propeller on a stick that flies in the air after a good twist? "The whirly is the simplest and perhaps the most amazing of our toys," says David Barnet of the guild, "because it flies. I know it preceded the Wright brothers because I remember reading that they did some experiments with simple propellers like this one. In fact, as we put on the handle, we test each one to see that it flies well. Two people can play catch by aiming the toy at an angle toward one another. It's also remarkably sturdy because it's made of maple." Cost: $4.

All work is signed only with the name of the guild because members feel it reflects their shared way of life and the wider search and struggle behind each finished piece. "We have an ongoing debate about the number of grooves for winding the string on our thrown top" (made of hardwood with a brass nail centered in the tip, $7), says David. "Should there be three? Turning and throwing a top is a science in itself. Some prefer to wind down near the tip and throw it upright; others wind up near the shoulder and throw upside down so that the spinning top has to right itself. We also try to make up interesting ribbon

277

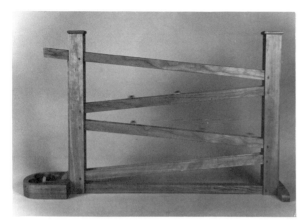

Marble game by Rochester Folk Art Guild

combinations on the Jacob's Ladder'' (six flat wooden blocks that magically somersault down ribbons that act as hinges).

The guild also makes that untiring twosome Mr. and Mrs. Flip, hand-painted acrobats who swing between two upright supports in reaction to a squeeze on the handles ($8); a jack-in-the-box whose hand-painted papier-maché head pops up out of a 4- by 4-inch-square varnished box ($28); and a marble run like those used by children in the Victorian era (hardwood 29 by 17 inches, $50). One of the hallmarks of the guild is a Noah's Ark of hand-carved basswood with removable hatch, cabin, deck, roof and hinged door ramp and hand-painted figures of Mr. and Mrs. Noah, a dove and twenty-four pairs of animals (22 by 14 inches, $550). The only toys that can't be shipped

Toy Noah's Ark by Rochester Folk Art Guild

are the 7-foot-long stilts, with two levels of footrests, for beginners and pros and nonskid rubber on tips and footrests (oak or ash, $30).

The guild's graphic arts department publishes a fine if limited selection of handmade books for the discriminating reader and collector to keep or share with youngsters. Produced by a variety of techniques including hand silkscreen, most are printed from original hand-scripted texts, some on handmade paper. Subjects include fairy tales, poems, songs and recipes.

Although there is no catalog, the guild's glass shop produces a wide range of hand-blown glass in clear and crackled textures ranging in price from $10 to $40, available by mail order. Wholesalers can visit anytime by appointment. For schedule of retail sales and open house dates, send self-addressed, stamped envelope.

Rochester Folk Art Guild
1445 Upper Hill Road
Middlesex, NY 14507
(716) 554-3539 or 554-6401
V   R   W   S   C   MO

Other Makers

Dick Schnacke, Mountain Craft Shop, American Ridge Road, Route 1, New Martinsville, WV 26155; (304) 455-3570, makes traditional folk toys.

Yesteryear Toy Co., P.O. Box 3283, Charleston, WV 25332; (304) 744-2162, makes hand-painted wooden toys.

Guys Folk Toys, Route 1, Sugar Grove, NC 38670.

Timbertoys of Vermont, RFD 1, Box 250, Fletcher Road, Fairfax, VT 05454; (802) 849-6156, makes toys in the Vermont tradition.

John Michael Linck, 2550 Van Hise Avenue, Madison, WI 53705; (608) 231-2808 makes hardwood toys, trains, chests and children's furniture.

R. Voake, Route 113, Thetford Center, VT 05075; (802) 785-2837, makes ridable wooden trucks and trains, rocking and rolling animals, Noah's Arks and building blocks.

Tramp Art *See under* **Carving**

TREENWARE

Virginia Petty's father taught her to whittle when she was 6. ''I used to carve pretty designs on tree limbs,'' she says. ''The first time I cut my finger, I walked around with my hand in my pocket so my parents wouldn't take my knife away. My mother, who is an artist, encouraged me. She'd spread a sheet on the floor and let me whittle away. Bowling Green, where I grew up, wasn't a craft-oriented community. The only people who carved were the older men around the town square. People teased and said that's where I belonged. I knew it was unusual for a girl to carve and was uncomfortable about that, but I truly enjoyed whittling. When I joined the Kentucky Guild in 1970, I went to shows as the Whistlin' Whittler because I was unsure of myself and my work. But after my work sold out the first day of a 4-day show, I quit hiding behind a business name. I'm still the Whistlin' Whittler, but now my sign and card read: Virginia Petty, The Whistlin' Whittler.''

Buckeye (treenware) biscuit bowl 10½ inches across and 5 inches deep by Virginia Petty

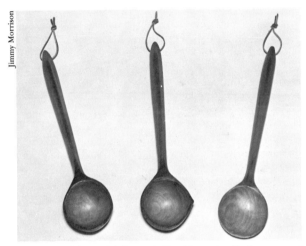

Treenware: (left to right) dipper, ladle with pouring lip for soups and stews and spaddle (part spoon, part paddle) for stirring thick sauces, by Virginia Petty

Like early settlers, Virginia makes treenware (which means ware from trees) household utensils: spoons, paddles, bowls and scoops like those made in the 1800s in Kentucky. The only difference is that her wood comes from beams and floor joists of homes and businesses that are being torn down. "The buildings are at least 100 years old," she says, "and most are much older than that. I use mainly old poplar because it develops a deep, rich color with aging, and tag each utensil with the age of the building it came from."

Her husband, Paul, is in charge of materials. In between farming 155 acres where they raise corn, tobacco, alfalfa, cattle and hogs, he locates and hauls home most of the wood Virginia uses, and in a pinch can be pressed into helping with the finish.

Although she makes bowls of sassafras, hackberry, cherry and poplar, Virginia prefers buckeye because it resists chipping along the grain, doesn't crack easily, and dough doesn't stick to the sides. After wood is sawed to the proper thickness, it's stored in the barn until seasoned.

"I bandsaw the outside shape of each object," says Virginia, "but from there on it's all by hand with curved gouges and a carver's mallet. I use a lot of sandpaper because I like to feel the wood, but sand only enough to remove roughness and soften the tool marks, yet still show the hand of the craftsman." Her honest spoons, ladles and scoops, a joy to hold and a pleasure to hang instead of stashing in a drawer, are signed, dated, rubbed with nontoxic finish so that they can be used for cooking, then strung with a leather thong for hanging. Ranging in size

Group of treenware bowls by William Farr Day

from a 4-inch scoop (which makes a great coffee measure, $6) to a 15-inch ladle with a bowl 2 inches deep ($20), they include a 15-inch paddle, part spoon and part paddle ($10). Her biscuit bowls, 10½ inches wide and 5 inches deep ($75), are a Kentucky tradition for making buttermilk biscuits every morning.

Virginia Petty
The Whistlin' Whittler
1684 Three Forks-Flatrock Road
Oakland, KY 42159
(502) 563-4324
R W S MO

Other Makers

William Farr Day, RR 1, Box 64, West Lebanon, IN 47991; (317) 893-4390, makes hand-hewn bowls of black walnut and wild black cherry, in the Swedish style found in Wisconsin and elsewhere in the North, which are shallow and without corners; and the English type found in Appalachia and Arkansas, which are deeper, with a flat bottom and defined sides. "I cut directly out of the log," says Bill, "using green material; then rip or split the block into two slabs, which are hewed with a foot adz to get rid of sawmarks. I then chop my bowls with two types of hand adz, scrape them with a carver's hook to eliminate the chop marks, then hand-sand them and soak the finished bowls in linseed oil for 48 hours." His round bowls (7½ to 23 inches) range from $25 to $225, while his rectangular models (8 by 7 inches to 21 by 15 inches) are $25 to $200.

Nancy Lou Webster, P.O. Box 148, Elgin, TX 78621.

James S. Young, Route 1, Box 221, Omaha, Arkansas 72662.

Lewis E. Everline, Charming Forge, Route 1, Womelsdorf, PA 19567.

William Schmidt and Diana Andra, 704 West 4th Street, Mansfield, OH 44906; (419) 525-0776 or 526-2056, also make wooden bowls ($25 to $250), dulcimer noters ($3) and wooden hairpins ($3.50). R W S MO

Trunks *See Petacas*

Ukeleles *See under* **Musical Instruments**

Utensils, Cooking *See* **Iron, Inlaid, and Whitesmithing** *and* **Iron Tools, Locks and Cooking Utensils**

HORSE-DRAWN VEHICLES

"Most of our clients have high-pressure jobs," says Barbara Evensizer, whose husband, John, builds horse-drawn vehicles by hand, using century-old tools. "They've found that spending a day on country back roads in a carriage can be very relaxing and rewarding." Stagecoaches, buggies, Stanhope gigs, Phaeton carriages, cutters, sleighs and fringe-topped surreys are only a few of their authentically crafted beauties. In addition to producing the vehicle at their shop, the Carriage Works in Oregon, they'll also deliver it, complete with horse and harness, anywhere in the world *and* train the new owner to drive it.

"As far as I'm concerned, nothing is impossible," says Barbara. Although it usually takes 6 months from order to delivery, she once delivered a surprise gift of a horse and buggy to movie director George Lucas's 40th birthday party with only 4 days' notice, plus a pony and pony cart for his daughter. She'd no sooner returned home than the donors, Courtney and Steve Ross (he is the president of Warner Communications) ordered a miniature donkey and wagon for their daughter.

The Evensizers' carriages were seen in the television mini-series "The Thorn Birds." Ski resorts use their cutters and sleighs; summer spas, their buggies; and their stagecoaches have become a popular attraction at amusement parks and dude ranches. Since opening in 1976, the Carriage Works has filled orders from all over the world. Their most satisfied customer may be the doctor in Texas who ordered a buggy so he could make house calls the old-fashioned way.

"As a young girl, I always wanted a horse," says Barbara, "and finally got one at the age of 15: an Arabian gelding

Single-seat buggy with top built for movie actor Slim Pickens by the Carriage Works

Surrey with fringe on top made for the W. R. Hearst, Jr., family by the Carriage Works

Barbara and John Evensizer
The Carriage Works
P.O. Box 64
Oakland, OR 97462
(503) 459-9100
V   R   C ($3)   S   MO

Other Makers

Montana Carriage Company, Inc., 7457 Highway 2 East, Columbia Falls, MT 59912; (406) 892-3178.

Justin Carriage Works, 5299 Guy Road, Nashville, MI 49073; (800) 533-3390.

named Spartacus. I'm not happy unless I ride or drive one every day. Luckily, we keep one of almost every breed at our ranch to sell with carriages.'' John, a Vietnam veteran, was a logger when they met and married. Their carriage trade began when they saw an old single-seat buggy in their neighbor's chicken coop, bought it for $300 and fixed it up so Barbara could take the children for rides. When they received an offer for it that tripled their investment, they sold the buggy and bought a wagon. Before they knew what was happening, they were in the restoration business. When they couldn't find enough good vehicles to restore, they started making their own.

Today their shop, billed as "No. 1 in the Carriage Trade," can make anything horse-drawn to custom specification with the same quality and precision as the original. "Making wooden wheels is the most colorful part," says Barbara. "It's exciting to smell the coal burning and to see the metal rim get hot enough to almost burn the wood when it's put on the wheel, then watch it contract and draw tight after it's immersed in cold water. The finish on our carriages takes many hours of sanding, but it's mirrorlike, which sets them apart from others made today."

Their two-wheel vehicles start at $275, while their four-wheel carriages start at $1,900, ranging to $26,000 for a stagecoach. The Carriage Works also restores antique vehicles and makes buggy wheels and spare parts for horse-drawn vehicles. "We keep a stockpile of old parts," says John. "If a part can't be repaired, we make a new one. We also build and rebuild wheels for light vehicles, but not for farm wagons."

The shop is open from 9 A.M. to 5 P.M. Monday through Saturday; tours by appointment only.

SHEEPHERDER WAGONS

When Basque sheepherders came to America to earn money in the sheep country around Idaho, Wyoming and Colorado, they lived in sheepherder wagons. Originally built on standard farm wagon frames and wheels, these homes on wheels were hauled by a team of horses into high pastures at the beginning of the summer, where a sheepherder lived in isolation for 6 months.

"Once a week or so, a boy from the ranch would take him light stores, news and fresh tobacco," says Jim Tolpin, who began building sheepherder wagons in 1974 after living in one for a year. "Other than that, the sheepherder's only company was the sheep dog or border collie. These wagons were built at different locations but were very much alike: about 11 to 13 feet long, 4½ feet wide at the base, stepping out to a 6-foot width over the wheels, with canvas spread over oak hoops in the style of covered wagons. The interior usually had a bed at the far end, a

Front of sheepherder wagon with canvas top on bent oak hoops by Jim Tolpin

281

table and a little pot-belly stove. After the advent of the auto, they were built on junked car frames. A real-life gypsy, Professor Shenandoah, came to my door with an old sheepherder wagon that he'd used to travel America. A few years later, he came by again with the stripped Model T chassis and asked me to build a wagon on it. That was my beginning in this business."

Sheepherder's and tinker's wagons were simpler versions of the more ornate gypsy types used in England. The first mention of a "cart with a stove" was in 1840, but it was not until about 1875 that the gypsy *vardo*, or van, was made by traditional English wagon and coach builders.

After Jim graduated from college, he apprenticed with several New England woodworkers, learning how to build everything from furniture to timber-framed houses. He began building sheepherder wagons when he found the experience enriching. "They are warm and snug, pleasantly lit and make a wonderful retreat *to* the road," he says, "because wherever the wagon stops is home."

He researched and came up with a design that keeps the form of the originals but allows them to be towed safely at modern highway speeds. New thick wall 2/3 channel iron for the chassis is professionally welded and rustproofed. Wood-spoked Model T wheels are restored to new condition with new bearings, seals, tires and tubes. Tongue-and-groove cedar is used for siding and roofs because it is lightweight and resists rot. Oak was chosen for flooring because of its beauty and resistance to wear, and for hoops because it's easily bent yet retains its form. Canvas is waterproofed heavy-weight marine quality because it's leakproof and mildew-resistant. Joint lines are cut to drain away water, surfaces bedded with marine

compounds, and nonrusting fasteners used throughout. The exterior is sealed with marine-grade paint, interiors hand-rubbed like furniture.

"I build them one at a time for special people," says Jim. "They have lots of handwork, even the undercarriage is nicely shaped and carved. Door panels are sometimes carved with flowers and most windows have stained and leaded panes. Interior walls are wainscotted, and warming ovens near the stove have punched copper panels. Several wagons have been built as mobile studios and galleries, one as a music studio that travels to students and another as a puppet theater."

The Sheepherder sells for $9,500. Canvas-roofed Bow-Tops come in a simple style ($12,500) and ornate model ($15,500), while the wooden-roofed and -sided Ledge type is $25,000.

Jim Tolpin
The Interwood Company
Box 681
Port Townsend, WA 98368
(206) 385-4338
V   R   S

WALLPAPER

When Bruce Bradbury was growing up in New England, he had a recurring dream of climbing through a secret attic door into a "large room of breathtaking beauty, with a door at the end that took me into another, then another, each different, each more beautiful than the last. Years later, I found a description of that world by the Pre-Raphaelite painter Burne-Jones: 'a beautiful romantic dream of something that never was, never will be . . . in a light better than any light that ever shone . . . in a land no one can define or remember, only desire.' " Bruce traveled to San Francisco, where he fell in love with Victorian architecture, then on to England, where he spent 2 years studying and copying intricate 19th century wallpaper designs, recording thousands of colors. One his return to San Francisco, he apprenticed with two wallpaper manufacturers to learn technique, then went into business as Bradbury and Bradbury.

"At first I was like a one-man band doing all the work alone," he says, "but as time went on, I realized no one single individual could design, print and distribute the complex work we're doing." Today, with seven assistants, he feels "more like a conductor, but the work we produce together far excels what I could do alone." Their goal is

Rear of sheepherder wagon by Jim Tolpin

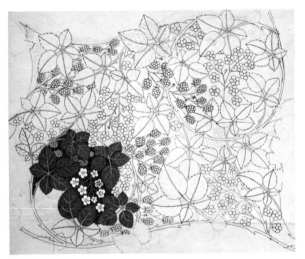

Raspberry Bramble, original hand-painted wallpaper drawn from nature by Bradbury and Bradbury Wallpapers

to resurrect the concept of art wallpaper and the wallpaper crafts studio of the late 19th century.

"Handpainted 'art' wallpaper," Bruce explains, "is an offshoot of the Victorian arts and crafts movement led by William Morris, which spread to America in the 1870s. Many leading artists and architects designed wallpapers as a means of spreading innovative ideas to a broader public. Proponents believed that wallpaper could be a valid art form; that art could move outside the limitations of a frame into an all-encompassing environment. Un-

fortunately, most of the art wallpaper companies were ruined by material shortages during World War I; the Second World War and the advent of the modern movement spelled doom for the few survivors."

In the artful Victorian interior, both walls and ceiling were segmented into elaborate ornamental combinations using wallpaper friezes, dadoes, ceiling papers, rosette fans, corner blocks and panels. "Victorians were not bound by the paltry taste of modernism," says Bruce. "Whatever they could imagine is what they would try to create."

Since 1976, Bruce has continued to add designs. In addition to reproducing historic wallpapers (often from scraps found under floorboards or molding), he finds antique designs in books that were designed but never made, and interprets Victorian styles with American motifs.

Separate stencils and silk screens are cut for each color, paint is mixed by hand, and paper is printed by the silk-screen process (an adaptation of Japanese stenciling) on tables 90 feet long. Bradbury offers forty wallpaper patterns and seven frieze designs in every conceivable Victorian style (for instance: Eastlake, Morris, Dresser and Neo-Grec). All may be ordered by mail. For those who want to create their own fantasies, Bradbury's catalog ($2) is a heady delight full of possible combinations. Rolls (15 feet long, 30 square feet) are $24 to $38; borders and friezes run $6 to $20 a yard; and embellishments are sold individually, one to a yard. If you send room measurements and a $50 deposit (credited toward your purchase), their design service will completely design your room from their existing collection of one hundred design combinations, tell you how much to order and what it will cost. They also serve as Victorian designers in creating new effects based on Victorian elements, but that costs a good bit more. Hand-printed samples of all designs are also available for a nominal charge.

Bradbury and Bradbury Wallpapers
P.O. Box 155
Benicia, CA 94510
(707) 746-1900
V (by appt.)   R   W   S   C   CC   MO

Iris Frieze, hand-painted wallpaper adaptation by Bradbury and Bradbury Wallpapers

WEATHERVANES

Early American weathervanes were most often cut from flat wooden boards, because they were accessible and inexpensive, then painted and decorated with metal. Although Paul Revere worked in metal, he cut his weath-

Rooster weathervane by Ivan Barnett

Indian with bow and arrow weathervane by J. Donald Felix

Whimsical striped horse weathervane by Ivan Barnett

Carved and gilded angel weathervane by C. H. Becksvoort

ervane, in the shape of a fish, from wood, then studded its surface with large copperhead nails. Coastal regions favored fish and ship motifs, while rural areas preferred animal shapes. Originally, weathervanes were placed on churches to ward off evil, and over the years, the predominant design was that of a fish, the secret symbol Christians once used to identify one another.

"Most early weathervanes didn't have directional markers," says Ivan Barnett. "Many were poorly made and often didn't work because their makers didn't understand the dynamics involved. The pivot point has to be one-third of the way from the bottom edge so that two-thirds of the weight is pushed by the wind. Most early vanes had primitive symbolic forms that were deceptively simple. They also had a strong sense of color, pattern and spirit. I try to capture that spirit in my designs."

While searching for a means of artistic expression after he graduated from the Philadelphia College of Art, Ivan found he reacted most positively to the two-dimensional shapes and colors of the primitive vanes in the Lancaster County farmland surrounding his studio. After a year of researching weathervanes in the major folk art collections of the United States and a winter apprenticing with Peter Renzetti (see Iron Hinges) to learn the basics of blacksmithing and construction, Ivan started making his own in 1974.

Since then, his whimsical weathervanes, known for their strong sense of color and design, have found their way into some of the most important American collections. Winterthur commissioned an original rooster design for its catalog and museum shop; Landis Valley Farm Museum in Pennsylvania ordered several cut from sheet iron; the White House decorated its 1981 Christmas tree with miniatures of his barnyard animal designs; the Smithsonian (where Ivan now lectures and conducts workshops annually) asked Ivan to reproduce a Triton weathervane for its catalog; for Colonial Williamsburg he produced weathervanes, garden and tree ornaments; and for the Museum of Fine Arts in Boston, a decorated copper weathervane like one in their collection.

Using only basic hand and machine-shop tools, Ivan cuts shapes from salvaged wood and metal, adding buttons, rivets and even steel shavings for detail. When asked how he achieves his antique patina, he answers, "Eighty percent of my finish is provided by Mother Nature."

His weathervanes, ranging in price from $275 to $600, include flying geese, polka-dotted birds and striped horses. In recent years, Ivan has expanded into other objects that have their roots in weathervane shapes, like table sculptures ($24 to $36), ornaments in sets of three and six ($15 to $18), garden stakes ($10), wall collages ($18 to $60) and mobiles ($140). A set of six barnyard animal decorations like those used on the 1981 White House Christmas tree is $45; and a Noah's Ark with removable roof and ramp comes in two sizes with forty free-standing tin animals ($500 and $1,000). If you're in Lancaster County, call Ivan and plan to visit his studio, 10 miles from Lititz. Color catalog $2.

Ivan Barnett
RD 1
Stevens, PA 17578
(717) 738-1590
V   R   W   C   S   MO

Other Makers

J. Donald Felix, P.O. Box 995, Hampton, NH 03842; (603) 474-2225, whose work twice received the Stevens Award from the League of New Hampshire Craftsmen, "captures life in a vane," using only his hands, hammers, an anvil and metal stakes to form his work. Like those of the town and city vane makers of the past, his vanes are designed to show a client's interests, profession and even logo. C ($1)

C. H. Becksvoort, Box 12, New Gloucester, ME 04260; (207) 926-4608, makes carved and gilded weathervanes.

Marilyn E. Strauss, Salt & Chestnut, Route 6A at Maple Street, West Barnstable, MA 02668; (617) 362-6085, has hand-hammered copper swell-bodied- and full-bodied-style weathervanes 2 to 4 inches thick.

COTTON, SILK AND WOOL WEAVING

During a 3-year apprenticeship at Ohio Village in Columbus, Ohio, Mary Beth Burkholder worked with warps 50 to 70 yards long for the most efficient production.

"I learned to make warps carrying 20 to 30 threads at a time," she says, "as professional weavers in 1810 would have, when weaving with extremely fine thread was the rule rather than the exception. The exacting techniques used by professionals for hundreds of years differ quite a bit from those used by many contemporary artisans. Speed and efficiency were as important as fine craftsmanship, which meant that fine, durable and beautiful fabrics had to be produced in as little time as possible. Achieving perfectly straight selvages and a perfectly even beat in the finished product were very important to the professional weaver, so that when two pieces of fabric were seamed together to form a large blanket or coverlet, the patterns would match exactly. The even rhythm and steady beat come from practice and concentration."

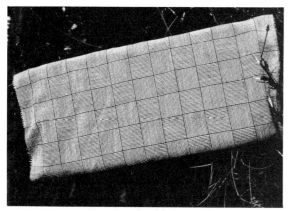

Cotton fabric in basket-weave pattern woven by Mary Beth Burkholder

Wool tweed woven by Mary Beth Burkholder

Assorted striped and plaid cotton fabrics woven by Mary Beth Burkholder

After serving as master weaver for an additional 4 years, Mary Beth went into business for herself, choosing as her firm's name Perfectly Warped. She continues to work with the natural fibers of cotton, linen, silk and wool, concentrating on rugs, blankets, tablecloths and fine yardage. She uses warps 8 to 40 yards long, and in making those warps still uses the technique of carrying many threads while measuring them, usually 16 to 20 threads at a time.

"Private and public restorations have difficulty finding usable period materials," explains Mary Beth. "Many are stained, worn or have not been cared for properly. In addition to being able to duplicate period fabrics in the historic manner like checks, windowpane checks, plaids, Bronson, spot weaves, bird's-eye, etc., I can weave an infinite variety using different patterns, colors and fibers. With all the possibilities, I could weave the rest of my life and never repeat the same fabric."

Born and raised in Wisconsin, where she earned a bachelor's degree in social work at the University of Wisconsin, Mary Beth moved to Ohio in 1972 where she now lives and works in a large Victorian house in Troy with her husband. Although she used counter-balance looms at Ohio Village, she now weaves on a 62-inch countermarche loom with overhead batten. "The action of the swinging overhead batten is essential," she says, "to achieving a perfectly steady even beat, and to weave for many hours without tiring."

Most of her yardage is done on commission, woven to the client's personal needs and specifications. Prices, which include shipping costs, vary depending on cost of materials and complexity of pattern. There is a minimum order of 4 yards on most fabrics. Cotton and linen are preshrunk and may be washed and dried in a machine. Her most frequently ordered fabric is wool, available in tweed suitable for winter coats, heavy jackets and vests (28 to 44 inches wide, $40 to $50 a yard) and wool shirting ($50 to $60 a yard). Linen, which she enjoys most in the finished product, can be ordered in a medium weight suitable for toweling, tablecloths and curtains ($40 to $50 a yard) or fine weight for toweling, clothing and napkins ($50 to $60). Silk is $50 to $60 a yard. Medium-weight cotton is $30 to $40 a yard; fine-weight is $40 to $50.

Orders require one-third deposit and take up to 6 weeks for delivery, depending on size of order.

Mary Beth Burkholder
Perfectly Warped
419 South Market Street
Troy, OH 45373
(513) 335-3795
V (by appt.)   R   S   MO

Other Makers

Kurt Wendt, 577 Lafayette Street, Denver, CO 80218; (303) 778-8739, does custom hand-spinning and hand-weaving.

Diane Jackson Cole, 9 Grove Street, Kennebunk, ME 04043; (207) 985-7387.

Marion Scannell, Waterford Weavers, 117B Boston Post Road, East Lyme, CT 06333; (203) 739-4001.

HOUSEHOLD LINENS

"Weaving was an important part of everyday life for settlers in the Mohawk Valley, second only to cooking," says Gene Valk, who specializes in early American patterns and weaving techniques. Valk's studio, Weefhuis (Dutch for "weaving house"), produces textiles for the home: cotton and linen napkins, runners and towels in old huck, Bronson, overshot, summer-and-winter and twill patterns as well as plaids, checks and stripes in plain weave. "We also adapt traditional patterns for modern use," says Gene, "like table mats, afghans and doll house miniatures."

Gene bought her first loom while in college and "through trial and error, b'guess and b'gosh" taught herself. After retiring as a librarian, she began weaving full time. Three of her antique looms are on permanent loan to nearby museums; many others are loaned to students. "Most of the kids in the neighborhood have woven a rug on one of my looms at one time or other," she says.

Gene was intrigued by the patterns of early weavers, and her greatest find was the pattern book owned by Franz Xavier Gärtner, who arrived in the area in the 1830s, the same time weaving factories came to Ephrata. "We believe that the ninety patterns were done by his father, who wrote the introduction to the book," says Gene, "and that he learned to weave from his father. If he had apprenticed to someone else, he would have made his own pattern book. There is a rough draft in the back of the book of an overshot pattern that he didn't know and had to learn. In Stone Arabia [near Palatine, New York], there is a coverlet with the same errors as the threading draft." Gene has translated the drawings into modern drafts (instructions for threading the patterns onto the shafts of a loom). "I use a lot of his patterns," she says, "working from a photocopy of the original manuscript, which is in a museum."

All of Gene's weaving is by hand-thrown shuttle and hemmed or fringed by hand. Each item is individually woven. "We do not weave on a wide warp, then cut several pieces from it. Orders for specific colors or textures are

Samples of different weaves created by Weefhuis Studio

accepted only if we have an appropriate warp on the loom." She and her two partners (who market work under the name Adirondack Handweavers) use natural fibers in cotton, linen, silk and wool, which is sometimes hand-spun (although on request they will use synthetic fibers for afghans and coverlets or for items washed frequently, like baby blankets).

Old huck (or huckaback) is a small all-over pattern whose motifs are created by warp floats on one side and weft floats on the other; the floats add texture and increase absorbency, one reason why huck toweling is used in roller

Woven table runner by Weefhuis Studio

Frank Ambrose

Assorted towels woven by Weefhuis Studio

towels. Gene recommends that dish towels be woven of linen and cotton or all linen, which in addition to being lint-free grows more lustrous with use and absorbs up to 30 percent of its weight without feeling wet. Barleycorn, or spot Bronson, and Atwater, or lace Bronson (used for household textiles, scarves and blankets), are related to huck but floats are distributed to form geometric patterns that resemble barley or corn grains. Swedish lace appears similar but is drafted more like huck, while leno is a lace weave that looks like hem-stitching when used as a border or hemming line.

Considering that a table mat takes from 30 minutes to 2 hours to weave, depending on weight of threads, it's surprising that they cost only $5 to $8, depending on technique of weave. Towels and runners the same width as mats are 25¢ to 40¢ an inch, while table runners range from 35¢ to 60¢ an inch. Napkins run from $4.50 to $6 each. Generous-sized towels range from $11.50 to $14.50 for cotton or cotton and linen, and 20 percent more for all linen. Shipping extra. Inquiries must include a self-addressed, stamped envelope.

Gene Valk
Weefhuis Studio
402 North Main Street
Gloversville, NY 12078
(518) 725-3371
V R S MO

Other Makers

Winters Textile Mill, P.O. Box 614, Winters, CA 95694, weaves coverlets, tablecloths and tea towels. C (with swatches, $1)

Coker Creek Handweavers, P.O. Box 8, Coker Creek, TN 37314; (615) 261-2157, makes place mats with natural or cork fringe, napkins and table runners 13 inches wide to any length.   C

Karen Jackson, P.O. Box 8, Jaffrey, NH 03452.

Nicole Shatswell, Heirloom Weavings, 34 Pleasant Street, Salem, MA 01970.

JACQUARD WEAVING

In the early 1800s, when Frenchman Joseph Jacquard invented an arrangement of holes in punched cards to control the operation of a loom, professional weavers in America were quick to adopt the complex technique for use in their work. After drawing the design on graph paper and planning colors, an expert transferred the pattern to punch cards, each of which contained information for one row.

The series of cards, attached to a belt on the loom, translated information mechanically to vertical rods leading to levers, which selectively lifted groups of warp threads, allowing the shuttle to pass. Although the process allowed far more intricate designs than before, the majority of weavers used only a few in their lifetime, at the most five or six. Because many coverlets contained a corner block listing the person for whom the coverlet was made, the name of the weaver, year and place it was woven, Jacquard spreads documented their own history.

In 1982, David Kline of York County, Pennsylvania, began making Jacquard coverlets like those made in his region 150 years ago, using wool yarns over a natural cotton background, each woven in a long strip, cut apart, then hand-sewn with a center seam.

"From the time I graduated from high school in 1949, until the company went bankrupt in 1974, I worked in weaving mills," says David, "as a loom cleaner, a cut boy taking rolls of cloth off the looms, a weaver and repairman fixing Jacquard looms. I tried other work but never enjoyed it, so my wife, Carole, and I decided that we would

J. David Allen & Son

Bird and Bush Border with Four Roses pattern, Jacquard weaving by David and Carole Kline

try to locate used looms and weave Jacquard coverlets like those made by Pennsylvania-Germans in the mid-1800s. We read everything we could find on the subject. I also had scraps of two coverlets made for my great-grandmother in 1842. My sisters had thrown them away, but I decided to keep them even though they were threadbare. I cut out the name blocks and gave them to my niece and nephews, then saved all the scraps in a box. In 1982 I used them to determine the count (3/8s) or size of the warp and weft in our coverlet. We had to pick

them apart, thread by thread, and have 1 yard of thread weighed in a textile lab to determine the right size of yarn. We bought two shaft looms from a mill, rented a building with no heat, water or bath, then bought a Jacquard attachment. We now have five: four in use and a spare.''

After cleaning and taking out 1,304 needles and 2,608 hooks and putting them back together again, they mounted the Jacquard and tied in the harness with 1,280 strings. "The tricky part," David found, "was remembering to change the cards at the right time." His solution, one Rube Goldberg would love, was a wired Model-T horn whose blast he couldn't ignore.

They looked at many coverlets before deciding on a design used by Andrew Kump of Hanover in 1838. "We liked the crispness of the weave, as well as the design: four roses with a bird-and-bush border," says David, "so we borrowed a coverlet from a dealer and took it to Philadelphia, where the motifs were painted on point paper and 2,200 cards punched. Eleven months after we began research, we sold our first coverlet in October 1983. Since then we've woven more than 500 and introduced another design with houses, a dog and cat up a tree, the town pump, geese on the border, with a body of four roses and geometric designs made by Seifert Brothers in Mechanicsburg in 1848."

A crib-size Jacquard is $125; double, $350; queen, $395; and king, $525. Both designs are in red, blue, green and natural. A block twill design coverlet, an authentic adaptation of one by Henrich Leisy dating from 1823 in blue and white, is not personalized with the corner block and sells for $165 in a double size. Like many Jacquard weavers, the Klines also weave ingrain carpet.

David and Carole Kline
Family Heir-Loom Weavers
RD 3, Box 59E
Red Lion, PA 17356
(717) 246-2431
V R MO

LINEN, TICKING, LINSEY-WOOLSEY AND CALAMANCO

The first cloth woven in America was probably linen, made from flax grown from seed brought by the early immigrants. The best table linens, sheets and underwear were made from the longest (called line) fibers; utilitarian linens came from the tow; and the rough outer fibers were made into rope. Fabric woven with a warp of linen

J. David Allen & Son

House Border, Jacquard weaving by David and Carole Kline

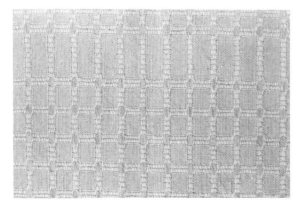

M's & O's pattern woven by Julia A. Lindsey

and a woof of wool became known as linsey-woolsey (called drugget in England). It was left its natural color for curtains, blankets and sheets and dyed for bed hangings, coverlets and upholstery. Mothproof, and lightweight yet warm, it was used for summer blankets, coats, winter petticoats (often striped with colorful dyes) and an extra layer of warmth on the bed in winter months. Quilted coverlets, most often made from blue, red or brown linsey-woolsey, were sometimes polished by hand or glazed with diluted gum arabic, rice water or egg white. Calamanco, often mistakenly called linsey-woolsey, was an all-wool worsted used for coverlets, curtains and clothing. Its pattern was woven into the fabric on the loom rather than quilted like linsey-woolsey. Both were quilted—only the fabric differed.

Julia A. Lindsey, whose hand-weaving studio is named, aptly enough, Lindsey Woolseys of Ohio, makes all three (linen, linsey-woolsey and calamanco), plus ticking, wool, cotton and overshot coverlets, rugs and pillows in fourteen patterns. Although her nickname as a child was Lindsey-Woolsey, she didn't considered a career as a weaver until 1971 when she was teaching art at an Indiana high school. "A student asked for suggestions for a weaving project," says Julie, "and I suggested linen. Since the budget didn't include funds to purchase linen, I searched out a 73-year-old woman I'd met at a conference who was a weaver, and discovered that every room in her house contained a loom. The next day I bought one, took my first lesson the following Saturday and have been weaving since."

Today, Julie's studio specializes in the reproduction of 18th and 19th century textiles with a focus on those that were originally woven in the home. "I complete careful research on each pattern before reproducing it," she says, "and try as much as possible to use traditional color as well as traditional materials. All weaving is done on a completely hand-operated four-harness loom, the same one I bought in Indiana."

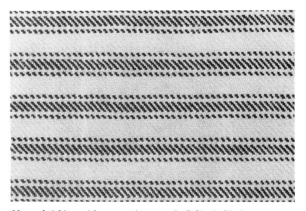

Natural ticking with navy strip woven by Julia A. Lindsey

Julie is one of the few weavers making ticking, a linen twill used to hold feathers in mattresses, bolsters and pillows. While most people are familiar with the blue-and-white striped kind, ticking came in a variety of colored stripes. The superfine was used for linings, gaiters and women's corsets, while coarser tickings (called ticks) were used to make feather mattresses, whose seams were gummed to seal in the down.

Lindsey's coverlets in overshot range in price from $200 to $1,200, while those in calamanco or linsey-woolsey cost $1,300 to $2,500. Overshot rugs are $200 and up, depending on size. Checked linen and ticking are $9 a square foot; fine linen, $15 a square foot; and pillows in overshot

Calamanco pattern woven by Julia A. Lindsey

or linen are $28 to $110, depending on size and fabric. Special retail orders require a 50 percent deposit at the time of order with the balance due on delivery. There's a 25 percent deposit for special wholesale commission and catalog orders. Brochure with yarn samples, $1.

Julia A. Lindsey
Lindsey Woolseys of Ohio
275 North Main Street
Germantown, OH 45327
(513) 855-6424
V (by appt.)   R   W   S   MO

Other Maker

The weaving shop of The Farmers' Museum, Inc., Lake Road, P.O. Box 800, Cooperstown, NY 13326; (607) 547-2593, specializes in 18th century coverlets, sheets, yard goods, tartans, 19th century wool and linen textiles and reproductions from the museum's collection. Also special orders.

NAVAJO WEAVING

Although Navajo Indians were fierce warriors, they were also highly intelligent traders, quick to adapt to the needs of the market. After the Pueblo Indians taught them to weave in cotton, the seminomadic Navajos switched to wool and wove blankets for wear, warmth and trade. Unlike cotton plants, sheep could be moved from one place to another; and since the tending of sheep was traditionally women's and children's work, Navajo weaving has usually been done by women.

Navajo wool is hand-spun, not on a spinning wheel, but on a simple spindle twirled in the right hand while the wool is held in the left, giving the yarn a left-hand twist, unlike machine-made yarn, which twists to the right. Created on upright looms with the most primitive tools, Navajo weavings range from sturdy room-size rugs to place-mat-size tapestries so finely woven that they're translucent when held to the light.

"Wool is spun down on the spindle so many times it is finer than dental floss," says Sande Bobb, who with her husband, Bill, updated Gilbert S. Maxwell's book, *Navajo Rugs—Past, Present and Future.* "Tapestries, which must have a minimum count of 80 wefts per running inch, can have as many as 126 weft threads per inch. As fine as linen, a small tapestry can be folded up and put in a man's pocket. Even more mind-boggling is that these complicated designs are woven directly onto the loom from the mind of the maker and not first planned on paper."

The earliest Navajo weaving (1700–1850) was woven

Two Grey Hills tapestry by Lynette Nez

in stripes of natural colors. During its classic period (1850–70), the Navajo Chief blanket (an irony, since the Navajos had no chiefs) became a status symbol among chiefs of other tribes and as presentation gifts to authorities. Woven first in black and white stripes, later with gray blocks within stripes, diamonds and corner designs, Chief blankets cost many horses or silver pesos. When red was added to the design, it came not from nature but from imported bayeta flannel, which was unraveled and respun. Once Germantown wools became available in 1880, Navajos began weaving gaudier blankets known as eye-dazzlers because of their bright colors and intricate designs. When factory-made blankets threatened the market, traders encouraged weavers to develop heavier textiles that could be used on the floor. But when traders began paying by the pound instead of for craftsmanship, the pragmatic Navajos beat sand into their wool to command a higher price.

Today, although no two Navajo rugs are alike, there

Burntwater rug by Cara Yazzie

Burntwater rug by Marie Watson

are more than a dozen distinct types: Two Grey Hills, in natural white, gray, black and brown; Ganado, similar in design but predominantly red with a black border; Burntwater, in soft pastel and vegetable shades; Crystal, in often heavy hand-spun yarn and rich, earthy vegetable colors banded in straight or wavy lines. The Teec Nos Pos, prized by collectors for its complex colors and intricate designs reminiscent of Persian oriental carpets, is usually woven from commercial yarn; Red Mesa, though similar, is not as colorful as Teec Nos Pos, and woven from hand-spun yarn. Chinle has stripes, bands and serrated designs like the old blankets, with no borders. Yei weavings, seldom larger than 3 by 5 feet, feature elongated figures against a white background, while Yeibichai designs feature rows of Navajo dancers. Sand-painting rugs (which originated in 1904) are usually square and depict designs drawn in sand at healing ceremonies. Pictorials, which often include modern subjects like cars and planes, are actually one of the oldest forms, dating to 1880 or perhaps 1865.

When rugs have borders, a "spirit line" can be seen in the design. "Navajos do not believe in enclosing something entirely," Sande explains. In traditional Navajo thought, it is unwise to enclose something totally without leaving an opening, which is why weavers frequently add a spirit line when rugs have borders so that the maker's creativity will be able to flow out and into the next weaving.

No longer sold by the pound, Navajo weaving is priced according to its craftsmanship: the finer the spinning, the tighter the weave, the more complex the design, the larger the size, the higher the price. A 2- by 3-foot rug can start at $200 and larger ones can cost up to $12,000, while a tapestry with 126 wefts to the inch may run as high as $21,000.

Makers

Navajo Arts and Crafts Enterprise, Postal Drawer A, Window Rock, AZ 86515; (602) 871-4090.

Sande and Bill Bobb, Cristof's, 106 West San Francisco, Santa Fe, NM 87501; (505) 988-9881.

Dan Garland, Garland's Navajo Rugs, P.O. Box 851, Sedona, AZ 86336; (602) 282-4070, located at the intersection of Highway 179 and Schnebly Hill Road.

Kalley Musial, P.O. Box 1335, Flagstaff, AZ 86002; (602) 839-4465.

NORWEGIAN-AMERICAN WEAVING

"When I first saw traditional Norwegian weavings," says Julie Brende, "I wasn't sure I liked them. I thought the patterns were automatic and that traditional weaving wasn't creative. But after studying antique weavings and trying several techniques, I realized how ignorant I had been and began to appreciate the beauty of the colors, patterns, designs and the many ways they could be combined."

Although her mother had a loom, Julie didn't become interested in weaving until after college, marriage and three children. She built herself a small frame loom, took classes in Milwaukee and Topeka, and after moving to Decorah, Iowa, studied weaving in the Norwegian tradition at the Norwegian-American Museum. Since then, she has won five top awards in the National Exhibition of Weaving in the Norwegian Tradition.

Norwegian-American *Akläe* weavings are done in strong geometric designs, often with stripes in borders at the top and bottom, with the bottom border usually wider than the top. Within these borders are stripes, overshot motifs and sometimes a section of crosses and celtic knots that may have represented immortality. Old Hag's Teeth, a common border, uses one color over alternating threads, and another color over the opposite threads.

"Most of the weaves I use," says Julie, "are hand-manipulated. The loom is threaded to a regular plain weave. The design is put in by hand instead of threading the warp with a pattern. The Norwegians liked the back of a weaving to be as neat as the front. On the Vestfold weavings, all the ends are sewn in, but the work is not reversible like the *Akläe*, woven with a tapestry technique known as single-interlocking, with wefts wound in one direction, from right to left, where each color meets another. The *Randäkle* type of *Akläe* uses only stripes, but the *Smettäkle* is a combination of border stripes with interlocking geometric designs in the center. The zigzag pattern used in many borders is *fjord og fjell,* meaning water and mountains. Designs include eight-petaled flowers, eight-pointed stars, celtic knots, crosses and diamonds. *Krokbragd,* the poor man's *Akläe,* a very thick, loom-controlled twill weave, is commonly done with three harnesses."

Vestfold weavings use linen or *fiskegarn* (a tightly twisted cotton yarn used for fish nets) for the warp and wool for the weft, worked in patterns separated by a stripe. A raised surface that looks like embroidery is made by laying in a double thread by hand. Double-weave technique uses wool for both the warp and weft. The loom is threaded with a double warp, one light and one dark. The design is woven

Smettäkle with border stripes and geometric designs of eight-petaled flowers, stars and diamonds woven by Julie Brende

293

Norwegian-American weaving by Julie Brende

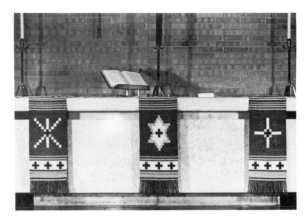

Akläe *altar hangings woven by Julie Brende*

where the piece will be seen," she explains, "the architecture and colors in the church; then try to find a technique that I can fit into the symbolism of a particular season." Approximate prices are $100 to $150 for a pastor's stole and $200 to $500 for an altar hanging.

Julie Brende
Nordic Handweaving
410 Home Park Boulevard
Waterloo, IA 50701
(319) 232-7339
R   S   MO

Other Makers

Äse Blake, 1771 Timberland Road Northeast, Atlanta, GA 30345.

Myrna Golay, RD 2, Box 55, Annandale, NJ 08801; (201) 735-9620.

Mary Temple, 1011 Cottage Place, St. Paul, MN 55112.

by picking up warp threads from the bottom warp and keeping them on top in areas of design. Picture-weaving uses linen warp or *fiskegarn* with a wool weft. Julie also employs the Brooks Bouquet and leno lace techniques.

A small Vestfold hanging is $20, while runners are $45 to $200. Woolen rugs 3 by 5 feet start at $200; scarves are $25 to $35; and shawls are $70 to $100. Julie is especially known for her church paraments (altar hangings, pulpit and lectern hangings and pastor's stoles), which she designs and weaves. "I first consider the environment

OVERSHOT COVERLETS

Overshot coverlets have been an American tradition for centuries. Evolving from the white-on-white "floating thread" linens of England, Scotland and Ireland, the overshot technique developed in this country as weavers experimented with floats of colored wool on a linen warp background. The overshot weft yarn that created the pattern was made of wool from sheep grown on the farm, and the linen, from flax grown in the fields. The earliest overshot used small repeat designs, first on smaller objects like shawls and later in larger areas of coverlets. Most often woven in strips approximately 26 to 40 inches wide (as wide as the loom or as wide as the weaver could reach), coverlets commonly had at least one seam joining the strips to make the desired width. Although contemporary weavers take pride in evenly matched seams, early southern weavers didn't worry about it, saying that an uneven pattern drove away evil spirits.

In most regions, women and children prepared, spun and dyed the wool and the women wove the coverlets, while in other areas the weaving was left to the local professional or itinerant weaver who traveled with his own pattern books. Pattern drafts (instructions) for coverlets were passed from generation to generation, handwritten on long strips of paper and kept in safe places like family Bibles. These drafts, resembling sheets of music, were sometimes kept so secret that certain patterns were woven only in certain parts of the country.

In 1980 a group of weavers in Kansas started Heirloom Fibers to preserve weaving techniques and to meet the demand for traditional textiles. "We were concerned with the number of old coverlets that were being cut up for decorative items," says Linda Stoker, co-owner with Linda Middlemas. "Right away we received requests from dealers and collectors for rare crib-size coverlets as well as those large enough for today's beds. Because there are so many variables involved (like patterns, color combinations, etc.) we decided to custom-make overshot coverlets and not stockpile ready-made sizes."

Stoker and Middlemas use 100 percent virgin wool fibers in colors as close as possible to the vegetable-dyed tones used a century ago. Authentic 18th and 19th century patterns (like Nine Snowball, Conestoga and Lee's Sur-

render) are hand-woven on floor looms in standard and custom sizes; Monmouth, Crown and Diamonds, Whig Rose and Four Blooming Leaf designs may be custom-ordered. Coverlets are carefully matched, joined by hand and hand-washed, then fringed if desired.

"We also cross-stitch a little piece of linen to one corner," says Linda, "which usually carries the name of the owner, the date it was made and the name of the weaver."

If requested, Heirloom Fibers also matches custom-dyed colors and patterns. Average delivery is from 4 to 8 weeks, longer for custom. Yardage 44 inches wide runs $120 a yard. Standard-size overshot coverlet prices range from $30 for 16- by 16-inch tops to $800 for one 100 by 104 inches. A sample packet with yarn, fabric swatches, pictures, brochure and order form is available for $3, deductible from the first order.

Heirloom Fibers
9800 West 100th Street
Overland Park, KS 66202
(913) 888-8476
V R W C S MO

Other Makers

Julia Lindsey, Lindsey-Woolseys of Ohio, 275 North Main Street, Germantown, OH 45327; (513) 855-6424, in addition to patterns mentioned also weaves the Shaker Dogwood pattern, Double Chariot Wheels, Tennessee Trouble and others. Prices run from $200 to $1,200.

Jessie Marshall, 3251 Main Street, Coventry, CT 06238.

Gene Valk, Weefhuis Studio 402 North Main Street, Gloversville, NY 12078; (518) 725-3371, makes afghans in the overshot coverlet patterns and miniature crib coverlets on a 1 inch to the foot scale for doll houses.

Ann Williams, 1601 Wendover Road, Charlotte, NC 28211; (704) 365-2402, makes hand-woven coverlets in traditional overshot patterns from $300 to $525.

Craig Evans, RFD 1, Box 16, East Calais, VT 05650; (802) 223-7234.

Tim and Maureen Rastetter, Rastetter Woolen Mill, State Routes 39 and 62, Star Route, Box 42, Millersburg, OH 44654; (216) 674-2103, make overshot coverlets in Morning Star, Whig Rose and Lovers Knot patterns in wool and cotton from $180 up.

Heir-Looms, Box 455, Imler, PA 16655.

Old Abingdon Weavers, P.O. Box 786, Abingdon, VA 24210. C (with fabric swatches, $3)

Assortment of overshot coverlets and pillows by Heirloom Fibers

RIO GRANDE WEAVING

Rio Grande, a general term for weaving done along the Rio Grande River from southern Colorado to Rio Abajo, south of Albuquerque, New Mexico, includes several traditional styles and methods: *sabanilla* and *jerga* (both types of yardage) and weft-faced blankets woven on two-harness treadle looms.

"*Sabanilla,* used as a base for *colcha* embroidery, sheeting, mattress ticking and light clothing," explains Lisa Trujillo, "is a fine wool balanced-weave fabric whose warp and weft are equally visible in the finished product. *Jerga,* the only twill weaving done on a four-harness loom, is a thicker, coarser fabric. Although it has been used in recent years as a term for floor covering, *jerga* includes a wide variety of utilitarian fabrics. Colonial *jerga* was woven in diamond (partridge eye) or herringbone weave, often in a plaid or check pattern."

"In our family," adds her husband, Irvin, a seventh generation weaver whose ancestors settled Chimayo in the early 1700s, "Rio Grande is a pattern dominated by horizontal stripes and bands. Originally woven as relatively large blankets, they were usually wool, although some cotton examples have been found in southern New Mexico. Many are all stripes, while others utilize tapestry techniques, placing design elements within the stripes. Other weft-faced designs include Saltillo, Vallero or Trampas-Vallero and Chimayo."

The Saltillo pattern, a simplified version of the Mexican serape design, has a formal defined border on all sides of a rectangle, a vertically oriented background and a central serrated diamond or lozenge. "Few weavers had the skill or time to weave them," says Lisa. "Late in the 19th century a variation that added eight-pointed stars became known as Vallero or Trampas-Vallero. A brilliantly colored

Rio Grande weaving: Chimayo influence on Saltillo weaving by Irvin L. Trujillo

Trampas-Vallero, Rio Grande weaving by Jacobo O. Trujillo

flamboyant pattern, it has been described as the last fling of native weaving. Some Valleros have a star in the center and one in each corner, while others place the stars in different arrangements. Most have strong border designs and chains of radiating diamonds around the center. Vallero weavings have a huge diversity of design and home-grown variations."

"Chimayo has its roots in Saltillo and Rio Grande," adds Irvin, "but has a system of design all its own. Because it incorporates all sorts of designs and symbols (like the roadrunner, New Mexico's state bird), it has been called pan-southwestern, which is pretty accurate."

The family homestead, the Centinela Ranch in the hills above Chimayo, once served as a sentinel or observation point against Indian attack. Irvin's father, Jake, patriarch of the clan, has been weaving since the 1920s and is recognized as one of the best in a village of weavers. He

La Primavera, Rio Grande weaving by Lisa R. Trujillo

never sketches a design in advance but draws from the picture in his mind, "because it takes longer to draw than weave it." Lisa and Irvin do all the dyeing; Lisa and Irvin's mother, Isabel, spin. For several weeks each year the family gathers natural materials (*chamisa, cota,* goldenrod, bindweed, black walnut hulls, plum roots, marigolds and *canaigre,* a dock plant) to use for dyeing. They are currently experimenting with ikat, for which yarn is wrapped in part to resist dye, producing a design when woven.

A large variety of traditional and contemporary blankets, rugs, bedspreads, shawls and pillows, ranging from $6 for smaller pieces to several thousand dollars for larger work and special orders, is for sale in their gallery. Also displayed are wood-carving and woodworking by son-in-law Marco A. Oviedo, a seventh generation woodworker expert in the styles of 17th through 19th century colonial and territorial New Mexico. Marco's wife, Pat, paints his *bultos* and *retablos.*

Centinela Traditional Arts
Box 4
Centinela Ranch
Chimayo, NM 87522
(505) 351-4755
V R C S CC MO

Other Makers

Ortega's Weaving Shop, P.O. Box 325, Chimayo, NM 87522; (505) 351-4215, designs, furnishes materials and threads the warps for sixty to one hundred weavers whose work is sold in the shop. Chimayo blankets start at $5 for the 10- by 10-inch doll's size and go up to $225 and above for one 54 by 84 inches. Rugs 26 by 45 inches are $40 and go up to $225 for 54 by 84 inches. Ortega's will also weave heavier blankets known as *fresadas* and will custom-dye. They also weave ponchos, capes, vests, coats, sashes, ties, bags and clergy stoles. R S C MO

John R. Trujillo, Box 18-A, Chimayo, NM 87522, sells hand-woven blankets, coats, purses and rugs.

Maria Vergara Wilson, Route 2, Box 46, La Madera, NM 87539; (515) 983-2745 is an expert in ikat weaving.

TABLE LINENS

In 1912, the national women's collegiate sorority Pi Beta Phi started a settlement school in Gatlinburg, Tennessee. At the time, the only industry in the mountainous area was logging. For most inhabitants, the economic situation was bleak. After the sorority realized that weaving and handcrafted objects were being made for personal

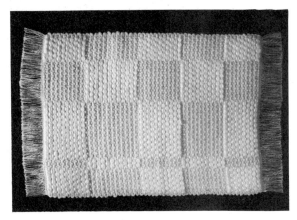

Pebble design table linen woven by the Arrowcraft Shop

Miss Olivia design table linen woven by the Arrowcraft Shop

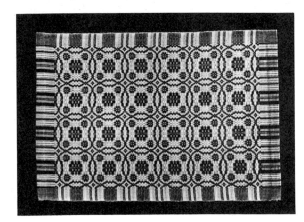

Whig Rose design table linen woven by the Arrowcraft Shop

use and for barter, they decided that if they could provide a sales outlet, women could work in their homes and sell through the shop. In 1925, the Arrowcraft Shop opened, selling simple items for everyday life like wooden bowls, furniture and baskets. A weaving designer was hired to set up a production weaving program. Its purpose: to teach local women how to weave or, if they already knew how, to teach them more sophisticated techniques. Most of the weavers made their own looms or inherited them. Designs and raw materials were provided by the shop. To be included in the program, women had to know how to make their warps, dress their looms, weave and finish all goods before bringing them in for sale. The same system is in use today.

"The caliber of the weaving is exceptional," says Janet S. Skinner, a former manager, "and the versatility and durability of the work make it unique. I feel that our table linens are the finest made in this country, both in quality and in the great variety offered, from casual to very formal. Our linens have been purchased for use in governor's mansions in several states and also exhibited in the Smithsonian. Because we also do commission work for interior designers, our crafts and weavings have been purchased for use in many decorator showcase houses.

"We have traditionally used wool, linen and cotton in our weaving. Our afghans are made from locally vegetable-dyed yarns; our stoles are available in mohair or acrylic; and our cotton tote bags in a variety of styles have become worldwide advertising for our shop."

Many of the weavers earn part or all of their family's income, while enjoying the freedom of working at home and at their own pace. "While working on a prototype for a new item," says Janet, "an Arrowcraft apprentice spent half a day plotting out the solution on paper only to discover that most of our weavers could solve it in their heads in a lot less time."

Their 16- by 16-inch fringed cotton napkins ($2.75) are available in white, natural and twelve colors, while their cotton/linen napkins are $4. Cotton place mats in plaid, stripe and plain texture range in price from $4 to $6.50; in cotton/linen, $5.75 to $8; and in linen, $6.50. Tablecloths in 41-inch squares are $40, while 41-inch-wide rectangles start at $1 an inch in length. Table runners may be custom-ordered in place-mat patterns 12 to 13 inches wide at 50¢ an inch; the 17-inch-wide Whig Rose pattern costs 70¢ an inch.

The shop represents the work of 150 craftspeople from the southern highlands in clay, blown and flat glass, wood, fiber, fabric, metal, paper and leather. Because it is a non-profit organization, it does not sell wholesale.

"However, many shops buy our weaving at our retail

and mark up their retail," says Janet. "We also act as agent for craftsmen, so that when customers see work they admire and want special sizes or colors, they can place commissions through us. All profits go to support Arrowmont School of Arts and Crafts, which is located near the shop."

Arrowcraft Shop
P.O. Box 567
Gatlinburg, TN 37738
(615) 436-4604
V   R   C   S   MO

WESTERN SILVER AND GOLD

"When I cowboyed in northeastern New Mexico, not many riders used silver except in bits and buckles, but in California and Nevada, quite a few working cowboys use a lot of silver and gold in their trappings," says S. Tracy White, who has made saddle and breast collar sets priced from $15,000 to $27,000.

Bridle *concha designed and crafted by S. Tracy White, engraved by Fran Harry*

Collar tips in 14-karat gold by S. Tracy White

"For the amount of work and hours involved," says Tracy, "I'd have made more money driving a UPS truck, but I learned a great deal. Working on those sets was the beginning of my three-dimensional pieces."

Before land was surveyed in the West, no one could hold title, so money was put into movables like cattle, horses, a saddle that cost 2 years' wages, custom-made boots and silver anywhere it would fit. Originally used at wear points on a saddle to protect the leather, silver was safer than currency, a way of carrying savings, and it looked good. Before long, cowboys were turning silver dollars and pesos into belt buckles, stirrups, spurs, hat bands, buttons, toe guards, collar tips, silver braid and scarf decorations. A "saddle bum" was often worth more from boots to hat than a farmer with 100 acres and a houseful of goods.

Saddle corner plate by S. Tracy White

299

"Even today," says Tracy, "a lot of cowboys may wear up to $3,000 worth of trappings, but they're good investments that last a long time." Collar tips, which fit over the points of a collar, may seem superfluous to outsiders, but "they keep shirts looking nice when the corners are frayed or the stays are lost. I use mine on cotton golf shirts when the dryer turns up the edges. Boot tips keep boots from getting scuffed. I also make a lot of *conchas*, buckle tips and keepers for chaps. Chaps are cowboy overalls that protect legs from brush and animals and also save wear on jeans. They come in different sizes: chinks are short, below the knee; shotguns are long, tight full-length leggings; batwings are loose and made of thicker leather. The buckle tip and keeper sets can get real fancy, especially for showing pleasure and for rodeos. The finely lined engraving is distinctly western. It's a more effective texture than chased silver because it hides scratches and takes more abuse than a plainer finish."

Before he started working on ranches, Tracy made gold and diamond jewelry, which was sold through Saks Fifth Avenue and Neiman-Marcus. Since then, he's gained a reputation for his elegantly designed and executed western jewelry and trappings, a wide range of gold and diamond jewelry, silver and gold designs and championship rings for the Snaffle Bit Futurity World Championship, National Finals Rodeo and National Cutting Horse Futurity. "Buckles had become too conventional," Tracy says. "They wanted something fancy, different. Prizes in some shows can be a quarter of a million dollars or more but they still like to win a ring."

A constant student, Tracy has as his goal "to make a piece as good as can be bought anywhere. However, the time it takes to learn, balanced against the number of people who appreciate it and are willing to pay what an object is worth does not always come out equal." Although few designers are secure enough to ask someone else to engrave their work, when Tracy found an engraver whose work was better than his, he suggested a collaborative relationship. "Just like I don't make the saddle my silver is on, he couldn't design and build pieces like I could. In my opinion Fran Harry was the finest western engraver ever. In the 2 years he worked with me before he passed away in 1984, I learned a great deal. Although his style has been used by almost everyone who is really good, he died relatively unknown without much to show for it after engraving for 45 years." Tracy is one of the few jewelers who gives equal billing to engravers of his work.

He does custom work of all kinds. A bridle *concha* designed by Tracy and engraved by Fran Harry sold for $2,600, and a futurity ring for $6,000, but he "can make anything anyone wants."

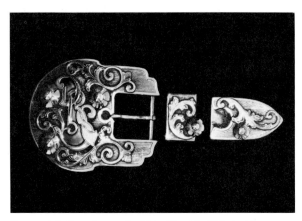

Engraved sterling silver and gold buckle set by Victoria Adams

S. Tracy White
208 Portola Avenue
Livermore, CA 94550
(415) 449-8577
R   MO

Other Makers

Victoria Adams, 2801 South Old Stage Road, Mt. Shasta, CA 96067; (916) 926-3291.

Perry Lukacovic, Western Silversmiths, 4661 West 130th Street, Hawthorne, CA 90250; (213) 675-6438 or 675-1744.

Victoria Trujillo Ramsey, P.O. Box 881, Taos, NM 87571; (505) 758-8553.

Larry B. Martinez, P.O. Box 892, Taos, NM 87571; (505) 758-4601.

Mark Drain, SE 3211 Kamilche Point Road, Shelton, WA 98584.

Robert Schaezlein, 1146 Clement Street, San Francisco, CA 94118; (415) 397-9744.

Whalebone Carving   *See* **Carving, Alaskan** *and* **Scrimshaw**

WHEAT-WEAVING AND STRAW HATS

Ancient peoples believed that a grain goddess lived in the fields. To insure a good crop the following year, they made good-luck "dollies" (a corruption of the word *idol*) from the last grain of the harvest. In spring, their seeds were the first sown, transferring fertility back to the fields. In the hope of insuring good harvests, almost every nationality immigrating to American farms did some form of wheat-weaving, often in the shape of hearts, angels and stars. With the invention of modern farm machinery, which crushed stalks in the reaping process, wheat-weaving was on the verge of becoming a lost art until it was revived in the 1950s. Since then, this folk craft has reappeared in almost every state.

In 1984, several years after graduating from West Virginia University with a degree in business finance, Beverly Robinson became a full-time wheat weaver. "I always liked braiding hair and working with my hands," she says, "so wheat-braiding was a natural. My basic materials are wheat and thread. After soaking the stalks in water until they become pliable, I plait, twist and tie them to form various traditional designs, like wheat plait, love knot, mini-Welsh fan, candy cane, flat ribbon trio, double hearts and friendship rings, then decorate them with ribbon bows or raffia ties. Small wheat decorations (5 inches) are $4 to $4.50, while medium-size are $9 to $11 depending on size and complexity of design.

"When I noticed the similarity of my wheat braids to those used in hats," says Beverly, "I researched traditional

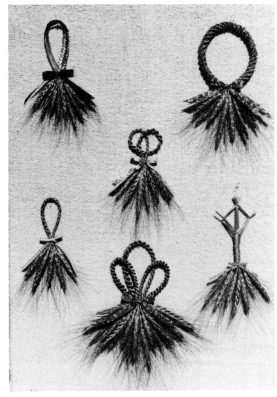

Assortment of wheat-weavings by Beverly Robinson

Regular-size hand-braided hats by Beverly Robinson

hats and have been making them ever since. Would it surprise you to know that the first straw hat in America was made by a 12-year-old named Betsy Metcalf of Providence in Rhode Island? People came from neighboring towns to see and order her bonnets, which cost half the price of imported hats. Betsy used oat straw, but hats can also be made from rush, cornshucks, palms or even grasses."

Beverly's hats are made from braided palm leaves, each handcrafted from a continuous hand-braided length. The braid is flattened, then shaped on a homemade hat block, hand-sewn and blocked. "Since each hat is formed individually by hand," says Beverly, "the sizes vary slightly. The adult size is 22 to 23 inches, which is an average ladies' hat size, but I can make them larger or smaller on request."

The hats are available in tan, the natural color of the palm, and decorated in palm trim braids in natural, brown or a combination of the two. "But they can be trimmed in any color or in a variety of materials," adds Beverly, "including ribbons, ribbon bows, silk flowers, dried flowers or material from a dress." Adult sizes with 2½- to 3-inch brims sell for $50 to $75, while miniatures for dolls (5½ to 6 inches wide) are $16 to $20. Beverly also fills special orders for hats to go with all periods of clothing. For ordering information and descriptions, send a self-addressed, stamped envelope.

Beverly Robinson
3332 Oakwood Avenue
Morgantown, WV 26505
(304) 599-3656
R W S MO

Other Makers

Barbara Mann, 500 Windsor Road, Asheville, NC 28804; (704) 254-4519, does traditional wheat-weavings from $1 to $50. For price list, send a self-addressed, stamped envelope.

June Kraft Garges, 1125 Sparrow Road, Audubon, PA 19403, makes rye straw hats.

WHIPS

"In the early days of the cattle industry in Florida and some parts of Georgia," Curly Dekle will tell you, "there were few towns. Our nearest neighbor was 2 miles away. There was no fence law, so the cattle just roamed the countryside. Each afternoon the men would go out into the woods and swamps to drive the cattle back to the house so they could be milked and penned for the night. To keep the cows on the move, the cowboys would crack those whips. You only had to hit a cow once or twice with the whip and she'd learn what cracking was all about. I had an 18-foot whip that could be heard a quarter of a mile away. If it was real still late in the fall, you could hear them a mile away. You'd hear those whips long before you saw the cows. Now it was the ladies' job to milk, and the cowpens or corral were almost a quarter of a mile from the house. When they heard the whips they knew it was time to get their pails and head for the corral."

Curly learned at an early age how to whip a horsefly off a cow's back without touching the hide and snap the head off a snake before it had a chance to strike. "That cracking noise comes from the tip breaking the sound barrier," he says. "Whips aren't meant to hurt. They just remind the cows to keep moving."

Close-up of the starting of a whip by Curly Dekle

As a teenager, he couldn't wait to join the rodeo circuit to wrestle steer and ride broncos, but one day while bucking stock in Indiana, he saw an act billed as an Australian bullwhip cracker.

"I got my whips out," he remembers, "and discovered I could do all kinds of things he couldn't. I was good and didn't know it." When an injury took Curly out of the bucking saddle, he turned to whip-cracking and went on to become National Bullwhip Champion. He can trip the trigger of a double-barreled shotgun and fire it, slice a straw held between his own lips or wrap his whip traveling at 700 mph around another person's body without hurting

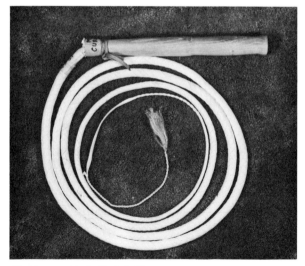
Florida cow whip by Curly Dekle

him. His secret (in addition to talent and agility) is in the whip, which he makes like no one else.

He starts his whips from the tip end instead of the handle as other whip makers do. "If you start at the handle end," he says, "you have to put a knot in the tip, which will affect your accuracy." In 50 years, Curly's never hit anyone or anything he didn't want to, proof that his system works.

Curly makes whips the way his father taught him as a boy, with a strip of deer hide less than an inch wide. After clamping it in a vise, he pulls with all his might. If the leather holds, he starts twisting. With a sharp pocketknife, he slashes the hide down the middle and starts braiding, making another split for a four-plait, on up to eight plaits. To make the "belly," the inner bulk that gives weight and shape, Curly adds latigo, heavier leather strips tanned by a different process. When he reaches the end, he attaches a lathe-turned hickory handle. "A drover's handle is braided on and fastened," explains Curly, "but Florida crackers like their handles separate and tied on with buckskin." He finishes leather whips by working in beef tallow with his hands.

Curly also makes whips out of nylon for use in stock pens and mud conditions. These cost the same as buckskin whips "because the thread comes in small strands and takes three times as long to make." Prices for whips are by the foot: from 6 to 10 feet is $5 a foot, up to 12 feet is $6 a foot and after that, $7 a foot.

J. P. "Curly" Dekle
P.O. Box 917
Macclenny, FL 32063
(904) 259-3877
R S MO

Wooden Molds   *See* **Molds for Baking** *and* **Iron, Cast**

Wycinanka   *See* **Papercuts, Polish**

Additional Resources State by State
Who Sell Traditional American Crafts

ALABAMA

Boggs Pottery
Prattville, AL 36067
Earthenware from local clay

Jerry Brown Pottery
Route 4
Hamilton, AL 35570
(205) 921-2597
Ninth generation potter making stoneware of local clay

Miller Pottery
Box 107
Brent, AL 35034
124-year-old family operation: stoneware from local clay

Tannehill Historical State Park Gift Shop
Route 1, Box 124
McCalla, AL 35111
(205) 477-6571
Baskets, pottery, wood and metal objects

ALASKA

Ahtna Lodge
P.O. Box 88
Glennallen, AK 99588
(907) 822-3288
Indian and Eskimo baskets, carvings, beadwork

Alaska Native Arts and Crafts Association, Inc.
425 D Street
Anchorage, AK 99501
(907) 274-2932
Eskimo and Aleut baskets, carvings, beadwork, skinsewing

Alaska Native Arts and Crafts Center of Fairbanks
1603 College Road
Fairbanks, AK 99701
(907) 452-8164 or 452-8119
Indian, Eskimo and Aleut baskets, carvings, beadwork, parkas, masks

Alaska Native Hospital Craft Shop
Box 7-741
Anchorage, AK 99510
(907) 279-6661, ext. 150
Indian, Eskimo and Aleut baskets, carvings, beadwork, skinsewing

Alaskan Ivory Exchange
700 West 4th Avenue
Anchorage, AK 99501
(907) 272-2215
Ivory, scrimshaw; Indian, Eskimo and Aleut baskets, carvings and beadwork

Alaska State Museum Gift Shop
Pouch FM
Juneau, AK 99811
(907) 456-2904 or 456-2901
Indian, Eskimo and Aleut baskets, carvings, beadwork

Alyeska Resort Gift Shop
P.O. Box 249
Girdwood, AK 99587
(907) 783-2711
Indian and Eskimo baskets, carvings

Anchorage Museum Shop
Anchorage Historical and Fine Arts Museum
121 West 7th Avenue
Anchorage, AK 99501
(907) 274-4326

ADDITIONAL RESOURCES STATE BY STATE

Anica Inc.
P.O. Box 565
Bethel, AK 99559
(907) 543-2108
Eskimo baskets, carvings

A.R.A. Services Airport Gift Shop
P.O. Box 60630
Fairbanks, AK 99706
(907) 474-9298
Eskimo carvings, dolls, mukluks, baleen, jewelry

Arctic Trading Post
P.O. Box 262
Nome, AK 99762
(907) 443-2686
Baskets, carvings, beadwork, skinsewing

Arctic Traveler's Gift Shop
201 Cushman Street
Fairbanks, AK 99701
(907) 456-7080
Yupik baskets, carvings, beadwork, dance fans, baleen boats, skinsewing of Indian Eskimo and Aleut cultures

Baranof Indian Eskimo Art, Inc.
Box 124
Sitka, AK 99835
(907) 747-6556
Indian, Eskimo and Aleut baskets, carvings, beadwork

Baranof Museum Store
The Baranof Museum
Box 61
Kodiak, AK 99615
(907) 486-5920
Alaskan native baskets, ivory carvings

Berry Sea Originals Gift Shops
2023 Arlington Drive
Anchorage, AK 99503
(907) 278-4406
Indian, Eskimo and Aleut baskets, carvings, dolls, etched baleen, scrimshaw ivory and jewelry

The Craft Market
401 5th Avenue
Fairbanks, AK 99701
(907) 452-5495
Indian and Eskimo objects

Eskimo Bow Drill Gallery
P.O. Box 812
Cooper Landing, AK 99572
(907) 595-1221
Ivory carvings, scrimshaw

The Gathering, A Collector's Gallery
28 Creek Street
Ketchikan, AK 99901
(907) 225-5987

N. G. Hanson Trading Company
Box 47
Kotzebue, AK 99752
(907) 442-3101
Eskimo baskets, carvings, beadwork

Sheldon Jackson Museum Shop
104 College Drive
Sitka, AK 99835
(907) 747-8615
Indian, Eskimo and Aleut baskets, carvings, beadwork, skinsewing

Mt. Juneau Trading Post, Inc.
151 South Franklin Street
Juneau, AK 99801
(907) 586-3426
Indian, Eskimo and Aleut objects

St. Lawrence Island Original Ivory Cooperative Ltd.
P.O. Box 111
Gambell, AK 99642
(907) 985-5826
Eskimo carvings, baleen boats

Savoonga Native Store
P.O. Box 100
Savoonga, AK 99769
(907) 984-6211
Eskimo baskets, carvings, beadwork

Scanlon Gallery
Box 8095
Ketchikan, AK 99901
(907) 225-4260
Baskets, carvings

Tauqsigniguik
P.O. Box 363
Barrow, AK 99723
(907) 852-3663
Ivory, baleen, skinsewing

Thiyaat Native Arts
Fairbanks Native Association
310½ First Avenue
Fairbanks, AK 99701
(907) 452-1648
Grass and birchbark baskets, carvings, dolls, masks, mukluks, ulus, beadwork

The Village Store and Gallery
P.O. Box 111
Eagle, AK 99738
Indian baskets, carvings, beadwork

ARIZONA

Colorado River Indian Tribes Library/Museum
Route 1, Box 23-B
Parker, AZ 85344
(602) 669-9211, ext. 213
Beadwork, Navajo rugs, kachina dolls, pottery, bows and arrows, cradleboards

Dawa's Hopi Arts and Crafts
P.O. Box 127
Second Mesa, AZ 86043
(602) 734-2430
Hopi overlay silver jewelry

Fine Apache Arts
P.O. Box 57
San Carlos, AZ 85550
(602) 465-2235
Apache camp dresses, crown dancer masks, peridot jewelry, tus jars, cradleboards, devil dancer dolls, beadwork

Garland's Navajo Rugs
Highway 179, P.O. Box 851
Sedona, AZ 86336
(602) 282-4070
Navajo rugs and sand paintings, baskets; Hopi kachina dolls

Gila River Arts and Crafts Center
Box 457
Sacaton, AZ 85247
(602) 562-3411
Southwest Indian jewelry, pottery, rugs, kachina dolls, beadwork, baskets

Hopi Arts and Crafts/Silvercraft Cooperative Guild
P.O. Box 37
Second Mesa, AZ 86043
(602) 734-2463
Jewelry, pottery, baskets, dolls, textiles

Hubbell Trading Post
P.O. Box 150
Ganado, AZ 86505
(602) 755-3475
Hopi kachinas, Navajo weavings

National Native American Cooperative
P.O. Box 5000
San Carlos, AZ 85550-0301
(in lobby of Caravan Inn Motel, 3333 E. Van Buren, Phoenix, AZ)
(602) 275-4740
Jewelry, baskets, wood and stone carvings, beadwork, rugs, pottery

Navajo Arts and Crafts Enterprise
Postal Drawer A
Window Rock, AZ 86515
(Junction 264 & Route 12 at Window Rock near AZ/NM state line)
(602) 871-4090
Rugs, jewelry, sand paintings, wood carvings, dolls, pottery

ARKANSAS

Arkansas Craft Gallery
100 Markham Street
Excelsior Hotel Lobby
Little Rock, AR 72201
(501) 371-0841

Arkansas Craftworks
P.O. Box 282
33 Spring Street
Eureka Springs, AR 72632
(501) 253-7072

Country Craftworks
Box 87H
Eureka Springs, AR 72632
(501) 253-9635

Guild Crafts
P.O. Box 227
600 Central Avenue
Hot Springs, AR 71901
(501) 321-1640

Seven Springs Craft Shop
P.O. Box 47
625 South 7th Street
Heber Springs, AR 72543
(501) 362-6222

Sycamore Creek Craft Shop
P.O. Box 800
Highways 5, 9 & 14 North
Mountain View, AR 72560
(501) 269-3896

ADDITIONAL RESOURCES STATE BY STATE

CALIFORNIA

American Indian Store
2778 Fletcher Parkway
El Cajon, CA 92020
(619) 461-2276
Sioux star quilts, ribbon shirts, quillwork, dance bustles, war bonnets, hair roaches, Pueblo pottery, jewelry

Appalachia
340 Village Lane
Los Gatos, CA 95030
(408) 354-6700
Crafts of Southern Appalachia

George N. Blake
P.O. Box 1304
Hoopa, CA 95546
(off Highway 96, Central Hoopa)
(916) 625-4619
Sinew-backed yew bows, elk antler carvings, canoes, pottery

Chief George Pierre Trading Post
P.O. Box 3202
Torrance, CA 90510
(620 The Village, Redondo Beach)
(213) 372-1048
Beadwork, jewelry, rugs, kachina dolls

De Luna Jewelers
521 Second Street
Davis, CA 95616
(916) 753-3351
Pottery, Navajo rugs, jewelry baskets, carvings, beadwork

The Indian Shop
1341 East Valley Parkway
Escondido, CA 92027
(619) 746-5522
Baskets; pottery; drums; pipes; dolls; Navajo rugs; Zuni, Hopi and Navajo silverwork

Intertribal Trading Post
523 East 14th Street
Oakland, CA 94606
(415) 452-1235
Beadwork, silver jewelry, Navajo rugs, moccasins

Pacific Western Traders
P.O. Box 95, 305 Wool Street
Folsom, CA 95630
(916) 985-3851
Baskets; hairpins; dance plumes; headdresses; musical instruments; pipes; dolls from Popo, Western Mono, Yurok, Wintun and Paiute tribes

Sacramento Indian Center Arts & Crafts Store
2612 K Street
Sacramento, CA 95816
(916) 442-0593
Beadwork, leatherwork, baskets, jewelry, dance capes, hair ties

Shaker Shops West
Five Inverness Way, South
Inverness, CA 94937
(415) 669-7256
Shaker furniture, boxes, rugs, tinware

CONNECTICUT

Appalachian House
Appalachia Volunteers, Inc.
1010 Post Road
Darien, CT 06820
(203) 655-7885
Quilts, weavings, wood carvings, pottery

Connecticut River Artisans Cooperative
Goodspeed Landing
(P.O. Box 155)
East Haddam, CT 06423
(203) 873-1661
Baskets, toys, quilts, weathervanes, floorcloths, weaving

Mystic Seaport Museum
Mystic, CT 06355
(203) 572-0711
Carving, boats, ironwork

Woodstock Pottery
Bradford Corner Road
Woodstock Valley, CT 06282
New England redware

DELAWARE

Winterthur Museum and Gardens
Winterthur, DE 19735
(302) 656-8591
Faithful reproductions of objects from their collections

DISTRICT OF COLUMBIA

American Indian Gallery
224 Missouri Avenue NW
Washington, DC 20011
(202) 723-3239
Cherokee belts, Navajo rugs, Nez Percé baskets, Ft. Peck quilts, baskets, pottery

Appalachian Spring
1655 Wisconsin Avenue NW
Washington, DC 20007
(202) 337-5780
Stoneware pottery, rugs, quilts, toys

Indian Craft Shop
Room 1023
U.S. Department of the Interior
Washington, DC 20240
(On C & E streets between 18th and 19th)
(202) 343-4056
Baskets, pottery, Navajo rugs, dolls, sand paintings, beadwork, carvings, Alaskan native crafts

National Trust for Historic Preservation Shop
1610 H Street NW (behind Decatur House)
Washington, DC 20006
(202) 842-1856

The Renwick Gallery Museum Shop
17th Street & Pennsylvania Avenue NW
Washington, DC 20006
(202) 357-1445
Wide range of the best traditional American crafts

FLORIDA

Artisan's Guild
806 University Avenue
Gainesville, FL 32601
(904) 378-1383

The Clean Sweep
600 S.W. 69 Way
Hollywood, FL 33023
(305) 963-3095
Brooms

Grassroots Art Guild
P.O. Box 175
Monticello, FL 32344
(904) 997-5639

Jolima Indian Crafts
1403 North 57th Avenue
Pensacola, FL 32506
(904) 455-0874
Pine straw baskets, breast plates, beadwork, wood and metal tomahawks

Miccosukee Gift Shop and Cultural Center
P.O. Box 440021
Tamiami Station
Miami, FL 33144
(U.S. 41, 38 mi. west of Miami)
Miccosukee patchwork dolls, skirts, shirts; carvings, baskets, beadwork

Seminole Arts and Crafts Center
6073 Sterling Road
Hollywood, FL 33024
(305) 583-3590
Palmetto dolls, baskets, beadwork, patchwork, wood carvings

Seminole Cultural Center
5221 Orient Road
Tampa, FL 33610
(813) 623-3549
Seminole patchwork, dolls, beadwork, moccasins, pouches, carvings

Suwannee River Crafts Guild
Route 1, Box 140
White Springs, FL 32096
Traditional crafts of rural north Florida

Ukrainian Cultural Center
2850 Taylor Street
Hollywood, FL 33020
(305) 925-8838
Decorated eggs, embroidery

GEORGIA

Anniston Museum Gift Shop
Anniston Museum of Natural History
4301 McClellan Boulevard
P.O. Box 1587
Anniston, GA 36202

Appalachian Gallery
Box 257
Young Harris, GA 30582
(404) 379-3807
Weaving, pottery, jewelry, stained glass

The Apple Basket
717 East Second Avenue
Rome, GA 30161
(404) 234-5411
Needlework, woodworking, pottery, baskets, quilts

Autumn Leaves
3-B Public Square
Dahlonega, GA 30533
(404) 864-7305
Quilts, woodcarvings, dolls, baskets

Clayton House Craft Shop
Stone Mountain Memorial Association
Box 778
Stone Mountain, GA 30086
Quilts, baskets, brooms, dolls, toys

The Co-op Craft Store
The Georgia Mountain Arts Products Association, Inc.
Box 67
Tallulah Falls, GA 30573
(404) 734-6810
Pottery, dolls, toys, brooms, quilts, rugs

The Co-op Craft Store
The Georgia Mountain Arts Products Association, Inc.
Clarkesville, GA 30523
(404) 754-2244

Craven's Pottery, Inc.
Route 1
Gillsville, GA 30543
Earthenware from local clay

Fort Mountain Village Shops
2007 Cherokee Trail
Chatsworth, GA 30705
(404) 695-5067
Several craft shops on U.S. 76 S.R. 52

Georgia Craft Galleries, Inc.
311 Green Street South
P.O. Box 1061
Gainesville, GA 30503
(404) 534-4272

Hewell's Pottery
Route 1
Gillsville, GA 30543
Earthenware from local clay

North Georgia Handcrafts, Inc.
110 North 3rd Avenue
Chatsworth, GA 30705
(404) 695-7245
Handmade crafts of the region

Okefenokee Heritage Center Gift Shop
Route 5, Box 406-A
North Augusta Avenue
Waycross, GA 31501
(912) 285-4260
Quality handmade crafts

Rabun Gap Crafts
Rabun Gap, GA 30568
(404) 746-5343
Pottery, weaving, woodcarving

Soquee River Pottery
P.O. Box 568
Cornelia, GA 30531
Wood-fired stoneware

Stone Mountain Arts & Crafts Center
943 South Main Street
Stone Mountain, GA 30083
(404) 469-0328
13 shops featuring pottery, weaving, candles, etc.

Tekakwitha Indian Arts & Crafts Shop
P.O. Box 338
Helen, GA 30545
(404) 878-2938
Baskets, masks, carvings, dolls, beadwork

Toy Museum of Atlanta Gift Shop
2800 Peachtree Road NW
Atlanta, GA 30305
(404) 266-8697
Dolls, toys for children

Unicoi State Park Craft Shop
P.O. Box 256
Helen, GA 30545
(404) 878-2201
Split oak baskets, gourd crafts, quilts, pottery, dolls

Wilson's Pottery
Cornelia Highway
Lula, GA 30554
Earthenware pottery

ILLINOIS

Cedarhurst Art Center
Mitchell Museum
26th and Old Union Road
Mount Vernon, IL 62864
(618) 244-6130
Pottery, weavings, stained glass, baskets

Country Cousin
8 West First Street
Hinsdale, IL 60521
(312) 655-1567
Rag rugs, quilts, tin lighting fixtures

The Country Store
28 James Street
Geneva, IL 60134
(312) 232-0335
Handmade toys, gameboards, coverlets

Rustic Revival
672 North Dearborn
Chicago, IL 60610
(312) 337-5932
Twig furniture, folk art

INDIANA

Blue Duck Country Shop
1280 North 200 E
Lebanon, IN 46052
(317) 482-5471

Conner Prairie Pioneer Settlement
13400 Allisonville Road
Noblesville, IN 40606

Haarer's Quaint Shop
Box 52
Shipshewana, IN 46565
(219) 768-4787

Handmade in the U.S.A.
P.O. Box 31
Charlestown, IN 47111
Cornhusk dolls, rag dolls, pewter, bandboxes, decorated eggs

Roadside Gallery
208 West Main
Centerville, IN 47330
(317) 855-3398
Southern folk pottery, ceramics, carvings, whirligigs

IOWA

Amana General Store
South Amana, IA 52334
(319) 622-3513
Amana pottery made and sold on premises

Broom and Basket Shop
Amana, IA 52203
(319) 622-3315
Amana brooms and West Amana baskets

Candlestick
Colony Candle Works
Main Street
Amana, IA 52203
(319) 622-3879
Handmade candles

Moccasin Tracks Trading Post
105 South Broadway
Toledo, IA 52342
(515) 484-5749
Ribbonwork shirts and skirts; Mesquakie and Sioux dolls; Mesquakie old-style moccasins; beadwork, dance sets, pipes, buckskin dresses

Norwegian-American Museum Shop
Decorah, IA 52101
(319) 382-9681
Crafts by Norwegian-American artisans

Old Fashioned General Store and Gift Shop
High Amana, IA 52203
(319) 622-3797
Handcrafts made in the Amanas

The Original Amana Furniture and Clock Shop
Amana, IA 52203
(319) 622-3291
Furniture made by the old guild of Amana cabinetmakers

Vanberia
217 West Water
Decorah, IA 52101
Scandinavian-American crafts

West Amana Store
West Amana, IA 52357
(319) 622-3104
Handmade quilts and folk art by local artisans

KANSAS

The Arrow Smiths
Route 1, Box 224
Wakarusa, KS 66546
(913) 761-2200
Arrowheads, custom silver and crafts from various tribes

Indian Museum Gift Shop
Mid-America All-Indian Center
650 North Seneca
Wichita, KS 67203
(316) 262-5221
Jewelry, rugs, pottery, kachina dolls, beadwork, baskets, Navajo dolls

Kansas Museum of History Shop
6425 Southwest 6th
Topeka, KS 66615
(913) 272-8681
Work of Kansas folk artists

KENTUCKY

Appalachian Arts and Crafts
Main at Center Street
Berea, KY 40403
(606) 986-1239
Stoneware pottery, woven yardage, rugs, baskets, quilts

Berea College Crafts
CPO 2347
Berea, KY 40404
(606) 986-9341, ext. 473, 512, or (800) 824-4049
Fine furniture reproductions, pottery, toys, brooms, weavings

Campus Crafts, Inc.
Annville, KY 40402
(606) 364-5457
One-of-a-kind sturdily woven rugs, placemats

Churchill Weavers
P.O. Box 30
Lorraine Court
Berea, KY 40404
(606) 986-3126
Baby blankets, throws, ties, shawls, scarves

David Appalachian Crafts
David, KY 41616
(606) 886-2377
Quilts, pillows, white oak split baskets

Kentucky Hills Industries
Pine Knot, KY 42635
(606) 354-2813
Cherry and walnut furniture, wooden kitchen items, hand-loomed rugs and placemats, white oak split baskets, cornshuck dolls and baskets

The Saltbox
859 High Street
Lexington, KY 40502
Pierced tin lanterns; other lighting fixtures in copper, brass and pewter; hand-forged hardware; frakturs; *candles; baskets; redware pottery*

MAINE

Abacus Handcrafter's Gallery
8 McKown Street
Boothbay Harbor, ME 04538
(207) 633-2166
Fine American crafts, museum-quality jewelry

Robert Abbe Museum of Stone Age Antiquities
Box 286
Bar Harbor, ME 04609
(207) 288-3519
Penobscot Indian jewelry; quill and clam shell jewelry; birchbark, sweetgrass, Micmac, and split ash baskets of all sizes

Amicus Cooperative Gallery
P.O. Box 1484
Kennebunkport, ME 04046
(Route 35 at the light)
Baskets, pottery, weaving, sweaters, stained glass

The Apple Core
Routes 2 and 4
Wilton, ME 04294
(207) 645-4461
Handcrafted toys, moccasins, buckets, baskets, candles

Aroostook Micmac Council's Basket Bank
P.O. Box 930
Presque Isle, ME 04769
(8 Church Street)
(207) 764-1972
Wood splint baskets: potato, pack, fishing, cradle, sewing, fancy

Basket Barn
Route 27 and River Road
Boothbay, ME 04537
(207) 633-5532
Baskets, pottery, quilts, ironware

Beaumont Pottery
293 Beech Ridge Road
York, ME 03909
(207) 363-5878
Salt-glazed stoneware

Blue Hill Yarn Shop
Blue Hill, ME 04614

Edgecomb Potters Gallery
Route 27
Edgecomb, ME 04556
(207) 882-6802
High-quality porcelain

Especially Maine
U.S. Route 1
Kennebunkport, ME 04046
Toys, decoys, Maine stoneware, candles

The Good Earth
Ocean Avenue
Kennebunkport, ME 04046
(207) 967-4635
Decorative stoneware, pottery for cooking and serving

Hands On
112 Main Street
Ellsworth, ME 04605
(207) 667-7089
Pottery, metal, wood, textiles

Island Artisans
Bar Harbor, ME 04609
(207) 288-4214
Stoneware, porcelain, jewelry, hand-weaving

Maine Potters' Market
9 Moulton Street
Old Port
Portland, ME 04101
Cooperative gallery featuring earthenware, stoneware, porcelain

No Necessities
Route 1
East Belfast, ME 04915
(207) 338-5219
Maine-made patchwork, quilts, braided rugs, woodwork

North Country Textiles
South Penobscot, ME 04476
(207) 326-4131
Hand-woven and knitted clothing, linens, blankets

Nutmeg Pottery
Nutmeg Road
Swanville, ME
(207) 338-5416
Functional stoneware, porcelain pottery

Options in Wood
Herrick Road
Brooksville, ME 04617
(207) 326-4124
Adirondak furniture, toys

Chief Poolaw Teepee Trading Post
1 Center Street
Indian Island
Old Town, ME 04468
Penobscot sweetgrass baskets, moccasins, beadwork, wood carvings, dolls, war clubs, Passamaquoddy baskets

Rackliffe Pottery, Inc.
Blue Hill, ME 04614
(207) 374-2297
Ovenproof redware

Rowantrees Pottery
Blue Hill, ME 04614
Functional earthenware

Song of the Sea
47 West Street
Bar Harbor, ME 04609
(207) 288-5653
Dulcimers, lyres, harps, whistles

Times 10 Cooperative Gallery
420 Fore Street
Old Port Area
Portland, ME 04101
(207) 761-1553
Natural Maine wool yarn, sweaters hand-loomed in Maine

Tomah Baskets
Box 1006
Houlton, ME 04730
(207) 532-6054
Split ash and Micmac baskets

Unique 1
2 Bayview, Camden, ME 04843
and
4 Cottage, Bar Harbor, ME 04609
Natural Maine wool yarn, Maine wool sweaters

Wabanaki Arts
P.O. Box 453
Old Town, ME 04468
(207) 827-3447
Penobscot carved canes, war clubs, totem poles, stone tomahawks, baskets, beadwork, quillwork

Wildlife Gallery
Bayview Street
Camden, ME 04843
(207) 236-9568
Decoys, nautical carvings

Yankee Artisan
178 Front Street
Bath, ME 04530
(207) 443-6215
Baskets, candles, dolls, knitwear, pottery, quilts, braided rugs

MARYLAND

Americana Marketplace
5000 Berwyn Road
College Park, MD 20740
(301) 474-2720
Folk art

Antique Cupboard
812 West Main Street
Emmitsburg, MD 21727
(301) 447-6558
Painted grain furniture, dower chests, fireboards

Appalachiana, Inc.
10400 Old Georgetown Road
Bethesda, MD 20014
(301) 530-6770
Stoneware pottery, rugs, baskets, quilts, glass

Smokehouse Country Crafts
8537 Hollow Road
Middletown, MD 21769
(301) 371-7466
Tallow candles, baskets

Tomlinson Craft Collection
519 North Charles Street
Baltimore, MD 21201
(301) 539-6585

MASSACHUSETTS

A.J.P. Coppersmith
34 Broadway
Wakefield, MA 01880
(617) 245-1223
Reproductions of early lighting fixtures

Bluebird Indian Crafts
32 Varney Street
Lowell, MA 01854
(617) 937-1818
Porcupine quillwork, bustles, beadwork, dance accessories

Brother Jonathan
Route 20, Box 415
Sturbridge, MA 01566
(617) 347-7061
Quilts, tin, furniture

Cedar Swamp Stoneware Company
Box 701
30 Perseverance Way
Hyannis, MA 04601
(617) 771-6633
Stoneware in sponge or decorated with cobalt blue, redware

The Gifted Hand
32 Church Street
Wellesley, MA 02181

Historic Deerfield, Inc., Museum Store
Deerfield, MA 01342
(413) 774-5581
Fine reproductions of early crafts

Leverett Artists and Craftsmen
Leverett Center
Leverett, MA 01054
(413) 549-6871

Little Flower Trading Company
P.O. Box 294
Gay Head, MA 02535
(617) 645-9055
Beaded, feathered and quilled jewelry; sweetgrass, grapevine and honeysuckle baskets; Gay Head pottery; Wampum beads

Old Sturbridge Village
Museum Gift Shop
Sturbridge, MA 01566
(617) 347-3362
Tinware, ironware, candles, theorems, pottery, baskets, brooms

Progress Pottery
R.F.D. 1, H. Vinton Road
Sturbridge, MA 01566

Shaker Workshops
P.O. Box 1028
Concord, MA 01742
(617) 646-8985
Shaker furniture, boxes, carriers, baskets

Three Feathers
190 Wood Street
Middleboro, MA 02346
(617) 947-6453
Finger-woven bags, moccasins, beadwork, baskets, quillwork

Williamsburg Blacksmiths, Inc.
Goshen Road
Williamsburg, MA 01096
(413) 268-7341
Hand-forged iron hardware, latches, sconces

MICHIGAN

American Country House
1063 South State
Davison, MI 48424
(313) 653-0140

Henry Ford Museum and Greenfield Village
Museum Store
P.O. Box 1970
Dearborn, MI 48121
(313) 271-1620, ext. 308

Indian Earth Arts & Crafts Store
124 West First Street
Flint, MI 48502
(313) 239-6621
Pottery, quillwork, black ash baskets, quilts, beadwork, moccasins

Indian Hills Trading Company
1681 Harbor Road
Petoskey, MI 49770
(616) 347-3789
Porcupine quill boxes, traditional drums, beadwork, baskets, pipes

Moon Bear Pottery
257 Elizabeth Street
Rockford, MI 49341
(616) 866-2519
Pottery, clay and bronze

North American Indian Association of Detroit, Inc.
360 John Road
Detroit, MI 48226
(313) 963-1710
Beadwork, porcupine quillwork, ribbon shirts

Porcupine Patch
1737 West Sheridan Road
Petosky, MI 49770
Porcupine quill boxes, beadwork, wood carvings, leatherwork

Sweetgrass Arts & Crafts
206 Greenough Street
Sault Sainte Marie, MI 49783
(906) 635-6050
Quill and birchbark boxes, black ash baskets, beadwork, sweetgrass pots, dance shawls, quilts, wood carvings

MINNESOTA

Chippewa Indian Craft and Gift Shop
Red Lake Indian Reservation
Goodridge, MN 56725
(218) 378-4210 or 378-4322
Carved peace-pipe bowls with decorated stems, effigies, drums, cradleboards

Lady Slipper Designs
Highway 71 South
Bemidji, MN 56601
(218) 751-0763
Birchbark, willow and black ash baskets; beaded charms; moccasins

The Mille Lacs Indian Trading Post
Mille Lacs Indian Museum
P.O. Box 192, Star Route
Onamia, MN 56359
(612) 532-3632

Pipestone Indian Shrine Association
Pipestone National Monument
Box 727
Pipestone, MN 56164
(507) 825-5463
Pipestone carvings, pipes, war clubs, arrowheads, effigies; beaded pipe bags

Pipestone Lady Arts and Crafts Shop
Box 107
Columbia Avenue
Prior Lake, MN 55372
(612) 445-1408
Peace pipes, jewelry, breastplates, hair ties, chokers

Woodland Indian Crafts
1530 East Franklin Avenue
Minneapolis, MN 55404
(612) 874-7766
Ribbon shirts and blouses, beadwork, moccasins, bone chokers, baskets, quilts, war clubs, shawls

MISSISSIPPI

Mississippi Crafts Center on the Natchez Trace Parkway
P.O. Box 69
Ridgeland, MS 39157
(601) 856-7546
Weaving, quilting, pottery, blown and leaded glass, wood carving, toys, games and furniture, jewelry, basketry

315

ADDITIONAL RESOURCES STATE BY STATE

MISSOURI

Engler Woodcarvers
1401 West Highway 76
Branson, MO 65616
(417) 334-4595
Wooden indians up to 7 feet tall, carousel horses, spirit faces.
The work of over seventy wood-carvers

Miniature Museum of Kansas City Foundation
Museum Shop
5235 Oak
Kansas City, MO 64110
(816) 333-2055
Miniatures

O'Dell House
466 South O'Dell
Marshall, MO 65340
(816) 886-3663
Whirligigs, quiltwork, crochet, silhouettes

Ozark Mountain Collectables
Route 2, Box 126-C
Nixa, MO 65714
(417) 725-3134
Weathervanes, folk art, whirligigs

MONTANA

Blackfeet Crafts Association
P.O. Box 51
Browning, MT 59417
(Sales shop on U.S. 89 in St. Mary)
Beadwork, dolls, moccasins

Blackfeet Trading Post
P.O. Box 626 (U.S. 2)
Browning, MT 59417
(406) 338-2050
Ribbon shirts, dance costumes, moccasins, beadwork, baskets,
pottery, shawls

Buffalo Chips Trading Post
Billings, MT 59002

Coup Marks
Box 532
Ronan, MT 59864
(406) 246-3216 or 644-2267
Ribbon shirts, moccasins, beadwork, dolls, shawls, drums, stick
game sets, wing dresses, cradleboards

Flathead Indian Museum Trading Post
P.O. Box 464 (Highway 93)
St. Ignatius, MT 59865
(406) 745-2951
Moccasins, beadwork, dance costumes

Northern Cheyenne Arts and Crafts Association
Lame Deer, MT 59043
Buckskin and beadwork accessories, moccasins, jewelry

Northern Plains Indian Crafts Association
P.O. Box E
Browning, MT 59417
Buckskin vests, gloves and moccasins; beadwork; dolls; native-
tanned hides

NEVADA

Earth Window
Nevada Urban Indians, Inc.
917 East 6th Street
Reno, NV 89512
(702) 329-2573 or 786-5999
Beadwork, buckskin and leather items, jewelry

Fortunate Eagle's Round House Gallery
7133 Stillwater Road
Fallon, NV 89406
(702) 423-2220
Ceremonial pipes, silverwork, beadwork, wood carvings

Pueblo Grand de Nevada
Lost City Museum of Archeology
P.O. Box 807
Overton, NV 89040
Major outlet for Moapa Indian Reservation jewelry, rugs, dolls,
clothing

Stewart Indian Museum Trading Post
5366 Snyder Avenue
Carson City, NV 89701
(702) 882-1808
Baskets, silver and turquoise jewelry, beadwork, pottery,
kachinas

The Tepee
MGM Grand Hotel Shopping Arcade
Suite 8, 3645 Las Vegas Boulevard, South
Las Vegas, NV 89109
(702) 735-5333
Navajo, Zuni and Hopi jewelry, pottery, baskets, rugs, beadwork

NEW HAMPSHIRE

Clinton Village Glassworks/Block Island Glass
Route 21 and Old Hancock Road
Antrim, NH 03440
(603) 588-2736
Hand-blown glass goblets, candlesticks and bottles; cast glass

Concord Arts & Crafts*
36 North Main Street
Concord, NH 03301
(603) 228-8171

Cooper Shop
Peacham Road
Center Barnstead, NH 03225
(603) 776-7191
Painted grain furniture, boxes, frames

Country Artisans Crafts Gallery
15 Court Street
Keene, NH 03431
(603) 352-6980
Pottery, weaving, quilts, jewelry, toys

Exeter Craft Center*
61 Water Street
Exeter, NH 03833
(603) 778-8282

Franconia League of N.H. Craftsmen*
Glaessel Building, Box 428
Franconia, NH 03580
(603) 823-9521

Hanover League of N.H. Craftsmen*
13 Lebanon Street
Hanover, NH 03755

New Hampshire Farm Museum, Inc.
Country Store
P.O. Box 644, Route 16, Plummber's Ridge
Milton, NH 03851
(603) 652-7840
Hand-woven rugs; painted and stenciled items; hand-knit sweaters, mittens and hats; wood carvings

North Conway League of N.H. Craftsmen*
Box 751, Main Street
North Conway, NH 03860
(603) 356-2441

* League of New Hampshire Craftsmen member retail shop.

Olde Nutfield
80 Candi Road
Chester, NH 03036
(603) 887-3879
Colonial crafts, especially theorems made from old patterns

Sandwich Home Industries*
Center Sandwich, NH 03227
(603) 284-6831

Sharon Arts Center*
RFD 2, Box 361, Route 123
Sharon, NH 03458
(603) 924-7556

The Stocking Stuffer
4488 Highland Avenue
Milton Mills, NH 03887
(603) 652-4488
Specializes in decorative painting

Strawbery Banke
Box 300
Portsmouth, NH 03801
Faithful reproductions of early New England crafts

Valley Artisans
Goboro Road
Epsom, NH 03234
(603) 736-8200
Baskets, folk art, weaving, glass, pottery, leather, dolls

NEW JERSEY

The Bramble Patch
13 North Main Street
Mullica Hill, NJ 08062
(609) 478-6242
Quilts, rag rugs, pottery, weaving

Lone Bear Indian Craft Company
300 Main Street, #3F
Orange, NJ 07050
Woodland Indian craftwork, beading, war bonnets, headdresses

Navajo Textiles and Arts
1184 Main Street, #73
River Edge, NJ 07661
(201) 695-9171
Navajo rugs, wedding baskets, pottery, jewelry

Peters Valley
Layton, NJ 07851
(201) 948-5200
Craft community located in Delaware Water Gap National Park, whose shops feature many traditional crafts

NEW MEXICO

Acoma Pottery
P.O. Box 22
San Fidel, NM 87049
(505) 552-9411
Acoma pottery

Jeffrey Adams, Inc.
555 Canyon Road
Santa Fe, NM 87501
New Mexico furniture, spurs, branding irons

Aguilar Indian Arts
Route 5, Box 318C
Santa Fe, NM 87501
Black and red pottery, nativity sets, Black Buffalo figurines

Apache Mesa Gallery & Gifts
P.O. Box 233
Jicarilla Inn, Highways 64 & 44
Dulce, NM 87528
(505) 759-3663
Jicarilla woven sumac and willow baskets, Jicarilla micaceous pottery, beadwork, ribbon shirts; Pueblo pottery; Navajo rugs

Carl's Indian Trading Post/White Buckskin Gallery
Box 813
East Kit Carson Road & Dragoon Lane
Taos, NM 87571
(505) 758-2378
Navajo rugs, sand paintings, Papago baskets, Pueblo pottery, Taos Pueblo drums, Zuni and Navajo fetishes, southwestern Indian silver and turquoise jewelry

Centinela Traditional Arts
Box 5, Centinela Ranch
Chamayo, NM 87522
(505) 351-2180
Rio Grande weaving, wood carving, Spanish colonial furniture

Christof's
106 West San Francisco
Santa Fe, NM 87501
(505) 988-9881
Navajo rugs, weavings, carvings

Indian Pueblo Cultural Center, Inc.
2401 12th Street NW
Albuquerque, NM 87102
(505) 843-7270
Pueblo pottery, basketry, wood carvings, textiles, drums, stone carvings, silver and turquoise jewelry, Navajo rugs, sand paintings

Institute of American Indian Arts Shop
1369 Cerrilus Road
Santa Fe, NM 87501
(505) 988-6281

Jicarilla Arts and Crafts Shop/Museum
P.O. Box 507
Dulce, NM 87428
(505) 759-3515
Beadwork, baskets and leatherwork by Jicarilla Apache tribe

The Kiva Shop
57 Old Santa Fe Trail
Santa Fe, NM 87501
Indian pottery, baskets, rugs, kachina dolls, fetishes, beadwork

Lilly's Gallery
P.O. Box 342
Acoma Pueblo, NM 87034
(505) 552-9501
Traditional handcrafted Acoma pottery

Lopez & Ortiz Woodcarving Shop
Cordova, NM 87523
(505) 351-4572

Museum of International Folk Art
Museum of New Mexico
P.O. Box 2087
Santa Fe, NM 87503

Native American Art Gallery
2113 Charlevoix NW
Old Town, Albuquerque, NM 87104
(505) 843-9332
Indian pottery, beadwork, baskets, carvings

Navasya Gallery of Contemporary Fine Art
115 Don Gaspar
Santa Fe, NM 87501
(505) 984-1111
Ceremonial pipes, pottery, beadwork, jewelry

Oke Oweenge Arts and Crafts
P.O. Box 1095
San Juan Pueblo, NM 87566
(505) 852-2372
Traditional ceremonial dance clothes, pottery, rattles, carvings, dolls, beadwork, baskets, jewelry

Oklahoma Indian Crafts Co.
2801 Rodeo Road, Suite B-195
Santa Fe, NM 87505
(505) 983-2115
Warbonnets, headdresses, beadwork, war shirts, costumes, featherwork

Old Cienega Village Museum
Route 2, Box 214
1525 Camino Sierra Vista
Santa Fe, NM 87501

Popovi Da Studio of Indian Art
San Ildefonso Pueblo
Santa Fe, NM 87501
(505) 455-2456
Pottery by San Ildefonso craftsmen and other Pueblos; Navajo, Hopi and Zuni jewelry; Jemez and Papago basketry; Navajo rugs

Pueblo of Zuni Arts and Crafts
P.O. Box 425
Zuni, NM 87327
(505) 782-4481 or 782-5531
Zuni turquoise, shell, coral, jet and silver jewelry; pottery; fetishes

Rhonda Holy Bear
P.O. Box 70
Chamisal, NM 87521
(505) 587-2018
Plains and other tribal dolls in authentic costume

Ta-Ma-Ya Co-op Association
Santa Ana Pueblo
Star Route Box 37
Bernalillo, NM 87004
(505) 867-3301
Pottery, Pueblo embroidery, weaving, gourd rattles and dippers, wooden and straw inlaid crosses

Tehn-Tsa Indian Arts and Crafts
P.O. Box 471
Taos, NM 87571
(505) 758-0173
Kachina dolls, beadwork, pottery, jewelry

Teresita Naranjo
Route 1, Box 455
Santa Clara Pueblo
Espanola, NM 87532
(505) 753-9655
Santa Clara black and red pottery, wedding vases, ceremonial bowls

Carol Vigil
P.O. Box 443
Jemez Pueblo, NM 87024
Carved and painted Jemez pottery

Zuni Craftsmen Cooperative Association
P.O. Box 426
Zuni, NM 87327
(505) 782-4425
Zuni silver and turquoise jewelry, beadwork, fetishes

NEW YORK

Akwesasne Crafts & Creations
Box 2
Mohawk Nation
Hogansburg, NY 13655
Traditional Mohawk crafts: beadwork, porcupine quillwork, fancy splint and sweetgrass baskets, ribbon shirts, cornhusk dolls

Alaska Shop Gallery of Eskimo Art
31 East 74th Street
New York, NY 10021
(212) 879-1782
Baskets, carvings, beadwork

American Indian Community House Gallery
591 Broadway, 2nd Floor
New York, NY 10012
(212) 219-8931
Pottery, baskets, beadwork, wood carvings, dolls, Navajo rugs, Iroquois cornhusk dolls, kachina dolls, carved pipes, jewelry

American Indian Crafts
719 Broad Street
Salamanca, NY 14779
(716) 945-1225
Seneca beadwork, masks, rattles and cornhusk dolls; Ute pottery; Mohawk baskets; Zuni and Navajo jewelry

Black Bear Trading Post
Route 9W, P.O. Box 47
Esopus, NY 12429
(914) 384-6786
Baskets, pottery, beadwork, pipes, war clubs

Canyon Trading Company
J.F.K. International Airport
International Arrivals Building, East Wing
Jamaica, NY 11430
(212) 656-7474
Indian baskets, carvings, beadwork, pottery, moccasins, jewelry

Chrisjohn Family Arts and Crafts
RD 2, Box 315
Red Hook, NY 12571
(914) 758-8238
Masks, bone jewelry, pipes, wood carvings, cornhusk dolls

ADDITIONAL RESOURCES STATE BY STATE

The Farmers' Museum, Inc.
Lake Road, P.O. Box 800
Cooperstown, NY 13326
(607) 547-2593
Textiles, ironwork, tools, brooms

Iroquois Bone Carvings
3560 Stony Point Road
Grand Island, NY 14072
(716) 733-4974
Carvings, bone jewelry, Iroquois horn rattles, drums, beadwork

Museum of American Folk Art Shop
62 West 50th Street
New York, NY 10112
(212) 481-3080

Museum of Historical Society of Early American Decoration, Inc.
19 Dove Street
Albany, NY 12210
(518) 462-1676
Authentic reproductions of objects in the museum: theorems, fireboards, ornamented tin and wood, reverse paintings on glass, tinsel paintings, bridge's boxes, tinware

Museum of the American Indian
Broadway at 155th Street
New York, NY 10032
(212) 283-2420
Indian and Eskimo baskets, carvings, beadwork

Native American Center for the Living Arts, Inc.
25 Rainbow Mall
Niagara Falls, NY 14303
(716) 284-2427
Iroquois pottery, beadwork, baskets, carvings

Native Peoples Arts and Craftshop
P.O. Box 851, 210 Fabius Street
Syracuse, NY 13201
(315) 476-6425
Baskets, pottery, moccasins, ribbon shirts, lacrosse sticks

Onondaga Indian Trading Post
Nedrow, NY 13120
(315) 469-4359
Iroquois cornhusk dolls, turtle rattles, beadwork, baskets

Seneca-Iroquois National Museum Gift Shop
P.O. Box 442, Broad Street Extension
Salamanca, NY 14779
(716) 945-1738
Iroquois beadwork; splint, porcupine quill and sweetgrass baskets; wooden false-face masks; horn, gourd and turtle shell rattles; wampum and scrimshaw jewelry

United Nations Gift Center/Folk Arts and Handicrafts
U.S. Building, Room 414
42nd Street & First Avenue
New York, NY 10017
(212) 754-7000
Stoneware pottery, baskets, glass, Indian and mountain crafts

NORTH CAROLINA

Carolina Mountain Arts & Crafts Cooperative
P.O. Box 573
Murphy, NC 38906
Handmade traditional crafts

The Craft Shop
John C. Campbell Folk School
Brasstown, NC 28902
(704) 837-2775
Wood, fiber, metals, pottery

The Craft Shop of Piedmont Craftsmen, Inc.
300 South Main Street
Winston-Salem, NC 27101

Goodwin Guild Weavers
Blowing Rock Crafts, Inc.
Blowing Rock, NC 28605
(704) 295-3577
Coverlets, fringed tablecloths, runners, textiles

Medicine Man Craft Shop
P.O. Box 256
Cherokee, NC 28719

Moravian Book & Gift Shop
614 South Main Street
Winston-Salem, NC 27101
(919) 723-6262
Tinware, wooden toys, salt-glaze and slip pottery, folk art

Oakland Pottery
1257 Foushee Road
Ramseur, NC 27316
(919) 824-4416

Qualla Arts and Crafts Mutual, Inc.
P.O. Box 277
Cherokee, NC 28719
(704) 497-3103
Baskets of river cane, oak splints and honeysuckle; wood carvings; masks; beadwork; pottery; dolls; metalwork

Southern Highland Handicraft Guild
P.O. Box 9545
Asheville, NC 28805
(Showroom in Folk Art Center, Blue Ridge Parkway)
(704) 298-7928
Baskets, brooms, candles, pottery, ironwork, toys, carvings, furniture, dolls, weavings

Tuscarora Indian Handcraft Shop
Route 3, Box 273
Maxton, NC 28364
(919) 844-3352

Wayah'sti Indian Traditions
P.O. Box 130
Hollister, NC 27844
(919) 586-4519
Beadwork, stone pipes, pottery, bark craft, fans

NORTH DAKOTA

ArtMain
13 South Main
Minot, ND 58701
(701) 838-4747

Country Arts Collective
Block 6, 620 Main
Fargo, ND 58103
(701) 325-6525

Country Crafts
128 North Main
Elgin, ND 58533
(701) 584-2036

Five Tribes Cooperative
North Dakota Indian Affairs Commission
First Floor, State Capitol
Bismarck, ND 58505
(701) 224-2428

The Glass Box
North Dakota Heritage Center
Bismarck, ND 58505
(701) 224-2666

The Nordic Needle, Inc.
1314 Gateway Drive
Fargo, ND 58103
(701) 235-5231

Standing Rock Sioux Arts & Crafts
Fort Yates, ND 58538
(701) 854-7231
Beadwork, peace pipes, shawls, star quilts

Three Affiliated Tribes Museum
Arts and Crafts Division
New Town, ND 58763
(701) 627-4477
Beadwork jewelry, star quilts

OHIO

Benchworks Gallery
2563 North High Street
Columbus, OH 43202

The Columbus Museum
Designer Craftsman Shop
480 East Broad Street
Columbus, OH 42315
(614) 221-6801

Court Street Collection
64 North Court Street
Athens, OH 45701
(614) 593-8261

The General Store
Olde Circle #7
Circleville, OH 43113

Hale Farm & Village
2686 Oak Hill Road
Bath, OH 44210

Of Earth and Water
1717 Hankinson Road NE
Granville, OH 43023
(614) 587-3696
Hand-thrown functional pottery

Ohio Designer Craftsmen Gallery
1981 Riverside Drive
Columbus, OH 43221
(614) 486-7119
Ceramics, glass, jewelry, leather, wood, fiber, toys

Pincherry Pottery
519 Pincherry Lane
Worthington, OH 43085
(614) 885-1586
Functional stoneware pottery

Posterity Studio
2687 Osceola Avenue
Columbus, OH 43211
(614) 267-2323 or 263-1319
Hand-thrown functional stoneware

ADDITIONAL RESOURCES STATE BY STATE

The Rushcreek Craftsworks
8450 Main Street
Rushville, OH 43150
(614) 385-3412

Trisolini Gallery Shop
48 East Union Street
Athens, OH 45701
(614) 592-4224
Glass, toys, baskets, quilts, weavings

Warren County Historical Society
Gift Shop
105 South Broadway
P.O. Box 223
Lebanon, OH 45036
(513) 932-1817

OKLAHOMA

American Indian Handicrafts
P.O. Box 533
Meeker, OK 74855
(405) 279-3343
Ribbonwork blankets, shirts and shawls; beadwork

Bruce C. Caesar
P.O. Box 1183
Anadark, OK 73005
(405) 247-2303
Traditional nickel silver jewelry, Native American Church–type ornaments

Cherokee Arts & Crafts Center
P.O. Box 948
Tahlequah, OK 74464
(918) 456-6031
Traditional Cherokee "tear" dresses, ribbon shirts, buckbrush baskets, beadwork, wood carvings, pottery, Cherokee grass dolls, turtle shell rattles, silver and Oochelata stone jewelry

Cherokee National Museum Gift Shop
P.O. Box 515
TSA-LA-GI
Tahlequah, OK 74464
(918) 456-6007
Baskets, weapons

Choctaw Trading Post
1520 North Portland
Oklahoma City, OK 73107
(405) 947-2490
Silver and turquoise jewelry, moccasins, beadwork, pottery, baskets, rugs, elk and deer hides

Five Civilized Tribes Museum Trading Post
Agency Hill
Honor Heights Drive
Muskogee, OK 74401
(918) 683-1701
Beaded jewelry, baskets

Oklahoma Cherokee Artists Association
P.O. Box 182
Rose, OK 74354
(918) 868-3345 or 868-2933
Baskets, pottery, hand-weaving, grass dolls, wood carvings, finger-weaving, shell jewelry, silversmithing, beadwork

Oklahoma Indian Arts and Crafts Cooperative
P.O. Box 966
Anadarko, OK 73005
(U.S. 62, Southern Plains Indian Museum)
(405) 247-3486
Beadwork, war dance bustle ensembles, nickel silver jewelry and ornaments, dolls

Sac & Fox Tribal Minimart and Gift Shop
Route 2, Box 246
Stroud, OK 74079
(918) 968-2256
Beadwork, shawls, Sac & Fox traditional dresses, ribbonwork

Snake Creek Workshop
P.O. Box 147
Rose, OK 74364
(918) 479-8867
Mussel shell gorget necklaces

Ta-Fv Hokkolen, Two Feathers Indian Shop
1605 South Main
Broken Arrow, OK 74012
(918) 258-1228
Ojo-De-Dios ("God's eyes") moccasins, Seminole turbans, beadwork, ribbonwork, quillwork, ball sticks

Wewoka Trading Post
P.O. Box 1532
524 South Wewoka Avenue
Wewoka, OK 74884
(405) 257-5580
Beadwork, Seminole patchwork, Seminole ball sticks, wood carvings

OREGON

Red Bear Creations
358 North Lexington Avenue
Brandon, OR 97411-0007
Star quilts

PENNSYLVANIA

Artisans Cooperative
Box 216
Chadds Ford, PA 19317
(215) 388-1435
Rural crafts from throughout the U.S. Shops also in Philadelphia; Ardmore, PA; and Nantucket, MA

Brandywine River Museum
P.O. Box 141, Route 1
Chadds Ford, PA 19317
(215) 388-7601 or 459-1900
Traditional crafts from Berks County

Chester County Historical Society
The Museum Shop
225 North High Street
West Chester, PA 19380
Museum reproductions

Chriffo Craft Gallery
138 East Gay Street
West Chester, PA 19380
Delaware Valley craftspeople

The Creative Hand Cooperative
Zook House
Exton Square
Exton, PA 19341
(215) 363-7436

Dilworthtown Country Store
275 Brinton's Bridge Road
West Chester, PA 19380
(215) 399-0560

Gallery of Shoppes
Route 222, 1 mile east of Kutztown
Kutztown, PA 19530
(215) 683-8182
Quality handmade traditional crafts

Heart and Home
Farmers Market
Lancaster Avenue
Strafford, PA 19087
(215) MU8-8793
Folk pottery, redware, sgraffito, slipware, decorated boxes

A Little Gallery
P.O. Box 397
210 Main Street (Route 997)
Mont Alto, PA 17237
(717) 749-3831
Crafts of the Cumberland Valley: pottery, carving, Shaker furniture, weaving, decorative painting, theorems

Moravian Museum
Historic Bethlehem
Bethlehem, PA 18018

Old Eagle Studios
237 Bridge Street
Phoenixville, PA 19460
(215) 933-3080

Pennsylvania Designer Craftsmen Gallery
Route 209
Bushkill, PA 18324
(717) 588-9156
Frakturs, pottery, theorems, wood carving, weaving

Pennsylvania Farm Museum of Landis Valley
2451 Kissel Hill Road
Lancaster, PA 17601

Raintree Gallery Folk Art Carvers
204 North Poplar Street
Elizabethtown, PA 17022
(717) 367-2990

Sawtooth Folk Art
6 Marion Court
Lancaster, PA 17602
(717) 393-3884
Amish quilts, baskets, rag rugs

The Yellow Brick Road Craft Gallery
Avondale/New London Road
Avondale, PA 19311
(215) 268-8652
Handmade American crafts

RHODE ISLAND

Dovecrest Indian Trading Post
Summit Road
Exeter, RI 02822
(401) 539-2786
Bone jewelry, leatherwork, beadwork, pottery

Nishnabeykwa Productions
Box 874
Charlestown, RI 02813
(401) 364-9783
Traditional Woodlands pottery, beadwork, finger-woven sashes, beaded leather pouches

ADDITIONAL RESOURCES STATE BY STATE

SOUTH CAROLINA

Sara Ayers
1182 Brookwood Circle
West Columbia, SC 29169
(803) 794-5436
Pottery pipes, Catawba pottery

The City Market
The Four Corners of the Law
Broad and Meeting Streets
Charleston, SC 29401
Low-country baskets, regional crafts

Greenville County Museum of Art
The Sales Shop
420 College Street
Greenville, SC 29601
(803) 271-7570

SOUTH DAKOTA

Art Gallery
Friends of the Middle Border Museum
1311 South Duff, Box 1071
Mitchell, SD 57301
(605) 996-2122

Indian Originals
1510 Space Avenue
Rapid City, SD 57701
(605) 343-0479
Native American traditional costume

Lakota Artists
Northern Lights Gallery
31 Charles
Deadwood, SD 57732
(605) 578-1270

Lakota Jewelry Visions
P.O. Box 5158
Rapid City, SD 57709
(605) 358-0359
Traditional jewelry, dance accessories

Lamont Gallery
Dacotah Prairie Museum
21 South Main
Aberdeen, SD 57401
(605) 229-1608

Oyate Kin Cultural Cooperative
Marty, SD 57361
Beadwork, feather and leather work for dance outfits, Indian star quilts, ribbon shirts

Sioux Indian Museum and Craft Center
Paulette Montileaux
1002 St. Joe, Box 1504
Rapid City, SD 57709
(605) 348-8834

Starboy Enterprises
P.O. Box 33
Rosebud Sioux Reservation
Okreek, SD 57563
(605) 856-4517
Star quilts

Tipi Shop, Inc.
Box 1542
Rapid City, SD 57709
(Sales shop in Sioux Indian Museum)
(605) 343-8128
Beadwork, quillwork, parfleche boxes, willow baskets, dance costume accessories, pottery, dolls

Womens' Art Guild/Museum Store
Civic Fine Arts Center
235 West 10th Street
Sioux Falls, SD 57102
(605) 336-1167

TENNESSEE

Appalachian Center for Crafts
Route 3, Box 347A-1
Smithville, TN 37166
(615) 597-1418
Fiber, handmade paper, functional pottery, quilts, baskets, cornhusk dolls

Boones Creek Pottery
Route 13, Box 9
Johnson City, TN 37615
(615) 282-2801

The Country Store
Route 5, Box 215-B
Bluff City, TN 37618
(615) 538-8411
Mountain crafts

Craftwork Gallery
Box 5658
Greeneville, TN 37743
(615) 639-4681
Clay

Fall Creek Falls State Park Craft Shop
Route 3
Pikeville, TN 37367
(615) 881-3824

Great Smoky Arts & Crafts Community
Route 321 North
Gatlinburg, TN 37738
More than thirty shops along 8 miles of mountain road

Hunter Museum of Art Gift Shop
10 Bluff View
Chattanooga, TN 37403
(615) 267-0968
Earthenware and stoneware pottery, textiles, baskets, quilts, glass, dolls, mountain crafts

Jonesborough Designer Craftsmen
109 East Main Street
Jonesboro, TN 37659
(615) 753-6300

Museum of Appalachia Shop
P.O. Box 359
Norris, TN 37828
(615) 494-7680
Locally handmade crafts including white oak baskets

Possum Valley Farm Forge & Weavers
Route 2
Martin, TN 38237
(901) 587-3489 or 587-6250

TEXAS

Crazy Crow Trading Post
P.O. Box 314
107 North Fannin
Denison, TX 75020
(214) 463-1366
Silverwork, beadwork, warbonnets, moccasins

Marshall Pottery
P.O. Box 1839
Marshall, TX 75670
(214) 938-9201
Stoneware

Southwest Craft Center
300 Augusta
San Antonio, TX 78205
(512) 224-1848

Tique Indian Reservation Cultural Center
P.O. Box 17579, 122 South Old Pueblo Road
El Paso, TX 79917
(915) 859-3916
Wheel-thrown and molded hand-painted pottery, silver, jewelry

Tribal Enterprise
Alabama-Coushatta Indian Reservation
Route 3, Box 640
Livingston, TX 77361
(713) 563-4391
Coiled pine needle baskets, animal effigies, beadwork, pottery

UTAH

Grandma's Quilts
395 South Main
Logan, UT 84321
(801) 753-5670
Quilts, handcrafted textiles

Mormon Handicraft
Temple Square, 105 North Main
Salt Lake City, UT 84101
(801) 355-2141

Native Crafts
876 South 4th Street
Salt Lake City, UT 84111
(801) 355-2141
Beadwork, baskets, native tanned-hide dolls

Pioneer Center
391 North Main Street
Springville, UT 84663
(801) 489-6853
Baskets, rugs, Pueblo pottery, jewelry

Shoshone Buckskin and Beadwork
896 South 1000 East
Clearfield, UT 84015

Urshel Taylor's Indian Studio
447 Crestview Drive
Brigham City, UT 84302
(801) 723-6196 or 723-5897
Shoshone-Bannock and Washakie beadwork; native-tanned buckskin hides, white or smoked; moccasins; buckskin dolls

ADDITIONAL RESOURCES STATE BY STATE

VERMONT

Carriage House Crafts
Route 125
East Middlebury, VT 05740
(802) 388-4120
New England handcrafts

Cornwall Crafts
RD 2
Middlebury, VT 05753
(802) 462-2438
Braided rugs, wooden toys, Vermont handcrafts

The Craft House at Blueberry Hill
Goshen, VT 05733
(802) 247-3177
Quilts, pottery, glass, pewter

The Craft Shop
Putney Road
Brattleboro, VT 05301
Hand-knit sweaters, caps and mittens; dolls; moccasins

Green Mountain Spinnery
P.O. Box 54
Putney, VT
(802) 387-4528
100 percent virgin wool yarn made from New England fleece, handmade knitwear

The Log Cabin
Route 30
Newfane, VT 05345
(802) 365-4460
Quilts, glassware, ironware, sheepskin and deerskin items

Marlboro Craft Center
Route 9
Marlboro, VT 05344
(802) 254-9704
New England handcrafts: pottery, woodwork, quilts, toys, pewter

The Pottery Works
Sunshine Marketplace
Routes 100/103
Ludlow, VT 05149
(802) 228-8743
Functional ovenproof stoneware in earthy glazes

The Silk Purse & Sow's Ear
Routes 12 and 107
Bethel, VT 05032
(802) 234-5368
Vermont and New England crafts: quilts, toys, jewelry, weaving, glass

Vermont State Craft Center
Frog Hollow
Middlebury, VT 05753
(802) 388-3177
Showroom for the work of 300 Vermont craftspeople

Vermont State Craft Center at Windsor House
Main Street, P.O. Box 110
Windsor, VT 05089
(802) 674-6729
Features work of 250 craft professionals

James Walker Stoneware Pottery
P.O. Box 469
Arlington, VT 05250
(802) 375-9457

Weston Toy Works
Route 100
Weston, VT 05161
(802) 824-3073
Imaginative wooden toys, games and puzzles

VIRGINIA

American Naturals
917 North Lexington Street
Arlington, VA 22205
(703) 527-3270
Traditional clothing, dolls and quilts; bone/leather and bone/clay jewelry; shawls

Colonial Williamsburg
P.O. Box C
Williamsburg, VA 23187
A village of 18th century craftspeople whose baskets, pottery, silver, carving, pewter and printing are for sale in shops in the Historic Area and Craft House. A folk art shop, Sign of the Rooster, specializes in decoys, tinware, coverlets, needlework and quilts.

Fredericksburg Pottery
800 Sophia Street
Fredericksburg, VA 22401
(703) 371-1730

Handwork Shop, Inc.
7 North 6th Street
Richmond, VA 23219
(804) 649-0674
Stoneware pottery, forged iron, wood furniture, glass, rugs, baskets, quilts

Pamunkey Pottery and Crafts Trading Post
Route 1
King William, VA 23086
(804) 843-2851

Virginia Handcrafts, Inc.
2008 Langhorne Road
Lynchburg, VA 24501
(804) 846-7029
Pottery, jewelry, leather, wood, weaving, glass

Yorktown Creative Art Center
On the Hill
Alexander Hamilton Boulevard at Ballard
Yorktown, VA 23690
(804) 989-3076

WASHINGTON

Bainbridge Arts and Crafts
155 Winslow Way East
Bainbridge Island, WA 98110

Bead Lady/Cherokee Rainbows
315-B Roosevelt
Wenatchee, WA 98801
Beadwork, appliqué, moccasins, dance shawls, ribbonwork

Daybreak Star Arts Gallery
Discovery Park
P.O. Box 99253
Seattle, WA 98199
(206) 285-4425
Baskets, masks, silver jewelry, Navajo rugs

Indian Arts
P.O. Box 551
Suquamish, WA 98392
(206) 598-3213
Beadwork, totem poles, masks, paddles

Lelooska Family Gallery
5618 Lewis River Road
Ariel, WA 98603
(206) 225-9522 or 225-8828
Totem poles, dolls, masks, rattles

Lummi Indian Craftsmen
4339 Lummi Shore Road
Ferndale, WA 98248
(206) 384-5292 or 758-2522
Northwest Coast Salish wool blankets, cedar bark baskets

Makah Cultural Research Center
P.O. Box 95
Neah Bay, WA 98357
(206) 645-2711 or 645-2712
Woven baskets and mats, totem poles, masks, rattles

Marietta Band of Nooksak Indians
1827 Marine Drive
Bellingham, WA 98226
(206) 733-6039
Beadwork, knitwear, wood carvings, beaded moccasins

North by Northwest
630 Water Street
P.O. Box 656
Port Townsend, WA 98368
Baskets, carvings, beadwork

Potlatch Gifts
Northwind Trading Company
708 Commercial Avenue
Anacortes, WA 98221
(206) 293-6404
Coast Salish–style wood carving; knitwear; pottery; baskets

Sacred Circle Gallery of American Indian Art
607 First Avenue
Seattle, WA 98104
(206) 223-0072

Seattle Indian Arts and Crafts Shop
617 Second Avenue
Seattle, WA 98104
(206) 623-2252
Cowichan knitwear, Ute Mt. and Yakima pottery, totem poles, baskets, shawls, ribbon shirts, moccasins, soapstone carvings

Snow Goose Associates
4220 N.E. 125th Street
Seattle, WA 98125
(206) 362-3401
Indian, Eskimo and Aleut crafts; baskets; masks; carvings

Suquamish Museum
P.O. Box 498
Suquamish, WA 98392
(206) 598-3311
Suquamish/Puget Sound Salish items: baskets, clam baskets and basketry dolls; wooden bowls; canoe bailers; wood carvings

ADDITIONAL RESOURCES STATE BY STATE

WEST VIRGINIA

Cabin Creek Quilts
Box 383
Cabin Creek, WV 25035
(304) 595-3928
and
200 Broad Street
Charleston, WV 25301
Quilts, home furnishings, toys

The Cultural Center Shop
Cultural Center
Capitol Complex
Charleston, WV 25305
(304) 348-0690

Gibson Glass
Route 1, Box 102A
Milton, WV 25541
(304) 743-5232
Traditional glassblowing

Sycamore Pottery
Route 1, Box 8A
Kearneysville, WV 25430
(304) 725-4251
Traditional pottery

West Virginia Artists' and Craftsmen's Guild
32½ Capitol Street
Charleston, WV 25301
(304) 345-0289

WISCONSIN

Maple Plain Craft Shoppe
Route 3, Box 142A
Cumberland, WI 54829
(715) 822-8706
Moccasins, vests, beadwork, dolls

The Mineral Point Artisans Guild
Mineral Point, WI 53565
A village of craft shops: weaving, leather, folk art, woodworking

Oneida Nation Museum
P.O. Box 365
Oneida, WI 54155
(414) 869-2768
Beadwork, quillwork, leatherwork

Red Cliff Arts & Crafts Center
P.O. Box 529
Bayfield, WI 54814
(715) 779-5858
Wood carving, beadwork, birchbark items

Rowe Pottery Works, Inc.
404 England Street
Cambridge, WI 53523
(800) 356-5510
Salt-glazed stoneware

Wa-Swa-Gon Arts and Crafts
P.O. Box 477
Lac du Flambeau, WI 54538
(715) 588-7636
Beadwork, birchbark items, finger-weaving, carvings

Winnebago Public Indian Museum
P.O. Box 441
Wisconsin Dells, WI 53965
(608) 254-2268

WYOMING

Fort Washakie Trading Company
53 North Fork Road
P.O. Box 428
Fort Washakie, WY 82514
(307) 332-3557
Beadwork, quillwork, rawhide and smoked skin accessories, dolls, Native American Church articles, Navajo rugs, Papago baskets, Pueblo pottery

La Ray Turquoise Co.
P.O. Box 83
Cody, WY 82414
(307) 587-9564
Navajo, Zuni, Chippewa and Hopi silverwork; Ojibwa beadwork; Navajo rugs

Wyoming State Museum
Barrett Building
Cheyenne, WY 82002
Shoshone and Arapaho crafts and jewelry, Wyoming crafts

Acknowledgments

With special thanks to the following, whose support, cooperation and nominations of craftspeople made this book richer than it would have been without them.

Ralph Rinzler and Diana Parker, the Smithsonian Institution; Robert G. Hart and Myles Libhart, Indian Arts and Crafts Board, U.S. Department of the Interior; Ray Dockstadter, Alan Jabbour and Peter Bartis, American Folklife Center, Library of Congress; Robert Gray and James Gentry, Southern Highlands Handicraft Guild; Jeanne Dougherty, Alaska Native Medical Center Craft Shop; Robert Teske, National Endowment for the Arts; Elliot Wigginton, *Foxfire;* Henry Willett, Alabama State Council on the Arts and Humanities; Donald R. Friary, Historic Deerfield; Jonathan L. Fairbanks, Boston Museum of Fine Arts; Jo Ann Andera, Texas Folklife Festival; Frank G. White, Old Sturbridge Village; Jane C. Nylander, Strawbery Banke; Marion Nelson, the Norwegian-American Museum; Doris H. Fry, Museum of Historical Society of Early American Decoration, Inc.; Kathryn Boardman, Farmers' Museum, Cooperstown.

William Warmus, Paul Gardner, Jane Shadel Spillman and David Whitehouse, Corning Museum of Glass; Paul Norman Perrot, Virginia Museum of Fine Arts; Helen Drutt, Moore College; Edith Wylie, Craft and Folk Art Museum; Sylvia Ullman, American Crafts Gallery; Meredith Schroeder, American Quilter's Society; Hank Prebys, Henry Ford Museum; Larry Yerdon and Robert A. Guffin, Hancock Shaker Village; Lee Hall; Jackie Chalkley; Gail Stern, the Balch Institute for Ethnic Studies; John Rice Irwin, Museum of Appalachia; Sam Scherr, past president of the American Craft Council; Mary Ann Scherr, Parsons School of Design.

Gail Andrews Trechsel, Birmingham Museum of Art; Ellen J. Landis, Albuquerque Museum; Lonn Taylor and Orlando Romero, Museum of New Mexico; Michael Taylor, New Mexico State Monuments; Helen R. Lucero and Judith Sellars, Museum of International Folk Art; Cassie Vieira, Old Cienega Village Museum; Dian Magie and Tina Bucuvalas, Coconino Center for the Arts; Alice C. Merritt, Tennessee Crafts Fair; the librarians of C. Burr Artz Library, Frederick, MD; Carol Sedestrom, American Craft Enterprises, Inc; American Craft Library; Carlos Gutierrez-Solana, New York State Council on the Arts; Kathleen Kochkin-Youritzin, Empire State Crafts Alliance; George Boeck, Louisiana State Museum; Kay-Karol Horse Capture, Buffalo Bill Historical Center; Joe Wilson, National Council for Traditional Arts; Lloyd Herman, former director of the Renwick Gallery; Beatrix Rumford, Colonial Williamsburg; James Griffith, the Southwest Folklore Center, University of Arizona; Jeanette Zug, Moravian Museum; Dorothy O. Olson, National Crafts Planning Board; Judy Peiser, Center for Southern Folklore; Boston University's Program in Artisanry; Craig Gilborn, Adirondack Museum; Dr. Regina Perry, Virginia Commonwealth University; John Vlach, George Washington University; Drew Beisswenger, North Dakota Council on the Arts; Sally Moore.

John Berquist, Minnesota State Arts Board; Lynn Martin and Marilyn L. Nicholson, the State Foundation on Culture and the Arts, Hawaii; Christina Kreps, Alaska Native Arts & Crafts, Inc.; Jan Steinbright and Rose Atuk Fosdick, Institute of Alaska Native Arts, Inc.; Ann McMullen, American Indian Archaeological Institute, Inc.; Kathryne Olson, Pueblo Grande de Nevada Lost City Museum of Archeology; Leverett Craftsmen & Artists, Inc.

Michael Korn, Montana Folklife Project; Rebecca E. Sterling, Department of Culture and History, West Virginia; Terry Alliband, Southern Illinois University; Fred H. Bair, Jr., Society of Workers in Early Arts and Trades; Dan Burke, Ruth Draper and Carol Edison, Utah Arts

ACKNOWLEDGMENTS

Council; Scott Derks; Lyn Jackson, Pennsylvania Guild of Craftsmen; Liz Harzoff, Ohio Arts Council; JoAnn H. Stevens, Ohio Designer Craftsmen; Jonathan Shay, Mystic Seaport Museum; Peggy A. Bulger, Florida Folklife Programs; Fran Padgett, Kentucky Department of the Arts; Kim Madsen, Williston (North Dakota) Fiber Arts Guild; Becky Dietrich, A Little Gallery; Deborah Whitehurst, Arizona Commission on the Arts; Dona R. Bachman, Wyoming State Museum; Marian Johnson, Kodiak Historical Society; Elwood Mose, Nevada Indian Commission; Floyd Ballinger, Minnesota Historical Society; Jennie Chinn, Kansas State Historical Society; Carolyn Dodson, Southwest Parks and Monuments Association; Sandra Percival, Washington State Arts Commission; Herb Puffer, Pacific Western Traders; Jan Mahood, Nebraska Arts Council; Holly Duggan, Georgia Mountain Crafts, Inc.; Michael Malcé, Kelter-Malcé; Egle Victoria Zygas, Illinois Arts Council; Mary Greeley, Oregon School of Arts and Crafts; Pam Carter, Brandywine River Museum; Richard March, Wisconsin Arts Board; David S. Cohen, New Jersey Folklife and Ethnic History Programs; Patricia Mortati and William L. Fox, Nevada State Council on the Arts; John Alexander; Sven G. Froiland, the Center for Western Studies.

Betty Belanus and Geoff Gephart, Indiana Arts Commission; Altina Mirando; Caroline Garrett, Morehead State University; Nancy Sweezy; California Arts Council; Anne Gould Hauberg; Steve Ohrn, Iowa Arts Council; Ron Kley, Alonzo Wood Homestead, Maine.

Michael Durham, *Americana Magazine;* Joel Gardner, Office of Culture, Recreation and Tourism, Louisiana; Carolyn Hecker and Ronald Pearson, Maine Crafts Association; Maine State Commission on the Arts and Humanities; Maryland Arts Council; Ruth Burt, League of New Hampshire Craftsmen; Linda Morley, New Hampshire Folk Arts Program; Melissa Walker, New Hampshire Farm Museum; Joan Cravens, *Better Homes & Gardens;* Catherine Wallace, Maryland–National Capital Park and Planning Commission; Winifred Lambrecht, Rhode Island State Council on the Arts; Dennis Coelho, Wyoming Council on the Arts; Raymond Shermoe, Civic Fine Arts Association/Museum, South Dakota; Richard Siegesmund, Pennsylvania Council on the Arts; Shalom Staub, Pennsylvania Folklife Programs; Bud Leavitt, Bangor *Daily News;* Institute of Texan Cultures; United Maine Craftsmen; Carolyn Wagner, Laramie County Community College; Jennifer Dowley, Sacramento Metropolitan Arts Commission; Georgia Council for the Arts and Humanities; South Dakota Arts Council; Tennessee Arts Commission.

Index

Adams, Robert, 100
Adams, Stephen A., 51, 99
Adams, Victoria, 187, 300
Adirondack baskets, 1
Adirondack furniture, 94–96
Adirondack Handweavers, 287
Afghans, hand-woven, 298
African-American jewelry, 150–52
The Aged Ram, Essex, VT, 225
Ahern, Tom, 37
Ahnangnatoguk, Mary, 249
Akana, Elizabeth A., 212
Alaska Native Medical Center Craft
    Shop, Anchorage, AK, 3, 35, 248
Alaskan crafts. See Eskimo crafts
Albert, Barbara, 3
Albro, Donna W., 126, 257, 263
Alden, John, 64
Aleut baskets, 2, 3
Aling, Ralph, 226
Allen, Earl L., 215–16
Allen, Ray and Susan, 200
Allgood, John, 144
Alowa, Annie, 69, 248
Althaus, Evelyn, 80
Amana Colony crafts, 3–4
American Folk Art, Marietta, GA, 116
American Rug, Pittsfield, IL, 221
Amish crafts, 75, 209–10
Anderson, Eileen, 263–64
Anderson, John, 22
Andirons, 28, 144
Andra, Diana, 183, 280
Animal figures:
    carvings, 37–38, 41–42
    pottery, 203–4
The Antique Cupboard, Emmitsburg,
    MD, 79, 91, 94, 175
Appalachian Craftsmen, Inc.,
    Barboursville, WV, 215
Apple dolls, 70–71
Apple-picking basket, 4
Arch, Davy, 52, 53
Architectural ironwork, 139–41

Archuleta, Antonio J., 113
Archuleta, Felipe Benito, 234
The Arden Forge Co., West Chester,
    PA, 142–43
Armijo, Frederico, 113
Armstead, George B., Jr., 21
Arntzen, A. Eldred, 220
Arold, George, 31
Arrington, Noel, 116
Arrowback chairs, 46, 47
Arrowcraft Shop, Gatlinburg, TN, 298–
    99
Arrowhead Forge, Belfast, ME, 145
Art glass, 117
Ash-glazed pottery, 195–97
Athabascan crafts, 2, 248
Atkinson, Janie, 93
Auguah, Bruce, 132
Authentic Designs, West Rupert, VT,
    267
Autoharps, 175
Ayres, Roger A., 255

Babyboards, 208, 209
Baby clothes, crocheted, 67
Backenstose, Dan, Jr., 98
Backwoods Furnishings, Indian Lake,
    NY, 95
Baleen baskets, 2, 3
Ball, George, 27
Ball, Whitman, 27–28
Ball, William, Jr., 27
Ball and Ball, Exton, PA, 27–28
Baltimore Scrimshanders, Baltimore,
    MD, 240
Bandboxes, 24–25
Banjos, 176–77
Banks, Loretta, 273
Bannister-back chairs, 43–45
Baranko, Betty, 80
Barash, William S., 123
Barela, Patrocinio, 232
Bark cloth, 153–55
Barnet, David, 277

Barnett, Ivan, 284, 285
Barnett, Jean, 81
Barnstable Originals, Camden, ME,
    103–4
Barrett, David, 46, 49
Barretts Bottoms, Kearneysville, WV, 46,
    49
Barringer, C. Milton, 240
Barron, Sharon, 124
Barrow, Robert, 50
Basketry, 1–12
    beehives, 246–47
    Choctaw, 54–56
    cornhusk, 65
    fabric, 75
    Hopi, 131
Bastine Pottery, Noblesville, IN, 205
Baut, Eugene, 122
Baut, Gerhard, 122
Bayberry candles, 30, 31
Beadwork, 12–14, 62, 162, 209, 218
    Alaskan, 248
    Choctaw, 54, 55
Bean, W. G. (Glen), 38–39
Bean pots, 197–98
Beauchamp, Heather and Jack, 200–201
Beaulieu, Ron, 38
Beaumont, Gerard T., 198
Beavers, Anna, 3
Becksvoort, Christian H., 99, 108, 250,
    284, 285
Bed linens, 83–84, 288–89, 290
    coverlets, 294–95
    crocheted spreads, 67
    knotted spreads, 14–15
    quilts, 209–15
    rugs, 15–16
    See also Blankets
Beehives, 246–47
Beeswax candles, 31
Begay, Joe, 153
Bell, Bill, 62–63
Bellas Artes Gallery, Santa Fe, NM, 83
Belton, Kepka Hochmann, 79–80

INDEX

Belts:
  beaded, 12, 54, 55
  concha, 63
  Hopi, 131
Benson, Pat, 86
Benson, Ted, 136
Berg, Gudrun, 220
Berg, Martha, 92–93
Berry, George, 54, 55
Berry, Mariette and Ralph, 217
Berryman, Clifford, 260
Betty lamps, tinware, 266
Bigmeat family, 53, 54
Bigton, Else, 104–5
Birchbark baskets, 3
Birchbark canoes, 31–32
Bird carvings, 36–39
  decoys, 67–69
The Bird Store, Tyner, NC, 69
Bishop, Adele, 256
Bissell, June, 93
Bivens, John, 127
Black, Emma, 69
Black, Mary, 3
Black River Junction Co., Nicholson, PA, 227
Blake, Åse, 294
Blake, Buckeye, 187
Blanchard, Porter, 169
Blankets, 16–18
  Chilkat, 18
  Hopi, 131
  Lummi, 18–19
  Navajo, 291–93
  ribbonwork, 217, 218
  Rio Grande, 296–97
Bleil, Dave, 249
Blue Star Tipis, Missoula, MT, 262
Blumenstein, Rita, 249
Boats, 240–42
  birchbark canoes, 31–32
  kayaks, 247
  models, 20–21, 192–94
Bobb, Bill and Sande, 291–92
Bobbin lace, 160–61
Boggis, Ed, 57
Boggs, Brian, 46
Bohemian braid rugs, 222, 223
Bokenkamp, Mark, 127, 128, 141, 146, 147, 273–74
Bolster, Jane, 256, 257
Bonework, 21–22
  scrimshaw, 239–40
Bonifacio, F., 272
Bonner, Thomas, 69
Bookbinding, 23
Books, handmade, 22–23, 278
Boots, 162–67
  mukluks, 248
  See also Moccasins; Shoes
Bosals, 168
Boston Scrimshanders, Boston, MA, 240
Botnick, Ken, 23

Bottles, cornhusk, 65
Boundweave rugs, 227–29
Bourdon, Betsy, 18
Bourdon, Robert, 145
Bowen, Renee, 104
Bowie knives, 158–59
Bowls, 181
  Norwegian-American, 105
  treenware, 279, 280
Bowman, Jim, 164
Boxes:
  bone, 21–22
  leather-covered, 186–87
  paper-covered bandboxes, 24–25
  Shaker, 25–26
  straw inlay, 258
  tin, 264–66
Boyt, David, 179
Bradbury, Bruce, 282–83
Bradley, Irma and James, 52
Bradley, Susan, 227
Braided horsehair, 135
Braided rugs, 220–21
Brain-tanned hides, 161–63
Brandau, Judith, 138–39
Branding irons, 26–27
Branford Craft Village, Branford, CT, 245
Braskie, Brian, 48–49
Brass items, 27–28
Brasstown carving, 37–38
Break-A-Day Country Store, Concord, NH, 221
Breed, Allan, 43–45
Breininger, Barbara and Lester, 203–4
Brende, Julie, 293–94
Brennan, Judson, 127
Bretschneider, Christopher and Gordon, 58, 60
Brett, Bill, 133–35
Brewster, Delbert, 132–33
Brewster, Ellis, 187
Briggs, Barbara J., 73
Brion, Mary Louise, 213–15
Brock, Kathleen, 87
Bronze stenciling, 257
Brooms, 4, 28–29, 65
Brown, Julia, 227
Brown, Mrs. Mary C., 15
Brunner, Hattie, 41
Buchanan, Curtis, 50
Buck, Sandra, 93
Buckets, wooden, 64
Buckles, silver, 63, 300
Buck Mountain Stenciling, Calais, VT, 93
Buckskin clothing, 62
Buechner, Thomas, III, 117
Buffalo Enterprises, East Berlin, PA, 62
Buggies, 280–81
Building, timber-frame construction, 135–36
Bull's-eye glass, 117–19

Bultos, 231–36, 297
Bunchgrass Folk Toys, Pullman, WA, 206–7
Burkhart, Dane, 109
Burkholder, Mary Beth, 227, 285–86
Burleigh, Cindy, 217
Buttons, pewter, 188, 191
Bybee Pottery, Waco, KY, 204–5

Cabot Chair Shop, Cabot, VT, 46, 49, 50
Cahn, Marjorie, Gallery, Los Gatos, CA, 213
Calamanco, 290
Calderwood, Carol, 116
Calhoun, Al and Rita, 37
Camp, Michael, 51, 100
Campbell, John C., Folk School, Brasstown, NC, 158
Campbell, Marion H., 100
Campos, Foster S., 58, 59
The Candle Cellar and Emporium, Fall River, MA, 30–31
Candles, 29–31
Candlesticks, ironwork, 146
Canepa, Peter Anthony, 114
Canoes, 31–32
Canterbury chairs (Shaker), 48
The Cape Cod Bullseye Glass Co., Barnstable, MA, 119
Capes:
  feather, 87–88
  Hopi, 131
Carleton, Carolyn and Vincent, 226
Carlson, Laurie, 73–75
Carousels, 32–34
The Carpenter's Boatshop, Pemaquid, ME, 242
Carriages, 280–81
The Carriage Works, Oakland, OR, 280–81
Carrillo, Charles M., 236
Carter, Maybelle, 175
Carter Canopies, Troutman, NC, 161
Cartwright-Jones, Catherine, 156–57, 253
Carvings, 34–43, 54–57, 104–5, 297
  bultos, 231–34
  decoys, 67–69
  dolls, 77
  Northwest Indian, 275–77
  scrimshaw, 239–40
  Spanish colonial furniture, 111–13
  treenware, 278–80
  wooden molds, 171–73
Cast iron, 142
Caswell, Bill, 181
Cates, Jerry D., 255
Cayford, Nancy Good and Philip, 91–92
Cedar fans, 38
Centinela Traditional Arts, Chimayo, NM, 297
Cerbone, Vincent, 43–44

Chadwick, Robert A., 21–22
Chadwick, Robert N., 21
Chain carvings, 42
Chairs, 43–52
  Adirondack, 95
  arrowback rocker, 98
  Norwegian-American, 104–5
  veneered, 115
  willow, 115–16
  See also Furniture
Challis, John, 179
Chamberlain, James, 28
Chandeliers:
  ironwork, 144
  tin, 266–67
  See also Lighting fixtures
Chandler, Rolla E., 246–47
Chaps, 300
Charles, Nick, 35
Charming Forge, Womelsdorf, PA, 280
Cherokee crafts, 52–54
  baskets, 10–11
  cornhusk dolls, 73
Chests:
  leather-covered, 186–87
  Norwegian-American, 105
  Pennsylvania-German, 77–79
  Shaker, 108
  Spanish colonial, 112
  See also Furniture
Childress, Lestel and Ollie, 11–12
Chilkat dance robes, 18
Chiltoskey, Goingback, 52, 53
Chimayo blankets, 296–97
Chinese Chippendale furniture, 96–97
Ching, Douglas, 183
Choctaw crafts, 54–56
Christmas ornaments, 56, 285
  cornhusk, 71
  fabric, 75–76
  glass, 120
  low-country baskets, 5
  pewter, 190
  tin, 270
Chriswill Forge, North Lawrence, OH, 144–45
Chronister, Liz, 87
Chruszch, Angeline, 80
Churchill, Delores, 3
Churns, 64
Cigar-store indians, 56–57
Cioffi, Suse F., 65
Claggett, David L., 267
Clark, Howard, 23, 184–85
Clark, Kathryn, 23
Clark, Shawn Mitchel, 116
Clay, Jackie (Mrs. C. E.), 15
Cleveland, Katherine, 3
Cleveland, Royce, 178
Clocks, 58–60, 105
Clothespin dolls, 76
Clothing, 138–39, 155–58, 248, 297
  brain-tanned leather, 162–63

Clothing (Continued)
  period reproductions, 60–62
  ribbonwork, 217–18
Coffey, Mrs. H. L., 161
Coffin guitars, 177–78
Coker Creek Crafts, Coker Creek, TN, 12
Coker Creek Handweavers, Coker Creek, TN, 227, 288
Cola, Elena, 160
Colcha embroidery, 81–83
Cole, Diane Jackson, 287
The Colonial Keeping Room, Fairfield, ME, 249
Composition dolls, 74
Conchas, 62–63, 153
Conner, P., 242
Continuum Studio and Craft Workshop, Bloomdale, OH, 29
Cook, Bertha (Mrs. D. W.), 14–15
Cookie cutters, 54–56, 264–65
Cookie molds, 171–73
Coopered items, 64
The Cooper's Trade, Williamsburg, VA, 64
Copenhaver, Laura, Industries, Inc., Marion, VA, 161
The Copper Rooster, Export, PA, 99
Cornelison, Walter, 204
Cornhusk crafts, 65, 71–73
Cotton fabrics, hand-woven, 286–88
Country Crafts, Landisville, PA, 31
Country Cuttings, Middletown, MD, 245
Country furniture, 97–99
The Country Iron Foundry, Paoli, PA, 90, 142
Counts, George and Goldie, 73
Coverlets, hand-woven, 17
Cowboy trappings, 165, 299–300
  boots, 163–64
  hats, 65–67
Cowhide chair seats, 51–52
Cox, Mike, 127
Cox, Sally, 67
Cox, Sheila Barron, 86, 87
Cozza, Laurie, 256
Cradleboards, 208, 209
Cramer, James, 75–76
Creations, Milford, NJ, 81
Creative Quilting, Bethlehem, PA, 214–15
Crèche, cornhusk, 71, 72
Creedon, Elizabeth, 84
Crewel embroidery, 83–84
Crochet, 67
  rugs, 222–23
Crochet hooks, 183
Crockett Bros. Boatyard, Oxford, MD, 242
Crosses:
  pewter, 190–91
  straw inlay, 257–58
  tinware, 270

Crouse, G. Atlee, 133
Crouse, Lawrence, 109–10
Crystallized tin, 269
The Cuklas of Hammer Song, Boonsboro, MD, 269
Culhane, Shelley, 83–84
Cullum, Peter, 50
Cupboards, Norwegian-American, 105
Currituck Decoy Co., Goldsboro, NC, 68
Curtis, Lemuel, 58
Cutts, Edmund A., 242
Cutts & Case, Inc., Oxford, MD, 242
Cutwork embroidery, 84, 85

Dahl, Mark, 255
Dalton, Kathleen and Ken, 12
Damm, Anne and Edward, 182
Davis, Gene, 255
Davis, Jack, 190
Davis, Marylou, 126
Davis, Steve, 129
Dawson, Richard, 34
Day, William Farr, 180–81, 279, 280
Deacon, Belle, 3
Deacon, Edna, 3
Decoys, 67–69
The Decoy Works, Davie, FL, 69
DeCurtins, Jim, 267
Dekle, J. P. "Curly", 302–3
de la Cruz, Alejandro, 107
deLesseps, Michael, 193–94
Delgado, Francisco, 270–71
Delgado, Ildeberto "Eddie", 271
Dentzel, Gustav, 32
Dentzel, Michael, 33
Dentzel, William H., II, 34
Dentzel, William H., III, 32–34
Derr, Peter, 145
Desks, 99, 109, 112, 114, 115
  See also Furniture
Deuel, Helen, 67
Dickel, Philip, 3
Dickenson, Levi, 28
Digman, Gail, 260
Dillon, Don, 171–73
The Dockyard, South Freeport, ME, 194
Doering, Mavis, 10–11
Dolega, Stan, 162
Dolls, 69–77, 131, 275–76
  cornhusk, 65, 71–73
  straw hats for, 302
  teddy bears, 260–61
  See also Toys
Dolmetsch, Arnold, 179
Door hardware, 142–43, 147–49, 267
  brass, 27–28
Doormats, cornhusk, 65
Dorr, Elke, 244–45
Douthit, Charlotte, 249
The Dovetail Joint, Rockford, IL, 50
Dowd, William, 179
Dower chests, 77–79

Doyle, J. Michael, 119
Doyle-Schectman, Deborah, 71
Drain, Mark, 255, 300
Drake, Peter Garrison, 111
Drake, Phillips, 111
Drums, Choctaw, 54
Dulcimer noters, 280
Dulcimers, 178–79, 181–82
Dunn, Charlie, 164
Dupont, Gerry, 239–40
Dupuy, Roy L., 39
Dyeing of yarn, 251–53

Eagle carvings, 38–39
Early American furniture, 99–101
Earthenware, 194–95, 199–203
Edens, Marion C., 227, 253
Edouart, August, 243
Edwards, Ian F., 109
Egg baskets, 6, 7
Eggs, decorated, 79–80
Ehlers, Anna, 18
Eighteenth century furniture, 99–100
Ellis, Annabell, 5
Ellison, Lucinda, 124
Ellison, Nancy, 220, 252–53
Embroidery, 80–87
    See also Needlework
Emmett, Robert, 96
Enfield chairs, 48, 49
Erickson, George, 245
Erickson, Peter, 245–46
Ero, Graham, 242
Eskimo crafts, 155–56
    baskets, 2–3
    carvings, 34–35
    dolls, 69
    skin-sewing, 247–49
    See also Indian crafts
Euston, Charles, 90, 147
Euston, Pat, 90
Evans, Craig, 295
Evensizer, Barbara and John, 280–81
Everline, Lewis E., 280
The Exemplarery, 86
Ex Ophidia Press, Cottondale, AL, 23

Fabrics:
    hand-woven, 16–19, 62, 83, 131–32,
        285–99
    horsehair, 135
    kapa cloth, 153–55
    knitted, 155–58
    rugs, 220–29
    See also Embroidery; Leatherwork;
        Yarn, spinning and dyeing
Family Heir-Loom Weavers, Red Lion,
    PA, 225, 289
The Farmer's Museum, Inc.,
    Cooperstown, NY, 143, 147, 150
Farrell, David and Mary, 199–200
Fat lamps, 145

Feather baskets, 6
Featherwork, 87–90, 208
Federal period furniture, 100–101
Fehrenbach, Esta, 65
Felix, J. Donald, 284, 285
Fellenbaum, Tom, 179, 182
Fellers, Gerald, 267
Fiant, Jeffrey M., 50
Fiddles, 178
Fiedler, Ronnie, 51–52
Figureheads, 38–39, 56–57
Fine, Jody, 171
Fine Wood Works, Northport, AL, 111
Fireplace accessories, 28, 90–91, 267
Fisher, Elizabeth, 210
Fishermen's mittens, 158
Flintlock guns, 126–28
Flintridge Woodshop & Fibers, Sister
    Bay, WI, 253
Floorcloths, 91–93
Folk dolls, 75–76
Foltz, Carl Ned, 204
Ford, R. F., 255
Ford, Susan, 240
The Forge, Brook Park, OH, 145
Forgey, Marylee, 221
Forslund, Carl, 173
Fort Washakie Trading Co., Fort
    Washakie, WY, 12–13
Four Winds Craft Guild, Nantucket,
    MA, 8
Frakturs, 93–94
Frames, 43, 125, 126
Franklin Glassworks, 120
Frankson, Alex and Elaine, 3
Frazier, Rosie, 55
Frederick, Carol, 263
The Freedom Quilting Bee, Alberta, AL,
    215
French hand-sewing, 138–39
Fretwell, Forest, 253–55
Friday, Mary, 3
Friedrich, Wenzel, 101–2
Frost, Edward, 224
Frost, Lindsay E., 25
Frye's Measure Mill, Wilton, NH, 26
Furniture, 94–116
    crewel upholstery, 83–84
    dower chests, 77–79
    gametables, 117
    inlaid, 137, 138
    rosemaling decoration, 218–20
    spinning wheels, 253
    See also Chairs
Furs, 247–49

Gagne, Kerry P., 100
Galipeau, Janice, 209, 275
Gamble, Kae, 215
Gameboards, 116–17
Games:
    Choctaw, 54

Games (Continued)
    marbles, 170–71
    puzzles, 205–7
Gametables, 117
Gammage, M. E. "Manny", 65–67
Garcia, Nancy Brown, 14, 209
Garges, June Kraft, 302
Garland, Dan, 293
Garrett, Robert "Bud", 170–71
Gärtner, Franz Xavier, 287
Gaston, Jerry "Gotcheye", 255
Generations in Crochet, Memphis, TN,
    67
Gerakaris, Dimitri, 139–41
Gerard Originals, Methuen, MA, 120
Getz, C. R. and D. E., 127
G-H Productions, Adolphus, KY, 12
Gibson, Charles, 119
Gilbert, Scott, 12
Ginette, Eric, 46, 49, 50
Glass, 117–23, 278
The Glass Depot, San Rafael, CA, 123
Glen, Clifford and Leonard, 177
Glessing, Ernestine, 18
Goblets, metalwork, 170
Goehring, W. R., 97–98
Golay, Myrna, 294
Gold items, 169–70, 299–300
Gold stenciling, 257
Gomes, David, 183
Gonzales, Elidio, 113
Good & Co., Floorclothmakers, Dublin,
    NH, 91–92
Goodpasture, Lynn, 92, 255–56
Goodwin, Virginia, 161
Goosehill Farm Crafts, Orwell, VT, 71
Gordy, D. X., 198–99
Gordy, W. T. B., 198
Goss, Donald, 147
Gottilly, Doris Rockwell, 77
Gottshall, David and Marie, 126, 217
Gottshall, Walter L., 42
Gourdcraft Originals, Cleveland, GA,
    124
Gourds, 123–24
Graining, 124–26
Grass baskets, 3, 4–5
Gray, Dennis, 222, 225–26
Gray, Diana, 222–23, 225–26
Green, Slim, 231
Green Mountain Crafts, Morehead, KY,
    26
Greeves, Jeri, 12–13
Grell, Richard, 51
Grier, Fred, 38
Griffiths, John W., 242
Grimes, Nina, 215
Groff, Marjorie Cannon, 215
Gruwell, Miriam, 124
Guitars, 177–78
Guns, flintlock, 126–29
Gunstocks, hornwork, 133

Gurshin, Christopher, 174
Guys Folk Toys, Sugar Grove, NC, 278
Gwaltney, John, 159–60

Hairpins, wooden, 280
Hale Farm and Village, Bath, OH, 120–22
Hale Kuku O Moanalua, 154–55
Hale Naua III, 'Aiea, HI, 39, 40
Halford, Monica, 174, 217, 234–35
Hall, Carl D., 255
Hall, Clyde M., 207–9, 285
Hall, R. M., 255
Halwas, Stefanie, 71
Ham, Marion N., 224
Hamady, Walter, 23
Hamilton, Aubrey, 124
Hammered dulcimers, 178–79
Hammer Song, Boonsboro, MD, 265
Hammerworks, Worcester, MA, 267
Hampshire Pewter Company, Wolfeboro, NH, 189
Hand, David, 116
Hands and Hearts Stenciling, Rockford, IL, 93
Hangings, Norwegian-American weaving, 294
Hannah, Duncan, 56–57
Hannah, Marilyn, 57
Hannah, Pat, 56
Hardanger, 84, 85
Hardware, 142–44, 147–50
    brass, 27–28
Harn, Robert, 128
Harness, 166, 253–55
    horsehair, 133–35
    rawhide, 167–69
    See also Saddles
Harpsichords, 179–80
Harris, Paul and Susan, 28–29
Harry, Fran, 300
Hartley, Wilma (Mrs. Cecil), 15
Hartwigs, Gerhard, 58
Harvey, Charles, 26
Harvey, Joanne, 86
Hastrich, James, 104
Hatband, horsehair, 135
Hatchets, 160
Hathaway, Carl G., 242
Hats:
    cowboy, 65–67
    straw, 300–302
Haubrick, Liana, 1
Hawaiian crafts, 154–55
    carvings, 39–40
    featherwork, 87–88
    quilts, 210–12
The Hawaiian Quilter, Kaneahe, HI, 212
Hayes, Gordon, 255
Hayes, Herman L., 42

Hayne & Son Forged Hardware, Candler, NC, 145
Head, Trude, 94, 237
Heartwood Quilts, Newmarket, NH, 215
Hedebo, 84, 85
Hedge, Carolyn, 256, 257
Heilman, Carl, 250–51
Heirloom Fibers, Overland Park, KS, 295
Heir-Looms, Imler, PA, 295
Heirloom Weavings, Salem, MA, 288
Heisey, R. L., 136–38
Heitz, Ken, 95
Hejna, John J., 80
Helige Ande Arts, West Newbury, MA, 217
Heller, Marilyn, 139
Hepplewhite, George, 100–101
Herget, Dee, 237–39
Heritage Lanterns, Yarmouth, ME, 267
Heritage Rugs, Lahaska, PA, 227
Hex signs, 129–30
The Hiding Place, Ingram, TX, 52
Hieba, Betty, 263
High Point Crafts, Tully, NY, 29
Hill, John H., 126
Hill, Rupert, 96
Hinges, iron, 142–43
Hobbles, 168
Hoffman, Beatrice H., 272–73
Hogscraper candlesticks, 146
Hogsed, Ethel, 38
Holmes, David J., 23, 179–80
Holmes, Evan, 188
Holmes, Lydia, 187–88
Holzer, Joyce, 256, 257
Homeyard, Illoyna Sotack, 80–81
Hooked rugs, 223–25
Hoole, Bill, 115–16
Hoop-back chairs, 47
Hopf, Claudia, 236–37
Hopi Arts and Crafts Guild, Second Mesa, AZ, 131–32
Hopi crafts, 131–32
Horn, Judy, 73
Hornwork, 132–33
    furniture, 101–2
Horse-drawn vehicles, 281–82
Horsehair items, 133–35
Horton, Gail Fischer, 223–24
Horton Brasses, Cromwell, CT, 28
Hotchkiss, Sara, 227
Hought, Gail, 135
Household items:
    iron, 143–45
    linens, 287–88
    tinware, 264–67, 268–69
    treenware, 279–80
Houser, Betsy and Dick, 221
Houses, timber-frame construction, 135–36
Howe, Lenore, 48–49

Howe, Margery Burnham, 161
Hoyt, Ivan, 129–30
Huart-Wourms, Rosemarie, 185
Hubbard, Frank, 179
Hudson, Clarissa, 18
Humphrey, Lynn, 115–16
Hungerford, Rebecca, 189–90
Hunter, Dard, 184
Hurn, Gail E., 210
Hurwitz, Daniel, 141–42
Hutchinson, Robert D., 182

Ideal Toy Company, 260
Ikat weaving, 297
Indian crafts:
    beadwork, 12–14
    Cherokee, 10–11, 52–54
    Chilkat dance robes, 18
    Choctaw, 54–56
    featherwork, 88–90
    jewelry, 152–53
    leatherwork, 161–63
    Lummi, 6, 18–19
    Morning Star quilts, 212–13
    Pomo baskets, 8
    quillwork, 207–9
    ribbonwork, 217–18
    stone pipes, 191–92
    tepees, 261–62
    tomahawks, 273–75
    totem poles, 275–77
    See also Eskimo crafts; Hawaiian crafts
Ingersoll, Ian, 49, 108
Ingrain carpet, 225
Inlay, 136–38
    ironwork, 145–47
Innisfree Weaving Center, Inc., Berea, KY, 227
The Interwood Company, Port Townsend, WA, 282
Ironwork, 139–51, 267
    branding irons, 26–27
    firebacks, 90
    tomahawks, 274
    See also Metalwork
Isackson, Emma, 3
The Island Scrimshander, Mackinac Island, MI, 240
Istaboli equipment, 54
Ivory, carvings, 34–35

Jackson, Dorica, 18
Jackson, Karen, 288
Jackson, Mary A., 5
Jacquard weaving, 288–89
James, Bill, and Fran, 6, 18–19
James, Ned, 141
James, William J., Co., Denmark, ME, 51
Janus Press, West Burke, VT, 22–23
Jarrow, Judy, 221
Jensen, Lucia Tarallo, 87–88

INDEX

Jensen, Rocky Ka'iouliokahihikolo'Ehu, 39–40
Jensen Turnage Pottery, Lanexa, VA, 200
Jenson, Karen, 219–20
Jewelry, 35, 63, 151–53
  beadwork, 12–14
  Hopi, 132
  Western-style, 300
Jischke, George, 253
Johnson, Carolyn, 25, 26
Johnson, Jack Lowell, 25–26
Johnston, Gladys Daniels, 93
Jones, Anita Romero, 234
Jones, David, 189
Jones, Ray, 164
Joyner, Tony, 124
Jugs, pottery, 195–97
Jugtown Mountain Rugs, Topanga, CA, 220–21
Jugtown pottery, Seagrove, NC, 194–95
Justin Carriage Works, Nashville, MI, 281

Kachinas, 131
Kakalia, Deborah U., 211–12
Kalona Kountry Kreations, Kalona, IA, 210
Kamahinaokalani'ehukapuaoka'iouli, Natalie, 88
Kamaka Ukelele, Honolulu, HI, 183
K & M Forge, McConnellsville, NY, 145
Kane, Michael, 8
Kapa cloth, 153–55
Karen's Krafts, Milan, MN, 220
Kashin, Muffy, 70–71
Kauainui, Mrs. Sarah, 88
Kauffman, Mabel, 210
Kayaks, 247
Kearney, Lisa, 262–63
Kear's Broom Shop, Gatlinburg, TN, 29
Kekuewa, Mary Louise, 88
Kelly, Philip B., 266
Kelly, Tom, 91
Kennedy, Doris Finch, 259–60
Kennedy, Norman, 16–18
Kent, Virginia, 24
Kentucky rifles, 126–27
Kepka's Kraslice, Ellsworth, KS, 80
Kilbourn & Proctor, Inc., Scituate, MA, 58
Kilgore, Mr. and Mrs. Allen, 73
King, Don, 231
King, Donald, 127
King, Edna, 55
King, Nancy, 55
Kingeekuk, Amelia, 35, 69, 248
Kingeekuk, Floyd, 35, 69
Kingeekuk, Ruthelle, 248
King's Saddlery, Sheridan, WY, 231
Kiracofe, Brian, 240
Kiracofe, Daniel, 240

Kiracofe, Gary, 240
Kirklin, Jerry, 127
Kirkpatrick, Will, 69
Kitchen utensils, 144
  baking molds, 171–73
  ironwork, 146, 150–51
  tinware, 264–66
Klein, Alois, 107
Kline, Carole, 288–89
Kline, David, 225, 288–89
Knitted rugs, 223
Knitwear, 155–58
Knives, 158–60
  horn-handled, 133
Knopp, Steven, 96–97
Knot In Vane, DeKalb, IL, 17, 69
Knotted bed coverings, 14–15
Knouss, Alice, 76
Knox, Jan, 215
Koopus, Jeff, 50
Koyuk, Isaac, 35
Kraatz, Michael, 117–19
Kraatz Russell Glass, Caanan, NH, 119
Kramer, Peter, 105–7
Krause, Marika, 220
Krauss, Beatrice, 154
Krug, G., & Son, Inc., Baltimore, MD, 141
Kump, Andrew, 289
Kunkle, Robert, 58–60
Kybee-Grubber, Doris, 18

Lace, 160–61
  crocheted, 67
  Irish, 138–39
  tatted, 258–60
Ladderback chairs, 45–46, 52
Ladies Aid of the Methodist Church, Chebeague Island, ME, 158
Laidman, Virginia and William, 31
Laity Woodcarvers, Lancaster, PA, 69
Lakota Jewelry Visions, Rapid City, SD, 152–53
LaLena, Constance, 225
Lalioff, Steven M., 164–65, 187
Lally, Barbara, 80
Lamb, David, 107–8
Lamps, 43, 188
Lampwork, 119–20
Landsverk, Halvor, 105
Lankford, Robin, 117
Lanterns, pierced tin, 269–70
Larsen, Angela, 249
Larsen, Angela, 249
Lathrop, Jim, 229–31
Latches, iron, 147–49
Lathrop, Jim, 229–31
Latourelle, Norton, 42
Lavery, Robert M., 119
Lavoie, Gerard, 119–20
Lea, Barbara, 101
Lea, James A., 50, 100–101
Lead crystal, 120
Leaded glass, 117–19

Leatherwork, 161–69
  petacas, 186–87
  saddles, 229–31
  skin-sewing, 247–49
  whips, 302–3
Lefko, Linda C., 125–26
Leis, feather, 87, 88
Lelooska, Don, 275–77
The Lelooska Family, Ariel, WA, 277
Leone, Ellen, 18
Leong, Hattie, 88
Leopold, F. W. "Dutch", 163–64
Leopold, Henry, 163
Leopold's Boot Shop, Morgan, TX, 164
Levin, Ed, 136
Lighting fixtures, 43, 188
  brass, 28
  ironwork, 144
  tinware, 264–67, 269–70
Linck, John Michael, 278
Lindsey, Julia A., 290–91, 295
Lindsey-Woolseys of Ohio, Germantown, OH, 290–91, 295
Linen fabrics, hand-woven, 286–91
Lingle, Doris, 69
Linsey-woolsey, 290
Little Bit of Bybee, Louisville, KY, 205
Liturgical items, 169–70, 270–71, 294
Livers, Kathleen, 93
Loch, Kay and Ron, 227
Logan, William T., 203
Lokanin, Margaret, 3
The Long Family, Phoenixville, PA, 204
Longhurst, Denise, 84–86
Loose, Thomas G., 145–47
Lopez, Eurgencio and Orlinda, 234
Lopez, Felix A., 233, 257–58
Lopez, George T., 234
Lopez, Jose Benjamin, 234
Lopez, Joseph and Krissa, 258
Lopez, Manuel, 235, 236
Lossiah, William, 52–54, 274–75
Low Country Candles, St. Simons Island, GA, 31
Lujan, Luisito, 234
Lujan, Maria T., 83
Lukacovic, Perry, 300
Lummi crafts, 6, 18–19
Lymburner, Janice, 123–24
Lynn, Paul D., 198

McAdams, Mrs. Eva, 62
McClure, Hal, 37
McConlogue, K. Kerchner, 94, 237
McDonald, Rosemarie, 256, 263
Mack, Daniel, 96
McKay, Mabel, 8
McLaughlin, Virginia Jacobs, 78–79, 91, 94, 174–75, 257
McLellan, Leigh, 23
McMahon, Theresa, 166
McMillan, Sandy, 263

Maine baskets, 6–7
The Maine Bucket Co., Auburn, ME, 64
Makepeace Chandlers, Dover-Foxcroft, ME, 31
Mandarino, Monte, 128
Mann, Barbara, 302
Mantle, Bob, 64
Marbles, flintrock, 170–71
Marbling, 255–57
Marquetry, 136–38
Marshall, Jessie, 15–16, 295
Marshall, Lila, 71, 72
Marshall, Samuel, 197
Marshfield School of Weaving, Plainfield, VT, 16–18
Martens, Susan, 93
Martha Wetherbee's Basket Shop, Sanbornton, NH, 9
Martin, Nora, 210
Martinez, Angelina Delgado, 236, 270–72
Martinez, Efren, 236, 271
Martinez, Eluid L., 233
Martinez, Larry B., 300
Martinez de Pedro, Linda, 236
Maryland Art Glass, Silver Spring, MD, 123
Masks, 248, 276–77
Maslach, Steven, 171
Mason, Sherry, 93
Massey, William, 69
Matfay, Larry, 35
Matfay, Martha, 3
Maxwell, Carol, 237
May, Warren A., 182
Mayac, Peter, 35
Mayac, Teddy, 35
Maynard House Antiques, Westborough, MA, 99
Mazyck, Mary, 5
Meaders, Cleater, 195–96
Meaders, Edwin and John Rufus, 196, 197
Meaders, Lanier, 196, 197
Meaders Folk Pottery, Byron, GA, 196
Meadowcroft, Eleanor, 42
Meadow Press, San Francisco, CA, 23
Medicine Man Craft Shop, Cherokee, NC, 192
Medicine Mountain Trading Co., Sturgis, SD, 161–63, 209
Messersmith, Joseph, 266–67
Messner, Charles, 264–65
Metalwork, 139–51
  brass, 27–28
  knives, 158–60
  liturgical, 169–70
  pewter, 187–91
  silver, 245–46
  See also Ironwork
Metcalf, Betsy, 301
Meyer, Heidi, 24

Michton, Morris, 260
Middlemas, Linda, 295
Milk pans, pottery, 197, 198
Miller, Anita, 227
Miller, Chris and Meredith, 99
Miller, Elmer, 255
Miller, Sara, 210
Miller, Steve, 23
Miller, Susan and Sven, 25
Milligrock, Lincoln, 35
Mill River Hammerworks, Turners Falls, MA, 141
Miniatures, 102–4, 202, 295
Mississippi Crafts Center, Ridgeland, MS, 54–56
Mittens, knitted, 158
Mix, Allean, 217
Mize, Robert R., 181–82
MJA Porcelain Dolls, Hope Valley, RI, 75
Moccasins, 12–13, 62, 162
Molds, for baking, 171–73
Montana Carriage Company, Inc., Columbia Falls, MT, 281
Moon, Arlin, 177, 178
Moore, Gates, 267
Moran, William F., Jr., 158–59
Moretti, Roberto, 122
Moretz, James L., 128–29
Morgalis, Annie, 80
Morgan, A. G., 27
Morgan, Nancy, 220
Morgan, Scott, 177–78
Morgan, Tom, 175, 177
Morning Star quilts, 212–13
Morrill, Benjamin, 58
Mosheim, Dan, 50
Mostrom, Jocelyn, 73
Mougin, Genevieve, 160
Mountain Craft Shop, New Martinsville, WV, 278
Mt. Lebanon chair, 49
Mounts, Aaron, 41
Mukluks, 248
Mule-ear chairs, 46, 47
Mummert, Becky, 204
Murals, 173–75
Musial, Kalley, 293
Musical instruments, 175–83
Musk Ox Producers' Co-operative, Anchorage, AK, 155–56
Myers, Butch, 167
Myers, J. R., Co., Richmond, VA, 167
Mystic Maritime Gallery, Mystic, CT, 21
Mystic Seaport Museum, Mystic, CT, 242

Nails, iron, 147
Nampeyo, Fannie, 131
Nantucket lightship baskets, 7–8
Narragansett beadwork, 14
Nash, Mary, 69

Natural Metals, Jackson, MS, 265
Nautical carvings, 38–39
Navajo Arts and Crafts Enterprise, Window Rock, AZ, 292
Navajo crafts, 62–63, 153, 291–93
Needlework, 138–39
  embroidery, 80–87
  knitwear, 155–58
  lace, 160–61
  quilts, 209–15
  rugs, 222–23
  tools, 183
Nejdl, Marjorie Kopecek, 80
Nelson, Billie, 220
Nelson, John Scott, 126
Nelson, Judy, 220
Nelson, Mark, 50
Neptune, Stan, 275, 277
Netting, 85, 160–61
Newell, Eddie, 7
New England Firebacks, Woodbury, CT, 90
New England pottery, 197–98
Nolan, Sara, 93
Norsk Husflid, Barronett, WI, 105
Norsk Wood Works, Barronett, WI, 105
North Country Dulcimers, Valencia, PA, 182
North Woods Chair Shop, Canterbury, NH, 48–49
Northwood Stoneware Pottery, Northwood, NH, 198
Norwegian-American crafts, 40–41, 104–5
  weaving, 293–94
Nowalka-Gilinsky, Magdalena, 186
Nutt, Craig, 110–11

Odden, Phillip, 104–5
Ohio glass, 120–22
Ohio Valley chairs, 48, 49
Oklahoma Indian Arts and Crafts Cooperative, Anadarko, OK, 90
Oktavec, William Anton, 237
Old Abingdon Weavers, Abingdon, VA, 295
Old Broom and Basket Shop, West Amana, IA, 4, 29
The Old Hickory Company, 94
Old Town Artisans, Tucson, AZ, 153
Oley Valley Blueware, Fleetwood, PA, 203
Oley Valley Redware, Fleetwood, PA, 203
Olson, Cecilia, 3
O'Neill, Bill, 122–23
Oosterman, William F., 42
Open Cupboard, Tenants Harbor, ME, 25
Orr, J. F., & Sons, Sudbury, MA, 98–99
Ortega, Eulogio and Zoraida, 234

INDEX

Ortega's Weaving Shop, Chimayo, NM, 297
Osmundsen, David W., 145
Overshot coverlets, 294–95
Oviedo, Marco A., 113, 233, 235, 236, 297
Oviedo, Pat, 233, 297
Owens, Vernon, 194

Pacific Western Traders, Folsom, CA, 8
Packbaskets, 1
Painting:
   frakturs, 93–94
   hex signs, 129–30
   murals, 173–75
   pottery, 198–99
   reverse, 216–17, 272–73
   rosemaling, 218–20
   stenciled, 255–56
   tepees, 261–62
   theorem, 262–63
   tinware, 268–69
   window-screens, 237–39
Pairpoint Glass Works, Sagamore, MA, 120
Palmer, Chlotiea, 62, 89, 261–62
Palmer, Dixon, 88–89, 262
Palmer, George, 89
Palota, Marie, 263
Panek, Bruce C., 265–66
Panijak, Rosalie, 69
Panzarella, Joe, 29
Paper, handmade, 184–85
Papercuts, 184–86
   scherenschnitte, 236–37
   silhouettes, 242–45
Papercuttings by Alison, Sarasota, FL, 237
Papier-mâché dolls, 77
Papp, Nora, 257
Paradis, Bob and Donna, 69
Park, Helen DuPree, 124
Parkas, 248
Parker Mountain Decoys, Center Barnstead, NH, 69
Parquetry, 136–38
Patched rugs, 225–26
Pate, Rowdy, 135, 167–69
Paton, Bruce L., 20–21
Pavila, Molly, 3
Peale, Charles Willson, 243
Peet, Beverly, 117
Pemaquid Floorcloths, Round Pond, ME, 92
Penayah, Caroline, 69
Perfectly Warped, Troy, OH, 227, 286
The Perishable Press, Mount Horeb, WI, 23
Perrera, Leimomi, 88
Peterkin, E. W., 166
Peterson, Dolores, 220
Peterson, Gene, 255

Petty, Virginia, 278–80
Pewter items, 169–70, 187–91
The Pewter Shop, Kansas City, MO, 189–90
Phillips, Charles Weston, 111
Picazio, Edward and Marianne, 216–17
Piedmont pottery, 199–200
Pierced tin, 269–70
Piggins, 64
Pilgrim Pewterers, Stow, MA, 187–88
Pingayuk, Mary, 69
Pins and Bobbins, Dallas, TX, 160
Pipestone Indian Shrine Association, Pipestone, NM, 192
Pistols, flintlock, 126
Pleasant Walk Folk, Myersville, MD, 261
Plimouth Plantation, Plymouth, MA, 242
Podell, Linda, 126, 256
Pomeroy, Sandra Pearl, 117
Pomo baskets, 8
Popcorn Studio, Murfreesboro, TN, 200
Porcelain dolls, 73–75
Porter, Rufus, 173
Potato baskets, 6, 7
Pottery, 122, 194–205
   Cherokee, 54
   Hopi, 131
   tile, 263–64
Potts, Bonnie Jean, 144–45
Potts, Ronald E., 144–45
Potts, Thomas, 90
Powder horns, 132, 133
Pratt, Cameron and Rick, 242
Pressed glass, 120
Pretty Voice Hawk, 152
Primitive carvings, 41–42
Pritchard, Mary, 154
Pulford, Florence, 213
Pumphret, Marcy, 240
Pure and Simple, Nashville, AR, 116
Putnam, Nol, 141
Puzzles, 205–7

Qiviut knitwear, 155–56
Quail Hill Designs, Clark, NJ, 224
Qualla Arts & Crafts Center, Cherokee, NC, 52–54, 73, 192, 274–75
The Queen Anne Parlour, Greenport, NY, 224
Quillwork, 207–9
The Quiltery, Boyertown, PA, 215
Quilts, 209–15
Quirts, 168

Rafter-Four Designs, Sandpoint, ID, 221, 222–23, 225–26
Rag dolls, 75–76
Rag rugs, 226–27
Raikes, Bob and Carol, 77
Rain parkas, 248
Raiselis, R. P., 64

Rakes, 215–16
Ramsey, Victoria Trujillo, 300
Ranier Metalcraft, Tacoma, WA, 190
Raphaela, 93
Rastetter, Maureen, 295
Rastetter, Tim, 226–27, 295
Rastetter Woolen Mill, Millersburg, OH, 226–27
Ratliff, B. Terry, 46
Rattles, ceremonial, 276–77
Rawhide, 167–69
Ray, Gail, 87
Red Clay Tile Works, Pittsburgh, PA, 264
Red Ozier Press, New York, NY, 23
Refsal, Harley, 40–41
Reilly, Michelle, 251–52
Religious objects, 231–36, 257–58
   See also Liturgical items
Renaissance Press, Annapolis, MD, 23
Rendon, Enrique, 234
Renna, Matthew, 37
Renzetti, Peter A., 142–43, 285
Reproductions:
   fabrics, 286
   footwear, 166–67
   furniture, 99–101, 107–15
   hardware, 142–43
   ironwork, 150
   leatherwork, 164–65
   miniature furniture, 102–4
   netted canopies, 161
   period clothing, 60–62
   petacas, 186–87
   pottery, 197
   ships, 240–42
   tinware, 266
Reredos, 234–36
Retablos, 232–36, 297
Revere, Paul, 283–85
Reverse painting, 216–17
   tinsel painting, 272–73
Reynolds, Kathi, 60–61
Reynolds, Martin F., 58
Rhein, Margaret, 185
Ribbonwork, 217–18
Richardson, Ben, 238
Rieman, Tim, 49
Rifles, 126–29
Rill, Stanley, 34
Rio Grande weaving, 296–97
Ritchie, Kati, 186
Rizetta, Sam, 179
Roach, Dianne Carol, 227–29
Roberson, Carole S., 62
Robinson, Beverly, 301–2
Robson, Joe W., 26, 108
Robson, Malcolm, 126
Robson Worldwide Graining, Ltd., Fairfax, VA, 126
Rochester Folk Art Guild, Middlesex, NY, 119, 277–78

Rocking chairs, 52, 98
  See also Chairs; Furniture
Rogers, Kevin, 120, 121–22
Romera, Orlando, 234
Romero, Emilio and Zenaida, 272
Rope:
  horsehair, 134–35
  rawhide, 168
Rose, Marion, 80
Rosemaling, 218–20
Rosenquist, Bill and Marilyn, 7–8
Roth, William James, 99
Rountree, Susan, 104
Rowantrees Pottery, Blue Hill, ME, 198
Rowden, Shalah, 217–18
Rowell, Mona, 263
Roybal, Max, 234
Rugs, 17, 220–29, 289, 290, 297
  embroidered, 16
  floorcloths, 91–93
  Norwegian-American, 294
Rummonds, Richard-Gabriel, 23
Rupp, Becky, 31
Rural Arts & Crafts Cooperative,
    Parkersburg, WV, 215
Russell, Susan, 117–19
Rustic Furnishings, New York, NY, 96
Ruta, Jadwiga, 185–86
Ryan, Julie, 220

Saari, Michael J., 145
Saddles, 229–31
  silver mountings, 299–300
  See also Harness
Saguto, D. A., 166–67
St. John, Richard, 101–2
Sakeva, Dora, 131
Salazar, David, 233
Salazar, Leon Jorge, 232–33
Salt & Chestnut, West Barnstable, MA,
    285
The Saltbox, Lancaster, PA, 267
Salt-glaze pottery, 194–95, 200–201
Salt O' Thee Earth Pottery, Guernsey,
    OH, 200–201
The Sampler, Plymouth, MA, 84
Samplers, 86–87
Sanborn, Ingrid, 217
Sanchez, James, 234
Sanchez, Joseph T., 234
Sand, Toland, 122
Sanders, Marian, 14
Sandom, Hans, 105
Sandoval, George, 111–13
Santee Sioux, stone pipe, 192
Santiago, Ethel, 215
Santos, 232–36
Sari, Peter, 255
Sawyer, David, 49–50, 51
Sayle, Bill and Judy, 8
Saylor, Duane, 69
Scadden, Walt, 145

Scannell, Marion, 287
Schaeffer, Mr. and Mrs. Ted, 169
Schaezlein, Robert, 255, 300
Schanz, Joanna E., 3–4
Schanz, Norman, 4
Scherenschnitte, 236–37
  See also Papercuts
Scherer, Bill, 109
Schimmel, Wilhelm, 41
Schmidt, William, 183, 280
Schnacke, Dick, 278
Schranks, 98
Schurig, Patricia, 67
Scott, Racheal Alexander, 209–10
Scow, Darlene R., 215
Scratch-carved furniture, 105–6
Screen Art, Baltimore, MD, 239
Scrimshaw, 8, 239–40
Sea grass baskets, 4–5
Seal gut baskets, 3
Seamstress cameos, 31
Selby, Cleland and Suzanne, 225
Self, Bob, 43
Sen, Wesley, 154–55
Seto, A. Ulu, 88
Settona Willow Co., Murrieta, CA, 115,
    116
Sexton, Sharon, 126
Sgraffito, 203–4
Shaker crafts, 8–9, 25–26, 48–49,
    107–9
Shatswell, Nicole, 288
Sheepherder wagons, 281–82
Sheets, Joyce, 260–61
Shenandoah furniture, 109–10
Sheraton, Thomas, 100, 101
Shew, Dick and Kay, 206–7
Shipcarver's Shop, Mystic, CT, 38
Ships, 240–42
  models, 20–21
Shirley, Earlon, 255
The Shoemakers (candles), Oley, PA, 31
Shoes, historic reproductions, 166–67
  See also Boots; Moccasins
Shona-Hah (Mary Smith), 275–76
Shoshone beadwork, 12, 13
Shoshone Buckskin and Beadwork,
    Clearfield, UT, 14
Shourds, Harry V., 69
Silhouettes, 242–45
Silk fabrics, hand-woven, 286
Silver, Mark, 127
Silver items, 245–46, 299–300
  conchas, 62–63
  harness decorations, 254–55
  Hopi, 132
  liturgical, 169–70
The Silvias, 30–31
Simmons, Harold B., 38
Simmons, Schtockschnitzler, 42
Simon, Barry and Lisa, 8, 240
Sioux crafts, 153, 161

Skeps, 246–47
Skinner, Arlene, 3
Skinner, Janet S., 298
Skin-sewing, 247–49
Skoog, Teresa A., 256, 257
Sleds, 249–50
Sleighs, 249–50
Slip-painted pottery, 201–4
Slippers, Alaskan, 248
  See also Boots; Moccasins; Shoes
Smart, Anna, 3
Smith, Bill, 96
Smith, Cathy, 161–63, 209
Smith, David T., 99, 126
Smith, Harry W., 102–4
Smith, Helen H., 69
Smith, Jerry Read, 179
Smith, Lena, 3
Smith, Mary (Shona-Hah), 275–76
Smith, Melbourne, 240–42
Smith, William B. "Bill", 1
Smiths, 274
Smith's Adirondack Crafts, 1
The Smithy, Wolcott, VT, 145
Smocking, 138–39
Smokehouse Country Crafts,
    Middletown, MD, 30
Snowden, Barry and Cheryl, 122–23
Snowshoes, 250–51
Snyder, Michael, 145
Snype, Henrietta, 5
Snype, Latrelle, 5
Solomon, Jeffie, 55
Solomon, Lela, 55
Song bows, 180–81
Soule, Toby, 93
Southern furniture, 110–11
Southern Highlands Handicraft Guild,
    Ashville, NC, 14, 15, 71
Southern mountain knives, 159–60
Southern mountain rifles, 128–29
Southern Plains Indian Museum Shop,
    Anadarko, OK, 14
Southwestern colonial ironwork, 148–49
Southwest Spanish Craftsmen, 112, 113
Spanish colonial furniture, 111–13
Spatterware, 204–5
Spaulding, Paul H., 143, 147, 150–51
Spekulaas molds, 171–73
Spencer, Dolly, 69
Spinning, 251–53
Spinning wheels, 253
Spiron, Charles, 68
Spongeware, 204–5
Spoons, 187–88, 190–91, 246
Spoor, Margaret Paradise, 77
Sprigged pottery, 202
Spring, John B., 242
Springerle molds, 171–73
Spring House Classics, Lebanon, PA, 98
Spurs, 253–55
Staffs, ceremonial, 277

INDEX

Stambaugh, Ron, 205
Stampers, Alyne, 54
Staples, Stephen C., 99
Starr, Penelope C., 123
Stauffer, John L., 64
Stauffer, J. Thomas, 189, 190
Stave Puzzles, Inc., Norwich, VT, 207
Steel, Terry, 141
Stenciling, 255–57, 262–63
Stennes, Elmer, 58
Stephen, James B., 128
Stessel, Beverly, 117
Stewart, Alex, 64
Stewart, David, 169
Stewart, Rick, 64, 181
Stoker, Linda, 295
Stoles, hand-woven, 298
Stoltzfus, Katie, 210
Stoltzfus, Lizzie, 210
Stoneham Pewter, Brookfield, NH, 189
Stone pipes, 191–92
Stoneware, 194–95, 199–200
Stools, 52
Stough, Alice, 158
Stoughton, Don, 90
Stoveplates, 90
Stove polish, beeswax, 31
Straus, Lonita, 243–44
Strauss, Marilyn E., 285
Straw hats, 300–302
Straw inlay, 257
Strawser, Barbara, 126
Strawser, Daniel G., 41–42
Streeter, Donald, 148
Stringed dulcimers, 181–82
Strode, Barbara and Jim, 190–91
Stromsoe, Randy, 169–70
Sturgill, Dan, 177
Sturgill, David A., 176–77, 178
Sturgill, John, 177
Summer-and-winter rugs, 227–29
Summers, Tom, 145
Sunflower, Cliff and Lois, 31
Svarney, Gertrude, 3
Swedish braid rugs, 223
Sweetland, J., 76

Table linens, 287–89, 297–99
  crocheted, 67
Tables:
  Chinese Chippendale, 96–97
  country-style, 98
  gametables, 117
  Queen Anne, 109
  Shaker, 108
  See also Chairs; Furniture
Tagarook, Greg, 3
Talin, Jim, 23
Talin, Pamela, 23
Talin Bookbindery, Brewster, MA, 23
Tallow candles, 30

Tanner, Gordon, 178
Tapia, Star, 187, 258
Tarbox, Sandra B., 91, 256
Tate, Pam and Randy, 69, 117
Tatting, 258–60
Tatting shuttles, 183
Taylor, Cledie C., 151–52
Taylor, Joyce, 52
Taylor, Roberta, 126
Teddy bears, 260–61
Teich, Peggy, 225
Temple, Mary, 294
Teneriffe embroidery, 85
Tepees, 261–62
Terrapin Paper Mill, Cincinnati, OH, 185
Terry, Eli, 58
Tertichny, Mrs. Boris, 80
Texas Hatters, Buda, TX, 67
Theorem painting, 262–63
Thlunaut, Jennie, 18
Thomas, Astrid, 256, 257
Thomas, Earlean, 12
Thompson, Agnes, 3
Thompson, Glen D., 231
Thompson, Let, 11
Three Feathers Pewter, Columbus, OH, 189
Thumb-back chairs, 46, 47
Thun, Candy, 175, 256
Ticking, linen, 290
Tierney, Louise J., 75
Tile, 263–64
Tilter chair (Shaker), 49
Timber-frame construction, 135–36
Timbertoys of Vermont, Fairfax, VT, 278
Tinsel painting, 272–73
Tinware, 257, 264–72
Tolpin, Jim, 281–82
Tomah, J. A., 1
Tomahawks, 273–75
Tomson, Bob and Gail, 265
Tools, 150, 215–16
Totem poles, 275–77
Touhey, Peter, 50
Towels, handwoven, 287–88
Toys, 277–78, 285
  puzzles, 205–7
  See also Dolls
Traditional Leatherwork Co., Noblesville, IN, 165
Tramp art, 42, 43
Treenware, 278–80
Troyer, Simon, 226
Trujillo, Irvin, 296
Trujillo, Isabel, 297
Trujillo, Jake, 297
Trujillo, John R., 297
Trujillo, Lisa, 296
Trunks, painted tin, 268–69

The Trust for Native American Crafts and Cultures, Greenville, NH, 32, 251
Tubby, Darryl, 55
Tucker, Lois, 268–69
Tucker-Jones Tavern Puzzles, Setauket, NY, 207
Tulipware, 201–3
Turley, Frank, 27, 148–49
Turley Forge, Santa Fe, NM, 149
Turner, Ellen, 77
Turner, Laura, 261
Turtlecreek Potters, Morrow, OH, 204
Twinrocker Handmade Paper, Brookston, IN, 184–85

Ukeleles, 182–83
Umiaks, 247–48
Ungolt, Josephin, 69
Unicorn Candles, Telford, PA, 31
Unique 1, Camden, ME, 158
Upholstery, crewel embroidered, 83–84

Vaillancourt, Henri, 31–32, 251
Valdez, Horacio E., 234
Valk, Gene, 287–88, 295
Van Antwerp, Glen, 38
Vandal, N., 100
Vanderhorst, Mary V., 5
Van Der Maas, Daniel A., 240
Van Dorpe, Pua, 155
Van Duren, Henry, 201
VanHoose, Ed, 96
Vanishing American Needle Arts, Mendon, UT, 86
Van Vliet, Claire, 22–23
Veneering, 113–15
Vergara-Wilson, Maria, 82–83
Vermont rockers, 46, 47
Vigil, Fred, 234
Village Antiques Shop, Blowing Rock, NC, 15
Village Lantern, North Marshfield, MA, 267
Village Pewter, Medina, OH, 189
Vitrix Hot Glass Studio, Corning, NY, 117
Voake, R., 278
Von Gunten, Walter, 237

Wabanaki Arts on the Penobscot Reservation, Old Town, ME, 209, 275, 277
Wagner, Dick, 255
Wagons, horse-drawn, 281–82
Wallpaper, 282–83
Walsh, Martha Link, 237, 245
Walz, Nancy and Ron, 30
Warbonnets, 88–89
Warm Valley Arts & Crafts, Ft. Washakie, WY, 62

Washington, Martha, 161
Waterford Weavers, East Lyme, CT, 287
Waterman Hill Studio, Quechee, VT, 71
Watts, Blanche, 5
Way Back When, Fort Wayne, IN, 76
Weapons:
    guns, 126–29
    knives, 158–60
    tomahawks, 273–75
Weathervanes, 283–85
Weber, David, 190
Webster, Nancy Lou, 280
Weefhuis Studio, Gloversville, NY, 287–88, 295
Weekley, Marie, 29
Weidner, Georg Adam, 202
Weinkauf, John A., 164
Weir, Beverly, 93, 94
Weldon, Charles, 231
Welker, Eugene L., 113–15
Wendt, Kurt, 287
Western Silversmiths, Hawthorne, CA, 300
Westmoore Pottery, Seagrove, NC, 199–200
Wetherbee, Martha, 9
Wetherbee's Basket Shop, Sanbornton, NH, 9
Weycouania, Stephan, 35
Wheaton Village Glasshouse, Millville, NJ, 119
Wheat-weaving, 300–302
Wheeler, Ellsworth H. "Bud", 197–98
Whips, 302–3
The Whistlin' Whittler, Oakland, KY, 279–80
White, Bill and Grace, 36–37
White, Cheryl and Ted, 189
White, S. Tracy, 299–300

White oak baskets, 10–12
The White Oak Forge, The Plains, VA, 141
Whitesmithing, 145–47
Whitley, Robert, 99–100
Whitten, Paul F., 8
Wiggins, David, 173–74, 257
Wiggins, Gerard, 174
Willard, Aaron, 58
Willard, Aaron, Jr., 58
Willard, Simon, 58
Williams, Ann, 295
Williams, D. R., 267
Williams, Levine and Susie, 251
Willis, J. Richard, 64, 182
Willow baskets, 3–4
Willow furniture, 115–16
The Willow Place, Roswell, GA, 116
Willow root baskets, Eskimo, 2
Willow Works, Magadore, OH, 116
Wilnoty, John Julius, 52, 53, 192
Wilson, Gene, 173
Wilson, John, 26
Wilson, Maria Vergara, 297
Wilson, Priscilla, 123–24
Wilson, Sadye Tun, 259–60
Window-screens, painted, 237–39
Windsor chairs, 49–51
Windy Hill Forge, Perry Hall, MD, 142
Winters Textile Mill, Winters, CA, 288
Wise, Lewis, 169
Wolfe, Eva, 52, 53
Wolf scarers, 35
Women's Exchange, Hartford, CT, 14
Wongittlin, Elmer, 34
Woodbury Blacksmith & Forge Co., Woodbury, CT, 147–48
Woodbury Pewterers, Woodbury, CT, 190

Woodcock-Lynn, Kathryn, 198
Woodstock Pottery, Woodstock Valley, CT, 198
Woody, Arval, 45
Woody's Chair Shop, Spruce Pine, NC, 45
Woolen fabrics, hand-woven, 16–18, 286
Wool yarn, 251–53
Worley, Mary, 16–18, 62
Worthing, Michelle, 25
Woven fabrics, 62, 83, 285–99
    blankets, 16–19
    boundweave rugs, 227–29
    Hopi, 131–32
    horsehair, 135
    ingrain carpet, 225
    rag rugs, 226–27

Yancey, Minnie B., 227
Yarbrough, Joyce A., 244
Yarn, spinning and dyeing, 251–53
Yeiser, Nancy, 25
Yesteryear Toy Co., Charleston, WV, 278
Yoder, Gerald H., 201–3
Yoder, Marjorie, 263
Yost, Judy, 240
Young, James S., 280
Young, Rita, 2
Younis, Paul, 271, 272
Younis, Vincent, 271, 272
Yupik Eskimos, grass baskets, 3

Zeh, Stephen, 6–7
Zeleny, Ray, 142
Zephier, Mitchell, 152–53
Zundel, Hazel and Wallace, 14

About the Author

Constance Stapleton, coauthor of *Antiques Don't Lie* (Doubleday) and *Barter* (Scribner's), was consultant to American Craft Enterprises, Inc., for the first and second Winter Market of American Crafts, the Rhinebeck Fair and the Pacific States Fair in San Francisco; to the Women's Committee of Smithsonian Associates for the first Washington Craft Show; and to the Renwick Gallery for The First National Forum on Collecting and Connoisseurship. Her articles have appeared in many national publications, including *Architectural Digest, Connoisseur, American Craft, Americana, McCall's, Woman's Day, Reader's Digest* and the *Washington Post.* She lives in Frederick, Maryland.